Cyber Forensic Frameworks for User-Centric Human Threat Intelligence Analysis

Seifedine Kadry
Lebanese American University, Lebanon

Mritunjay Rai
https://orcid.org/0000-0002-8911-4826
Shri Ramswaroop Memorial University, Barabanki, India

Padmesh Tripathi
Delhi Technical Campus, Greater Noida, India

IGI Global
Scientific Publishing
Publishing Tomorrow's Research Today

Vice President of Editorial	Melissa Wagner
Director of Acquisitions	Mikaela Felty
Director of Book Development	Jocelynn Hessler
Production Manager	Mike Brehm
Cover Design	Jose Rosado

Published in the United States of America by
IGI Global Scientific Publishing
701 East Chocolate Avenue
Hershey, PA, 17033, USA
Tel: 717-533-8845 | Fax: 717-533-7115
Website: https://www.igi-global.com E-mail: cust@igi-global.com

Library of Congress Cataloging-in-Publication Data

LCCN: 2025032060 (CIP Data Pending)
ISBN13: 9798337348988
Isbn13Softcover: 9798337348995
EISBN13: 9798337349008
British Cataloguing in Publication Data
A Cataloguing in Publication record for this book is available from the British Library.

Table of Contents

Detailed Table of Contents

This chapter introduces the Theory of Two-Sided Fact (TSF) and its operationalization through Multiple-Lens Analysis (MLA) as a transformative framework for cyber forensic intelligence. While traditional methods like anomaly detection, machine learning, and rational-choice models capture patterns, they often neglect symbolic, ideological, and affective dynamics. TSF addresses this by emphasizing the inseparability of objective structures and subjective meanings, situating cyber events as sociotechnical phenomena. Through MLA's structural, symbolic, historical, affective, and ideological lenses, analysts gain multidimensional insight into causality, escalation, and intervention. Ethical reflexivity remains central, ensuring balanced interpretation and enabling socially informed, contextually grounded responses to contemporary cyber threats.

People are just as important to cybersecurity as gadgets. Attacks frequently result from human error or manipulation. Common examples include insider misuse, phishing, and weak passwords. These dangers highlight the necessity of researching human behavior in relation to cyberthreats. Users are only marked as "safe" or "unsafe" in older models. However, actual conduct frequently lies in the middle of these two extremes. To deal with such situations, this chapter employs a fuzzy soft set (FSS) structure. Partial risk is represented using fuzzy sets, such as a user who

The advancement of cyber forensics—through AI-driven profiling, metadata analysis, and real-time surveillance—has enhanced digital investigations but raised significant legal and ethical concerns. This chapter explores the growing tension between state surveillance and individual privacy, focusing on the Indian legal framework, including the Justice K.S. Puttaswamy decision, and comparing it with global standards such as the GDPR, ECHR, and Budapest Convention. Key issues addressed include algorithmic bias, lack of consent, cross-border data sharing, and misuse of forensic tools against vulnerable groups. The chapter argues for a balanced, rights-based framework grounded in privacy-by-design, proportionality, and judicial oversight. It offers policy recommendations to ensure cyber forensic practices remain effective while upholding constitutional protections and international human rights norms.

In this day and age, cyberspace is rife with exposures generated by people - insider attacks, clever social engineering phishing schemes, and lurking advanced persistent threats, and each event not only tests company defences but also challenges the broader security framework of a nation. This chapter draws on an intersection of cyber forensics and human intelligence threat, with a forensic-first approach to provide a foundation to profile, investigate and pursue the people undertaking attacks. You'll observe how behavioural analytics, raw digital evidence, and advanced artificial intelligence work in concert to depict motivation, strategies, and actions intruders will employ, as well as their electronic footprints. Here are the sequential techniques to identify, pin blame, and mitigate these impacts and threats, which rely on forensic toolkits, network traffic examinations, and digital poison extraction, aka malware reverse engineering.

Increasing numbers of people using online resources without precautions is one of the main reasons hazardous computer apps evolve quickly. These days, Trojan horseback, malware, and worm authors do it for profit rather than fame. So, malware problem Computer security now prioritizes detection. Zero-day malware exploits undiscovered holes without detection. Deep learning models, which can analyze data in several dimensions and uncover features, are an effective threat detection and classification alternative. This chapter examines deep learning-based malware recognition and categorization for zero-day vulnerabilities and attack authentication. While studying model architectures, data sources, evaluation criteria, and real-world applications, we discuss asymmetrical evasion, comprehensibility, and statistical imbalance. The article also explores how graph-based models, self-encoder RNN, and CNN understand unfamiliar virus behaviors.

Artificial intelligence and cybersecurity convergence has fundamentally transformed the threat environment, in particular, the social engineering attacks. In this paper, a comprehensive holistic user-centered approach to detection and reduction of adversarial AI-assisted social engineering attacks is proposed with assistance of adversarial AI-determined menace insight. The proposed architecture takes into consideration the concepts of machine learning, behavioral analytics, and human-computer interaction to create a defense multilayer. The experiments prove that the rate of AI-generated phishing attacks and identification of deepfake-generated campaigns are high, respectively, 94.3 and 99.0, respectively. The viability of the framework is proven by the experiments that are founded on the real-life data and simulated AI-based attacks that are serious challenges to the framework. It is an original work of literature that bridges many gaps in the current threat intelligence models through the application of human-centered principles of design, adversarial artificial intelligence detection systems, and training systems that adapt to new developments. Interdisciplinary character of the framework brings along with the ethical considerations and policy orientation and human behavioral analysis besides the technical innovations and thus it is a holistic approach to the next-generation cybersecurity issues.

In this paper, we propose a forensic framework that is able to forecast downtime errors at the server level based on anomaly detection to system logs, converted into features according to machine learning (ML) algorithms. We used hybrid of ML model, based on Isolation Forest and One-Class SVM algorithms for encoding normal patterns of behaviour systems to annotate deviations from the norm. Detailed log file parsing of any log files of interest, feature extraction, and weighted scoring in combining anomalies were among the actions included in my approach. The hybrid model achieved 99.54% accuracy on real-world live-server log validation data and 95.08% in recall, consistent with individual models, making it a not-so-common occurrence. It identified high-risk periods and scheduled the preventive maintenance. This shows the practical way to bring into predictive IT operations log analysis using ML techniques, which in turn answers a very direct critical need for improved reliability of infrastructure. Future work will be pointed toward this dimension in view of limitations related to dataset scope and sensitivity of models to changes in log format.

Preface

The rapid expansion of digital technologies has fundamentally reshaped the nature of crime, security, and investigation. Cybercrime today is no longer confined to technical exploits or isolated system breaches; instead, it is increasingly driven by human intent, behavior, psychology, and social context. Attackers exploit trust, cognitive bias, ideology, and organizational weaknesses as effectively as they exploit software vulnerabilities. In this evolving threat landscape, cyber forensics must move beyond a purely artifact-centric approach and adopt user-centric, human-focused, and intelligence-driven frameworks. It is within this context that the edited volume Cyber Forensic Frameworks for User-Centric Human Threat Intelligence Analysis has been conceptualized.

This book provides a comprehensive exploration of modern cyber forensics through the lens of human threat intelligence. It integrates technical forensic methodologies with behavioral analysis, artificial intelligence, psychological profiling, legal frameworks, and ethical safeguards. The subject matter spans insider threats, social engineering, blockchain and cryptocurrency crimes, malware attribution, network forensics, adversarial AI, and decision-support systems. By emphasizing the human dimension of cyber threats, the book addresses a critical gap in existing literature, where technical solutions often overlook the motivations, behaviors, and social dynamics that drive cybercrime.

In today's world—characterized by digital transformation, remote work, cloud infrastructures, cryptocurrency adoption, and AI-driven automation—cyber threats have become more adaptive, persistent, and deceptive. Nation-state attacks, financially motivated cybercriminals, hacktivists, and malicious insiders increasingly operate across jurisdictions, exploiting both technological systems and human vulnerabilities. Simultaneously, advances in AI-based surveillance, behavioral profiling, and real-time monitoring raise serious concerns regarding privacy, bias, legality, and ethical accountability. This book situates itself precisely at this intersection of technology, human behavior, and governance, offering frameworks that are not only effective but also legally defensible and ethically responsible.

The target audience for this volume is broad and interdisciplinary. It is designed for academic researchers and postgraduate students in cybersecurity, digital forensics, computer science, artificial intelligence, and criminology. It also serves practitioners, including digital forensic analysts, cybersecurity professionals, incident responders, intelligence analysts, and law enforcement officials. Policymakers, legal professionals, and organizational leaders concerned with cyber risk, compliance, and governance will also find the discussions highly relevant. By combining theoretical foundations with applied frameworks and case-based insights, the book supports both scholarly inquiry and real-world implementation.

Each chapter in this edited volume contributes a distinct and essential perspective to the overarching theme of user-centric human threat intelligence:

CHAPTER OVERVIEW

Chapter 1: The Two-Sided Reality of Cyber Threat Actors: A Sociological MLA of Forensic Intelligence introduces an innovative theoretical framework using the Theory of Two-Sided Fact and Multiple-Lens Analysis. By incorporating structural, symbolic, historical, affective, and ideological perspectives, the chapter enriches forensic intelligence with sociological depth and ethical reflexivity.

Chapter 2: Fuzzy Soft Set-Based Decision Framework for Human-Centric Cyber Threat Analysis presents a mathematically grounded yet practical decision-support model. By leveraging fuzzy logic and soft set theory, the chapter demonstrates how uncertainty and vagueness in human behavior can be systematically modeled and ranked for effective threat assessment.

Chapter 3: Legal and Ethical Implications of Cyber Forensics reinforces the necessity of lawful, transparent, and reproducible forensic practices. It maps the forensic lifecycle to admissibility standards and data protection principles, offering operational guidance for privacy-preserving investigations.

Chapter 4: Psychological Dimensions of Social Engineering in Cybercrime complements earlier discussions by deeply examining cognitive and emotional vulnerabilities exploited in cybercrime and outlining integrated defensive measures that combine psychology, training, and technical controls.

Chapter 5: Network Forensics for Human-Driven Cyber Attacks highlights the role of network forensics in detecting adaptive, targeted attacks carried out by skilled human adversaries. The chapter emphasizes real-time monitoring, anomaly detection, and proactive incident response in complex network environments.

Chapter 6: Forensic-Centric Human Threat Intelligence: An Integrated Framework for Modern Cybercrime Investigation provides a unifying framework that integrates behavioral science, digital forensics, AI, and threat intelligence. It offers a structured methodology for profiling, attribution, and mitigation across diverse threat actors and critical infrastructure contexts.

Chapter 7: Reconciling Privacy Rights with Digital Investigations: Legal-Ethical Challenges in Cyber Forensics critically examines the tension between surveillance and privacy, with particular emphasis on the Indian legal context and global human rights frameworks, proposing a rights-based, proportional approach to cyber investigations.

Chapter 8: A Forensic Intelligence Approach for Profiling and Investigating Human-Driven Cyber Threats presents a forensic-first methodology that combines behavioral analytics, digital evidence, and AI to uncover attacker motivations, tactics, and operational patterns.

Chapter 9: Malware Analysis and Attribution in Human Threat Intelligence focuses on deep learning–based malware detection and attribution, addressing zero-day threats, evasion techniques, and the role of explainable AI in understanding malicious behavior.

Chapter 10: Adversarial AI-Driven Cyber Threat Intelligence: A Human-Centric Framework for Detecting and Mitigating AI-Augmented Social Engineering Attacks examines the emerging challenge of AI-powered deception, proposing adversarial AI frameworks that integrate human behavior modeling with machine intelligence.

Chapter 11: Anomaly Detection and Downtime Prediction in Server Logs Using Hybrid Machine Learning highlights the operational importance of predictive analytics in maintaining cyber resilience, demonstrating how early anomaly detection can prevent large-scale disruptions.

Chapter 12: Leveraging AI for Behavioural Analysis of Digital Forensic Artifacts in Cybercrime Investigations emphasizes memory forensics and AI-driven artifact analysis, showcasing how volatile evidence can be mapped to attack lifecycles for proactive threat hunting.

Chapter 13: Social Engineering and the Psychological Aspects of Cyber Crime explores how attackers manipulate human cognition and emotion. Through psychological theory, survey findings, and real-world case studies, the chapter underscores the importance of awareness, behavioral resilience, and multi-layered defense strategies in countering social engineering attacks.

Chapter 14: Forensic-Ready Approaches to Insider Threat Mitigation and Human Behavior Analysis focuses on one of the most damaging yet difficult-to-detect threat categories—insiders. The chapter integrates behavioral analytics, machine learning, access control mechanisms, and organizational policy to present a proactive, forensic-ready framework for insider threat prevention.

Chapter 15: Cryptocurrency and Blockchain Forensics: Tracing Digital Transactions expands on the technical foundations of blockchain forensics, examining transaction mapping, clustering, deanonymization, and AI-assisted tools, while critically discussing limitations such as privacy coins, mixers, and jurisdictional barriers.

Chapter 16: Blockchain Forensics for Cryptocurrency-Driven Cybercrime introduces the forensic challenges posed by decentralized financial systems. It explains how blockchain analysis, combined with user behavior profiling, enables the tracing of illicit transactions while addressing the legal and ethical complexities unique to cryptocurrency investigations.

Chapter 17: Legal and Ethical Considerations in Cyber Forensics establishes the foundational legal and ethical context for human-centric cyber forensic investigations. It examines constitutional protections, admissibility of AI-generated evidence, cross-border challenges, and privacy regulations such as GDPR, highlighting the necessity of balancing security imperatives with civil liberties and professional accountability.

In conclusion, Cyber Forensic Frameworks for User-Centric Human Threat Intelligence Analysis makes a significant contribution to the field by redefining cyber forensics as a multidisciplinary, human-centered discipline. It advances theoretical understanding, introduces innovative analytical frameworks, and provides actionable methodologies for addressing modern cyber threats. By integrating technology with human insight, law, and ethics, this book not only responds to current challenges but also shapes the future direction of cyber forensic research and practice. We hope this volume will inspire continued innovation, collaboration, and responsible advancement in the fight against human-driven cybercrime.

Chapter 1
The Two-Sided Reality of Cyber Threat Actors:
A Sociological MLA of Forensic Intelligence

M. M. Abdullah Al Mamun Sony
https://orcid.org/0000-0001-8169-2851
ChangeMaker Nexus Ltd., Bangladesh

ABSTRACT

This chapter introduces the Theory of Two-Sided Fact (TSF) and its operationalization through Multiple-Lens Analysis (MLA) as a transformative framework for cyber forensic intelligence. While traditional methods like anomaly detection, machine learning, and rational-choice models capture patterns, they often neglect symbolic, ideological, and affective dynamics. TSF addresses this by emphasizing the inseparability of objective structures and subjective meanings, situating cyber events as sociotechnical phenomena. Through MLA's structural, symbolic, historical, affective, and ideological lenses, analysts gain multidimensional insight into causality, escalation, and intervention. Ethical reflexivity remains central, ensuring balanced interpretation and enabling socially informed, contextually grounded responses to contemporary cyber threats.

1 INTRODUCTION

In recent decades, the accelerating complexity of digital technologies and the expansion of transnational cybercrime have posed unprecedented challenges to forensic intelligence. Investigators, analysts, and intelligence communities are confronted with vast flows of technical data, new forms of organized criminality

DOI: 10.4018/979-8-3373-4898-8.ch001

(Di Nicola, 2022), and the persistence of cyber-enabled ideological movements that resist conventional profiling (Lavorgna, 2023). The dominant response to this landscape has been to intensify the technical sophistication of forensic tools: more refined anomaly detection systems, advanced machine learning classifiers, and highly formalized models of risk assessment (Chen & Yuan, 2022; Liu et al., 2024). While these developments undeniably extend investigative capacity, they also reveal an enduring limitation—an epistemic bias that privileges technical artifacts and rational-choice assumptions while marginalizing the symbolic, cultural, and ideological dimensions of cyber behavior (Chen & Yuan, 2022). The consequence is an intelligence paradigm that excels at describing *how* certain actions occur within networks but remains less effective at explaining *why* actors mobilize, persist, or innovate in the ways they do.

This problem can be characterized as the persistence of technical bias in forensic intelligence. Analysts often rely on algorithmic models designed to process massive quantities of data with high statistical accuracy (Galante et al., 2023; Galyashina et al., 2025). Yet the epistemology of such models is oriented toward correlation rather than interpretation (Galante et al., 2023), treating behavior as a calculable function of rational incentives and system vulnerabilities (Oatley et al., 2020). In this sense, many forensic approaches remain tethered to a form of rational-choice reductionism: the assumption that cybercriminals, hackers, and digital activists act primarily as strategic calculators of risk and reward (Mushtaq & Shah, 2025; Oatley et al., 2020). While this model may capture some elements of cybercrime economics, it falls short when confronted with phenomena such as ransomware groups invoking geopolitical symbolism, hacktivist collectives animated by ideological grievances, or insider threats driven by resentment, alienation, or identity conflicts (Galyashina et al., 2025). Here, motivations are not reducible to utility-maximization; they are entangled with narratives of injustice, communal belonging, or symbolic recognition (Tyagi et al., 2024). Without adequate theoretical tools to integrate these dimensions, forensic intelligence risks constructing partial and misleading portraits of the actors it seeks to understand.

The inadequacy of this paradigm, however, becomes clearer when forensic intelligence is situated in the broader history of criminology and sociology. Criminological theories rooted in rational-choice and deterrence logics have long dominated policy frameworks, emphasizing calculation, opportunity, and risk environments (Ramadhan, 2024). In parallel, the technical disciplines that contribute to cyber forensics—computer science, data analytics, network engineering—naturally emphasize quantifiable evidence, traceable patterns, and computational modeling (Galyashina et al., 2025; Mushtaq & Shah, 2025). Yet the sociological insight, first articulated by classical thinkers such as Émile Durkheim, Max Weber, and Karl Marx, is that social action cannot be adequately understood without reference to shared meanings, normative orders, and historically situated structures of power (Giddens, 1976). Forensic intelligence, to the extent that it neglects these dimensions, risks reproducing the same epistemological divide that sociology itself has long wrestled with: the gulf between objectivist empiricism and interpretivist understanding.

It is precisely here that the Theory of Two-Sided Fact (TSF) becomes indispensable. Conceived as a sociological meta-paradigm, TSF advances the claim that every social phenomenon—including those manifests in digital environments—exists simultaneously as an objective structure and as a subjective meaning. These two dimensions are not simply additive layers but are constitutively relational: each derives its significance from its interplay with the other. A cyber intrusion, for instance, is not merely a technical breach of a system (objective fact) but also a communicative act, embedded within cultural codes and ideological narratives (subjective fact) (Arjun & Singh, 2025). Similarly, an encrypted data trail is not only a piece of objective evidence; it is also interpreted through professional norms, institutional mandates, and symbolic frames that shape how analysts "see" it (Arjun & Singh, 2025). By foregrounding this duality, TSF offers forensic intelligence a framework to move beyond its current technical bias and reductionism, enabling a richer, more holistic analysis of cyber phenomena.

The necessity of such a paradigm becomes evident when considering the shortcomings of existing forensic methodologies in addressing ideologically motivated cyber actors. Consider, for example, a collective of hacktivists who deface government websites with slogans referencing colonial histories and anti-imperial struggles (Dunn Cavelty et al., 2023). From a purely technical perspective, forensic intelligence may successfully trace the attack vector, identify vulnerabilities exploited, and estimate the sophistication of the malware deployed (Galyashina et al., 2025). From a rational-choice lens, analysts may attempt to calculate potential benefits accrued to the group—attention, disruption, or deterrence (Thompson, 2023). Yet such models fail to capture the deeper significance of the act as a symbolic contestation of authority, rooted in historical memory and ideological orientation. TSF, by contrast, requires analysts to situate the objective act of defacement within its subjective meaning context: why these slogans, why this target, why now? This interpretive dimension not only enriches understanding but also has practical implications for anticipating future threats (Huda & Sony, 2024), assessing potential escalation, and identifying underlying grievances that may be leveraged for prevention.

Moreover, TSF insists on contextual relativity as an epistemic anchor. It rejects the assumption that social phenomena can be universally defined or explained without regard to situational environments. In forensic intelligence, this means that the same technical pattern of cyber intrusion may acquire radically different meanings in different cultural or geopolitical contexts. A distributed denial-of-service (DDoS) attack carried out by environmental activists in Europe cannot be equated with a similar DDoS launched by political dissidents in an authoritarian regime (Kim et al., 2024). Both may involve identical technical signatures, yet the subjective meanings, motivations, and consequences are contextually distinct. TSF provides the tools to recognize and theorize this contextual variability, grounding forensic intelligence in the specificity of time, place, and culture rather than in abstract universals.

tThe call for a sociological meta-paradigm is not simply an academic exercise but a practical imperative. As digital environments increasingly become the battlegrounds of ideological, political, and cultural struggle, where forensic intelligence cannot afford to remain confined to its technical core. Cyber actors are not merely engineers of disruption; they are also meaning-makers, embedded in communities of belief and practice (Di Nicola, 2022; Sony et al., 2025). The symbolic dimensions of their actions—whether invoking religious imagery, nationalist rhetoric, or subcultural codes—are central to understanding their persistence and impact (Arjun & Singh, 2025). TSF equips forensic analysts with a conceptual language to engage with these dimensions without collapsing into moral judgment or cultural stereotyping. By reconceptualizing neutrality as a methodological discipline, TSF allows analysts to treat value-laden categories ("terrorism," "justice," "resistance") as data for interpretation rather than as predetermined conclusions. This reflexive stance expands the scope of forensic inquiry while preserving analytical rigor.

In this chapter, therefore, I propose to extend the Theory of Two-Sided Fact into the domain of forensic intelligence as a means of overcoming its current epistemological impasse. The chapter unfolds in four movements. First, I elaborate the theoretical foundations of TSF, clarifying its principle of dual relationality—the idea that objective and subjective dimensions always shape each other, its commitment to contextual relativity—the principle that social facts change meaning across cultures, histories, and environments, and its reconfiguration of value neutrality—a methodological stance that treats moral judgments as data rather than conclusions. Second, I articulate a methodological framework—the Multiple-Lens Analysis (MLA)—through which TSF can be operationalized in forensic practice. This framework introduces five interpretive lenses (structural, symbolic, historical, affective, ideological) that enable analysts to move fluidly between objective and subjective dimensions of cyber phenomena. Third, I illustrate the utility of this approach through case-based analysis, contrasting conventional forensic interpretations with those enabled by TSF. Finally, I reflect on the broader implications of TSF for the future of forensic intelligence, emphasizing its potential to reorient training, typology construction, and policy design toward a more holistic and reflexive model of analysis.

The argument is not that TSF replaces existing forensic methodologies, but rather that it provides an umbrella under which they can be integrated and expanded. By situating technical evidence within symbolic frameworks, and by embedding rational calculations within cultural and historical narratives, TSF enables forensic intelligence to grasp the full complexity of cyber phenomena. This, in turn, enhances both explanatory power and practical efficacy, equipping analysts to anticipate, interpret, and respond to threats in ways that are attuned to their sociotechnical reality. In an era where cyber conflicts are increasingly entangled with geopolitical struggles, ideological movements, and identity politics, such a paradigm is not merely useful—it is necessary.

2 THE LIMITS OF CURRENT FORENSIC PARADIGMS

The rise of digital technologies has fundamentally reshaped the terrain of forensic intelligence. Law enforcement agencies, intelligence services, and cybersecurity professionals now operate in an environment saturated with vast data flows, complex network architectures, and ever-evolving techniques of concealment and disruption (Arjun & Singh, 2025). To meet these challenges, forensic science has increasingly turned toward technical solutions, particularly those grounded in computational modeling, machine learning, anomaly detection, and biometric profiling (Arjun & Singh, 2025; Di Nicola, 2022; Galyashina et al., 2025). These frameworks, while powerful in their capacity to process immense datasets and identify patterns invisible to human observers, nevertheless embody specific epistemological commitments that circumscribe their analytical horizon. Put differently, they privilege what can be measured, quantified, and modeled, while relegating meaning, culture, and ideology to the margins of analysis. The result is a forensic paradigm that excels at describing the *how* of digital action but falters when tasked with explaining the *why*.

2.1 Current Forensic Frameworks

One of the most celebrated developments in contemporary forensic practice is the integration of machine learning algorithms (Tyagi et al., 2024). These systems are trained on large datasets of past cyber incidents and are designed to classify new events based on learned patterns (Hussein Jassim, 2025). For example, supervised learning models can distinguish between benign and malicious network traffic, while unsupervised models can identify anomalous behaviors that deviate from established baselines (Hussein Jassim, 2025; Mushtaq & Shah, 2025; Tyagi et al., 2024). Such techniques have revolutionized detection efficiency, allowing investigators to parse terabytes of network logs in real time. The epistemology here, however, is one of statistical correlation: significance is assigned based on recurrence, deviation, or probabilistic association.

Closely related is the domain of anomaly detection, which forms the backbone of intrusion detection systems (IDS) and security information and event management

(SIEM) platforms. These frameworks establish baselines of "normal" system behavior and flag deviations as potential threats (Hussein Jassim, 2025). The strength of anomaly detection lies in its capacity to uncover previously unknown attack vectors, thereby extending forensic capacity beyond signature-based methods that rely on predefined rules (Liu et al., 2024). Yet anomaly detection also inherits the epistemic limitation of treating deviation as inherently suspicious, irrespective of its contextual meaning. A sudden surge in traffic to a government website may be flagged as a denial-of-service attempt (Huda & Sony, 2024; Sony, 2023), but without contextual interpretation, it remains unclear whether the surge stems from malicious actors or from legitimate public interest following a political event.

A further technical frontier is biometric profiling, which extends forensic intelligence into the domain of human identification (Sammoud et al., 2022). Facial recognition, voice pattern analysis, and keystroke dynamics now provide investigators with tools to link digital traces to embodied individuals (Galyashina et al., 2025). In cyber forensics, biometric profiling can be employed to attribute attacks, identify insiders, or authenticate suspects (Hussein Jassim, 2025; Sammoud et al., 2022). The promise of such techniques lies in their apparent objectivity: biological and behavioral signatures appear resistant to manipulation (Sammoud et al., 2022). Yet here too the epistemic orientation is narrowly technical. By treating identity as a fixed, measurable trait, biometric systems often overlook the ways in which identity is performed, symbolized, and politicized within digital spaces (Huda & Sony, 2024).

Together, these frameworks reflect the technical rationality that underpins current forensic paradigms. They privilege calculability, precision, and prediction, aspiring to strip away ambiguity in favor of statistical certainty (Arjun & Singh, 2025; Galyashina et al., 2025). From the perspective of operational necessity, this orientation is understandable: investigators need timely, actionable insights rather than philosophical reflections on meaning. However, the danger lies in mistaking technical sophistication for analytical completeness. In privileging the quantifiable, current paradigms risk obscuring the symbolic, ideological, and cultural dimensions of cyber action—dimensions that are often central to understanding motivation, persistence, and escalation.

2.2 The Limits of Technical Bias

The first major limitation of current forensic paradigms is what may be termed technical bias: the privileging of artifacts, codes, and quantifiable traces at the expense of subjective orientations and symbolic acts (Bose, 2025). Machine learning models, for example, are agnostic to meaning; they register only correlations within data (Arjun & Singh, 2025). An algorithm may detect that certain forms of traffic are statistically associated with ransomware (Liu et al., 2024), but it cannot interpret the ideological statements embedded in a ransom note, nor the cultural symbolism of targeting hospitals versus banks (Hanna et al., 2025). Analysts, if reliant solely on algorithmic outputs, risk overlooking the communicative dimensions of such attacks.

The second limitation is the persistence of rational-choice reductionism. Many forensic approaches implicitly assume that cyber actors behave as strategic calculators of cost and benefit (Mushtaq & Shah, 2025). This is evident in models that estimate the expected value of attacks, calculate opportunity structures, or design deterrence strategies based on risk-reward logic (Hussein Jassim, 2025). While such models capture part of the truth—economic incentives are indeed relevant—they fail to account for actors motivated by ideology, grievance, or symbolic recognition (Ardichvili, 2022; Kim et al., 2024; Stibbe et al., 2025). A collective of hacktivists targeting multinational corporations may derive no direct financial benefit from their actions (Stibbe et al., 2025), but their sense of efficacy and identity may be deeply tied to the symbolic disruption of corporate power. To reduce such actions to rational calculation is to miss their constitutive meaning.

Third, current paradigms exhibit a *universalizing tendency* that neglects context. Machine learning models trained on global datasets may assume that cyber behavior is invariant across cultural and political environments (Stibbe et al., 2025). Yet the same technical act can carry radically different meanings depending on context. A data leak orchestrated by dissidents in an authoritarian regime may function as a form of political resistance (Booth, 1994), while a similar leak by employees in a liberal democracy may be interpreted as whistleblowing or personal vendetta (Bhambra, 2025). Without situating acts in their cultural and historical specificity, forensic analysis risks flattening distinctions that are critical for understanding.

2.3 The Ideological and Symbolic Blind Spot

Perhaps the most serious limitation of current forensic paradigms is their *blind spot for ideology and symbolism*. Digital acts are not only technical operations but also communicative gestures, saturated with meaning (Stibbe et al., 2025). Hacktivist campaigns often invoke historical grievances, religious imagery, or countercultural codes to frame their actions (Yar & Steinmetz, 2023). Cyberterrorist propaganda deploys aesthetic and symbolic strategies to recruit, mobilize, and inspire (Yar & Steinmetz, 2023). Even mundane cybercrimes may be embedded in subcultural identities, such as those cultivated in dark web forums or gaming communities (O'Boyle, 2022). These dimensions are not epiphenomenal; they are central to the reproduction of cyber collectives and to the persistence of their practices.

Technical frameworks, however, are ill-equipped to capture these dimensions. An anomaly detection system may flag a surge of traffic, but it cannot discern the political symbolism of defacing a national monument's website on the anniversary of independence. A biometric system may attribute an intrusion to an individual, but it cannot explain why that individual aligns with a particular ideological movement. Analysts trained to rely on such frameworks may therefore misinterpret the nature of threats, mistaking symbolic acts for rational crimes or overlooking the cultural resonance that sustains collective mobilization.

2.4 Illustrative Example: Misinterpreting Hacktivism

The dangers of these limitations can be vividly illustrated through the example of a hacktivist campaign misinterpreted as a purely financial crime. Consider a hypothetical scenario in which a collective of digital activists launches a coordinated campaign against multinational banks, disrupting services and leaking customer data (Gupta, 2025). From a technical perspective, forensic analysts identify the modus operandi: phishing emails, malware deployment, lateral movement, and data exfiltration (Galyashina et al., 2025). Machine learning models classify the incident as consistent with financially motivated cybercrime (Ramadhan, 2024), while anomaly detection systems highlight the deviations from normal banking traffic. On this basis, the campaign is initially understood as an attempt at financial gain.

However, a closer examination reveals a different picture. The leaked data are not monetized on dark markets but are instead released publicly alongside manifestos denouncing global financial institutions for perpetuating inequality and exploitation (Hasan & Sony, 2022). The group frames its campaign as a form of "digital direct action," drawing on anti-capitalist rhetoric and referencing historical protest movements (Rovira-Sancho, 2023). The symbolic choice of banks as targets reflects not opportunistic vulnerability but ideological opposition to financial capitalism (Yolles, 2024). To interpret the campaign solely as financial crime is to miss its constitutive meaning: an act of protest and resistance, performed through digital means.

Nevertheless, the misinterpretation has practical consequences. By framing the campaign as economically motivated, forensic intelligence agencies may prioritize financial disruption as the central risk, overlooking the potential for ideological escalation, recruitment, or alliance-building with other activist movements (Rovira-Sancho, 2023). Policy responses may focus narrowly on financial security rather than on addressing underlying grievances or monitoring ideological networks. The result is a forensic practice that is technically accurate (Tyagi et al., 2024) but substantively incomplete—capable of describing *how* the attack unfolded but blind to *why* it occurred and what it signified.

2.5 Toward a Broader Forensic Horizon

The limitations of current forensic paradigms thus underscore the need for a broader analytical horizon—one that integrates technical precision with interpretive depth. Machine learning (Hussein Jassim, 2025), anomaly detection (Liu et al., 2024), and biometric profiling (Sammoud et al., 2022) remain indispensable tools; their contribution to efficiency and accuracy cannot be denied. But they must be supplemented by frameworks that can capture the symbolic, ideological, and cultural dimensions of cyber phenomena. Without such supplementation, forensic intelligence risks reproducing a form of epistemological reductionism, treating complex social acts as mere technical events (Bose, 2025).

In these regards, the Theory of TSF provides precisely such a framework. By insisting on the inseparability of objective structures—material and institutional systems (laws, infrastructures, economic forces) that shape behavior—and subjective meanings—beliefs, perceptions, emotions, identities, and narratives actors use to interpret their world, TSF equips forensic intelligence to grasp the dual truth of cyber action: the technical event and the symbolic act, the artifact and the narrative, the trace and the interpretation. In the following sections, I elaborate this framework, showing how it can overcome the epistemological limits of current paradigms and reorient forensic intelligence toward a more holistic and reflexive practice.

3 THE THEORY OF TWO-SIDED FACT (TSF)

The Theory of TSF represents a significant reorientation in sociological thinking, advancing the claim that every social phenomenon is fundamentally constituted by a duality: objective structures and subjective meanings. These dimensions are inseparable, not merely additive, and their interrelation is constitutive of the phenomena themselves. Objective realities such as institutions, laws, infrastructures, or economic indicators acquire their significance only when interpreted through the subjective perceptions, beliefs, identities, and cultural narratives of actors (Buchanan et al., 1998; Letherby et al., 2012). Conversely, subjective orientations are always constrained and enabled by material conditions, structural arrangements, and institutional frameworks (Buchanan et al., 1998; Letherby et al., 2012). In foregrounding this inseparability, TSF challenges the long-standing epistemological divide between positivist traditions, which privilege measurable regularities, and interpretivist traditions, which emphasize meaning and lived experience. By integrating the strengths of both perspectives, TSF provides a meta-paradigm capable of capturing the complexity and nuance of contemporary social life, including phenomena in digital and cyber contexts that are increasingly global, symbolic, and contested.

At its core, TSF posits that objectivity and subjectivity are not independent layers that can be analyzed in isolation. Rather, they are relational dimensions whose meaning emerges from their mutual interplay (Table 1). This principle of dual relationality underscores that no sociological analysis is complete if it privileges one side over the other. The study of labor market inequality exemplifies this (Aksoy et al., 2024). Conventional positivist analyses focus on wage statistics, employment rates, and productivity measures (Häusermann et al., 2020), while interpretivist accounts foreground experiences of precarity, dignity, or alienation (Doody et al., 2016). TSF insists that neither perspective alone is sufficient. Wage statistics must be interpreted through cultural narratives surrounding work, gender, and generational aspirations, while subjective experiences of insecurity or exploitation cannot be fully understood outside of economic structures, labor regulations, and institutional dynamics. The resulting analysis reveals a dual truth: one inscribed in empirical regularities and the other embedded in interpretive frameworks. This relational perspective extends beyond the labor market to other domains, such as political protest (Häusermann et al., 2020). Authoritarian laws and restrictive institutions, understood as objective structures, cannot explain collective action without attending to symbolic repertoires—the set of cultural symbols, narratives, and communicative codes actors draw upon, shared memories of injustice, and identities forged in struggle. Simultaneously, symbolic protest only becomes effective when it resonates with concrete structural constraints. The dynamic interdependence of objective and subjective realities thus defines the analytical terrain of TSF.

Contextual relativity forms another cornerstone of TSF. Whereas many sociological paradigms treat context as a background variable, TSF elevates it to an epistemic anchor. Social facts are never isolated; they are always mediated by situational environments that shape both objective manifestations and subjective interpretations (Rafanell, 2013). A 10 percent unemployment rate, for example, carries divergent meanings depending on cultural, historical, and geographical contexts. In an industrialized Western economy, unemployment generates anxieties about consumer debt, healthcare, and social status, while in a rural agrarian community, it may correspond to seasonal labor patterns, subsistence economies, or extended family support networks. The "same" numerical fact is, in reality, two distinct phenomena, demonstrating how context transforms the interplay between objectivity and subjectivity. This emphasis on contextualization also guards against universalizing tendencies in policy and analysis, ensuring that social phenomena are examined in relation to the specific environments in which they are embedded.

Building on Weber's concept of value neutrality, TSF reconceptualizes neutrality as a methodological discipline rather than a detachment from moral or political concerns (Giddens, 1976). Judgments of social phenomena as "progressive" or "regressive," "good" or "bad," are themselves products of cultural, ideological, and historical processes, and thus constitute empirical objects of study. For example, debates surrounding digital surveillance technologies are often polarized: some view surveillance as a threat to privacy and civil liberties, while others see it as essential for public safety (Wörsdörfer, 2024). TSF treats these evaluations as data rather than conclusions, interrogating who articulates these judgments, in what contexts they gain legitimacy, and which institutional actors' benefit. This approach broadens the analytical horizon, enabling scholars to adopt a reflexive stance, acknowledging their own normative assumptions while resisting the imposition of universal moral categories.

TSF operationalizes contextual relativity through five interlocking lenses: *structural, symbolic, historical, affective,* and *ideological*. The *structural lens* highlights how infrastructures, institutions, and regulations shape both opportunities and constraints, while the *symbolic lens* attends to the narratives, languages, and visual codes through which events acquire meaning. The *historical lens* situates current phenomena within long-term trajectories of conflict, exclusion, and technological change; the *affective lens* foregrounds emotions and psychological intensities that animate behavior; and the *ideological lens* examines how value systems and political imaginaries filter and reframe objective facts. Together, these lenses constitute a multi-dimensional analytic scaffold, showing how cyber events—such as ransomware or hacktivist campaigns—are simultaneously technical, political, emotional, and symbolic phenomena whose interpretation shifts depending on the lens applied.

A major contribution of TSF lies in its ability to integrate individual agency, group dynamics, and competing factuality's within this lens-based architecture. Cyber actions are not reducible to structural imperatives or cultural codes alone; they are informed by perceived benefits, affective attachments, and ideological commitments. Likewise, collective mobilizations—from hacktivist groups to cybercrime networks—draw strength not only from material advantage but also from symbolic identification, loyalty, and shared narratives. This pluralism extends to interpretation itself: the same rise in phishing attacks may be framed structurally as law enforcement weakness, historically as the outcome of global inequality, affectively as a source of public fear, or ideologically as evidence of political failure. By holding these multiple truths in tension, TSF resists reductionism and fosters sophisticated, reflexive analysis.

As a meta-paradigm, TSF integrates what existing theories isolate: the determinism of structure, the conflictual dynamics of power, the symbolic construction of meaning, and the affective and ideological currents that underlie them all. In forensic intelligence and cyber analysis, this framework moves beyond technical traces to embrace the full spectrum of forces that shape digital events, enabling richer interpretations and more adaptive strategies (Di Nicola, 2022). By embedding objectivity and subjectivity within a single architecture, TSF equips scholars and practitioners to navigate the contested realities of contemporary life, where the dual truths of measurable structures and lived meanings are always co-constitutive.

Table 1. Key Elements of the Theory of Two-Sided Fact (TSF).

TSF Concept	Short Definition	Why It Matters for Cyber Forensics
Objective Structures	Material and institutional conditions (laws, infrastructures, economies).	Shows the systemic and technological conditions enabling cyber events.
Subjective Meanings	Beliefs, emotions, identities, and narratives shaping action.	Helps interpret motivations, symbols, and ideological signals in attacks.
Dual Relationality	Objectivity and subjectivity are inseparable and co-produced.	Prevents analysts from treating cyber incidents as purely technical events.
Contextual Relativity	Social facts change meaning across cultural and historical contexts.	Explains why identical attacks have different meanings in different regions.
Value Neutrality	Treat moral judgments as data, not conclusions.	Avoids bias when analyzing extremist messaging or political justification.
Five TSF Lenses	Structural, Symbolic, Historical, Affective, Ideological.	Provides a multi-layered method for decoding cyber threat behavior.

(Author Produces, 2025)

4 METHODOLOGICAL CORE: MULTIPLE-LENS ANALYSIS (MLA)

The Methodological Core of the Theory of TSF is anchored in a systematic approach that allows for the rigorous analysis of complex social phenomena: Multiple-Lens Analysis (MLA). This methodological innovation is designed to operationalize the duality of social facts—objective structures and subjective meanings—by providing distinct yet intersecting analytic perspectives. MLA does not merely offer alternative ways of examining a phenomenon; rather, it situates each lens in relation to the others, demonstrating that understanding emerges from the interplay of multiple dimensions (Cole et al., 2023). At the center of this framework is the recognition that contemporary social events, particularly in the cyber domain, cannot be fully understood through singular epistemologies or unidimensional metrics. Cyberattacks, hacktivist campaigns, disinformation operations, and digital activism are simultaneously material, symbolic, historical, affective, and ideological, and any analysis that ignores one of these dimensions' risks misinterpretation, misclassification, or inadequate response (Arjun & Singh, 2025; Di Nicola, 2022; Gupta, 2025; Hussein Jassim, 2025).

The first lens, structural, addresses the objective and institutional dimensions of social phenomena. It is concerned with the material, technological, organizational, and regulatory frameworks that shape both the possibilities and constraints of human action. In cyber contexts, the structural lens examines network architectures, digital infrastructures, regulatory regimes, security protocols, and economic systems that underpin cyber activity. For example, a ransomware attack on a healthcare system cannot be understood purely in terms of the malware itself (Hussein Jassim, 2025); the structural lens draws attention to the hospital's network configuration, the allocation of IT resources, the vulnerabilities in legacy software, and the broader institutional incentives that may have contributed to the susceptibility of the system. Similarly, in digital disinformation campaigns (Fritts & Cabrera, 2021), the structural lens focuses on social media platforms' algorithms, moderation policies, network connectivity, and data flows that enable the amplification of content. This lens underscores that objective realities—often the primary focus of technical cyber forensics—constitute only one side of the story, and that understanding these infrastructures is essential for interpreting the broader social significance of cyber events.

The second lens, symbolic, engages with the meanings, narratives, and communicative structures that actors use to interpret and enact social phenomena. Symbols are not superficial overlays but constitute the very medium through which social life is experienced and contested. In cyber incidents, symbolic dimensions may include the messaging embedded in a hacktivist operation, the iconography used in memes or digital protests, or the framing of a cyberattack as a form of political resistance rather than mere criminality. For instance, a group defacing government website may embed cultural references, ideological slogans, or historical allusions in their digital footprint—the trail of digital traces left behind by an actor during online activities (Rai et al., 2023). The symbolic lens allows analysts to decode these meanings, situating the technical event within the lived experience, cultural norms, and interpretive repertoires of participants and observers alike. By integrating symbolic analysis, MLA ensures that the subjective dimension of TSF—the ways in which actors perceive, narrate, and negotiate events—is not marginalized, allowing a more nuanced interpretation of cyber-social dynamics.

The historical lens adds temporal depth to MLA, emphasizing that contemporary phenomena are always situated within trajectories shaped by precedent, institutional memory, and cumulative experience. Social and cyber events are rarely isolated; they emerge from a confluence of historical processes that structure both objective conditions and subjective meanings. A cyberattack on critical infrastructure (Gupta, 2025), for instance, is best understood in relation to prior incidents, patterns of vulnerability, the evolution of cybersecurity practices, and historical relationships among actors, whether nation-states, corporate entities, or activist groups. Similarly, historical legacies influence the symbolic dimension: a campaign targeting a government database may evoke collective memories of political oppression or previous cyber conflicts, thereby shaping both interpretation and response. The historical lens anchors MLA in temporality, reminding analysts that the present is always conditioned by the past, and that the meaning of events is inseparable from the contexts in which they emerge and recur.

The affective lens addresses the emotional, psychological, and relational dimensions of social phenomena. Human behavior is not purely rational or ideologically motivated; it is suffused with affect, sentiment, and embodied experience. In cyber events, affective dynamics manifest in multiple ways: the fear engendered by ransomware, the collective exhilaration of a successful hacktivist campaign, the outrage generated by disinformation, and the anxiety provoked by perceived institutional failure. Affect shapes decision-making, mobilizes collective action, and mediates responses to structural conditions. For example, a healthcare organization may prioritize certain security protocols not only based on technical risk assessments but also in response to public fear, media scrutiny, or internal stress. Similarly, hacktivist communities often rely on affective cohesion—shared anger, indignation, or moral outrage—to sustain collective activity. By incorporating affect into analysis, MLA ensures that the emotional dimensions of social life, which are often invisible in technical or rational-choice frameworks, are foregrounded, allowing a more comprehensive understanding of both agency and structure.

The fifth lens, ideological, examines the frameworks of belief, normative commitments, and discursive formations that guide perception and action. Ideologies shape how actors interpret events, prioritize goals, and evaluate outcomes, providing coherence to both individual and collective behavior. In the cyber realm, ideological analysis reveals the motivations behind attacks, the narratives that justify them, and the interpretive frames through which observers evaluate their significance. For instance, a cyber campaign by environmental activists may target corporate websites (Tavakkoli et al., 2025), not for financial gain but to signal opposition to environmental degradation and to mobilize public awareness. Ideological framing informs both symbolic representation and affective engagement, demonstrating that beliefs and values are not peripheral but central to understanding social phenomena. By incorporating ideology into MLA, analysts capture the normative and moral dimensions that mediate both action and interpretation, providing a lens through which the interplay of structural, symbolic, historical, and affective factors can be contextualized.

The strength of MLA lies not in the isolated utility of each lens but in their systematic intersection, where structure, symbolism, history, affect, and ideology overlap to co-produce meaning. A cyber event—such as an attack on a financial institution—can thus be analyzed through multiple, intersecting dimensions: infrastructural vulnerabilities (structural), encoded community messaging (symbolic), precedent regulatory failures (historical), collective indignation or urgency (affective), and the grievances or principles motivating participants (ideological) (Figure 1). Conceptually, this integrative logic can be visualized as overlapping circles surrounding a central "event," where intersections reveal how infrastructures shape narratives, how history informs belief, and how emotion animates meaning. This multi-lens framework operationalizes TSF's core claim that objectivity and subjectivity are inseparable, offering a systematic guide for organizing observation, data collection, and interpretation in research and forensic intelligence alike.

Beyond theory, MLA provides methodological flexibility and practical utility (Figure 1). It accommodates mixed methods by situating quantitative data (traffic logs, intrusion metrics, usage patterns) within structural and historical analysis, while interpreting qualitative data (interviews, forums, narratives) through symbolic, affective, and ideological lenses. This pluralism avoids the reductionism of single-method approaches, ensuring that technical, emotional, and normative factors are analyzed together. Importantly, MLA also cultivates reflexivity by requiring analysts to scrutinize their own assumptions, biases, and normative commitments across all lenses. Its application extends beyond cyber events to political movements and digital governance, where the same five lenses reveal institutional constraints, symbolic repertoires, legacies of repression, collective emotion, and competing visions of freedom or security. In training and practice, MLA equips analysts to move beyond technical signatures toward socially informed intelligence, reducing misinterpretation and enabling more adaptive threat assessment. By embedding rigor, reflexivity, and multidimensionality, MLA transforms TSF's theoretical sophistication into a practical methodology for navigating the complexity of contemporary, interconnected worlds.

5 CASE-BASED ILLUSTRATIONS

To elucidate the practical utility of the Theory of TSF coupled with the MLA methodology, this section examines three empirical scenarios, demonstrating how traditional forensic approaches and TSF-MLA differ in explanatory depth, interpretive nuance, and predictive foresight. Each scenario highlights the limitations of conventional technical or rationalist paradigms (Table 2), while revealing how the integration of structural, symbolic, historical, affective, and ideological lenses can enrich sociological understanding and operational insight.

The first scenario concerns a hacktivist campaign targeting a multinational financial institution. Traditional forensic analysis tends to prioritize quantifiable digital footprints: IP addresses, timestamps, malware signatures, and transaction anomalies

(Oatley et al., 2020; Tavakkoli et al., 2025). Analysts typically interpret the activity through the lens of technical deviation or financial gain (Singh & Bajeje, 2025), assuming a rational-choice motivation. Under such frameworks, the campaign may be categorized simplistically as economically motivated cybercrime, prompting immediate but narrowly scoped responses, such as patching system vulnerabilities or tracing perpetrators through law enforcement channels (Siwakoti et al., 2024). These measures, while operationally necessary, risk mischaracterizing the social and symbolic drivers of the event, leading to reactive rather than proactive strategies.

Re-analyzing this scenario using TSF-MLA opens multiple dimensions of understanding. The structural lens situates the attack within institutional vulnerabilities, regulatory environments, and technological architectures, clarifying which system weaknesses were exploited. The symbolic lens interrogates the meanings encoded by the campaign itself: the choice of targets, the messages disseminated on social media, and the cultural narratives evoked to mobilize public attention. Historical analysis traces the lineage of previous hacktivist campaigns, revealing patterns of resistance against perceived corporate malfeasance. The affective lens accounts for emotional resonance among participants and the public, including outrage, solidarity, and moral indignation. Finally, the ideological lens situates the campaign within broader discourses on economic justice, digital sovereignty, and corporate accountability. By layering these lenses, TSF-MLA reframes the event not merely as a technical breach but as a complex social phenomenon whose significance emerges at the intersection of institutional vulnerability, collective meaning-making, and sociopolitical ideology. This multidimensional interpretation enables stakeholders to anticipate subsequent waves of activity, engage with underlying grievances, and design responses that are not solely reactive but culturally and structurally informed.

The second scenario involves the spread of disinformation during a national election cycle. Traditional forensic approaches focus on tracing information sources, algorithmic propagation, and network anomalies (Galyashina et al., 2025; Oatley et al., 2020). Analysts often reduce the phenomenon to patterns of dissemination and exposure metrics, seeking to identify manipulators and quantify impact on voter behavior (Sela et al., 2025). While technically precise, such analyses neglect the symbolic, historical, and ideological contexts that give the disinformation its traction. Without attending to these dimensions, interventions may focus narrowly on content removal or algorithmic filtering, addressing symptoms rather than root causes.

Applying TSF-MLA, however, uncovers a richer explanatory terrain. The structural lens identifies platform algorithms, content moderation policies, and communication infrastructures that facilitate viral spread. Symbolic analysis examines the narratives and memes deployed, assessing how they resonate with collective anxieties, partisan identities, or cultural frames of legitimacy. Historical analysis situates the event within longstanding political conflicts, recurring propaganda strategies, and electoral norms, revealing patterns that transcend individual campaigns. The affective lens captures the emotional arousal triggered by targeted messaging, including fear, anger, and in-group/out-group dynamics. Ideological analysis clarifies the underlying frameworks of authority, civic duty, and moral evaluation—judgments about right and wrong produced within specific cultural and ideological systems, that inform both producers and consumers of disinformation. The integrated TSF-MLA perspective illuminates not only how disinformation propagates but why it resonates, who it mobilizes, and how it interacts with existing political and social structures. This holistic approach allows policymakers, civil society actors, and platform designers to develop nuanced strategies that address structural vulnerabilities, narrative resonance, and ideological polarities simultaneously, moving beyond reactive content moderation toward systemic resilience.

The third scenario considers corporate insider threats, such as unauthorized data exfiltration by employees with privileged access. Standard forensic techniques emphasize log analysis, anomaly detection, and behavioral monitoring (Galante et al., 2023; Hussein Jassim, 2025; Tyagi et al., 2024), often relying on predefined thresholds or algorithms to flag suspicious activity (Akter et al., 2021). These approaches assume rational instrumental behavior—actors are expected to act to maximize personal gain or minimize risk. While effective at detecting overt breaches, such methods often fail to account for the subjective and relational dimensions that shape insider activity (Sela et al., 2025). Without attention to context, technical monitoring may produce false positives, misinterpret human behavior, or overlook emergent patterns of moral justification, peer influence, or organizational culture that drive actions (Galyashina et al., 2025; Kim et al., 2024).

TSF-MLA reconfigures the analytical gaze to encompass these complexities. The structural lens assesses organizational hierarchies, access controls, and reporting mechanisms, identifying latent vulnerabilities and opportunities for data misuse. Symbolic analysis explores the meanings that employees attach to corporate policies, norms, and ethical codes, revealing how perceived legitimacy or injustice may motivate behavior. Historical analysis examines prior incidents, cultural legacies of organizational trust, and sector-wide patterns of insider threats. The affective lens considers emotional states, stressors, loyalty, resentment, or fear that influence decision-making. Finally, the ideological lens interrogates broader assumptions about corporate governance, ethical responsibility, and professional identity that frame employees' perceptions and rationalizations. By intersecting these five lenses, TSF-MLA reconstructs insider threat not merely as a technical anomaly but as a socially embedded phenomenon whose causes and consequences are relationally constituted. This multidimensional understanding enables organizations to implement interventions that integrate structural safeguards, ethical education, cultural alignment, and emotional support, complementing technical controls with sociological foresight.

Overall, traditional forensic paradigms remain essential for technical verification and operational response but are limited by reductionist assumptions. TSF-MLA expands this scope by integrating structural, symbolic, historical, affective, and ideological dimensions, capturing both objective conditions and subjective meanings. This multidimensional approach not only explains how cyber events are produced and contested but also informs practical strategies—whether addressing cultural grievances in hacktivism, building resilience against disinformation, or fostering ethical culture in insider threat prevention. By embracing pluralism, reflexivity, and contextual sensitivity, TSF-MLA enables a shift from narrow, reactive analysis to holistic, anticipatory insight, offering a robust methodology for forensic intelligence, cybersecurity policy, and broader sociological inquiry in a digitally entangled world.

Table 2. Summary of Case-Based Illustrations Using TSF–MLA.

Scenario	Traditional Forensic Interpretation	TSF–MLA Interpretation	Added Value of TSF–MLA
Hacktivist Campaign Against Financial Institution	- Focus on IP traces, malware signatures, transaction anomalies. - Framed as financially motivated cybercrime. - Response: patch systems, pursue attribution.	- Structural: Targets linked to institutional vulnerabilities and public distrust. - Symbolic: Messaging frames action as resistance. - Historical: Continuity with past anti-corporate activism. - Affective: Outrage, solidarity, moral indignation. - Ideological: Discourses on economic justice and anti-corporate politics.	Reveals campaign as sociopolitical protest, not just a breach. Enables anticipation of future waves, understanding of grievances, and culturally informed intervention.
Election Disinformation Campaign	- Tracks content origin, propagation patterns, bot activity. - Measures exposure metrics and influence on voters. - Solutions: removal, filtering, correcting false content.	- Structural: Algorithms, platform incentives, and moderation policies shape spread. - Symbolic: Narratives, memes, identity cues resonate culturally. - Historical: Builds on long-standing political divisions and propaganda traditions. - Affective: Fear, anger, group belonging drive uptake. - Ideological: Competing visions of authority, legitimacy, nationalism.	Shows why disinformation works, not only how it spreads. Enables long-term resilience strategies addressing structural, emotional, and ideological vulnerabilities.

continued on following page

Table 2. Continued

Scenario	Traditional Forensic Interpretation	TSF–MLA Interpretation	Added Value of TSF–MLA
Insider Threat / Data Exfiltration	- Log audits, anomaly detection, behavioral thresholds. - Assumes rational self-interest and risk-benefit calculation. - Technical monitoring as primary solution.	- Structural: Hierarchies, access privileges, weak oversight. - Symbolic: Employee perceptions of fairness, recognition, or betrayal. - Historical: Prior conflicts, trust erosion, sector norms. - Affective: Stress, resentment, loyalty shifts. - Ideological: Views on corporate ethics, governance, or personal responsibility.	Interprets insider behavior as socially embedded. Supports interventions combining technical controls with cultural alignment, emotional support, and ethical training.

(Author produces, 2025)

6 THEORETICAL AND PRACTICAL CONTRIBUTIONS

The Theory of TSF, when integrated with the MLA framework, represents a profound reorientation in the conceptualization and practice of cyber forensic intelligence. Traditional approaches often privilege the observable and measurable—code signatures, anomaly logs, or attack vectors—treating cyber incidents as discrete, technical occurrences (Galante et al., 2023; Galyashina et al., 2025). While these approaches yield operational precision, they risk reductionism (Oatley et al., 2020), overlooking the sociocultural, ideological, and interpretive dimensions that shape both the production and reception of cyber events. TSF challenges this limitation by asserting that every cyber incident is fundamentally a two-sided fact: it is simultaneously constituted by objective structures—technological systems, regulatory frameworks, organizational architectures—and subjective interpretations—motivations, cultural meanings, and ideological narratives. This duality is not additive but relational; the objective and subjective dimensions co-construct one another, such that neither can be fully understood in isolation.

In theoretical terms, TSF reframes cyber forensic intelligence by shifting the analytical gaze from isolated technical phenomena to sociotechnical events. Cyberattacks are not merely the outcome of algorithmic exploitation or rationalized instrumental behavior; they are embedded in complex networks of meaning, history, emotion, and ideology (Di Nicola, 2022; Gupta, 2025). Analysts adopting the TSF lens are encouraged to move beyond the question of "what happened" to interrogate "why it happened" and, crucially, "under what symbolic and ideological conditions" the event emerged. This shift extends the explanatory reach of forensic intelligence, situating attacks within broader social processes and patterns rather than treating them as anomalous or purely opportunistic acts. For instance, a distributed denial-of-service attack on a financial institution might be understood not merely as a disruption of services but as a manifestation of broader ideological contestation, drawing upon cultural narratives about economic inequity, corporate accountability, or political dissent. By foregrounding these dual dimensions, TSF offers a theoretical scaffold for analyzing cyber phenomena as socially and technologically embedded events, rather than as disjointed technical incidents.

From a practical standpoint, TSF-MLA yields multiple benefits for cyber forensic practice. First, it enables the development of more nuanced typologies of threat actors. Traditional typologies often rely on binary or linear categories: financially motivated versus politically motivated, insider versus outsider, skilled versus unskilled. By incorporating structural, symbolic, historical, affective, and ideological lenses, analysts can construct multidimensional profiles that reflect not only technical capabilities but also interpretive frameworks, emotional drivers, cultural identities, and ideological commitments. For example, a hacktivist group might be simultaneously driven by ethical commitments, community pressures, historical grievances, and perceived personal benefit (Singh & Bajeje, 2025; Tavakkoli et al., 2025). Recognizing these intersecting dimensions allows forensic practitioners to anticipate not only immediate behaviors but also potential shifts in strategy, alliances, and target selection.

Second, TSF-MLA contributes to more effective prevention and de-radicalization strategies. In conventional frameworks, interventions often prioritize technological fortification or legal deterrence, which, while necessary, address only one side of the problem (Huda & Sony, 2024; Sony, 2023). TSF encourages a holistic view: preventive measures should attend to both structural vulnerabilities and the subjective interpretations that motivate actors. By understanding the symbolic repertoires, ideological narratives, and affective investments of threat actors, organizations and policymakers can design interventions that mitigate risk without alienating communities or inadvertently reinforcing adversarial narratives. For instance, engagement strategies might combine technical security measures with culturally informed dialogue, ethical guidance, or community-based monitoring initiatives that address grievances and reduce the allure of radicalized action. This integrated approach bridges the gap between reactive security and proactive sociotechnical strategy.

Third, TSF-MLA promotes ethically conscious analysis. Traditional forensic intelligence can inadvertently pathologize actors, reducing complex motivations to simplistic categories of "malicious" or "deviant." By foregrounding the duality of objective structures and subjective meanings, TSF encourages reflexivity: analysts are prompted to interrogate their own assumptions, biases, and interpretive frameworks. This reflexive stance prevents over pathologizing, recognizing that behaviors labeled as threatening may emerge from legitimate grievances, culturally grounded moral frameworks, or historically situated practices. For example, participation in a hacktivist campaign may be interpreted not solely as criminality but also as a strategic response to perceived injustice, a performance of moral identity, or an articulation of communal solidarity (Gupta, 2025; Singh & Bajeje, 2025). Ethically aware forensic analysis acknowledges these complexities, enabling practitioners to differentiate between harmful behavior and socially situated protest, thereby refining both operational response and policy guidance.

Additionally, TSF-MLA enhances the foresight capabilities of forensic intelligence. By tracing events through structural, symbolic, historical, affective, and ideological lenses, analysts can identify patterns that would remain invisible under purely technical paradigms. Structural analysis reveals systemic vulnerabilities and institutional constraints; symbolic analysis deciphers meaning-making and narrative resonance; historical analysis situates events within temporal trajectories; affective analysis gauges emotional intensity and relational dynamics; ideological analysis interprets the frameworks that justify or legitimize action. When these lenses intersect, forensic practitioners gain anticipatory insight into potential escalation points, secondary consequences, and emergent behaviors. For example, an emerging disinformation campaign may initially appear low-risk based on technical metrics alone (Stibbe et al., 2025). TSF-MLA, however, reveals its alignment with existing social grievances, historical conflicts, and affective mobilization, enabling preemptive intervention that addresses underlying drivers rather than solely symptoms.

Moreover, the TSF framework contributes to the development of policy and organizational norms that are attuned to the complex realities of cyber environments. Policymakers can leverage TSF insights to craft regulatory responses that are sensitive to both structural constraints and social interpretations, avoiding one-size-fits-all solutions that may prove ineffective or counterproductive. Similarly, corporate security teams can design protocols that integrate technical safeguards with culturally informed communication, ethical oversight, and context-sensitive monitoring. In essence, TSF operationalizes the principle that effective cyber governance requires simultaneous attention to objective and subjective dimensions, ensuring that measures are not only technically sound but socially legitimate.

The theoretical contributions of TSF-MLA extend beyond immediate operational benefits. By bridging positivist and interpretivist traditions, the framework advances the sociological understanding of cyber phenomena as intrinsically dual in nature. It affirms that measurable technical events and interpretive social meanings are inseparable in their production and consequences, thereby challenging reductionist approaches that privilege one domain over the other. In doing so, TSF-MLA cultivates a more comprehensive epistemology for forensic intelligence, in which complexity, pluralism, and contextual specificity are not limitations but core analytic strengths.

In practice, the integration of TSF with MLA allows cyber forensic analysts to move along a continuum from detection to understanding, from reactive response to proactive engagement. By systematically applying structural, symbolic, historical, affective, and ideological lenses, analysts can identify not only immediate threats but also underlying sociotechnical processes that generate and sustain them. This expanded perspective enhances the predictive power of forensic intelligence, informing interventions that are not merely punitive but preventative, culturally resonant, and ethically attuned.

Furthermore, the theoretical and practical contributions of TSF-MLA represent a paradigm shift in cyber forensic intelligence. The framework transforms the analyst's perspective: cyberattacks and digital threats are no longer treated as isolated technical anomalies but as complex sociotechnical events embedded in historical, cultural, affective, and ideological perspectives. The framework provides practical benefits by enabling nuanced actor typologies, informing prevention and de-radicalization strategies, and fostering ethically reflexive analysis. By integrating multiple lenses and emphasizing the relational co-production of objective structures and subjective meanings, TSF-MLA equips forensic intelligence with the conceptual sophistication and methodological rigor necessary to navigate the complexity of contemporary cyber environments. In an era defined by interconnectivity, digital transformation, and socio-political contestation, TSF-MLA offers both a theoretical anchor and a practical roadmap, ensuring that forensic intelligence operates with depth, foresight, and ethical responsibility.

7 ETHICAL CONSIDERATIONS: UNDERSTANDING MOTIVATIONS AND LEGITIMIZING ACTIONS

The integration of the Theory of TSF with MLA in cyber forensic intelligence carries profound ethical implications. By foregrounding the inseparability of objective structures and subjective meanings, TSF-MLA situates analysts in a position of interpretive power. This power is not merely technical but deeply epistemic: forensic practitioners do not simply document observable events (Tyagi et al., 2024); they actively participate in constructing narratives, framing the significance of actions, and shaping the interpretation of social phenomena within digital environments.

Ethical considerations, therefore, are not ancillary to the analytical process but constitute a central dimension of responsible practice.

One foundational principle in this regard is reflexive neutrality. Drawing on Weberian sociology, TSF reconceptualizes neutrality not as detachment or apolitical observation but as disciplined reflexivity (Giddens, 1976). Analysts must continuously interrogate their own assumptions, methodological choices, and interpretive frameworks to mitigate the influence of cognitive, cultural, or institutional biases. Reflexive neutrality requires acknowledging that every lens—structural, symbolic, historical, affective, or ideological—carries embedded assumptions that shape which facts are foregrounded and which are marginalized. For instance, a structural lens emphasizing network vulnerabilities may inadvertently overstate the determinative power of technical systems, while an ideological lens focusing on extremist narratives may overemphasize the intentionality of actors. Recognizing these potential distortions demands a commitment to reflexivity, wherein analysts critically examine how their epistemic positioning affects the construction of knowledge and the identification of threats.

Reflexive neutrality also addresses the ethical risks inherent in interpreting subjective dimensions. When analysts examine motivations, beliefs, or cultural narratives, there is a fine line between understanding and over-ascribing meaning. Misinterpretation can lead to unjust profiling, stigmatization of communities, or policy recommendations that are punitive rather than preventive. For example, interpreting participation in a hacktivist campaign solely as ideological extremism may obscure structural grievances that motivate collective action (Romagna & Leukfeldt, 2024), while interpreting it solely as a rationalized financial pursuit may ignore the symbolic and affective dimensions that sustain engagement (McGregor). Ethical practice, therefore, requires careful calibration: motivations must be analyzed as social facts without prematurely legitimizing or delegitimizing the actors involved (Mirchandani, 2005). TSF-MLA provides a structured methodology to maintain this balance by systematically intersecting multiple lenses, ensuring that interpretations are grounded in empirical evidence and contextual specificity rather than personal or institutional biases.

A second ethical consideration lies in the distinction between understanding motivations and legitimizing actions. TSF-MLA emphasizes that analyzing the subjective meanings behind cyber incidents is not equivalent to endorsing those actions (Lund et al., 2025). Forensic analysts must navigate this tension consciously (Oatley et al., 2020). Understanding a cyberattack' s ideological grounding, emotional resonance, or historical antecedents provides insight into causation and potential intervention points (Stoddart, 2007; Thompson, 2023), yet such understanding does not entail moral approval. Ethical responsibility entails maintaining this boundary, ensuring that sociological interpretation does not collapse into advocacy or justification (Ramadhan, 2024). In practice, this requires transparent documentation of analytic assumptions, careful differentiation between description and evaluation, and constant reflection on how interpretive choices might influence decision-making, public perception, or policy outcomes.

Moreover, ethical responsibility extends to the social consequences of meaning-making itself. Analysts are not neutral observers; their reports, classifications, and narratives shape institutional responses, media framing, and legal judgments (Akter et al., 2021). The interpretive authority exercised in forensic intelligence has tangible effects on individuals, communities, and broader social systems (Galante et al., 2023). For example, categorizing a cyber event as "terrorism" versus "politically motivated protest" has profound implications for law enforcement responses, resource allocation, and community relations (Singh & Bajeje, 2025). TSF-MLA requires that analysts recognize this power and act with a heightened sense of ethical accountability. Reflexivity is essential, but it must be operationalized through explicit ethical protocols, peer review, and ongoing dialogue about the social impact of analytic outputs.

Another dimension of ethical responsibility concerns the avoidance of reductionism and over pathologizing. Traditional forensic paradigms often reduce actors to their instrumental behaviors, risk profiles, or demographic characteristics, inadvertently framing them as inherently deviant or dangerous (Oatley et al., 2020). TSF-MLA mitigates this risk by integrating structural, symbolic, historical, affective, and ideological lenses, emphasizing the co-production of behavior and meaning. This approach recognizes that actions emerge from the intersection of personal incentives, group dynamics, institutional constraints, and cultural narratives. Ethical analysis, therefore, entails resisting simplistic causal attributions and instead presenting a nuanced account that situates actors within broader social and technological contexts (Galyashina et al., 2025). This not only enhances analytic accuracy but also ensures that interventions are proportionate, culturally informed, and socially responsible.

Furthermore, ethical considerations in TSF-MLA extend to the responsible handling of sensitive information. Cyber forensic analysis often involves access to personal data, communication records, or ideological expressions (Galante et al., 2023). Analysts must navigate privacy concerns, data protection regulations, and the potential for misuse of information (Hussein Jassim, 2025; Oatley et al., 2020). TSF encourages a dual-lens approach even in data ethics: objective considerations involve compliance with legal and technical standards for data security, while subjective considerations require reflection on the social and cultural implications of data interpretation. Ethical practice demands that analysts consider both the immediate operational needs and the broader societal impact of how information is collected, interpreted, and disseminated.

Finally, TSF-MLA underscores the ethical imperative of anticipatory responsibility. Understanding cyber phenomena as sociotechnical events equips analysts with foresight, enabling them to anticipate potential escalation, social mobilization, or policy consequences. Ethical responsibility entails using this foresight not merely to protect organizational interests but to prevent harm, reduce social conflict, and promote socially constructive outcomes. For example, recognizing that a disinformation campaign is intertwined with historical grievances and ideological narratives allows policymakers to design interventions that address underlying causes rather than solely suppressing symptoms (Huda & Sony, 2024; Mollah et al., 2024). Ethical foresight, in this sense, is inseparable from analytic rigor: the more accurately analysts interpret dual-sided facts, the more responsibly they can anticipate consequences and guide interventions.

Subsequently, ethical considerations in TSF-MLA are both foundational and operational. Reflexive neutrality safeguards against bias, overinterpretation, and unintended legitimization of harmful actions. Distinguishing understanding from endorsement preserves analytic integrity and moral clarity. Recognizing the social consequences of interpretation ensures that analysts exercise power responsibly, avoiding over pathologizing and reductionism. Finally, anticipatory responsibility integrates ethical foresight into practice, aligning technical and sociological insights with broader societal well-being. By embedding these principles within the methodological core of TSF-MLA, cyber forensic intelligence achieves not only greater analytical sophistication but also ethical legitimacy, reinforcing the discipline's commitment to rigorous, responsible, and socially attuned practice in an increasingly complex digital environment.

8 SYNTHESIS AND CONCLUSION

This chapter has mapped a broad intellectual trajectory, moving from the limitations of conventional forensic paradigms to the theoretical, methodological, practical, and ethical contributions of the Theory of Two-Sided Fact and its operationalization through Multiple-Lens Analysis. TSF challenges dominant assumptions in cyber forensic intelligence that cyberattacks and online mobilizations can be fully explained through technical metrics or objective data alone. While existing approaches—whether rooted in machine learning, anomaly detection, or rational-choice models—are effective at identifying empirical patterns, they often overlook the symbolic, ideological, and affective forces that shape digital behavior. By emphasizing the inseparability of objective structures and subjective meanings, TSF establishes a meta-paradigmatic framework for understanding cyber phenomena as sociotechnical events that are simultaneously measurable, interpretable, historically situated, and ethically consequential.

The framework rests on several key principles. The principle of dual relationality posits that objective conditions and subjective interpretations are mutually constitutive, resisting reductionist binaries such as structure versus agency or fact versus meaning. Contextual relativity situates all events within their temporal, spatial, cultural, and historical settings, ensuring analytic sensitivity to specificity rather than universalization. TSF also redefines value neutrality, shifting it from detached observation to disciplined reflexivity, in which moral claims are treated as empirical phenomena rather than endpoints. Together, these principles provide a rigorous and adaptive epistemic foundation for navigating the complexities of contemporary digital life.

Operationalizing TSF through MLA translates these principles into a systematic yet flexible methodology. By employing structural, symbolic, historical, affective, and ideological lenses, analysts can examine cyber events across both objective and subjective dimensions. This layered analysis reveals how institutional structures, cultural narratives, emotional dynamics, historical legacies, and ideological framings interact to shape outcomes. Beyond descriptive richness, MLA generates actionable insights into causality, escalation risks, and intervention points. Case studies demonstrate how traditional forensic methods often misinterpret cyber incidents when divorced from sociotechnical and symbolic contexts—for instance, reframing hacktivist campaigns from being merely financially motivated to expressions of identity, ideology, and strategic agency.

Theoretical and practical contributions follow from this reconceptualization. TSF redirects attention from the question of "what happened" to the deeper inquiries of "why it happened" and "under what symbolic and contextual conditions." This enables richer typologies of threat actors, informs prevention and de-radicalization strategies, and supports ethically conscious analysis. By bridging technical forensics, behavioral psychology, and sociological theory, TSF creates a meta-paradigmatic orientation that fosters cross-disciplinary dialogue and integrative analytic practice.

Ethical considerations are central to this framework. Reflexive neutrality ensures analysts remain critically aware of their biases and interpretive authority, while distinguishing understanding from endorsement prevents analytical missteps that conflate explanation with justification. Moreover, by recognizing the social consequences of meaning-making, TSF-MLA underscores that forensic analysis has real-world effects on communities, policy, and justice. Ethical foresight is thus woven into analytic rigor, equipping practitioners to anticipate not only technical vulnerabilities but also the broader cultural and political implications of cyber events.

Synthesizing these dimensions, TSF-MLA emerges as a significant advancement in forensic intelligence. It reframes cyber incidents as emergent, co-constructed phenomena shaped by actors, institutions, and sociohistorical forces. It broadens forensic analysis from anomaly detection to comprehensive interpretation, while embedding ethical reflexivity to guard against bias and unintended harm. The framework provides a conceptual and methodological compass for navigating digital complexity, offering tools to anticipate threats, analyze their layered causes, and design proportionate and socially informed interventions.

Overall, TSF-MLA represents a transformative approach to cyber forensic intelligence. By integrating objective and subjective dimensions, contextual sensitivity, and ethical responsibility, it provides a holistic and reflexive toolkit for analyzing sociotechnical phenomena. This framework not only strengthens scientific rigor but also grounds forensic practice in social responsibility, ensuring analysts remain attuned to the human, cultural, and ideological dynamics that define the digital age. In an era of global interconnection, TSF-MLA charts a path toward predictive, contextually sophisticated, and ethically grounded forensic intelligence capable of illuminating the dual truths at the heart of contemporary cyber life.

9 EXECUTIVE SUMMARY

Cyber forensic investigations have traditionally focused on the technical side of cyber incidents—logs, malware, algorithms, anomalies, and digital traces. While these tools remain essential, they often overlook the human dimensions of cyber threats: emotions, ideology, symbolic expression, historical grievances, and cultural meaning. This chapter introduces the Theory of Two-Sided Fact (TSF) to address this gap. TSF argues that every cyber event has two inseparable sides: an objective/technical side and a subjective/human meaning side. Understanding both is necessary for accurate interpretation, attribution, and prevention.

To operationalize TSF, the chapter presents Multiple-Lens Analysis (MLA)—a practical method using five lenses: structural, symbolic, historical, affective, and ideological. These lenses help analysts move beyond "what happened" to understanding why it happened, how meaning was constructed, and under what evolving conditions an event unfolded. Through cases involving hacktivism, disinformation, and insider threats, the chapter demonstrates how TSF–MLA reveals deeper motives and patterns missed by traditional approaches. The framework enhances threat actor profiling, improves prevention and de-radicalization strategies, and promotes ethically responsible analysis grounded in reflexive neutrality. TSF–MLA ultimately reframes cyber forensics as a sociotechnical practice—one that integrates digital evidence with human meaning to produce richer, more anticipatory intelligence

10 REFERENCES

Aksoy, B., Carpenter, C. S., & Sansone, D. (2024). Understanding Labor Market Discrimination Against Transgender People: Evidence from a Double List Experiment and a Survey. *Management Science*, mnsc.2023.02567. Advance online publication. DOI: 10.1287/mnsc.2023.02567

Akter, S., McCarthy, G., Sajib, S., Michael, K., Dwivedi, Y. K., D'Ambra, J., & Shen, K. N. (2021). Algorithmic bias in data-driven innovation in the age of AI. *International Journal of Information Management*, *60*, 102387. https://doi.org/https://doi.org/10.1016/j.ijinfomgt.2021.102387. DOI: 10.1016/j.ijinfomgt.2021.102387

Ardichvili, A. (2022). The Impact of Artificial Intelligence on Expertise Development: Implications for HRD. *Advances in Developing Human Resources*, *24*(2), 78–98. DOI: 10.1177/15234223221077304

Arjun, E., & Singh, P. (2025). Future Directions in Digital Forensics and Cybersecurity. In *Securing the Digital Frontier* (pp. 333-365). https://doi.org/https://doi.org/10.1002/9781394268917.ch15

Bhambra, G. K. (2025). Empires, Famine, and the Significance of the Political Economy of Colonialism: From the Mughal Empire to British Colonial Rule in India. *Archives Européennes de Sociologie*, *66*(1), 1–24. DOI: 10.1017/S0003975625000050

Booth, W. J. (1994). On the idea of the moral economy. *The American Political Science Review*, *88*(3), 653–667. DOI: 10.2307/2944801

Bose, M. (2025). Bias in AI: A Societal Threat: A Look Beyond the Tech. In Pandey, R., Srivastava, N., Prasad, R., Prasad, J., & Garcia, M. B. (Eds.), *Open AI and Computational Intelligence for Society 5.0* (pp. 197–224). IGI Global., DOI: 10.4018/979-8-3693-4326-5.ch009

Buchanan, J. T., Henig, E. J., & Henig, M. I. (1998). Objectivity and subjectivity in thedecision making process. *Annals of Operations Research*, *80*(0), 333–345. DOI: 10.1023/A:1018980318183

Chen, H., & Yuan, Y. (2022). The impact of ignorance and bias on information security protection motivation: A case of e-waste handling. *Internet Research*, *33*(6), 2244–2275. DOI: 10.1108/INTR-04-2022-0238

Cole, B., Bradley, A. V., Willcock, S., Gardner, E., Allinson, E., Hagen-Zanker, A., Calo, A. J., Touza, J., Petrovskii, S., Yu, J., & Whelan, M. (2023). Using a multi-lens framework for landscape decisions. *People and Nature*, *5*(4), 1050–1071. https://doi.org/https://doi.org/10.1002/pan3.10474. DOI: 10.1002/pan3.10474

Di Nicola, A. (2022). Towards digital organized crime and digital sociology of organized crime. *Trends in Organized Crime*. Advance online publication. DOI: 10.1007/s12117-022-09457-y

Doody, S., Chen, V. T., & Goldstein, J. (2016). Varieties of Entrepreneurial Capitalism: The Culture of Entrepreneurship and Structural Inequalities of Work and Business Creation. *Sociology Compass*, *10*(10), 858–876. https://doi.org/https://doi.org/10.1111/soc4.12407. DOI: 10.1111/soc4.12407

Dunn Cavelty, M., Eriksen, C., & Scharte, B. (2023). Making cyber security more resilient: Adding social considerations to technological fixes. *Journal of Risk Research*, *26*(7), 801–814. DOI: 10.1080/13669877.2023.2208146

Fritts, M., & Cabrera, F. (2021). AI recruitment algorithms and the dehumanization problem. *Ethics and Information Technology*, *23*(4), 791–801. DOI: 10.1007/s10676-021-09615-w

Galante, N., Cotroneo, R., Furci, D., Lodetti, G., & Casali, M. B. (2023). Applications of artificial intelligence in forensic sciences: Current potential benefits, limitations and perspectives. *International Journal of Legal Medicine*, *137*(2), 445–458. DOI: 10.1007/s00414-022-02928-5

Galyashina, E. I., Komissarova, Y. V., & Solovieva, N. A. (2025). Forensic Methods for Detecting Criminal Attacks on Business Models of Industrial Companies Using Artificial Intelligence. In Inshakova, A., Matytsin, D., & Baltutite, I. (Eds.), *LegalTech and Legal-AI in Business: Major and Promising Sectors of Economy* (pp. 415–427). Springer Nature Switzerland., DOI: 10.1007/978-3-031-93474-2_36

Giddens, A. (1976). Classical Social Theory and the Origins of Modern Sociology. *American Journal of Sociology*, *81*(4), 703–729. DOI: 10.1086/226140

Gupta, S. (2025). Hacking the System. In *The Techno-Legal Dynamics of Cyber Crimes in Industry 5.0* (pp. 121-148). https://doi.org/https://doi.org/10.1002/9781394242177.ch7

Hanna, M. G., Pantanowitz, L., Jackson, B., Palmer, O., Visweswaran, S., Pantanowitz, J., Deebajah, M., & Rashidi, H. H. (2025). Ethical and Bias Considerations in Artificial Intelligence/Machine Learning. *Modern Pathology*, *38*(3), 100686. https://doi.org/https://doi.org/10.1016/j.modpat.2024.100686. DOI: 10.1016/j.modpat.2024.100686

Hasan, M. K., & Sony, M. M. A. A. M. (2022). Covid-19, Social Change, and Society 5.0. In *The Palgrave Handbook of Global Social Change* (pp. 1-19). Springer International Publishing. https://doi.org/DOI: 10.1007/978-3-030-87624-1_48-1

Häusermann, S., Kemmerling, A., & Rueda, D. (2020). How Labor Market Inequality Transforms Mass Politics. *Political Science Research and Methods*, *8*(2), 344–355. DOI: 10.1017/psrm.2018.64

Huda, M. N., & Sony, M. A. A. M. (2024). A Review of the MFS Regulatory Framework to Control IFF in Bangladesh. *Essays of Faculty of Law University of Pécs, Yearbook of [year] 1*(1), 105-124. https://doi.org/https://doi.org/10.15170/studia.2024.01.08

Hussein Jassim, A. (2025). A comprehensive study of Cybercrime and Digital Forensics through Machine Learning and AI. *Al-Rafidain Journal of Engineering Sciences*, *3*(1), 369–395. DOI: 10.61268/hff1pp49

Kim, Y., Hakak, S., & Ghorbani, A. (2024). Detecting Distributed Denial-of-Service (DDoS) attacks that generate false authentications on Electric Vehicle (EV) charging infrastructure. *Computers & Security*, *144*, 103989. https://doi.org/https://doi.org/10.1016/j.cose.2024.103989. DOI: 10.1016/j.cose.2024.103989

Lavorgna, A. (2023). Unpacking the political-criminal nexus in state-cybercrimes: A macro-level typology. *Trends in Organized Crime*. Advance online publication. DOI: 10.1007/s12117-023-09486-1

Letherby, G., Williams, M., & Scott, J. (2012). *Objectivity and Subjectivity in Social Research*. SAGE Publications Ltd. https://digital.casalini.it/9781446271414

Liu, R., Shi, J., Chen, X., & Lu, C. (2024). Network anomaly detection and security defense technology based on machine learning: A review. *Computers & Electrical Engineering*, *119*, 109581. https://doi.org/https://doi.org/10.1016/j.compeleceng.2024.109581. DOI: 10.1016/j.compeleceng.2024.109581

Lund, B., Orhan, Z., Mannuru, N. R., Bevara, R. V. K., Porter, B., Vinaih, M. K., & Bhaskara, P. (2025). Standards, frameworks, and legislation for artificial intelligence (AI) transparency. *AI and Ethics*, *5*(4), 3639–3655. Advance online publication. DOI: 10.1007/s43681-025-00661-4

McGregor, C. Learning to lack? Towards a psychoanalytic interpretation of climate anxiety as a political emotion in education for climate justice. *Environmental Education Research*, 1-25. https://doi.org/DOI: 10.1080/13504622.2025.2543005

Mirchandani, R. (2005). Postmodernism and Sociology: From the Epistemological to the Empirical. *Sociological Theory*, *23*(1), 86–115. https://doi.org/https://doi.org/10.1111/j.0735-2751.2005.00244.x. DOI: 10.1111/j.0735-2751.2005.00244.x

Mollah, M. A., Rana, M., Amin, M. B., Sony, M. M. A. A. M., Rahaman, M. A., & Fenyves, V. (2024). Examining the Role of AI-Augmented HRM for Sustainable Performance: Key Determinants for Digital Culture and Organizational Strategy. *Sustainability (Basel)*, *16*(24), 10843. DOI: 10.3390/su162410843

Mushtaq, S., & Shah, M. (2025). Threats to the Digital Ecosystem: Can Information Security Management Frameworks, Guided by Criminological Literature, Effectively Prevent Cybercrime and Protect Public Data? *Computers*, *14*(6), 219. https://www.mdpi.com/2073-431X/14/6/219. DOI: 10.3390/computers14060219

O'Boyle, N. (2022). Actors: An Introduction to Symbolic Interactionism. In O'Boyle, N. (Ed.), *Communication Theory for Humans: Communicators in a Mediated World* (pp. 27–50). Springer International Publishing., DOI: 10.1007/978-3-031-02450-4_2

Oatley, G., Chapman, B., & Speers, J. (2020). Forensic intelligence and the analytical process. *Wiley Interdisciplinary Reviews. Data Mining and Knowledge Discovery*, *10*(3), e1354. https://doi.org/https://doi.org/10.1002/widm.1354. DOI: 10.1002/widm.1354

Rafanell, I. (2013). Micro-situational Foundations of Social Structure: An Interactionist Exploration of Affective Sanctioning. *Journal for the Theory of Social Behaviour*, *43*(2), 181–204. https://doi.org/https://doi.org/10.1111/jtsb.12012. DOI: 10.1111/jtsb.12012

Rai, M., Tyagi, N., Tripathi, P., Kumar, N., & Kumari, P. (2023). Advancement in agricultural techniques with the introduction of Artificial Intelligence and Image Processing. In *Smart Village Infrastructure and Sustainable Rural Communities* (pp. 47–68). IGI Global., https://doi.org/https://doi.org/10.4018/978-1-6684-6418-2.ch006 DOI: 10.4018/978-1-6684-6418-2.ch004

Ramadhan, S. (2024). Harnessing machine learning for money laundering detection: A criminological theory-centric approach. *Journal of Money Laundering Control*, *28*(1), 184–201. DOI: 10.1108/JMLC-04-2024-0083

Romagna, M., & Leukfeldt, R. E. (2024). Becoming a hacktivist. Examining the motivations and the processes that prompt an individual to engage in hacktivism. *Journal of Crime and Justice*, *47*(4), 511–529. DOI: 10.1080/0735648X.2023.2216189

Rovira-Sancho, G. (2023). Activism and affective labor for digital direct action: The Mexican #MeToo campaign. *Social Movement Studies*, *22*(2), 145–162. DOI: 10.1080/14742837.2021.2010530

Sammoud, A., Hamdi, O., Chalouf, M.-A., & Montavont, N. (2022). The Contributions of Biometrics and Artificial Intelligence in Securing the IoT. In *Intelligent Security Management and Control in the IoT* (pp. 197-221). https://doi.org/https://doi.org/10.1002/9781394156030.ch8

Sela, A., Neter, O., Lohr, V., Cihelka, P., Wang, F., Zwilling, M., Phillip Sabou, J., & Ulman, M. (2025). Signals of propaganda—Detecting and estimating political influences in information spread in social networks. *PLoS One*, *20*(1), e0309688. DOI: 10.1371/journal.pone.0309688

Singh, N. K., & Bajeje, S. (2025, 2025//). Hacktivism or Cyber Warfare? Decoding the Motivations Behind Cyber Attacks Targeting Israel. Artificial Intelligence Based Smart and Secured Applications, Cham.

Siwakoti, Y. R., Bhurtel, M., Rawat, D. B., Oest, A., & Johnson, R. (2024). Your IP Camera Can Be Abused for Payments: A Study of IoT Exploitation for Financial Services Leveraging Shodan and Criminal Infrastructures. *IEEE Transactions on Consumer Electronics*, *70*(4), 7562–7573. DOI: 10.1109/TCE.2024.3482708

Sony, M. M. A. A. M. (2023). A review of online business regulatory framework to reduce IFF in Bangladesh. *Essays of Faculty of Law University of Pécs, Yearbook of [year], 1*(1), 167-182. https://doi.org/https://doi.org/10.15170/studia.2023.01.10

Sony, M. M. A. A. M., Amin, M. B., Ashraf, A., Islam, K. M. A., Debnath, N. C., & Debnath, G. C. (2025). Bias in AI-driven HRM systems: Investigating discrimination risks embedded in AI recruitment tools and HR analytics. *Social Sciences & Humanities Open*, *12*, 102082. https://doi.org/https://doi.org/10.1016/j.ssaho.2025.102082. DOI: 10.1016/j.ssaho.2025.102082

Stibbe, D., Ruiter, S., Steenbeek, W., & Moneva, A. (2025). Rational Choice on a Hacker Forum: The Effect of Risk and Reward Cues on Target Selection for Account Hijacking. *Deviant Behavior*, 1-22. https://doi.org/DOI: 10.1080/01639625.2025.2459699

Stoddart, M. C. J. (2007). Ideology, Hegemony, Discourse: A Critical Review of Theories of Knowledge and Power. *Social Thought & Research*, *28*, 191–225. https://www.jstor.org/stable/23252126. DOI: 10.17161/STR.1808.5226

Tavakkoli, N., Çetin, O., Ekmekcioglu, E., & Savaş, E. (2025). From frontlines to online: Examining target preferences in the Russia–Ukraine conflict. *International Journal of Information Security*, *24*(1), 64. DOI: 10.1007/s10207-025-00981-w

Thompson, J. B. (2023). *Studies in the Theory of Ideology 4. The Theory of Structuration: An Assessment of the Contribution of Anthony Giddens*. University of California Press., https://doi.org/doi:10.1525/9780520312234-006

Tyagi, A. K., & Kumari, S. (2024). *Richa*. Artificial Intelligence-Based Cyber Security and Digital Forensics. In Artificial Intelligence-Enabled Digital Twin for Smart Manufacturing., https://doi.org/https://doi.org/10.1002/9781394303601.ch18

Wörsdörfer, M. (2024). Mitigating the adverse effects of AI with the European Union's artificial intelligence act: Hype or hope? *Global Business and Organizational Excellence*, *43*(3), 106–126. https://doi.org/https://doi.org/10.1002/joe.22238. DOI: 10.1002/joe.22238

Yar, M., & Steinmetz, K. F. (2023). *Cybercrime and Society*. SAGE Publications Ltd. https://digital.casalini.it/9781529615524

Yolles, M. (2024). Diagnosing Market Capitalism: A Metacybernetic View. *Systems*, *12*(9), 361. DOI: 10.3390/systems12090361

Chapter 2
Fuzzy Soft Set-Based Decision Framework for Human-Centric Cyber Threat Analysis

Ajoy Kanti Das
http://orcid.org/0000-0002-9326-1677
Tripura University, India

Ebenezer Aquisman Asare
http://orcid.org/0000-0003-1185-1479
Northeastern University, USA

Samia Daas
University of Batna 2, Algeria

Iqbal M. Batiha
Al Zaytoonah University of Jordan, Jordan

Adam Sandow Saani
http://orcid.org/0009-0007-4286-6055
Tamale Technical University, Ghana

Nageswara Rao Lakkimsetty
http://orcid.org/0009-0006-0146-8889
American University of Ras Al Khaimah, UAE

Abdollah Arasteh
Babol Noshirvani University of Technology, Iran

ABSTRACT

People are just as important to cybersecurity as gadgets. Attacks frequently result from human error or manipulation. Common examples include insider misuse, phishing, and weak passwords. These dangers highlight the necessity of researching human behavior in relation to cyberthreats. Users are only marked as "safe" or "unsafe" in older models. However, actual conduct frequently lies in the middle of these two extremes. To deal with such situations, this chapter employs a fuzzy soft set (FSS) structure. Partial risk is represented using fuzzy sets, such as a user who is "moderately risky." Different facets of user behavior and actions are described

DOI: 10.4018/979-8-3373-4898-8.ch002

by soft sets. When combined, FSSs provide a versatile approach to researching Human-Centric Cyber Threats (HCCT). This chapter provides a basic explanation of fuzzy sets, soft sets, and ." It demonstrates how they aid in the clear analysis of cyber risks. A methodical framework for making decisions is created. A fuzzy soft decision matrix is used to store user behaviors. Low, medium, and high-risk scores are created by combining these numbers. Phishing, insider risks, and sloppy passwords are examples of case studies. Every example demonstrates how FSSs produce more realistic and understandable outcomes. Additionally, an algorithm is presented and its performance is compared in this chapter. For specialists, these are straightforward and transparent, in contrast to machine learning (ML) black boxes. A discussion of the framework's advantages concludes the chapter. It can scale effectively, deal with unpredictability, and change with the times. However, it relies on expert-assigned weights and the quality of the data. In the future, ML for adaptive weights will be added. Real-time cyber monitoring systems can also make advantage of it. It will increase security and transparency when used with explainable AI and blockchain.

1. INTRODUCTION

Both people and technology are essential to the cyber world. The majority of attacks are the result of human error rather than sophisticated hacking. This issue is demonstrated by phishing, weak passwords, and insider attacks. Older systems simply consider technology and disregard human behavior. Attackers now take advantage of human emotions and behaviors (Ali et al., 2025). We require models that analyze human behavior and deal with ambiguity. Partial truths are difficult for classical frameworks like logic and probability to grasp. They only categorize users as "safe" or "unsafe," which is overly strict. In practice, user behavior frequently falls in the middle between these two extremes. This type of uncertainty can be modeled using fuzzy and soft set theories. A fuzzy soft set (FSS) framework for improved cyber risk analysis is formed by their combination. Clear and adaptable human-centered security decisions are supported by this concept.

Models based on FSSs aid in the management of intricate and unpredictable cyber hazards. They use soft sets and fuzzy logic to analyze ambiguous data and human behavior. These models provide more robust and lucid results for cybersecurity choices. Recent research employs sophisticated MCDM techniques with bipolar and FSS. Additionally, they use specialized aggregation algorithms to include expert viewpoints into risk assessments. These models enhance the precision and comprehension of HCCT assessment (Hussain et al., 2024; Ali and Yang, 2024; Zhang et al., 2020).

The human element, which is frequently the weakest link in cybersecurity, is the emphasis of fuzzy-based frameworks (Gozon et al., 2021). By incorporating organizational and individual behaviors, they forecast risk. Flexible decision-making is enhanced by new models such as multi-fuzzy N-soft sets (Fatimah and Alcantud, 2021; Korkmaz et al., 2024). These models aid in identifying social media threats and cyberbullying. For real-time intrusion detection, explainable fuzzy systems offer unambiguous and comprehensible rules (Al-Qudah, 2024; Gu et al., 2024). Flexible and expert-based risk analysis is made possible by neutrosophic fuzzy soft expert models. Additionally, fuzzy approaches outperform standard models in capturing shifting risk trends (Korystin et al., 2024).

Zadeh's fuzzy set theory from 1965 marked the beginning of the study of fuzzy soft sets. It made it possible for truth to exist on a spectrum rather than a binary. An early customizable approach for FSS-based decision-making was presented by Feng et al. (2010). Later, Shagari and Azam (2020) created an understandable, step-by-step algorithm for practical application. Wen (2023) and Dey et al. (2020) added hesitant and weighted hesitant FSS. Expert hesitancy and varying opinion weights in decision-making are handled by these models. For further flexibility, Al-Shami, Alcantud, and Mhemdi (2023) introduced the $(a,)$- FSS model. The hypothesis was subsequently developed by Alsager and Alharbi (2024) using cubic type-2 FSS. When taken as a whole, these studies created a solid foundation for managing ambiguity in decision-making.

Fuzzy N-soft expert sets were developed by Ali and Akram (2020) to integrate the opinions of numerous experts. This concept was further upon by Akram et al. (2023) utilizing Pythagorean fuzzy N-soft sets. Both confidence and skepticism in expert opinions are captured by their model. T-spherical fuzzy softrough sets were suggested by Akram and Martino (2022) for more in-depth uncertainty analysis. Fermatean fuzzy bipolar soft sets were created by Ali and Ansari (2021) to manage dual-sided data. Intuitionistic fuzzy hypersoft expert sets for difficult decision problems were introduced by Ihsan et al. in 2023. Complex, bipolar complex, and image fuzzy soft models were applied to networks and systems by Jan et al. (2023a). In order to facilitate expert judgment, Li et al. (2024) concentrated on human-centered fuzzy Best–Worst techniques. The goal of all these investigations is to develop models that are both strong and easy to use and comprehend.

These days, fuzzy logic and FSSs are crucial to cybersecurity. Fuzzy inference was employed by Gusmão et al. (2018) and Alali et al. (2018) to evaluate information system hazards. Compared to straightforward yes/no techniques, their models produced more accurate results. In order to improve management, Božanić et al. (2023) used fuzzy reasoning to rank security concerns. A fuzzy blockchain model was developed by Yazdinejad et al. (2023) to defend IoT systems from intrusions. Ge et al. (2023) investigated cyber-threat behavior using explainable models. Almutairi (2023) used deep learning to identify attacks instantly. Strong validation is required, as demonstrated by the unreliable work that Hang et al. (2022) published and then withdrew. For cyber risk, Ali, Razzaq, and Manahil (2025) developed bipolar complicated intuitionistic fuzzy soft models. These studies demonstrate how sophisticated fuzzy models are increasingly being used in cybersecurity analysis.

Tripathi et al. (2023) talked about how smart agriculture is supported by ML. They demonstrated how farmers may forecast crop health and productivity using data-driven models. Rai et al. (2023) described how image processing and artificial intelligence enhance farming. They introduced new instruments that identify crop conditions and soil quality. Beemkumar et al. (2023) concentrated on deep learning and the Internet of Things for activity recognition. They examined smart gadgets using CNNs and time series data. Vasani et al. (2024) investigated ML for predicting psychology and emotion recognition. They explained how digital data can be used by AI systems to interpret human emotions.

In the context of Industry 5.0, Arora et al. (2024) investigated emotional intelligence. Singh et al. (2024) talked about Industry 5.0 systems and emotional intelligence. Advances in face expression identification were presented by Singh, Pandey, Rai, and Saxena (2024). To effectively identify emotions, they employed deep learning algorithms. Tripathi et al. (2024) explored deep learning in healthcare under Industry 5.0. They described how AI helps with medical decision-making and patient care.

FSSs are utilized in numerous intricate systems outside of cybersecurity. Jan et al. (2023b) used complicated fuzzy soft data to study digital systems and networks. Fuzzy soft decision-making was used in smart car systems by Li and Tang (2025). These studies demonstrate the versatility and applicability of fuzzy soft approaches across numerous domains.

The theoretical backbone of this study is rooted in FS theory (Zadeh, 1965), SS theory (Molodtsov, 1999), and their fusion into FSSs (Maji et al., 2001), which are well-suited for modeling complex, uncertain, and MCDM problems in digital security assessments and cyber risk evaluation. Extensions such as intuitionistic FSs (Atanassov, 1986), neutrosophic sets (Smarandache, 2005), and FSMSs further enhance decision models under uncertainty, making them highly relevant to integrating health technologies, infrastructure design, and community values in EC systems. For MCDM, Das and Granados (2022a) created a fuzzy parameterized intuitionistic fuzzy soft multiset theory. Their research on FP-intuitionistic multi-fuzzy N-soft sets enhanced MCDM models' adaptability (Das and Granados, 2022b). To further this study, they later presented IFP-intuitionistic multi-fuzzy N-soft sets (Das and Granados, 2023a). Weighted fuzzy soft multisets were suggested by Das (2018) as a novel MCDM tool. Previously, preference fuzzy rough relations and intuitionistic fuzzy rough relations were studied by Das (2016) and Das & Granados (2023b).

Their collaborative study presented a fuzzy soft group MCDM technique in 2021. It employed weighted average ratings to enhance MCDM theory and practical analysis (Das and Granados, 2021). New operations on FSSs were proposed by Das et al. (2022). They demonstrated how these operations aid in the efficient resolution of MCDM issues. Weighted hesitant bipolar-valued FSSs were later introduced by Das et al. (2023). These sets provide a more thorough method of contrasting and assessing several choices. A fuzzy MCDM model was also created by Das et al. (2025b) to investigate how human activity affects the water quality of urban rivers. An important addition to environmental MCDM research is this work. It assessed the Gomati and Haora Rivers' contamination levels. Water contamination was also graded using FSS models and weighted hesitant FSS (Das et al., 2024a; 2024b; 2025a). Mukherjee and Das's work is also used in the development of fuzzy soft multi-set theories in MCDM (2016a). In their 2015 work, interval-valued intuitionistic fuzzy soft multi-sets were applied to practical MCDM situations (Mukherjee and Das, 2015b). Additionally, they investigated the application of intuitionistic FSSs with interval values in investment decision-making (Mukherjee and Das, 2015a).

In 2022, they also developed Einstein operations on fuzzy soft multisets and MCDM (Mukherjee & Das, 2022). In their 2023 book, they go into greater detail about the theoretical underpinnings and practical applications (Mukherjee & Das, 2023). Mukherjee & Das focus even further on the topological and relational paradigm of fuzzy and rough sets (2015c; 2016b). Granados et al. (2022) introduced the continuous neutrosophic distributions with neutrosophic parameters that give a possibility to represent the uncertainty probabilistically. Granados et al. (2023) proposed the weighted neutrosophic soft multiset approach, which Das et al. (2025c) have recently thoroughly examined. Das et al. (2025d) recently introduced the fuzzy logic decision-support system to streamline the concept of an adaptive inventory management system within the retailing context. Das et al. (2025e) have developed a new weighted hypersoft expert system MCDM paradigm. They provide helpful strategies on how to deal with uncertainty, make decisions more precisely, and address difficult real-life problems (Das et al., 2025f). Das et al. (2025g) investigated how urban river water is impacted by human activity. Fuzzy logic applications in multicultural marketing were investigated by Das et al. (2026a). Das et al. (2026b) examined smart luxury goods co-branding in a different study. They made decisions using a neutrosophic multi-criteria method. Neutrosophic sets were also used in environmental recovery by Das et al. (2026c). A generalized interval-valued neutrosophic rough soft set structure was presented by Mukherjee et al. (2026). Together, these works have strengthened the theoretical foundation and practical usefulness of FSS theory in complex domains like digital security assessments and cyber risk evaluation.

This chapter aims to:

- Introduce the mathematical foundations of fuzzy sets, soft sets, and FSSs in simple terms.
- Develop a decision framework for analyzing HCCT.
- Present mathematical models and algorithms for risk evaluation.
- Provide illustrative case studies to show practical implementation.
- Compare the FSS-based framework with other decision-making methods.
- Discuss applications in cyber forensics and future research directions.

2. HCCT LANDSCAPE

2.1 Cybersecurity Shifts: From Technical To Human Threats

Earlier generations of cybersecurity primarily revolved around technical defenses such as firewalls, intrusion detection systems, and malware scanners. While these remain essential, attackers increasingly bypass them by targeting human weaknesses.

- Phishing Attacks: Over 80% of breaches involve phishing, where individuals are deceived into revealing credentials.
- Insider Threats: Disgruntled employees or careless insiders cause unintentional or malicious breaches.
- Password Practices: Weak, reused, or default passwords remain a leading vulnerability.
- Social Engineering: Attackers exploit psychological manipulation to gain trust or access.

These threats demonstrate gradual behaviors rather than binary states. A user might be partially vigilant against phishing but still vulnerable to sophisticated spear-phishing.

2.2 Uncertainty In Human-Centric Threat Intelligence

The uncertainty challenge arises because:

- Human behavior is context-dependent (a user may act securely at work but insecurely at home).
- Threat data is often incomplete (e.g., not all user activities are logged).
- Risk levels are subjective (security analysts may disagree on classifications).

Traditional crisp models fail in this domain. For example:

- Crisp classification: "User is high-risk (1)" or "low-risk (0)."

- Reality: "User is moderately risky (0.6)."

Thus, we require mathematical models that can represent degrees of risk. This motivates the use of FSS theory.

2.3 Psychological And Cognitive Factors In Hccts

Cyberthreats rely on human behavior and thought. People make mistakes because of their habits, emotions, or stress. These human factors are incorporated into our fuzzy soft model in a straightforward mathematical way.

2.3.1. Curiosity and Urgency

When people are in a hurry or are curious, they click on phony links. The phishing susceptibility value in our model illustrates this. More danger and an emotional reaction are associated with higher values.

2.3.2. Overconfidence

Some people believe they are always safe when using the internet. They are more likely to make mistakes because of this mindset. This shows up as a low awareness score in the model.

2.3.3. A habit

Passwords are reused because they seem simple and secure. This behavior is a typical risk factor. The fuzzy value for password weakness is increased.

2.3.4. Anxiety

Stress causes people to act without thorough thought. Users disregard warnings while they are preoccupied. High levels of stress raise the attention risk value in our model.

2.3.5. Disengagement from Morality

Some insiders defend destructive behavior. They don't think rules matter to them. This is captured by an ethical conduct parameter in the model.

2.3.6. Relation to the Model

The fuzzy membership value is altered by each human aspect. We blend them using basic weights. One final risk score is then determined by the model.

$$R(u_i) = \sum \omega_j \times \mu(u_i, a_j)$$

This section makes a connection between math and human behavior. It illustrates how habits and feelings impact cyber risk. Our methodology aids in the explanation and mitigation of human mistake in cyberthreats.

3. MATHEMATICAL PRELIMINARIES

3.1 Fuzzy Sets

An element is either a part of a set or it is not in classical set theory. For instance, a user may or may not be reckless. This binary concept is too rigid to comprehend how people behave online. People frequently have conflicting or unclear motives and behaviors. Zadeh (1965) suggested fuzzy sets as a solution. Rather than having rigid borders, fuzzy sets permit partial membership. They are helpful for characterizing partially dangerous behaviors in HCCT assessments.

3.1.1 Mathematical Definition

A fuzzy set F in a universe of discourse U is defined as:

$$F = \{(x, \mathbf{u}_F(x)) \mid x \in U\}$$

where:

- U: Universe of elements (e.g., set of users, network events, or behaviors).
- $x \in U$: An individual element (such as a user or activity).
- $\mathbf{u}_F(x) \in [0, 1]$: The membership function assigns each element a value between 0 and 1, representing the degree of belongingness to the fuzzy set F.

If $\mathbf{u}_F(x) = 0$, the element does not belong to the set.
If $\mathbf{u}_F(x) = 1$, the element fully belongs to the set.
If $0 < \mathbf{u}_F(x) < 1$, the element partially belongs to the set.

This formula measures how much a user's behavior fits a certain risk pattern. A value close to 1 means strong association (high risk), while 0 means no association.

3.1.2 Example With Human-Centric Cybersecurity

Let the universe be U = {Alice, Bob, Carol}. Suppose the fuzzy set F represents "careless users."

F = {(Alice, 0.2), (Bob, 0.8), (Carol, 0.5)}

- Alice has a 0.2 membership degree in being careless → She is mostly careful.
- Bob has 0.8 → He is highly careless.
- Carol has 0.5 → She is moderately careless.

This representation allows us to quantify human behavior, which is often ambiguous, into analyzable numbers.

3.1.3 Membership Functions

The membership function $\mathbf{u}_{\mathbf{F}}(x)$ is the backbone of fuzzy sets. It maps elements to values in [0,1]. In cybersecurity contexts, it can be derived from:

- User activity logs (e.g., number of failed logins).
- Expert judgment (security experts assigning risk scores).
- Statistical data (probabilities mapped to fuzzy values).

Common membership functions

- Triangular: Captures gradual belonging with a peak.
- Trapezoidal: Allows a flat "high-risk" region.
- Gaussian: Smooth representation of uncertainty.

3.1.4 Classical vs. Fuzzy Sets in Cybersecurity

Table 1 highlights the key differences between classical sets and fuzzy sets in addressing uncertainty within cybersecurity.

Table 1. Comparison of classical sets and fuzzy sets in the cybersecurity context

Aspect	Classical Set	Fuzzy Set
Belonging	User is either careless or not careless	User can be partially careless
Representation	Binary (0 or 1)	Continuous [0, 1]
Handling Uncertainty	Not possible	Naturally handled
Example	Bob = careless (1), Alice = not careless (0)	Bob = 0.8, Alice = 0.2

This flexibility makes fuzzy sets particularly suitable for HCCT intelligence, where behaviors often exist on a spectrum rather than extremes.

3.1.5 Operations On Fuzzy Sets

Just like classical sets, we can perform operations, but in fuzzy logic, they are generalized.

- Union (OR):

$$\mathbf{u}_{F \cup G}(x) = max(\mathbf{u}_F(x), \mathbf{u}_G(x))$$

- Intersection (AND):

$$\mathbf{u}_{F \cap G}(x) = min(\mathbf{u}_F(x), \mathbf{u}_G(x))$$

- Complement (NOT):

$$\mathbf{u}_{F^c}(x) = 1 - \mathbf{u}_F(x)$$

Example in Human Threat Analysis

- F: careless users.
- G: socially influenced users (those who fall for phishing).

Suppose:

$$F = \{(Alice, 0.2), (Bob, 0.8), (Carol, 0.5)\}$$

G = {(Alice, 0.6), (Bob, 0.4), (Carol, 0.9)}

- Union ($F \cup G$): Degree of being either careless or socially influenced.

$$F \cup G = \{(Alice, 0.6), (Bob, 0.8), (Carol, 0.9)\}$$

- Intersection ($F \cap G$): Degree of being both careless and socially influenced.

$$F \cap G = \{(Alice, 0.2), (Bob, 0.4), (Carol, 0.5)\}$$

- Complement (F^c): Degree of being careful.

$$F^c = \{(Alice, 0.8), (Bob, 0.2), (Carol, 0.5)\}$$

3.1.6 Advantages In The Hcct Context

- Captures Human Uncertainty: HCCTs often arise from partially risky behaviors.
- Integrates Expert Knowledge: Security analysts can define membership functions based on intuition.
- Quantifies Non-Binary States: A user can be moderately suspicious, not just innocent or guilty.
- Supports Hybrid Models: Can be combined with soft sets, neural networks, or Bayesian analysis.

3.2 Soft Sets

Soft set theory was developed by Molodtsov (1999) to address decision-making uncertainty. Soft sets do not require precise membership definitions, in contrast to classical sets. They depict ambiguous or imprecise data by associating parameters with subsets of a universe. Soft sets are helpful in HCCT research because of their adaptability. They aid in simulating ambiguous human behavior, user decisions, and attack trends.

Definition:

Let:

- U be a universal set, called the universe of discourse (e.g., set of all users in a system).
- A be a set of parameters (e.g., behaviors, activities, or attributes related to security).
- F be a mapping $F{:}A \rightarrow P(U)$, where $P(U)$ is the power set of U.

Then, a soft set over U is defined as:

$$(F,A) = \{(a, F(a)) \mid a \in A\}$$

Here, for each parameter $a \in A, F(a) \subseteq U$ represents the subset of elements from the universe that are related to the parameter a.

Example 1: User-Centric Cybersecurity Behavior

- Universe (Users):

$$U = \{Alice, Bob, Carol\}$$

- Parameter Set:

$$A = \{a_1, a_2\}$$

where:

- a_1= "uses strong passwords,"
- a_2= "falls for phishing emails."
- Mapping F:

$$F(a_1) = \{Alice, Carol\}, F(a_2) = \{Bob\}$$

Thus, the soft set is:

$$(F,A) = \{(a_1, \{Alice, Carol\}), (a_2, \{Bob\})\}$$

Interpretation:

- Alice and Carol use strong passwords.
- Bob is the one who falls for phishing emails.
- This captures the relationship between users and security-related parameters without forcing binary (yes/no) classification.

Properties of Soft Sets

- Parameter-Driven Representation:

Each soft set depends on a chosen parameter set. Different parameter sets can yield different soft sets for the same universe.

- Partial Information Handling:

Not all parameters need to be considered. Missing parameters simply do not appear in the soft set.

- Non-Uniqueness:

Two different soft sets may represent the same universe, but with different parameter perspectives.

Operations on Soft Sets:

Operations extend soft sets into a decision-making framework. For two soft sets (F, A) and (G, B) over the same universe U:

- Intersection:

$$(F,A) \cap (G,B) = (H,A \cap B)$$

where $(a) = F(a) \cap G(a)$, for all$a \in A \cap B$.
Meaning: Identifies users that satisfy both conditions.

- Union:

$$(F,A) \cup (G,B) = (K,A \cup B)$$

where

$$K(a) = \begin{cases} F(a), a \in A \setminus B \\ G(a), a \in B \setminus A \\ F(a) \cup G(a), a \in A \cap B \end{cases}$$

Meaning: Combines user behaviors across parameter sets.

- Complement:

For a soft set (F,A), the complement is defined as:

$$(F,A)^c = (F^c,A)$$

where $F^c(a) = U \setminus F(a)$.
Meaning: Identifies users not satisfying the given parameter.

Example 2: Threat Behavior Analysis

- Universe of Users:

$$U = \{Alice, Bob, Carol, David\}$$

- Parameters:

$$A = \{a_1, a_2, a_3\}$$

where:

- a_1= "uses public Wi-Fi for banking,"
- a_2= "ignores software updates,"
- a_3= "clicks suspicious links."
- Mapping F:

$$F(a_1) = \{Bob, Carol\}, F(a_2) = \{Alice, Bob\}, F(a_3) = \{David\}$$

So, the soft set is:

$$(F,A) = \{(a_1, \{Bob, Carol\}), (a_2, \{Alice, Bob\}), (a_3, \{David\})\}$$

Remark:

- Bob appears in both a_1 and a_2, suggesting he is highly vulnerable.
- Carol uses public Wi-Fi unsafely.
- Alice delays updates but avoids phishing.
- David falls for suspicious links.

Advantages of Soft Sets in HCCT Analysis

- Handles ambiguity: Not every user fits strictly into “safe” or “unsafe.”
- Parameter-based modeling: Analysts can choose relevant behavioral parameters for different contexts.

- Customizable: Parameters can be added or removed dynamically.
- Decision-friendly: By applying operations, one can filter out risky users, identify overlaps in vulnerabilities, and prioritize threats.

3.3 FSSs

Fuzzy set concepts are used in the notion of FSSs to extend soft sets. Fuzzy sets utilize membership degrees, whereas soft sets use parameters to manage ambiguity. Both concepts are combined to manage several unknown qualities. A fuzzy degree of belonging exists for each attribute in a FSS.

Formally, let:

- U = universe of discourse (a set of objects under consideration).
- $A \subseteq E$ = a subset of parameters (where E is the full set of attributes or descriptors).
- F = a fuzzy set-valued mapping $F{:}A \rightarrow F(U)$,where $F(U)$ denotes the family of fuzzy subsets of U.

Thus, a FSS over U is written as:

$$(F,A) = \{(a, F(a)) \mid a \in A\}, where F(a) = \left\{(x, u_a(x)) \mid x \in U\right\}.$$

Here:

- $u_a(x) \in [0, 1]$ is the membership value showing the degree to which object x satisfies the parameter a.
- A higher value of $u_a(x)$ indicates a stronger association, while values close to 0 indicate a weak or negligible association.

Intuitive Meaning

- In soft sets, an element either belongs to a parameter (YES/NO).
- In fuzzy sets, an element belongs to a set partially (0 to 1).
- In FSSs, both are combined: each parameter describes a fuzzy classification of the objects.

This is extremely useful in HCCT analysis, because human behavior and vulnerabilities are rarely binary — people are not just "vulnerable" or "not vulnerable," but somewhere in between.

Example 1: Phishing Susceptibility

Suppose we analyze employees in a company for susceptibility to phishing attacks.

- Universe of discourse:

$U = \{Alice, Bob, Carol\}$

Parameter set:

$A = \{a_1 = \text{"phishingsusceptibility"}\}$

- Fuzzy membership function:

$F(a_1) = \{(Alice, 0.3), (Bob, 0.9), (Carol, 0.6)\}$

Remark:

- Alice has low vulnerability (0.3),
- Bob is highly vulnerable (0.9),
- Carol is moderately vulnerable (0.6).

Thus, the FSS:

$(F,A) = \{(a_1, \{(Alice, 0.3), (Bob, 0.9), (Carol, 0.6)\})\}.$

Example 2: Multi-Parameter Threat Analysis
Now suppose we extend the model to multiple human-centric cyber risk parameters:

- Parameters:

$A = \{a_1 = \text{"phishingsusceptibility"}, a_2 = \text{"passwordhygiene"}, a_3 = \text{"malwarea-wareness"}\}$

- Fuzzy mappings:

$F(a_1) = \{(Alice, 0.3), (Bob, 0.9), (Carol, 0.6)\}$

$F(a_2) = \{(Alice, 0.8), (Bob, 0.2), (Carol, 0.7)\}$

$F(a_3) = \{(Alice, 0.5), (Bob, 0.4), (Carol, 0.9)\}$

Interpretation:

- Bob is highly vulnerable to phishing (0.9) but maintains relatively poor password hygiene (0.2).
- Alice has strong password hygiene (0.8) but moderate malware awareness (0.50.50.5).
- Carol shows balanced vulnerabilities but is most aware of malware (0.90.90.9).

The FSS becomes:

$$(F,A) = \{(a_1, F(a_1)),\ (a_2, F(a_2)),\ (a_3, F(a_3))\}.$$

Table 2. Tabular Representation

Employee	Phishing (a_1)	Password Hygiene (a_2)	Malware Awareness (a_3)
Alice	0.3	0.8	0.5
Bob	0.9	0.2	0.4
Carol	0.6	0.7	0.9

This representation is compact, intuitive, and can be extended to hundreds of users and parameters in HCCT analysis.

Operations on FSSs

As fuzzy sets have operations (union, intersection, complement), FSSs support similar operations but parameter-wise.

- Union:

$$(F,A) \cup (G,B) = (H, A \cup B)$$

where

$$H(a)(x) = max(F(a)(x), G(a)(x)).$$

- Intersection:

$$(F,A) \cap (G,B) = (H, A \cap B)$$

where

$H(a)(x) = min(F(a)(x), G(a)(x)).$

- Complement:
- $(F,A)^c = (F^c,A), F^c(a)(x) = 1 - \mathbf{u}_a(x).$

These operations allow modeling of combined risks, overlapping vulnerabilities, and inverse security measures in HCCT intelligence.

Example of Union and Intersection

Suppose:

- Set F models phishing susceptibility.
- Set G models malware susceptibility.

For Bob:

$F(a_1)(Bob) = 0.9,$

$G(a_3)(Bob) = 0.4.$

- Union (overall susceptibility to phishing or malware):

$H(a)(Bob) = max(0.9, 0.4) = 0.9$

Intersection (simultaneous susceptibility):

$H(a)(Bob) = min(0.9, 0.4) = 0.4$

This shows that Bob is strongly vulnerable overall (0.9), but his joint vulnerability to phishing and malware is only moderate (0.4).

Relevance to HCCT Analysis

- Flexibility: Handles imprecise behaviors like "sometimes careless," "often cautious."
- Multi-criteria: Allows inclusion of multiple attributes (social engineering risk, device hygiene, awareness level).
- Decision support: Can combine vulnerabilities across parameters to prioritize users needing training or monitoring.

- Realistic modeling: Unlike binary risk assessment, FSSs capture degrees of threat, matching human unpredictability.

3.4 Why FSSs For Hccts?

- Fuzzy sets capture uncertainty in user behaviors.
- Soft sets capture multi-parameter dependencies.
- Combined, FSSs provide a decision-support system that balances technical and behavioral threat indicators.

Table 3 explains key mathematical ideas in simple terms and shows how each concept is used to assess human-related cybersecurity risks.

Table 3. Key Mathematical Ideas and Their Meanings in Cybersecurity

Mathematical Element	Purpose in the Model	Cybersecurity Interpretation
Membership Function (u(x))	Defines degree of belonging	Measures how risky a user's behavior is
Union / Intersection	Combine or overlap fuzzy sets	Identify users with multiple vulnerabilities
Fuzzy Soft Decision Matrix	Collects fuzzy values under parameters	Represents risk across users and behaviors
Aggregation Formula	Computes overall threat score	Calculates a single risk score per user
Weight Vector (w)	Assigns importance to parameters	Emphasizes critical behaviors (e.g., phishing)

The mathematical foundation described above provides the tools for modeling uncertainty in user behaviors. The next section applies these tools to develop a practical decision-making framework, transforming fuzzy and soft data into actionable cyber risk evaluations.

4. FSS-BASED DECISION FRAMEWORK

The proposed FSS-Based Decision Framework (FSSDF) consists of the following stages:

Step 1: Define the Universe and Parameters

- Universe $U = \{u_1, u_2, \ldots, u_n\}$: set of users/entities.
- Parameters $A = \{a_1, a_2, \ldots, a_n\}$: attributes describing threats.

Examples of parameters:

- a_1: password strength.
- a_2: phishing susceptibility.
- a_3: insider activity.
- a_4: awareness of security policies.

Step 2: Construct FSSs

For each parameter a_i assign fuzzy values:

$$F(a_i) = \left\{ (u_j, u_{a_i}(u_j)) \mid u_j \in U \right\}$$

Step 3. Build the Decision Matrix

A decision matrix represents all fuzzy soft values: Table 4 presents the fuzzy soft decision matrix, showing how different users exhibit varying degrees of vulnerability across key cybersecurity factors.

Table 4. Fuzzy soft decision matrix for cybersecurity factors

User	a_1 (Password)	a_2 (Phishing)	a_3 (Insider)	a_4 (Policy Awareness)
u_1	0.6	0.3	0.4	0.7
u_2	0.4	0.8	0.7	0.2
u_3	0.9	0.5	0.2	0.6

Step 4. Aggregation of Threat Scores

The aggregation formula below combines all behavior-based risk factors into a single user score. This score directly reflects how likely a user is to cause a cyber-incident.

Assign weights *wi* to parameters such that:

$$\sum_{i=1}^{n} \omega_i = 1$$

We employed a group decision strategy to minimize subjectivity in weight assignment. The significance of each component was discussed and agreed upon by experts in behavioral science and cybersecurity. This group approach guarantees equitable weight values and helps counteract individual prejudice. Additionally, we propose ML and adaptive techniques to automatically update weights with new data. These procedures improve the fuzzy soft decision framework's dependability, transparency, and data-drivenness.

The total threat score for each user is found using the formula below.

Threat score for user *j*:

$$T(u_j) = \sum_{i=1}^{n} \omega_i \cdot u_{a_i}(u_j)$$

Decision rules:

- $T(u_j) \geq 0.7$:High Risk.
- $0.4 \leq T(u_j) < 0.7$: Medium Risk.
- $T(u_j) < 0.4$: Low Risk.

Step 5: Ranking Users

Sort users according to $T(u_j)$. This ranking helps cyber forensic analysts prioritize monitoring and mitigation.

Figure 1 illustrates the overall process flow from human behavior data collection to FSS formulation, aggregation, and decision-making.

Figure 1. Conceptual Structure of the Fuzzy Soft Decision Framework

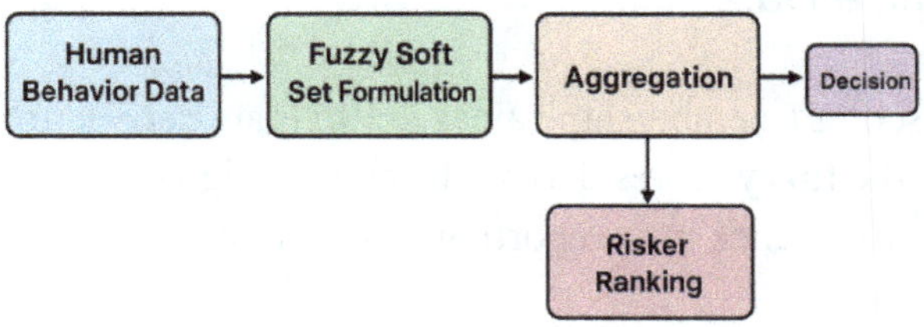

Conceptual Structure of Fuzzy Soft Decision Framework

5. ILLUSTRATIVE CASE STUDIES

To demonstrate the applicability of the FSSDF, this section presents extended case studies in HCCTs.

5.1 Step-by-Step Simulation: Detecting Human Error in Phishing Attacks

HCCTs often come from human mistakes, such as clicking on phishing emails or ignoring security warnings. To show how the fuzzy soft decision framework works in a real situation, this section presents a simple simulation on human error detection in phishing attacks.

Step 1: Description of the Scenario

A medium-sized organization wants to find out which employees are more likely to fall for phishing emails. The security team collects behavioral data such as how often employees click suspicious links, how quickly they report phishing attempts, and whether they complete security training. These human-related factors are important for assessing cyber risk.

- Universe $U = \{u_1, u_2, u_3, u_4\}$: employees.
- Parameters $A = \{a_1,\ a_2,\ a_3\}$:
  - a_1: Click rate on phishing links.
  - a_2: Reporting rate of suspicious emails.
  - a_3: Completion of cybersecurity training.

Step 2: Sample Data

The fuzzy scores (membership values in [0,1]) are derived from campaign data: Table 5 shows the fuzzy scores derived from campaign data, reflecting each user's behavior in terms of click rate, reporting, and training effectiveness.

Table 5. Fuzzy scores of users based on campaign data

User	a_1 (Click Rate)	a_2 (Reporting)	a_3 (Training)
u_1	0.8	0.3	0.5
u_2	0.4	0.6	0.7
u_3	0.2	0.9	0.9
u_4	0.7	0.2	0.3

Interpretation:

- u_1 clicked phishing links 80% of the time → high susceptibility.
- u_3 reported most phishing emails and completed training → low risk.

Step 3: Fuzzy Membership Mapping

Each value is converted into a fuzzy membership value between 0 and 1. This value shows how strongly a behavior belongs to the "risky" category.

Assign weights:

$\omega_1 = 0.5$ (clickrate), $\omega_2 = 0.3$ (reporting), $\omega_3 = 0.2$ (training)

Threat score:

$$T(u_j) = \sum_{i=1}^{3} \omega_i \cdot u_{a_i}(u_j)$$

$$T(u_1) = 0.5(0.8) + 0.3(0.3) + 0.2(0.5) = 0.4 + 0.09 + 0.1 = 0.59$$

$$T(u_2) = 0.5(0.4) + 0.3(0.6) + 0.2(0.7) = 0.2 + 0.18 + 0.14 = 0.52$$

$$T(u_3) = 0.5(0.2) + 0.3(0.9) + 0.2(0.9) = 0.1 + 0.27 + 0.18 = 0.55$$

$$T(u_4) = 0.5(0.7) + 0.3(0.2) + 0.2(0.3) = 0.35 + 0.06 + 0.06 = 0.47$$

Decision Results

- u_1: Medium Risk (0.59)
- u_2: Medium Risk (0.52)
- u_3: Medium Risk (0.55)
- u_4: Medium Risk (0.47)

Observation: All users fall into a medium risk band, but u1 shows the highest priority for further training.

5.2 Case Study 2: Insider Threat Analysis

A financial organization suspects insider threats. Parameters include access anomalies, file transfer activities, and compliance with policies.

- Universe $U = \{u_1, u_2, u_3\}$.
- Parameters $A = \{a_1, a_2, a_3, a_4\}$
  - o a_1: Unauthorized access attempts.
  - o a_2: Data transfer volume.
  - o a_3: Login time anomalies.
  - o a_4: Compliance with security policies.

Fuzzy Matrix: Table 6 presents the fuzzy evaluation matrix for insider threat analysis, capturing user behavior across access attempts, data transfer, login anomalies, and policy compliance.

Table 6. Fuzzy scores of users for insider threat analysis:

User	a_1	a_2	a_3	a_4
u_1	0.6	0.5	0.7	0.3
u_2	0.2	0.8	0.4	0.7
u_3	0.9	0.6	0.8	0.2

Weights

$W = (0.25, 0.35, 0.25, 0.15)$

Threat Scores:

$T(u_1) = 0.25(0.6) + 0.35(0.5) + 0.25(0.7) + 0.15(0.3) = 0.15 + 0.175 + 0.175 + 0.045 = 0.545$

$T(u_2) = 0.25(0.2) + 0.35(0.8) + 0.25(0.4) + 0.15(0.7) = 0.05 + 0.28 + 0.1 + 0.105 = 0.535$

$T(u_3) = 0.25(0.9) + 0.35(0.6) + 0.25(0.8) + 0.15(0.2) = 0.225 + 0.21 + 0.2 + 0.03 = 0.665$

Results:

- u_3: High Risk (0.665)
- u_1, u_2: Medium Risk (~0.54)

Observation: The fuzzy soft framework identifies u3 as the most suspicious insider.

5.3 Case Study 3: Password Negligence

Password negligence is analyzed for employees.
Parameters:

- a_1: Strength of password.
- a_2: Frequency of reuse.
- a_3: MFA (multi-factor authentication) usage.

Decision Matrix: Table 7 presents the fuzzy decision matrix for password negligence, evaluating employees based on password strength, reuse frequency, and multi-factor authentication usage.

Table 7. Fuzzy Decision Matrix for Password Negligence Analysis:

User	a_1	a_2	a_3
u_1	0.4	0.7	0.2
u_2	0.6	0.5	0.5
u_3	0.9	0.2	0.8

Weights

$W = (0.4, 0.4, 0.2)$

Scores

$$T(u_1) = 0.4(0.4) + 0.4(0.7) + 0.2(0.2) = 0.16 + 0.28 + 0.04 = 0.48$$

$$T(u_2) = 0.4(0.6) + 0.4(0.5) + 0.2(0.5) = 0.24 + 0.2 + 0.1 = 0.54$$

$$T(u_3) = 0.4(0.9) + 0.4(0.2) + 0.2(0.8) = 0.36 + 0.08 + 0.16 = 0.60$$

Results

- u_3: Highest priority for security training (0.60).
- u_1: Lower but still concerning risk (0.48).

6. ALGORITHMIC REPRESENTATION OF THE FRAMEWORK

To formalize, we propose the following decision-making algorithm:

Algorithm 1: Fuzzy soft decision framework for human threats

Input:

- Universe $U = \{u_1, u_2, \ldots, u_m\}$.
- Parameters $A = \{a_1, a_2, \ldots, a_n\}$.
- Fuzzy membership values $u_{a_i}(u_j)$.
- Weights ω_i.

Steps:

1. Construct a fuzzy soft decision matrix M.
2. Normalize membership values (optional if scales differ).
3. For each user u_j:

$$T(u_j) = \sum_{i=1}^{n} \omega_i \cdot u_{a_i}(u_j)$$

4. Rank users based on $T(u_j)$.
5. Classify risk levels:
   - High Risk: $T(u_j) \geq 0.7$.
   - Medium Risk: $0.4 \leq T(u_j) < 0.7$.
   - Low Risk: $T(u_j) < 0.4$.

Output: Ranked list of users with risk categories.

Complexity Analysis

- Constructing fuzzy soft matrix: O(mn).
- Aggregation: O(mn).
- Ranking: O(mlogm).

Thus, total complexity:

$O(mn + mlogm)$

Efficient even for large enterprise datasets.

7. COMPARATIVE ANALYSIS

The FSS framework can be compared with other approaches: Table 8 presents a comparative analysis of different approaches against the FSS framework in terms of uncertainty handling, flexibility, human-centricity, and interpretability.

Table 8. Comparative analysis of different approaches with the FSS framework

Method	Handles Uncertainty	Parameter Flexibility	Human-Centric	Interpretability
Classical Probability	Limited (requires distributions)	Moderate	Weak	Moderate
Bayesian Networks	Strong	Strong	Weak	Complex
ML (Black Box)	Strong	Strong	Weak	Low
Crisp Decision Trees	Weak	Strong	Weak	High
FSSs	Strong	Strong	Strong	High

Observation:

- ML models (e.g., neural networks) may predict risks but lack interpretability.
- FSSs are transparent, flexible, and well-suited to human-centric forensic analysis.

8. MATHEMATICAL MODELING OF FSS IN HCCT ANALYSIS

HCCT analysis often deals with ambiguous, incomplete, and conflicting information. For example, a suspicious login attempt could be harmless (user traveling abroad) or malicious (credential theft). To mathematically capture this uncertainty, FSSs provide a structured way to model threats.

8.1 Recap Of Soft Sets

Let

- U = universe of discourse (set of cyber entities, e.g., users, devices, sessions),
- E = set of threat-related attributes (e.g., "suspicious login", "unusual file transfer", "phishing attempt").

A soft set is defined as:

$$F = \{(e, F(e)) \mid e \in E\}$$

where F(e) ⊆ U.
This means for each attribute e, we have a subset of suspicious entities.

8.2 FSS

In a FSS, instead of crisp membership, each element has a degree of belonging between 0 and 1.
Formally:

$$F: E \rightarrow F(U)$$

where $F(U)$ is the set of all fuzzy subsets of U.
For each attribute $e \in E$,

$$F(e) = \{(u, \mu_F(e)(u)) \mid u \in U\}$$

with $\mu_F(e)(u) \in [0,1]$ being the degree to which entity u satisfies attribute e.

8.3 Example: Suspicious User Behavior

- Universe $U = \{u_1, u_2, u_3\}$ (three users).

- Attributes $E = \{e_1, e_2, e_3\}$:
  - e_1: "Multiple failed logins"
  - e_2: "Accessing sensitive files"
  - e_3: "Unusual login time"

Define FSS F:

$$F(e_1) = \{(u_1,0.8),(u_2,0.6),(u_3,0.2)\}$$

$$F(e_2) = \{(u_1,0.4),(u_2,0.7),(u_3,0.9)\}$$

$$F(e_3) = \{(u_1,0.5),(u_2,0.3),(u_3,0.8)\}$$

Here:

- u_1 has a high chance of a brute-force attack (0.8) but a lower unusual access (0.4).
- u_3 shows data theft suspicion (0.9) and unusual time usage (0.8).

This mathematical modeling quantifies threat suspicion under uncertainty.

8.4 Operations

- Union:

$$(F \cup G)(e)(u) = max\left(\mu_F(e)(u), \mu G(e)(u)\right)$$

- Intersection:

$$(F \cap G)(e)(u) = min\left(\mu_F(e)(u), \mu G(e)(u)\right)$$

- Complement:

$$(F^c)(e)(u) = 1 - \mu_F(e)(u)$$

These operations allow combining multiple intelligence sources (e.g., logs + anomaly detection + forensic tools).

9. DECISION-MAKING FRAMEWORK USING FSSS

HCCT analysis aims to rank threats or users and take action.

9.1 Framework Outline

- Identify Universe (*U*): set of users, systems, or network nodes.
- Define Attributes (*E*): suspicious patterns (phishing, failed logins, malware activity).
- Construct FSS (*F*): assign membership scores using detection models.
- Weight Attributes: assign importance *we* to each attribute *e*.
- Aggregate Scores: compute risk index for each entity.
- Rank Entities: Classify them into high/medium/low risk.

9.2 Weighted Fuzzy Soft Decision Model

Each attribute $e \in E$ is assigned a weight ω_e such that:

$$\sum_{e \in E} \omega_e = 1$$

The aggregated score of entity u is:

$$S(u) = \sum_{e \in E} \omega_e \cdot \mu_F(e)(u)$$

where $\mu_F(e)(u)$ is the membership value.

Figure 2 presents the operational workflow of the HCCT analysis process. It's showing how raw data are transformed into actionable intelligence through fuzzy soft computation.

Figure 2. Workflow of HCCT Analysis

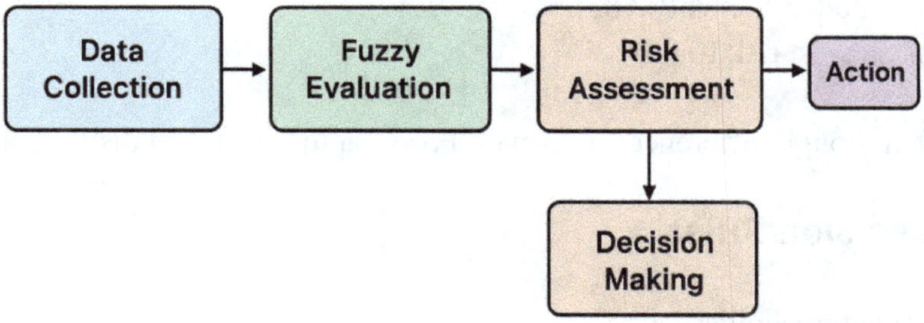

Workflow of Human-Centric Cyber Threat Analysis

9.3 Example: Computing Threat Scores

From the Section 8 example, assume weights:

v ω_{e_1} = 0.4,

v ω_{e_2} = 0.35,

v ω_{e_3} = 0.25.

Now compute $S(u)$:

For 1:

$S(u_1)$ = (0.4)(0.8) + (0.35)(0.4) + (0.25)(0.5) = 0.32 + 0.14 + 0.125 = 0.5
85

For 2:

$S(u_2)$ = (0.4)(0.6) + (0.35)(0.7) + (0.25)(0.3) = 0.24 + 0.245 + 0.075 = 0.56

For 3:

$S(u_3) = (0.4)(0.2) + (0.35)(0.9) + (0.25)(0.8) = 0.08 + 0.315 + 0.20 = 0.595$

Thus, ranking:

- u_1 : highest risk (0.595),
- u_2: moderate risk (0.585),
- u_3: lowest risk (0.56).

Even though differences are small, FSSs capture nuanced distinctions.

9.4 Decision Rules

Define thresholds:

- $S(u) \geq 0.7 \rightarrow$ High Risk (Immediate Action).
- $0.5 \leq S(u) < 0.7 \rightarrow$ Medium Risk (Monitor Closely).
- $S(u) < 0.5 \rightarrow$ Low Risk (No action).

This provides a clear, human-centric decision pathway.

10. CASE STUDY: HUMAN-CENTRIC THREAT INTELLIGENCE SYSTEM

To illustrate, let us build a cyber forensic model for detecting insider threats in an organization.

10.1 Scenario

An enterprise network monitors employee activity. Suspicious indicators include:

- e_1: Unauthorized USB usage
- e_2: Large file transfer at midnight
- e_3: Accessing payroll database without role
- e_4: Multiple failed login attempts

Universe $U = \{u_1, u_2, u_3, u_4\}$ (four employees).

10.2 Constructing FSS

Suppose monitoring tools give membership values:

v $F(e_1) = \{(u_1, 0.7), (u_2, 0.2), (u_3, 0.5), (u_4, 0.9)\}$

v $F(e_2) = \{(u_1, 0.4), (u_2, 0.6), (u_3, 0.8), (u_4, 0.3)\}$

v $F(e_3) = \{(u_1, 0.2), (u_2, 0.7), (u_3, 0.9), (u_4, 0.4)\}$

v $F(e_4) = \{(u_1, 0.8), (u_2, 0.5), (u_3, 0.6), (u_4, 0.7)\}$

10.3 Attribute Weights

Experts assign importance:

v $\omega_{e_1} = 0.25,$

v $\omega_{e_2} = 0.25,$

v $\omega_{e_3} = 0.3,$

v $\omega_{e_4} = 0.2.$

10.4 Risk Computation

For each user:

$u_1 : S(u_1) = (0.25)(0.7) + (0.25)(0.4) + (0.3)(0.2) + (0.2)(0.8)$
$= 0.175 + 0.1 + 0.06 + 0.16 = 0.495$

$u_2 : S(u_2) = (0.25)(0.2) + (0.25)(0.6) + (0.3)(0.7) + (0.2)(0.5)$
$= 0.05 + 0.15 + 0.21 + 0.1 = 0.51$

$u_3 : S(u_3) = (0.25)(0.5) + (0.25)(0.8) + (0.3)(0.9) + (0.2)(0.6)$
$= 0.125 + 0.2 + 0.27 + 0.12 = 0.715$

$u_4 : S(u_4) = (0.25)(0.9) + (0.25)(0.3) + (0.3)(0.4) + (0.2)(0.7)$
$= 0.225 + 0.075 + 0.12 + 0.14 = 0.56$

10.5 Results

Ranking:

- u_3 (0.715) → High risk (potential insider threat).
- u_4 (0.56) → Medium risk.
- u_2 (0.51) → Medium risk.
- u_1 (0.495) → Low risk.

Thus, u_3 should be investigated first.

10.6 Human-Centric Integration

Unlike traditional rigid models, this approach allows:

- Explainability: Why u_3 is flagged (due to high weights on sensitive access + large transfers).
- Flexibility: The security team can adjust weights (e.g., during a phishing campaign, give login attempts more weight).
- Transparency: forensic investigators see exact numerical reasoning.

11. ADVANTAGES, LIMITATIONS, AND FUTURE DIRECTIONS

11.1 Advantages

1. Handles Uncertainty: FSSs model vague and incomplete intelligence data.
2. Human-Centric: Security analysts can fine-tune attribute weights.
3. Scalable: Can handle large sets of users and threat attributes.
4. Flexible Decision Support: Works with dynamic environments (IoT, cloud, enterprise).
5. Integration with AI: Can be combined with ML anomaly detectors.

11.2 Limitations And Practical Challenges

The fuzzy soft model is useful but faces some real-world challenges. These must be understood for better use and improvement.

11.2.1. Data Quality

The model needs correct and complete data. Missing or wrong data give poor results. Use clean, updated, and verified data.

11.2.2. Computational Load

Large data increase system work and time. Big organizations face slow calculations. Use fast computers or cloud tools to solve this.

11.2.3. Changing Threats

HCCTs change very fast. A fixed model may soon become outdated. Update model weights and data often.

11.2.4. Expert Dependence

Model weights depend on expert opinion. Different experts may give different results. Combine expert views with data-based methods.

11.2.5. Model Complexity

Too many fuzzy rules make the model hard to explain. Keep it simple and easy to read. Show results with graphs or short labels.

11.2.6. Scalability

Big companies need the model to handle many users. Use modular design and batch processing. Cloud systems can help scale it easily.

These limits show where the model can improve. Better data, speed, and updates will make it stronger.

11.3 Future Directions

Cyber risks are always evolving due to advancements in technology and time. Additionally, the fuzzy soft model needs to develop and change. Explainable AI (XAI) enables consumers to comprehend the rationale behind decisions. It displays the behavior that resulted in a high or low risk. This enhances human-AI system trust. The system can learn from fresh data thanks to adaptive risk modeling. When user behavior shifts, it automatically adjusts the fuzzy weights. The model becomes intelligent and self-learning as a result.

Quantification of uncertainty reveals the model's level of confidence in each outcome. It gives each fuzzy score an additional degree of confidence. This aids analysts in determining when a choice is reliable. Blockchain and deep learning can be used with fuzzy logic in hybrid AI models. Better accuracy and a more robust cyber protection result from this. The model will eventually be able to explain, learn, and adjust on its own. It will become more dependable, transparent, and prepared for emerging cyberthreats.

12. CONCLUSION

This chapter demonstrates how important human behavior is to cybersecurity. Antivirus software and firewalls are useful but insufficient. A lot of attacks begin with carelessness or basic human error. Phishing, insecure passwords, and insider abuse are a few examples. Instead of breaching systems, attackers frequently deceive individuals.

We suggested the FSS Decision Framework as a solution. It investigates human behavior and how risk varies with behavior. Only "safe" or "unsafe" labels are used in traditional models. Risk levels range from 0 to 1 in our fuzzy soft model. This makes it easier to understand actual human behavior.

Soft sets and fuzzy sets are combined in the model. Soft sets employ parameters, while fuzzy sets display partial truth. When combined, they create a powerful decision-making tool for cybersecurity professionals. Phishing, password, and insider threat studies all benefit from the model's effectiveness. It makes decisions using straightforward reasoning, basic math, and simple principles.

It is simpler to comprehend than outdated or machine models. Although powerful, ML frequently functions as a "black box." The fuzzy soft model is adaptable, transparent, and explicable. It provides results that are trustworthy and readable by specialists.

Comparative Illustration

The sole words on older models are "safe" and "unsafe." Users who are "partly risky" are missed. For these individuals, the fuzzy soft model provides middle values (Table 9).

REFERENCES

Akram, M., Ali, G., & Alcantud, J. (2023). A novel group decision-making framework under Pythagorean fuzzy N-soft expert knowledge. *Engineering Applications of Artificial Intelligence*. Advance online publication. DOI: 10.1016/j.engappai.2023.105879

Akram, M., & Martino, A. (2022). Multi-attribute group decision making based on T-spherical fuzzy soft rough average aggregation operators. *Granular Computing, 8*, 171–207. DOI: 10.1007/s41066-022-00319-0

Al-Qudah, Y. (2024). *A robust framework for the decision-making based on single-valued neutrosophic fuzzy soft expert setting*. International Journal of Neutrosophic Science., DOI: 10.54216/ijns.230216

Al-Shami, T., Alcantud, J., & Mhemdi, A. (2023). New generalization of fuzzy soft sets: $ (a, b) $-Fuzzy soft sets. *AIMS Mathematics*. Advance online publication. DOI: 10.3934/math.2023155

Alali, M., Almogren, A., Hassan, M., Rassan, I., & Bhuiyan, M. (2018). Improving risk assessment model of cyber security using fuzzy logic inference system. *Computers & Security, 74*, 323–339. DOI: 10.1016/J.COSE.2017.09.011

Ali, G., & Akram, M. (2020). Decision-Making Method Based on Fuzzy N-Soft Expert Sets. *Arabian Journal for Science and Engineering, 45*, 10381–10400. DOI: 10.1007/s13369-020-04733-x

Ali, G., & Ansari, M. (2021). Multiattribute decision-making under Fermatean fuzzy bipolar soft framework. *Granular Computing, 7*, 337–352. DOI: 10.1007/s41066-021-00270-6

. Ali, Z., Razzaq, A., and Manahil, K. (2025). Enhancing Cybersecurity Risk Assessment Techniques Based on Bipolar Complex 0Intuitionistic Fuzzy Soft Robust Aggregation Operators: A Comprehensive Approaches. Journal of Intelligent Decision Making and Information Science. https://doi.org/.DOI: 10.59543/jidmis.v2i.13475

Ali, Z., & Yang, M. (2024). Improving Risk Assessment Model for Cyber Security Using Robust Aggregation Operators for Bipolar Complex Fuzzy Soft Inference Systems. *Mathematics*. Advance online publication. DOI: 10.3390/math12040582

Almutairi, L. (2023). Deep Learning based Frameworks for Real-time Cyber Threat Analysis. *Journal of Engineering and Applied Sciences (Asian Research Publishing Network)*. Advance online publication. DOI: 10.5455/jeas.2023110109

Alsager, K., & Alharbi, H. (2024). Exploring Symmetry in Industrial Decision-Making: A New Framework Based on Cubic Type-2 Fuzzy Soft Sets. *Symmetry*. Advance online publication. DOI: 10.3390/sym16111491

Arora, S., Rai, M., & Gupta, M. (2024). Importance of Industry 5.0 in understanding emotional intelligence. In Kumar, N., Pal, S. K., Agarwal, P., Rosak-Szyrocka, J., & Jain, V. (Eds.), *Human-machine collaboration and emotional intelligence in Industry 5.0*. IGI Global., DOI: 10.4018/979-8-3693-6806-0.ch011

Beemkumar, N., Gupta, S., Bhardwaj, S., Dhabliya, D., Rai, M., Pandey, J. K., & Gupta, A. (2023). Activity Recognition and IoT-Based Analysis Using Time Series and CNN. In Goel, N., & Yadav, R. (Eds.), *Handbook of Research on Machine Learning-Enabled IoT for Smart Applications Across Industries* (pp. 350–364). IGI Global Scientific Publishing., DOI: 10.4018/978-1-6684-8785-3.ch018

. Božanić, D., Tešić, D., Puška, A., Štilić, A., and Muhsen, Y. (2023). Ranking challenges, risks and threats using Fuzzy Inference System. Decision Making: Applications in Management and Engineering. https://doi.org/.DOI: 10.31181/dmame622023926

Das, A. K. (2016). On partially included intuitionistic fuzzy rough relations. *Afrika Matematika*, *27*, 993–1001. DOI: 10.1007/s13370-016-0395-2

Das, A. K. (2018). Weighted fuzzy soft multiset and decision-making. *International Journal of Machine Learning and Cybernetics*, *9*, 787–794. DOI: 10.1007/s13042-016-0607-y

Das, A. K., Das, R., Das, S., Debnath, B. K., Granados, C., Shil, B., & Das, R. (2025c). A comprehensive study of neutrosophic SuperHyper BCI-semigroups and their algebraic significance. *Transactions on Fuzzy Sets and Systems*, *4*(2), 80–101. DOI: 10.71602/tfss.2025.1198050

Das, A. K., Das, R., Datta, R., & Granados, C. (2025e). An Innovative Approach to Group Decision-Making Based on Weighted Hypersoft Expert System. In Smarandache, F., Jdid, M., & Leyva-Vazquez, M. (Eds.), *Neutrosophic and Plithogenic Inventory Models for Applied Mathematics* (pp. 483–518). IGI Global Scientific Publishing., DOI: 10.4018/979-8-3693-3204-7.ch019

Das, A. K., & Granados, C. (2021). An advanced approach to fuzzy soft group decision-making using weighted average ratings. *SN Computer Science*, *2*, 471. DOI: 10.1007/s42979-021-00873-5

Das, A. K., & Granados, C. (2022a). A new fuzzy parameterized intuitionistic fuzzy soft multiset theory and group decision-making. *Journal of Current Science and Technology, 12*(3), 547–567. DOI: 10.14456/jcst.2022.42

Das, A. K., & Granados, C. (2022b). FP-intuitionistic multi fuzzy N-soft set and its induced FP-Hesitant N soft set in decision-making. *Decision Making: Applications in Management and Engineering, 5*(1), 67–89. DOI: 10.31181/dmame181221045d

Das, A. K., & Granados, C. (2023a). IFP-intuitionistic multi fuzzy N-soft set and its induced IFP-hesitant N-soft set in decision-making. *Journal of Ambient Intelligence and Humanized Computing, 14*, 10143–10152. DOI: 10.1007/s12652-021-03677-w

Das, A. K., & Granados, C. (2023b). Preference intuitionistic fuzzy rough relation and its theoretical approach. *Journal of the Indian Mathematical Society, 90*(3-4), 199–212.

Das, A. K., Granados, C., & Bhattacharya, J. (2022). Some new operations on fuzzy soft sets and their applications in decision-making. *Songklanakarin Journal of Science and Technology, 44*(2), 440–449. DOI: 10.14456/sjst-psu.2022.61

Das, A. K., Gupta, N., Das, R., Das, S., Das, R., Granados, C., & Debnath, B. K. (2026a). Fuzzy Logic-Driven Strategies for Diversity and Inclusion in Multicultural Marketing. In Tarnanidis, T., Sousa, B., Vlachopoulou, M., Papachristou, E., & Kittu Manda, V. (Eds.), *Diversity and Inclusion-Driven Marketing for Multicultural Marketplaces* (pp. 189–236). IGI Global Scientific Publishing., DOI: 10.4018/979-8-3373-2111-0.ch009

Das, A. K., Gupta, N., Das, R., Granados, C., & Das, S. (2026c). Neutrosophic Sets for Decision-Making in Natural Disasters and Environmental Recovery. In Ezaier, Y., Gaamouche, R., & Lahby, M. (Eds.), *Computational Intelligence and Optimization Methods for Sustainable Water Management* (pp. 119–162). IGI Global Scientific Publishing., DOI: 10.4018/979-8-3373-2700-6.ch004

Das, A. K., Gupta, N., Fujita, T., Das, S., Granados, C., Debnath, B. K., & Das, R. (2026b). Advanced Co-Branding Strategies for Smart Luxury Products: A Multi-Criteria Decision-Making Approach Using Neutrosophic Sets. In Tarnanidis, T., Sousa, B., Vlachopoulou, M., Papachristou, E., & Kittu Manda, V. (Eds.), *Co-Branding Strategies for Smart Luxury Products* (pp. 203–258). IGI Global Scientific Publishing., DOI: 10.4018/979-8-3373-3010-5.ch006

Das, A. K., Gupta, N., & Granados, C. (2023). Weighted hesitant bipolar-valued fuzzy soft set in decision-making. *Songklanakarin Journal of Science and Technology, 45*(6), 681–690. https://sjst.psu.ac.th/journal/45-6/10.pdf

Das, A. K., Gupta, N., Granados, C., Das, R., & Das, S. (2024b). Neutrosophic Approach to Water Quality Assessment: A Case Study of Gomati River, the Largest River in Tripura, India. *Neutrosophic Systems with Applications*, *22*, 1–12. DOI: 10.61356/j.nswa.2024.22386

Das, A. K., Gupta, N., Mahmood, T., Tripathy, B. C., Das, R., & Das, S. (2024a). Assessing anthropogenic influences on the water quality of Gomati River using an innovative weighted fuzzy soft set based water pollution rating system. *Discover Water*, *4*, 73. DOI: 10.1007/s43832-024-00136-3

Das, A. K., Gupta, N., Mahmood, T., Tripathy, B. C., Das, R., & Das, S. (2025a). An efficient water quality evaluation model using weighted hesitant fuzzy soft sets for water pollution rating. In Kumar, A., Kumar, P., Rathee, S., & Kumar, B. (Eds.), *Mechatronics: Concepts, Tools, Applications, and New Trends* (1st ed., p. 17). CRC Press., DOI: 10.1201/9781003494478-10

Das, A. K., Gupta, N., Mahmood, T., Tripathy, B. C., Das, R., & Das, S. (2025b). An innovative fuzzy multi-criteria decision making model for analyzing anthropogenic influences on urban river water quality. *Iran Journal of Computer Science*, *8*, 103–124. DOI: 10.1007/s42044-024-00211-x

Das, A. K., Gupta, N., Mahmood, T., Tripathy, B. C., Das, R., & Das, S. (2025g). Anthropogenic Impacts on Urban River Water Quality for Rating Water Pollution Using an Effective Fuzzy Soft Multi Criteria Group Decision Making Model. *Iraqi Journal of Science*, *66*(9), 3921–3937. DOI: 10.24996/ijs.2025.66.9.32

Das, A. K., Mahmood, T., Das, R., & Das, S. (2025d). Optimizing Inventory Levels in Retail: Fuzzy Logic-Based Decision Support Systems for Adaptive Inventory Management. In Jana, S., Basu Mallik, B., Sarkar, A., & Jana, C. (Eds.), *Applications of Fuzzy Logic in Decision Making and Management Science. Information Systems Engineering and Management* (Vol. 29). Springer., DOI: 10.1007/978-3-031-77719-6_8

Das, A. K., Patra, S., & Granados, C. (2025f). An innovative approach to hesitant bipolar fuzzy soft sets in multi-criteria group decision-making. Adv. in Comp. *Int.*, *5*, 4. DOI: 10.1007/s43674-025-00082-0

. Dey, A., Senapati, T., Pal, M., and Chen, G. (2020). A novel approach to hesitant multi-fuzzy soft set based decision-making., 5, 1985-2008. https://doi.org/.DOI: 10.3934/math.2020132

Fatimah, F., & Alcantud, J. (2021). The multi-fuzzy N-soft set and its applications to decision-making. *Neural Computing & Applications*, *33*, 11437–11446. DOI: 10.1007/s00521-020-05647-3

Feng, F., Jun, Y., Liu, X., & Li, L. (2010). An adjustable approach to fuzzy soft set based decision making. *Journal of Computational and Applied Mathematics*, *234*, 10–20. DOI: 10.1016/j.cam.2009.11.055

Ge, W., Wang, J., Lin, T., Tang, B., & Li, X. (2023). Explainable cyber threat behavior identification based on self-adversarial topic generation. *Computers & Security*, *132*, 103369. DOI: 10.1016/j.cose.2023.103369

Gozon, F., Vaczi, D., & Tóth-Laufer, E. (2021). Fuzzy-based Human Factor Centered Cybersecurity Risk Assessment. 2021 IEEE 19th International Symposium on Intelligent Systems and Informatics (SISY), 83-88. https://doi.org/DOI: 10.1109/SISY52375.2021.9582520

. Granados, C., Das, A.K., Das, B. (2022). Some continuous neutrosophic distributions with neutrosophic parameters based on neutrosophic random variables. Advances in the Theory of Nonlinear Analysis and its Applications, 33(2): 293-308. https://doi.org/DOI: 10.31197/atnaa.1056480

. Granados, C., Das, A.K., Osu, B. (2023). Weighted neutrosophic soft multiset and its application to decision making. Yugoslav journal of operations research, 33(2): 293-308. https://doi.org/DOI: 10.2298/YJOR220915034G

Gu, X., Howells, G., & Yuan, H. (2024). A soft prototype-based autonomous fuzzy inference system for network intrusion detection. *Inf. Sci.*, *677*, 120964. DOI: 10.1016/j.ins.2024.120964

Gusmão, A., Silva, M., Poleto, T., Silva, L., & Costa, A. (2018). Cybersecurity risk analysis model using fault tree analysis and fuzzy decision theory. *International Journal of Information Management*, *43*, 248–260. DOI: 10.1016/J.IJINFOMGT.2018.08.008

Hang, F., Xie, L., Zhang, Z., Guo, W., & Li, H. (2022). RETRACTED ARTICLE: Artificial intelligence enabled fuzzy multimode decision support system for cyber threat security defense automation. *Journal of Computer Virology and Hacking Techniques*, *19*, 257–269. DOI: 10.1007/s11416-022-00443-0

Hussain, A., Ullah, K., Pamučar, D., & Simić, V. (2024). Intuitionistic fuzzy Sugeno-Weber decision framework for sustainable digital security assessment. *Engineering Applications of Artificial Intelligence*, *137*, 109085. DOI: 10.1016/j.engappai.2024.109085

Ihsan, M., Saeed, M., & Rahman, A. (2023). An intuitionistic fuzzy hypersoft expert set-based robust decision-support framework for human resource management integrated with modified TOPSIS and correlation coefficient. *Neural Computing & Applications*, •••, 1–25. DOI: 10.1007/s00521-023-09085-9

Jan, N., Gwak, J., & Pamučar, D. (2023a). A robust hybrid decision making model for Human-Computer interaction in the environment of Bipolar complex picture fuzzy soft Sets. *Inf. Sci.*, *645*, 119163. DOI: 10.1016/j.ins.2023.119163

Jan, N., Gwak, J., Pei, J., Maqsood, R., & Nasir, A. (2023s). Analysis of Networks and Digital Systems by Using the Novel Technique Based on Complex Fuzzy Soft Information. *IEEE Transactions on Consumer Electronics*, *69*, 183–193. DOI: 10.1109/TCE.2022.3226819

Korkmaz, E., Riaz, M., Deveci, M., & Kadry, S. (2024). A novel approach to fuzzy N-soft sets and its application for identifying and sanctioning cyber harassment on social media platforms. *Artificial Intelligence Review*, *57*, 14. DOI: 10.1007/s10462-023-10640-y

Korystin, O., Korchenko, O., Kazmirchuk, S., Demediuk, S., & Korystin, O. (2024). *Comparative Risk Assessment of Cyber Threats Based on Average and Fuzzy Set Theory*. International Journal of Computer Network and Information Security., DOI: 10.5815/ijcnis.2024.01.02

Li, H., & Tang, T. (2025). Deconstruction of Intelligent Vehicle Cyber-Physical System Based on Fuzzy Soft Set and Multi-Attribute Group Decision Making. *IEEE Transactions on Intelligent Transportation Systems*, *26*, 5167–5181. DOI: 10.1109/TITS.2025.3530938

Li, Y., Tsang, Y., Lee, C., & Chen, Z. (2024). A Survey of Fuzzy Best-Worst Group Decision-Making Process Toward Human Centricity. *IEEE Transactions on Fuzzy Systems*, *32*, 3302–3318. DOI: 10.1109/TFUZZ.2024.3379555

Maji, P. K., BISwas, R., and Roy, A. R. (2001). Fuzzy soft sets. *Journal of Fuzzy Mathematics*, *9*(3), 589–602.

Molodtsov, D. (1999). Soft set theory: First results. *Computers & Mathematics with Applications (Oxford, England)*, *37*(4–5), 19–31.

Mukherjee, A., & Das, A. K. (2015a). Application of interval valued intuitionistic fuzzy soft set in investment decision making, *2015 Fifth International Conference on Advances in Computing and Communications (ICACC)*, Kochi, India, 2015, pp. 61-64, https://doi.org/DOI: 10.1109/ICACC.2015.37

Mukherjee, A., & Das, A. K. (2015b). Interval valued intuitionistic fuzzy soft multi set theoretic approach to decision making problems, 2015 International Conference on Computer, Communication and Control (IC4), Indore, India, 2015, pp. 1-5, https://doi.org/DOI: 10.1109/IC4.2015.7375640

Mukherjee, A., & Das, A. K. (2015c). Relations on intuitionistic fuzzy soft multi sets. In Kim, K. (Ed.), *Information Science and Applications. Lecture Notes in Electrical Engineering* (Vol. 339). Springer., DOI: 10.1007/978-3-662-46578-3_71

Mukherjee, A., & Das, A. K. (2016a). Application of fuzzy soft multi sets in decision-making problems. In: Nagar, A., Mohapatra, D., Chaki, N. (eds) Proceedings of 3rd International Conference on Advanced Computing, Networking and Informatics. Smart Innovation, Systems and Technologies, vol. 43. Springer, New Delhi. https://doi.org/DOI: 10.1007/978-81-322-2538-6_3

Mukherjee, A., & Das, A. K. (2016b). Topological structure formed by intuitionistic fuzzy rough relations. *Journal of the Indian Mathematical Society*, *83*(1-2), 135–144.

Mukherjee, A., & Das, A. K. (2022). Einstein operations on fuzzy soft multisets and decision making. *Boletim da Sociedade Paranaense de Matematica*, *40*, 1–10. DOI: 10.5269/bspm.32546

Mukherjee, A., & Das, A. K. (2023). Essentials of fuzzy soft multisets: Theory and applications, Springer Nature Singapore Pte Ltd., 1-151. ISBN: 978-981-19-2759-1, https://doi.org/DOI: 10.1007/978-981-19-2760-7

Mukherjee, A., Das, A. K., Gupta, N., Patra, S., Mahmood, T., Das, S., & Das, R. (2026). A novel generalized interval-valued neutrosophic rough soft set framework for enhanced decision-making: Application in water quality assessment. *Transactions on Fuzzy Sets and Systems*, *5*(1), 1–25. DOI: 10.71602/tfss.2026.1194037

Rai, M., Tyagi, N., Tripathi, P., Kumar, N., & Kumari, P. (2023). Advancement in Agricultural Techniques With the Introduction of Artificial Intelligence and Image Processing. In Khan, M., Gupta, B., Verma, A., Praveen, P., & Peoples, C. (Eds.), *Smart Village Infrastructure and Sustainable Rural Communities* (pp. 47–68). IGI Global Scientific Publishing., DOI: 10.4018/978-1-6684-6418-2.ch004

Shagari, S., & Azam, A. (2020). *An algorithm for fuzzy soft set based decision making approach*. Yugoslav Journal of Operations Research., DOI: 10.2298/yjor190715026m

Singh, S., Pandey, J. K., Rai, M., & Saxena, A. K. (2024). Advancements in Facial Expression Recognition Using Machine and Deep Learning Techniques. In Rai, M., & Pandey, J. (Eds.), *Machine and Deep Learning Techniques for Emotion Detection* (pp. 149–166). IGI Global Scientific Publishing., DOI: 10.4018/979-8-3693-4143-8.ch007

Singh, S., Rai, M., Pandey, J. K., & Saxena, A. K. (2024). Emotional intelligence and collaborative dynamics in Industry 5.0 for human–machine interactions. In Kumar, N., Pal, S. K., Agarwal, P., Rosak-Szyrocka, J., & Jain, V. (Eds.), *Human-machine collaboration and emotional intelligence in Industry 5.0* (pp. 1–15). IGI Global., DOI: 10.4018/979-8-3693-6806-0.ch010

Smarandache, F. (2005). Neutrosophic set: A generalization of the intuitionistic fuzzy sets. *International Journal of Pure and Applied Mathematics*, *24*, 287–297.

Tripathi, P., Kumar, N., Paroha, K. K., Rai, M., & Panda, M. K. (2024). Applications of Deep Learning in Healthcare in the Framework of Industry 5.0. In Khan, M., Khan, R., Praveen, P., Verma, A., & Panda, M. (Eds.), *Infrastructure Possibilities and Human-Centered Approaches With Industry 5.0* (pp. 69–85). IGI Global Scientific Publishing., DOI: 10.4018/979-8-3693-0782-3.ch005

Tripathi, P., Kumar, N., Rai, M., Shukla, P. K., & Verma, K. N. (2023). Applications of Machine Learning in Agriculture. In Khan, M., Gupta, B., Verma, A., Praveen, P., & Peoples, C. (Eds.), *Smart Village Infrastructure and Sustainable Rural Communities* (pp. 99–118). IGI Global Scientific Publishing., DOI: 10.4018/978-1-6684-6418-2.ch006

Vasani, V. P., Chandra, U., Sahu, G., Boyineni, S., Dhamodaran, S., Kumbhkar, M., Rai, M., & Gupta, S. (2024). Introduction to Emotion Detection and Predictive Psychology in the Age of Technology. In Rai, M., & Pandey, J. (Eds.), *Using Machine Learning to Detect Emotions and Predict Human Psychology* (pp. 1–16). IGI Global Scientific Publishing., DOI: 10.4018/979-8-3693-1910-9.ch001

Wen, X. (2023). Weighted hesitant fuzzy soft set and its application in group decision making. *Granular Computing*, *8*, 1583–1605. DOI: 10.1007/s41066-023-00387-w

Yazdinejad, A., Dehghantanha, A., Parizi, R., Srivastava, G., & Karimipour, H. (2023). Secure Intelligent Fuzzy Blockchain Framework: Effective Threat Detection in IoT Networks. *Computers in Industry*, *144*, 103801. DOI: 10.1016/j.compind.2022.103801

Zadeh, L. A. (1965). Fuzzy sets. *Information and Control*, *8*(3), 338–353.

Zhang, H., Xie, J., Song, Y., Ge, J., & Zhang, Z. (2020). A novel ranking method for intuitionistic fuzzy set based on information fusion and application to threat assessment. *Iranian Journal of Fuzzy Systems*, *17*, 91–104. DOI: 10.22111/IJFS.2020.5113

Chapter 3
Legal and Ethical Implications of Cyber Forensics

S. Ida Evangeline
https://orcid.org/0000-0003-2997-7897
Government College of Engineering, Tirunelveli, India

ABSTRACT

This chapter examines the legal and ethical foundations of cyber forensics in user-centric human threat intelligence. It argues that technical success is not sufficient: investigations must be anchored in clear legal authority, proportionate scope, and transparent, reproducible methods to remain admissible and worthy of trust. The chapter first defines core concepts and differentiates forensic investigation from incident response and threat intelligence. It then maps the lawful bases for digital search and seizure—warrants, consent, and limited exigency—showing how particularity and minimisation shape defensible collection. A lifecycle model links identification, preservation, collection, examination, analysis, reporting, and presentation to admissibility standards, while privacy and data-protection principles translate into operational choices on purpose limitation, data minimisation, retention, and security of processing. Practical guidance is offered on consent, monitoring, and transparency, including trauma-informed practice and safeguards for privileged or sensitive data.

DOI: 10.4018/979-8-3373-4898-8.ch003

1. INTRODUCTION: WHY LEGAL–ETHICAL RIGOR MATTERS IN CYBER FORENSICS

Cyber forensics now sits at the centre of user-centric human threat intelligence, where investigators must reconstruct digital activity that is intimate, distributed, and often encrypted, while protecting the rights and dignity of the very people whose data is examined (Rai et al. 2023). The stakes are unusually high. On one side lies the imperative to prevent harm, attribute misconduct, and preserve organizational resilience. On the other lies the risk that intrusive collection, opaque analytics, or lax procedure will erode public trust, contaminate evidence, or infringe fundamental liberties. This chapter begins from the premise that forensic success cannot be measured solely by the quantity of artifacts recovered or the apparent conclusiveness of an attribution. It must be measured by the lawfulness of the methods used, the fairness of the process followed, and the reliability and contestability of the findings produced (Kim et al. 2023).

The legal and ethical frame for cyber forensics is not an afterthought but a working architecture. Rule-of-law constraints, due process guarantees, and evidentiary standards define what may be gathered and how it must be handled if it is to be admitted and believed (Tripathi et al. 2023). Ethical principles—proportionality, necessity, purpose limitation, data minimization, transparency, and accountability—translate these constraints into everyday investigative choices: whether to image an entire device or target a partition; whether to deploy remote acquisition; how to treat bystander or privileged material; when to disclose monitoring; and how to document each step so it is intelligible to non-technical decision-makers. In a user-centric setting, these choices are magnified by power asymmetries between institutions and individuals, by the blurred boundaries of consent in workplaces and platforms, and by the ease with which automated tools can amplify bias or convert preliminary signals into premature conclusions (Fernando, 2021).

Time pressure and technical complexity do not dissolve these responsibilities. Rapid triage during an incident, cross-border data flows in cloud environments, or the use of AI-assisted classifiers to prioritize leads all create operational need, but they also raise predictable legal questions about authority, scope, and particularity, and predictable ethical questions about fairness and explainability. Meeting these challenges requires disciplined governance: clear investigative charters, defensible chains of custody, tool validation and version control, human-in-the-loop oversight for automated inferences, and reporting that is precise, neutral, and appropriately qualified.

This chapter is written for investigators, counsel, cybersecurity leaders, auditors, regulators, and policymakers who must make or review these decisions. It does not offer tool tutorials or exhaustively catalogue technical artifacts; instead, it provides a principled map for aligning investigative practice with legal doctrine and applied ethics in mixed public-private contexts. The discussion proceeds by defining core concepts of cyber forensics and human threat intelligence, examining the sources of legal authority for digital search and seizure, detailing the evidence lifecycle and admissibility requirements, and analysing privacy, consent, monitoring, automation, cross-border conflicts, professional ethics, and governance. It concludes with horizon issues and a reform agenda that prepare practitioners for emerging stresses—quantum-resistant ecosystems, decentralized platforms, and biometric-behavioural data—without compromising the commitments that make forensic evidence trustworthy and worthy of trust.

2. CORE CONCEPTS AND WORKING DEFINITIONS

Cyber forensics, as used in this chapter, refers to the disciplined acquisition, preservation, examination, analysis, and presentation of digital evidence in a manner that is legally authorised, ethically defensible, and technically reproducible. It spans endpoints such as laptops and mobiles, cloud platforms and software-as-a-service environments, enterprise servers and network devices, and extends to operational technologies including industrial control systems and connected sensors. Although tools and data formats vary across these environments, the governing idea is constant: evidence must be collected and interpreted in a way that can be explained, verified, and challenged without degrading the underlying rights of individuals or the integrity of proceedings (Khan et al. 2022).

It is useful to distinguish cyber forensics from adjacent practices that often occur in the same incident. Incident response is focused on rapid containment, eradication, and recovery after a breach or insider event. Threat intelligence seeks to understand adversary capabilities, infrastructure, and intent, frequently at an ecosystem level and sometimes without any case-specific attribution. Forensic investigation is narrower and more formal. Its purpose is to answer case-bounded questions—who acted, what occurred, when and how it happened, and whether policies or laws were violated—using methods that satisfy evidentiary standards. In practice, these domains overlap. Triage artefacts gathered during response may later be promoted to evidence, and intelligence cues may guide forensic search strategies. The moment material is intended for use in disciplinary or judicial fora, however, forensic rigour and documentation requirements attach.

Within user-centric human threat intelligence, the unit of analysis is often a person situated within an organisational or platform context. This vantage point foregrounds concepts that protect users while enabling investigation. Expectation of privacy defines whether and to what extent an individual could reasonably anticipate monitoring or inspection, which in turn shapes the lawfulness of collection in workplaces or managed devices. Purpose limitation and data minimisation require that only information strictly necessary to answer defined questions is accessed and retained. Proportionality connects investigative scope to risk and harm, asking whether less intrusive alternatives exist and whether they have been considered (Sharma et al. 2023).

The digital evidence lifecycle provides the backbone of definitions that matter in court and in audits. Identification concerns locating potentially relevant sources and segregating volatile from non-volatile data so that time-sensitive information is not lost. Preservation entails legal holds and technical safeguards that prevent alteration, including the use of write blockers and cryptographic hashing. Collection refers to the act of imaging or exporting data in a manner that is complete for the chosen scope and that records the context of acquisition, such as time synchronisation settings and tool versions. Examination and analysis take raw artefacts and turn them into findings, through repeatable workflows which do not suffer from bias and articulate alternate explanations. Reporting and presentation render technical results into correct, neutral reports with artefacts whose provenance can be established.

Three legal constructs frame the question as to whether these steps will pass scrutiny. Authority identifies the legal ground for access, which can be warrants for access, statutory powers, and informed consent, and how extensive and specific the search can be (Beemkumar et al. 2023). Admissibility controls the admissibility of evidence to be received by a tribunal and is based upon rules that test decisions of relevance, authenticity, and reliability and the absence of unfair prejudice. Chain of custody is the documentary trail of possession and control and can determine who handled the evidence, when and why and prove that the item in question is the same item collected.

Technical vocabulary also always has an ethical weight. Remote acquisition refers to the acquisition of data over a network link instead of the seizure of physical media; oftentimes essential in the cloud, this raises increased questions of over collecting as well as cross border transfer. Tool validation refers to the process of testing software and hardware on known data sets and following up on limitations, aiding in the reduction of automation bias, as well as reproducibility. Metadata contains data such as timestamps, geolocation and system descriptor information that may reveal a lot more about a person than the content itself; its processing needs to respect the same privacy safeguards as content data. Privileged or confidential information e.g. communications with counsel, whistleblower submissions require segregation and protective controls so that they do not taint an investigation (Haque et al. 2023).

These concepts are not just a bunch of pieces of terminology. They operate as operational guardrails in a context where personal data and organisational secrets are found side by side, where a misstep is made at any point and evidence will be useless or unlawfully acquired. By grounding the remainder of the chapter in these definitions, the discussion that follows can treat legal authority, evidence handling, privacy, consent, automation, jurisdiction, and professional duty with a shared vocabulary that is both practically oriented and normatively clear.

3. LEGAL AUTHORITY FOR DIGITAL SEARCH AND SEIZURE

Every forensic action rests on a threshold question: what is the lawful basis to access, copy, analyse, and present another person's digital data. Unlike physical searches, digital searches touch vast amounts of intimate information in a single step. Establishing clear authority before collection is therefore not a procedural nicety but a precondition for admissibility, fairness, and institutional legitimacy.

The most familiar source of authority is a warrant or comparable judicial order. In digital contexts, particularity carries special weight because a single device can hold years of communications, location trails, health records, and financial histories. Scope should be framed in terms that can be operationalised: accounts, date ranges, applications, or artefact classes rather than an open-ended demand for "all contents." A defensible warrant plan anticipates the difference between on-scene triage and off-site imaging, records the tools and filters to be used, and explains why a narrower approach will suffice or why a broader capture is strictly necessary. Courts are increasingly attentive to protocol: whether segregated review teams will screen privileged or irrelevant material, whether keyword or hash lists will confine examination, and whether search steps will stop once the sought evidence has been located (Chen & Dong, 2023).

Consent-based access is common in workplaces and incident response. For consent to carry legal and ethical weight it must be informed, voluntary, and limited to an agreed scope. A blanket clause in an employment contract may not justify intrusive examination where there is a serious power imbalance or where personal data on a mixed-use device is not segregated. Consent can be withdrawn, and collection should stop when that happens unless a separate legal power applies. Third-party consent raises further complexity. A system administrator may authorise access to enterprise logs, but cannot necessarily waive an individual's rights over personal containers on a bring-your-own-device handset. Family members, account delegates, and shared-drive collaborators each have partial control that does not automatically extend to full-content searches. Where the facts are contested, the safer course is to secure independent legal authority rather than rely on broad interpretations of consent.

To clarify the operational distinctions and common pitfalls associated with each legal basis for digital evidence collection, Table 1 summarises key features of warrants, informed consent, statutory powers, and exigent circumstances. This comparative framework assists practitioners in selecting the appropriate authority type based on context, scope, and risk.

Table 1. Comparison of Legal Authority Types for Digital Investigations.

Legal Basis	Scope Limitation	Consent Required	Common Use Cases	Key Risks
Warrant	High	No	Criminal investigations	Over-collection, delay
Informed Consent	Medium	Yes	Workplace probes, BYOD contexts	Coercion, withdrawal handling
Statutory Power	Variable	No	Regulator/agency access	Vagueness, oversight lapses
Exigent Circumstance	Narrow & Urgent	No	Imminent threats	Overreach, lack of record

Exigent circumstances sometimes permit immediate action to prevent imminent harm or loss of life, but volatility of data alone rarely justifies bypassing normal procedures. If emergency powers are used, the team should take the least intrusive steps compatible with the risk, preserve volatile artefacts using minimal capture, and document the factual basis, decision-makers, and time limits applied. Follow-on authorisations should be obtained promptly, with a clear separation between material collected under exigency and material collected under later authority (Vasani et al. 2024).

A large share of relevant evidence now resides with service providers. Access to provider-held data raises questions that turn on both law and contract. Content and communications may require a higher threshold than basic subscriber or transactional records. Preservation requests can prevent routine deletion while the appropriate order is sought. Some jurisdictions impose notice requirements on targets or account holders unless a court authorises delayed notice; others allow secrecy orders that must be narrowly tailored and time-bound. Providers also enforce their own policies on customer privacy and law-enforcement process, which means investigators should plan for lead times, format constraints, and the need to particularise requests so that overbroad demands are not rejected or narrowed unilaterally (Adel, 2022).

Enterprises often rely on internal policies to support examinations of corporate systems. Acceptable use policies, onboarding acknowledgements, and device management terms are important, but they do not eliminate the need for proportionality. Investigations should begin with artefacts the organisation already controls—centralised logs, access records, and security telemetry—before escalating to invasive imaging of endpoints or personal spaces. Bring-your-own-device arrangements require even greater care. Containerisation and mobile device management profiles that separate business from personal data make it possible to collect what is necessary while respecting areas where users retain a reasonable expectation of privacy. In multinational organisations, works council obligations and local labour protections may also constrain monitoring and require prior consultation or transparency.

Cross-border storage complicates authority. Cloud architectures distribute data across regions, and the legal power to compel production may be limited by jurisdiction, blocking statutes, or data-localisation rules. Investigators should map where target data likely resides, then choose pathways that respect both the requesting and the hosting state's laws. Mutual legal assistance, executive agreements, or provider production under recognised mechanisms may be appropriate depending on the case and timeframe. When parallel proceedings or overlapping regulators are involved, coordination prevents inconsistent orders and preserves the integrity of privilege and confidentiality claims.

Particularity and minimisation are not only judicial requirements; they are also ethical commitments that limit collateral intrusion. A written search protocol should explain how the team will narrow collection, isolate sensitive categories, and cease examination when objectives are met. Filter teams or independent reviewers can screen for legally protected material before investigators see it. Timeboxing, artefact-scoped imaging, and targeted exports from cloud applications reduce the risk of turning a defined inquiry into a fishing expedition. Automated triage and AI-assisted ranking may prioritise review, but they cannot substitute for legal thresholds; a high anomaly score is not itself authority to go wider or deeper.

Documentation is the bridge between authority on paper and authority in practice. Approvals, timestamps, tool versions, decision logs, and deviations from plan should be recorded in real time. Where authority depends on consent, the request language, the information provided to the user, and any scope clarifications must be preserved. Where authority depends on a court order, service and return details, provider correspondence, and any narrowing negotiated must be kept with the case file. This record is what allows a tribunal to test claims of lawfulness and what allows external auditors or regulators to assess compliance without re-running the investigation.

Many suppression failures arise from the same predictable errors: beginning wide and justifying later, treating incident response sweeps as if they were evidentiary collections, letting convenience drive cloud exports beyond what an order permits, or assuming enterprise ownership of an account collapses individual rights entirely. The remedy is cultural as much as legal. Teams should be trained to ask, at each turn, what authority applies now, what the minimum necessary step is, and how the action will appear when reconstructed by someone who was not in the room. When authority is uncertain, pause and seek counsel rather than normalising risk in the name of speed.

Legal authority in digital investigations is thus a living constraint that shapes scoping, tooling, sequence, and reporting from the first preservation letter to the last page of testimony. Treating it as such equips investigators to act with confidence and equips courts, boards, and the public to accept the results as both effective and just (Kim et al. 2023).

4. DIGITAL EVIDENCE LIFECYCLE AND ADMISSIBILITY

A defensible investigation follows a lifecycle that turns raw digital artefacts into findings capable of resisting scrutiny in courts, tribunals, and internal proceedings. The lifecycle is not a rigid checklist but a series of interdependent stages—identification, preservation, collection, examination, analysis, reporting, and presentation—each of which must be executed with legal authority, ethical restraint, and technical rigour. To aid understanding and operational clarity, Table 2 provides a structured overview of each lifecycle stage, highlighting its core activities, associated legal requirements, and ethical considerations. This reference supports disciplined investigative practice aligned with both evidentiary standards and human rights principles. When a misstep occurs early, later diligence cannot fully cure it; admissibility is therefore the cumulative result of many ordinary, careful decisions. To visually reinforce the sequential nature and interdependence of these stages, Figure 1 illustrates the digital evidence lifecycle as a linear process. This helps investigators map their activities to legal and ethical checkpoints throughout the forensic workflow.

Table 2. Evidentiary Lifecycle and Legal-Ethical Considerations.

Stage	Key Activities	Legal Requirement	Ethical Concern
Identification	Locate relevant sources	Authority	Avoid scope creep
Preservation	Prevent data alteration	Legal hold, immutability	Timely action to avoid spoliation
Collection	Acquire data within scope	Warrants, consent logs	Intrusiveness, privileged material
Examination	Parse and filter data	Tool validation, documentation	Privacy, bias minimization
Analysis	Build timelines, hypotheses	Chain of custody continuity	Confirmation bias, fairness
Reporting	Translate to neutral narrative	Authenticity, admissibility	Transparency, explainability

Figure 1. The Digital Evidence Lifecycle.

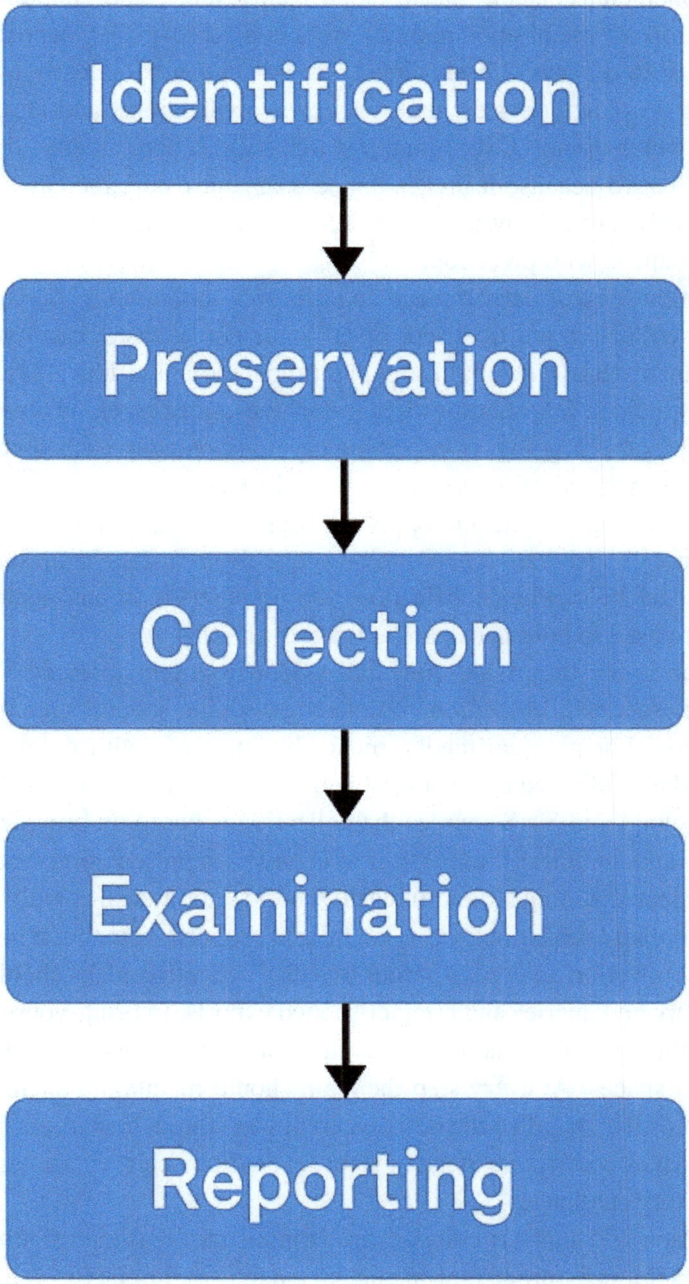

Identification begins with scoping what sources are likely to hold probative data and separating volatile from non-volatile elements so that short-lived information is not lost. In user-centric investigations this often means prioritising live memory captures, ephemeral chat messages, cloud audit events, and endpoint telemetry before they roll off retention windows (Arora et al. 2024). The identification plan should be tied to the lawful basis already established and to clearly framed questions: which accounts, devices, time windows, applications, and artefact classes matter, and which do not. Over-breadth at this stage is both an ethical risk and an evidentiary hazard because it invites unnecessary intrusion, increases the chance of handling privileged or bystander content, and creates volumes of data that are difficult to manage with precision.

Preservation secures data in place and prevents spoliation while authority and logistics for collection are finalised. Legal holds notify custodians not to alter or delete relevant material and should be explicit about scope and duties. Technical preservation may include snapshotting virtual machines, freezing cloud object versions, enabling immutable logging, or exporting cryptographically hashed point-in-time copies. Time synchronisation is so critical; if clocks on the system are out of sync, timelines will be out of sync and opposing counsel will question the reliability of event sequences. Preservation needs to be auditable so that the team should record who started each hold, when notifications were sent and what automatic or manual controls were used to hold data stable (Tyagi et al. 2024).

Collection is the time when potential evidence is transformed to actual evidence, and is successful based on completeness within scope, contaminated, and documentation. For physical media, bit for bit imaging (with write blockers) is still the standard, followed by hash verification (using algorithms which have been tested). For cloud and SaaS sources the collection is based on provider APIs, export formats and audit trails; the task is to acquire a representation that is faithful, containing metadata, context and integrity checks, not a cosmetically convenient summary. Remote acquisition can be lawful and proportionate, but it heightens the risk of over-collection and cross-border transfer; collection plans should therefore implement targeted queries and artefact-scoped exports. In bring-your-own-device settings, containerisation enables the capture of business data without intruding into personal spaces. At every step the team should maintain a chain-of-custody log that records who handled the item, where it was stored, how it was transported, and which hashes confirm its identity. Gaps, even if innocent, create fertile ground for admissibility challenges.

Examination and analysis convert raw captures into reasoned findings. Examination refers to structured, tool-mediated parsing of artefacts—registry hives, application databases, logs, media, network traces—using validated software whose version, configuration, and known limitations are recorded. Analysis is the interpretive work that builds timelines, tests hypotheses, and considers alternative explanations. Because user-centric evidence often intertwines personal behaviour with organisational systems, analysts must apply minimisation strategies that avoid reading more than necessary and use segregation in case privileged or confidential material is encountered. AI-assisted triage or classification may help prioritise review, but the human examiner remains responsible for verifying outputs, explaining the method, and disclosing error rates or uncertainty. Reproducibility is central. A peer with similar tools and instructions should be able to arrive at the same artefact-level observations, even if interpretations differ at the margins.

Reporting translates technical findings into accurate, neutral narratives that non-specialists can evaluate. A sound report states the authority for the investigation, the scope and questions posed, the sources consulted, the methods used, and the results obtained, along with any constraints, anomalies, or limitations. Terminology should be precise and careful about certainty levels. If timestamps were normalised across time zones or adjusted for clock drift, the method should be stated. If certain applications alter files upon opening, that behaviour should be documented and accounted for. Where appropriate, the report should describe the steps taken to minimise intrusion and handle sensitive classes of data. The aim is not advocacy but clarity, enabling decision-makers to understand what the evidence shows, what it does not show, and how confident the investigator is about each conclusion (Ratul et al. 2024).

Presentation is the moment where admissibility principles are tested. Although rules vary across jurisdictions, four recurring tests dominate. Relevance asks whether the item makes a material fact more or less probable. Authenticity requires that the proponent show the item is what it purports to be, which in digital cases often involves hash values, tool output, witness testimony about collection, and contextual corroboration. Integrity and reliability examine whether the evidence has been altered or could have been altered and whether the methods used are scientifically or technically sound (Singh et al. 2024a). Fairness ensures that probative value is not outweighed by unfair prejudice, confusion, or needless cumulativeness. In common-law courts, expert testimony on specialised matters may be evaluated under standards that consider testability, error rates, peer acceptance, and general reliability of methods. Regardless of forum, a consistent theme is that transparent process and documented controls make it easier for adjudicators to accept digital evidence without needing to master every technical detail.

Several recurring pitfalls jeopardise admissibility and can be anticipated. Mixing incident-response artefacts gathered without evidentiary controls into the forensic set invites arguments that collection was opportunistic or contaminated. Exporting from cloud dashboards that reformat or re-timestamp events, instead of using raw API pulls with checksums, exposes the record to authenticity challenges. Failing to isolate privileged legal advice or whistleblower submissions risks tainting the investigation and, in some systems, may trigger exclusion. Using tools without validation or failing to record versions and settings undermines reproducibility, especially when proprietary algorithms are involved. Losing sight of minimisation harms credibility; a tribunal may admit the evidence but criticise the process, weakening its persuasive value and inviting regulatory consequences.

The lifecycle therefore operates as a chain whose strength is measured at its weakest link. If identification is disciplined, preservation is timely, collection is complete within scope, examination is methodical, analysis is transparent, reporting is neutral, and presentation is candid about limitations, the result is evidence that decision-makers can trust. In user-centric human threat intelligence this is also a discipline that serves as an ethical safeguard to ensure that an effort to understand what is harmful behaviour is not itself harmful behaviour (Mishra et al. 2024).

5. PRIVACY, DATA PROTECTION, AND PROPORTIONALITY

Privacy is not a barrier to cyber forensics but rather the situation in which forensic work is legitimized. Data protection law gives that intuition concrete form by setting out principles to apply to all stages of the evidence lifecycle: investigations must be lawful, must be necessary to address defined purposes, must be proportionate to those purposes, must be limited to what's necessary, must be kept no longer than necessary, must be secured against misuse, and must be accountable to documentation and oversight. In user-centric, human threat intelligence, where the investigative lens is in many cases occupied with a particular person, in the context of a complex platform or workplace, these principles do not exist outside of the technical process. They guide the form of it - what is collected, how they are treated, who may access them and when it has to be deleted.

The starting point is the understanding of purpose. An investigation that begins with a vague aim predictably grows in scope and intrusiveness. A written statement of purpose, tied to specific questions and grounded in the lawful authority already established, disciplines later choices about sources, time windows, and artefact classes. Purpose limitation then requires that data collected for the investigation is not quietly repurposed for unrelated goals, such as product development, profiling, or broad workforce analytics. Where secondary use is contemplated, fresh legal analysis and ethical review are needed, and in many settings renewed consent, impact assessment, or both will be appropriate (Katkuri, 2025).

Data minimisation is the practical expression of proportionality. It compels investigators to prefer targeted over bulk methods and to choose the least intrusive source that will credibly answer the question. In an enterprise email matter, for example, it may be sufficient to examine headers, audit logs, and limited date ranges rather than ingest years of content. In a mobile device context, containerised business data can often be extracted without touching personal galleries, messaging apps, or health information. Minimisation also applies to the manner of review. If keyword filters, hash lists, or artefact-scoped exports can exclude categories that are plainly irrelevant or sensitive, they should be applied and their parameters recorded. A proportional approach is not only ethically superior; it reduces downstream risk by limiting the quantity of data that must be safeguarded and defended.

Certain data categories heighten obligations. Health information, biometrics, precise location traces, communications content, data about minors, and materials covered by professional or legal privilege carry elevated sensitivity. When such data is in scope because it is genuinely probative, additional controls are warranted. Segregation of review teams prevents privileged or whistleblower material from contaminating the fact-finding group. Role-based access, least-privilege permissions, and time-boxed access windows reduce unnecessary exposure. Encryption at rest and in transit, controlled key management, tamper-evident logging, and secure evidence vaults protect against unauthorised access or exfiltration. Where tools derive behavioural inferences from metadata—such as movement patterns or social graphs—those outputs should be treated with the same care as content, since the privacy impact can be as great or greater (Singh et al. 2024b). Figure 2 illustrates a conceptual escalation of ethical risk based on data sensitivity. It visually reinforces the importance of applying stricter safeguards and proportionality measures as forensic investigations move from basic metadata to more intimate or third-party information.

Figure 2. Ethical Risk Escalation in Cyber Forensics.

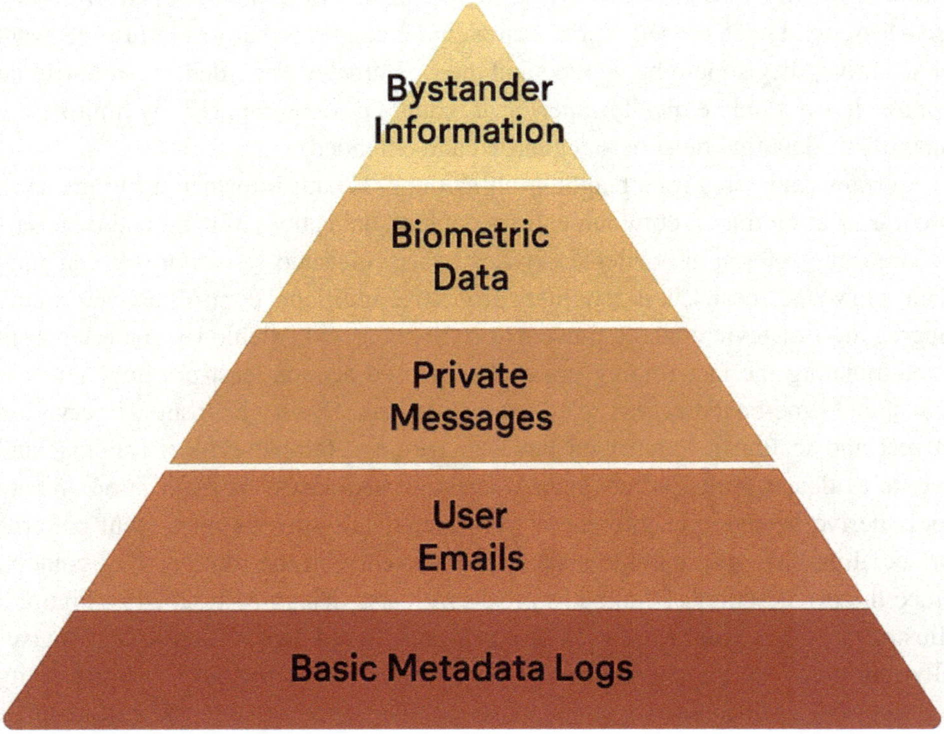

Retention and deletion policies are central to data protection, yet investigations often treat them as an afterthought. The lawful hold that preserves data for the duration of a matter is a narrow exception to the general rule of storage limitation. It should be scoped, renewed only as necessary, and lifted without delay when the litigation or disciplinary risk has abated. Evidence repositories should track matter identifiers and retention dates so that automatic alerts prompt review. Where regulations or case strategy require long retention, measures like encryption with segregated keys, access review, and periodic re-justification of continued storage can mitigate the risk of prolonged retention. When deletion occurs, it should be irreversible at the level that matters for the particular storage medium, and accompanied by an auditable record that shows what was deleted, when, and under whose authority (Malik et al. 2024).

Transparency presents a persistent tension between investigative effectiveness and user rights. In many jurisdictions, individuals are entitled to be informed about monitoring and data processing, particularly in employment and platform contexts. Generic notices in acceptable use policies and privacy statements may satisfy baseline transparency, but covert steps may still be justified in narrow circumstances where notice would jeopardise evidence or enable harm. Even then, secrecy should be the exception and subject to time limits and post-fact notice where safe. Where investigators rely on consent, transparency is inseparable from validity. Consent obtained through boilerplate or under conditions of dependency is vulnerable to challenge; consent obtained for one purpose is not a blank cheque for another. Records of what was explained, what scope was agreed, and how withdrawal would operate are therefore part of the evidentiary file, not merely HR documentation.

Proportionality, understood as a structured balancing test, offers a method for reconciling these pressures. The analysis should begin by defining the legitimate aim and the specific harms the investigation seeks to prevent or remediate. It should in turn establish the intrusiveness of contemplated measures along a continuum, ranging from review of telemetry of enterprise systems to targeted collection from defined accounts or time ranges to full disk imaging or remote acquisition. The inquiry tasks are whether each intrusive step is necessary to achieve the aim, whether a less intrusive alternative could do, and whether the anticipated probative value outweighs the collateral impact of its effect on privacy and other rights. Documentation of this reasoning before collection locks in discipline; revisiting this reasoning as facts evolve guards against scope creep.

Cross context data flows require special attention because privacy obligations go with the data. When evidence moves out of its original environment but from a user's device to a forensic workstation; from an export of a service as a software as a service (SaaS) to an on-premises vault or from one country to another - the legal basis and safeguards should be appropriate to the new context. Technical measures such as hashing, sealing and cryptographic proofs are used to support authenticity and there are contractual and organisational measures such as access controls, confidentiality undertakings and review protocols which constrain use. In a multinational context, transfer impact assessments and suitable transfer processes may be necessary; legal details differ in each jurisdiction and yet the ethical consideration remains the same: when investigators investigate in a legal grey area they should not do so simply because it is expedient.

Security of processing is more than a compliance box to tick, it is the moral equivalent of collection. Evidence systems are tempting targets because they consolidate sensitive information with detailed timelines and attributions. A defensible security posture therefore includes having forensic networks isolated from production, strict oversight by administrators, multi-factor authentication of all evidence platforms, immutable logging with frequent review, and tested incident response plans that include the possibility of a breach of the evidentiary store itself. Toolchain security should be given the same care. Where proprietary tools are used, their update channels, plugin ecosystems and output verification steps should be scrutinised; where open source tools are used, version pinning and reproducible builds reduces the risk of unnoticed drift (Tatipatri & Arun, 2024).

Data subject rights add complexity of operations but they bring in accountability as well. Requests for access, correction or erasure may come in during a hold. The appropriate response is to honour the right to the extent that is compatible with legal obligations to preserve evidence, which often means that processing and documenting the conflict is reduced to the extent that it is the case of deletion. Clear workflows are agreed with legal counsel and the data protection function which allows consistent handling and takes away the impression of arbitrariness. Whereas, the investigation of a person exonerating him or making certain data irrelevant, the fairness suggests proactive narrowing or deletion instead of waiting for a request.

Finally, proportionality is maintained by governance. Decision logs recording alternatives considered and reasons for rejection sign-offs by counsel and data protection officers for high-risk steps periodic audits of active matters to ensure practice matches policy Training supports the concept of privacy being an operational requirement, rather than an obstacle imposed by another team. When investigators internalise that mindset, they ask better questions, collect cleaner data and produce results that are not only technically accurate, but that were obtained in a way that respects the people behind the artefacts (Admass et al. 2024).

6. CONSENT, MONITORING, AND TRANSPARENCY IN PRACTICE

Consent in cyber forensics is less a signature and more a sustained, intelligible conversation about purpose, scope, and limits. Treating it as a living process rather than a one-time form is essential because digital investigations evolve. New facts emerge, hypotheses narrow or widen, and tools reveal artefacts that were not anticipated at the outset. A defensible approach therefore begins by explaining, in plain language, why an investigation is being undertaken, what specific data sources are in scope, how long processing will last, who will have access, and what safeguards apply to sensitive categories such as privileged communications or health information. Consent obtained under conditions of dependency, such as an employment relationship, demands extra care; voluntariness cannot be presumed when the person believes refusal might cost them their job or reputation. To mitigate that imbalance, organisations should separate the requestor from the decision-maker, offer a genuine opportunity to ask questions, and provide alternatives where appropriate, such as targeted collection from enterprise containers instead of full-device imaging (Tripathi et al. 2024). Revocation must be real. If the person withdraws consent, investigators should stop processing unless a separate, pre-existing legal authority justifies continued collection, and the case file should record the time, the circumstances, and the adjusted plan.

Documentation is the backbone of valid consent. It is not enough to record that consent was given; the record should capture the exact language presented, the language of communication, any interpreter involvement, comprehension checks, and the answers to scope questions the person actually asked. Where forms are long or technical, layered notices help: a short front page summarises purpose and scope, with links to fuller explanations and policies. In places where people have different literacy and accessibility needs, consent artefacts should be designed to be clear and inclusive, using both readable typography and accessible formats and examples that help to ground abstract terms such as "metadata," "audit log," or "enterprise container" in concrete behaviours that people understand (Bhambri & Khang, 2024).

Monitoring policies stand or fall on the issue of transparency. In workplaces and platforms, baseline notice in the form of acceptable use policies, login banners, or privacy statements is often given. These must communicate that security telemetry and limited content review may occur for defined purposes such as threat detection, policy enforcement and incident investigation. Yet generic notice is limited. If a specific investigation does require steps more intrusive than routine monitoring, such as remote live acquisition, review of personal folders on a mixed-use device or capturing private messages on a continuous basis, some fresh and specific transparency is warranted unless it jeopardises evidence or safety. Even where such covert measures are justified they should be limited in time and scope, be subject to appropriate oversight and subject to post-fact notice where risk has passed. In some jurisdictions, works councils, unions or regulatory authorities need to be consulted prior to the introduction of new monitoring technologies; integrating these requirements into the governance calendar eliminates the temptation to make changes by the seat of one's pants.

Covert techniques require special restraint. Their ethical defensibility rests on the principles of necessity and proportionality; investigators should be able to explain why less intrusive alternatives could not achieve the aim, the importance of delay which would lead to material harm and the way in which intrusion to collateral sites will be minimised. Timeboxing, event-driven triggers, and artefact-scoped filters are practical controls that keep covert steps tethered to the investigative question. Decisions to use deception—such as seeded content or honeypot resources—should be rare, be approved at a higher level than routine actions, and be documented with the same care as overt measures so that later reviewers can evaluate fairness (Akhtar et al. 2024).

User-centric threat intelligence often involves people in vulnerable positions: whistleblowers, victims of harassment, minors on educational platforms, or employees in precarious roles. Consent and transparency norms bend towards protection in these contexts. Trauma-informed practice reduces re-victimisation by focusing questions on what is necessary, limiting repeated interviews, and avoiding unnecessary exposure to the same harmful material. Where guardianship or capacity is in question, investigators should obtain assent from the person and consent from a legally authorised representative, while adjusting the scope to the least intrusive set of artefacts that can answer the defined questions. When a person is a suspect, fairness requires recognising procedural rights—access to counsel, caution against self-incrimination, and clarity about the consequences of agreeing to a search—rather than using the language of "consent" to mask compulsion.

Third-party and bystander data are unavoidable in modern systems and demand deliberate handling. Chats, shared drives, group calendars, and collaborative documents intertwine multiple people's information in a single artefact. When only one participant has consented, investigators should prefer techniques that isolate the consenting party's contributions or that rely on enterprise logs and headers rather than full-content review. If privileged, confidential, or unrelated sensitive material is encountered, segregation protocols should divert it to a separate review track or seal it entirely, with access limited to a small, independent team. Redaction and selective export are tools of ethics as much as law, not cosmetic steps performed at the end.

Targeted search strategies connect consent, monitoring, and transparency to daily practice. Anchoring queries to articulated hypotheses, defined time windows, and specific applications reduces drift. Stopping rules—commitments to cease examination when the objective evidence is found—preserve proportionality and demonstrate good faith. Where automated triage or ranking is used to prioritise review, investigators should be transparent, at least internally, about how the model works, what data it used for training, and what error characteristics it exhibits. The fact that a classifier flags an artefact does not expand authority; it merely allocates attention. Human review, with explicit checks for false positives in sensitive categories, protects both fairness and accuracy.

Finally, transparency is also outward-facing. Stakeholders beyond the investigation team—legal, HR, data protection officers, executives, and, in some cases, regulators—should be able to reconstruct why particular steps were taken and how risks to individuals were addressed. Decision logs, approvals, and communications with the data subject become part of that accountability record. When the matter closes, organisations should consider post-fact debriefs, including lessons for policy and training. If the investigation exonerates a person, it is both ethically sound and reputationally wise to narrow or delete their data and to inform them, where appropriate, that the matter has been resolved. Consent, monitoring, and transparency thus operate not as separate checkboxes but as a single, continuous discipline that keeps user-centric forensics lawful, humane, and trustworthy (Kalinin et al. 2024).

7. AUTOMATION, AI-ENHANCED FORENSICS, AND FAIRNESS

Automation now permeates digital investigations. Classifiers flag suspicious artefacts, anomaly detectors surface unusual login patterns, entity-resolution models stitch identities across platforms, and language models summarise message clusters or suggest investigative hypotheses. These systems promise speed and consistency but also present a second evidentiary layer which needs justification in its own right: not only that the artefacts be authentic and lawfully obtained, but also that the analytical process that took them to the top of the pyramid be reliable, explainable, and fair. Treating the outputs of AI as though they are neutral facts opens the way to error. Toward the end of this article, we have two parameters to consider: accuracy and rights.

The main technical danger is automation bias, the tendency of humans to overtrust the suggestions of machines, particularly when they are under pressure of time. A triage model which prioritizes devices based on "likelihood of policy violation" can determine the entire course of a case if investigators accept its ordering without challenge. Countermeasures are practical in nature and cultural. Models should be documented for purpose, training data provenance, known limitations, and typical failure modes. Versioning, configuration snapshots and random seed capture allow for later reproduction of outputs. Calibration should be measured and reported, so that a score can be interpreted as a meaningful probability rather than a meaningless ordinal label. Human - in - the - loop check points should force an analyst to explain in words how independent (or independent from the model) artefacts support or do not support the model's suggestion. When an output is adopted, the recording should indicate the reasoning and not just the score (Bhimavarapu, 2026).

Fairness is an even trickier issue because the datasets used in investigations seldom contain explicit demographic information; while the attributes that the tools of forensic science are working with could represent proxies such as language, location, device type, or work schedule. A classifier which down -ranks communications or flags atypical working hours that are not in English may inadvertently target minority populations or shift workers. The ethical response starts upstream, in the data selection, and includes downstream, in the impact assessment. Training sets should be examined for gaps in coverage and for historical artefacts which indicate previous patterns of enforcement and not behaviour. Where this is not possible because of privacy considerations, fairness could still be investigated indirectly by testing performance in operationally relevant strata, e.g. languages, regions, device classes, or network segments. If error rates differ, thresholds and workflows should be adjusted to reduce disparate impact such as requiring more corroboration before escalating cases originating from higher equation error strata.

Explainability is often presented as a single requirement, but its audience differs between investigators, courts, and affected individuals. Investigators need operational transparency—why this logon sequence was flagged and which features contributed—so they can decide what to do next. Courts need methodological transparency—how the model was trained, validated, and controlled—so they can determine whether the outputs are reliable enough to influence findings. Individuals need decisional transparency—what the model did in their case and how to challenge it—so they are not subjected to unreviewable inferences. Local explainability techniques can help, but they should not be used to mask fundamentally opaque pipelines. If a model cannot be defended without revealing trade-secret internals, organisations should anticipate the legal and ethical consequences: independent validation by a neutral expert, disclosure under protective orders, or the choice to rely on more interpretable methods where rights are at stake (Zangana & Omar, 2025).

Law governs automated inference even when statutes do not mention algorithms. Admissibility standards require demonstrable reliability, which implies tested error rates, documented validation against known-truth datasets, and stability of outputs across reasonable perturbations. Chain-of-custody principles apply to models too: the version used, the weights or rules at the time of analysis, the feature extraction code, the pre-processing steps, and any post-processing filters should be frozen alongside the evidence so results can be replicated later. When tools are updated mid-investigation, the team should avoid re-scoring historical artefacts unless the change is documented, justified, and its impact on earlier decisions is reviewed. Where models generate synthetic artefacts or reconstructions, their outputs should be clearly marked as inferential and kept separate from direct evidence.

Privacy and AI intersect in two directions. Training on internal archives or case data can create leakage, allowing later models to memorise sensitive strings or authorship patterns. Technical safeguards include data minimisation in training, differential privacy for certain tasks, and strict separation between evidentiary stores and model-development environments. At inference time, model prompts and outputs can themselves reveal sensitive information; logs must therefore be treated as part of the evidence file and subject to the same access and deletion controls. When third-party AI services are used, contractual terms should prohibit secondary use, require regionally appropriate processing, and mandate security attestations; otherwise, investigators risk exporting confidential evidence into uncontrolled ecosystems.

Operational discipline keeps AI in proportion. Thresholds should be tuned to the investigation's tolerance for false positives and false negatives, with explicit recognition that different phases may warrant different trade-offs. Early triage might prefer recall to avoid missing critical leads, paired with mandatory human corroboration before any intrusive step. Later confirmation should prefer precision to avoid unwarranted escalation. Stopping rules matter: once direct artefacts answer the question, continuing to widen AI-driven search because it is easy undermines proportionality. Red-team exercises that attempt to mislead models, induce spurious correlations, or exploit out-of-distribution weaknesses reveal fragility before it affects real people.

Fairness is finally a governance problem. A register of approved analytic models, with purpose, validation status, oversight owners, and sunset dates, prevents uncontrolled proliferation. Case templates that include fields for documenting AI use and its influence on decisions convert abstract principles into repeatable practice. Periodic audits can sample closed matters to test whether automation altered outcomes in ways that correlate with protected or vulnerable groups. When issues are found, remediation should include model retraining or retirement, retrospective case review where appropriate, and transparent communication to stakeholders. In this way, AI becomes an assistant to forensic judgement rather than its unexamined substitute, improving speed and consistency without eroding the fairness that gives investigative results their legitimacy (Albtosh, 2025).

8. CROSS-BORDER EVIDENCE AND JURISDICTION

Digital investigations rarely respect territorial lines. Cloud providers shard data across regions for resilience and performance; employees work remotely from multiple countries; platforms route traffic through content delivery networks; and a single user's footprint may span personal devices, corporate systems, and third-party services hosted in several jurisdictions. The result is that questions of "where" evidence is located and "whose law" governs access arise before a single artefact is collected. Cross-border issues are not exotic edge cases; they are the default setting of user-centric cyber forensics, and they shape authority, scope, timing, and admissibility from the outset.

The first challenge is ontological rather than legal: data does not sit still. A mailbox presented as "EU-hosted" may include attachments stored in object storage replicated to another region; logs visible in a dashboard may be aggregated from microservices whose raw traces live elsewhere; and caches or backups can place fragments in jurisdictions no one anticipated. Because the location of processing and the location of controllership are not the same, investigators should disentangle three coordinates before planning collection: where the relevant data was or is processed at rest, who controls the system that can deliver it on demand, and where the data subject is located. Each point can pull in a different legal direction. A provider may be willing to produce content under one country's order because it is subject to that country's jurisdiction, while the same production could contravene another country's privacy or secrecy laws because the data concerns a resident there or was stored on its soil. Recognising this triangle early prevents later conflict and supports a collection strategy that is both effective and respectful of comity. Figure 3 visualizes the three-point tension in cross-border digital evidence scenarios: where data is stored, who controls it, and where the data subject resides. Understanding this jurisdictional triangle is key to lawful and defensible collection strategies in multinational investigations.

Formal inter-State mechanisms are at the centre even there. Mutual legal assistance pathways provide for one state to request evidence from another state using designated authorities so that local rights and privileges are used prior to production. These mechanisms may be slow in comparison to incident response timelines but they have the benefit of conferring legitimacy and usually the clearest path to admissibility. Newer instruments and executive agreements in some regions allow law-enforcement or regulatory orders to be served directly on foreign providers, bypassing older diplomatic routes under defined safeguards. In corporate or civil cases letters of request and recognised channels of discovery are used with a similar purpose. The practical question is not whether one can force data but which route will provide reliable evidence without a jurisdictional clash tarnishing the case or a sanction against the organisation (Zhang & Gong, 2024).

Figure 3. Cross-Border Jurisdiction Triangle.

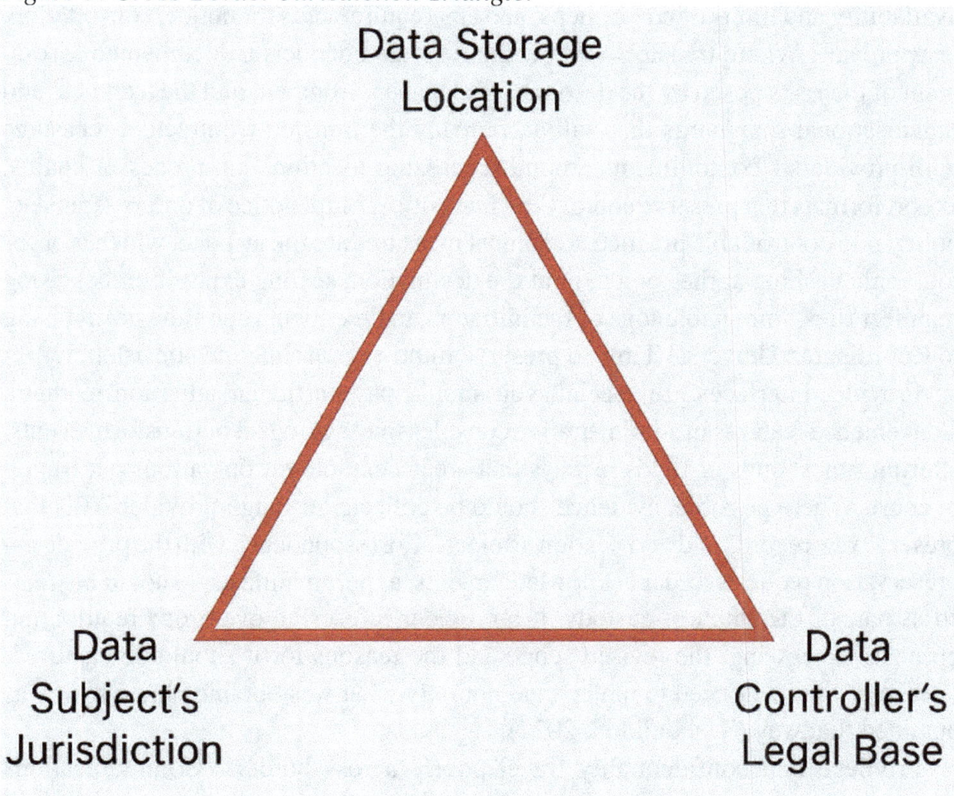

Enterprise investigations complicate matters because private actors are neither courts nor consulates, yet their actions can have cross-border legal consequences. A multinational employer may be able to access logs and content under its contractual terms with a provider, but doing so from one country may violate blocking statutes or labour protections in another. Works councils or data-protection authorities may demand prior consultation when new monitoring or export practices are introduced. Internal policies that authorise examination of corporate systems do not extinguish constitutional or fundamental rights that attach to individuals in certain jurisdictions. The operationally sensible move—collect from the place with the easiest access—can be legally reckless if it triggers localisation penalties or undermines later admissibility. The better discipline is to map the relevant legal regimes, decide the forum or fora in which results must stand, and align collection with the most demanding of those regimes that is still practicable.

A defensible cross-border playbook begins with scoping that is sensitive to geography. Investigators define the precise questions to be answered and identify the minimal set of accounts, time windows, and artefacts that bear on those questions.

Counsel in each implicated jurisdiction confirms the lawful basis for collection, the availability and limits of covert steps, and any requirements for notice, consultation, or approvals. Where transfers will occur, the team conducts a documented assessment of the risks posed by the destination's legal environment and the technical and organisational safeguards that will accompany the transfer. Contractual measures with providers - commitments around processing location, sub processor chains, export formats that preserve context and integrity, prompt notice of orders - translate policy into controllable practice. Technical measures are the last one, which is cryptographic hashing at the source, or at the destination, sealing export bundles using manifest files, immutable logs of the initiators and recipients and time normalising to Coordinated Universal Time to preserve multi-region timeline consistency.

Provider interfaces are special, you should pay particular attention to them. Convenience features in administrative consoles may aggregate or transform events, altering timestamps or fields in ways that are acceptable for operations but fragile in court. Where possible, evidence should be collected through provider APIs that preserve raw records and verification artefacts. Correspondence with the provider—preservation requests, order acknowledgements, export manifests—should be treated as part of the chain of custody. If a provider refuses an overbroad request and proposes narrowing, the revised scope and the reasons for it should be captured; later reviewers will need to understand not only what was obtained but why it was obtained that way (Sachoulidou, 2024).

Privilege and confidentiality travel poorly across borders. Communications with in-house counsel that are protected in one jurisdiction may not enjoy the same status in another; professional secrecy rules may protect categories of data that do not exist elsewhere; and whistleblower protections can restrict access to reports or identities except under defined safeguards. Without careful segregation, a single collection can pull in protected material whose review is unlawful in the country of origin or whose exposure undermines the investigation's integrity. Screening teams, privilege logs suited to each forum, and, where necessary, neutral reviewers create the buffer that keeps the merits team from seeing what it ought not to see. When courts or regulators are involved in multiple countries, parallel proceedings raise the risk of inconsistent orders and uncoordinated disclosures. Proactive coordination between counsel means that duplication is avoided and the spectacle of one tribunal discovering that material has been quietly exported under the colour of a different legal process is avoided.

Cross-border reality also puts proportionality to the test. The fact that data can be pulled from a global dash board does not mean that it should be pulled, and the fact that a home state order reaches a foreign provider does not make obligations to consider the impact on non-parties in the host state cease. Narrowing down by date, artefact type and custodians; preferring logs and metadata where content may not be necessary; and sequencing collection so that early, less intrusive steps may inform decisions on whether and how to take later, more intrusive ones, are not only ethical practices but also the surest way to show respect for the host state's interests. Where encrypted stores or end-to-end communications are in scope, investigators should deal with and not avoid the legal questions that decryption or capture of communications at the client end raise. Workarounds using jurisdictional grey zones may win tactically but may cost the legitimacy of the overall effort.

Finally, the cross-border dimension has its end at its beginning: with documentation that allows decisions to be reconstructed by third parties. Decision logs should explain why one pathway was chosen over another, how conflicts of law were analysed, what safeguards were attached to each transfer, and how objections or constraints from providers or authorities were dealt with. When the matter is closed, lessons learnt in relation to data-residency claims, responsiveness of providers and safeguards performance should be fed back into governance so that future cases start on a better footing. In an era where the individual at the hub of an investigation may live in one country, use a device bought in another, and store their life in several others, jurisdiction is not an obstacle to be set aside, it is the structure to place around it, to facilitate, if respected, cyber-forensics as a way to yield results that are not only technically sound but also lawful in whichever area they have to be defended (Alsaraireh, 2025).

9. PROFESSIONAL ETHICS AND STANDARDS OF PRACTICE

Professional ethics in cyber-forensics is not a code that one hangs on the wall, it is a code that is operational, that guards against whether an investigation will have credibility when it is reconstructed by outsiders. At their core are duties of competence, honesty, impartiality, confidentiality and respect for persons. Competence requires more than the knowledge of tools; it is an attitude of using current knowledge of platforms, artefact development and legal standards, and to refuse or request supervision in matters beyond knowledge. Honesty and impartiality means that investigators report what the evidence supports rather than what they believe their stakeholders want to see, distinguish observation from inference, and recognize uncertainty, error margins, and alternative explanations. Confidentiality restricts the disclosure of information to those who have a legitimate need to know, persisting beyond the life of the case - forensic curiosity is not license to browse nor is it license to share stories between friends - evidence stores have to be protected as if they were attractive targets - because they are.

Standards of practice put these duties into routine practices that can be repeated. Validated methods, version pinned tools and written standard operating procedures mean that investigator discretion is limited to the junctures where judgement really adds value. Peer review and technical quality assurance - second-examiner checks on critical artefacts, re-run of important queries, independent hash verification - are not expressions of distrust in a team but expressions of respect for the stakes of the work. A documentation culture is also an ethical practice: decision logs, chain-of-custody records, and notes about methods make it transparent for later review and ensure a colleague would be able to reproduce steps with no guess work. When deviations from protocol occur—and they will in messy real-world contexts—ethical practice requires recording what changed, why it changed, and what controls were used to mitigate new risks (Quang Huy & Kien Phuc, 2025).

Conflicts of interest are often subtle in user-centric contexts. An investigator embedded within a security team may face pressure to protect the organisation's reputation; a consultant may be tempted to shade conclusions to preserve a commercial relationship; an expert witness may be offered terms that tie compensation to outcome. Ethical independence demands that investigators and experts refuse contingent fee arrangements, disclose relationships that could appear to bias judgement, and accept that neutrality may sometimes cost a client. Where organisational structure creates unavoidable tensions, firewalls—separate reporting lines, independent counsel oversight, and review by a governance committee—can insulate the forensic function from operational or public relations priorities.

Certification and continuing education matter because technology and law move quickly. Formal credentials do not guarantee virtue, but they signal baseline proficiency and a willingness to submit to third-party standards. Ongoing training should include not only new tool features but also platform behaviour, cloud provider export semantics, cross-border legal developments, and human factors such as interviewing, trauma-informed practice, and cognitive bias mitigation. Mentorship and after-action reviews institutionalise learning, turning individual experience into shared organisational memory.

Communication is an ethical act. Reports must be written in neutral language that distinguishes between facts, interpretations, and assumptions, and that calibrates confidence without exaggeration. Visual aids are often helpful, but when they are absent—as in this chapter's constraints—the obligation to write clearly is even higher. Testimony requires the same discipline. Experts should answer the question asked, avoid advocacy, and be candid about limitations, including the possibility that an alternative explanation fits the data. Where proprietary tools or models are used, ethical testimony prepares the tribunal for what can be disclosed, what has been validated independently, and what the known error characteristics are, rather than hiding behind claims of trade secrecy (Patrick et al. 2025).

Ethics also govern what happens when things go wrong. If potentially exculpatory material has been missed, if there was a misconfigured the result of a collection, or if the scope of a collection was beyond authority, the duty is to surface the issue and consider impact on collection promptly along with rectifying the record. Internal paths for escalation, and policies of non-retaliation to ensure that concerns can be raised, provide a good and healthy environment for forensic work, without which errors can fester and become credibility crises. Whistleblowing channels to independent bodies may be required in extreme cases of failure of internal governance.

This means that professional ethics are supported by governance that sees beyond the individual case. A code of conduct specific to the right risk profile of an organisation, an ethics committee or designated officer to offer advice on difficult choices, periodic audits of closed matters, and statements about the principles of investigation to the public foster accountability. In a human threat intelligence setting that is user centered, this governance should be explicit in protecting vulnerable populations, making proportionality analyses for intrusive steps, and in the need for additional safeguards for sensitive data classes. When investigators work within this framework the outcome is not slower or timid practice, but it is work that is more trusted, more resilient to challenge and more worthy of the people whose digital lives it touches (Dhaundiyal et al., 2025).

10. GOVERNANCE, DOCUMENTATION, AND ACCOUNTABILITY

Governance gives cyber - forensics an institutional spine. And without a coherent framework, even the most skilled practitioners drift into ad hoc choices that are hard to defend later. Effective governance starts with an investigation charter specifying mandate, scope and limits, roles and responsibilities amongst investigators, legal counsel, data protection officers and HR, not to mention thresholds for approval for intrusive activities such as full disk imaging, remote live acquisition or covert monitoring. Standard operating procedures are the translation of the charter into the daily practice and they stipulate how the verification of the authority is carried out, how the scoping and the proportionality are recorded, how the chain of custody is preserved, how privileged or confidential material is separated. Because user-centric investigations often involve vulnerable people, the framework should expressly mandate trauma-informed practice, minimisation and other safeguards regarding sensitive classes of data.

Documentation is the thread that binds principle and proof. A defensible case file includes the lawful basis for each action, the articulated investigative questions, the narrowing criteria used at collection, the versions and configurations of tools, and a complete chain-of-custody record with hash values and storage locations. Decision logs capture why alternatives were rejected, how proportionality was assessed, and when stopping rules were applied. Where automation or AI influenced triage or prioritisation, the file should identify the model version, validation status, salient parameters, and the human judgement that adopted or rejected the suggestion. Deviations from SOPs are inevitable; governance requires that each deviation be acknowledged, explained, and counterbalanced by compensating controls rather than quietly normalised (Katkuri, 2025).

Accountability operates at several layers. Case-level accountability relies on peer review of critical artefacts, second-examiner verification of timelines or attributions, and counsel sign-off before major escalations. Function-level accountability uses quality assurance audits of closed matters to test whether methods were reproducible, whether minimisation was honoured, and whether documentation would survive scrutiny from a regulator or court. Board-level accountability recognises that high-impact investigations can entail strategic, legal, and reputational risk; periodic briefings to a designated oversight committee keep leadership informed without compromising independence. When jurisdictional issues arise or when works councils and regulators have consultation rights, governance should schedule those engagements early and record outcomes in the case file.

Risk management integrates forensics into the wider control environment. A register of investigative risks—over-collection, cross-border transfer conflicts, tool reliability, privilege taint, evidence store compromise—assigns owners, mitigation measures, and review cadences. Data protection and legality impact assessments are triggered for high-risk steps, documenting necessity, safeguards, and residual risk. Evidence platforms are treated as critical systems, with isolated networks, strong authentication, immutable logging, and rehearsed incident response plans that contemplate the possibility of a breach of the evidentiary store itself. Vendor governance applies the same discipline to outside labs and cloud providers via contracts that require raw format exports, audit cooperation, security attestations, and notice of lawful demands (Quang Huy & Kien Phuc, 2025).

Closure is a governance event, not just an administrative step. Upon conclusion, the team should validate that findings are backed by reproducible artefact-level observations, deliver a neutral report that contextualises confidence and limitations, and make retention and deletion decisions that are linked to the legal hold. Whereas, where one person is exonerated or where material is no longer relevant, narrowing or deletion is evidence of fairness and mitigates residual risk. Lessons learned - on the responsiveness of providers, tool behaviour or cross-border friction - are captured in a feedback loop that updates SOPs, training and model registries. If there have been errors, there should be accountability for it, including prompt disclosure to decision-takers, corrective action and, where relevant, notification to affected people/regulators.

Transparent governance does not slow down investigations, it helps them to be more credible and efficient. By requiring documentation of authority, purpose, proportionality, and method as they are exercised, the organisation equips investigators to act with confidence, equips reviewers to test the work without having to re-run it, and reassures the people whose data is touched that the search for truth was conducted within clear and humane boundaries.

11. HORIZON ISSUES AND REFORM AGENDA

The technical substrate of cyber - forensics is developing much faster than the doctrines that govern it. Post-quantum cryptography, default end-to-end encryption, ephemeral messaging, and on-device AI will make wholesale capture harder and increase the premium on targeted, consent-aware, and context-rich. Decentralised platforms and edge architectures have the artefacts spread across peers rather than providers, compounding the authority, chain of custody and authenticity. At the same time, biometric and behavioural signals, such as keystroke dynamics, gait, voice and micro-interaction patterns, hold out the promise of attribution on the one hand, and the threat to dignity and equality on the other. These trends will not abolish forensics, they will dictate a change in approach from bulk acquisition of data to judicious reconstruction using smaller slices of data that are better documented.

Authenticity will be a key evidentiary issue as the number of synthetic media and automated content generation grows. Deepfakes, voice clones, text generated by huge models - we are now on the edge of the question of what is true and what is not. The response cannot be based solely on human expertise; it must incorporate provenance infrastructures, cryptographic signing at capture, and regular preservation of context - device attestations, model versions, prompts, and processing metadata - that enable subsequent examiners to distinguish source from synthesized. Courts and regulators will demand that testing standards and disclosure requirements include generative pipelines as part of the evidence and not as opaque auxiliaries (Nargis et al., 2025).

Privacy-preserving forensics: From research to practice Selective disclosure through secure enclaves, auditable queries against provider-side datasets, privacy budgets in investigations and controlled use of differential privacy or redaction-by-default may provide probative answers without exposing unnecessary data. Where organisations use AI technologies for triage or correlation purposes, model registries, independent validation, and impact assessments should be mandatory, and structured rights of affected individuals to dispute automated inferences that materially affect an investigation.

Cross-border reality demands legal harmonisation. Mutual assistance must be faster and more predictable, with template protocols for cloud exports that preserve raw logs, time bases, hashes, and minimal necessary context. Data-localisation and blocking statutes should be recalibrated to allow narrow, rights-respecting investigative transfers subject to audited safeguards. Enterprise monitoring rules in labour and platform settings should require proportionality analyses, time limits, and post-fact notice where safe, balancing security with autonomy rather than treating one as the exception to the other.

The reform agenda is concrete. Legislatures and courts should require written search protocols, minimisation plans, and stopping rules for digital warrants; mandate disclosure of tool versions, validation results, and known error rates; and recognise a qualified right for independent experts to examine methods under protective orders. Professional bodies should embed trauma-informed practice, bias mitigation, and AI governance into certification and continuing education. Organisations should fund methodologically open research on emerging artefacts, create forensic ombud roles with authority to halt disproportionate steps, and publish anonymised post-mortems to raise the field's baseline. If practitioners, providers, and policymakers adopt these reforms together, cyber forensics can remain both effective and worthy of trust in a future where the boundary between person and platform is ever more porous (Conti & Turrin, 2025).

12. CONCLUSION

Cyber forensics earns public confidence only when its technical success is matched by legal fidelity and ethical restraint. Across this chapter, the same theme recurs: trustworthy results are not the product of clever tools alone but of principled choices made, recorded, and reviewable at every stage. Authority is secured before action; scope is tied to defined questions; evidence is preserved, collected, and examined with methods that others can replicate; privacy is treated as an operational requirement rather than an inconvenient afterthought; and explanations are written for people who were not in the room when decisions were taken. In a user-centric human threat intelligence setting—where the investigative lens often rests on identifiable individuals—these commitments do more than protect rights. They improve accuracy by keeping inquiries tightly aligned with purpose, reduce noise by limiting over-collection, and enhance credibility when findings must withstand challenge.

If there is a single operational lesson, it is discipline. Discipline means starting narrow and widening only when facts demand it; distinguishing incident response artefacts from evidentiary collections; running chain-of-custody and validation as habits rather than heroics; and applying stopping rules once the probative objective has been met. Discipline also means treating automation as an assistant, not an oracle. Models can prioritise attention, but they cannot supply legal thresholds or moral justification. Their versions, training assumptions, and error characteristics belong in the case file, and their outputs must be corroborated by artefacts whose provenance is clear.

The worldwide distribution of data makes jurisdiction architecture. Sound cross-border practice starts with mapping where the data sits, who controls it, and where the forum has to be persuaded, and then determining the pathways to ensure respect for the most demanding applicable regime. Provider APIs, raw exports and sealed transfer bundles guarantee integrity; talks to works councils, regulatory boards and local counsel guarantee legitimacy. Privilege and confidentiality ride with evidence and need separation by design, not as an after-the-fact patch.

Professional ethics is what helps hold these strands together. Competence, impartiality, and confidentiality are not buzz words; they are daily habits that are enforced by peer review, second examiner checks, and a communication style that separates observation from inference and calibrates confidence without overstatement. When errors happen, as they inevitably will in complex and time-pressured investigations, the ethical response is to surface them as soon as possible and correct the record publicly and learn, where possible, to public shame.

Governance is turning an ideals into muscle memory. Investigation charters, proportionality assessments, decision logs, model registries and periodic audits to make sure that what ought to happen usually does. Evidence platforms are secured as critical systems. Retention is ended when justification is ended. As matter draws near, exoneration leads to narrowing down or deletion and learning is brought back into policy and training. None of this slows practice down, on the contrary it prevents rework, reduces disputes and makes testimony easier because it is anchored in transparent process.

The issues surveyed with regards to the horizon - post-quantum ecosystems, decentralised platforms, pervasive encryption, synthetic media, and biometric - behavioural signals - don't change the foundation. They increase the premium placed on methods of targeted collection, provenance and privacy preservation, and call for regulatory reforms to make digital warrants, model disclosures and cross-border cooperation faster and fairer. Yet the core remains: legality, proportionality, reproducibility and human dignity continue to be the conditions under which cyber -forensics is still worthy of belief.

For investigators, counsel, regulators, and leaders, the practical mandate is clear: implement governance now, write protocols now, validate tools now, train for bias, trauma-informed practice, and explainable automation now. When the next case comes -- and it's inevitable -- you'll be less able to act swiftly and justly if you don't know a particular platform, but you'll be more able to if your institution has already decided to make legality and ethics the structure of your forensic craft.

Despite the fact that the legal-ethical frameworks are matured, cyber-forensics still struggles with practical and conceptual challenges. These include solving jurisdictional conflicts in real-time investigations, explainability, and fairness in AI-assisted inference operations, and also chain of custody integrity in decentralized or encrypted environments. Future work should focus on scalable methods for evidence collection that are privacy preserving, international harmonisation of data access protocols and empirical studies on the effects of forensic governance on the results of the investigation. Advancements in these frontiers must be done with cross-disciplinary work by technologists, legal scholars, ethicists and frontline investigators.

REFERENCES

Adel, A. (2022). A conceptual framework to improve cyber forensic Administration in Industry 5.0: Qualitative study approach. *Forensic Science*, *2*(1), 111–129. DOI: 10.3390/forensicsci2010009

Admass, W. S., Munaye, Y. Y., & Diro, A. A. (2024). Cyber security: State of the art, challenges and future directions. *Cyber Security and Applications*, *2*, 100031. DOI: 10.1016/j.csa.2023.100031

Akhtar, M. A. K., Kumar, M., & Nayyar, A. (2024). Transparency and accountability in explainable AI: Best practices. In *Towards ethical and socially responsible explainable ai: Challenges and opportunities* (pp. 127–164). Springer Nature Switzerland. DOI: 10.1007/978-3-031-66489-2_5

Albtosh, L. (2025). Automated Evidence Collection and Analysis Using AI. In *Integrating Artificial Intelligence in Cybersecurity and Forensic Practices* (pp. 143–186). IGI Global Scientific Publishing.

Alsaraireh, N. (2025). Digital Forensics in the Age of Cybercrime: Challenges and Future Directions. In *Tech Fusion in Business and Society: Harnessing Big Data, IoT, and Sustainability in Business* (Vol. 2, pp. 555–564). Springer Nature Switzerland. DOI: 10.1007/978-3-031-84636-6_48

Arora, S., Rai, M., & Gupta, M. (2024). Importance of industry 5.0 in understanding emotional intelligence. In *Human-Machine Collaboration and Emotional Intelligence in Industry 5.0* (pp. 205–219). IGI Global. DOI: 10.4018/979-8-3693-6806-0.ch011

Beemkumar, N., Gupta, S., Bhardwaj, S., Dhabliya, D., Rai, M., Pandey, J. K., & Gupta, A. (2023). Activity recognition and IoT-based analysis using time series and CNN. In *Handbook of Research on Machine Learning-Enabled IoT for Smart Applications Across Industries* (pp. 350–364). IGI Global. DOI: 10.4018/978-1-6684-8785-3.ch018

Bhambri, P., & Khang, A. (2024). Managing and monitoring patient's healthcare using AI and IoT technologies. In *Driving Smart Medical Diagnosis Through AI-Powered Technologies and Applications* (pp. 1–23). IGI Global Scientific Publishing. DOI: 10.4018/979-8-3693-3679-3.ch001

Bhimavarapu, U. (2026). Deep Learning for Digital Forensics: Advancing Criminal Investigations. In *AI-Driven Policing and Urban Security in Smart Cities* (pp. 155-170). IGI Global Scientific Publishing.

Chen, C., & Dong, B. (2023). Digital forensics analysis based on cybercrime and the study of the rule of law in space governance. *Open Computer Science*, *13*(1), 20220266. DOI: 10.1515/comp-2022-0266

Conti, M., & Turrin, F. (2025). Cyber Forensics for Cyber-Physical Systems. In *Encyclopedia of Cryptography, Security and Privacy* (pp. 498–500). Springer Nature Switzerland. DOI: 10.1007/978-3-030-71522-9_1722

Dhaundiyal, R., Anand, P., Bhargava, D., & Das, L. (2025). Navigating cyber forensics: Investigative techniques and challenges. In *Intelligent Computing and Communication Techniques* (pp. 269–274). CRC Press. DOI: 10.1201/9781003635680-42

Fernando, V. (2021, April). Cyber forensics tools: A review on mechanism and emerging challenges. In *2021 11th IFIP International Conference on New Technologies, Mobility and Security (NTMS)* (pp. 1-7). IEEE. DOI: 10.1109/NTMS49979.2021.9432641

Haque, E. U., Abbasi, W., Murugesan, S., Anwar, M. S., Khan, F., & Lee, Y. (2023). Cyber forensic investigation infrastructure of Pakistan: An analysis of the cyber threat landscape and readiness. *IEEE Access : Practical Innovations, Open Solutions*, *11*, 40049–40063. DOI: 10.1109/ACCESS.2023.3268529

Kalinin, O., Gonchar, V., Abliazova, N., Filipishyna, L., Onofriichuk, O., & Maltsev, M. (2024). Enhancing Economic Security through Digital Transformation in Investment Processes: Theoretical Perspectives and Methodological Approaches Integrating Environmental Sustainability. *Natural and Engineering Sciences*, *9*(1), 26–45. DOI: 10.28978/nesciences.1469858

Katkuri, S. (2025). Securing the Digital Frontier: Legal Analysis of Cybersecurity, Data Privacy and Cyber Forensics in India. *The Indian Journal of Public Administration*, *71*(1), 75–91. DOI: 10.1177/00195561241284886

Khan, A. A., Shaikh, A. A., Laghari, A. A., Dootio, M. A., Rind, M. M., & Awan, S. A. (2022). Digital forensics and cyber forensics investigation: Security challenges, limitations, open issues, and future direction. *International Journal of Electronic Security and Digital Forensics*, *14*(2), 124–150. DOI: 10.1504/IJESDF.2022.121174

Kim, K., Alshenaifi, I. M., Ramachandran, S., Kim, J., Zia, T., & Almorjan, A. (2023). Cybersecurity and cyber forensics for smart cities: A comprehensive literature review and survey. *Sensors (Basel)*, *23*(7), 3681. DOI: 10.3390/s23073681 PMID: 37050740

Malik, A. W., Bhatti, D. S., Park, T. J., Ishtiaq, H. U., Ryou, J. C., & Kim, K. I. (2024). Cloud digital forensics: Beyond tools, techniques, and challenges. *Sensors (Basel), 24*(2), 433. DOI: 10.3390/s24020433 PMID: 38257526

Mishra, A. K., Hemamalini, V., & Tyagi, A. K. (2024). Digital forensics with emerging technologies: Vision and research potential for future. *Conversational Artificial Intelligence*, 675-697.

Nargis, T., Thomas, A. C., Rao, R. R., Dsouza, R., Dsouza, R., & SM, S. (2025, April). Cyber Forensic Evidence Protection System Using Blockchain Technology. In *2025 8th International Conference on Trends in Electronics and Informatics (ICOEI)* (pp. 614-619). IEEE.

Patrick, H. A., Gujjar, P. J., Prasad, G. M., Kumar, R., & Kumar, N. H. (2025). Issues and Challenges in Emerging Cyber Forensics and Traditional Cyber Forensics Methods. *Cyberology*, 90-102.

Quang Huy, P., & Kien Phuc, V. (2025). Insight into how legal and ethical considerations of artificial intelligence enhance the effectiveness of cyber forensic accounting. *Journal of Global Information Technology Management, 28*(2), 136–166. DOI: 10.1080/1097198X.2025.2480972
Quang Huy, P., & Kien Phuc, V. (2025). Insight into how legal and ethical considerations of artificial intelligence enhance the effectiveness of cyber forensic accounting. *Journal of Global Information Technology Management, 28*(2), 136–166. DOI: 10.1080/1097198X.2025.2480972
Rai, M., Tyagi, N., Tripathi, P., Kumar, N., & Kumari, P. (2023). Advancement in agricultural techniques with the introduction of Artificial Intelligence and Image Processing. In *Smart Village Infrastructure and Sustainable Rural Communities* (pp. 47–68). IGI Global. DOI: 10.4018/978-1-6684-6418-2.ch004

Ratul, M. H. A., Mollajafari, S., & Wynn, M. (2024). Managing Digital Evidence in Cybercrime: Efforts Towards a Sustainable Blockchain-Based Solution. *Sustainability (Basel), 16*(24), 10885. DOI: 10.3390/su162410885

Sachoulidou, A. (2024). Cross-border access to electronic evidence in criminal matters: The new EU legislation and the consolidation of a paradigm shift in the area of 'judicial' cooperation. *New Journal of European Criminal Law, 15*(3), 256–274. DOI: 10.1177/20322844241258649

Sharma, D., Mittal, R., Sekhar, R., Shah, P., & Renz, M. (2023). A bibliometric analysis of cyber security and cyber forensics research. *Results in Control and Optimization, 10*, 100204. DOI: 10.1016/j.rico.2023.100204

Singh, S., Pandey, J. K., Rai, M., & Saxena, A. K. (2024b). Advancements in Facial Expression Recognition Using Machine and Deep Learning Techniques. In *Machine and Deep Learning Techniques for Emotion Detection* (pp. 149–166). IGI Global Scientific Publishing. DOI: 10.4018/979-8-3693-4143-8.ch007

Singh, S., Rai, M., Pandey, J. K., & Saxena, A. K. (2024a). Emotional Intelligence and Collaborative Dynamics in Industry 5.0 for Human-Machine Interactions. In *Human-Machine Collaboration and Emotional Intelligence in Industry 5.0* (pp. 190-204). IGI Global.

Tatipatri, N., & Arun, S. L. (2024). A comprehensive review on cyber-attacks in power systems: Impact analysis, detection, and cyber security. *IEEE Access : Practical Innovations, Open Solutions*, *12*, 18147–18167. DOI: 10.1109/ACCESS.2024.3361039

Tripathi, P., Kumar, N., Paroha, K. K., Rai, M., & Panda, M. K. (2024). Applications of Deep Learning in Healthcare in the Framework of Industry 5.0. In *Infrastructure Possibilities and Human-Centered Approaches With Industry 5.0* (pp. 69–85). IGI Global Scientific Publishing. DOI: 10.4018/979-8-3693-0782-3.ch005

Tripathi, P., Kumar, N., Rai, M., Shukla, P. K., & Verma, K. N. (2023). Applications of machine learning in agriculture. In *Smart Village Infrastructure and Sustainable Rural Communities* (pp. 99–118). IGI Global. DOI: 10.4018/978-1-6684-6418-2.ch006

Tyagi, A. K., Kumari, S., & Richa. (2024). Artificial Intelligence-Based Cyber Security and Digital Forensics: A Review. *Artificial Intelligence-Enabled Digital Twin for Smart Manufacturing*, 391-419.

Vasani, V. P., Chandra, U., Sahu, G., Boyineni, S., Dhamodaran, S., Kumbhkar, M., & Gupta, S. (2024). Introduction to Emotion Detection and Predictive Psychology in the Age of Technology. In *Using Machine Learning to Detect Emotions and Predict Human Psychology* (pp. 1–16). IGI Global Scientific Publishing. DOI: 10.4018/979-8-3693-1910-9.ch001

Zangana, H. M., & Omar, M. (2025). Introduction to Digital Forensics and Artificial Intelligence. In *Digital Forensics in the Age of AI* (pp. 1–30). IGI Global Scientific Publishing.

Zhang, H., & Gong, X. (2024). The research on an electronic evidence forensic system for cross-border cybercrime. *The International Journal of Evidence & Proof*, *28*(1), 21–44. DOI: 10.1177/13657127231187059

KEY TERMS AND DEFINITIONS

Admissibility: The set of legal tests determining whether evidence can be received by a tribunal (typically relevance, authenticity, reliability, and fairness).

Authenticity: Demonstrating that an item is what it purports to be, often via hashes, provenance records, and credible testimony.

Automation bias: The tendency to over-trust automated recommendations, mitigated by validation, corroboration, and documented reasoning.

Blocking statute / data localisation: Laws that restrict export of certain data or require storage within a jurisdiction, affecting collection strategy.

Bystander/third-party data: Information about people not under investigation that may appear in shared artefacts; requires minimisation and, where possible, redaction.

Chain of custody: The documented history of evidence handling—who collected, transferred, stored, and examined it—showing integrity over time.

Collection: The act of acquiring data within authorised scope using methods that maintain integrity and context (e.g., imaging, API exports).

Comity: Respect for other jurisdictions' laws and interests when planning cross-border evidence collection.

Cross-border transfer: Movement of evidence across national boundaries, requiring lawful mechanisms, safeguards, and documentation.

Cyber forensics: The disciplined acquisition, preservation, examination, analysis, and presentation of digital evidence in a legally authorised, ethically defensible, and technically reproducible manner.

Data minimisation: Limiting collection and processing to the smallest amount of data necessary to answer defined questions.

Decision log: A contemporaneous record of key choices, alternatives considered, approvals, and deviations from plan.

Digital evidence: Any data with probative value that is stored or transmitted in digital form, including content, metadata, and system artefacts.

Evidence lifecycle: The end-to-end process of identification, preservation, collection, examination, analysis, reporting, and presentation of evidence.

Exigent circumstances: Limited emergency conditions allowing immediate action to prevent serious harm; subject to minimisation and prompt follow-up authority.

Expectation of privacy: What an individual can reasonably expect to remain private in a given context, shaping lawfulness of monitoring and search.

Explainability: The ability to articulate how a model or tool produced a given output, at levels suitable for investigators, courts, and affected individuals.

Hash (cryptographic): A fixed-length fingerprint of data used to verify integrity and identity of evidence.

Human-in-the-loop: A governance pattern where humans review, verify, and remain accountable for automated or AI-assisted outputs.

Informed consent: Voluntary, specific, and informed agreement by a person to a defined scope of collection; revocable unless another legal basis applies.

Least privilege: Granting investigators only the access they need for defined tasks, for the shortest necessary time.

Legal authority: The lawful basis to access and process data for an investigation (e.g., warrant, statutory power, informed consent).

Legal hold: A directive suspending routine deletion for identified custodians/ sources to preserve potentially relevant data.

Metadata: Descriptive data about data (timestamps, geolocation, device IDs) that can be probative and privacy-sensitive.

Model registry: A controlled inventory of analytic/AI models with versions, validation status, purpose, owners, and sunset dates.

Mutual Legal Assistance (MLA/MLAT): Formal state-to-state processes for obtaining evidence across borders with local rights protections.

Particularity: The requirement that searches be narrowly scoped to specific accounts, artefacts, time ranges, or locations, avoiding open-ended collection.

Preservation: Legal and technical steps to prevent alteration or loss of potentially relevant data (e.g., legal holds, snapshots, immutable logs).

Privileged material: Legally protected communications (e.g., attorney–client) that require segregation and restricted handling.

Proportionality: Balancing investigative aim against intrusiveness, choosing the least intrusive method likely to achieve the purpose.

Purpose limitation: Using collected data only for the specific, stated investigative purpose unless fresh lawful basis is obtained.

Remote acquisition: Collecting data over a network without seizing physical media; lawful and proportionate use requires tight scoping and safeguards.

Reproducibility: The ability for a competent peer to obtain the same artefact-level results using the documented methods and versions.

Retention and deletion: Policy-driven timelines and irreversible deletion procedures applied when legal justification ends.

Search protocol: A written plan that details scope, sources, filters, handling of sensitive classes, and safeguards before collection begins.

Security of processing: Technical and organisational measures to protect evidence (isolation, access control, encryption, immutable logging).

Segregation (taint/filter team): Use of an independent team to screen and withhold privileged or out-of-scope material from investigators.

Stopping rule: A pre-defined commitment to cease examination once the investigative objective is met, preventing unjustified expansion.

Storage limitation: Retaining evidence only as long as necessary for legal, regulatory, or case needs, then securely deleting it.

Tool validation: Testing and documenting that forensic tools perform as intended, including known limitations and error characteristics.

Transparency: Providing clear, timely information about monitoring and investigative processing, subject to narrow, time-bound exceptions.

Write blocker: Hardware or software that prevents modification of a source drive during acquisition.

Chapter 4
Psychological Dimensions of Social Engineering in Cybercrime

Sonu Sharma
https://orcid.org/0009-0004-3836-590X
Poornima University, Jaipur, India

Bright Keswani
https://orcid.org/0000-0003-1464-0431
Poornima University, Jaipur, India

Ashish Avasthi
https://orcid.org/0000-0003-3069-1984
Poornima University, Jaipur, India

Sangita Gupta
https://orcid.org/0009-0009-3751-8317
Poornima University, Jaipur, India

Sumit Kumar Kapoor
https://orcid.org/0009-0005-6291-3176
Poornima University, Jaipur, India

Nikhil Kumar Goyal
https://orcid.org/0009-0007-4532-8033
Poornima University, Jaipur, India

ABSTRACT

This chapter reflects on social engineering as an important aspect of cybercrime, based on the psychology principles that make it possible to manipulate and deceive the individual in digital realities. It explains cognitive and emotional loopholes that attackers use, i.e. trust, fear, authority and curiosity, and discusses some commonly-used attack vectors, i.e. phishing, pretexting and impersonation. The discussion points out both the personal and corporate other results, that vary between financial loss and psychological trauma and loss of reputation. The idea is that there is a synergy between human psychology and technological systems that cybercriminals are able to adjust their tactics to the changing systems. The chapter also discusses defense measures, involving awareness training, psychological resilience and technical measures, as well as legal and ethical issues.

DOI: 10.4018/979-8-3373-4898-8.ch004

1. INTRODUCTION

1.1 Cybercrime in the Modern Era

Cybercrime has elevated the single and incidence-based computer misuse to an international systematized and very lucrative business. In the previous decades, individuals hackers driven by curiosity or fame were the main perpetrators of attacks. Cybercrime today is fuelled by monetary gain or political interest and even attempts by states to do the same. Attackers use the enormous digital landscape that is the internet, a connected network of billions of devices, cloud-based work, and communication infrastructure, to target individuals and organisations in large volumes. Cybercrime is no longer focused just on technical skills; the approach figured in social, cultural and psychological measures in order to overcome security protocols (Abroshan, Devos, Poels, & Laermans, 2021).

The emergence of digital banking, e-commerce, and telework has increased the targets of the criminals. Due to poor authentication mechanisms, human carelessness, and cognitive failures, malicious parties will always take advantage to access the system even though it is solid technologically. Indeed, some of the worst attacks in recent years have not been caused by sophisticated malware or zero-day attacks but instead by tricked employees clicking on malicious links or improperly sharing confidential information. Therefore, cybercrime indicates the paradox of the fact that technology continuously evolves on the one hand and, on the other hand, the human aspect always stays under threat of attack.

In addition, cybercrime is not confined to one country; therefore, a comprehensive way of controlling it or prosecuting it is impossible. Criminals in one region of the world can assault the victims located thousands of kilometers with little chance of being detected. This has led to the formation of dark web marketplaces where stolen data and phishing kits together with hacking services get sold off as commodities. The impact of this process of professionalization of cybercrime is that even those with very little technical knowledge can actually deliver effective attacks using purchased social engineering tools. This dynamic rides more strongly in view of the fact that cybercrime needs to be looked beyond a technological issue and more as a human dilemma (Wang, Zhu, & Sun, 2021).

1.2 Role of Human Psychology in Cybersecurity

Core to social engineering is human psychology. Cybercriminals also know that firewalls, intrusion detection systems, and encryption can inhibit the access of a digital system but that people could frequently be cajoled or coerced to give access. Human psychology is rife with predictable tendencies- to be inclined toward authority and fear negative outcomes, or being driven to act impulsively in cases of urgency etc. These trends are used bases on creating attack tactics by the attackers

As an example, an employee can be sent an email that looks like it comes directly from their manager seeking to authorize an urgent financial transfer. Even when the employee is uncertain, psychological fear that he or she may upset a supervisor or hold up a critical assignment can overcome rational care. Similarly, curiosity can be made use of by attractive texts such as "Click to see who viewed your profile." The effectiveness of such psychological triggers is in their ability to evade rational reasoning and manipulate the most instinctive responses in people and, hence, these triggers are highly capable of being used in cybercrime (Goyal, 2025).

Observations on the behavioral science justifies the notion that human beings are susceptible to psychological manipulations like the confirmation bias, scarcity effect and anchoring. Cybercriminals will use these prejudices to build convincing messages. As an example, the time-sensitive offerings (You're about to be suspended in 24 hours unless you act now") drive a desperate action on the part of the victims who may not know whether they are actually talking to a legitimate representative.

1.3 Why Social Engineering Matters More Than Technology

Although technology is extremely important in securing digital infrastructures, most of the cyber attacks are initiated by humans. Social engineering attacks Appearance of sophisticated defenses among the individuals is misleading because social engineering attacks get around it by attacking people rather than the sophisticated defenses in place. Whatever the level of encryption their organization uses or its firewall, one employee clicking on a rogue link or submitting his/her login credentials can undermine the entire system. This fact has transformed the paradigm of the cybersecurity approach not into exclusively technological one but with the awareness of the human aspect being primarily concerned (Albladi & Weir, 2020).

It is demonstrated consistently that more than 90 percent successful cyberattacks include social engineering. Phishing emails, deceitful phone calls, and imitation scammers do not involve much technical knowledge but can be quite effective since they are predicated on the human weakness to trust. Unlike technical exploits, which can take a deep understanding of the vulnerabilities to exploit, social engineering is based on human to human interaction, communication, and psychology- skills that are quick to learn and scale.

Moreover, social engineering is much cheaper to use and much more successful in attackers point of view. It is almost free to launch a phishing campaign to thousands of individuals and a few victims can get considerable financial awards. This enables social engineering to be not only profitable, but also sustainable to the cybercriminals. On the attackers side, it is usually easier to take advantage of human than beating a machine (Hughes-Lartey et al., 2021).

2. FOUNDATIONS OF SOCIAL ENGINEERING

2.1 Evolution of Social Engineering Attacks

An art of manipulating people into taking actions or disclosing information that is confidential can be termed as social engineering. In contrast to technical hacking, the use of hacking techniques of social engineering involves harnessing human trust, emotions and the ability to make decisions. It can also be termed as hacking the human mind because it can encourage the use of psychology instead of code to end up with its objectives (Montañez et al., 2020).

Figure 1. Scenario of social engineering attacks

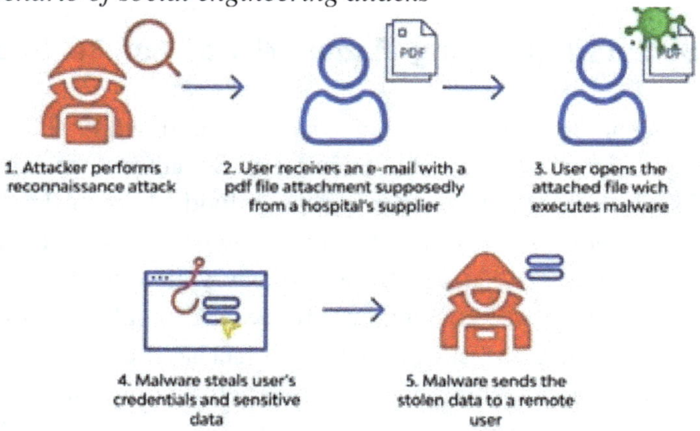

The principle is not new since deception is an aspect that has always been present in human history. Persuasion and manipulation has been a tool used by con artists, spies and fraudsters to obtain what they want personally. In the cyber age, though, social engineering has fallen to a larger scope. Attackers no longer rely on physical interactions to scam people; instead, they prefer the use of email, instant messaging, phone calls, as well as social media to cheat victims. Increased anonymity of the net creates attackers the comfort of impersonating other anomalous people or entities.

Social engineering has come to be more professionalized over time. Attackers have adopted more elaborate procedures, phishing kits, psychological profiling, etc. in order to target their victims in a more informative manner. Using both technical automation (such as widespread phishing email) and psychological maneuvers (such as time pressure, fear, or incentive) has made social engineering one of the most effective cybercrime tactics. It is exceptionally harmful due to its flexibility: attackers are continuously changing their strategies in order to exploit new technologies and societal trends (Goyal et al., 2025a).

2.2 Core Principles of Manipulation and Deception

The strength of any social engineering attack is based on general tenets of human behavior. Robert Cialdini is a well known psychologist whose work on persuasion distinguishes major influences that an attacker can use: authority, scarcity, reciprocity, consistency, liking, and social proof. In such cases, an attacker assumed the role of an IT administrator (authority) and requests a password reset. Equally, the false limited-time bargains (scarcity) make people want to be fast without first checking it.

Deception has the use of layering these principles The steps that might be involved are a relationship with the victim (liking), followed by asking minor favours (consistency) and finally to a major request like confidential access. Those psychological triggers do not go through logical thinking but appeal to instinctive reactions that human beings have acquired over the evolution period (Gratian et al., 2018).

2.3 Human Factors as the Weakest Link in Security

With all of these billions of dollars spent on cybersecurity technology, the most unsecure part is still the human being. Companies make the mistake of believing that they can easily dupe the employees to leak out sensitive information. Human vulnerabilities are unlike software vulnerability in that software can be patched with a simple update, but human cannot, at least not by dumping knowledge into them.

Attackers use normal human behaviors: they trust, they are curious, and people want to help. Employees may also pass information through telephone when they think that the caller represents a technical support. Likewise, curiosity may steer one to open a suspicious attachment to have a look at what is in it.

In addition, social engineering is successful since people are usually under pressure. Employees are subject to poor judgments in workplaces because they may be pressured and in a hurry. Where attackers can exploit this is through the use of urgency, whether that be, "act before the next 30 minutes" or some other. Even well trained IT experts may succumb to such tricks in cases when they are diverted or tired. In that way, the ``human factor is not only a vulnerability but an intended goal in the majority of cyberattacks"(Govindankutty, 2021).

3. PSYCHOLOGICAL ASPECTS OF CYBERCRIME

3.1 Cognitive Biases Exploited in Attacks

Cognitive biases are decision-impacting systematic errors of thinking. Social engineers use such biases in order to make their attacks more successful. An example is the urgency bias where human beings arrive at a decision after a shorter period and they are typically less rational. The emails used in phishing may use a warning about a suspension of accounts in case they are not acted on immediately, using this bias in the hope of getting the target to comply quickly.

Confirmation bias is another example in which the individuals will seek information that confirms their current beliefs. By sending messages that seem legit to the victims, attackers use this tactic when they send faked messages that are seen as expected by the victim- for example a packaging delivery notification to someone who ordered online. Since it validates their perceptions, the victim will be less likely to question the message (Ferreira et al., 2015).

3.2 Trust, Authority, and Obedience in Manipulation

Human relationships are based on trust, which in the cyberspace causes trouble. Social engineers tend to drive confidence within a short time through pretense or through acts that imitate valid communication patterns As an example, an attacker could spoof the email address so as to pretend to be a trusted peer. After winning trust, the victim will tend to provide information or even do things they would not normally do (Goyal et al., 2025b).

The aspect of authority is an important element of obedience. Society instills in children since young to respect the people in authority, such as teachers, the managerial level and the authorities as well. This is something that is exploited by attackers who make such commands to seem as though it is coming directly through someone who is in authority. To cite a more familiar example, a scam email sent by a company CEO requiring an immediate bank transfer is likely to short-circuit regular verification procedures due to the employees feeling that they need to comply.

In hierarchically positioned organizations further enhancing the concept of obedience. In these environments, the employees are trained to obey orders without questioning particularly when they are under pressure. This is used by cybercriminals to create scenarios, which appear to be a workplace of authority and urgency. This combination of trust and manipulation of authority, guarantees behind the scenes adherence, even with otherwise hesitant persons (Cialdini, 2006).

3.3 The Role of Fear, Curiosity, and Greed in Victim Behavior

The emotions of humans are strong drive forces that supersede the rational thought. Fear is one of the best weapons of social engineering. Very often, hackers spam with threatening messages suggesting that a user will lose their account, be sued or their personal information will be published in case they do not follow the steps within a short period. Fear leads to panic; this causes victims to agree without making any confirmation.

The other exploitable emotion is curiosity Due to human nature, we are prone to search new information, particularly when it looks more personal or specialized. Phishing messages are sent out like: See who viewed your profile, or Exclusive confidential document which attracts the victims with their curiosity in clicking the malicious links. In the case of highly security conscious persons, he or she may be compelled or tempted to explore out of curiosity (Ajzen, 2020).

Victims are also motivated to act by greed as well as the incentive of rewards. Examples of scams are that they promise a lottery win or investment or an unusually low price, and they exploit the desire to make personal profit. The victims with the belief that they can make any gain financially often suppress their doubts making them good targets.

Table 1. Cognitive Biases, Attack Examples, and Defensive Measures

Cognitive Bias	Attack Example	Why Victims Fall	Defense Strategy
Authority Bias	CEO fraud/BEC	Trust in hierarchy	Verification protocols, call-backs
Urgency Bias	Phishing deadlines	Time pressure reduces reasoning	Pause-and-verify training
Scarcity Effect	Limited-offer scams	Fear of missing out	Awareness of manipulation triggers
Confirmation Bias	Delivery notice scams	Message fits expectations	Habitual skepticism
Familiarity Heuristic	Impersonated colleagues	Known names increase trust	Email domain validation

4. TYPES OF SOCIAL ENGINEERING ATTACKS

4.1 Phishing, Spear Phishing, and Whaling

The most common and the most named type of social engineering is phishing, which means using a deceptive message driven to look like they came with the blessing of trusted agents. Such messages are usually emails but also sms (smishing) or social media messages where some victims are fooled into clicking malicious links, downloading an infected file or giving away sensitive information like passwords or even credit card details. Fear and urgency are the flourishing environments of phishing. A typical one is an email saying that unless the user confirms his/her information, the account will be closed down or suspended immediately. In the condition of victims, it is the individual action of the epistemological status in which one acts without thinking (Burgoon & Buller, 1996).

Figure 2. Spear phishing and whaling phishing

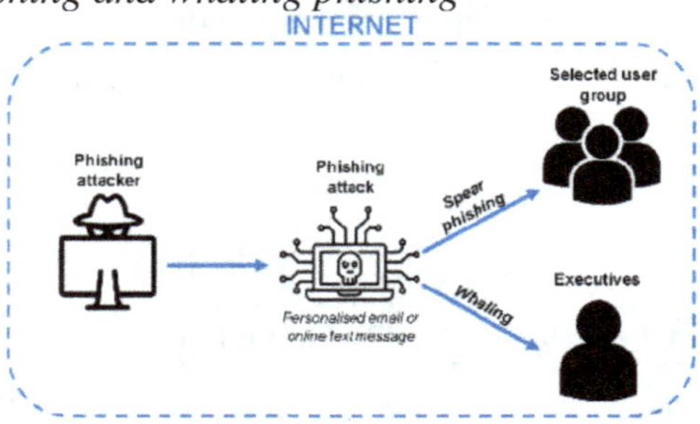

More sophisticated versions have come into being Spear phishing focuses on particular individuals, usually to make the message sound more authoritative by drawing on personal information someone has posted on social networks or has been leaked in databases. To give an example, an email could have alluded to an on-going project rendering it indistinguishable with earnest business email messages.

Real life scenarios reveal the handicaps. Business Email Compromise (BEC) scams have defrauded organizations billions of dollars around the world with the fraudsters acting as company executives to execute fraudulent transfers. Phishing is effective because of its versatility- it updates along with technology and can create believable automated messages and even deep fakes of voices. Some of the methods used in defense are multi-factor authentication, spam services, and most effective of all, constant user awareness training that equips the person to detect suspicious indicators and confirm requests through alternate channels (Dhillon et al., 2020).

4.2 Pretexting, Impersonation, and Baiting

Pretexting is the act of using a false scenario (the pretext) in order to persuade victims to provide information and/or to take actions that they would otherwise not. Unlike phishing which is often impersonal and by the hundreds, pretexting needs strategic planning, and acting. As an example, a scammer may impersonate an IT worker requiring the user to confirm user credentials or a bank official who needs personal information. Authority and legitimacy overcome the resistance and get the target to be cooperative.

4.3 Tailgating, Dumpster Diving, and Physical Exploitation

Attackers use physical access as well; social engineering is not an Internet phenomenon only. Tailgating is a situation in which someone who is not permitted into a secure building gains access because the employee does not check to ensure the person with whom he or she is talking is allowed in. An example is when one is almost carrying a load of boxes and he/she requests the employee to hold the door forgetting there are access controls. Once inside intruders may pilfer data, plant malware or obtain intelligence with no one knowing.

An additional hidden risk is dumpster diving Sensitive material, e-mails sent and printed, invoices, access codes, etc, are not removed properly. Criminals swoop on this information as it may be discarded in trash cans and help them with identity theft or create a convincing pretext. As an example, there is waste related to financial data that can be used to identify fictitious suppliers or coerce employees into making fraudulent transfers (Goyal et al., 2025c).

4.4 Emerging Trends: Deepfakes, AI-driven Social Engineering

Develops in artificial intelligence have brought new fields in social engineering. Deepfakes-framevariing audio recording, audio-video, or image AI-generated to sound like they are being spoken by a trusted party. As another example, AI-generated voices of CEOs were used by criminals to order employees to authorize fraudulent money transfer and cause losses of millions of dollars. On the same note, deep fake videos may be used in disinformation efforts, which diminish trust in real-life communications (Collins & Miller, 1994).

Automated social engineering can be generated using the power of AI as well. Chatbots are able to carry on lifelike conversations that adjust to the responses of victims as they occur. Through social media, attacks can also extract personal background information about a cyber victim and, with the help of AI, send specifically personalized messages that do not arouse suspicion. These tools make attacks large and powerful with minimal human intervention of the attacker.

The consequences are grave Because of the development of VR and AR technologies, the next generation of attacks could involve the use of immersive manipulative environments, which will make it even challenging to human victims to discern what is real and what is fake. These threats need to be fought on both technical and psychological fronts: using detection tools to automatically detect tampered media, to use digital watermarking to prove authenticity, and to educate people to question and be resilient to manipulation (Serchan et al., 2013).

4.4.1 Adaptive AI Persuasion Models and Next-Generation Threats

AI is transforming social engineering from static, scripted messages into *dynamic, adaptive persuasion systems.*

A. Adaptive Persuasion Engines

Modern attackers use AI models that:

- Profile targets using digital footprints from social media, breaches, and online behavior.
- Adjust tone, urgency, and emotional cues in real-time.
- Generate personalized pretexts based on personality traits inferred from writing style.

B. Multi-Agent Social Engineering Bots

New attackers deploy swarms of AI agents that mimic entire teams of coworkers or customer support units, reinforcing false legitimacy.

C. Socio-Technical Mitigation

Defensive AI focuses on:

- Detecting subtle anomalies in message style.
- Authenticity verification markers (cryptographic signatures).
- Predictive models that identify psychological risk states (fatigue, distraction).

AI arms both sides—attackers and defenders—requiring new hybrid strategies that combine *technical detection with psychological preparedness.*

5. CASE STUDIES OF PSYCHOLOGICAL EXPLOITATION

5.1 Corporate Data Breaches Caused by Social Engineering

Because businesses trust each other and constantly communicate as well as rely on ongoing work processes, their corporate environments are vulnerable to social engineering attacks. Attackers are aware that employees, contractors, and vendors may each provide an entry point into a corporate network. The best known breach is probably the Target data breach of 2013 that led to the theft of 40 million such records as credit and debit cards. Investigations that subsequently followed showed that attackers logged in using stolen credentials of a third-party HVAC contractor. The criminals did not directly hit the strong network security in Target; instead, by exploiting a smaller less secure vendor the cybercriminals exploited that access to move inside Target systems. This example illustrates that even very secure companies may fall victim to the hackers who may use human connections and interpersonal trust chains.

A more dramatic case is the one of the Ubiquiti Networks fraud of 2015. Spear phishing emails were used by the attackers to convince the employees of the finance department to issue wire transfers to overseas accounts, in the name of the top executives. More than 40 million dollars went into vain before the fraud was discovered It is interesting to see that no malware, zero-day exploit, or brute force was used, instead all of the attack was based on psychological pressure, exploitation of authority, and the ability of employees to listen to the commands of those who seem to lead them. It was technology-savvy social engineering that was sophisticated (Handoko & Putri, 2018).

5.2 Financial Frauds and Identity Theft Scenarios

Financial fraud driven by social engineering is now one of the most lucrative areas of cybercriminals. Such deceptively straightforward scams as the perennially popular Nigerian Prince phishing mail still grab hold of casualties with sultry dreams of getting rich. These frauds take advantage of greed, hope and in certain cases loneliness. In victims, the expectation to receive a reward convinces them to give bank details or send fees toward processing. Although they become well-known in the sphere, they remain active due to the targeted population such as vulnerable groups and powerful psychological stimulations (Mitnick & Simon, 2003) .

Fraudulent behavior takes place in more sophisticated ways using personalization. As an example, in 2016 the Austrian aerospace business FACC lost about 50 million euros, after the attackers corresponded to the name of the CEO in an email and ordered employees to transfer money under the pretext of the purchase of a project.

Figure 3. Identity Theft process

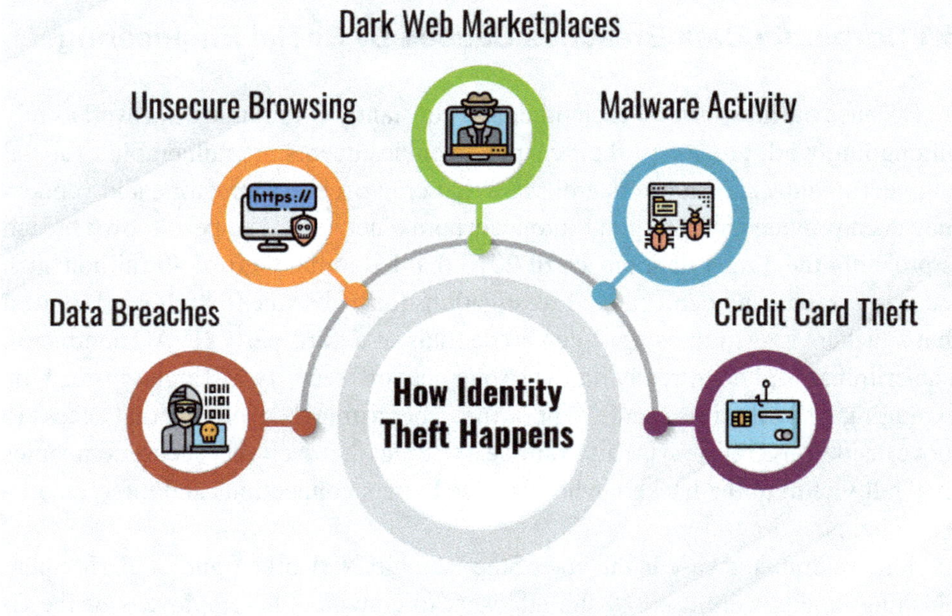

Another evolving accomplishment of social engineering is identity theft. The attackers tend to accumulate pieces of information by phishing, pretexting or imitating a customer service, claiming to call. After they include such information as names, addresses, and identification numbers, they blend it together to pose as the victims. Using stolen identities, perpetrators open credit cards, get loans, or exercise tax fraud. Machine failures were also a part of the root cause in the Equifax breach of 2017, but a large portion of the subsequent fallout was phishing messages to consumers under the guise of Equifax assistance in remedying the situation- instead, the scammers were able to gather more personal information.

The financial sphere is the most susceptible one due to the huge amount of money involved. Banks and payment related services are under constant phishing and impersonation attacks. Criminals are aware of the fact that one successful adventure can cause tremendous financial gains. The scenarios justify the necessity of multi- layered verification systems and the need to educate the consumers how not to provide sensitive information in response to unsolicited messages (Goyal, 2025).

5.3 Psychological Profiling in Advanced Persistent Threats (APTs)

The most advanced social engineering is usually found in Advanced Persistent Threat (APT) campaigns. In contrast to opportunistic malpractices, APTs are focused, sustained campaigns, frequently perpetuated by adequately-funded criminal societies or governments. Social engineering in this situation does not describe the simple process of deceiving an individual into clicking on a link, it describes months or even years of building trust, learning behaviors and taking advantage of psychological weaknesses.

One of them is the Operation Aurora campaign (2009-2010) that targeted such companies as Google, Adobe, and Juniper Networks. Attackers generated email based spear phishing that included malicious URLs that shared interests with individual workers. Attackers as well managed to maximize the chances of interaction by personalizing messages to the professional realities of targeted individuals.

The breach of RSA Security in 2011 makes the threat even more vivid. The emails sent to employees had the title, 2011 recruitment Plan and had an excel attachment which contained a malware. The topic was selected to make use of the curiosity and the professional interest because recruitment is applicable to almost any business. Once exploited, the malware gave attackers an opportunity to enter RSA SecurID authentication systems, sabotaging the security of many entities across the world. This was not haphazard phishing- this was surgical psychological targeting (Rodríguez Priego et al., 2020) .

5.3.1 Contemporary Case Studies Highlighting Cognitive Biases in Real Attacks

Recent cyberattacks increasingly blend *advanced technology with predictable human behaviors*, demonstrating how cognitive biases drive real-world victim decisions. The following cases offer contemporary insight:

A. 2023 MGM Resorts Attack (Vishing + Cognitive Overload)

In 2023, the MGM Resorts ransomware incident demonstrated how attackers exploit *cognitive overload* and *authority bias*. Criminals impersonated IT personnel, calling the helpdesk and convincing staff to reset privileged login credentials.

Key psychological triggers:

- **Authority** ("I'm from corporate IT; this is urgent.")
- **Cognitive strain and distraction** (timing calls during peak workload).
- **Helpfulness bias**, where staff wanted to quickly resolve the problem.

B. 2024 Deepfake CFO Scam (Adaptive Persuasion + Authenticity Bias)

A global engineering firm lost millions after employees received a *deepfake video call* from a supposed CFO. Modern AI models replicate voice tone, facial movement, and speech rhythm with near-human precision.

Psychological mechanisms exploited:

- **Authenticity bias**: humans trust vivid audiovisual input.
- **Time pressure**: demands for urgent fund transfer.
- **Familiarity heuristic**: visual similarity to a known leader.

C. WhatsApp Parent-Impersonation Scams (Emotion-Driven Urgency)

In multiple 2024 incidents, attackers cloned voices of teenagers using public social media posts. Parents received calls saying, *"Mom, dad, I'm in trouble—send money."*

Triggers exploited:

- **Fear and loss aversion**
- **Emotional urgency**
- **Heuristic thinking overriding rational verification**

D. Experimental Findings: Click Behavior Under Cognitive Load

Recent behavioral cybersecurity studies show:

- People under *stress*, *time pressure*, or *interruptions* are *3× more likely* to click malicious links.
- *Multitasking employees* exhibited the highest susceptibility.
- Alerts lose effectiveness after repeated exposure ("security habituation").

These findings highlight why psychology—not technology—remains the central battlefield in cyber deception.

5.4 Lessons Learned from Case Studies

Together, these case studies reveal that social engineering is not on the fringe of successes of many cyberattacks. In fact, across industries, criminals are always able to play on our predictable human instincts: obedience to authority, curiosity, greed, fear, and trust. In corporate breaches, financial frauds and state-sponsored espionage, what all the cases have in common is the human weakness.

The lessons are multiple-pronged The first thing that organizations have to do is to embrace a comprehensive approach to cybersecurity that takes into consideration not only technical solutions but also psychological sensitivities. Employee training is also not limited to stating rules but to providing reasons why a human being is prone to be toyed around with and giving good examples of such manipulative examples. Second, the plans of incident response should include the psychological needs of the victims of the incident and promote disclosure and eliminate the feeling of being ashamed about having fallen to a scam. Lastly, governments and regulators need to acknowledge social engineering as an important conduit of cybercrime and include psychological resilience as a part of the overall strategy of cybersecurity (Yasin et al., 2021).

6. IMPACT ON INDIVIDUALS AND ORGANIZATIONS

6.1 Emotional and Psychological Impact on Victims

Social engineering attacks do not only leave financial scars; they take a serious toll on the psychology of their victims. Feelings of shame, guilt and embarrassment are so strong in people who fall into such schemes. The victims even blame themselves by regretting they should have identified the red flags. Such self-blame may develop a chain of silence: rather than report the attack immediately, people hide the fact to avoid being judged by the colleagues, families, or the police. Resistance to speak puts work behind the process of acting and in most cases allows attackers to perpetrate the exploitation.

In most of the victims, it leaves permanent anxiety and fear. Following an event, they can become overly paranoid and doubt everything, every email, phone call or online message. This state of hyper-alertness is taxing on minds and can leave a broad-side of doubt upon the general faith with the usage of technology. Among severe ones, victims characterize symptoms that are close to those of post-traumatic stress disorder (PTSD) when they get reminded of the incident, e.g. similar scam messages, that cause panic or distress (Leary, 1996).

It is especially hurtful that romance scams take advantage of romantic attachments. Victims put more than financial resources in their relationships that prove to be constructed: they usually devote trust, affection, and even years of emotional input. The unfolding of the betrayal usually results into depression, withdrawal and lack of belief in further relationships. Victims of such scams tend to withdraw to prevent the humiliation and this increases their loneliness and open them up to further exploitation.

6.2 Organizational Losses and Reputation Damage

To corporations, social engineering assaults can be disastrous. Unlike individuals who usually incur their short-term losses, firms endure not only financial destruction but reputational plight in the long-term. When an effective phishing campaign is launched or a Business Email Compromise (BEC) attack is tricked, the result could be the loss of millions of dollars in a short time. In addition to direct losses, organizations spend more in legal arms-war, regulatory fines, and technical cleaning of infected systems.

What is possibly even more harmful is the loss of customer confidence. In most industries like banking, healthcare and e-commerce, trust is the basis of customer relationship. A single breach by a manipulated employee (e.g., that employee has activated his or her) can destroy that trust. As in the case of 2013 breach of Target, the company had to settle millions of dollars in addition to losing customers as they shopped less during subsequent quarters in the future. An unauthentic trust once severed requires years to restore (Lahcen et al., 2020).

Social engineering incidences are also characterized by loss of operations After an attack, organizations have to use staff and resources in the damage weeks, forensic inquiries and policy revamping. Employees can become too conservative and the speed of work and decision-making process will be slower. Such delays can be life even in life-threatening sectors such as healthcare, where systems or personnel may be paralyzed by a fear of error. Therefore the organizational cost of social engineering is not merely in monetaryial terms, but by interfering with functioning and credibility of the enterprise (Metzger et al., 2020).

6.3 Long-term Behavioral Effects of Social Engineering

The post-response of the social engineering attacks rest engaging the individuals and organizations in a changed manner. Security fatigue is one of the consequences of security, especially to individuals. Some employees or users become hardened after multiple warnings were issued, training sessions, and simulation phishing tests. They change their state, which instead of alertness to become resigned—"Attackers are going to get me, anyway." This exhaustion negates the effectiveness of awareness campaigns, putting a premium on training that is interesting, varied and with a psychological understanding of what works.

Other victims on the opposite end of the spectrum become over-cautious. They can abstain to access valid emails, open online bank accounts or even embrace new technologies. Though caution is part of vulnerability reduction, too much paranoia can slow the pace of personal and workplace efficiency. Such as, an employee that fails to respond toactual client messages due to the fear that it is a phishingattack, may harm business relationships.

As the outcomes of a successful social engineering attack usually, a tightening of the organizational security. Some of the typical responses are multi-factor authentication, required verification of any financial transfers, and tightened monitoring. Although such steps are enhanced security, they might also create tensions between usability and security. A procedure with more steps will be perceived as a barrier to efficiency by employees and/or may come across as a lack of trust. Such strain may lead to unwillingness to adhere to regulation and instead instigate a form of resistance that runs counter-productively to safety by creating workarounds, i.e., shortcuts that do not follow the official procedures (Goyal et al., 2025d).

The medium term effect is the change of culture where the culture of trust becomes vulnerable. Trust is core to digital ecosystems- trusting platforms, trusting communication and trusting between human beings. The trust is corroded by social engineering causing the society to be more cynical, business more bureaucratic, and people more anxious. It will take long-term transparency, communication, and psychological resilience programs that are not limited to technical solutions (Robert & Timothy, 1970).

6.4 Addressing the Psychological Aftermath

Because social engineering can produce longer-term consequences, the remediation should not solely be technical. Victims both individuals and employees need their psychological support in gaining back the confidence. Stigma can be decreased with counseling services, open discussions about cybercrime, and peer-support groups which will help encourage victims to come forward. Organisations that subject the victims to empathy and not blame are more likely to facilitate a culture of openness where you have situations reported early.

Training programs need to develop beyond technical indicators of phishing and into the emotional indicators. Explaining cognitive biases to employees would make them understand how to recognize when they are being manipulated. The kind of simulations that ought to be employed should be real but encouraging to the employees to become resilient without causing terror or exhaustion.

Within the society, government and the institutions can facilitate the victims by educating people and offering assistance to victims. As an example, national cybercrime hotlines and websites can help to get instant advice. Laws should be changed in such a way that they recognize that cybercrime not only affects people financially but psychologically, and they need to be treated as a whole (Gass, 2015).

6.5 Cultural and Ethical Variability in Susceptibility to Manipulation

Susceptibility to cyber deception varies across populations due to cultural, ethical, and socioeconomic factors.

Influential Cultural Factors

- **Collectivist cultures** show higher trust in authority and social conformity, increasing vulnerability to hierarchical scams.
- **High power-distance societies** are more prone to authority-driven manipulation.
- **Individualist cultures** often face more curiosity-based attacks (clickbait, exploration).
- **Digital literacy gaps** amplify susceptibility across all age groups.

Ethical Considerations

- Awareness campaigns must avoid stereotyping cultural groups.
- Privacy norms differ between cultures, affecting how users evaluate requests for information.
- Socioeconomic stress increases vulnerability to reward-based scams.

Understanding these variations allows organizations to design culturally aligned training and interventions.

7. DEFENSE MECHANISMS AND COUNTERMEASURES

7.1 Building Psychological Resilience Against Attacks

The best defense against social engineering is not technology-but it is psychology. Fear, curiosity, urgency, and authoritative status are some of the emotional triggers on which attackers base their success, and people should be trained to handle these emotional conditions. Psychological resilience involves the development of capacity to ponder, think and doubt instead of acting on a suspicious request.

The process of creating a skeptic culture is one of them. It is important to make sure that the employee and individuals should be asked to confirm information prior to doing anything with it, even when it originates in a trustworthy source. As an example, consider the case when a worker receives an urgent email message sent by a CEO with a request to transfer money to his/her account, resilience will help the worker not to obey the request instantly, but to find other method to verify its correctness, by phone, or any other secure method. Such a straightforward stop and check mechanism is a blow to the manipulation ability of urgency and authority (Myers, 2012).

The other thing of resilience is realization of rational prejudice. Knowledge about the existing biases like confirmation bias, scarcity effect, and authority bias, and how they affect decision-making, can help a person train himself/herself to identify occasions when certain biases are being used. As an example, when an email states something like, "Act now or you will lose it forever," resilience training will assist the person in recognizing that as a scarcity bias tactic. Consciousness turns auto responses into voluntary rational choices.

7.1.1 Practical Organizational Strategies for Reducing Vulnerability

To strengthen human defenses, organizations should implement:

A. Psychological Resilience Programs

- Workshops teaching emotional regulation under urgency.
- Stress-reduction modules for high-pressure teams.

B. Cognitive Fatigue Monitoring

- Detecting overload indicators (rapid clicking, unusual errors).
- Limiting sensitive tasks during peak fatigue periods.

C. Human-in-the-Loop Verification

- Mandatory callback verification for financial transfers.
- Dual-authorization for sensitive data changes.

D. Environment-Based Prevention

- Decluttering digital interfaces to reduce cognitive load.
- Highlighting risky content with visual cues.

These interventions convert cybersecurity from a technical function into a *holistic human-centered system.*

7.2 Security Awareness Training and Behavioral Conditioning

A major part of the defense strategy against social engineering is training programs. The training of traditional cybersecurity training may lack elements of the psychological manipulation that needs to be explicitly addressed in awareness programs. Effective training will be a combination of knowledge, practice and reinforcement in an attempt to turn awareness into a habituated cautious behavior.

As an example, an organization may run phishing simulations, where they send safe but fake phishing emails to employees and see how many of them are fooled by the ruse. Employees greeted with the click of the link are subjected to immediate feedback and more training programs. With time, repetition will lead to desensitization as employees get used to stopping to consider each clicking. Such drills will serve as behavioral reinforcement in the same manner in which other drills condition individuals to counteract emergencies (Kabay et al., 2012).

Training should also be situational and ongoing. A one-off workshop or exercise is insufficient since attackers are continually evolving. Rather, organizations should have recurring courses that address emerging trends like deepfakes, smishing (smart-phone phishing) as well as voice phishing (vishing). It is also important that employees should be aware of the organizational user-related consequences of a breach. As an example, one phishing click can undermine an entire company reputation, and this promotes the importance of individual responsibility all the more.

Gamification reinforces behavioral conditioning also. One can effectively fight against security fatigue by making awareness training interactive in the form of challenges, quizzes, or competitions. Positive reinforcement, including recognition of the employees who shut down simulated phishing attacks, can drive a proactive security culture. To overcome this challenge of employees being weak links, awareness training can help turn this around when it is implemented regularly and in an imaginative way and engage the employees, they also become the first stop defence.

7.2.1 Behavioral Economics and Cybersecurity Training

Modern cybersecurity training draws increasingly from *behavioral economics*, which examines how humans make decisions under uncertainty and cognitive constraints.

Core Behavioral Principles for Training

- **Nudge Theory**: Subtle design changes—such as default security settings—guide safer behaviors without forcing them.
- **Choice Architecture**: Presenting security options in clear, low-friction formats increases compliance.

- **Loss Aversion Messaging**: Training framed around *potential loss* increases attention more than neutral information.
- **Instant Feedback Loops**: Immediate correction after phishing simulations reconditions decision patterns.

Practical Applications in Organizations

- Embedding "Are you sure?" prompts when sending sensitive data.
- Designing email clients that highlight external senders visually.
- Using micro-learning modules—short 2–5-minute lessons that build retention.
- Reward-based conditioning: recognizing employees who report threats.

This blended psychological–economic approach shifts security from one-time lectures to *habit formation*, the key determinant of long-term resilience.

7.3 Technical Tools to Support Human Vigilance

Technology is another crucial element that supports the reduction of the effectiveness of social engineering as the focus shifts to psychology. Humans are not perfect observers and therefore automated systems that warn about suspicious activity before it reaches the human eye must be included as part of the defenses.

Among the basic instruments is spam (email) filtering. Increased protection means when the messages receive advanced spam filters to check the links, attachments or the discrepancy in the senders messages. Machine learning improves these filters because it can discover subtle patterns that are typical in phishing emails. Even though no filter is 100 percent effective, it significantly lowers exposure, by separating most messages containing malicious content out of the inbox.

The second significant tool is the multi-factor authentication (MFA). Even in the event that an attacker manages to trick a victim into providing login information, MFA blocks unauthorized logins because a second authentication factor is also needed (a mobile token or a repeat biometric test). MFA does nothing to prevent the original fraud, but places a layer in between the stolen credentials and the hacking of the system (Washo, 2021).

Organizational systems are also beginning to take on Zero Trust Architecture (ZTA), in which no user and no device is trusted. Access is restricted only through on-going verification, which makes most attempts at social engineering with stolen credentials less effective. Also, malicious attachments or scripts may be identified by endpoint protection tools and blocked, eliminating the most common payloads of phishing attacks.

Lastly, anomaly detection systems that employ AI techniques can learn to pick out abnormal activities (e.g. sudden high volume of money transfers, or log-ins at unusual times or unexpected places) and raise red flags. These systems serve as the digital guardrails, keeping manipulation out of the hands of a full-blown breach. With a merged human vigilance and technical safeguards, the organizations come up with multi-tiered defenses that minimize dependency on one method over another.

7.4 Legal and Policy Perspectives

Besides the organizational controls, there is a need to adopt wider laws and policies to address social engineering. Given that most attacks are cross-border, victims can find it difficult to pursue justice and attackers can take advantage of jurisdictions that have poor enforcement of cybercrimes. International collaboration is thus a necessity International mechanisms and agreements of criminal laws such as the Budapest Convention on Cybercrime have given a basis of unification about criminal laws as well as assisting in cross border investigations; however enforcement is patchy.

National governments can also contribute by issuing the regulations and compliance requirements. As an example, a General Data Protection Regulation (GDPR) set out by the European Union requires organizations to enforce data protection measures, in compliances which lead to indirect reinforcement of social engineering protection mechanisms. Finance and healthcare sectors are the most regular examples where regulators require awareness training and reporting of incidents to reduce the risk (You & Lee, 2019).

Their policies should also touch upon the new threats of the AI-based social engineering. Such Deepfakes as fake accounts impersonation and phishing malicious bots pose legal questions as they are not always clear whose responsibility the case is most likely to be. Are organizations supposed to be held responsible should an employee be rendered a victim of a deepfake CEO call? Are AI-produced frauds to be punished according to existing fraud legislation, or are criminals of a new type of crime that needs new types of violations? These are very urgent questions to the policymakers.

Also essential are protection policies to the victims Others are afraid to report scams because of stigma or the fear of witnesing admonition. Regulations must be welcoming to informing policies through providing some forms of protection, resources and straightforward avenues of support. Government-led campaigns to raise awareness of the subject can also help to destigmatize victimhood and focus on resilience. Policies, thus are not only linked with punishment but the establishment of an ecosystem of prevention, support and accountability (Albahar & Almalki, 2019).

8. FUTURE DIRECTIONS AND CHALLENGES

8.1 AI and Automation in Social Engineering

Artificial intelligence (AI) and automation are the upcoming trend that will transform the social engineering business. In the past, criminals had to spend time and resources to gather information about victims, create messages and put scams into action. With AI though they are being automated on a mass scale. Artificial intelligence is now able to gather large amounts of data about a victim in social media, record databases and breach databases, constructing an incredibly detailed profile. With these profiles, attackers can design targeted phishing or pretexting messages that can connect with each individual with respect to their habits, interests, and weaknesses.

Or to provide the example illustrating precise grammar and tone, an email sent by a natural language processing (NLP) model can be written in a style with which a victim is familiar. Equally, AI-designed chat bots are capable of continuing a conversation with a potential victim changing their responses accordingly to ensure they remain reputable. This means that people can increasingly never know what is veritable and fake.

Deepfake is another technology that I is making possible and is creating new verification problems. Voice-cloning technology enables the attackers to convincingly fake executives or even family members over the phone, and deepfakes can be issued over video conference to give fraudulent orders. In 2019, an energy company based in the UK lost almost 250,000 due to voice spoofing backfired by AI-generated mimicking voices of the CEO who requested an urgent transfer. It is easy to see how these incidences will lead to a future in which visual and aural illusion can hardly be told apart.

Protecting against social engineering using AI is a demanding task that needs equally sophisticated security tools. Cybersecurity systems should also include applications of AI-based abilities to detect fine grains in anomalies, say, variations in metadata values or peculiarities in behavioral patterns. What is more, is that the public education campaigns that should welcome people to a world where seeing is not believing should teach them to trust methods of verification, other than using their eyes and ears. Identifying and implementing technical countermeasures is only part of the challenge; what is also needed is a restructuring of human beliefs to consider this new digital reality in the realm of trust (Campbell, 2019).

8.2 Psychological Warfare in Cyberspace

With the digital interactions more and more becoming interlocked with the areas of politics, economics and culture, social engineering is emerging into a psychological warfare. Manipulation is being used by nation-states and organized groups not only to steal but also to create disinformation, propaganda and destabilizations. They are not like the traditional scams directed at individuals because they are a large-scale attempt to exploit psychological weaknesses in a uniform way across entire societies.

The spread of fake news and misinformation through the social media is one such example. Competitors may make use of this time during elections to push fake stories intended to divide the population, to destabilize faith in democratic processes, and provoke rivalry. The tricks take advantage of such cognitive biases as confirmation bias where individuals tend to trust information that confirms their prior beliefs. By increasing the loudness of divisive narratives, the attackers make the society live in a cloud of mistrust and confusion which loosens social bond.

A final dimension is cyber psychological operations (PsyOps), in which the attackers are specific in their intent to demoralize or intimidate people. As an example, hoax warnings of upcoming online invasion, terrorist attacks, or economic fall- out may create panic and destroy the trust of populations in authorities. And of course, the problem of misinformation regarding the vaccines during the COVID-19 pandemic demonstrated directly how the psychological manipulation in the online space can lead to apparent real-life implications regarding health outcomes (Montañez et al., 2020).

The task of defenders is gigantic. Defence against psychological warfare needs coordination between the government, technology corporations and the people. Fact-checking efforts, rapid response efforts and random digital literacy campaigns are vital but struggle to stem the tide of the tsunami that is disinformation. Simultaneously, democratic societies must maintain a proper balance between counter measures and the freedom of expression so that in fighting to counter manipulation we do not also end up muzzling legitimate conversations. It is not only a problem of cyber technologies and security but also one of national security and social stability in the future of social engineering.

8.3 Towards a Human-Centric Cybersecurity Framework

The future in defense will reside outside of technical solutions and into one of a more human-centric approach to cybersecurity given the psychological aspect of social engineering. Customary security systems focus on firewalls, encryption and intrusion detection, but criminals circumvent these by attacking the human mind.

The defense of the future needs the combination of psychology, education and culture as well as technology.

The next step is to instill cybersecurity awareness in day-to-day life and not only in the organizations. As a larger proportion of everyday functions--banking, shopping, healthcare, education--migrate to the digital realm, citizens require lifelong and continuing skills training in digital literacy. Jus like you teach traffic safety or financial literacy, cybersecurity awareness, like verifying your sources, doubting urgency, or using safe authentication should also be part of core education.

Organizations need also to realize that blame culture erodes security. Employees who fear being punished when they become victims are not keen to report the incidences and this gives the attackers more time to exploit the breaches. A human centric approach puts an emphasis on psychological safety and promotes open reporting and focuses on viewing incidents as a learning opportunity. Workshops, encouraging counseling, and the reward of employee vigilance helps in developing an atmosphere where employees feel they are free to take their responsibility.

Last, technological design has to be based upon human psychology. Security software cannot present too many messages or complicated procedures that promote risk exposures. Rather, systems should be self-explanatory, or they have to direct their users into an easy flow toward safe behavior. Such functionality as smooth multi-factor security that enables people to focus on completing the task, contextual security queries and verification aided by AI harnesses the human behavioral patterns with technology. A human focus response accepts the fact that, technology is not the answer to social engineering and only through enhancing human judgment and strength can society exist to become stronger facing the changing threats.

8.4 Ethical and Legal Challenges of the Future

With the current changes in defenses, there is a need to change ethical and legal frameworks. One of the problems is in measuring liability. Where a sophisticated deepfake scam engages an employee, who should take responsibility; the employee, the organization, or the platform that enabled the manipulation to occur? Legal frameworks more often than not lack certainty and leave victims exposed and culprits feeling empowered.

Another ethical issue exists in the application of AI to defense. Although phishing can be detected with the help of AI, there are some privacy issues which can be caused by AI, as it can monitor personal messages as well. Finding a balance between effective defense and personal rights will become one of the outstanding debates of the upcoming decades. Too much and intrusive supervision will compromise trust between the employer and employees and where there is little to no monitoring, organizations stand to lose.

There is also the spectrum of social engineering weaponization by governments. The methods of social control dangled over the heads of citizens in the homeland can also be applied in authoritarian systems to control and keep populations in line. The laws that target the fight against misinformation are easy to transform into the ones that follow the ideas of censorship. The international community will have to come up with measures that prevent abuse but still allow action to be taken in response to pertinent cyber threats.

The last aspect to be discussed is the ethics of treatment of victims. People who become victims of scam are often looked down upon as irresponsible or naive. This discourages reporting in addition to the ingenuity of modern manipulation being despoid. Ethical doctrines should lay particular stress on compassion, remedial, and education as social engineering works on universal human nature, rather than on the personal failings of the victim.

8.5 Integrating Cognitive Science with AI-Based Detection Systems

Future research must unite cognitive psychology with advanced AI models to create next-generation defenses.

Key emergent areas include:

- **Cognitive–AI Fusion Systems** capable of predicting when users are in a psychologically vulnerable state.
- **Emotionally aware intrusion detection** that recognizes manipulation attempts.
- **Neuro-behavioral modeling** to understand how attention, fatigue, and stress shape digital risk.
- **Adaptive defense agents** that adjust alerts based on user mental load and decision patterns.

The next stage of cyber defense is not only technological—it is *deeply human-centered.*

CONCLUSION

Social engineering is one of the most common and dangerous types of Internet fraud due to their ability to target not machine but human psyche. Unlike technical exploits that can be aided by software updates or tightened by eliminating firewalls, social engineering takes advantage of classic psychological mechanisms of trust, fear, curiosity, authority and greed. In this chapter, these human weaknesses have been demonstrated to be exploited by cybercriminals in many ways including phishing and identity theft and other more advanced tools and techniques such as advanced persistent threats and large-scale disinformation campaigns. The case studies presented above demonstrate that not even the most technologically sophisticated organizations are immune to targeted attacks since hackers will exploit the weakest link which is the people.

The psychological repercussion of such attacks is disturbing. To the individuals, being victimized by manipulation results in shame, guilt, and long-term emotional trauma. To organizations, the impact is compounded by economic losses, loss of reputation and breakdown in trust amongst the stakeholders. This is because the mesh of digital ecosystem grows increasingly interconnected, with social engineering events having further effects on the victim far beyond themselves as severity snowballs to the entire society and erodes the trust in interactions via the digital medium not to mention democracy as a whole.

It is vital to have a multidimensional approach to countering such a widespread threat. Mental toughness, cognitive stimulation education, and behavior modification need to make a person alert about the manipulation. Meanwhile, there are protective means like multi-factor authentication, artificial intelligence in detecting anomalies and zero trust systems that can add a security blanket. The support of the legal and policy frameworks is mutually dependent, as it needs to work across-borders to protect the victim and provide ethical barriers to abuse. The upcoming evolution of social engineering is quite inevitably determined by the future of artificial intelligence and deepfakes that have the ability to increase the context where deceptions operate and the verisimilitude of those deceptions. These tools are also changing and soon, the border between believability and falsity will become even simpler as resilience and verification will be the foundations of digital trust.

Social engineering can serve as a reminder that cybersecurity is a human issue, as much as it is technical. Our defense against it has to be at two levels, our digital protections and our psychological awareness. Battlefield lies, on the one hand, in networks and systems, and on the other hand, it lies in the perceptions, feelings, and choices of individuals. Through creating cultures of questioning, compassion and strength, as well as embracing the insight of human psychology into cybersecurity procedures, communities can reduce the harm caused by manipulation. What we really wage war against, thus, in the fight against social engineering is not only information but also trust, which is the basis of our digital future.

REFERENCES

Abroshan, H., Devos, J., Poels, G., & Laermans, E. (2021). Phishing happens beyond technology: The effects of human behaviors and demographics on each step of a phishing process. *IEEE Access : Practical Innovations, Open Solutions, 9*, 44928–44949. DOI: 10.1109/ACCESS.2021.3066383

Ajzen, I. (2020). The theory of planned behavior: Frequently asked questions. *Human Behavior and Emerging Technologies, 2*(4), 314–324. DOI: 10.1002/hbe2.195

Albahar, M., & Almalki, J. (2019). Deepfakes: Threats and countermeasures systematic review. *Journal of Theoretical and Applied Information Technology, 97*(X), 3242–3250.

Albladi, S. M., & Weir, G. R. S. (2020). Predicting individuals' vulnerability to social engineering in social networks. *Cybersecurity, 3*(1), 7. DOI: 10.1186/s42400-020-00047-5

Burgoon, J. K., & Buller, D. B. (1996). Interpersonal deception theory. *Communication Theory, 6*(3), 203–242. DOI: 10.1111/j.1468-2885.1996.tb00132.x

Campbell, C. C. (2019). Solutions for counteracting human deception in social engineering attacks. *Information Technology & People, 32*(5), 1130–1152. DOI: 10.1108/ITP-12-2017-0422

Cialdini, R. B. (2006). *Influence: The psychology of persuasion*. Harper Business.

Collins, N. L., & Miller, L. C. (1994). Self-disclosure and liking: A meta-analytic review. *Psychological Bulletin, 116*(3), 457–475. DOI: 10.1037/0033-2909.116.3.457 PMID: 7809308

Dhillon, G., Abdul Talib, Y. Y., & Picoto, W. N. (2020). The mediating role of psychological empowerment in information security compliance intentions. *Journal of the Association for Information Systems, 21*(1), 152–174. DOI: 10.17705/1jais.00595

Ferreira, A., Coventry, L., & Lenzini, G. (2015). Principles of persuasion in social engineering and their use in phishing. In T. Tryfonas & I. Askoxylakis (Eds.), *Human Aspects of Information Security, Privacy, and Trust: Third International Conference, HAS 2015* (pp. 36–47). Springer. DOI: 10.1007/978-3-319-20376-8_4

Gass, R. H. (Ed.). (2015). *International encyclopedia of the social & behavioral sciences* (2nd ed.). Elsevier.

Govindankutty, M. S. (2021). Is human error paving way to cyber security? *International Research Journal of Engineering and Technology, 8*, 4174–4178.

Goyal, N. K. (2025). Security and privacy in IoT, fog, and blockchain networks. In Sathio, A., Rind, M., Awan, S., & Junejo, A. (Eds.), *Energy-efficient deep learning approaches in IoT, fog, and green blockchain revolution* (pp. 371–398). IGI Global., DOI: 10.4018/979-8-3373-0300-0.ch015

Goyal, N. K. (2025). Weaponizing misinformation and cyberattacks on supply chains. In Bukhari, S., & Zafar, I. (Eds.), *Mass media and impact of fake news on supply chains* (pp. 177–210). IGI Global Scientific Publishing. DOI: 10.4018/979-8-3373-2175-2.ch007

Goyal, N. K., Dandotiya, M., Kumari, M., Kaloria, S., & Anushya, A. (2025a). AI-Powered Haptic Devices for Patient Rehabilitation. In Mamodiya, U., Kalam, A., Bossoufi, B., Awad, M., & Somwanshi, D. (Eds.), *Integrating AI With Haptic Systems for Smarter Healthcare Solutions* (pp. 143–170). IGI Global Scientific Publishing., DOI: 10.4018/979-8-3373-2307-7.ch007

Goyal, N. K., Dandotiya, M., Kumari, M., Sheikh, M. F., & Sharma, S. (2025c). Emerging Job Roles in the Tourism Sector Leveraging Artificial Intelligence. In Silic, M., Luthia, M., Ahmad, F., & Chakraborty, P. (Eds.), *Empowering Sustainable Performance and Competitive Advantage in Tourism* (pp. 89–126). IGI Global Scientific Publishing., DOI: 10.4018/979-8-3373-4546-8.ch004

Goyal, N. K., Dandotiya, M., Qurashi, J. A., Kumari, M., & Sharma, S. (2025b). AI-Driven Predictive Analytics for Disease Management. In Ouaissa, M., Ouaissa, M., Imad, M., Qurashi, J., & Farooq, M. (Eds.), *Utilizing AI of Medical Things for Healthcare Security and Sustainability* (pp. 231–276). IGI Global Scientific Publishing., DOI: 10.4018/979-8-3373-0690-2.ch008

Goyal, N. K., Kumari, M., Kushwah, V., Dandotiya, M., & Vijay, A. (2025d). Evaluating blockchain security: Trade-offs in consensus mechanisms. *IET Conference Proceedings,* 2024(38), 80–88. https://doi.org/DOI: 10.1049/icp.2025.0775

Gratian, M., Bandi, S., Cukier, M., Dykstra, J., & Ginther, A. (2018). Correlating human traits and cyber security behavior intentions. *Computers & Security, 73*, 345–358. DOI: 10.1016/j.cose.2017.11.015

Handoko, H., & Putri, D. A. W. (2018). Threat language: Cognitive exploitation in social engineering. *In Proceedings of the International Conference on Social Sciences, Humanities, Economics and Law (ICSSHEL)*. DOI: 10.31219/osf.io/zxgm6

Hughes-Lartey, K., Li, M., Botchey, F. E., & Qin, Z. (2021). Human factor, a critical weak point in the information security of an organization's Internet of things. *Heliyon, 7*(3), e06522. DOI: 10.1016/j.heliyon.2021.e06522 PMID: 33768182

Kabay, M. E., Robertson, B., Akella, M., & Lang, D. T. (2012). Using social psychology to implement security policies. In *Computer Security Handbook.* DOI: 10.1002/9781118820650.ch50

Lahcen, R. A. M., Caulkins, B., Mohapatra, R., & Kumar, M. (2020). Review and insight on the behavioral aspects of cybersecurity. *Cybersecurity*, *3*(1), 10. DOI: 10.1186/s42400-020-00050-w

Leary, M. R. (1996). *Self-presentation: Impression management and interpersonal behavior*. Routledge.

Metzger, M. J., Hartsell, E. H., & Flanagin, A. J. (2020). Cognitive dissonance or credibility? *Communication Research*, *47*(1), 3–28. DOI: 10.1177/0093650215613136

Mitnick, K. D., & Simon, W. L. (2003). *The art of deception: Controlling the human element of security*. Wiley.

Montañez, R., Golob, E., & Xu, S. (2020). Human cognition through the lens of social engineering cyberattacks. *Frontiers in Psychology*, *11*, 1755–1773. DOI: 10.3389/fpsyg.2020.01755 PMID: 33101096

Myers, D. (2012). *Social psychology*. McGraw-Hill.

Robert, O., & Timothy, B. (1970). Distraction increases yielding to propaganda by inhibiting counterarguing. *Journal of Personality and Social Psychology*, *15*(3), 344–358.

Rodríguez-Priego, N., Van Bavel, R., Vila, J., & Briggs, P. (2020). Framing effects on online security behavior. *Frontiers in Psychology*, *11*, 2833–2844. DOI: 10.3389/fpsyg.2020.527886 PMID: 33192769

Wang, Z., Zhu, H., & Sun, L. (2021). Social engineering in cybersecurity: Effect mechanisms, human vulnerabilities and attack methods. *IEEE Access : Practical Innovations, Open Solutions*, *9*, 11895–11910. DOI: 10.1109/ACCESS.2021.3051633

Washo, A. H. (2021). An interdisciplinary view of social engineering: A call to action for research. *Computers in Human Behavior Reports*, *4*, 100126. DOI: 10.1016/j.chbr.2021.100126

Yasin, A., Fatima, R., Liu, L., Wang, J., Ali, R., & Wei, Z. (2021). Understanding and deciphering of social engineering attack scenarios. *Security and Privacy*, *4*(4), e161. DOI: 10.1002/spy2.161

You, L., & Lee, Y. H. (2019). The bystander effect in cyberbullying on social network sites. *Telematics and Informatics*, *45*, 101284. DOI: 10.1016/j.tele.2019.101284

Chapter 5
Network Forensics for Human-Driven Cyber Attacks

T. C. Swetha Priya
https://orcid.org/0000-0002-0644-4329
Stanley College of Engineering and Technology for Women, India

ABSTRACT

Network Forensics is a part of Digital Forensics that helps in monitoring and analysis of Computer network traffic for gathering information, evidence, or intrusion detection. This helps in capture, analysis and interpretation of network traffic to uncover evidence of malicious activities and to support incidence response efforts. Unlike the automated Cyber intrusions, human-driven attacks are often carried out by skilled adversaries such as hackers, Cyber Criminals and malicious users. Such attacks are targeted, persistent and are adaptive in nature. Such attacks exploit not only the vulnerabilities in technology but also the human behavior and strategic planning bypassing the traditional security measures. Human-driven attacks try to exploit specific vulnerabilities making their detection demanding. This chapter focuses on how Network forensics provides a methodological framework and technical tools for monitoring, capturing, analyzing and reconstructing the network activities thereby enabling incident response and helps the analysts to trace the origin, method and impact of attacks. It also helps in mitigating human-driven cyber threats. Human-driven attacks typically follow a structured format. This chapter highlights the forensic techniques such as packet inspection, traffic flow analysis, anomaly detection, etc. With the integration of Machine learning and Artificial Intelligence (AI) technology into network forensic systems, the ability to detect indicators of advanced persistent threats has enhanced. Such techniques play a crucial role in environments where the attackers actively evade detection by misleading that as legitimate traffic

DOI: 10.4018/979-8-3373-4898-8.ch005

through encryption, spoofing or data exfiltration. This chapter explores the basic forensic process that involves systematic collection, preservation, and analysis of evidence collected from network traffic. Generally, human-driven cyber attacks follow a sequence of phases such as reconnaissance, intrusion, data collection, and exfiltration. Because tampered evidence will not be valid, the forensic investigators must preserve the evidence through a proper chain of custody which is essential for acceptance before the court of law. Network forensics provides incident response and threat identification in a proactive manner by continuously monitoring network behaviour using forensic tools that flags anomalies and suspicious behaviour in real-time enabling the organizations to respond spontaneously before damage occurs. This chapter also identifies and addresses the challenges in network forensics by providing the solutions across distribute environments in real-time.

1. INTRODUCTION

Network Forensics is a branch of digital forensics that focuses on monitoring, capturing, analyzing and preserving the evidence collected from network traffic for finding the source and the type of cyber incidents. This plays a major role in the identification of malicious activities, responding timely to the data breaches, reconstructing the evidence and supporting legal investigations based on the network evidence data. Unlike other Digital Forensics that deals with collecting the evidence in static form, Network forensics works in an environment that is dynamic making it relevant for real-time data analysis and faster decision-making. = A huge amount of cyber threats are common in real world because of the automated malicious software. Apart from these, human-driven attacks have become increasingly widespread and dangerous. Human-driven cyber attacks are attacks that are done by individuals or group of people who are skilled professionals involving the human intervention and sufficient planning. Some examples of such human-driven cyber attacks are social engineering, phishing, insider threats, whaling etc. Such threats are dangerous and challenging in nature as they involve taking advantage of human behaviour, trust and vulnerabilities making it difficult for prediction using common tools. Identifying human-driven attacks is complicated when compared to the automated attacks. As it involves manipulating human behaviour, the attackers may use encrypted communications over network, may pass through various networks by exfiltrating the data slowly to avoid detection or may fragment the forensic evidence (Guan, 2014).

This chapter focuses on providing a clear understanding about the Network Forensics, the challenges that are faced while collecting dynamic evidence from networks by highlighting the threats posed by the human-driven cyber attacks. It also focuses on process of network forensics, the tools and techniques for detection of human-driven threats in the context of Network Forensics.

2. OVERVIEW OF HUMAN-DRIVEN CYBER ATTACKS

Most of the cyber attacks now-a-days are automated or are driven by malicious softwares. But still a growing class of more sophisticated attacks that leverages human behavior either by user manipulation or misuse of the right to use by legitimate insiders. Human Driven attacks are those in which the humans are offenders or they may be the vulnerable point of attack. Such attacks will take the advantage of the behavioural, social and psychological aspects of a human rather than depending on the vulnerabilities of software. Such attacks are highly targeted and are persistent in nature. Human-driven cyber attacks involve manual inspection and interaction to adapt dynamically by avoiding detection of the identity of an individual involved in such attacks.

The most common types of Human-driven Cyber attacks are classified as shown below:

a. Human errors

Some of the mistakes such as setting up weak passwords, phishing, outdated software installation, missing software updates and security patches can lead to entry of attackers into the network.

b. Social Engineering

Social Engineering is a technique in which the cybercriminals try to use some deceiving tactics by establishing trust or fear to trap the individuals into revealing sensitive information such as passwords, personal information to gain control of the computer systems in order to steal bank account numbers, pin numbers to gain access to the individual's financial information. Some of the common Social Engineering techniques are Phishing, Pretexting, Smishing, Vishing, scareware, Tailgating etc. Phishing is a technique in which the attackers impersonate that they are trusted by sending Emails, SMS, or phone calls to make the victims reveal sensitive information or by clicking malicious links. Pretexting is a method where attackers create a situation to mimic the individuals to disclose sensitive information to compromise security. Smishing is the attack that uses fake SMS messages to trick recipients to reveal the sensitive information. Vishing is an attack where the malicious attackers use phone calls or voice messages to trick recipients to reveal the sensitive information such as credit card numbers, login credentials or other bank account information. Scareware is a software used to make the victim afraid of fake alerts or tactics in order to make victim take immediate action such as downloading fake softwares. Tailgating is gaining physical access in an unauthorized manner in order to access secure areas following a person without getting noticed.

c. Insider Threats

The inside employees, partners or competitors whether maliciously or unintentionally cause harm through sabotage or stealing data.

d. Lacking Awareness and Training

Individuals who lack sufficient awareness about cyber security and cyber threats may be vulnerable to social engineering, malwares, and phishing.

e. Phishing

Phishing is a technique in which the attackers impersonate that they are trusted by sending emails, sms, or phone calls to make the victims reveal sensitive information or by clicking malicious links. Some of the types of Phishing attacks are Smishing, Vishing, etc. Smishing is the attack that uses fake SMS messages to trick recipients to reveal the sensitive information. Vishing is an attack where the malicious attackers use phone calls or voice messages to trick recipients to reveal the sensitive information such as credit card numbers, login credentials or other bank account information.

f. Malware Infections

Downloading malicious software or executing them by clicking external links may lead to malicious attacks.

g. Whaling Attack

Whaling is a type of cyber attack that especially targets high-level professionals like CEOs or other senior level employees in an organization to trap them to reveal sensitive information such as granting access to systems with confidential information and frighten them to involve in scams.

h. Ransomware-as-a-Service Attack

Ransomware as a Service is one of the Cybercrime where ransomware will be used as a source to launch attacks by cyber criminals. Some of the ransomware attacks are LockBit, BlackCat, Conti, Darkside etc., Such attacks have become global actors in various sectors such as Healthcare, education, government etc. Such attacks are human driven especially by the ransomware groups that try to target or exploit the weak controls of the system.

Change Healthcare, a subsidiary of united health Group has become a victim of ransomware incident in year 2024. It is one of the organizations that process huge amount of data of US medical claims. The attackers have implemented data exfiltration and encrypted the critical systems and forced the organization to pay approximately 22 dollars as ransom in order to get the organization's own data. This attack has happened by exposing the major vulnerabilities in the areas such as patient-billing, report generation and supply chains.

Colonial Pipeline Cyberattack attack is considered to be one of the disruptive ransomware attack in the history of Infrastructure base in U.S in the year 2021. It was executed by DarkSide ransomware group. They have gained access to the network using a compromised VPN account as the network lacks multi-factor authentication due to the lack of Multi-factor authentication. This has led to the shortage of fuel across US East coast causing a shutdown of the operations, price surge, affecting transport and commercial sectors. This has revealed the importance of better authentication practices and preparedness of cyber resilience.

Microsoft Blue Screen of Death (BSOD) attack has caused Global Outage on July 2024. This attack has caused millions of Windows OS crash with a blue screen. This has affected hospitals, airlines, retail services, and government operations in several countries. It was caused by a defective security update by CrowdStrike. The error occurred due to the human error in coding, testing and deployment. The error has occurred due to bypassing the validation checks. It has affected operational and financial loss by halting ATMs, PoS, and disrupting essential public services. As it has occurred due to the oversight in update management, it comes under the Human driven attack.

3. INTRODUCTION TO NETWORK FORENSICS

Network Forensics is a sub-branch of digital forensics that facilitates the analysis over the network irrespective of the type of network. It focuses on network evidence such as traffic, protocols and network usage logs for monitoring, capturing, analysing and interpretation of the network communications to uncover the evidence of the network intrusions, security incidents and cybercrimes from several electronic devices such as networks, computers, cloud platforms, smart phones and IoT devices (Joshi et al., 2016; Javed et al., 2022). Network Forensics is investigating network traffic patterns and communications that are transmitted over different networks. It focuses mainly on the data in movement. Traditional digital forensics focuses on creating image of media and memory and analysing data in a step-by-step manner. But network forensics deals with volatile and dynamic information. Network Forensics is used in the investigation of data theft, suspicious network connections, Distributed Denial of Service (DDOS) attacks, and network tapping. The primary goal of network forensics is detection of unauthorized activity by reconstructing cyber attack incidents and finally preserving the digital evidence that plays a critical role in legal proceedings. Network Forensics is helpful in the investigation of cases such as hacking, Malwares, insider threats, data breaches and Denial of Service (DOS) attacks.

Network Forensics faces several challenges that make it difficult for collecting, analyzing and interpreting the network data to identify malicious activities (Shrivastava, 2016).

a. Voluminous data

Networks generate vast amounts of data by making it difficult for storing, processing and analyzing that data.

b. Data Veracity

Another major challenge faced by digital forensics is the speed at which the data is being transmitted making it more complex requiring specialized tools and techniques for capturing and analyzing real time network traffic.

c. Data privacy regulations

Changing data privacy regulations makes it difficult for Investigators to collect suspicious network traffic from networks crossing the boundaries. Investigators have to comply with such regulations that are limiting scope of investigation.

d. Complex Network Topologies

Modern networks are complex as they involve different types of network topologies such as cloud infrastructure networks, virtual machines and containerized applications. Such networks create complexity in identifying and tracing the attacker's path.

e. Data Integrity

Maintaining the integrity of the captured network data traffic is crucial in the maintenance of validity of evidence. Investigators have to protect the network data from tampering or modifications while collecting, storing and analysing the evidence until it is submitted in the court for legal proceedings.

f. Difficulty in interpretation

Analyzing network traffic is a complex task that requires special tools and techniques for interpretation of results and identification of malicious activities identified over a network.

g. Privacy and Encryption

The widespread implementation of protocols such as Virtual Private Networks (VPN) and SSL/TLS has made it difficult for examining content making it necessary to perform metadata analysis to recover the encrypted network traffic by taking legal permissions for decryption of network traffic.

Network forensics plays a major role in organizations for the detection of intrusions and suspicious communications to identify the attackers who have penetrated into defense systems and to know how much data has got exfiltrated. Law enforcement agencies depend on network evidence such as malicious payloads, data transfer records and control information for reconstructing the attack paths, correlate diverse events, attack timelines for supporting prosecution of criminals. Network forensics helps in preventing the incident from occurring by blocking malicious IPs and enhancing the intrusion detection systems. Network Forensics plays a major role in modern Cyber investigations.

4. SOURCES OF NETWORK-BASED EVIDENCE

Every organization has a different network environment that ranges from small healthcare organization to large financial institutions. But the network infrastructure, topologies and equipment are common for any type of organizations. The value of network-based evidence depends on the type of investigation, configuration of devices, and the type of network topology. The evidence from multiple sources may help in providing unique information which can be correlated further to solve the case investigation.

This section discusses about the various types of evidences that can be used as part of network evidence.

a. Cables

Physical cables involve LAN connections between stations or between switches and routers. Network cables can consist of twisted pair cables, coaxial cables and Fiber-optic cables. The network forensic investigators can tap the physical wires to copy and store the network traffic that is being transmitted across the wire.

b. Signals through air

The most common way of data transmission is in the form of Radio Frequency (RF) signals, Infrared (IR) Waves via wireless networking. Transmission through wireless signals is easy as it requires less setup costs avoiding cables. The investigators gain access to traffic over such wireless networks to get the encrypted information by obtaining the key to access or break the encryption process to access evidence content. Using such data, the investigators can gain a lot of information such as the networks in which the suspected criminals have traversed, IP addresses, MAC Addresses, unauthenticated systems that are attacking Wireless network. Investigators perform statistical analysis on the network traffic by analyzing the patterns.

c. Switches

Switches are multi-port bridges that connect multiple stations or networks together to form a Local Area Network (LAN). These switches aggregate the traffic from various other segments. Data travels from one station to another traversing through many switches. Switches maintain Content Addressable Memory (CAM) table that stores a mapping between ports and network card MAC address. Switches provide investigators to capture network traffic.

d. Routers

Routers are the devices that connect several networks together facilitating packet transmission between network segments having diverse addressing schemes. Routers help in internetworking globally over various geographies through WAN. Routers help in filtering packets by denying transmission of packets over some routes. Forensic investigators can identify suspicious packets by tracing the path with the help of routing tables. Routers also maintain log of traffic that is denied. Logs stored on router may be volatile or gets erased during rebooting process.

e. Authentication Servers

Authentication servers are centralized servers that manages user accounts, successful logins, failed login attempts, and other suspicious events. Forensic Investigators analyze such logs to know about the brute force attacks on password-guessing, suspicious logins at odd hours or changed privileges.

f. Name Servers

Domain Name System (DNS) is a mechanism that maps MAC addresses to IP addresses. DNS servers have log that stores the queries for IP address and hostname resolutions. Such DNS logs helps investigators to reveal the timestamps at which connection attempts are made from internal systems to external systems along with the websites, external mail servers etc.

g. DHCP Servers

Dynamic Host Configuration Protocol (DHCP) is used to configure IP addresses to stations dynamically. Instead of manual configuration of IP addresses, the DHCP allows automatic assignment of IP addresses reducing the manual work. Investigators start suspecting the person by inspecting the IP addresses and identifying who allotted the IP address and for how much time it was leased or when it was renewed. DHCP logs help investigators to know which physical network card is assigned to which IP address.

h. Firewalls

Firewalls are the specialized routers that decide whether the traffic should be forwarded to or should be dropped out based on the IP addresses. Firewalls alert the system by blocking it to not enter to a particular network. Firewall logs help investigators to identify denied traffic, changes in system settings, errors and other events.

5. NETWORK FORENSICS INVESTIGATION PROCESS

Network Forensic Investigation process involves set of stages. These stages are vital for effective investigation of network security incidents and evidence gathering. The phases are discussed as shown below:

i. Evidence Collection

The evidence has to be first collected from various sources such as routers, switches, servers and systems. This data may also consist of packet capture, network traffic logs, network file systems, and other information. This data is used to identify whether the activity is normal, malicious or suspicious. But the evidence collection process must acquire evidence by taking the factors such as privacy, consent, and jurisdictional constraints. As network capture may expose sensitive personal or organizational data, it must follow proper rules and regulations while capturing such information. Clear policies and consent mechanisms must be imposed during monitoring and evidence reconstruction. Also, in cloud-based environments jurisdictional conflicts also arise if data is transmitted or is stored across different regions. Ethical and lawful network forensics require strict adherence to not only technical aspects but also ethical and legal aspects.

ii. Preservation

Preservation of the collected evidence is important to maintain and protect the integrity of evidence and chain of custody. It means the network devices have to be secured from data loss or modification.

iii. Examination and Analysis

Examining the data gathered is important to identify suspicious activities, anomalies, and reasons for attacks. Analyzing the data helps in determining the main cause for the network incident to happen. It also helps in understanding the methods and tools used by attackers and reconstructing the incident timelines.

iv. Reporting

Once the examination of data is completed, the findings have to be documented clearly in a concise manner. This report includes the type of incident, methods used, evidences collected, and the conclusions about the criminals. This document helps in legal proceedings and further in prevention and taking remedial measures.

6. TRADITIONAL FORENSIC MODELS

a. Cyber Kill Chain Model

It is a traditional forensic model that provides a linear framework to outline the sequential steps of a cyber attack that occurs from an external entity. The steps followed in this model starts from gathering information to successful completion of attack. It is mostly used by network forensic investigators to break down the attack into several stages in order to identify what happens at every stage and to detect key indicators that led to the compromise of the attack. It also helps in knowing who has entered into the network, movements across the network and stole the data from network. KillChain focus on the actions taken by the attackers from external sources. It works well for the traditional cyber attacks but is not efficient for the human-driven cyber attacks. But, the human-driven cyber attacks follow human behavior and psychological manipulation. As they do not follow the technical sequence, killChain model is not adequate to capture such human driven attacks.

b. Diamond Model of Intrusion Analysis

Diamond Model is a traditional model that helps the forensic investigators in analyzing the incident clearly. There are four key elements in this model. They are adversary, capabilities, Infrastructure, and the victims. The adversary is the attacker system, the capabilities are the tools and techniques, infrastructure is the systems and the networks involved in the incident and the victim is the target system or network. This model will help the experts in finding the links between these key elements and identify the threats and to determine how the attackers operate. But this model does not cover human-driven cyber attacks that occur within an organization such as misuse of internal resources, taking over legitimate user accounts, leaking the organization information etc. This model is not efficient in capturing the human behavior which is crucial in network forensics.

c. MITRE ATT&CK Framework

This framework provides a detailed list of tools and techniques for identifying the cyber attack at different stages. It helps the forensic investigators in identifying the logs, network incidents and alerts to the already known attacker behaviors. This model helps in determining the attack by comparing the determined data with the global threat data. This model also helps in threat identification and planning the defense mechanism before attack occurs. It mainly focuses on technical attacker incidents but is not much efficient in identifying the human attack behaviours or intentions behind human-driven attacks such as social engineering, human mistakes, revenge scenarios at workplace environment etc.

Although such traditional techniques may lay basic foundations for intrusion attack analysis, they only concentrate on attackers technical activity but not on the human behaviors. Human-drive cyber attacks such as credential theft, password hacking, software misuse and social engineering require even more sophisticated methods to identify the context, intent and human risk attribution in reconstructing the incidents in forensic process.

7. NETWORK FORENSIC TOOLS FOR HUMAN-DRIVEN CYBER ATTACKS

i. Wireshark

Network forensics has become important in cyber security for monitoring, capturing and analysing the network traffic for investigating complicated cases and uncovering security incidents and breaches. By examining the captured packets, logs and communication patterns, it is easy to reconstruct events that lead to an incident. Wireshark is a powerful tool that acts as a network packet analyzer. A network analyzer examines network traffic information, by capturing packet data. Wireshark is a tool used by network administrators for examining networking problems, security incidents and network protocol implementations. The investigators can perform real-time forensic analysis based on this data and helps them in understanding the situation and stop attack by collecting evidence and information to avoid further incidents. It is a free open-source tool that helps users in capturing and troubleshooting network traffic (Asassfeh et al.,2024). Figure 1 demonstrates the Wireshark tool home page.

Fig 1. Wireshark Packet Analyzer

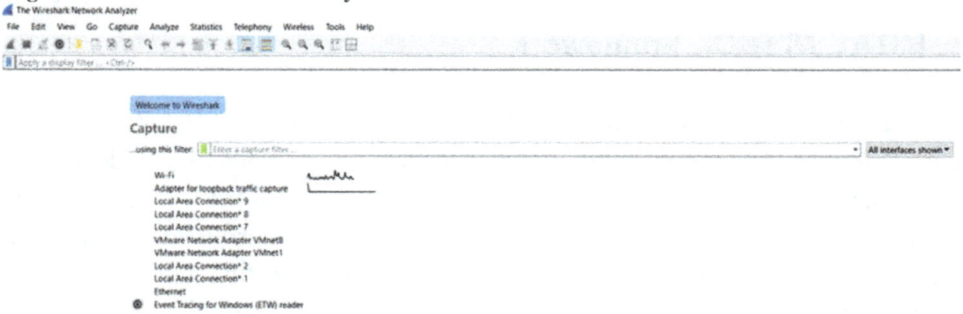

Figure 2 shows how live packet capturing is performed on network.

Fig 2. Live Packet Capture using Wireshark

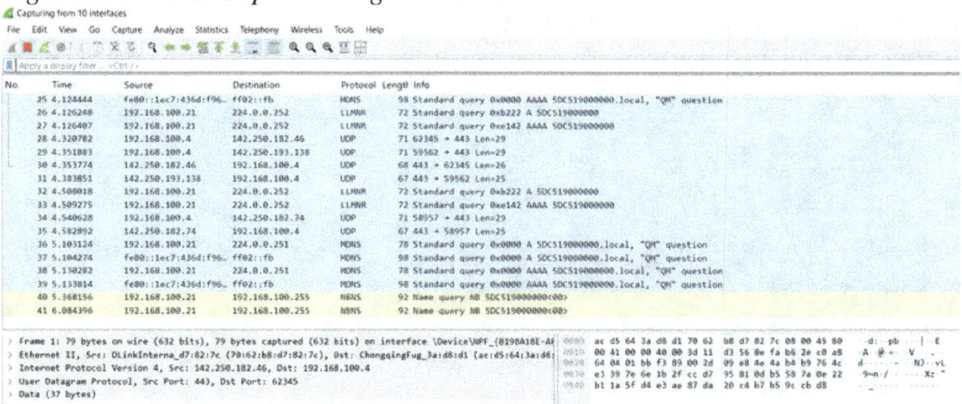

Figure 3 shows how to view the captured packet traffic.

Fig 3. Viewing and analyzing the captured traffic for packet analysis

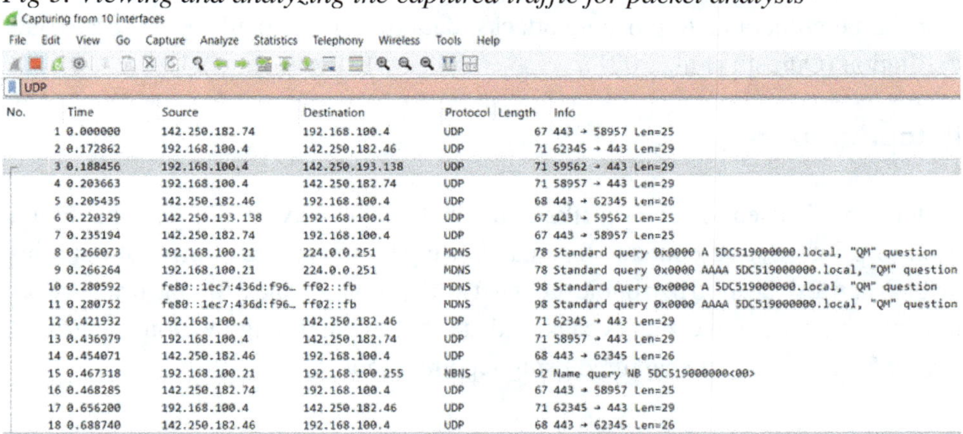

Wireshark tool also provides a powerful filtering capability to narrow down the captured traffic. Filters allow investigators to display only the relevant packets required for investigation based on specific criteria. At the top of the Wireshark window, there's a display filter bar where we can enter filters. For example, if ip-.addr == 192.158.1.1 displays all packets with the IP address 192.168.1.1. If filter is set to tcp.port == 80 it displays packets that are using TCP port 80 (HTTP) and if filter is set to http then it shows only HTTP packets. Figure 4 demonstrates the filtering capability of Wireshark.

Fig 4. Filtering capability of Wireshark

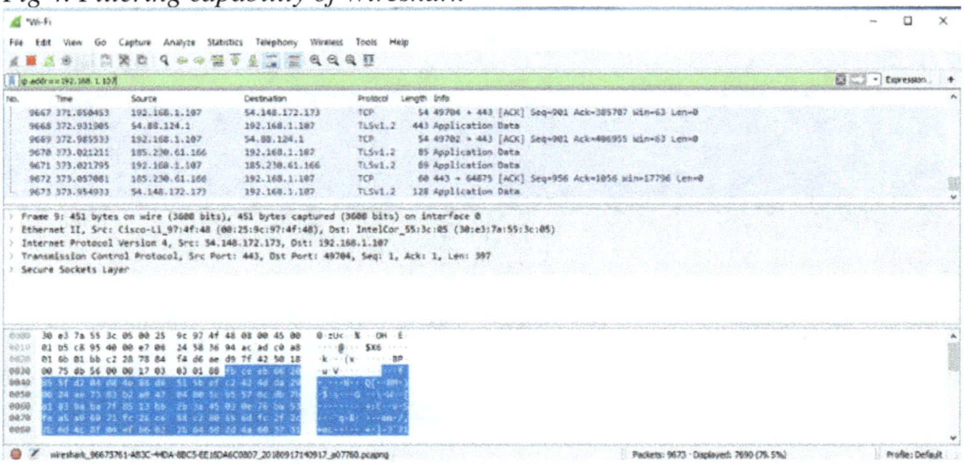

Wireshark tool helps to identify misconfigured network devices and protocols that can be vulnerable to phishing attacks, data breaches, email spoofing and data exfiltation (Qureshi et al., 2021).

ii. tcpdump

tcpdump is used to capture, filter, and analyze the network traffic. This tool is used to print or store contents for analysis. tcpdump captures traffic at data link layer. It can also be used to troubleshoot network problems and examine raw network information. tcpdump captures packets that are flowing through various interfaces. Figure 5 shows the data captured using tcpdump tool.

Fig 5. Packet capturing using tcpdump

```
suse1:~ # tcpdump
tcpdump: verbose output suppressed, use -v or -vv for full protocol decode
listening on eth0, link-type EN10MB (Ethernet), capture size 96 bytes
20:38:29.013544 IP text-lb.esams.wikimedia.org.http > 192.168.198.128.54543: FP
 659455554:659455554(0) ack 3797162379 win 64240
20:38:29.013961 IP 192.168.198.128.54543 > text-lb.esams.wikimedia.org.http: F
1:1(0) ack 1 win 51120
20:38:29.014324 IP text-lb.esams.wikimedia.org.http > 192.168.198.128.54543: .
ack 2 win 64239
20:38:29.015350 IP 192.168.198.128.40566 > 192.168.198.2.domain: 16599+ PTR? 12
8.198.168.192.in-addr.arpa. (46)
20:38:29.043034 IP 192.168.198.2.domain > 192.168.198.128.40566: 16599 NXDomair
 0/1/0 (95)
20:38:29.043533 IP 192.168.198.128.57315 > 192.168.198.2.domain: 34584+ PTR? 19
2.174.198.91.in-addr.arpa. (45)
```

Figure 6 shows the capturing of data from a particular ethernet interface using tcpdump options.

Fig 6. Packet capturing of an Ethernet interface using tcpdump

```
suse1:~ # tcpdump -i eth0
tcpdump: verbose output suppressed, use -v or -vv for full protocol decode
listening on eth0, link-type EN10MB (Ethernet), capture size 96 bytes
20:39:28.014065 IP 192.168.198.1.netbios-ns > 192.168.198.255.netbios-ns: NBT U
DP PACKET(137): QUERY; REQUEST; BROADCAST
20:39:28.014840 IP 192.168.198.128.56851 > 192.168.198.2.domain: 18867+ PTR? 25
5.198.168.192.in-addr.arpa. (46)
20:39:28.027418 IP 192.168.198.1.49733 > 224.0.0.252.llmnr: UDP, length 22
20:39:28.027850 IP 192.168.198.128.50611 > lhr14s24-in-f19.1e100.net.https: P 2
912329209:2912329246(37) ack 1375935787 win 18760
20:39:28.034322 IP lhr14s24-in-f19.1e100.net.https > 192.168.198.128.50611: . a
ck 37 win 64240
20:39:28.037196 IP6 fe80::2cfe:5154:6c0d:fafd.65460 > ff02::1:3.llmnr: UDP, len
gth 22
20:39:28.039057 IP 192.168.198.1.65460 > 224.0.0.252.llmnr: UDP, length 22
20:39:28.051576 IP 192.168.198.2.domain > 192.168.198.128.56851: 18867 NXDomair
 0/1/0 (95)
20:39:28.051744 IP 192.168.198.128.35496 > 192.168.198.2.domain: 58919+ PTR? 1.
198.168.192.in-addr.arpa. (44)
20:39:28.077704 IP 192.168.198.2.domain > 192.168.198.128.35496: 58919 NXDomair
 0/1/0 (93)
20:39:28.077903 IP 192.168.198.128.56215 > 192.168.198.2.domain: 59223+ PTR? 2.
198.168.192.in-addr.arpa. (44)
```

As the resources such as CPU cycles, disk space etc are limited, it is necessary to filter packets during packet capture for proper analysis. Figure 7 demonstrates how tcpdump can be used to display traffic only from eth0 interface by ignoring TCP port 80 traffic.

Fig 7. Packet Filtering using tcpdump

```
# tcpdump -nni eth0 'not (tcp and port 80)'
tcpdump: verbose output suppressed, use -v or -vv for full protocol decode
listening on eth0, link-type EN10MB (Ethernet), capture size 65535 bytes
12:49:33.631163 IP 10.30.30.20.123 > 10.30.30.255.123: NTPv4, Broadcast,
    length 48
12:49:38.197072 IP 192.168.30.100.57699 > 192.168.30.30.514: SYSLOG local2.
    notice, length: 1472
12:49:38.197319 IP 192.168.30.100.57699 > 192.168.30.30.514: SYSLOG local2.
    notice, length: 1472
12:49:38.197324 IP 192.168.30.100 > 192.168.30.30: udp
12:49:38.197327 IP 192.168.30.100 > 192.168.30.30: udp
12:49:38.197568 IP 192.168.30.100.57699 > 192.168.30.30.514: SYSLOG local2.
    notice, length: 1472
12:49:38.197819 IP 192.168.30.100.57699 > 192.168.30.30.514: SYSLOG local2.
    notice, length: 1472
12:49:38.197825 IP 192.168.30.100 > 192.168.30.30: udp
```

iii. Network Mapper (Nmap)

Nmap is a free open-source utility for network discovery and auditing security incidents. Nmap is a network scanner that is used to identify hosts and services over a computer network by analysing the responses. Nmap can scan large networks very quickly. It runs on almost all types of Operating Systems. Figure 8 demonstrates the execution of Nmap tool on Windows OS.

Fig 8. Demonstration of Nmap on Windows

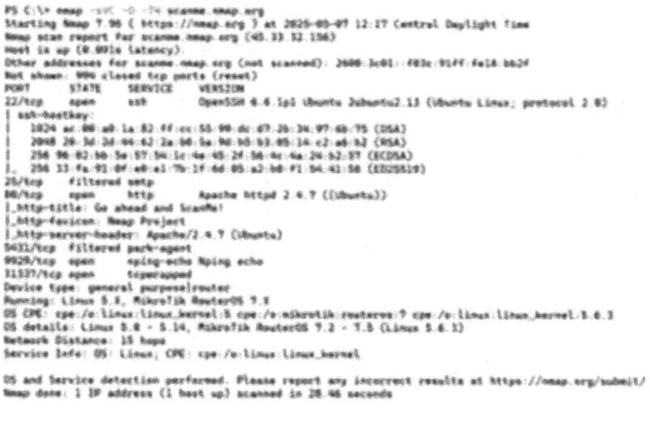

iv. Network Miner

It is a Network Forensic Analysis Tool (NFAT) designed for Windows. It is a passive oacket capturing tool that helps in the detection of Operating Systems (OS), hosts, ports etc. This tool also helps in parsing the packet capture (PCAP) files for performing the offline analysis. It also extracts the emails, certificates and files that are exchanged over the network by parsing the PCAP files or using packet sniffing directly on the network. Figure 9 illustrates the files extracted from sniffed network traffic using Network Miner tool.

Fig 9. Displaying files extracted from sniffed network to disk

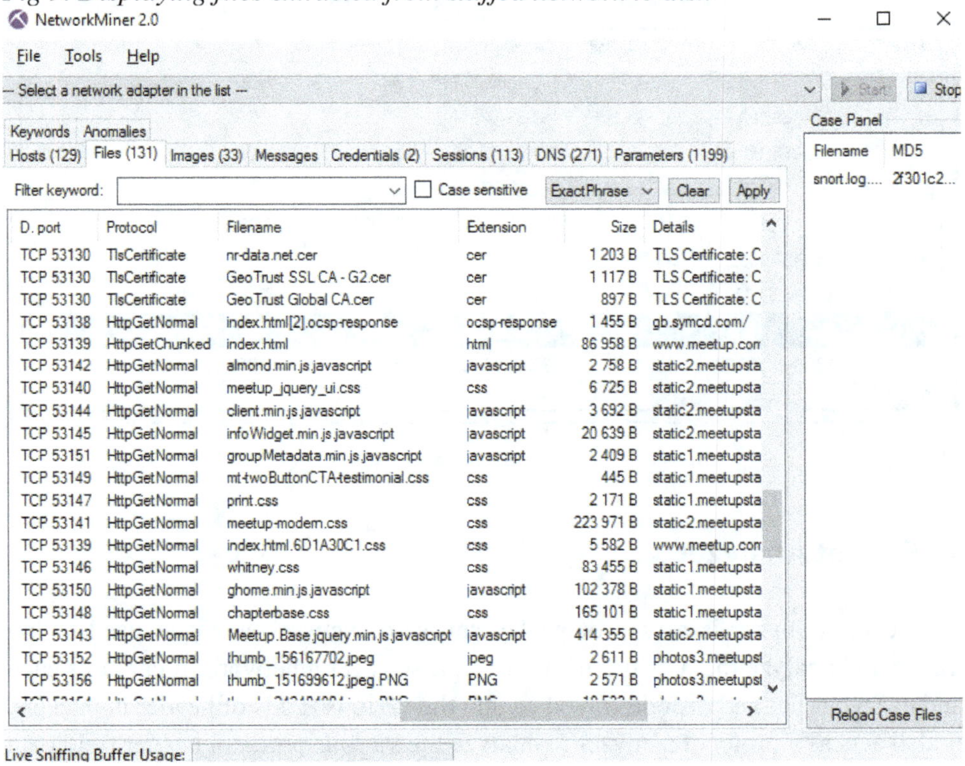

v. CapLoader

CapLoader is a tool that is designed for handling large amount of captured network traffic. This tool displays the list of TCP and UDP traffic flows. The users can filter the traffic based on the loaded PCAP files. This tool also helps in extracting, searching, sorting and filtering the data flow form PCAP files. Figure 10 shows the demonstration of CapLoader tool.

Fig 10. Demonstration of CapLoader tool

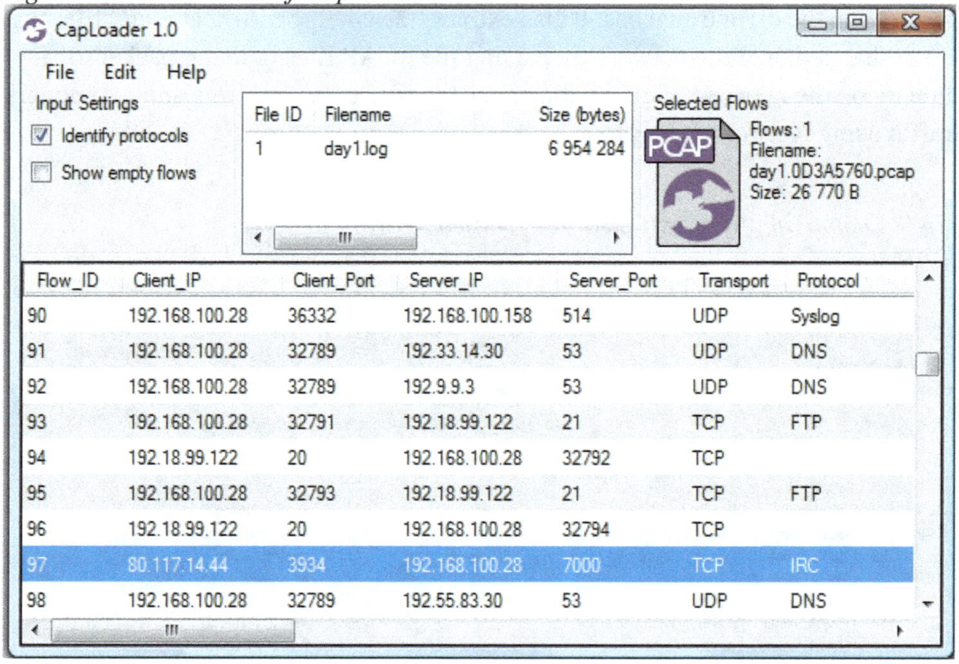

vi. Packet Analyzer

Packet Analyzer is a type of packet sniffer or network analyzer used to log traffic and analyze the network traffic that passes over a network. It captures each and every packet and decodes raw data and the various fields of header in packets. It also acts as a protocol analyzer to analyze the various protocol header field data and identify useful information required for network forensics. It is used to detect and analyze various network intrusions, network misuse, and network problems (Sikos et al., 2020).

vii. NetFlow

NetFlow is a traffic analyzer used to collect and analyze the data flow from the network devices such as routers, switches etc providing information on traffic patterns that can be used for Network Forensics.

viii. Aircrack-ng

Aircrack-ng is a software suite that consist of a collection of tools for Wireless LANs such as packet sniffer, Wired Equivalent Privacy (WEP) cracker, Wi-Fi-Protected Access (WPA) PSK cracker. This tool works with any controller and has ability to sniff any version of 802.11 traffic such as 802.11a, 802.11b, 802.11g etc. This is an in-built tool in many Linux distributions such as Kali Linux OS. This tool is mainly used in penetration testing and in security audits. Figure 11 demonstrates how to crack WEP and WPA-PSK Keys using Aircrack-ng Tool.

Fig 11. Cracking WEP and WPA-PSK Keys using Aircrack-ng Tool

```
                              Aircrack-ng 1.0


              [00:00:18] Tested 1514 keys (got 30566 IVs)

KB    depth   byte(vote)
 0    0/  9   1F(39680) 4E(38400) 14(37376) 5C(37376) 9D(37376)
 1    7/  9   64(36608) 3E(36352) 34(36096) 46(36096) BA(36096)
 2    0/  1   1F(46592) 6E(38400) 81(37376) 79(36864) AD(36864)
 3    0/  3   1F(40960) 15(38656) 7B(38400) BB(37888) 5C(37632)
 4    0/  7   1F(39168) 23(38144) 97(37120) 59(36608) 13(36352)

                      KEY FOUND! [ 1F:1F:1F:1F:1F ]
     Decrypted correctly: 100%
```

8. ANALYZING HUMAN BEHAVIOR THROUGH NETWORK DATA

A critical approach in Network Forensics is to understand the human behaviour by analysing network data in the detection and investigation of security incidents. By analysing the behavioural patterns associated with attacks such as social engineering, phishing, privilege misuse, unauthorized login activities and data exfiltration techniques, the forensic investigators can identify malicious activity in an efficient manner. Such identification may not be possible through other existing logs (Pilli et al.,2010).

Phishing attacks can sometimes lead to abnormal network access patterns. Forensic analysts can uncover unauthorized logins from IP addresses and login attempts. The logs related to authentication and the packet captures can be correlated in order to find the victim systems. They use the network forensic tools to detect unprivileged access to accounts by detecting unusual commands in systems and identify abnormal transferring of files. Privilege escalation and unauthorized movement can also be identified by analysing the internal traffic flows between different kinds of networks. Irregular logins and geo-tagged locations indicate compromised events. Network Forensic analysis correlates the login time with the location at which the incident happened. It also identifies session hijacking if any user logs in from two different locations at a time.

Network Forensics helps in examining the anomalies in outbound traffic, Suspicious DNS query patterns. Data gathered from tools like Packet analyzer, tcpdump, NetFlow, Nmap help in tracing the abnormal activities and reconstructing the sessions for further analysis. By exploiting the behavioural analysis in Network Forensics, Forensic investigators can detect and respond to threats with high accuracy even when an illegitimate user exhibits a legitimate behaviour.

a. AI driven Network Intrusion Detection (NIDS)

Previously the reconstruction of slow, human driven attacks used to take several hours to several days. But AI-driven models will facilitate the detection of anomalous patterns based on the conventional signatures, sequence embeddings that are useful for timeline construction in forensics. Transformer model architectures provide modelling for long-range dependencies in flow/time-series telemetry (Tripathi et al., 2023).

Network Forensics has now-a-days shifted from packet capture analysis to AI-augmented, context-rich reconstruction that integrates the temporal, relational, and identity based characteristics. Recent research has emphasized more on sequence-based deep models for telemetry, Graph-aware deep models, Human behaviour analytics (UEBA) and identity fusion to surface the human-centric anomalies. Graph Neural Networks have become major detection and correlation tool by modelling hosts, accounts, and flows as graphs to help revealing lateral movement and multi-host campaign that has become central to human-driven intrusions (Tripathi et al., 2024).

GNN embeddings helps the forensic specialists to cluster the group of campaign narratives and prioritizing the nodes for collection of evidence from packets or hosts. Transformer or the GNN hybrid variants can provide a compact and explainable artefact that can be used to store the raw captures for accelerating triage, reconstructing the attacker paths, and providing support to generate the summary of chain-of-custody aware evidence (Rai et al., 2023 ; Beemkumar et al., 2023).

b. Human Behavior Analytics (UEBA)

Human Behavior Analytics can be implemented using the User and Entity Behavior Analytics (UEBA). UEBA has gained high relevance in the field of Network Forensics for investigating human driven cyber attacks such as password cracking, insider threats, and socially engineering attacks. They have evolved as major behavioral baseline generators which have integrated the identity-awareness, temporal patterns and factors involving context. Modern UEBA platforms integrated data from multiple sources such as identity management, access management logs, network activity, recent access history, working hours, location history in order to build a dynamic and individualized behavioural profile for each user or entity. Machine learning models such as anomaly scoring, session based embeddings techniques are capable of detecting the deviations such as unusual logins, abnormal data access sequences and irregular network movements. It helps in early detection of human driven anomalies in forensic investigations. UEBA helps in providing metadata in action in order to guide investigation process. Metadata such as user-session identifiers, abnormal activity deviation scores will help investigators to examine the case in depth. It also saves time by narrowing the packet-level and log-level analysis focusing only on high risk human behavior rather than running through huge amount of raw network traffic. Integrating the behavioural analytics with forensic analysis raises important ethical and privacy considerations. UEBA helps not only in identifying what exactly happened in network it also helps in identification of who did the incident and how the incident has happened in order to prosecute the human-driven cyber attacks.

9. CHALLENGES AND CONSIDERATIONS

Network Forensics helps the organizations gather evidence to support legal investigations and prove the cyber criminal guilty and accountable for the security incident happened. Quick recovery of data helps companies to retrieve data from the network security breaches (Buric et al.,2015).

a. Legal aspects

Network Forensics operates by integrating technology and law, so understanding the importance of legal aspects is necessary to conduct the investigation in an ethical and lawful manner. Investigators must have a proper legal warrant in order to capture and monitor some network traffic. Even the search and seizure requires proper warrant. Handling the network data that crosses national and international boundaries also violate international laws if proper authorization is not taken. Organizations need to perform forensic investigation by following some regulatory frameworks such as HIPAA, PCI-DSS etc. Unauthorized use of packet sniffers or deep packet inspection tools may cause legal issues making the evidence invalid for legal prosecution at court. At the court, the network forensic investigators must testify the documentation and the methods used for collecting evidence in order to prove the cyber criminal as guilty.

b. Ethical Aspects

While legal aspects assure that the investigation is done by following regulatory laws, ethical considerations play a crucial role in assuring that the investigation is done in a fair manner with respect to individual rights. Investigators may sometimes come across personal, sensitive or confidential data. Ethically they must limit their data gathering to only what is required for investigation by avoiding irrelevant information. Another aspect of ethical consideration is informed content. Individuals in corporate companies must be informed about the network monitoring to provide transparency and build trust by preventing the misuse of network forensic tools. Investigators must also maintain integrity as tampering evidence may be a violation to ethical concerns. During investigation, the investigators must keep the sensitive data such as business secrets, trade secrets or any personal information in a confidential manner to avoid unauthorized access and disclosure. Investigators must document every step involved in investigation process by providing a clear chain of custody ensuring the accountability on all actions taken. These ethical aspects have to be considered during network forensic investigation.

c. Privacy Aspects

With the advancement of technology, many problems related to privacy and security arises. Sometimes investigators may obtain sensitive information without permission from concerned individuals or organizations violating the right to privacy. So, proper agreements or regulations must be negotiated between either parties for using the information without malicious intent. It is very important to ensure that the investigators must consent to right to privacy by giving at most respect to individuals avoiding bias to discrimination. Because bias can mislead the case to false conviction. So, it is crucial for policy makers to formulate rules and laws to protect individual's right to privacy (Tiwari et al., 2021).

d. Scalability

Several operational challenges have found limitations on the effectiveness of the current investigation mechanisms in the context of network forensics for human-driven cyber attacks. Scalability is one of the major concerns as the data that is captured may have large amounts of network data such as proxy logs, packet captures, identity events, behavioural traces etc., Scalability becomes a major barrier as most of the human-driven attacks will be identified slowly that may take days, weeks or several months. Managing that much data may pose scalability issues and demands for huge amount of storage, computational overhead and network bandwidth. Traditional forensic methods try to gather data from historical data efficiently but with few delays in reconstruction of events. But with the advancement of technology, cloud-based and hybrid environments has complicated the scalability where data is distributed across multiple platforms or globally. Intelligent data filtering and scalable analytics pipelines help the investigations to be complete and resource-intensive.

e. False Positives

Human-driven attacks that involve malicious actions may sometimes be falsely assumed to resemble legitimate user behaviour. Sometimes AI-based detection systems may sometimes identify unusual user actions to be suspicious. This leads to false alerts creating alert fatigue among the forensic analysts creating a overhead on manually verifying each case in order to differentiate between genuine and benign anomalies. High false positive rates will slow down the investigations but increases the risk of identification of actual attacks. Improving forensic investigation accuracy requires a more context-aware and better detection models. Incorporating multi-layered behavioural context enhances the ability of the model in differentiating malicious behaviour from original behaviour. In order to lessen the false positive rates, advanced methods like human-centric threat modelling, explainable AI, and adaptive base lining can be used for detection of human driven attack forensics.

10. CONCLUSION

With the increase in cyber threats in the modern era, understanding the human-driven attacks has become crucial. Such attacks involve social engineering, insider threats, intrusions that exploit human vulnerabilities more than the technical vulnerabilities. Addressing such threats may be far more difficult as they involve both human and electronic evidence. This chapter focuses on Network Forensics which is a key discipline for cyber threat investigations involving human intervention. It also discusses about the network forensic investigation process by gathering various sources of network evidence for reconstructing the events and identifying the potential methods used by attackers. The chapter mainly focused on analyzing human behaviour through network data by identifying patterns of misuse and deception. Understanding the user actions, communications and access patterns helps in understanding human behavior revealing the motivation for attack. It also emphasizes the legal, ethical and privacy concerns involved in Network Forensics investigation process. Compliance with such concerns can help in efficient defending and justice in legal proceedings. Network Forensics can provide proper tools and techniques to counter the human-driven cyber attacks by integrating the behavioural insights with technical knowledge in a lawful manner.

REFERENCES

Asassfeh, M., Al-Mousa, M. R., Al-Dweikat, H., Al-Mashagbeh, M. H., Afaneh, S., Samara, G., . . . Al Daoud, E. (2024, December). An overview of tools and techniques in network forensics. In 2024 25th International Arab Conference on Information Technology (ACIT) (pp. 1-7). IEEE. DOI: 10.1109/ACIT62805.2024.10876996

Buric, J., & Delija, D. (2015, May). Challenges in network forensics. In 2015 38th International Convention on Information and Communication Technology, Electronics and Microelectronics (MIPRO) (pp. 1382-1386). IEEE. DOI: 10.1109/MIPRO.2015.7160490

Guan, Y. (2014). Network forensics. In *Managing information security* (pp. 313–334). Syngress. DOI: 10.1016/B978-0-12-416688-2.00011-8

Javed, A. R., Ahmed, W., Alazab, M., Jalil, Z., Kifayat, K., & Gadekallu, T. R. (2022). A comprehensive survey on computer forensics: State-of-the-art, tools, techniques, challenges, and future directions. *IEEE Access : Practical Innovations, Open Solutions*, *10*, 11065–11089. DOI: 10.1109/ACCESS.2022.3142508

Joshi, R. C., & Pilli, E. S. (2016). *Fundamentals of Network Forensics*. Springer. DOI: 10.1007/978-1-4471-7299-4

Pilli, E. S., Joshi, R. C., & Niyogi, R. (2010). Network forensic frameworks: Survey and research challenges. digital investigation, 7(1-2), 14-27.

Qureshi, S., Tunio, S., Akhtar, F., Wajahat, A., Nazir, A., & Ullah, F. (2021). Network forensics: A comprehensive review of tools and techniques. *International Journal of Advanced Computer Science and Applications*, *12*(5). Advance online publication. DOI: 10.14569/IJACSA.2021.01205103

Shrivastava, G. (2016, March). Network forensics: Methodical literature review. In 2016 3rd International Conference on Computing for Sustainable Global Development (INDIACom) (pp. 2203-2208). IEEE.

Sikos, L. F. (2020). Packet analysis for network forensics: A comprehensive survey. *Forensic Science International Digital Investigation*, *32*, 200892. DOI: 10.1016/j.fsidi.2019.200892

Singh, S. (2024). *Pandey, J. K. Rai, M. Saxena, A.K. "Advancements in Facial Expression Recognition Using Machine and Deep Learning Techniques", Machine and Deep Learning Techniques for Emotion Detection*. IGI Global., DOI: 10.4018/979-8-3693-4143-8.ch007

Tiwari, A., Mehrotra, V., Goel, S., Naman, K., Maurya, S., & Agarwal, R. (2021, October). Developing trends and challenges of digital forensics. In 2021 5th International Conference on Information Systems and Computer Networks (ISCON) (pp. 1-5). IEEE. DOI: 10.1109/ISCON52037.2021.9702301

Tripathi, P., & Kumar, N. (2024). *Paroha, K.K. Rai, M. Panda, M.K. "Applications of Deep Learning in Healthcare in the Framework of Industry 5.0", Infrastructure Possibilities and Human-Centered Approaches With Industry 5.0*. IGI Global., DOI: 10.4018/979-8-3693-0782-3.ch005

Chapter 6
Forensic-Centric Human Threat Intelligence:
An Integrated Framework for Modern Cybercrime Investigation

J. V. P. Udaya Deepika
https://orcid.org/0000-0001-6593-4443
Sreenidhi Institute of Science and Technology, India

T. Venkat Narayana Rao
https://orcid.org/0000-0002-1996-1819
Sreenidhi Institute of Science and Technology, India

G. Seshu Kumari
Sreenidhi Institute of Science and Technology, India

ABSTRACT

Cyber threats today are increasingly driven by human intent, showing greater sophistication and stealth that traditional forensic models, focused mainly on digital traces, struggle to address. "Cyber Forensic Framework: Forensic-Centric Human Threat Intelligence Analysis" introduces an innovative framework that integrates behavioral science, cyber forensics, artificial intelligence, and human threat intelligence. This structured, forensic-centric approach empowers investigators, analysts, and cybersecurity professionals to detect, attribute, and mitigate threats from insiders, hacktivists, cybercriminals, and nation-state actors. By combining technical evidence with behavioral insights and threat intelligence, the book offers a comprehensive view of modern cybercrime. Through real-world case studies and

DOI: 10.4018/979-8-3373-4898-8.ch006

applied examples, it equips experts in academia, law enforcement, and cybersecurity with practical strategies to prevent and respond to complex threats across civilian domains and critical infrastructure environments.

1.INTRODUCTION

Cybercrime has become one of the most significant worldwide threats in the era of hyperconnected society, affecting both individuals and corporations, as well as national governments. Conventional solutions to cybersecurity which place their emphasis on technical security like firewalls, antivirus programs and intrusion identifications systems do not always serve to prevent the current high stakes of sophistication of cyber criminals.

Due to this, there is an urgent need of a more broad based approach where the human aspect of causing such attacks is taken under consideration. An approach that enables such combination can be referred to as a forensic-centric human threat intelligence (HTI) framework and focuses on digital forensics and human behavioral analysis to provide law enforcement with a tool to investigate and predict cyber threats more successfully.

Whereas the traditional threat intelligence is focused on determining evil artifacts such as malicious IP addresses or malware signatures, a forensic-centric HTI model goes deeper, addressing the behavioral, psychological, and social views of the threat actors. It will establish not only a way of how an attack was carried out, but (Williams & Lee, 2022) also a reason of why and who did it. The collected information by examining communication records, social media patterns, darknet communications, and previous attack trends can be used by the investigators to construct threat actor profiles with very complex data including their motives, alliances, and what they might do next.

Digital forensics is the key in this framework since it is able to gather and maintain a legally acceptable form of digital evidence. When used along with threat intelligence, this kind of data proves to be an effective source of mapping (Chen & Zhao, 2024) cyberattacks and knowing how and why a certain attacker does what they do. Instead of relying on post-attack investigations only, this combined response can enable the proactive detection and prevention of the attack before it happens.

Human aspect of cybercrime, which is normally ignored in technical defensive systems, consists of insiders and discontented employees, hacktivists and state-based attackers. The intentions can be seen through the understanding of the psychological traits and linguistic patterns, as well as through the observation of the social behavior that the technical signs would be no longer able to reflect. Such human intelligence assists in providing security personnel and law enforcement agencies an idea on what to expect given the profile of an attacker and the socio-political background.

Cybercrime on international level complicates the investigations since most jurisdictions may have different laws and restrictions regarding the exchange of data. Forensic-oriented HTI framework also encourages (NIST, 2023) the standardization of evidence management, cross-border collaboration, and intelligence exchanges. This is not only effective in making sound investigations but also making sound prosecutions that are legal.

To sum up, the model of investigating cybercrimes as a consequence of forensic science and human threat intelligence combination is more comprehensive. It adds perspective, depth, and foresight which are essential qualities in fighting the contemporary threats to the digital world. This combined model is a significant development in cybersecurity and digital forensic practices because it is based on it.

Recent advances in global cybersecurity emphasize integrating AI-driven behavioral analytics and human–AI collaboration within forensic investigations. The proposed HTI model aligns with these 2024–2025 developments, enhancing predictive accuracy, real-time decision-making, and adaptive intelligence in complex cybercrime scenarios (Vasani et al., 2024; Arora et al., 2024).

2. SURVEY ON THREAT INTELLIGENCE (TI)

Companies have become interested in pro-active and holistic ways of detecting and responding to cybercrimes. Two disciplines are essential in this endeavour, Threat Intelligence (TI), and Digital Forensics. TI is the systematic gathering and leveraging of information about past or potential cyberattacks, and its focus on Indicators of Compromise (IOCs), attacker Tactics, Techniques and Procedures (TTPs), motives and threat actor profiling. Its major purpose is prevention in the form of assistance to the strategic decisions making and the ability of early detection of threats.

Digital Forensics on the other hand is retrospective. It entails gathering, retaining and processing digital evidence to know what happened, how it was done and (Kumar et al., 2023) who did it. TI seeks to prevent attacks before they can take place whereas forensics is used to assign and prosecute crimes once they have been committed.

With the ineffectiveness of purely static blacklists came a new development of advanced threat intelligence systems with real-time data feeds, darknet monitoring, honeypots and automated scoring systems. Models such as the Lockheed Martin Cyber Kill Chain and the MITRE ATT&CK rose to become the standard followed by the industry in monitoring the actions of the attackers throughout the attack lifecycle. Nevertheless, these models are technical focused and usually overlook the psychological motive and human behavior. Thus, threat intelligence is not always contextual, especially in dynamic threat environments, where social awareness and analysis by individuals who are available in time are necessary to address cybersecurity successfully.

2.1. Digital Forensics

The investigation process that follows after the incident happens is critically dependent on Digital Forensics that finds hidden malware, establishes the timeline of the attacks, and restores deleted or encrypted information. EnCase, ftk, sleuth kit, and volatility are popular disk imaging, memory analysis as well as file recovery tools. Lawful compliance-including (Chen & Zhao, 2024) maintenance of the chain of custody, application of approved tools- are crucial to court admission. Despite being successful, traditional forensics methods are prone to focus more on technical artifacts such as IP addresses and timestamps thus falling short on such aspects as behavioral and psychological trappings of cybercriminals.

Conversely, Threat Intelligence (TI) is the capability of anticipating threats through profiling the adversaries, tactics and their intentions. Though TI and digital forensics are effective at the present time in their respective senses, they have been traditionally operating separately, therefore establishing threat assessment silos. A combination of the two disciplines enables investigators to not only know how an attack happened but also the perpetrators and the reason behind it. The above mixed method is especially useful in the detection of insider threats, APTs, and cyber terrorism which requires more than technical indicators. An amalgamation of both will give a more human and intelligent solution to cybersecurity.

2.2 Psychology of Human Behavior in Cybercrime Psychology, Motivation and Profiling

A human driven phenomenon is modelled as a way of enhancing threat intelligence and forensic investigation of cybercrime. Cybersecurity has conventionally been based on such technical components as vulnerability, malware, and system compromise, yet rarely addresses psychological and social aspects of offenses. Cybercriminals are not ordinary rash people who act according to their own will, have incentives and decision-making patterns. Psychology and behavioral profiling, implemented in combination with technical investigations, can provide the insight on the intent of the attackers that technical evidence cannot bring.

Some of the motives that have been mentioned in cybercriminology include financial gain, ideology, revenge, curiosity or social approval. Insiders are either motivated by workplace dissatisfaction (or financial gain), script kiddies are usually motivated by peer acceptance, and Hacktivists are usually guided by a political or religious idea (Harris, 2018). Such theories as Routine Activity Theory and General Strain Theory can be used to understand an opportunity, stress, and rationalization influence on criminal behavior in cyberspace.

Behavioral profiling relies on the writing style and time and the reuse of tools and online communication patterns in order to assist in attribution. Natural Language Processing (NLP) and Social Network Analysis (SNA) are two areas of linguistic forensics that may reveal emotional expressions and personality features as well as connections between threat actors (Anderson, 2021). Nevertheless, profiling has its threats like misinterpretations and false attributions unless it is backed by forensic evidence.

Human-centric analysis is particularly unique in relation to man-in-the-middle sophisticated dangers such as Advanced Persistent Threats al-APTs and insider attacks, during which long-term strategies or minor modifications in behavior can cause intent to show up in advance of technical indications happening. A digital forensics approach combined with behavioral profiling will form a more predictive and comprehensive one, and it is important to note that Human Threat Intelligence is what the proper attribution and proactive defense against contemporary cyber threats should rely on.

2.3. The existing Frameworks and their gaps within them

There are numerous frameworks used to write the mantra of digital investigating and cybersecurity in the proactive threat hunting and reacting. The most pronounced of them are Lockheed Martin Cyber Kill Chain, MITRE ATT&CK, and the Diamond Model of Intrusion Analysis. Such frameworks assist security professionals in planning cyberattack stages including the ones of reconnaissance, exploitation, and post-attack activities. As an example, the (Williams & Lee, 2022) Cyber Kill Chain encompasses a linear description of seven steps of an attack, which helps the defense to track and comprehend the breach points. MITRE ATT&CK is a catalog of adversary tactics and techniques catalogued based on reality incidents, whereas the Diamond Model is based on the interplay between the adversary, infrastructure, capability and victim. Such frameworks can offer nice technical details about the habits of cyberattacks.

Their major drawback however is the fact that they are not integrated into human centered intelligence. They are cast in terms of highly technical information such as IPs, hashes, or system logs but do not take into consideration psychological aspects such as driver of psychological (Chen & Zhao, 2024) motivation, or social backgrounds of the attackers. Because of the dynamics of cybercrime, such as more social engineering, tailored attacks, and attacks based on ideologies, it is becoming as crucial to learn the reason why attacks are made as how attacks are made.

The existing digital forensic tools, such as Autopsy, FTK, and Volatility, are very good in recovering technically, but do not have capabilities to add behavioral or psychological profiling. They are more responsive, and tend to overlook key inputs of human intelligence resources such as dark eBay activity, linguistics tendencies, or emotional clues.

Such a gap is especially hazardous in a scenario where we see cyber operations combined with psychological ones, such as in the case of Advanced Persistent Threats (APTs) or hybrid war. As such, there is an increased need of a forensic-oriented integrated model that combines technical evidence as well as behavioral analysis. A model of this would enhance accurate attribution, greater early threat identification and be in congruence with the contemporary intelligence practices that factor intent, context and human behavior in addition to digital footprints. Recent studies highlight that autonomous threat detection and the misuse of large language models (LLMs) are transforming the landscape of Threat Intelligence. Integrating AI-driven analytics into HTI enhances predictive accuracy, situational awareness, and adaptability against evolving cyberattacks (Tripathi et al., 2024; Singh et al., 2024).

2.4. Comparative Analysis Of Forensic And Human Threat Intelligence (HTI) Model

Albeit emerging, there are a few promising researches that are being conducted regarding integrating the Human Threat Intelligence (HTI) and Digital Forensics in the investigation of cyber crimes. The mix and level of sophistication of the contemporary cyberattacks are pushing towards the joint analysis of the technical and behavioral vectors. Studies indicate that a combination of forensic artifacts (access logs of files, command executions, and the patterns of malware) with psychological knowledge and words used in emails, forums, or chatrooms may be effective to better understand threats and their attribution.

As an example, Xu et al. (2020) showed that there is a collaboration network or influence patterns among attackers, which was revealed with the help of integrating Social Network Analysis (SNA) into traditional digital forensics. This relational mapping was useful in foretelling future moves and determinate the gravity of threat makers. Natural Language Processing (NLP) has been used on phishing emails, dark web messages and malware code comments to identify linguistic fingerprints that, when coupled with behavioral signatures and forensic timelines, provides substantial attribution capabilities.

Behavioral profiling has also been incorporated into Security Information and Event Management (SIEM) systems, where it automates those alerts when human intent or the behavior of a user is out of the ordinary. In spite of these achievements, challenges are there. Text or social media text is usually not very amenable to the tools used in forensics. The combination of these data types necessitates high end parsing and correlation engines as well as computing power. In addition, there are ethical and legal issues of privacy, prejudice and assumed emotional states that make broader implementation more difficult.

3. THE RESEARCH PROBLEM AND AIMS OF THE RESEARCH

Even with the tremendous progress in cybersecurity technologies, comparable situations taking place in cybercrime investigation and its detection remain difficult to accomplish currently in contemporary cybersecurity attacks where the attacks contain human-related aspects, including insider threat, hacktivism, and social engineering. The current models largely deal in technical data which are IP addresses logs, malware signature however neglect to identify the psychological, linguistics and behavioral variables of cyber users. This causes a serious shortcoming of investigative precision and restrains the possibility of accusing a definite individual or gathering of cyberattacks. Furthermore, there is no interconnection between digital forensics and human threat intelligence, which leads to a disparate analysis and missed potential to interfere at an early stage.

To deal with this challenge, the current study introduces the Forensic-Centric Human Threat Intelligence (HTI) Framework that integrates digital evidence data with some behavioral profiling, language, danger actor mapping. The main goals include: (1) To come up with an integrated model which correlates human intent with forensic artifacts; (2) To improve the accuracy of attribution (Chen & Zhao, 2024) during cybercrimes investigation; (3)To aid in proactive threat identification and (4)To improve on a standardized approach that can be customized to law enforcement and cybersecurity teams. This study seeks to devise a more comprehensive and forward-looking way of dealing with cybercrime by linking the field of forensic science to that of behavioral threat intelligence.

3.1. The Downsides to the Current Methods of Investigating Crime in the World of Computers

The existing tools of investigation of cybercrime are primarily based on technical examination and concentrate on IP addresses, logs and network files hashes, and system abnormalities. They can be useful in determining the roots of a breach but would tend to be unhelpful in the case of multidimensional attacks like Advanced Persistent Threats (APTs), insider attacks, and social engineering. Technical artifacts may re-implement the dynamics of an intrusion, but will hardly provide us with information on who initiated the attack and why. With the now more organized, anonymous, and globally dispersed cybercriminals, technical evidence is becoming more difficult to be attributed.

Lack of situational awareness regarding the actions and motives of the attackers is a big setback. A trusted access point is capable of stealing important data with minimal or no technical evidence. On the same note, psychological-based phishing attacks are not likely to raise system warnings. Conventional digital forensics tends to ignore emotional and linguistic and behavioral evidence that helps in giving the much-needed context. IP tracing and geolocation becomes a useless investigative tool with anonymisation tools like VPNs, tor, and cryptocurrency protection. There are far more useful human-centric indicators such as typing behavior, time-of-day behavior and language style, which are underused.

The other problem is the lack of interconnectivity between the forensic and the behavioral intelligence tools. Structured data forensic platforms, such as FTK, Autopsy, and Sleuth Kit, have a tendency to be combined with digital evidence, and behavioral tools, including the Natural Language Processing and social network mapping (Anderson, 2021), are rarely compatible with them. Such is a fragmented practice that isolates the technical what of the human why leading to a reactive investigation that predicts and preempts future attacks.

Legal and jurisdictional barriers also do not positively contribute to cross-border cybercrime collaboration. Altogether, the investigative scene focuses too much on the technical examination and without attention to the human motive and motivation. An effective solution to the problem of achieving accurate attribution, proactive detection, and effective interventions in the current investigation of cybercrime requires a forensic-centric approach of Humane Threat Intelligence (HTI), a blend of digital forensics and behavioral science.

3.2. The Problems with the Behavioral Attribution together with Analysis of Intentions

Attribution of behavior is now critical in cybercrime investigation particularly in that the suspects are now using indirect deceptive and socially engineered techniques. Behavioral analysis is founded around inferred proceedings like motivations, communication styles, mental tendencies and emotional triggers unlike technical forensics, which is identified on quantifiable and testable data. These attributes tend to be highly subjective and variable depending on the circumstances, and thus they become biased and misinterpretable unless approached with rigid procedures and cross-validations.

Anonymity is the root of the problem of behavior attribution. Hackers most of the time hide the identity and place of origin through the use of VPN, Tor, proxies, encrypted messaging software, and cryptocurrencies. Although in some cases, behavioral patterns can be identified, (Chen & Zhao, 2024) they can be similar, shared and/or intentionally copied during false flag operations which makes attribution unreliable. The attackers can also change their digital track to confuse the investigators on their identity, intent, or geopolitical affiliation.

Attacker motivation is even more problematic to analysis due to the variety of motivations they have. The threat actors can either be motivated by profit, revenge, activism, nationalism, or terrorism and their motives usually vary as time progresses. It becomes hard to foresee the intentions when motives are dynamic or intentionally camouflaged. To give an example, financially-driven cybercriminals can pose as hacktivist groups in order to dodge the scrutiny. One more critical drawback lies in the inability of the behavioral intelligence systems (e.g., NLP, AI, the social network analysis) to integrate with the forensic tools. The majority of existing tools are used in isolation - very few of them can be tested against the forensics such as system logs or malware activity. Besides, not all cybersecurity experts are trained in the background of psychology, which results in gaps in skills related to reading human-centric data.

Finally, obstacles to behavioral attribution include anonymity, malicious intent, and multi-factored motivation, and the tool sets are divided. Multidisciplinary combining forensics precision, behavioral (NIST, 2023) science, and AI-driven analytics is required to defeat these. It is with such integration that cyber investigations can achieve the pedigree of the contemporary human-driven threats.

3.3. Research Questions

With the ever-increasing sophistication, and magnitude of the cyber threats, the older concepts of investigations find it hard to withstand the changes. The forensic based Human Threat Intelligence (HTI) model should be deliberated through mindful research questions to cover existing gaps, at least in the areas of attributions, behavior analytics, and advance warning of threats. These are some of the questions reflected in the background and design of the proposed combined story.

The initial research question is the following: How to combine effectively digital forensic artifacts and those showing human behavior on the one hand to improve on attributing the cyber threat? Although forensic tools help reveal technical evidence, like traces of malware, logs of file accesses and network traffic, they are unlikely to reveal the attacker and her/his goals. Human threat intelligence on the other hand, watches for communication habits, psychology, and social. The combination of the two areas may allow profiling of threat actors in a more detailed and complete manner.

The second one is: What behavioral indicators were the most reliable in practice in cybercriminal profiling? This captures the detection of reoccurring patterns e.g. a (Smith & Johnson, 2020) particular writing style, use of time zones, emotional tone or platform preferences within the offender profile which can be used to influence predictive modelling.

The third question is: Is it possible to proactively identify or forecast the threats, or do they (Kumar et al., 2023) appear in forensic-behavioral model of hybrid? In contrast to reactive techniques of traditional forensics, behavioral indicators possess the potential to provide early warning evidences (Brown, 2019) which can be combined into monitoring and report the evidences to the system.

The fourth research question is as follows: Which is the best framework to be utilized in integrating forensic tools and behavioral intelligence systems? The (Williams & Lee, 2022) latter implies the development of an interoperable, scalable and legally acceptable architecture that is able to integrate current tools and datasets.

Collectively, these questions should provide an answer to the feasibility and success of a forensic-focused (Chen & Zhao, 2024) HTI model, a systematic approach to a complete and people-oriented way to investigate cybercrimes.

3.4. Research Objectives

This study will seek to address the shortcomings of the existing models of cybercrime investigation through the development of an elaborate forensic-based Human Threat Intelligence (HTI) framework. The model suggested above will combine evidence of digital forensics and behavioral analysis, creating a more predictive, contextual, and strategic response to cyber threats identification and remedies. The traditional models are inclined to separate technical indicators and the human-oriented information like motivations, relationship with others, and use of language. This paper will cover such a gap by establishing a multi-tiered model that integrates the concept of digital forensics and psychological profiling of cybercrime.

The initial goal is to develop an approach that can match technical forensic artifacts, such as system logs, malware activity and access traces with more human-focused indicators, e.g., language style, online behaviour and usage of social media platforms. This unified strategy will advance the attribution of the threat actors, especially those involving anonymity and false flags as well as social engineering. Not only will it be able to tell how an attack has been effected, but who and why.

The second goal aims at improving threat forecasting proactively. Unlike the current forensic tools mostly post incident based, the proposed framework will have behavioral cues into post incident based precursor events or so-called early warning systems (EWS). This can help security operations centers (SOCs) and law enforcement take appropriate measures against the threats before they grow to become full-scale attacks.

The third is to ensure that the framework is scalable and adaptable to those situations in various legal whose organizational contexts require their scaling or adaptability. The model will have a modularised interoperable architecture capable of supporting (Anderson, 2021) a global privacy regime, including cross-jurisdictional legal disparities and technical infrastructures. The claims of the framework in terms of accuracy, speed and completeness will be tested and validated using real life and simulated case studies.

Finally, this study attempts to design a new paradigm to investigate cybercrime, something linked with technical strength, (Smith & Johnson, 2020) but also human-aware that will involve strategic, evidence-based, and psychology-focused responses to such threats. Ethical implications and privacy remain vital in implementing forensic-centric HTI frameworks. Handling behavioral and psychological data must comply with global standards like GDPR and DPDP (2023). Incorporating privacy-preserving methods such as federated learning and differential privacy ensures ethical intelligence analysis (Anderson, 2021; Tripathi et al., 2023).

4. HTI QUALITY OF HUMAN THREAT INTELLIGENCE (HTI)

HTI is an emergent cyber security discipline which is involved in studying and comprehending the human aspects of cybersecurity threats. Whereas the heavy emphasis of the traditional threat intelligence is the technical indicators such as malware activities, network anomalies, and system vulnerabilities, HTI aims to discern, comprehend, and project cyber threats through identifying and understanding behavior, motivation, intention, and psychology of attackers. It takes human-centric data, like language patterns, communication habits, social affiliations, psychological triggers, and cultural markers into account to obtain an understanding of who an attacker is, why they are doing what they are doing, and the ways in which they can act in the future. The fact that is unusual about the HTI is that it has been applied in cases where the pure technical evidences could not give a detailed attribution e.g. in the instance of an insider attack (with the ideological motive), ideological-based attacks, and the socially-engineered attacks.

By means of HTI, the investigator is able to extract useful intelligence with regard to structured or unstructured data such as emails, forums, addresses in the dark web, and any social media data. It complements the conventional digital forensics and mapping and layers on top a measure of intent and personality profiling. As attacks are increasingly becoming less direct (with malware attacks giving way to social engineering attacks), the merging of HTI into the investigation setups of cybercrime is of upmost importance both inking back and proactive defence mechanisms.

4.1 What does the term human threat intelligence stand for?

Human Threat Intelligence (HTI) is a new and significant area in cybersecurity which is dedicated to the human-side of cyberattacks. On the contrary to a traditional threat intelligence, where focus is too much on technical indicators, such as malware signatures or certain IP addresses, HTI aims at identifying and anticipating the behavior, motivation, and psychology of the threat actors. This enables cybersecurity professionals to not only study the impacted systems, but also the motivation and acts of an aggressor, which results in enhanced attribution and preventative security.

The inclusion of HTI includes the systematic gathering and comprehensions of all types of behavioral, psychological, sociocultural, and linguistic information. It might involve dialect, tone of emotion, time-zone inclination, Internet alliances and interaction in the manner presented on a social media site or hidden Internet platform. These can be indicators, which portray an attacker, ideology, risk appette, and target. An example can be use of politically loaded phrases, which may show a hacktivism activity, and presence of urgency and greed, which may depict a money-based attack.

HTI is particularly useful to detect insider threats, i.e., abuses by trusted persons who have access, and that would be otherwise missed by conventional forensics tools. It supplements advanced persistent threat (APT) detection as well, as it locates long-range trends of behavior and language use. Moreover, social engineering attacks can be addressed much better with HTI, e.g. through sentiment analysis or impersonation detection: since they are based on the psychological weakness of a person and not on the technical vulnerability, the former can be prevented by such methods.

Also, HTI amplifies threat attribution by determining the pattern of repeat offenders and basing legal and policy decisions on behavioral information. It allows identifying the emergent threats earlier as it analyzes behavior before breach happens.Summing up, Human Threat Intelligence is an extension of cybersecurity to a human factor. With cybercriminals increasingly mastering how to use the social context to their advantage, it is no longer that HTI becomes a part of what digital forensics must use to create resilient, intelligence-driven cyber defense systems.

4.2 Behavioral and Psychological Threat Actors Profiling

HTI is important in helping to profile cybercriminals both in terms of their behavior and psychology since it identifies their motives, choice decision making processes and patterns. Whereas traditional digital forensics responds to what and how of an attack, the latter tries to answer the who and why. It is supported by forensic psychology, criminology and behavioral research and based on it, the investigators can make conclusions concerning the emotion state and character traits, along with the bias of attackers. It proves very useful most especially when the technical indicators are hidden and therefore it is possible to make a more certain attribution and sometimes predict future behavior.

Pathological behaviors are also likely to be exhibited by cybercriminals including the choice of language, time of activity, likes and dislikes about hardware and software, how to communicate on forums or the dark web. As an example, the action of a nation-state-sponsored actor may be stealthy and professional whereas a hacktivist may demonstrate (Kumar et al., 2023) impulsive, emotionally elastic, and ideology-driven behavior. With such methods as Natural Language Processing (NLP) and sentiment analysis, one can find some evidence of psychological conditions like aggression, narcissism, or paranoia. Geographic origin or working habits may also be gleaned through time-of-day activity and typing patterns.

HTI also gives the ability to detect insider threats and is notoriously hard to trace down via more traditional cybersecurity tools. The employees or the contractors who are motivated by vengeance or the spread of ideology would demonstrate a tonal shift in communication, lesser involvement, or higher levels of confidentiality. Such patterns may indicate unethical and illegal potential breach as long as they are monitored ethically and legally.

Behavioral profiling should however, be used with care. It is only probabilistic and is prone to cultural misunderstanding, which makes the necessity of confirming results with solid evidence of digital forensics.

In conclusion, HTI supplements and complements investigation of a cybercrime with digital artifacts, by offering a humanistic, prognostic perspective on a threat actor, adding to their attribution as well as proactive response. Incorporating emotion detection and predictive psychology strengthens behavioral profiling accuracy. Using affective computing and linguistic sentiment analysis enables investigators to uncover hidden motivations, emotional states, and stress cues behind insider threats or disinformation campaigns (Vasani et al., 2024; Sonia Arora et al., 2024).

4.3 Sources and Methods of Human Threat Intelligence

The precision and versatility of the tools and the data sources that are relied upon to gather and analyse behavioral indicators of cyber threats is essential to human threat intelligence (HTI). As opposed to traditional cybersecurity solutions which analyses network flow or malware signatures, HTI tools target psychology, behavioural and linguistic patterns left by the adversary. These devices employ massive amounts of unstructured, semi-structured data to draw out intelligence regarding who the attackers were, the motivation behind the incident and how they go about their actions.Typical data sources of HTI are social media, dark web message boards, pastebin dumps, phishing emails, ransomware notes, malware comments and online chats. These forums disclose ideological orientation, associations, emotional signals and even hints to the origin or nature of an attacker. To choose a few examples, language features may indicate level of education or region of origin, and interactions in a common forum may indicate the presence of group affiliation or recruitment attitudes.

High-tech tools facilitate the process: Natural Language Processing (NLP) is beneficial when the aim is to extract tone, sentiment, and use of vocabulary whereas sentiment engines can be used to find emotional triggers or change of motivation. Social Network Analysis (SNA) identifies threat attacker connections, identifies influential groups to attack, and tracks misinformation or a series of coordinated attacks. ML models will help discover the behavior anomalies and identify all the possible insider attacks. Moreover, HTI platforms usually associate indicators of actions with technical records in real-time with Threat Intelligence Platforms (TIPs) and Security Information and Event Management (SIEM) systems. Although these technologies are potent, they should be utilized in an ethical manner without interfering with the standards of privacy and data protection.

In conclusion, tools and sources of HTI are of core value towards behavioral threat analysis in increasing attribution, (Smith & Johnson, 2020) forecasting, and investigation of cybercrime in case used in conjunction with digital forensics in a moderate manner.

4.4. The Relations between HTI and Digital Forensics and Threat Intelligence

Multifunctionality is an essential concept that is taking shape in the field of cybersecurity; Human Threat Intelligence (HTI), digital forensics, and conventional threat intelligence demonstrate the aptitude of this approach. Digital forensics is retrospective, as it determines what has happened by analyzing the evidence, whereas HTI is proactive as it determines the reasons why actors have taken certain actions and the profiles of threat actors in terms of the psychological characteristics. Traditional threat intelligence is beneficial in that it records indicators of compromise (IOCs), tactics, and attack patterns on a wide scope of threats.

Incorporation of these three disciplines is an opportunity that has been used to make the studies richer and multi-layered. Technical activity traces (e.g. file modifications, access records) can now be correlated with behavioural pointers including linguistic patterns in phishing emails, emotional prose in forums or time-zone activity. As an example, digital forensics may identify an exfiltration of data, but it is only HTI that can show that it was conducted by a disgruntled insider as part of a personal motive-- critical information to prevent it in the future and even to prosecute. Threat intelligence itself may be able to connect TTPs (tactics, techniques, procedures) that have occurred frequently to known actors but the use of HTI proves these attributions correct by way of behavioral fingerprints or other indicators, such as language or ideology. Technically, HTI can be implemented into SIEM, TIPs and forensic systems having AI and machine learning possibility to process structured data (logs, packets) and unstructured (emails, forums, dark web offshoot). The visualization tools such as social network mapping and link analysis can improve the knowledge about the relations between actors and threat time scale.

Although there are potential problems that can occur (data interoperability, privacy concerns, and skill deficiency of analysts), the capability of augmented attribution, proactive defense, and investigation context (Chen & Zhao, 2024) can be realized by integrating them. Collective the term HTI, digital forensics and threats intelligence jam a more predictive, intelligence-based, i.e., strategic modus operandi in cybercrime investigations.

5 . CYBERCRIMES AND INVESTIGATION DIGITAL FORENSICS

Digital forensics forms part and parcel of the study of cybercrimes over the past few decades and which enables an investigator to retrieve, examine and present their electronic evidence in a format that is defensible and legally acceptable. It is used as the backbone of deriving the source, extent, and character of digital attacks including data attacks, intrusions and insider threat and malware attacks. By carefully examining these devices, networks and storage media, digital forensics can find valuable data clues like access logs, deleted files, timestamps, browsing histories, registry entries and even containers that have been encrypted and many other pieces of data that can recreate events and can be produced in court proceedings.

Digital forensics adds the indisputable, traceable aspects to the behavioral and psychological know-how anchoring it in technical reality in the context of Forensic-Centric Human Threat (HTI). To use the example, the forensic logs will come in handy to show when breach was hit and which files were accessed and HTI will provide clues on who did it and the possible intent. Digital Forensics has the advantage of proving or disproving behavioral hypotheses through empirical evidence, which makes the results of the investigations contextually rich and technically sound.

5.1. Digital forensics have major processes and tools.

Digital forensics is an important component of the investigation of cybercrime as it serves to define, discover, collect, retain, examine, and report digital evidences on the basis of standard and legally acceptable procedures. The procedure starts with the collection of data using digital media like hard drives, USB, network logs and memory dump. The imaging is performed using time stamps and tools that guarantee integrity of the data, after which preservation tools such as hashing, secure storage and documentation are carried out to maintain the chain of custody. When the evidence is captured, the evidence is then examined by the investigators to collect deleted files, malware traces, user action, timestamps, and system events that portray bad activity through the use of the detection tools. The last process is reportage whereby findings are written to the letter in case of law enforcement or court proceedings.

Particular forensic tools play a very significant role in such work. Disk imaging, metadata monitoring and analysis of user activity are performed by such tools as FTK (Forensic Toolkit) and EnCase. Autopsy and The Sleuth Kit are two open-source platforms which can help explore file systems, and Volatility is a memory forensics platform commonly used to discover active processes, files and hidden malware within the memory. Mobile and cloud data, e.g. chats encrypted via Signal, GPS records and synchronized contents, typically are processed with tools like Cellebrite or Oxygen Forensic Detective.

The use of digital forensics is worth stating that they transform raw data into intelligence. Forensic evidence can be used to prove behavioral insights and this can be done by combining it with Human Threat Intelligence (HTI). As an example, forensic (Kumar et al., 2023) evidence such as file access records may corroborate or refuted the misgivings about internal players. Therefore, digital forensics not only tells how and what happened but integrated with HTI can be used to reveal who and why carried out the attack.

5.2 Cybercrime Investigation

Digital forensics plays an important role in looking into a broad variety of cybercrimes that include the technical evidence-gathering process and the association of criminal activity with possible menacing actors. It is important during the incident of network intrusions, phishing, data breach, ransomware, insider risk, and Advanced Persistent Threats (APT). Different incidents produce unique digital traces, which forensic procedures can be used to define timelines of events, the systems that may have been compromised (Williams & Lee, 2022) and the damage that has taken place. In network forensics, net analysts analyze data streams, packet captures and firewall records using network forensics tools like Wireshark or NetWitness to determine how and where intrusions occurred and how unauthorized data could be removed or unusual communication patterns exist on the network. A tool such as Volatility can be used in forensic memory to detect malware or rootkits that only exist in RAM, and very important in analysing ransomware or in-memory threats.

Malware forensics is the reverse engineering of malicious programs in order to determine their payload, encryption techniques and persistence mechanisms, that can be used to develop signature-based detection, or profile threat actor tactics, techniques and procedures (TTPs). During a phishing attack investigation, email header, attachment, and fake sender information is examined to determine how the attackers tricked the victims into manipulation. Digital forensics is also important in the area of identifying insiders when the right users take advantage of the access rights. Because such activities might not create alarm, investigators will have to search user logs, file access patterns and data transfers. Mobile and cloud forensics can also permit forensic access to information in virtualized systems and encrypted messaging and cloud storage, extending the reach of forensics. To conclude, digital forensics offers irreplaceable information on cybercrime. Combined with the concept of Human Threat Intelligence (HTI), it allows it to offer a full picture of the threat landscape and is therefore considerably improved.

5.3. The limitations and the integration part of human intelligence.

Digital forensics has been found to be very effective in the investigations of cybercrimes but has shortcomings, especially in the attribution of intent, profiling the actors and predicting future threats. Traditional forensics are good at finding technical answers to questions like attack vectors, vulnerabilities used, and data stolen but commonly fail to answer the most important questions, i.e. who did the attack, why and how future, similar incidents can be foreseen. This technical discrepancy underlines a considerable significance of adopting Human Threat Intelligence (HTI) into the investigation.

There is the failure to derive a motive or psychological context, a major weakness. Although the forensic tools can trace back a phishing mail or detect the malicious code, they cannot detect the intent of the attacker whether they are after money, vengeance, ideology, or (Miller, 2021) money. Malicious users indeed pose a great challenge to detect since they work within the valid credentials. Such threats are not generally caught early since they lack behavioral signs such as when one raises the tone of their voice or when they express dissatisfaction.

The delayed process of digital forensics is also its other disadvantage. The majority of forensic transformations are reactive and look at gathering evidence and re-constructing an event. Although such a reactive model is useful as far as the legal side is concerned, it lacks prevention abilities. HTI provides an additional proactive layer, which is the analysis of early behavioral indicators of possible pre-attack planning, e.g. dark web activity, language, or suspicious internet usage.

Lastly, digital forensics are usually confined within data silos and thus they do not consider external intelligence such as emotional sentiment, language, or psychological profiling. With HTI, investigations have more context-who and why in addition to what and how-which results in improved attribution, proactive detection, and strategic threat reduction. he integration of AI-based image recognition and time-series analysis enhances forensic validation and behavioral correlation. Using machine learning-enabled IoT analysis supports anomaly detection, event reconstruction, and visual confirmation of threat activities, thereby strengthening evidential accuracy in HTI-driven investigations (Beemkumar et al., 2023; Tripathi et al., 2024).

6. HUMAN THREAT INTELLIGENCE (HTI) FRAMEWORK

The proposed Forensic-Centric Human Threat Intelligence (HTI) Framework refers to the differences between the established digital forensics and human behavior analysis to provide an integrated solution to solving cybercrimes. As traditional cyber investigations aim at providing answers to the question of how an attack is perpetrated through technical evidence, such as IP address, system logs, and malware signatures (Kumar et al., 2023), they usually cannot answer the questions of who and why. This shortcoming is tackled by the HTI framework, which involves the help of digital forensic artifacts and the utilization of behavioral analysis methods i.e. psychological profiling, linguistic analysis, behavioral tracking, etc. This is due to the enhancement of the attribution, prediction as well as prevention of the threat due to the integration.

This is composed of four related layers on which it is constructed namely the Data Collection and Acquisition, Forensic Processing, Behavioral, and Human Intelligence Correlation), and Threat Attribution and predictive intelligence. At the first level, they gather structured and unstructured data (e.g., logs, traffic, metadata, and chat logs, emails and dark web monitoring Such sources allude to the fact that technical and behavioral indicators are captured in an organisational manner. This framework is primarily designed to support multidisciplinary users, including law enforcement agencies, corporate cybersecurity teams, and intelligence units, enabling unified analysis and evidence correlation across operational contexts. By defining this scope, the framework ensures adaptability and precision in both investigative and preventive cybersecurity functions (Sonia Arora et al., 2024).

The tools used in the Forensic Processing layer include Autopsy, FTK and Volatility, which recover the technical evidence to recreate events. The further analysis uses metadata containing pieces of information about the geolocation and timestamps. The Behavioral Correlation layer puts the writing pattern, and online behaviour through Natural Language Processing (NLP), sentiment analysis and Social Network Analysis (SNA) that pick up on psychological aspects, motives, and ideological leanings of the writer (Chen & Zhao, 2024).

Lastly, the layer of Threat Attribution and Predictive Intelligence integrates said fragments of knowledge so that adversaries could be identified or predicted. Machine learning increases the identification of anomalies/insider threats. In addition to the post-incident analysis, proactive capability of the framework enables detection of high-risk behaviors early enough. Such a twofold model is reactive and proactive, which makes the HTI framework an evidence-based, future-ready, and human-conscious solution to detecting and handling modern cyber threats.

7. METHODOLOGY

The methodology of the studied research presents the structural approach to the design, implementation and verification of the suggested Forensic-Centric Human Threat Intelligence (HTI) Framework. The study is multi-disciplinary and hybrid in that it demonstrates the mixing of technical manifestations of forensics investigations with behavioral and psychological assessment of threats. The methodology allows both scenario-based and empirical verification of the framework since it incorporates digital evidences with human-focused signs. The given approach facilitates both qualitative ideas and metrics to evaluate performance, soundness, and performance in the real-world applications in linking cybercrimes.

The approach is framed in such a way that it addresses topics such as the collection, processing, analysis, correlation and critiquing within both behavioral and forensic scopes. It tests on experimental data sets, artificial attack scenarios and actual cases of citation in testing or experimenting on the impacts and results of the framework under different threat conditions. Digital forensics tools and behavioral analytics tools are applied to complement one another in an effort to guarantee methodological rigor combined with multi-dimensional insight.

7.1 Design and Architecture Framework

The infrastructure of the discussed proposal of the Forensic-Centric Human Threat Intelligence (HTI) Framework is conceptualised as the multi-level modular system where the digital forensic skills are cross-ended with the human behavior and psychological profile. It has 4 high level tiers: Data and acquisition of data (1), Forensic processing (2), Behavior and the intelligence correlation involving human beings (3), and, threat attribution and predictive intelligence (4). All the layers are interoperable (Smith & Johnson, 2020) and perform different tasks so that there are no hindrances to the flow of data and feedback between the processes. This is the first layer through which information is generated based on structured sources, structured sources include system logs, memory dumps and access records and unstructured sources, which include phishing emails, chat messages and dark web forums. With this dual-source approach, this framework will be able to capture what was being done as well as how the attacker was acting.

The second level is forensic processing, which involves the usage of standard tools that include, but are not limited to, FTK, Autopsy, and Volatility in order to isolate digital artifacts and recreate the timeline of the incident. At the same time, the third layer analyses behavior through Natural Language Processing (NLP), sentiment analysis and social network mapping to reveal the level of linguistic patterns, emotional tracts, and social connections that contain indication of attacker intent or psychological characteristics. Lastly, the fourth layer compiles everything that has been fed into it to form a threat actor profile which allows the attribution of identities as well as future action prediction. The modularity of the framework also allows using it in a reactive (post-incident investigation) and proactive (behavioral threat detection) way that can lead to the overall intelligence-based investigation of the cybercrime.

7.2 Evaluation and measuring of statistics

The efficiency of the proposed Forensic-Centric Human Threat Intelligence (HT) framework relies in a high extent on the quality and variety of the data that it was developed and validated with. To podulate the pure cases of cybercrimes, the study will adopt the hybrid method of collecting the research data, entailing simulated and observed data. Such structured data consists of such things as system logs, media captures of network traffic, memory dumps, registry data, and file system information such as metadata all of which a digital forensics investigator would come across after an incident. These data are produced with the help of sandboxed settings in which malicious activities like phishing, privilege escalation, and data exfiltration are executed in the constrained environment. The tools used to capture activity to analyze it include Wireshark, Sysmon, and Volatility.

At the same time, unstructured behavioural data is gathered in support of the HTI component. This is composed of phishing mails, false dark web conversations, hacker forums posts, and user interaction histories that are created to resemble manipulative opinion and linguistic prints. They consist of Natural Language Processing (NLP) models of capturing features, which are expected, depending on the writing style, the sentiment, and the psychological indicators. Ethically, any of the real-world data sets that we are using (public breach repositories, leaked forums and such) are anonymized, and only used in an academic process, by institutional policies on privacy and data usage.

The forensic lab terrain used in the execution of the experiment is virtualized providing the needed space in which malicious code and threat actor simulations can be deployed and tested safely and have the interaction tracked. The proposed framework does not require processing of both the forensic and behavioral data-sets together,but rather separately and then correlating with each other. This two-tube configuration guarantees the verisimilitude and the integrity of data as well as permits the deliberate trial and error, which makes it perfect to certify the capabilities of the framework in attribution, profiling, and advanced threat watch.

7.3 Data and Apparatus

Quality and the richness of the utilized data have been valued as factors that can determine the success of the proposed Forensic-Centric Human Threat Intelligence (HTI) framework in its development and validation. Since the study aims at simulating real-life situations around cybercrimes, a mixed approach of simulated and real world data collection will be implemented in this research study. Examples of the structured data are system logs, traffic captures, memory dumps, registry data and metadata of the file system- the type of data a digital forensics investigator may see afterwards. The creation of such datasets occurs through the use of sandboxed environments, within which the later phishing, privilege escalation and data exfiltration can be used to create a controlled attack scenario. Activity is recorded with tools such as Wireshark, Sysmon, Volatility to analyze the activity.

Simultaneously, unstructured behavioral data are also generated in order to assist with the HTI component. This contains simulated phishing emails, pseudo dark web chats, attacker forums posts, and user interaction history that is supposed to resemble psychological signs and language fingerprints. It employs the usage of an NLP model that is intended to be used to extract writing-style features, sentiment, and psychological markers. Ethically, any textual data used in the real world, be it a community archive of breaches or a compromised bulletin board, is anonymized and is applied purely as further academic reference, under the appropriate guidelines of organizational cautions on interpersonal privacy and utilization of information.

The virtualized forensic laboratory forms a containment around the experimental design that allows the testing and implementation of malicious code, simulated threat actor and tracking interaction to be conducted securely. It is possible to process the forensic and behavioral datasets independently and relate them in the suggested framework. The two-stream design guarantees the veracity and integrity of data and enables an experimental setup to be controlled, thus it is an ideal method of testing the abilities of the framework in terms of attribution, profiling, and proactive threat detection.

To enhance clarity and engagement, a conceptual flowchart or diagram should be introduced at this point. The visual should illustrate the interaction between forensic data acquisition, behavioral intelligence correlation, and predictive analytics, showing how digital and human intelligence converge to support attribution and proactive threat detection (Tripathi et al., 2023). This addition will help readers visualize the dynamic interconnections between layers and processes within the HTI framework.

8. CASE STUDY

Insider Threat at The Bank- EXAMPLE TO CASE STUDY 1.

A new generation of data breaches occurred in the case of one of the largest financial institutions where sensitive information about customers was being exported. Initial forensic examination of the traditional type showed that the access of the data was performed by valid employee credentials outside the working hours. Malware and malice of external intrusion was however absent. Following the Forensic-Centric HTI Framework, on the one hand, the investigators gathered and analyzed the behavioral indicators, and on the other hand, the investigators gathered and analyzed the forensic artifacts. The analysis of time and files access logs displayed the stable work by the employee of the middle rank in the late nights at several weeks. At the same time, the Natural Language Processing (NLP) and sentiment analysis of internal email messages and chat conversations of the employee were conducted. The results revealed a greater attitude of dissatisfaction, passive aggressive communication trait and the emotions were unreliable. Social network mapping has shown connection to referral clubs in other organization, as well as handfuls and opponents. Combining the cross section of the behavioral red flags and the forensic access patterns, the framework aided in concluding the breach as that of an insider that did so based on personal grievances and possibly, financial incentives. It was a two-tiered model that allowed the organization to provide discipline and legal measures as well as to more rigorous internal monitoring policies in order to stop any more insider events. These findings validate the effectiveness of integrating behavioral and forensic analysis, supporting the practical viability of the proposed Forensic-Centric HTI framework in enhancing attribution accuracy and proactive threat response.

Social Engineering Ransomware Infection in Healthcare Organization EXAMPLE TO CASE STUDY 2.

A ransomware attack penetrated one of the regional assistants to the healthcare sector that resulted in encrypted records of patients and several days of interruptions. Investigation by the forensics concluded that attack originated from phisihing email with harmful macro file. For the purpose of analysis, analysts used the HTI Framework to analyze the style of communication of an attacker, as extracted by the email and the ransom note. There was more formal tone, cellabrair grammar (like failure to use proper grammar most of the time) and Eastern European time-zone activity which coincided with a known European threat group in linguistic profiling. The continued research of dark web sites revealed the same rhetoric and requests made by an actor historicized before. The use of behavioral mapping and forensic tracebacks ensured that the team was able to make the reasonable scope of certainty stating that the attack belonged to an affiliate group of ransomware-as-a-service. The combination of human intelligence and digital forensics assisted the organization to form individual decisions regarding identity of the threat actor, recovery plans as well as legal reporting and this also enabled the organization to improve its future email filtering policies and staff training on phishing awareness. The second case further demonstrates how the HTI model's multi-layered design—combining digital evidence with behavioral profiling—improves investigative depth, contextual understanding, and predictive threat identification in real-world cybercrime scenarios

9. FUTURE SCOPE

Future studies of Forensic-Centric Human Threat Intelligence (HTI) will be aimed at the levels of automation, analysis, and practicality. Misinformation and social engineering, combined with technical exploits and AI-driven approaches, has become the dominant concern of cybercriminals, and so HTI needs to adapt to this challenge. By incorporating artificial intelligence and machine learning into the HTI systems, digital forensic artifacts and behavioral indicators can be gathered and processed in an integrated automated system (Miller, 2021). This change helps in the rapid and more in-depth identification of a threat, allowing Security Operations Centers (SOCs) and law enforcement personnel to identify not only network-based anomalies but psychological and linguistic changes in online communications.

This is further enhanced by recent advancements on AI-based behavioral analytics, which make it possible to model threats in real-time and find anomalies quickly. Differential privacy and federated learning are privacy-preserving techniques that are used to maintain adherence to ethical data standards and to guarantee the accuracy of an analysis (Singh et al., 2024; Arora et al., 2024). Continuous behavioral modelling is another opportunity that can be pursued, based on social media live streams, public forums, and the dark web. These dynamic adaptive models have the capability to revise the threat profiles on-the-fly and enhance defenses towards spear phishing, business email compromise (BEC), and insider threats. With the changing behavioral signs, the future interface will focus on algorithmic frameworks aimed at deceleration of false positives at high predictive efficacies (Harris, 2018). The cross-jurisdictional collaboration will also be enhanced with the integration of global threat feeds and APIs of forensics and standardize the attribution practices.

The HTI will still be developed in terms of legal and ethical considerations. The motive and intent can be determined using HTI frameworks in international legal procedures, which tend to have greater significance than technical traces. Digital evidence can also be reinforced by behavioral cues like ideological speech or psychological patterns, and legal argument support. As the world becomes more privacy conscious, next-generation HTI systems should address privacy-sensitive technologies, such as secure NLP and differential privacy, as a means to attain responsible data management (Anderson, 2021).

HTI also faces the likelihood of spreading to hybrid realm of threats such as the psychological warfare, the propaganda conducted through the internet as well as the coordination disinformation. A collaboration of HTI and media forensics and cognitive security will assist in unveiling the manipulative stories and safeguarding the information honesty of the society. Found on the convergence of forensic science, behavioral profiling, and automated analytics, the HTI framework is going to be needed in the development of resilient and ethically based cybersecurity systems.

10. CONCLUSION

The framework suggested would overcome a significant issue in the investigation of contemporary cybercrimes because of incorporating both digital forensics and behavioral analysis into a holistic human threat intelligence (HTI) framework. Where traditional methods seem to be lacking is in the ability to formulate what and why attackers use, what their motives are, their intentions, and their psychology. This framework ensures the bridging of the divide, since denormalized forensic evidence is compared to the behavioral indicators as expressed within language patterns, emotional tones and social affiliations. The layer structure grants it capability in both the reactive and proactive (Brown, 2019) areas, supporting afterincidentanalysis and the ability to detect threats early and profile the malicious actors. The incorporation of AI-driven implementations and natural language processing also makes it all-the-more flexible in the real life setting. This is validated and found to be more accurate to assign and burrow deep into exploration by means of validation of measurements and virtual instances of case studies. With cyber threats growing in sophistication and human determinism setting into play, the partnership between HTI and forensics allows the consolidation of a potential intelligent and future-oriented strategy to cybertb threats analysis and response.

REFERENCES

Anderson, A. (2021). Behavioral linguistics in cyber attribution: A forensic perspective. *Journal of Cyber Intelligence*, *14*(2), 55–72.

Arora, S., Rai, M., & Gupta, M. (2024). *Importance of Industry 5.0 in understanding emotional intelligence*. IGI Global., DOI: 10.4018/979-8-3693-6806-0.ch011

Beemkumar, N., Gupta, S., Bhardwaj, S., Dhabliya, D., Rai, M., Pandey, J. K., & Gupta, A. (2023). Activity recognition and IoT-based analysis using time series and CNN. In Goel, N., & Yadav, R. K. (Eds.), *Machine Learning-Enabled IoT for Smart Applications Across Industries* (pp. 350–364). IGI Global., DOI: 10.4018/978-1-6684-8785-3.ch018

Brown, T. (2019). Human-centric threat modeling for digital investigations. *International Journal of Cyber Behavior*, *7*(1), 22–39.

Chen, L., & Zhao, Y. (2024). Integrated forensic intelligence systems: Bridging behavioral and technical evidence. *Forensic Computing Review*, *12*(3), 101–118.

Harris, J. (2018). Psychological dimensions of cyber offenders: A criminological review. *Cyberpsychology and Crime*, *9*(4), 41–59.

Kumar, S., Patel, R., & Mehta, V. (2023). Modern digital forensics for advanced threat landscapes. *Journal of Digital Security*, *5*(2), 77–95.

Miller, D. (2021). AI-supported forensic automation in cybercrime investigations. *Journal of Advanced Security Analytics*, *11*(3), 33–49.

MITRE. (2023). *ATT&CK®: Knowledge base of adversary tactics and techniques*. Retrieved from https://attack.mitre.org/

NIST. (2023). *Digital forensics and cloud investigation standards*. National Institute of Standards and Technology.

Singh, S., Pandey, J. K., Rai, M., & Saxena, A. K. (2024). *Advancements in facial expression recognition using machine and deep learning techniques. Machine and Deep Learning Techniques for Emotion Detection*. IGI Global., DOI: 10.4018/979-8-3693-4143-8.ch007

Smith, A., & Johnson, T. (2020). Modern threat actor behavior and predictive profiling. *Cyber Threat Review*, *6*(2), 89–104.

Tripathi, P., Kumar, N., Rai, M., & Panda, M. (2024). *Applications of deep learning in healthcare in the framework of Industry 5.0*. IGI Global., DOI: 10.4018/979-8-3693-0782-3.ch005

. Vasani, V. P., Chandra, U., Sahu, G., Boyineni, S., Dhamodaran, S., Kumbhkar, M., Rai, M., & Gupta, S. (2024). *Emotion detection and predictive psychology in the age of technology*. IGI Global. DOI: 10.4018/979-8-3693-1910-9.ch001

Williams, K., & Lee, R. (2022). Multilayer threat intelligence and attribution models. *Journal of Cyber Operations*, *8*(1), 15–29.

Xu, Z., Li, H., & Chen, P. (2020). Human-centric cyber threat intelligence for predictive risk management. In *Proceedings of the ACM Workshop on Artificial Intelligence and Security* (pp. 95–104).

Chapter 7
Reconciling Privacy Rights With Digital Investigations:
Legal-Ethical Challenges in Cyber Forensics

Shashank Solanki
https://orcid.org/0009-0002-5923-0516
Christ University, India

ABSTRACT

The advancement of cyber forensics—through AI-driven profiling, metadata analysis, and real-time surveillance—has enhanced digital investigations but raised significant legal and ethical concerns. This chapter explores the growing tension between state surveillance and individual privacy, focusing on the Indian legal framework, including the Justice K.S. Puttaswamy decision, and comparing it with global standards such as the GDPR, ECHR, and Budapest Convention. Key issues addressed include algorithmic bias, lack of consent, cross-border data sharing, and misuse of forensic tools against vulnerable groups. The chapter argues for a balanced, rights-based framework grounded in privacy-by-design, proportionality, and judicial oversight. It offers policy recommendations to ensure cyber forensic practices remain effective while upholding constitutional protections and international human rights norms.

DOI: 10.4018/979-8-3373-4898-8.ch007

1. INTRODUCTION

1.1 Background and Context

Global digitalization has caused a significant shift in crime detection and state security practices and worldwide intelligence society. Central to this change is cyber forensics software, and it is used to locate, preserve, examine, and display electronic evidence. There has been a change over the years of cyber forensics as a reactive investigative instrument to a proactive one aimed at continuous monitoring and interpretation of the online behavior of a person.One of the emerging trends is what is known as user-centric human threat intelligence, which prioritizes the online behavior of an individual. It does not just evaluate technological systems but evaluates metadata, browsing patterns, communication traces, and behavioral cues, which can be determined with the help of Artificial Intelligence to find potential threats (Lyon, 2014).

In line with the above development, most states have developed their own capacity to spy, by use of interception systems, spyware, biometric authentication, and combined data platforms. Face recognition systems, Central Monitoring System (CMS) and metadata-based surveillance are some of the tools that have led to the controversy of the extent of the state authority in cyberspace in India. In the world, predictive policing, algorithmic border screening and social scoring systems all exhibit the same type of tension between security demands and personal autonomy.

These technological innovations have been advancing at a higher pace compared to the legal and ethical institutions that monitor it. Consequently, digital inquiries are often done in a normative vacuum where issues of due process, informed consent, proportionality, data integrity, and privacy are not resolved. It is particularly acute in the democracies where constitutional values demand safeguarding of individual rights such as privacy and freedom of arbitrary action of the state. The question is not whether cyber-forensic tools are to be applied, but how they may be applied in line with principles of justice and governance (Zuboff, 2015).

This theme is closely connected with the overall theme of privacy, governance, and forensic accountability in this book. The growth of forensic surveillance technologies poses some basic questions regarding the way the states regulate digital evidence, the way the accountability of oversight institutions can be ensured, and the way the privacy of individuals in high-surveillance conditions may be preserved in any meaningful way. This intersection needs to be understood in order to formulate regulatory frameworks that will sustain security as well as constitutional values.

1.2 Purpose of the Paper

This paper will attempt to critically explore the legal and ethical conflict between state-led digital investigative actions and safeguarding the rights of personal privacy. It assesses the method of the Indian legal system in dealing with this balance at the present time and contrasts it with methods used internationally to regulate the same. The thesis statement is that although the use of cyber forensic tools is indispensable in combating various modern crimes, including cyberterrorism, money laundering, financial fraud, disinformation, cyber-espionage, and state-sponsored surveillance, they tend to conflict or override legal security and ethics (Sabillon et al., 2017).

The paper evaluates the sufficiency of the existing law in India such as the Information Technology Act, 2000 and the evidentiary rules of the Indian Evidence Act, in controlling the digital investigation procedures. It also looks at the importance of the judiciary especially the understanding of privacy as a basic right in Justice K.S. Puttaswamy v. Defining constitutional boundaries to surveillance and forensic intrusions. Union of India. Moreover, the paper is based on the global best practices in the framework of the GDPR, ECHR, and the Budapest Convention to place the Indian regulatory stance in perspective and determine potential reform directions (Miron et al., 2020).

Central Research Question:

What must India do to balance digital forensic investigation and constitutional privacy and due process protection?

1.3 Methodology

The research will be based on a doctrinal legal approach that is based on analyzing statutory systems, judicial rulings, and legal commentary. It involves comparative analysis of Indian laws in response to the international standards established in the European Union, the United States, and other common law jurisdictions (Wachter et al., 2017).

Besides, the research combines cross-disciplinary articles on forensic science and AI ethics, as well as surveillance analysis and data governance to put all the analysis of the impact of technological processes on legal interpretation and operational responsibility into perspective. This interdisciplinary strategy guarantees that these technical facts and legal-ethical consequences are analyzed simultaneously.

2. BASICS OF PRIVACY IN DIGITAL JURISPRUDENCE

The spread of digital investigative and surveillance technologies has made the struggle between the State security goals and the individual rights to privacy more acute. In the cyber forensic context, invasive technological devices that can retrieve, steal or scrutinize online information are often used in areas where there is no sufficient legal protection. This section will look at the Indian constitutional Jurisprudence of privacy, legal boundaries in digital surveillance, and the privacy protection in India in comparison to the EU and the United States (Sengupta et al., 2025).

2.1 Privacy as Constitutional Autonomy in India

Privacy in India has become a vital part of individual freedom in the Constitution although this is not stated explicitly.

2.1.1 Article 21 and the Evolution of Privacy Jurisprudence

Judicial interpretation has been used to extend the right to privacy to Article 21 which has assured the right to life and personal liberty. The historic case in Justice K.S. Puttaswamy (Retd.). v. Privacy has become a fundamental right that is defined by the Union of India (2017) as part of Part III of the Constitution (Bhawna and Mahajan, 2024).

The conceptualization of privacy in the ruling held privacy as inclusive of:

- **Informational Privacy**
- **Decisional Autonomy**
- **Bodily Integrity**

The Court placed privacy in the constitutional morality which would be on par at greater heights than statutory or administrative restrictions and overturned the previous rulings that refused privacy the rightful status of a basic right.

2.2 Privacy Tests and Legal boundaries to the digital surveillance

2.2.1 The Test of Proportionality: Legality, Necessity and Proportionality

The main contribution of the Puttaswamy judgment is that it has introduced the three-fold proportionality test as an examination of any State measure that constrained privacy (Garrett & Rudin, 2023):

1. Legality- The intrusion should be backed by the legislation.
2. Necessity The invasion must have a justifiable State end.
3. Proportionality- The intrusion level should be the least restrictive.

The test is specifically applicable to online surveillance instruments like:

- Metadata collection systems,
- Real time interception structures,
- Algorithms profiling Systems in cyber forensics.

As an illustration, the Information Technology Act, 2000, Section 69 permits governmental interception and decryption of the digital information. It has however been criticized as lacking in independent oversight creating the fears of disproportionate State surveillance.

2.3 Comparative Approaches to Digital Privacy Governance

2.3.1 European Standards: GDPR and ECHR

The European Union model which is headed by the General Data Protection Regulation (GDPR) adheres to powerful principles like purpose limitation, transparency, lawfulness, and data minimization. Unauthorized digital forensic extraction either in the absence of informed consent or without judicial authorization typically breaches GDPR unless it is done under specific narrow law-enforcement exceptions necessitating Data Protection Impact Assessments (DPIA) (Alenezi et al., 2019).

Also, the European Convention on Human Rights (ECHR) shields against arbitrary surveillance of the confidential life of individuals in Article 8. In cases like the Zakharov v. Russia (2015) and v. Big Brother Watch. In the ECtHR case of United Kingdom (2021), the Court overturned mass surveillance schemes because no sufficient judicial and oversight protection was available.

2.3.2 U.S. Fourth Amendment Jurisprudence

Several amendments in the United States protect against unreasonable searches and seizures by the Fourth Amendment. In Carpenter v. The Supreme Court of the United States (2018) decided that the warrantless acquisition of cell-site location data did not comply with privacy rights because of intrusiveness of metadata surveillance (Franke et al., 2013).

The broad exceptions contained in expansive surveillance authorities in the USA PATRIOT Act, FISA, and CLOUD Act, however, are indicative of a reasonableness-based and not rights-based model.

2.3.3 Implications for Indian Legal Reform

The privacy system in India is not well established as a result of:

- The absence of a large-scale privacy law in the manner of GDPR,
- There is less judicial regulation of digital surveillance,
- Lack of mechanism of algorithmic accountability (Karabiyik and Akkaya, 2018).

Key reform measures include:

- Judicial warrants of computer intrusions,
- Surveillance agencies audit trails and transparency reports,
- Domestic law and cross-border standards of evidence-sharing harmonization.

Table 1. Comparative Governance of Digital Privacy and Forensic Access

Jurisdiction	Legal Basis	What Counts as Privacy	When Digital Forensics Is Allowed	Oversight Body
India	Article 21 + Puttaswamy	Informational privacy as part of constitutional liberty	Broad government discretion under IT Act & executive powers	Oversight weak; judicial review limited
European Union	GDPR + ECHR	Strong data subject control & decisional autonomy	Only under strict necessity with DPIA & safeguards	Independent Data Protection Authorities (DPA)
United States	Fourth Amendment + CLOUD Act	Reasonable expectation of privacy	Warrants generally required, but national security exceptions exist	FISA Courts & federal judiciary

3. USER-CENTRIC THREAT INTELLIGENCE AND DIGITAL FORENSICS

The exploding digital worlds have entirely transformed the nature of crime and criminality, occasioning the necessity of the transformation of the investigative methods and processes of evidence gathering and investigation to become intelligence-led and dynamic. As the requirement to discuss cyber-enabled crimes on cyber forensics increases, a paradigm shift is being witnessed in cyber forensics, that is, data extraction focus moving off device, to behavioural profile focus on the user. This section of the paper entails a critical analysis of the instruments, methods and theoretical determinants of the contemporary digital forensics wherein the implication of the same in lieu of privacy, consent, and legal liability are given particular attention in this paper.

3.1 Cyber Forensic Tools and Techniques

The contemporary cyber forensics is carried out with the help of a complex of high-tech solutions which makes it possible to locate, trace and attribute the criminal act in the virtual world. These tools like powerful as they are in the scope of the investigations cause enormous issues with the aspects of personal rights, data safety, and ethical use (Garfinkel, 2010).

Arificial Intelligence-Based Behavioral Profiling

The concept of Artificial Intelligence (AI) has assumed centre stage in the process of forensic intelligence especially in the profiling of any potential threat basing on the identified behavioural patterns discovered. These systems use the machine learning concept to analyse user actions on the digital space e.g. studying the browsing history (in case of browsing history), keystroke pattern (in the case of keystroke dynamics), geolocation data (in the case of geolocation data), interaction with social media (in the case of social media), to detect an anomalous behavior that is an indicator of ill intent. The most recent trends in AI-based user behaviour modelling indicate that more and more attempts are made to use massive behavioural data and adaptive recognition algorithms (Rai et al., 2023). Despite the fact that this enhances predictive policing, it creates critical concerns on bias in algorithms and lack of transparency and violation of due process. In countries that have less regulatory authority over AI systems, such profiling mechanisms may not be meaningfully reviewed by any courts and/or aware users, which does not enforce any values of legality or responsibility.

Metadata and Traffic Analysis

Metadata often also known as data about data consists of sets of data in the form of timestamps, IP address generation of file and device identifiers among others. The contextual intelligence that cyber forensic investigations may invoke about digital interactions without necessarily looking at the content concerned is often based on metadata; so networks of affiliation and the flow of traffic is a frequent exercise of counter-terrorism and cybercrime analysis. But metadata has not been stripped of privacy connotations. As it was perceived by the U.S. Supreme Court in Carpenter v. United States (2018), a comprehensive system of location metadata is a search that should be authorized by the court in accordance with the Fourth Amendment and require authorization by the court to proceed with the search (Cyber security and digital forensics, 2021).

Digital Evidence Extraction

Forensic examiners usually use imaging and extraction tools in order to retrieve information (including deleted files, encrypted data and logs) in digital devices. Common techniques are disk cloning, volatile memory and mobile forensic acquisition. Tools like EnCase, FTK (Forensic Toolkit) and Cellebrite have such purposes. This kind of evidence is however admissible and sound when the chain of custody is under guard, the data protection norms within jurisdictions are observed and the procedure of evidence handling is able to meet the internal provisions, as per the domestic laws, in this case, Sections 65A and 65B of the Indian Evidence Act, 1872.

3.2 Emerging Trends in Human-Centric Threat Intelligence

A significant change in the response mechanism to the cyber threats is the jump to human-oriented versus hardware-oriented forensics analysis. This change implies the heightened attention to the user as the primary point of attack with the regards to cyber risk: as an insider threat, a social engineering victim or an unintended actor (Tripathi et al., 2024).

Shift from Device-Based to User-Behavior-Centric Forensics

Traditional digital forensics was primarily focused on searching storage and system logs so as to find the digital artefacts following an incident. Under a user-centric model, the action would be to target forensics at the behaviour, trends and motivations of individual users, often in real time. This is the user actions surveillance in business networks at every moment, the biometrics in regards to such behaviors of various parties, and identity correlations in platforms. The aim is to have the capability of generating personalised and predictive threat intelligence. Even though this will make people more responsive in the context of security due to the heightened awareness of possible threats, it also encroaches the areas of individual autonomy, especially in the cases of uninformed consent or the substantial legal basis (Ekundayo, 2024).

3.3 Emerging Forensic Technology and Evidence Integrity

The contemporary forensic landscape currently encompasses a number of new hi-tech technologies, which will guarantee reliability and authenticity of the digital evidence; nevertheless, there are also new risks that can be posed by the same.

Blockchain-Based Chain-of-Custody Verification

Forensic logging systems should include blockchain-based ones that create a stable history of evidence extraction, storage, and transfer. Decentralizing the chain-of-custody trail, blockchain reduces risks of tampering and enhances admissibility in legal proceedings, particularly in the case of cross-border cybercrime where inter-agency cooperation must be among the mandates.

Deepfake and Synthetic Media Detection

The spread of deepfake and AI-generated synthetic material require specialized forensic algorithms to check the authenticity of digital audio-visual messages. The detection of pixel-level anomalies, compression artifacts and behavioural motion abnormalities are pattern recognition systems based on ML that are being trained to achieve promising accuracy (Tripathi et al., 2023). But, the antagonistic AI models are constantly advanced, and it is doubtful that the existing forensics counter-measures are enough.

Risks of Generative AI Fabricated Evidence

Generative AI systems are capable of generating fake chat logs, screenshots, biometric voice and video evidence that is impossible to distinguish between and real human communication. This puts the principle of evidentiary reliability in question requiring new evidentiary standards, expert authentication measures, and even a change in the scope of admissibility aimed at by legislation (Tripathi et al., 2024).

Figure 1. Conceptual Diagram of User-Centric Digital Forensic Process Flow

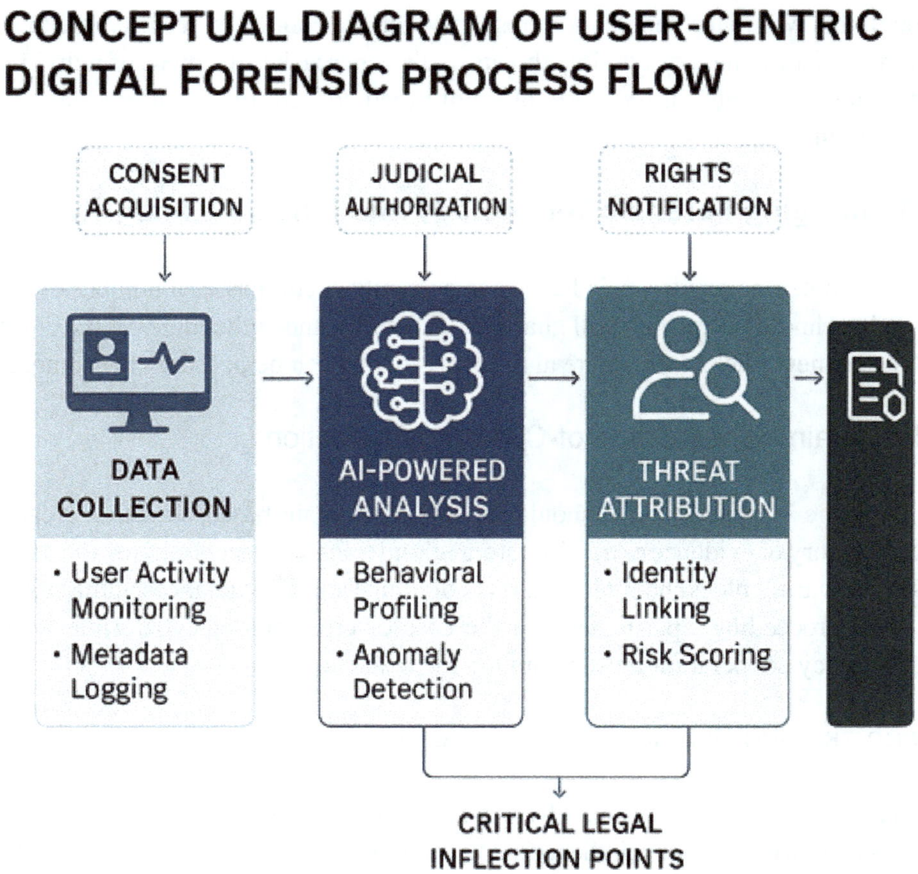

It should be a graphical representation (which would be placed here) of how information moves in a user centric forensic investigation, as it moves through the phases of data collection (user activity monitoring, metadata logging), AI based analysis (behavioral profiling and anomaly detection), threat attribution (identity association and threat scoring) and its final part either as evidence extraction or enforcement action. In this model, special attention should be paid to such legally significant inflexion points as the consent obtaining, court permission, and the notice about the rights..

4. THE CYBER FORENSIC ISSUES ON LEGAL MATTERS

4.1 The digital evidence presented by the prosecution must be admissible in court

The issue of admissibility of digital evidence is a primary one especially in countries like India whereby there has been a slow pace of adaptation of the procedure. Sections 65A and 65B are contained in Indian Evidence Act, 1872 to provide a governance on electronic evidence. The section 65B demands that an electronic record presented in court should be accompanied by certificate stating its validity and integrity. In Anvar P.V. v. P.K. Basheer (2014), the Supreme Court made the requirement of the certificate to be obligatory, whereas in Arjun Panditrao Khotkar v. The certificate was later submitted later when it was unavailable, as Kailash Kushanrao Gorantyal (2020) permitted it to be submitted later. Though this decision introduced procedural flexibility, it did not address the issue of forensic soundness in its entirety, along with the guarantee of the absence of interventions to digital evidence between the moment of acquisition and court hearings (Ferguson et al., 2020).

Digital data are capable of all the above unlike physical evidence where the evidence may be duplicated, altered, or planted without leaving the damage visible. It is thus necessary to have an effective chain of custody. Nonetheless, India does not have standard papers that are universally accepted and would guarantee similar and non-manipulated treatment of digital content that is confiscated. Such a loophole can undermine the fair trial provisions in Article 21 of the Indian Constitution because the courts can give undue credence to baked investigative agency assertions without strong verification instruments.

Chain-of-Custody Best Practice Steps (Recommended Forensic Workflow):

1. **Acquisition:** Obtain the original device through suitable imaging and hashing to obtain verifiable digital fingerprints.
2. **Storage:** Data on storage of acquired information in sealed and encrypted, and access-controlled locations.
3. **Transfer Logging:** The digital log records all the time and place of access, duplication or movement of the evidence.
4. **Checking:** Checking by an independent forensic analyst to make sure that the original integrity was intact by hash-matching.
5. **Presentation in court:** Filing with full audit trail to prove that no unauthorized modification.

The steps increase the evidentiary credibility and decrease the use of institutional trust alone.

4.2 Algorithmic Opacity and Due Process

The use of AI and machine learning in cyber forensics is on the rise in data analysis and behavioral profiling as well as predictive mapping of threats. Nevertheless, most of these tools are based on proprietary algorithms, the inner logic of which is not publicly available, as well as the weighting of inputs. This black box issue severely limits the options of the accused to object against the evidentiary foundation of digital leads, which is questionable about the equality of arms and due process. Audit and explainability of algorithms In order to mitigate these risks, the algorithm audit and explainability standards, which demand that the rationale of models, sources of training data, and error rates be disclosed to courts, could be important to ensure procedural fairness without undermining technological utility (Arora, Rai, and Gupta, 2024).To handle such concerns, global jurisprudence has been cautiously aware of the issue by requiring disclosure of the logic behind models, the data used to train them, and their error rates to the court (Arora, Rai, For instance, in State v. The court (Loomis, Wisconsin Supreme Court, 2016) recognized the dangers of bias due to obscure risk assessment instruments. The court highlighted the principles of transparency and fairness even though they were still used. The same should be applied to the forensic environment, where algorithmic outputs could also affect guilt determinations in themselves (Singh et al., 2024).

4.3 Real Case-Based Example: The Bhima Koregaon Forensic Controversy

The case of Bhima Koregaon can show the impact of misusing digital forensics. Several activists were accused of UAPA on the basis of the electronic files that have supposedly been found in their devices. Arsenal Consulting was hired to perform an independent forensic investigation into these matters in 2021 and 2022, which found that the incriminating documents were remotely installed with advanced malware tools (NetWire and Elcomsoft). The malware could create, modify, and delete files on its own without user intervention, which means that the accused did not know or control the evidence against him or her (Singh et al., 2024).

The state failed to seek independent validation and response to results of potential evidence manipulation, which casts serious due process concerns. The case highlights the necessity of legal protection, such as the appointment of forensic experts in the court, the adversarial testing of the digital evidence, and the legally assured rights to the independent forensic examination. It also points at the risks of the overreach of the state by using technology, involving the liberties of Articles 19 and 21 of the Indian Constitution (Investigating cyber law and cyber ethics, 2011).

5. ETHICAL DILEMMAS IN DIGITAL INVESTIGATIONS

The intertwining of cyber forensic techniques with the contemporary system of investigation and user-friendly forms of human threat intelligence has started a series of intricate moral issues. These dilemmas are created not only because the technological progress is far ahead of the regulatory framework but also because the normative uncertainty surrounding the practice of digital surveillance exists. The fundamental conflict is between the pragmatic effectiveness of the digital forensic tools and the constitutional obligations toward civil rights, especially the right to privacy, the right to speech, the equality principle, and the right to a trial. This paper critically discusses three key areas of ethical dilemma that have arisen in the field of digital forensic science; informed consent, profiling bias and democratic accountability. It is necessary to enhance the human-ethical aspect as cyber forensics is not a vacuum but has direct impact on the number of people whose rights are lived and the trust in the law of society.

5.1 Informed Consent and Surveillance

Informed consent is one of the main pillars of the democratic legal systems as it justifies the state intervention in human areas. In digital forensic investigations, however, consent is not clear, is usually pressured, or simply not provided at all. The legality of consent as one that is voluntary, informed, specific, and unambiguous is hard to enforce when it comes to the aspects of real-time monitoring, metadata harvesting, or insidious extraction at the device level. In many cases, surveillance is performed in a passive mode, using automated scrapers or spyware or through the use of remote access tools without the knowledge or consent of the subject (Krishna et al., 2018). As an example, the malware-used in the Bhima Koregaon case, India, to insert and extract the evidence posed a big question whether the data obtained was consensual, original or altered. Such issues are intensified by the fact that people are not digital-savvy and do not understand their rights, which creates a framework defect of legal and ethical consent norms (Khosla, 2020).

Among other things, the GDPR has provided a significant point of reference in the entire world since it mandates positive and withdrawable consent even in cases of investigations. Article 23, however, has exceptions to do with law enforcement, which can be broadened and abused under national security reasons. In terms of ethics, these exceptions should be heavily restricted, such as judicial supervision, time-related constraints, disclosure, and need and proportionality standard to ensure they are not abused (Rai et al., 2023).

5.2 Profiling Bias and Discrimination

An important ethical issue that appears to arise is profiling bias, where the use of forensic tools is based on algorithmic models, behavioural prediction systems or classification methods that are not properly tested concerning the issue of systemic unfairness. These systems can be replicated and enhanced in the absence of protective tools, which may reproportionate and promote social hierarchies and discriminatory state practices (Mann & Matzner, 2019). As a matter of fact, online surveillance and targeting of the digital forensics have systematically targeted journalists, minority groups, and political dissidents, as witnessed in India among Dalit activists, Muslim academics, and anti-CAA activists. This type of selective surveillance boosts inequalities in structures instead of being justice (Reddy & Venter, 2009).

This presents a serious human-ethical aspect: profiling is in direct contradiction with the constitutional rights of equality before the law (Article 14 of the Indian Constitution) and these procedures of fairness in Articles 20 and 21. The disproportionate focus of algorithmic or investigative approaches to specific groups does not only breach nondiscrimination principles but damages the due process, by making the suspects determined in advance instead of independent evidence developing. This threatens to make cyber forensics a device of objective investigation a technology of exclusion in the digital realm (Beemkumar et al., 2023).Moreover, algorithms that are based on the past often encode past discriminating trends. Indicatively, in the United States, predictive policing tools have unfairly identified areas inhabited by African-Americans as dangerous neighbourhoods, resulting in increased policing and further inflating so-called prejudices (Christin, 2017). In a similar case, in the United Kingdom, the implementation of automated facial recognition systems in public areas has been observed to be used in inaccurately identifying ethnic minorities more than others. Bringing such systems to the forensic space without contextual protection would lead to the institutionalization of discriminatory results in the justice process (Vasani et al., 2024).

The author underlines that in the situation where personal information is input into security and predictive systems, the evaluation should be based on human dignity and overall societal social harm not just technical efficiency (Mantelero 2018). This implies that the process of ethical consideration and regulatory boundaries should be incorporated during the actual process of designing and implementing forensic technologies, rather than added later on.

Therefore, ethical cyber forensics requires:

(1) impartial algorithmic audits,
(2) rights-based impact assessment,
(3) clear guidelines of the selection of surveillance targets, and
(4) enforceability of avenues of challenge and redress

5.3 Civil Liberties and Democratic Accountability

The swift increase in surveillance resources in the name of forensic legitimacy is a significant threat to the liberties of democracy, in particular, the freedom of speech, freedom of gathering, and opposition. Although stopping cybercrime and terrorism may be a valid state interest, these should meet the constitutional concerns of legality, necessity, and proportionality as highlighted in Justice K.S. Puttaswamy v. Union of India. In several jurisdictions, however, the use of digital forensic tools has been used to spy on civil society actors, political opposition and journalists. The Pegasus spyware revelation is one of the international cases in which the practice of state surveillance had invaded the personal conversations of the rights defenders, thus undermining the democratic role of the press and the other accountability institutions.

The more profound ethical problem is institutional: the control systems are not robust, the monitoring is mostly post-factum and not proactive, and secrecy advocacies restrict the transparency and remedies (Tripathi et al., 2023). This means that forensic surveillance should be conducted in a system of judicial oversight, popular responsibility, and oversight institutions to ensure that practice fits with constitutionalism and the rule of law (Wakili and Bakkali, 2024). Any limitation on rights should, as explained in the proportionality doctrine, be both legal, undertake a legitimate objective, and apply the least restrictive resources. Several modern surveillance regimes in the field of forensics fail to meet these requirements and endanger the credibility of democracy.

Figure 2. Infographic – Ethical Risks in Digital Investigations

Despite the fact that the digital investigations are critical aspects that guarantee governance and security, their ethical connotations are full of agitating concerns that ought to be analyzed in a systematic manner. This paper identifies three core fears (a) gathering of data without prior knowledge, particularly under coercive conditions, (b) discriminatory algorithms based on biased data sets that in most instances discriminate against vulnerable groups of people, and (c) systematic suppression of civil liberties through surveillance, which tends to send a chilling effect to dissent and free expression. Together, these threats dictate the necessity of the development of powerful accountability schemes and ethical surveillance frameworks in order to make sure that the digital investigation approaches support human dignity and democratic principles.

6. CASE STUDY: LEGAL SCRUTINY OF PRIVACY AND SURVEILLANCE

6.1 Justice K.S. Puttaswamy (Retd.) v. Union of India (2017): Establishing Privacy as a Constitutional Right

The historic decision in Justice K.S. Puttaswamy (Retd.). v. The case of Union of India, (2017) 10 SCC 1, which was decided by a Constitution Bench of nine Supreme Court of India judges, has set the stage of legal proceedings in India with regard to the right to privacy. The Court unanimously claimed that the right to privacy is a basic right that it guaranteed under Article 21 of the Constitution of India which is in turn implicit in the protections granted in Articles 14 and 19, and interconnected with the guarantees of life and personal liberty (Kumar & Pande, 2022).

This ruling reversed previous stands of MP Sharma v. Safar and Kharak Singh v. (1954). Both of which had rejected privacy as a fundamental right, State of UP (1962). The Court also formulated a more organised criterion, the Doctrine of Proportionality., to assess the degree and extent to which the State can restrict this right in acknowledging privacy as a core attribute of human dignity and autonomy.

Doctrine of Proportionality

1. **Legality:** It should be on a legal basis.
2. **Legitimate State Aim:** The invasion should have a legitimate government purpose.
3. **Proportionality:** The least restrictive means should be employed in order to accomplish such an end.

This criterion now plays the key role in assessing digital forensic procedures and surveillance by the state, which impacts techniques like imaging devices, metadata analysis, decryption, and behavioural profiling. The acknowledgment of informational privacy has a direct effect on the data collection, storage, and analysis, especially in the circumstances when the subjects are not accused or even involved in a formal investigation (Awan et al., 2021).

Digital Surveillance and Cyber Forensics Applied Implications

The implications of Puttaswamy to the cyber forensic practitioners are worthwhile. Digital search or surveillance can no longer be done without statutory approval of the same restricting unrestrained executive powers under the general provisions such as the provisions of Section 69 of the IT Act, 2000. Judicial checks are necessary in forensic practices especially in mass surveillance, automated analytics, as well as obscure data-profiling systems.Later rulings, like the case of Anuradha Bhasin v. The case of internet shutdowns and the litigation of the current Pegasus spyware by civil society organizations, including the Internet Freedom Foundation, indicates that the judiciary is worried about technological breaches and their constitutional scope (Chaure & Mane, 2023). Puttaswamy is therefore a constitutional precedent of balancing technological control and individual rights.

6.2 Schrems II (CJEU, 2020): Transnational Surveillance and Data Sovereignty

Commissioner of Data Protection v. The CJEU struck down the EU-US Privacy Shield Framework in Facebook Ireland Ltd and Maximillian Schrems (Case C-311/18), widely referred to as Schrems II because it does not adequately address surveillance laws in the U.S. and fails to provide any effective legal remedy to the EU citizens (Akter et al., 2021). The decision raised the question of the safety of data that is transferred out of the EU, which should be afforded an equivalent protection in comparison with the one that is guaranteed under the GDPR and the EU Charter of Fundamental Rights, as the former allowed blanket and non-transparent surveillance without allowing the foreigners to pursue any redress. The concept of data sovereignty was supported by Schrems II and required data exporters to carry out transfer impact evaluations and to implement additional protection mechanisms, including encryption or contractual restrictions.

The implications of this ruling are quite significant in cross-border cyber forensics and global investigations involving the use of MLATs or the Budapest Convention on Cybercrime. The court ruling continues to state that cooperation systems must not infringe on personal privacy and need to be in line with the regional constitutional safeguards.

6.3 Bhima Koregaon Surveillance Case: Digital Evidence and State Power

Bhima Koregaon case was a case in which digital evidence that was used to incriminate various activists was alleged to have been planted by means of a remote malware intrusion. The documents were subsequently not written by the accused, as independent forensic examination by third-party digital security researchers later revealed indicators of deliberate spyware installation on the computers of the accused. This cast dire doubts concerning the integrity of digital evidence, due process and the possibility of the use of cyber-forensic processes to develop artificial stories of criminality.

As highlighted in the case, the constitutional significance of authenticating and evaluating digital evidence, judicial review of the investigation procedures, and the absence of technological devices to undermine the freedom of individuals are emphasized.

6.4 Pegasus Spyware Investigations: Expanding the Surveillance Debate Globally

The Pegasus spyware leaks proved that the governments of India, France, Mexico, and a number of other nations had supposedly purchased a military-level hacking device that was able to compromise smartphones, steal information, and provide real-time tracking. This monitoring was done without transparent legal systems and in most instances without a judicial warrant or any other checks. The Pegasus scandals demonstrated the high level of spyware, which is capable of going around encryption and conventional privacy protection in futility.

Comparative Reflection

Although both Puttaswamy and Schrems II discuss the constitutional provisions against excessive surveillance, the cases of Bhima Koregaon and Pegasus demonstrate the practical difficulties of implementing these provisions in the situations when surveillance technologies are working quietly. This distinction may mostly be attributed to judicial control: Schrems II shows a continuing supranational regulatory control, whereas the Indian cases reveal behind-schedule or far-reaching institutional control. Bhima Koregaon and Pegasus both highlight the importance of independent verification as a prerequisite, without external technical verification, digital evidence can be subject to manipulation, and constitutional rights will be hard to protect.

7. OVERSIGHT MECHANISMS AND REGULATORY GAPS

The avalanche in the development of cyber forensic technologies and its application in the operations of state surveillance and investigation have drastically overtaken the current legal systems, especially in places like India. The lack of effective and enforceable control systems has facilitated the unrestrained growth of surveillance authority, bringing up the issue of the right to privacy, due process and democratization in accountability. This section is a critical analysis of the current vacuum in regulation in the Indian regulatory environment and its comparison with the best practices on the international front to demonstrate the urgency of institutional reform.

7.1 India's Data Protection Legal Vacuum

India is at a crucial crossroad in establishing a powerful regulation strategy on online privacy and cyber inquiries. Even though the right to privacy as a fundamental right was realised by the Supreme Court in Justice K.S. Puttaswamy v. Union of India (2017), The legislative and institutional frameworks that are necessary to implement this right in cyber forensic cases are inadequate. The Digital Personal Data Protection Act, 2023 (DPDP act) was a much-awaited change, but its relevancy to the surveillance by state authorities and cyber forensic evidence gathering is unintelligible. The Act does not include particulars regarding state surveillance or extraction of forensic information. Moreover, Sections 17 and 18 allow the Central Government to exempt state agencies even in case of wide exemption on grounds of national security, national sovereignty, or national order (Balogun and Zhu, 2013). These exceptions do not provide any procedural protections, judicial checks, and balances, and thus weaken the very principles of necessity, legality, and proportionality that the modern data protection regimes are based on.

Regulation remains based on piecemeal and obsolete provisions in the absence of an elaborate statutory framework. The Information technology act 2000 and the Information technology (Reasonable security practices and procedures and sensitive personal data or information) rules 2011 mainly govern the private organizations and offer no enforceable protection against the abuse of powers by the state in a forensic investigation. Similarly, Indian Computer Emergency Response Team (CERT-IN) established under Section 70B of the IT Act, is a technical cybersecurity response team, not one that deals with privacy or rights-based regulation. The 2022 directives issued by CERT-IN that mandated the retention of long-lasting user logs of five years were not done in a transparent manner and they lacked the integration of protection mechanisms such as limiting purpose, data minimisation and independent audit measures (Dushyant et al., 2022). Additionally, the institutional checks on investigative and intelligence agencies can be undermined because the proposed Data Protection Board of the DPDP Act is not structurally independent, and surveillance powers are broad, without any accountability and judicial review.

7.1.1 *Institutional Reform Recommendation: Establishment of a National Digital Forensics Oversight Authority*

As a way to deal with this oversight gap, there is need to have a National Digital Forensics Oversight Authority (NDFOA), as an independent statutory body. The Authority should have:

- Authority to assess and authorise digital surveillance warrants and guarantee their adequacy and regularity to necessity and proportion.
- Require certification of forensic tools and investigative software, such as AI-based systems, to be accurate, reliable, and auditable and lack any bias.
- Authority to periodically audit digital forensic labs, state cyber cells and intelligence activities requiring data extraction.
- Ability to effect independent verification of electronic evidence, such as chain-of-custody controls and anti-tampering.

This institutional framework would make the cyber forensic activities transparent and independently checked and conscious of the rights of the subjects as opposed to being purely security-centred (Tripathi et al., 2023).

7.2 International Best Practices and Institutional Frameworks

Comparatively, some jurisdictions like the European Union have embraced an integrated regulatory framework that places rights of individuals against justifiable investigative needs. The GDPR creates principles of a legal data processing, whereas the Law Enforcement Directive (Directive (EU) 2016/680) gives certain protection to the situation of criminal investigation (Chan et al., 2013). This is enforced through the European Data Protection Board (EDPB) which provides binding guidelines and ensures that the rules are applied consistently in all Member States. On the same note, international organizations, such as the UN Special Rapporteur on the Right to Privacy, have also raised issues relating to the use of intrusive surveillance devices and the necessity to have them checked by courts and with restrictions based on their rights.

The Budapest Convention on Cybercrime (2001) still continues to support the importance of procedural protection like judicial review, proportionality, and human rights protection in the process of collecting electronic evidence (Aleman, 2004). These frameworks prove that good cyber forensics do not have to be achieved at the cost of civil liberties, but instead, responsibility frameworks enhance investigative legitimacy and trust by the citizens.

Table 2. Oversight and Accountability Mechanisms Across Jurisdictions

Jurisdiction	Oversight Body	Mandate	Enforcement Powers	Notable Gaps
India	CERT-IN, Proposed Data Protection Board	Incident response, not rights protection	Limited enforceability	Lack of comprehensive law
EU	Data Protection Authorities (DPAs)	GDPR enforcement	Significant fines, remedies	Cross-border enforcement complexities
USA	FTC, FISA Courts	Market regulation & national security	Civil penalties, surveillance court approvals	Secrecy and lack of transparency

8. RECOMMENDATIONS FOR A PRIVACY-COMPLIANT FORENSIC FRAMEWORK

Cyber forensic practice is undergoing significant growth in volume and sophistication, and it is necessary that the ethical and legal context of digital investigations serves as a guardian of privacy rights and accountability (Mantelero, 2018). The table below is a summary of the proposed reforms in four major areas.

Table 3. Recommendations for a Privacy-Compliant Forensic Framework

Reform Domain	What Should Be Done	Why This is Necessary
Legal Reforms	Have an all-inclusive data protection regime that controls lawful collection, storage, and processing of forensic evidence; mandate that judicial warrants be taken when forensic intrusion is sought with limited and reviewable national security exceptions; revise the provisions in the IT Act, 2000 and the Indian Evidence Act, 1872 (including Sections 65A and 65B) to incorporate cloud storage, encrypted communication, and AI-driven evidence; provide statutory chain of custody and digital authentication guidelines.	Asures transparency, defines what digital evidence can be admitted, imposes state restraint and prevents random encroachment on privacy. It also improves the reliability of evidence and the confidence of the court.
Ethical and Procedural Safeguards	It is required that agencies using agencies using data-intensive or AI-based forensic tools conduct Privacy Impact Assessment (PIA) related to Article 35, GDPR; it is required that forensic algorithms used be independently audited, including third-party review, explainability requirements, and it is required that the affected individuals have the right to challenge automated determinations.	Adds the principles of necessity, proportionality and minimisation of data to the investigations. Stopps unfair or murky digital profiling and defends due process.
Institutional Mechanisms	Create a Digital Forensic Oversight Board, composed of judicial, scientific, civil society and data protection professionals, to assess the legality and proportionality of forensic surveillance, and have the ability to audit and make binding recommendations. Establish a Grievance redressal office (Ombudsman Office) that will have the power to order data destruction, pay compensation or take disciplinary measures against illegal surveillance (Mantelero, 2018).	Brings accountability and enhances trust of the people and brings about time-limited corrective measures when rights are violated. Eliminates the abuse of forensic powers by state authorities.
International Cooperation	Negotiate accession to the Budapest Convention on Cybercrime with the required reservations to mitigate the sovereignty issues; include privacy-by-design, enforceable timelines of MLAT, and data protection against the secondary misuse into bilateral and multilateral agreements; draw upon the examples of the frameworks formulated by the Council of Europe and the UN Special Rapporteur on the Right to Privacy.	Enables efficient cross border investigations and at the same time prevents disproportionate surveillance by shared data or its misuse. Weighs between control of cyber-crime and protection of fundamental rights.

9. CONCLUSION

The blistering development of cyber forensics and digital investigation opportunities has essentially changed the interdependence between state monitoring and personal rights. As noted in this chapter, the modern forensic tools, including metadata analysis and algorithmic profiling to more sophisticated evidence extraction methods, are legal and ethically constrained that is underdeveloped and applied unevenly. Although these instruments make investigation more efficient and help in law enforcement goals, they cause considerable threats to the basic constitutional rights, especially privacy, informational self-determination and due process. The law established in Justice K.S. Puttaswamy v. Union of India confirms that any invasion of digital communications should be of a quality that meets the criteria of legality, necessity, and proportionality as a result placing the constitutional burden of responsibility on the state to offer justification to its application of surveillance measures (Obermeyer et al., 2019).The analysis shows that the current statutory provisions, such as the Information Technology Act, 2000, and the Indian Evidence Act, are not yet sufficiently clarifying, protecting, or procedural to handle these new challenges. Without an extensive data protection law or independent forensic management authority, the systemic threats to the rights protection remain (Rowe, 2016). The GDPR and the European Convention on Human Rights are seen as comparative perspectives because the enforceable rights, accountability of algorithms, and transparency of the institutions are critical in controlling digital investigations. These paradigms indicate that protection of privacy is not the impediment of security but a prerequisite of lawful rule.

To balance the situation, digital forensics must be reformulated based on privacy-by-design approaches, compulsory judicial warrants, the disclosure of algorithm decision-making, and creating an independent mechanism of control. This kind of action does not undermine national security, on the contrary, it strengthens social confidence and enhances constitutional effectiveness. Cyber forensics should be not only technically efficient, but also with open respect to the human dignity and democratic principles. To sum up, the future of the digital justice lies in the ability to combine the technological change with the legal and ethical systems that respect the rights. Since digital evidence is still changing the way criminal cases are adjudicated and preventive police are developed, law studies, policymaking, and forensic practice will have to advance in tandem to make certain that technological advancement promotes, as opposed to decreases, individual freedom. This principled balance between the effectiveness of investigations and the preservation of civil liberties is the way of the just digital future.

REFERENCES

Akter, S., McCarthy, G., Sajib, S., Michael, K., Dwivedi, Y. K., D'Ambra, J., & Shen, K. (2021). Algorithmic bias in data-driven innovation in the age of AI. *International Journal of Information Management, 60*, 102387. DOI: 10.1016/j.ijinfomgt.2021.102387

Aleman, J. (2004). The ethnic in the canon; or, on finding Santa Anna's "Wooden leg.". *Melus, 29*(3/4), 165. DOI: 10.2307/4141849

Alenezi, A., Atlam, H. F., & Wills, G. B. (2019). Experts reviews of a cloud forensic readiness framework for organizations. *Journal of Cloud Computing (Heidelberg, Germany), 8*(1), 11. Advance online publication. DOI: 10.1186/s13677-019-0133-z

Arora, S., Rai, M., & Gupta, M. (2024). Importance of Industry 5.0 in understanding emotional intelligence. In *Human-machine collaboration and emotional intelligence in Industry 5.0*. IGI Global., DOI: 10.4018/979-8-3693-6806-0.ch011

Awan, S. A., Rind, M. M., Dootio, M. A., Khan, A. A., Shaikh, A. A., & Laghari, A. A. (2021). Digital Forensics and Cyber Forensics Investigation: Security challenges, limitations, open issues, and future direction. *International Journal of Electronic Security and Digital Forensics, 1*(1), 1. DOI: 10.1504/IJESDF.2022.121174

Balogun, A. M., & Zhu, S. Y. (2013). Privacy Impacts of data encryption on the efficiency of digital forensics technology. arXiv (Cornell University). https://doi.org//arxiv.1312.3183DOI: 10.48550

Beemkumar, N., Gupta, S., Bhardwaj, S., Dhabliya, D., Rai, M., Pandey, J. K., & Gupta, A. (2023). Activity recognition and IoT-based analysis using time series and CNN. In Goel, N., & Yadav, R. K. (Eds.), *Handbook of research on machine learning-enabled IoT for smart applications across industries* (pp. 350–364). IGI Global., DOI: 10.4018/978-1-6684-8785-3.ch018

Bhawna, N., & Mahajan, S. (2024). Artificial Intelligence Perspective on Digital Forensics. IGI Global, 33–44. DOI: 10.1002/9781394196470.ch3

Chan, L., Law, N., & Siu, W. (2013). A confidence map and pixel-based weighted correlation for PRNU-based camera identification. *Digital Investigation, 10*(3), 215–225. DOI: 10.1016/j.diin.2013.04.001

Chaure, S., & Mane, V. (2023). *Digital Forensic Framework for Protecting Data Privacy during Investigation*. ICST Transactions on Scalable Information Systems., DOI: 10.4108/eetsis.4002

Christin, A. (2017). Algorithms in practice: Comparing web journalism and criminal justice. *Big Data & Society*, *4*(2), 205395171771885. DOI: 10.1177/2053951717718855

Cyber security and digital forensics. (2021). In Lecture notes on data engineering and communications technologies. DOI: 10.1007/978-981-16-3961-6

Dushyant, K., Muskan, G., Annu, N., Gupta, A., & Pramanik, S. (2022). Utilizing Machine learning and deep Learning in CybeSecurity: an innovative approach. Wiley, 271–293. https://doi.org/DOI: 10.1002/9781119795667.ch12

Ekundayo, N. F. (2024). Big data and machine learning in digital forensics: Predictive technology for proactive crime prevention. *World Journal of Advanced Research and Reviews*, *24*(2), 2692–2709. DOI: 10.30574/wjarr.2024.24.2.3659

Ferguson, R., Renaud, K., Wilford, S., & Irons, A. (2020). PRECEPT: A framework for ethical digital forensics investigations. *Journal of Intellectual Capital*, *21*(2), 257–290. DOI: 10.1108/JIC-05-2019-0097

Franke, K., Hjelmås, E., & Wolthusen, S. D. (2013). Advancing digital forensics. In IFIP advances in information and communication technology (pp. 288–295). DOI: 10.1007/978-3-642-39377-8_34

Garfinkel, S. L. (2010). Digital forensics research: The next 10 years. *Digital Investigation*, *7*, S64–S73. DOI: 10.1016/j.diin.2010.05.009

Garrett, B. L., & Rudin, C. (2023). Interpretable algorithmic forensics. *Proceedings of the National Academy of Sciences of the United States of America*, *120*(41), e2301842120. Advance online publication. DOI: 10.1073/pnas.2301842120 PMID: 37782786

Investigating cyber law and cyber ethics. (2011). In Advances in information security, privacy, and ethics book series. DOI: 10.4018/978-1-61350-132-0

Karabiyik, U., & Akkaya, K. (2018, November 22). Digital forensics for IoT and WSNs. arXiv.org. https://arxiv.org/abs/1811.09239

Khosla, M. (2020). Democracy and decolonization: How India was made. *International Journal of Constitutional Law*, *18*(3), 1031–1035. DOI: 10.1093/icon/moaa078

Krishna, P. V., Gurumoorthy, S., & Obaidat, M. S. (2018). Social network forensics, cyber security, and machine learning. In SpringerBriefs in applied sciences and technology. DOI: 10.1007/978-981-13-1456-8

Kumar, K., & Pande, B. P. (2022). Applications of Machine Learning Techniques in the Realm of Cybersecurity. Wiley, 295–315. DOI: 10.1002/9781119795667.ch13

Lyon, D. (2014). Surveillance, Snowden, and Big Data: Capacities, consequences, critique. *Big Data & Society*, *1*(2), 2053951714541861. Advance online publication. DOI: 10.1177/2053951714541861

Mann, M., & Matzner, T. (2019). Challenging algorithmic profiling: The limits of data protection and anti-discrimination in responding to emergent discrimination. *Big Data & Society*, *6*(2), 205395171989580. DOI: 10.1177/2053951719895805

Mantelero, A. (2018). AI and Big Data: A blueprint for a human rights, social and ethical impact assessment. *Computer Law & Security Review*, *34*(4), 754–772. DOI: 10.1016/j.clsr.2018.05.017

Miron, M., Tolan, S., Gómez, E., & Castillo, C. (2020). Evaluating causes of algorithmic bias in juvenile criminal recidivism. *Artificial Intelligence and Law*, *29*(2), 111–147. DOI: 10.1007/s10506-020-09268-y

Obermeyer, Z., Powers, B., Vogeli, C., & Mullainathan, S. (2019). Dissecting racial bias in an algorithm used to manage the health of populations. *Science*, *366*(6464), 447–453. DOI: 10.1126/science.aax2342 PMID: 31649194

Rai, M.. (2023). Advancement in agricultural techniques with the introduction of artificial intelligence and image processing. In Khan, M. A. (Eds.), *Smart village infrastructure and sustainable rural communities* (pp. 47–68). IGI Global., DOI: 10.4018/978-1-6684-6418-2.ch004

Reddy, K., & Venter, H. (2009). A forensic framework for handling information privacy incidents. In IFIP advances in information and communication technology (pp. 143–155). DOI: 10.1007/978-3-642-04155-6_11

Rowe, N. C. (2016). Privacy Concerns with Digital Forensics. In Advances in public policy and administration (APPA) book series (pp. 145–162). DOI: 10.4018/978-1-4666-9905-2.ch008

Sabillon, R., Serra-Ruiz, J., Cavaller, V., & Cano, J. J. (2017). Digital Forensic analysis of cybercrimes. *International Journal of Information Security and Privacy*, *11*(2), 25–37. DOI: 10.4018/IJISP.2017040103

Sengupta, A., Kumar, P., & Sahani, A. K. (2025). Ensuring the privacy of digital forensic reports using searchable symmetric encryption. In IFIP advances in information and communication technology (pp. 25–40). DOI: 10.1007/978-3-031-71025-4_2

Singh, S., Pandey, J. K., Rai, M., & Saxena, A. K. (2024). Emotional intelligence and collaborative dynamics in Industry 5.0 for human-machine interactions. In *Human-machine collaboration and emotional intelligence in Industry 5.0*. IGI Global., DOI: 10.4018/979-8-3693-6806-0.ch010

Singh, S., Pandey, J. K., Rai, M., & Saxena, A. K. (2024). Advancements in facial expression recognition using machine and deep learning techniques. In *Machine and deep learning techniques for emotion detection*. IGI Global., DOI: 10.4018/979-8-3693-4143-8.ch007

Tripathi, P., Kumar, N., Paroha, K. K., Rai, M., & Panda, M. K. (2024). Applications of deep learning in healthcare in the framework of Industry 5.0. In *Infrastructure possibilities and human-centered approaches with Industry 5.0*. IGI Global., DOI: 10.4018/979-8-3693-0782-3.ch005

Tripathi, P., Kumar, N., & Rai, M.. (2023). Applications of machine learning in agriculture. In Khan, M. A. (Eds.), *Smart village infrastructure and sustainable rural communities* (pp. 99–118). IGI Global., DOI: 10.4018/978-1-6684-6418-2.ch006

Vasani, V. P., Chandra, U., Sahu, G., Boyineni, S., Dhamodaran, S., Kumbhkar, M., Rai, M., & Gupta, S. (2024). Introduction to emotion detection and predictive psychology in the age of technology. In *Using machine learning to detect emotions and predict human psychology*. IGI Global., DOI: 10.4018/979-8-3693-1910-9.ch001

Wachter, S., Mittelstadt, B., & Floridi, L. (2017). Why a right to explanation of automated Decision-Making does not exist in the General Data Protection Regulation. *International Data Privacy Law*, *7*(2), 76–99. DOI: 10.1093/idpl/ipx005

Wakili, A., & Bakkali, S. (2024). A Theoretical framework for Harnessing Machine Learning for Digital Forensics in Online Social Networks. In Lecture notes in networks and systems (pp. 200–214). DOI: 10.1007/978-3-031-52388-5_19

Zuboff, S. (2015). Big other: Surveillance Capitalism and the Prospects of an Information Civilization. *Journal of Information Technology*, *30*(1), 75–89. DOI: 10.1057/jit.2015.5

Chapter 8
A Forensic Intelligence Approach for Profiling and Investigating Human-Driven Cyber Threats

Vikas Sharma
https://orcid.org/0000-0001-8173-4548
Department of Computer Applications, SRM Institute of Science and Technology, Delhi, India

Puneet Chauhan
https://orcid.org/0009-0000-1652-8764
Swami Vivekanand Subharti University, Meerut, India

Tarun Kumar Vashishth
https://orcid.org/0000-0001-9916-9575
IIMT University, Meerut, India

Sanjukta Vidyant
Shobhit University, Meerut, India

Kewal Krishan Sharma
https://orcid.org/0009-0001-2504-9607
IIMT University, Meerut, India

Kajal Chaudhary
https://orcid.org/0009-0000-6713-6509
IIMT University, Meerut, India

Pushpendra Kumar Verma
https://orcid.org/0000-0003-2777-5626
School of Computer Science and Applications, IIMT University, Meerut, India

ABSTRACT

In this day and age, cyberspace is rife with exposures generated by people - insider attacks, clever social engineering phishing schemes, and lurking advanced persistent threats, and each event not only tests company defences but also challenges the broader security framework of a nation. This chapter draws on an intersection

DOI: 10.4018/979-8-3373-4898-8.ch008

of cyber forensics and human intelligence threat, with a forensic-first approach to provide a foundation to profile, investigate and pursue the people undertaking attacks. You'll observe how behavioural analytics, raw digital evidence, and advanced artificial intelligence work in concert to depict motivation, strategies, and actions intruders will employ, as well as their electronic footprints. Here are the sequential techniques to identify, pin blame, and mitigate these impacts and threats, which rely on forensic toolkits, network traffic examinations, and digital poison extraction, aka malware reverse engineering.

1. INTRODUCTION

In a world where cyberspace is dominated by human creativity and psychological intent, cyber threat attacks diligently contain a human component, and no longer just automated scripts or malware. Today's most harmful threat activity is human-driven, either from malicious insider risks with well-developed access, social engineers with an understanding of human psychology, or advanced persistent threat (APT) groups with long-term intent. Threats may impede or avert operations for organizations and can ultimately compromise national security and critical infrastructure. Generally, cybersecurity capabilities cannot easily defeat potentially sophisticated human-enabled threats. This chapter articulates a forensic intelligence approach through the development of a structured framework for investigating human-enabled cyber threats as a combination of cyber and human-centric threat intelligence that addresses the research problem, which is outlined below.

1.1. Overview of Human-Driven Cyber Threats

Human-enabled cyber threats fall into an increasingly sophisticated and generally more dangerous class of cyber threats. Actions taken by individuals or groups can include thought, targeted actions, and consideration of surrounding conditions. These threats depend on the human adversary's cognitive capacity, social engineering skills, and the planning that goes into the attack (considered as time) within a set timeframe. Human-enabled cyber threats may include but are not limited to: insider threats (whether active insider or passive insider), phishing attacks, business email compromises, and advanced persistent threats (APTs). Each of these threats includes steps taken by human adversaries to maintain covert access to networks over long-timeline engagements. Human-enabled cyber-attacks are not designed simply to gain unauthorized access to systems; they often seek to avoid detection, to manipulate human behavior patterns, extract sensitive data, serve as a strategic disruption to operations. One of the most substantive challenges of human-enabled cyber threats is their deceptiveness and unpredictability to stakeholders. For example, insiders are people, and people may include current disgruntled employees, counter groups, or individuals through trusted agency status, with approved or authorized access to sensitive corporate resources, data, and activities that can be exploited to steal resources, sabotaging operations internally, or facilitating constant access to external and unwanted adversaries. APTs (Advanced Persistent Threats), usually attributed to nation-state groups or organized cybercriminal groups, involve social applications, malware, and stealth in the form of persistence to communicate, gain access, and compromise targets to conduct espionage, sabotage, or theft of data. Increasingly, people are embracing a digital world not only in their personal and professional lives, but increasingly in their daily lives. Cloud services, remote work, and intertwined devices are accelerating the risks of human-driven cyber threats as attackers take advantage of the most vulnerable area in cybersecurity - human behavior. Humans are invariably weaker defenders of information security than traditional defences (firewalls, antivirus software and detection, intrusion systems). A hybrid approach is therefore required for human-driven cyber threats, utilising digital forensics, behavioural analysis, and threat intelligence employed in human-driven cyber threat reconstructions. This chapter will demonstrate that we can neither solely rely on purely technical defences or operational mitigative strategies alone, and that successful designs for the nature of human-driven cyber threats must also explore human based strategies, such as psychological and motive analysis, and behavioural indicators. The forensic intelligence approach to human-driven cyber threats presented in this chapter seeks to connect technical evidence to intent by establishing an overall approach to profiling, investigating, and mitigating the most identical and complex human-driven cyber threats currently in existence (Aburub & Almomani, 2025).

1.2. Need for Forensic Intelligence in Cybersecurity

As cyber threats become more and more multifaceted and human-centric, the traditional methods of cybersecurity that focus on only technical defense methods are becoming insufficient. Traditional tools, such as firewalls, intrusion detection and prevention systems, and antivirus systems, are primarily designed to identify known threats and respond to predetermined attack signatures. However, human-generated cyberattacks, such as insider threats, social engineering exploits, or advanced persistent threats (APTs), can often circumvent these modes of protection because of their stealthy, adaptive, and contextual nature. In these instances, it was equally as important to understand the attacker's intent, behaviour and how they operate than it was to detect the technical indicators of compromise. Here forensic intelligence has an important function within modern cybersecurity frameworks.

Forensic intelligence can be viewed as the integration of digital forensics and threat intelligence; whereby the objective of the forensic process is to establish, not only the mode by which an intrusion has occurred, but who perpetrated the intrusion and their purpose. Forensic intelligence provides a layer of proactive intelligence, in addition to the reactive investigation process. Forensic intelligence combines the elements of forensic evidence collection, behavioural and contextual profiling, and pattern recognition techniques to identify the human dimension of a cyber event. Security teams can identify if the behaviours generated an anomaly based on knowledge of typical user behaviours, determine who or where a malicious act originated, relate incidents across a number of sources, and more accurately conclude who the threat group was that perpetrated the cyber-attack. Ultimately, forensic intelligence will help security teams address the growing capacity of cyber threats that are, increasingly targeted, persistent, and organized, more effectively. This is vital for organizations bound by regulatory regimes or organizations seeking to prosecute malicious groups. This in itself allows for multi-party dynamics as mankind and organisations have a directionally defined intelligence led threat understanding. (Binbeshr et al, 2025), The following sections progressively discuss the structure of forensic intelligence and its practical application in dealing with human driven cyber threats. Section 2 discusses the behavioural and technical nature of such a threat, while section 3 introduces the concept and components of forensic intelligence. Section 4 & 5 give methodologies and frameworks for profiling and investigation, followed by section 6 on correlation and attribution techniques. Section 7 gives practical evidence of case studies, section 8 discusses critical challenges, while section 9 finishes with emerging trends and future directions.

2. UNDERSTANDING HUMAN-DRIVEN CYBER THREATS

Human driven cyber threats denote a fundamental change in cyber security. In what is generally meant by threat hunting this threat type has moved from being opportunistic automated attacks to more deliberate attacks that are planned in a unique way and style by individual entities or groups of people with certain aims. Systemically, human-driven threats are a composite of both technology and human observation and manipulation. Most malware spreads in an opportunistic and automated way across the internet through bots executing a pre-programmed cyber-attack. But human-driven threats add an additional layer of dangerous behaviour, that when eagle-eyed against your users and systems, exhibit technical capabilities with the motivation to psychologically manipulate system users. Because human-driven threats demonstrate both technical and psychological capabilities in their attacks, they are more poisonous and formidable opportunities for attackers to attack digital systems with both some digital exploitation and human-conducted manipulation. This is critical for every organization to understand; the nature of a threat, the motivation for the attack, and if it has been acted out and executed. At its core, human-driven cyber threats include the intent and motivation of the attacker - from monetary gain from theft of information, to corporate espionage, to sabotage, or ideologically oriented disruption. The biggest examples of human-driven threats to the cybersecurity domain are through insider threats (individuals with either active or past employment where they misuse their access to steal proprietary information or damage organizational systems), phishing and spear-phishing attacks (social engineering with the direct goal of tricking users into revealing information or click on malicious links), and advanced persistent threats (APTs) when attackers remain present inside the cyber systems to manipulate, gain intelligence, or steal information. Most of these actually occur simultaneously, as the multi-dimensional threat, combining social engineering and/or human behaviour to exploit a technical and/or digital vulnerability, and simultaneously, the multi-dimensional threat may compromise even the best-prepared defences (Sharma et al., 2025).

Figure 1. Architectural Layout of Human Driven Cyber Threats

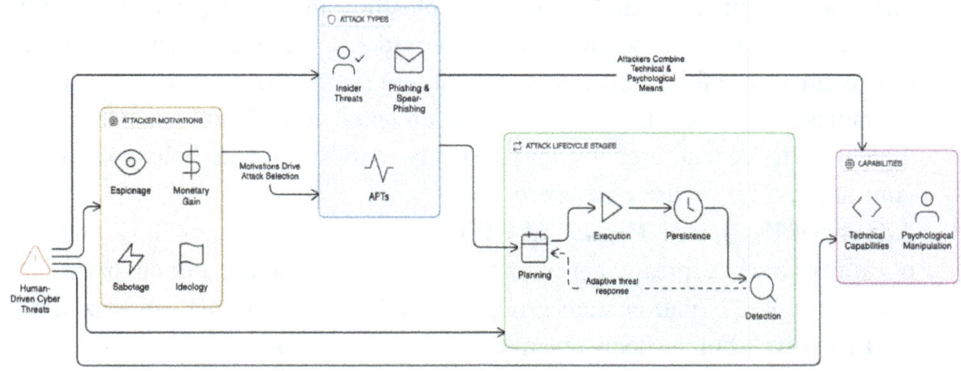

2.1. Categories of Human-Driven Threats

Human-driven cyber threats encompass a plethora of attack types with respect to the execution of the threat that hinge on human intent, human strategy, and ongoing human manipulation. Human cyber threats rely on human intelligence and decisions anchored in critical thinking and cannot be effectively executed by automated or randomly executed malware. Human cyber threats oftentimes exploit the social, psychological, and procedural vulnerabilities, weaknesses, and/or errors within organizations. Significant categories of human-driven cyber threats can be identified as insider threat, human engineering, and advanced persistent threats/ TTP's. Each threat type presents unique detection and de-escalation challenges.

1. **Insider Threats:** They are some of the hardest to detect and prevent because they are often conducted by those with legitimate access to internal systems. Insider threats can be malicious; they can arise from personal grievance, ideology, or financial incentives, and can be unintentional, where employees expose data unintentionally from carelessness or poor cybersecurity hygiene. Insider threat groups usually operate from inside the organization and bypass perimeter defences and remain undetected for extended periods of time (Mohamed, 2025). In 2024, a senior IT administrator at a financial firm misused legitimate credentials to transfer confidential trade data to a competitor. Forensic analysis later revealed evidence of unauthorized access logs and metadata trails consistent with insider data theft.
2. **Social Engineering Attacks:** Leverage human psychology rather than technology vulnerabilities to access information or systems. The most recognized type of attack is phishing, which entices users to click on a maleficent link or engage in some sharing of credentials through convincing communication. More specific social engineering attacks are spear phishing and whaling which are more targeted and typically used for specific individuals within an organization such as executives or IT administrators and thus are more readily permissible. Other examples of social engineering evolve around pretexting, baiting, and tailgating which use trust, fear, urgency, and curiosity to induce victim behaviour that is contrary to their security protocols.
3. **Advanced Persistent Threats (APTs):** They are sustained, stealthy, high opportunity attacks typically perpetrated by attackers present in our environments who are typically nation-state groups or well-funded criminal organizations. APTs involve a human decision-making process throughout the attack lifecycle, beginning with reconnaissance, moving to initial infiltration, lateral movement, and ending with data exfiltration. Attackers adjust to their environments, use custom malware, exploit zero-day vulnerability, utilize not only legitimate tools but also potentially other active legitimate credentials, and stay hidden. APTs typically have malicious purposes including cyber espionage, theft of intellectual property, or disruption of critical infrastructure (Aljumaiah et al., 2025). A nation-state APT group exploited an energy utility's SCADA systems, maintaining persistence for months through custom malware and encrypted channels to disrupt grid operations.

The descriptions above show how people, whether maliciously or through some psychological manipulation, play a human agency role in modern cyber threats.

Understanding the risk, action, and behaviours of each of these types is relevant as we consider threat defence and the deployment of focused efforts beyond only technical defences and controls to include behavioural monitoring, awareness training, and forensic intelligence.

2.2. Behavioural Patterns of Human Attackers

It is important to understand the behaviour of human attackers in order to detect, profile or respond to three different types of cyber threats that could stem from a deliberate human action. With automated attacks, we can predict the next action because it typically follows a fault scripted series of predictable steps and multiple planned paths for the same exploit. In contrast, human attackers have cognitive flexibility and emotional and strategic drivers (Vashishth et al., 2023). Human attackers do reconnaissance of their targets, customize the approach they will use, and adjust their movement depending on the multiple ways they are responded to as their incrementation of movement plan is implemented in real time. When organizations understand the behavioural signatures and psychological traits of human attackers, they can create enhanced and proactive threat detection (Vashishth et al., 2026). Human adversaries typically go through a cycle of reconnaissance, engagement, exploitation, and evasion. In the reconnaissance stage, the adversaries are observing the target environment to collect information about the environment's structure, systems, users, and weaknesses. Reconnaissance methods can be scanning for open ports, analyzing social media accounts of employees, or analyzing open-source metadata on target files. At this point the adversaries are functioning as invisible observers, collect as much intelligence as possible, without any alarms going off. In the engagement and exploitation phase, they interact with the environment or system users, such as if there is a spear-phishing email, impersonating a person of trust, or testing known credentials against the network. Human adversaries will typically test what they can get away with, such as what exists in the environment, and also watch how the environment reacts to them, to avoid creating any alerts. Skilled groups, will use deception and manipulation, both of which are key characteristics of social engineering, to get users to breach their security protocols, or ask users to give up sensitive information. APT groups conduct the lay out their operations by hours of the day, utilize intertwined obfuscation, and exhibit behaviours that suggest team-based collaborative configurations (McIntosh et al., 2024).

3. FORENSIC INTELLIGENCE: CONCEPT AND COMPONENTS

Forensic intelligence is a developing discipline at the intersection of digital forensics and threat intelligence, created to confront the increasing intricacy and human-centric nature of today's cyber threats. Unlike traditional digital forensics, which tends to be reactive and often emphasizes post-incident investigation, forensic intelligence is a proactive use of analysis that allows for anticipating, detecting, and attributing cyberattacks to human groups as shown in figure 2.

Figure 2. Forensic Intelligence: Core Components and Integration

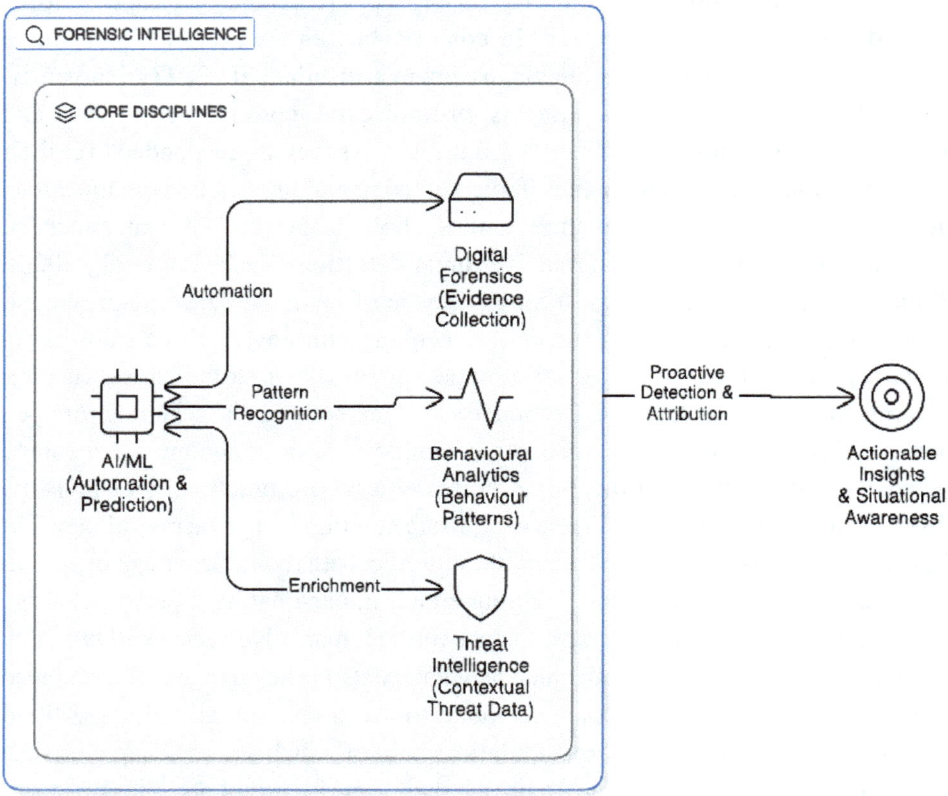

3.1. Core Components

The success of forensic intelligence as a proactive approach to identifying and combating human-driven cyber threats hinges on coherence between the disciplines and each discipline's unique capabilities brought to the forensic intelligence investigation and analysis process. Forensic intelligence uniquely blends the core disciplines of digital forensics, behavioural analytics, threat intelligence, and artificial intelligence/machine learning (AI/ML) into a consolidated approach to detecting, profiling, and attributing complicated cyber incidents. Each of the core disciplines work together to turn raw data into actionable insights, and thus affecting the situational awareness of the cybersecurity landscape.

1. **Digital Forensics:** This is the core block for forensic intelligence. It is the planned collection, preservation, analysis, and examination of digital evidence from various sources such as hard drives, memory dumps, network logs, mobile devices, and cloud environments. The function of digital forensics in a cyber event is to help build timelines for the locations of the event, systems and data failed, follow the digital footprints of the attacker, restore hidden or erased files, and various other pieces of intelligence. Digital forensics is essential to investigations in both the internal and legal arenas and attention is paid to the integrity and admissibility of the evidence (Eltayeb, 2024).
2. **Behavioural Analytics:** Behavioural analytics can analyze patterns of individuals' behaviours, like log-in habits, frequency of access to data, data usage using commands, and paths taken to log-in. This analytical component can identify patterns that identify anomalies from previously established behavioural patterns and can indicate insider threats, compromised accounts, or even malicious changes to data. Moreover, behavioural analytics is instrumental in establishing the normal behaviour continually present in the presence of both anomalous and suspicious behaviour; and in high noise complex environments the distinction of both becomes much more of a challenge.
3. **Threat Intelligence:** Threat intelligence consists of contextual information on both known and emerging threats, attacker TTPs (tactics, techniques, procedures), IOCs (indicators of compromise), and threat group profiles. Threat intelligence is used by forensic analysts to correlate evidence collected with known threat incidents in the real world so that evidence can be attributed with more speed and understanding on the intent of the group. It focuses on strategic intelligence (long term trends and motivations), operational intelligence (current events/processes of campaigns and behaviours), and tactical intelligence (known tools and IOCs). It should improve the relevance and value of forensic investigation.
4. **Artificial Intelligence/Machine Learning (AI/ML):** The disciplines of Artificial Intelligence and Machine Learning assist and supplement the functions of forensic intelligence, encompassing automated data analysis, pattern recognition, and tracking of threats on a scale. These technologies help discern attack vectors previously unknown, aggregate data of similar incidences, generate a prediction on the movements of attackers, prioritize alerts based on risks to the entities, etc.

AI/ML affords enormous value where there are in existence copious quantities of security data, causing analysts to dampen blueprint noise, concentrating on large incidents, enhance their incident response times, etc. Additionally, these models learn over time, whereby the adaptability of the model allows it to grow and better (Lodhi and Kassem, 2024).

3.2. Role of AI in Enabling Forensic Intelligence

Artificial Intelligence (AI) plays a significant role in transforming forensic intelligence, since it enhances and strengthens traditional methods of analysis, it permits faster, deeper, and more accurate analysis of complex cyber incidents. Attacks generated and executed by human guided threats are continually applying more pressure to today' s systems, resulting in malignant acts, which require modes of analysis to be applied on a forensic basis. The traditional methods of forensic analysis cannot cope with the vastness, speed and intricacies relating to detection and analysis of human guided attacks. This is one of the areas where AI has a great advantage, in that it achieves information at a speed, comprehensiveness, and it brings to life latent patterns, as well as providing intuitive and actionable insights that analysts may miss due to time pressures in the analysis. The ability to embed AI into a particular forensic intelligence framework can have a positive impact on investigations and efforts to prevent or counter new emergent threats. One of the most significant uses of AI in forensic intelligence will be in automating the data analysis process. Cyber incidents generate huge quantities of unstructured data, i.e. logs, packets, system events, access data, and user activity around data which is not amenable for intensive scrutiny by humans. AI systems can automatically analyze and correlate these datasets faster than human analysts cannot, to flag anomalies, find indicators of compromise (IOCs), and build a timeline of the attack with little human analysis. This not only provides a faster incident response, but also reduces the chance that an investigator will miss a subtle but important piece in the digital evidence. AI also has potential in behavioural profiling and anomaly detection because it can learn the normal behavior patterns of the users, the systems, and the network traffic over time. This could assist the forensic investigator to establish relationships between different incidences, as they seek linkages to threat groups and campaigns (Aziz et al., 2024).

4. PROFILING CYBERCRIMINALS: METHODS AND TOOLS

The profiling of cybercriminals is the process of systematically discovering, classifying, and interpreting the behavioural, technical, and psychological characteristics of individuals or groups that conduct cyber-attacks. Whereas automated malware or opportunistic attacks are unintentional threats that take advantage of an opportunity, threats originating from humans are intentional, targeted, and planned.

4.1. Behavioural Profiling of Cyber Groups

Behavioural profiling of cyber groups is an important part of forensic intelligence that aims to identify and understand threat groups based on their behaviours, habits, mental processes, and operational techniques within a digital context. Behaviour profiling does not look at pure signature detection or technical forensics Specifically, it looks at how a person behaves, how they make decisions rather than simply what they do. This is very useful for identifying persistent human-driven threats (i.e. insider threats, social engineering, advanced persistent threats) that tend to evade the traditional detection mechanism by pretending to be legitimate users or adapt over time. The main objective of behavioural profiling is to review the tactics, techniques, and procedures (TTPs) used by attackers at different stages of the cyber kill chain - including how they gain initial access, then escalate, move laterally and exfiltrate data. For example, a sophistically cybercriminal may have a penchant for phishing attacks as an intrusion vector, other cybercriminals may prefer shortcomings in a cloud service, while even others may prefer brute force attacks. Not only can these choices speak to the attacker's level of technical ability, but also to their preferred approach and strategic objectives. In cases where we can associate behaviours across incidents, we can comparatively use common behaviours to categorise attacks likely perpetrated by the same person or group, even if the tools are different. Another aspect of behavioural profiling is the time component. For various reasons, many cyber groups are tied to certain time zones suggesting an area they may operate from. Some cyber groups will only act during regular hours blending in to practises of normal activity, whereas others may act during holidays or off-hours aiming for a vulnerability in security monitoring. Time of action, when coupled with logs and other usage details can reveal strong contextual evidence about the areas they operate from and their operating habits. In insider threat detection, behavioural profiling can include variance from expected user behaviours. Similarly, behaviour relating to word use, interface preferences, selection of tools, and errors in technique like a floating tendency to typo commands or repeat a number of attempts at a type of technique will also point to psychological traits (skill level, patience, adaptability). In this sense, the behaviours represent a sort of "fingerprint" that can be useful when relating to attribution and a tool for pre-emptive defence (Rabzelj et al., 2023).

4.2. Psychological and Sociotechnical Profiling

Psychological and sociotechnical profiling looks deeper into the thinking, motivations, and contexts of cybercriminal behaviours. Behavioural profiling examines how cybercriminals act while looking at psychological and sociotechnical profiling provides understanding regarding why threat groups act that way. It also looks at personality, cognitive types, emotional triggers, ideology, and the sociotechnical context in which these groups operate.

1. **Psychological profiling:** It is all about investigating the internal motivations of the cybercriminal such as greed, revenge, ideology, thrill-seeking, or recognition. For instance, if an insider engages in data theft or sabotage based on their perceived injustice with the organization, that is an expression of revenge. Again, state-sponsored hackers or hacktivists, may act upon political or ideological beliefs against certain organizations or nation-states to support a cause. Profiling assists in determining the suspect based on motivations as well as the nature of the target and attack types that are acquired. The other dimension of psychological profiling is assessing the personalities involved based upon personality characteristics that include degree of risk tolerance, attention to detail, and persistence and decision-making skills.
2. **Sociotechnical Profiling:** The individual as relative to the greater world of technology, social aspects, and culture is the key determinant. This includes the technical tools that are available to them, whether or not they are involved in social media groups or have a set of contacts in the cybercriminal arena, the ideologies that they are aware of, as well as whether they are employed and the socioeconomic conditions. For example, where the economic opportunity is remote but the levels of technical education are high, they are more apt to be financially oriented by the nature of their criminality. Sociotechnical profiling also lends itself to the understanding of social engineering techniques employed by the cybercriminal in manipulating effects, revealing how those actors are assessing and taking advantage of the weaknesses of their victims. Such findings lead to a better understanding of how user awareness training etc. applied to defensive design helps in the interception of phishing, pretexting and baiting attacks (Gelman et al., 2024).

For example, in one forensic case, a threat actor culpable for revenge became involved with technical means, employing criminal intent through awareness of social networks, utilizing those to circumstantially place information, relative to their former employers creating public image harm through awareness of political entities, of favourable connections with social media. Here, sociotechnical profiling led to the correlation of postings, login time behaviours, malware codes and led to the attribution to a known insider.

4.3. OSINT (Open-Source Intelligence) and SOCMINT (Social Media Intelligence)

OSINT and SOCMINT are enormously useful methodologies for theorizing and pinpointing cyber-attacks of human origin. Their entire premise is the systematic collection of publicly-available data which is analysed giving intelligent actionable information about cyber threat groups, their motives, and their modus operation.

1. **OSINT:** This term refers to the gathering of information from publicly available sources like news articles, blogs, technical forums, public code repositories, domain registrations, leaked databases, and sourced satellite images. In software engineering, cyber security and digital forensics, OSINT makes it possible for investigators to collect background information on suspects, follow digital assets like domain names and IP addresses, catalogue linked threat groups on hacking forums, and track whether a suspect has previous involvement in a cyber incident. For example, if the malware used in an attack matches malware discussed in a forum, OSINT tools can help connect the forum user to a known alias or real name which helps ensure accurate attribution. OSINT can also be used to preempt incident involvement as threat detection. Investigators can use OSINT to characterize hacker channels, or the darknet markets and paste sites where threat groups often release stolen credentials or boast of exploits.
2. **SOCMINT:** A specific type of OSINT centred on intelligence collected from social websites like Facebook, Twitter (X), Instagram, Reddit, or Telegram. Cyber criminals and those who are considered an insider threat often exhibit some level of intent, behaviour changes, or operational details with social media—on purpose or by accident. Take for example an employee who is unhappy with their current work situation—they might demonstrate this through social media posts with dissatisfaction or related behaviours of revenge or vendetta-like tendencies! Hacktivist groups posting about their upcoming leak or campaign will provide cues about timing, targets, or methods. SOCMINT has the power to facilitate insights about the attacker's social network using sentiment analysis, keyword tracking, geolocation tag tracking, and social graph analysis, that help to trace the movements of potential attackers and an understanding of their influence/reach.

The result is thus an elegant union between OSINT and SOCMINT which gives a complete profile for the forensic investigation of an attacker which both yield technical indicators of compromise (IOCs), but their complementary behavioural and contextual signifiers. This hybrid intelligence will yield rewards for investigations of concerns such as phishing, ransom ware, or spurious disinformation operations.

4.4. Use of Machine Learning and Pattern Recognition

The use of machine learning (ML) and recognitive solutions are essential for forensic intelligence and detection, profiling, predicting of cyber threats of human origin. . These are scalable and adjustable solutions which are capable of analyzing huge amounts of data quickly, detecting unusual habit patterns in attacker behavior, which will improve both the speed and accuracy of cyber investigations. Some of the uses of machine learning are prefaced.

1. **Anomaly Detection in User Behavior:** Machine learning has a significant role in identifying anomalies in user behaviour that indicate potential human threats. This role consists of analyzing an extensive amount of log data to detect anomalous actions that deviate from expected actions of users. For example, if an employee accesses sensitive data in the middle of the night or massively downloads files, machine learning algorithms can indicate that this is worth further investigation, which is an example of detecting insider threat early.
2. **Classification of Malicious and Benign Activities:** Malignant activities, and benign activities, are categorized based on the historical attack data in ML at a high level. Using supervised learning techniques, a labelled dataset is the training data, which serves as the historical data. The models learn the differences between benign operations and malignant operations, i.e., attacks we do not see, phishing attempts, malware, etc. The classification, using machine learning, enables the system to be trained to auto classify the malignant activities/benign activities, with a high degree of accuracy, and enable response to an event without human intervention or oversight (Voigt et al., 2024).
3. **Discovery of Unknown Threats and Zero-Day Attacks:** Unsupervised learning combines clustering and anomaly detection models to identify previously undiscovered cyber threat. When looking at raw unlabelled data, these models group similar patterns and will draw attention to abnormal activities that may be a zero-day attack or some kind of new threat technique. The investigations based on this proactive threat hunting model will surely make identifying occurring cybercriminal's threat tactics that are emerging out much sooner (Yulianto et al., 2024).
4. **Threat Group Correlation across Multiple Data Sources:** Machine learning allows some correlate disparate information sources such as endpoint devices, network traffic logs, forensic logs, even if they exist on the dark web or the deep

web or extract information from social media. Therefore, forensic investigators will have the power of aggregating and triangulating multidimensional data for each threat group, making it easier for investigator's to be able to create better characterizations of each threat group.

These individual applications bring together how pattern recognition, and multiple uses of machine learning, help to better solidify it's a requirement and fundamentally work out that this is forensic intelligence, and other software is being integrated as we portray all of the human-driven cyber-threats faster, smarter, and effectively.

5. DIGITAL FORENSICS FRAMEWORK FOR HUMAN-CENTRIC ATTACKS

The continuous evolution of cyber threats has rendered imperative the establishment of a digital forensics' framework for human based attacks which is indispensable in understanding, mitigating, and preventing security incidents which stem from human behaviour. A practical digital forensics framework for human based attacks synthesises the technological, behavioural, and psychological factors which trace behaviour, identify persons, and acquire digital evidence and renders that evidence reasonable and acceptable from both legal or organizational perspective.

5.1. Evidence Collection and Preservation

Evidence collection and retention provide the bedrock for a digital forensic investigation particularly pertinent to human based cyber threats where purposeful acts may generate complex traces. The integrity, authenticity and admissibility of digital evidence depend on the method in which it is collected, retained, and documented. Human based cyber incidents such as insider data theft, social engineering and misuse of access privileges require careful pre-planned handling of the incidents to ensure that the digital effluvia neither change nor are discarded. The first stage in the evidence collection process lies in identifying and securing potential sources of digital data. Potential sources include but are not limited to server, end-use and third-party log files, emails, file access, web browsing histories and session and other digital activity related meta data. In cases where there is an extensive network-based breach element, packet captures (PCAPS), alerts from an Intrusion Detection System (IDS) and firewall logs will be the critical digital evidence. Analysts have a limited window of time to prevent the destruction or alteration of evidence, particularly when dealing with insider threats or ongoing attacks. Once the initial step has occurred, the next phase is acquisition, or creating forensic images of the impacted systems, using tools like FTK Imager, EnCase, or Autopsy. These tools will ensure that a bit-by-bit copy of the storage media is created without modifying the original, and hash values (e.g., MD5 or SHA-256) will be calculated to ensure that the integrity of the copied data is confirmable throughout the investigation process. Furthermore, documentation provides a basis for ensuring findings to be presented in a court of law or as part of some internal disciplinary hearing (Rawat et al., 2025).

5.2. Log and Metadata Analysis

Log and metadata analysis is integral to investigations of human tenure threats (i.e., human-driven threats) because they provide the richest context around user behavior, system activity, and activities indicative of compromise. Logs are the digital tracks left behind by legitimate users and bad groups alike. Logs, produced by the operating system, application, server, network device, or security appliance, essentially "log" the events that a user or entity has taken, such as login attempts, file accesses, privilege escalations, software installations, and network communications. When we aggregate log entries over time or by user ID, we can see patterns of unauthorized behaviours over time, as well as the temporal aspect of an event, and understand the user account or user associated with the bad activity. Logs and metadata both contain vital context around aberrant HT activity. If logs chronicle user actions; then we say that metadata represents context around a given digital artifact (including creation time, digital origin, file access history, and ownership information) that is not present in the contents themselves. In this regard, metadata could provide information about the individual and/or IP address that sent an email, path taken by the mail server, or the creation time. Understanding the metadata content allows investigators to rule in or rule out the actual source of a phishing attempt or insider leak. They can also build a better timeline for human-oriented attacks by recovering log files and metadata in sequence for behavior reconstruction.

5.3. Network Traffic and Endpoint Monitoring

Traffic monitoring and endpoint monitoring are important components of forensic investigations into human-driven cyber threats. Traffic monitoring and endpoint monitoring provide investigators with visibility into organizational data flow and individual device behaviours to allow forensic analysts to discover, track and understand malicious actions while they happen or after the incident. Traffic monitoring refers to the observation of and analysis of data packets traveling across the organization's network in a constant, ongoing manner. During traffic monitoring, investigators may observe unusual communication patterns such as anomalous or unexpected outbound connections, large amounts of data transferred to external servers that are not known or confirmed, and network traffic directed toward domains or IP addresses that the investigator has already determined to be non-good. Investigators see this type of flow data in human-driven attacks such as phishing and insider threats, where human beings typically will slowly exfiltrate data (e.g., files) from an organizational system, or establish a command-and-control (C2) connection and maintain any level of persistence to return to the compromised host or system. EDR allows investigators to understand the behavior of the compromise, and better move to map out the attack path and trace back to the communication endpoints and compromised assets. Endpoint monitoring requires monitoring and analyzing user devices, such as desktops, laptops, or phones. Many advanced monitoring tools now operate a menace intelligence feed and a behavioural baseline, allowing it to identify anomalies from regular operations that might point to human involvement- a suspicious increase in network activity from a specific endpoint or lateral movement across several hosts (Rojas et al., 2024).

Table 1. Summary of Key Stages in the Digital Forensics Framework

Stage	Objective	Key Tools / Techniques	Outcome / Deliverable
Evidence Collection and Preservation	To securely acquire and preserve digital data without altering its integrity.	FTK Imager, EnCase, Autopsy, BitLocker imaging tools.	Verified digital copies and hash-validated storage of evidence.
Log and Metadata Analysis	To identify behavioural anomalies and correlate system, user, and application activity.	ELK Stack, Splunk, SIEM systems, metadata extraction tools.	Detection of suspicious activity patterns and correlation of events.
Network Traffic and Endpoint Monitoring	To detect and trace malicious activity, data exfiltration, and lateral movements.	Wireshark, Zeek, Suricata, EDR systems (CrowdStrike, SentinelOne).	Identification of attack paths and compromised devices.
Behavioural Correlation and Profiling	To map attacker behaviour and intent using digital footprints and activity patterns.	Behavioural analytics engines, AI/ML anomaly detection models.	Attacker behavioural signature and motive profiling.

Table 1. summarizes the key stages in the digital forensics framework for human-centric attacks, outlining objectives, representative tools, and resulting outcomes at each stage, from evidence collection to attribution and reporting.

6. INVESTIGATIVE TECHNIQUES AND CORRELATION STRATEGIES

Investigatory techniques and correlational methods/models form the foundation for discovering the full extent of human-based cyberattacks and allow cybersecurity professionals to collate unrelated pieces of digital evidence and create a single construct.

6.1. Mapping Digital Clues to Attacker Behaviour

Analyzing digital clues against attacker behaviours helps provide insights into human groups associated with cyber intrusions. The idea in both cases is to put multiple technical artifacts that were recorded/sourced, which on their own appear as isolated, in relation to a human behavioural trait or tactical decision-making process exhibited by cyber-attackers. The day job is to not just answer what happened, but more importantly, answer why something happened, and who may be associated, based on how the digital breadcrumbs lay out. In the example of one foreign IP accessing a VPN, there began to be activity of repeated failed logins which were followed by a successful login around 4:00 a.m., the suspected result of a 'brute force' attack with credential theft. If this began with someone initial demonstrating lateral movement to sensitive directories, exfiltrating to a cloud-share external repository, while would definitely infer a degree of decision making related to reconnaissance, this may be also be suggest-hole theft of sensitive data. Forensic investigators also process for persistence such was discovered in the above examples by examining trace suggestions of scheduled tasks or registry alteration. This can also give clues as to how long an attacker was willing to expect to hold persistence access and how (un)observable they wanted to be and increase possibility of rating the ability of experience and threat it represented. Also informative was providing observations of examples where persistence error was tracked and attributed to user identity trail such deleting logs, obfuscation of activity via encrypted tunnels, as it would suggest some analogy of extended cognitive delayed gratification and a knowing that their badness was higher risk.

6.2. Timeline Reconstruction and Chain-of-Custody

When conducting a digital forensic investigation, the two important areas of emphasis are timeline reconstruction and chain-of-custody. Each is a fundamental aspect of a digital forensic investigation and both are especially relevant in human-initiated cyber threat incidents. The purpose they serve is to build a timeline of events while also showing that the digital evidence is credible, legally admissible, and uncontaminated during the forensic investigation. The timeline reconstruction phase results in the reconstruction of the sequence of digital events leading up to, during, and after the cyber incident. Timeline reconstruction uses data from the original system's journal logs, access records, and network packets; file timestamps from files relating to the compromise; web browser history and cached files; and possibly memory dumps or disk snapshots. The job of a forensic analyst is to establish the timeline for determining, among other things, when the attack occurred, how the attacker moved through the compromised system, and if able, what data was compromised during the attack. An example of the timeline reconstruction would be to correlate the user's access at 2:13 a.m. with the execution of suspicious script at 2:15 a.m., then outbound data transfer at 2:17 a.m. and one could show unauthorized activity occurring. Timelines are extremely important in highlighting legitimate or administrative actions taken by LDAP system administrators, compared to nefarious actions made by criminals, posing as regular operational activity. A proper chain-of-custody is critical in establishing if evidence has been altered or tampered with, or if it has been contaminated, otherwise, you put the investigation at risk and lack the ability to use it legally. These two processes are closely related. While establishing the timeline sketch establishes the what and when of an incident, a chain-of-custody establishes the how of evidence collection methods. Many forensic tools perform the majority of the timeline creation as part of the evidence collection process. Also, many forensic tools keep the chain-of-custody secure either by providing a tamper-evident log or some access log. Investigators not doing the timeline risk missing valuable clues, and if you don't have a proper chain-of-custody, no matter how compelling the evidence is, it will not hold up legally (Vashishth et al., 2025).

6.3. Attribution Techniques for Identifying Attackers

Attribution in cybersecurity refers to identifying the individual, group, or nation state responsible for a malicious cyberattack. This step is also one of the more complex and important parts to cyber investigations, especially involving human based attacks, which there is a broad range of motivations, methods, and footprints for attribution analysis. For attribution the techniques used are a combination of technical intelligence, behavioural intelligence, and contextual intelligence, with the aim to reasonably attribute the attack to a group shown in figure 3. For example, one basic technique of attribution would be using the IP address traceback technique, which consists of tracing hostile traffic or command-and-control communication from the endpoint back to its origin. While attackers often use proxy servers, VPNs, and bots to disguise the origin of attacks, forensic analysts can often identify patterns of use, shared IP addresses, or breach misconfigurations that eventually lead to the specific group behind the attack. Examining how malware from an incident is compared against known repositories, or databases (like VirusTotal or MITRE ATT&CK), can help facilitate connections to known threat groups, particularly Advanced Persistent Threats (APTs). Along with the above process, behavioural and linguistic analysis helps tie data back to an attribution. Analysts not only look for commonalities in code comments, but they look at the sort of communication language used in phishing emails, and they even examine documented times of the attacks – to deduce what specific hours the groups conducted the attack.

Figure 3. Attribution Techniques in Cyber World

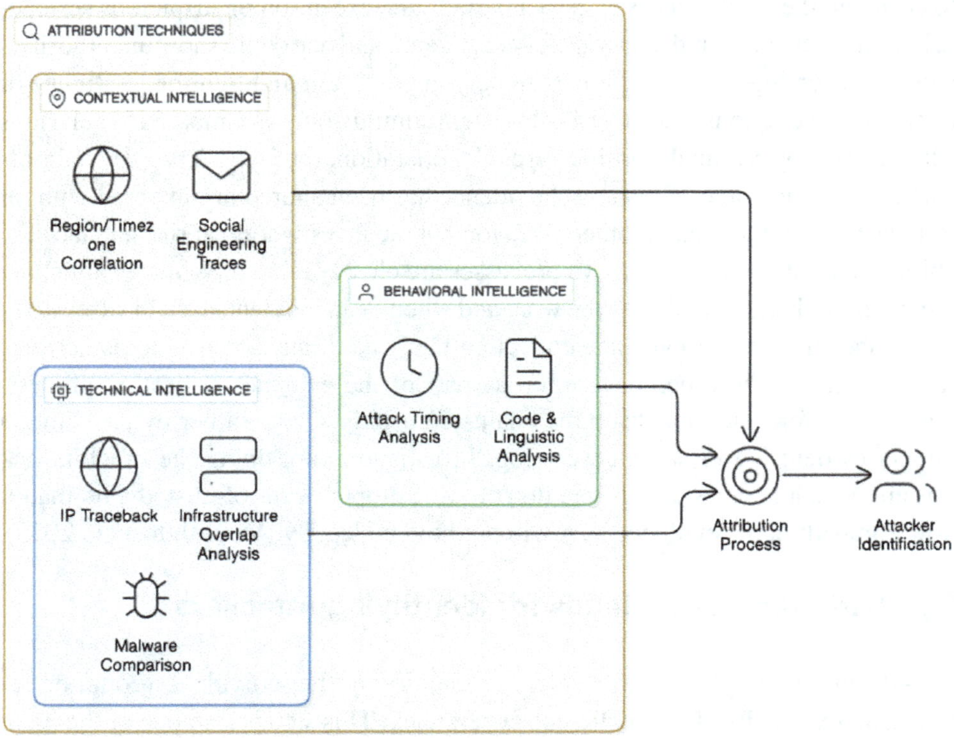

7. REAL-WORLD CASE STUDIES

Current case studies offer critical fire power in understanding how, why and the effects of human launched cyberattacks, and show that forensic intelligence can be of great aid in attacking, identifying, and frustrating these efforts. It is by studying known and documented cyberattacks that behavior patterns relative to the techniques of attack and a knowledge of how well the forensic means can be carried out and the knowledge of the lessons learned, which in turn can better prepare the forces involved for future problems of this nature with regard to conclusions and the effects of the same.

7.1. Case Study 1: Insider Data Exfiltration in a Financial Institution

In this case study, a large institutional bank experienced a data breach approximately 12 months after a trusted employee stole sensitive information on their customers and clients. The insider, a mid-level IT administrator who received a company sponsored education that paid for their college tuition, exploited their privileged access, took advantage of their knowledge of internal systems to avoid detection protocols, and transferred customer data to an external cloud storage site overnight over the course of several months. The insider transferred client information including personally identifiable information, transaction logs, and company strategy papers outside an approved framework. The bank initiated an internal review process after anomalous data access logs were revealed in internal audit logs through the internal automated tracking system that indicated off-hours (often outside their required hours) data access to files that were not part of their job description. Forensic investigators consulted with IT security and began a thorough investigation of the system access logs, network logs, and data access logs. They used log correlation tools and endpoint detection systems to reverse engineer the attack. They found the employee had used remote desktop software programs, encrypted USB devices, and cloud-based storage solutions to exfiltrate data. The technique most important in reconstructing the exfiltration timeline was a forensics tool that utilized metadata analysis and specific point of time activity. Investigators then also employed behavioural analytics tools as a means of comparing usage or activity by the employee and benchmarking it against normal usage or activity profiles and found some definite anomalies and other activity which clearly compromised safety and documented efforts made by the employee to eliminate their digital fingerprints.

7.2. Case Study 2: Nation-State APT Attack on Critical Infrastructure

The intent of the aggressors was to disrupt the national distribution of power by gaining access to the SCADA systems (Supervisory Control and Data Acquisition) of one of the large utility providers. This operation extended over a time period of many months with very carefully coordinated operations relative to the phishing, privilege escalation, lateral movements, and custom malware used. At the point where access was accomplished, the aggressors then used the credentials of the victim to move laterally across the systems in question, ultimately arriving at the control network segments which contained the elements controlling the real time grid operations. The aggressors installed malware which allowed them to give unsanctioned orders to the circuit breakers and relays whereby power could be disrupted in large regions of the U. S. The first on-site investigation was undertaken across a multi-stage program by digital forensic teams and national cyber security agencies to conduct a forensic examination of their networks involving network traffic analysis, memory dumps, and malware reverse engineering. The malware included a sophisticated plethora of components designed to disable safety systems and hide malware from monitoring software. They organised attack timelines providing details of the attack process we reconstructed and ultimately identified several phases to the attack related to a fully documented APT group and its clearly defined TTPs (tactics techniques and procedures) associated with a hostile nation state. Attribution techniques involving analytical techniques for coding based on language structure, IP origin and reuse of infrastructure provided for appropriate attribution of the campaign to a known threat group. In conclusion, this case showed how critical infrastructure was susceptible to state-sponsored cyber operations and demonstrated the necessity for cross-sector co-operation and collaboration with regard to the sharing of intelligence across sectors. This case also demonstrated the need for forensic readiness which comprises logging, EDR (endpoint detection and response) and continuous behaviour monitoring solutions pre-deployment. The incident accelerated reforms regarding cyber security governance for the critical sectors including regular threat simulation, employee awareness related to cyber risk, and the use of AI intrusion detection systems for future guard against and determination of more advanced attacks as this one.

8. CHALLENGES IN PROFILING AND INVESTIGATION

Profiling and investigating human-directed cyber threats, present many challenges, because of the changing levels of attack vector complexity, sophistication of threat group, and constantly changing digital environments. Some of the key challenges are:

1. **Complexity of Human Behavior:** Human directed threats are ultimately unpredictable because the attackers' motives and behaviour are shaped by psychological and sociocultural groups. Human attackers have the ability to be unpredictable, e adapt, improvise, and adjust their tactics at any point during an attack, rendering profiling difficult for human attackers because their behaviour is likely to not follow a repeatable pattern or observable trend.

2. **Insider Threats and Trust Exploitation:** Inside attacks are different because they happen inside the trusted environments. Employees, or partners can use their permitted access to steal data or harm systems. It is difficult to separate any malicious activities from accepted behaviours as insiders operate in legitimate areas of activity. People analysing this have to have the relevant context and, at times, sophisticated behavioural analysis tools.
3. **Lack of Unified Data Sources:** Inconsistent or siloed data often affects investigators as they attempt to gather forensic evidence from a number of disparate sources. Investigators are required to pull evidence together from logs, emails, social media, access and more. When the sources of information are separate, inaccuracies in reconstruction can occur and overall profiles may be inaccurate as behavioural patterns are unable to be accurately determined.
4. **Attribution Complexity:** Every time an attack or incident happens that may involve the identification of the person or group responsible, some measure of human intelligence is required along with technical intelligence. Attackers regularly include false flags within their exploitation, or they'll replicate a known group to trick investigators. Intentional ambiguity increases confusion for investigators and increases the likelihood that an attacker will be considered a legal threat under the wrong attribution - with both legal repercussions and political fallout.
5. **Legal and Ethical Issues:** Profiling will require access to some potentially sensitive information on individuals and we will mention how privacy issues arise; how important it is to be aware of data protection issues. The difficulty in this process will be carried out in a thorough analysis or should be against legal and ethical standards and obligations such as GPDR in order to decide on a legitimate defence. Legal and ethical requirements can be constraining on surveillance activities or retention of data.

9. EMERGING TRENDS AND FUTURE DIRECTIONS

The trends referred to already in the movement towards more intelligent and integrated and anticipatory forensic intelligence which is cyber in nature relates to something other than the technical evolution to something which is more concerned with ethical governance and global interdependency.

1. **Integration of AI and Behavioural Analytics:** One of the major emerging trends in cyber forensic intelligence is the use of artificial intelligence (AI) and machine learning (ML) to develop profiles based on the indicative behaviour of the attackers which is applied. AI and ML can cope with large databases, deter-

mine strange actions, and predict future actions predicated on previous actions. The ongoing development of the AI models will in a short time enable near real time profiling of cybercriminals more effectually with less false positives than heretofore been the case (Breitinger and Jotterand, 2023).

2. **Expanding Threat Intelligence Sharing:** The amount of collaborative platforms for real time threat intelligence sharing continues to expand across companies, sectors, and governments. There are important roles for this trend to continue to develop, including the collaborations to reduce the time to discovery of the attackers, create a consistent pattern of their tactics, and ultimately diminish the global spread of cybercrime. The future directions will continue centring on an automated disclosure trust-based ecosystem that integrates with blockchain to give tamperproof intelligence exchange.
3. **Zero Trust and Identity-Centric Security Models:** Many of the forensic methodologies are borne of the more current adoption of zero trust, wherein no user or device is trusted by default. As profiling becomes more and more important there will be a shift of the focus onto continuous authentication, user identity verification and baseline specific behaviours that might show user anomalies in real time and inform of the investigation. The future investigations may focus on the identification of possibly compromised identities using identity-centred telemetry, as well as the permissions and access control mechanisms adapting to user behaviour.
4. **Forensic Readiness by Design:** Organizations are beginning to build in the forensic readiness in design of systems. This means that not only do organizations specify the evidence collection capability but that it also includes different types of activity logging, attack traceability capability within architecture design of IT systems. In the future organizations will be required more to forensic preparedness to comply and mitigate risk (Shahani and Rafique, 2025).
5. **Ethical and Legal Evolution:** As cyber forensic tools become ever more powerful and invasive, ethical, and legal frameworks will increasingly define how we will develop and deploy such tools. Future trends may include the establishment of global ethical principles to the forensic intelligence space, clearly defined laws around digital privacy, and frameworks that describe responsible AI use when profiling subjects and in the investigation process.

10. CONCLUSION

The evolution of human-attacked cyber threats calls for a productive and multifaceted approach to incident response, cybersecurity, and digital forensics. This chapter has examined the fundamental nature and types of human-based attacks and emphasised the importance of understanding the attacker as a person, their motives, and behavioural traits, as well as decision-making through formal and informal profiling methods. With information from forensic intelligence through the application of AI, behavioural analytics and open-source intelligence investigators can formally ascribe threats, map behaviours, and attributes. Digital forensics frameworks facilitate this as they encapsulate evidence acquisition, network and endpoint monitoring, metadata retention, and memory forensics, enabling investigators to call upon timelines, document sequence of behaviours, and provide unimpeachable chains of custody. Real-world case studies demonstrate the application of investigatory tools, strategies, and techniques for suitably responding to insider threat and nation-state attacks. The case studies also illustrate enduring gaps for groups that challenge attribution, admissibility of evidence, and ethical languages for requestor or mandate. The growing complexity of tactics used by cybercriminals points toward productive areas for further work in predictive forensics, AI-based profiling of people, and global cooperation on international expectations for threat intelligence sharing, whilst managing ethical and legal ramifications.

REFERENCES

Aburub, F., & Almomani, A. (2025). Data-Driven Cyber Defense Leveraging Business Intelligence. In Complexities and Challenges for Securing Digital Assets and Infrastructure (pp. 457-482). IGI Global Scientific Publishing. DOI: 10.4018/979-8-3373-1370-2.ch020

Aljumaiah, O., Jiang, W., Addula, S. R., & Almaiah, M. A. (2025). Analyzing cybersecurity risks and threats in IT infrastructure based on NIST framework. *J. Cyber Secur. Risk Audit*, *2025*(2), 12–26. DOI: 10.63180/jcsra.thestap.2025.2.2

Aziz, M. T., Mahmud, T., Datta, N., Maskat Sharif, M., Khan, N. U. A., Yasmin, S., . . . Andersson, K. (2024, March). A state-of-the-art review of machine learning in cybersecurity data science. In International Conference on Innovations in Cybersecurity and Data Science Proceedings of ICICDS (pp. 791-806). Singapore: Springer Nature Singapore. DOI: 10.1007/978-981-97-5791-6_57

Binbeshr, F., Imam, M., Ghaleb, M., Hamdan, M., Rahim, M. A., & Hammoudeh, M. (2025). The Rise of Cognitive SOCs: A Systematic Literature Review on AI Approaches. *IEEE Open Journal of the Computer Society*, *6*, 360–379. DOI: 10.1109/OJCS.2025.3536800

Breitinger, F., & Jotterand, A. (2023). Sharing datasets for digital forensic: A novel taxonomy and legal concerns. *Forensic Science International Digital Investigation*, *45*, 301562. DOI: 10.1016/j.fsidi.2023.301562

Eltayeb, O. (2024). The Crucial Significance of Cyber Threat Intelligence in Mitigating Cyber Attacks. *Journal of Ecohumanism*, *3*(4), 2422–2434. DOI: 10.62754/joe.v3i4.3767

Gelman, H., Hastings, J. D., Kenley, D., & Loiacono, E. (2024, December). Toward an Insider Threat Education Platform: A Theoretical Literature Review. In 2024 International Conference on Computer and Applications (ICCA) (pp. 01-06). IEEE. DOI: 10.1109/ICCA62237.2024.10928083

Lodhi, K., & Kassem, M. A. (2024). Revolutionizing forensic science: the role of artificial intelligence and machine learning. International Journal of Data Science, 10-18.

McIntosh, T. R., Susnjak, T., Liu, T., Watters, P., Ng, A., & Halgamuge, M. N. (2024). A game-theoretic approach to containing artificial general intelligence: Insights from highly autonomous aggressive malware. *IEEE Transactions on Artificial Intelligence*, *5*(12), 6290–6303. DOI: 10.1109/TAI.2024.3394392

Mohamed, N. (2025). Artificial intelligence and machine learning in cybersecurity: A deep dive into state-of-the-art techniques and future paradigms. *Knowledge and Information Systems*, *67*(8), 1–87. DOI: 10.1007/s10115-025-02429-y

Rabzelj, M., Bohak, C., Južnič, L. Š., Kos, A., & Sedlar, U. (2023). Cyberattack graph modeling for visual analytics. *IEEE Access : Practical Innovations, Open Solutions*, *11*, 86910–86944. DOI: 10.1109/ACCESS.2023.3304640

Rawat, R., Borana, K., Gupta, S., Ingle, M., Dibouliya, A., Bhardwaj, P., & Rawat, A. (2025). Enhancing OSN Security: Detecting Email Hijacking and DNS Spoofing Using Energy Consumption and Opcode Sequence Analysis. *Informatica (Vilnius)*, *49*(2).

Rojas, L., Sánchez, A. G., Cruz, P. A., Mendoza, C. B., Vander Peterson, C., Gómez, D. F., & Vargas, J. R. (2024). Evaluation of Collective Intelligence Mechanisms for Multi-Stakeholder Cybersecurity Risk Management in Supply Ecosystems.

Shahani, S. A., & Rafique, A. A.Shahbaz Ali ShahaniAdnan Ahmed Rafique. (2025). AI-Driven Cybersecurity Risk Management: Leveraging Machine Learning for Automated Threat Detection, Real-Time Risk Assessment, and Regulatory Compliance Auditing. *Annual Methodological Archive Research Review*, *3*(5), 242–257. DOI: 10.63075/z8wh7360

Sharma, V., Vashishth, T. K., Tiwari, D., Sethi, P., & Sharma, S. (2025, April). Enhancing cybersecurity: A machine learning approach for phishing website detection. In AIP Conference Proceedings (Vol. 3278, No. 1). AIP Publishing. DOI: 10.1063/5.0261903

Vashishth, T. K., Kumar, B., Panwar, R., Kumar, S., & Chaudhary, S. (2023, August). Exploring the Role of Computer Vision in Human Emotion Recognition: A Systematic Review and Meta-Analysis. In 2023 Second, International Conference on Augmented Intelligence and Sustainable Systems (ICAISS) (pp. 1071-1077). IEEE. DOI: 10.1109/ICAISS58487.2023.10250614

Vashishth, T. K., Sharma, V., Samania, B., Sharma, R., Singh, S., & Jajoria, P. (2025). Ethical and Legal Implications of AI in Cybersecurity. In Machine Intelligence Applications in Cyber-Risk Management (pp. 387-414). IGI Global Scientific Publishing.

Vashishth, T. K., Sharma, V., Sharma, M. K., Sharma, R., Sharma, K. K., & Sharma, S. (2026). AI-Driven Threat Detection and Incident Response: Advancing Cybersecurity with Machine Learning. In Improving Threat Detection, Network Security, and Incident Response with AI (pp. 51-82). IGI Global Scientific Publishing.

Voigt, L. L., Freiling, F., & Hargreaves, C. J. (2024). Re-imagen: Generating coherent background activity in synthetic scenario-based forensic datasets using large language models. *Forensic Science International Digital Investigation*, *50*, 301805. DOI: 10.1016/j.fsidi.2024.301805

Yulianto, S., & Ngo, G. N. C. (2024, September). Automated Threat Hunting, Detection, and Threat Actor Profiling Using TIRA. In 2024 International Conference on ICT for Smart Society (ICISS) (pp. 1-7). IEEE.

Chapter 9
Malware Analysis and Attribution in Human Threat Intelligence

S. Manjula
Madanapalle Institute of Technology and Science, India

Amit Karbhari Mogal
https://orcid.org/0009-0008-4183-2264
MVP Samaj's CMCS College, Udoji Maratha Boarding Campus, India

C. S. Sandeep
https://orcid.org/0000-0003-3269-7984
Jawaharlal College of Engineering and Technology, India

L. R. Sujithra
https://orcid.org/0009-0003-9806-268X
Sri Eshwar College of Engineering, India

J. A. Jevin
https://orcid.org/0009-0008-8511-9698
Koneru Lakshmaiah Educational Foundation, India

Sachin Vasant Chaudhari
https://orcid.org/0009-0005-8856-8905
Sanjivani College of Engineering, India

V. Bhoopathy
https://orcid.org/0000-0003-2175-6328
Sree Rama Engineering College, India

ABSTRACT

Increasing numbers of people using online resources without precautions is one of the main reasons hazardous computer apps evolve quickly. These days, Trojan horseback, malware, and worm authors do it for profit rather than fame. So, malware problem Computer security now prioritizes detection. Zero-day malware exploits undiscovered holes without detection. Deep learning models, which can analyze data in several dimensions and uncover features, are an effective threat detection and classification alternative. This chapter examines deep learning-based malware

DOI: 10.4018/979-8-3373-4898-8.ch009

recognition and categorization for zero-day vulnerabilities and attack authentication. While studying model architectures, data sources, evaluation criteria, and real-world applications, we discuss asymmetrical evasion, comprehensibility, and statistical imbalance. The article also explores how graph-based models, self-encoder RNN, and CNN understand unfamiliar virus behaviors.

1. INTRODUCTION

Intentionally damaging the operating system kernel or other security-sensitive applications or data without the user's knowledge or agreement is the goal of malicious software. A wide variety of malicious software exist, including but not limited to computer viruses, worms, and PUP (Bilot et al., 2024). Numerous businesses and individuals across the globe are being impacted by cybercrime that employs this type of software. New assaults on the online have been created by undiscovered varieties of current malware that obscure their activity to elude detection. There have been several harmful activities on the web (Guo, 2023). Because there are no days between an unknown malware's first attack and its discovery, it is referred to as zero-day malware, which means fresh malware. This kind of attack is also known as a zero-day attack (Nikolopoulos & Polenakis, 2017). Static and dynamic analysis is the two primary methodologies to malware detection that are routinely used. In static analysis, features are extracted from a program's binary by using the file's syntax and structural attributes (Venkatraman & Alazab, 2018). In contrast, specific program activities can only be extracted by dynamic analysis of the file that is executed while the program is running.

Theoretically, static analysis benefits from information pertaining to structural qualities, such as sequences of bytes "signatures" and abnormalities in file content, make it faster and more effective than dynamic analysis. Runtime information, such a processor's state, might be used for dynamic analysis through the use of a control flow graph, which may make it more resistant to malware that obfuscates its messages. Several earlier investigations have found that combining the two methods yields superior outcomes. Malware authors use a plethora of metamorphic and polymorphic obfuscation strategies to stay undetected (Aboaoja et al., 2022). Among these methods are a number of approaches that involve inserting dead code, rearranging subroutines, transposing codes, replacing instructions, integrating codes, and reassigning registers (Zahoora et al., 2022). Furthermore, packers make sure that the code can only be examined during runtime by obfuscating the entire program (Malhotra & Bajaj, 2016).

2. UNDERSTANDING ZERO-DAY MALWARE

Android, developed and owned by Google, is widely used, with over 2.5 billion devices running the OS (R. Kumar et al., 2020). This includes wearable, smart phones, and in-car applications. Because of this, effective approaches for detecting Android malware are required since it becomes easier for malware writers to start attacks (Su et al., 2018). Identity theft, financial loss, and the infiltration of sensitive information are just a few of the major issues that might arise when malicious programs manage to infiltrate a device (Kansal, 2025). Threats to the security of pedestrians and drivers can potentially affect Android-powered vehicles equipped with in-car systems or autonomous driving (Nguyen et al., 2018). There are so many applications in the marketplace that it would be impossible to manually check their legitimacy. Attempts at large-scale detection automation using ML methods have been made in earlier research (Pudukotai Dinakarrao et al., 2019). But knowing Android malware inside and out is usually required to manually generate input characteristics for these detectors. Until new malware is found and reverse-engineered, detection features can be improved, leaving them more vulnerable to zero-day attacks (Sayadi et al., 2020). We aim to separate these domain insights from the learning process and input data in this work. When it comes to zero-day vulnerabilities in particular, our methodology is compelling for practical implementation and maintenance. As there is currently no way to prevent this type of attack, the most dangerous kind of malware is known as zero-day—the term for malware that is discovered only before an attack is about to happen. Because of this, cases can arise where an entirely new family of malware has infected Android devices. Lastly, we offer an ensemble learning-based strategy to improve the efficiency of conventional malware detectors, taking into account that present-day HPC barely capture a handful of micro architectural components when they're running. By doing so, they can address the issue of detecting zero-day malware in real-time (Rahman, 2017).

3. MALWARE DISCOVERY PROCEDURES

Malware detection procedures can be broadly classified into two types: mark-based and conduct-based. I think it would be a good idea to examine exam strategies (Agarkar & Ghosh, 2020).

3.1 Static Method

The use of pre-characterized marks is crucial to static malware analysis strategies. Some examples of document fingerprints are static strings, MD5 or SHA1 hashes, file metadata, and so on.

3.2 Dynamic Method

A malware-based strategy that is both dynamic and responsive to changes in the environment is able to classify threats in real time.

4. TYPES OF MALWARE

Malware classification helps shed light on the reasoning and techniques underlying the infection. Depending on its function, malware falls into one of numerous categories. Here are the lessons:

Virus: Here we have the most basic program format. It can be defined as any program that copies itself or alters other programs without the user's knowledge or consent.

Worm: This malicious software closely resembles the virus. Worms, on the other hand, can replicate and spread to other computers across a network.

Trojan: The malicious software that masquerades as legitimate software falls under this category. This course's principal infection vector is social engineering, which involves convincing consumers that they are downloading legitimate software.

Adware: This particular kind of virus is just designed to display adverts on infected computers. Adware is often considered a kind of spyware, and it's quite improbable that it will cause significant damage.

Spyware: It is a good word for the malicious software that plagues espionage operations. Spyware often records your online activities and searches in order to display targeted ads and then sells this information to other parties.

Root kit: Because of how it works, an attacker can get unauthorized access to the data. One potential use is to grant administrative privileges to an unauthorized user. Root kits are notoriously difficult to identify and remove because they constantly conceal their presence and are often undetectable on the system.

Backdoor: Malware in the form of a backdoor gives hackers an extra, covert entrance to the system. On its own, it doesn't inflict much damage, but it opens up more opportunities for attackers. This is why backdoors are never employed in isolation. In most cases, they are a precursor to other forms of malware.

Key logger: Passwords, credit card details, and other sensitive information can be stored by this type of malware since it records every key the user presses.

Ransom ware: Malicious software like this encrypts all of the user's data and then demands payment in order to decrypt it. Typically, a computer affected by ransom ware is "frozen" since the user is unable to access any files, and the desktop background displays the demands made by the attacker.

Remote Administration Tools: An attacker can access the system and perhaps make changes just like if they were physically there with this form of malware. It seems like it would be easy to explain using the example of Team Viewer, but someone is trying to trick you (Chumachenko & Technology, 2017).

5. MACHINE LEARNING TRADITIONAL APPROACHES

Over the last decade, there has been a proliferation of studies and applications of ML approaches for malware classification and identification. There have been three significant advancements that have contributed to the success and stability of ML techniques.

Figure 1. Taxonomy of features used by traditional M.L approaches.

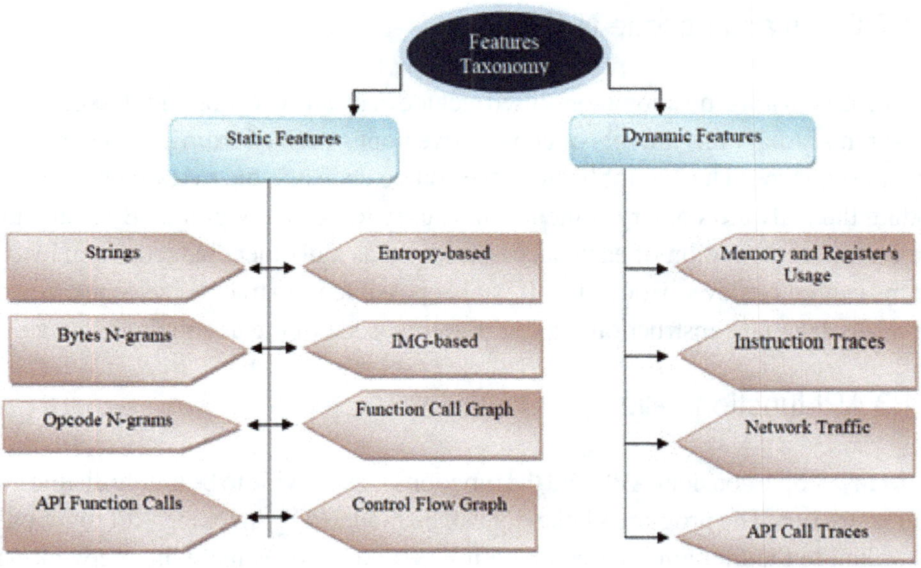

Feature taxonomy is presented in Figure 1. In the same way as different kinds of malware analysis methods fall into two categories, so do the types of features: the first is static features and the second is dynamic features. Listed below are the various feature types (Gibert et al., 2020).

5.1 Static features

Running a program is not necessary to extract static characteristics. The content of the binary executable or the assembly language source file retrieved through disassembly or recompilation is the primary source from which Windows Portable Executable files derive their static attributes. However, these properties are extracted during the disassembly of Android applications' APK.

5.1.1 String analysis

In computer programming, string analysis is extracting all strings that can be printed from an executable. An array of strings representing characters is called a string. Learning a program's inner workings is as easy as searching for strings. These strings might include data like the URLs the program accesses, the paths to files it has viewed or changed the names of application menu items, and much more besides. The Strings program finds ASCII and Unicode strings inside an executable, ignoring context and formatting (Cen et al., 2024).

5.1.2 Bytes and opcode N-Grams

Features that are most commonly used include malware detection and classification. Is n-grams. Anagrams are sets of consecutive nouns derived from a predetermined textual sequence. The assembly language source code and the bytes sequences encoding the malware's binary content can be used to extract N-grams. By analyzing the unique combination of each successive byte as a distinct characteristic, bytes-grams can be retrieved from files. It is also possible to extract these sequences of assembly language instructions from the source code of the assembly language.

5.1.3 API function calls

Many people consider APIs and the functions they provide to be highly distinctive characteristics. The program's behavior can be modeled by invoking API functions, according to the literature. Basic operating system services including networking, security, file management, etc. constitutes the foundation of API functions and system calls. The execution of specific API functions offers crucial information about malware behavior, since program cannot access system resources without them.

5.1.4 Entropy

To conceal the harmful intent of the executables, malware developers frequently use a variety of obfuscation techniques. To hide harmful portions from static analysis, compression and encryption are the two most used methods. As a result, the ability to identify executable files that contain encrypted or compressed code portions is of significant importance to the information security sector. This has made use of entropy analysis, since files with code segments that have been compressed or encrypted typically have higher entropy than the native code. In information theory, the entropy of a bytes sequence represents its statistical variety. If the entropy of the inspected segment is zero, it means that there is precisely one instance of the same character (He et al., 2021).

5.2 Dynamic features

The execution of malicious code allows for the retrieval of dynamic features during runtime. Dynamic analysis involves keeping an eye on the malware and seeing what API functions are triggered or what instructions are performed as it runs or examines the system after the infection has run. Adjustments to variables, memory values, and registers as well as process creation and file/registry manipulation are all laid bare.

5.2.1 Register's usage and Memory

At runtime, the contents of memory might represent the behavior of a program. Differentiating between good and bad programs is as simple as watching the values stored in various registers as the program runs.

5.2.2 Instruction traces

An instruction set called a dynamic instruction trace is called by the CPU as a program executes. With dynamic instruction tracing, unlike static tracing, the programs are executed in the exact order they are defined in the binary file. Since code packers and encrypters are unable to conceal or obstruct the code instructions from static analysis, dynamic traces are more trustworthy than static ones in portraying the program's behavior (Hamid et al., 2023).

5.2.3 API call traces

The Windows API gives developers access to the Windows registry, the ability to start, stop, and create services, and the management of user accounts. Windows also has access to a number of other essential resources, such as file devices, threads, processes, and error handling. As a result, researchers have examined Windows API call logs to learn how malicious programs behave(Barros et al., 2022).

6. TYPES OF DEEP LEARNING

6.1 Malware Detection with Deep Learning Based Method

One subfield of machine learning is the field of artificial intelligence called deep learning, often known as deep neural networks. Such ML methods are an effort to mimic how the human brain learns. The human brain, like any other neural network, is composed of neurones. Axons and dendrites connect every cell in the brain at synapses. Similar to how neurons in the human brain communicate with one another, these ANN connections are designed to transfer weights. Both the real human brain and a model of it created using an artificial neural network are shown in Figure A2 of Appendix B. The most crucial aspect to think about when comparing deep neural networks to regular ones is the quantity of DNN layers. The characteristics of data can be taught to them. The procedure is finished by giving a DL algorithm a big number of samples once feature engineering has learnt the most acceptable features (Rama et al., 2019). Next, the algorithm generates data, sorts it, or returns an identity. DL was utilized by numerous fields due to the large amount of data that needed to be sorted and processed. With the proliferation of the internet, deep networks are finding more and more applications in fields as diverse as healthcare, image processing, speech processing, and cyber security. Figure 2 shows how this domain can be further classified into different sub domains based on its attributes. Every aspect of PE files is important for determining the level of maliciousness in a certain file. The characteristics of the PE file, including its header and imports, are crucial in determining if the file is harmful or not. Utilized LSTM to choose the best PE characteristics. A model based on DL was trained to detect malicious PE files using these ideal attributes (Tayyab et al., 2022).

Figure 2. Types of Deep Learning

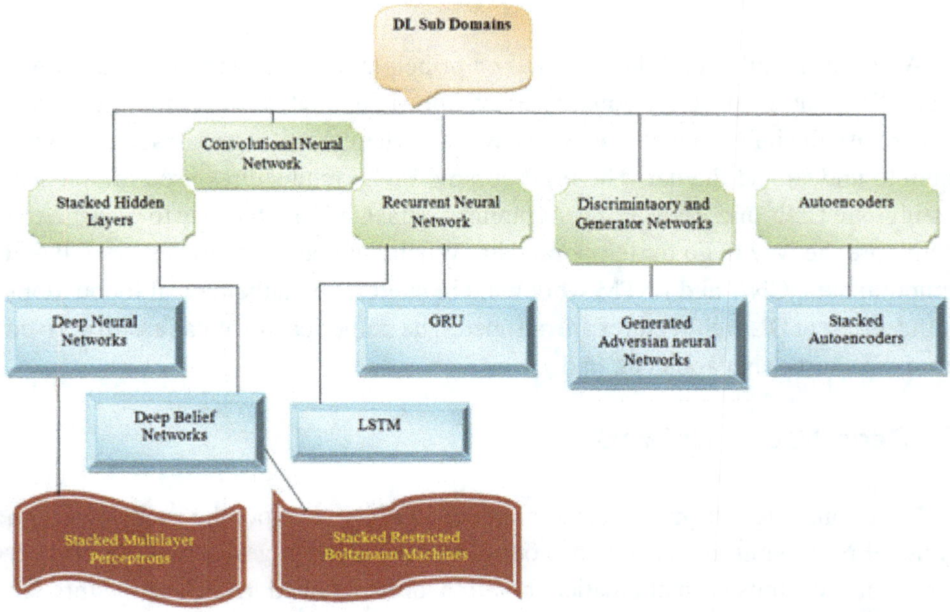

Used SAE to identify malware by feeding them Windows API calls extracted from PE files. A greedy layer-wise training technique was utilized by the SAEs model for unsupervised feature learning. Following that, the parameters were fine-tuned using supervised methods. In terms of training and testing accuracy, the model with three hidden layers and 100 neurons per layer outperformed ANN, SVM, Naïve Bays, and Decision Tree. A technique that modifies raw inputs in order to identify malevolence was used in reference. From security inputs, the expose model selects generic short strings. In this category of strings you may find registry keys, murexes, malicious URLs, and more. After that, it figures out whether they're bad guys. The feature extraction process in expose is powered by a convolution kernel from a neural network (S. Ali et al., 2022). The architecture is comprised of the classifier, components for feature detection, character embedding, and notional components. In comparison to these baselines, expose achieved a detection rate gain of 5-10% with a false-positive rate of 0.1%; this was a significant improvement over manual feature extraction approaches.

7. DEEP LEARNING ARCHITECTURES FOR MALWARE DETECTION

As a sub-module of AI, DNN draws on principles similar to those of the human brain. Without the need for domain expert knowledge, DL systems may automatically revise the inferred meaning with new data when given large datasets, allowing them to understand the dat. The most common DL architectures used in practical settings are CNN and RNN. For geographical data, CNN are the way to go, whereas RNNs are the way to go for temporal data. When it comes to analyzing spatial and temporal data, CNN and LSTM work hand in hand. The mathematical foundations of the different DL architectures are outlined. The numerical formulas are all derived from the source (Nhlapo et al., n.d.).

7.1 Deep Neural Network

Nodes and edges form a directed graph in a FFNN. Without the need to create a cycle, FFN transmits data from one node to another along edges. A massive number of neurons, or units in mathematical notation, are contained in each of the three or more levels that make up an MLP FFN. These layers include the input layer, the hidden layer, and the output layer. The number of hidden layers is determined using a hyper parameter tuning technique. Data is sent forward from one layer to another without considering the values from the preceding layer. Neurons in each layer are also highly related. You can mathematically formulate an MLP with n hidden layers like this shown in equation 1.

$$S(x) = S_m\left(S_{m-1}\left(S_{m-2}\left(\;\left(S_1(c)\right)\right)\right)\right) \tag{1}$$

Concealed layer is defined by H. Usually DNN are used to describe this method of overlaying hidden layers. The diagram in Figure3 depicts a DNN design featuring n layers that are not visible. $Ittakesinputc = c_1, c_2, \ldots, c_{k-1}, c_k andoutputl = l_1, l_2, \ldots, l_{x-1}, l_x$ Another non-linear activation procedure used by each of the hidden layers is ReLU. This aids in lessening diminishing and mistakes states difficulty with gradients (Li et al., 2017).

Figure 3. Architecture of DNN with n hidden layers

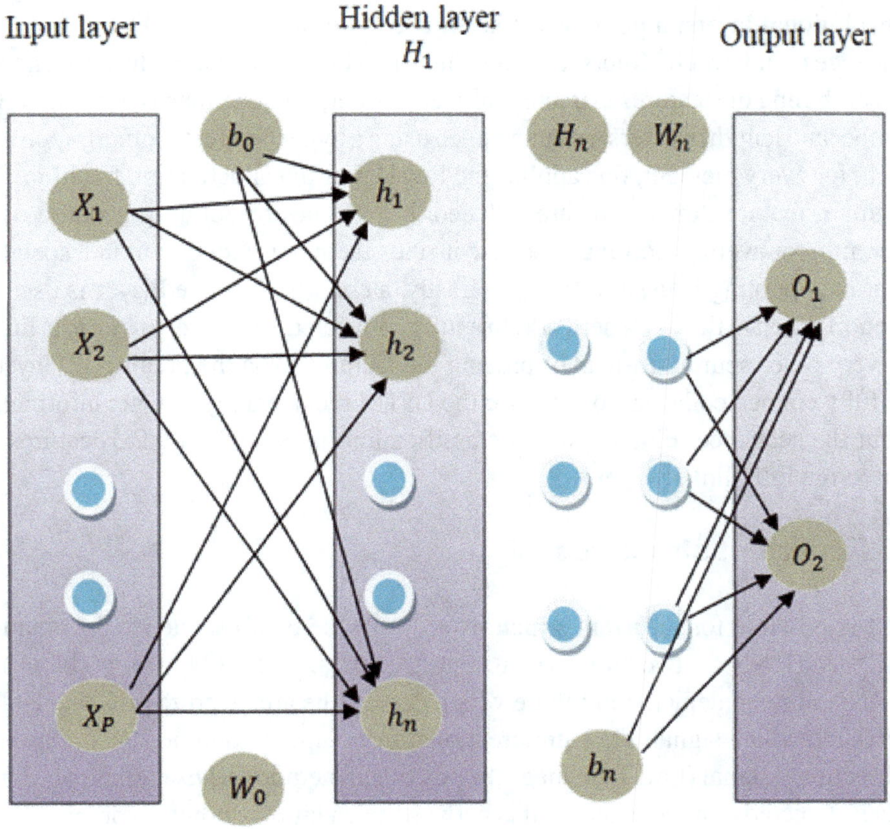

The problem with error gradients and the state of vanishing is mitigated as a result. Using ReLU, which is more efficient, can speed up the entire training process. The mathematical definition of ReLU is shown in equation 2.

$$u(c) = max(0, c) \tag{2}$$

When x stands for input.

7.2 Convolutional Neural Network

The field of image processing makes extensive use of convolutional networks, also known as CNN, as a supplement to classical FFN. The hidden levels, links, and units are not entirely displayed in Figure 2. The input features, denoted as m, and the reduced feature dimension, p, are proportional to the pooling length, in liters. In this study, a CNN with three layers—a fully connected layer, a pooling layer, and a convolution layer—was utilized. A CNN network typically consists of many 1D convolutional layers, a pooling 1D layer, and fully linked layers. Data from a 1D sequence is slid over by filters in a convolutional 1D layer to extract the best features. By combining the features extracted from each filter, a feature map is generated. The number and length of filters are determined using a hyper parameter tuning approach. Then, for every element, this applies the ReLU non-linear activation function. The optimum feature dimensions are reduced in a 1D layer pooling procedure using max, min, or average pooling. Because it finds the maximum output in a specified area, max pooling is used in this job. Lastly, a completely linked layer is used for categorization in the CNN network. In a fully connected layer, every neuron is linked to every other neuron. Instead of passing the features from the pooling 1D layer to the fully connected layer, you can use the LSTM recurrent layer to get information about the sequence. Finally, in this classification process, the LSTM features are sent to the fully linked layer.

7.3 Recurrent structures

It is possible for recurrent structures to learn the data's sequence information. LSTM and RNN are two famous recurrent structures. An LSTM memory block and an RNN unit are depicted in Figure which depicts the architecture of CNN. Unlike a FNN, in which signals flow unidirectional from input to output, RNN allows for bidirectional signal flow. To manage the positional memory, RNN is employed when data is depicted as a sequence. In this network, each layer's output is combined with the input from the layer below it before being sent back into the same layer. In terms of time, it regulates the signal's data. RNNs are the ideal network to use when the data pattern evolves over time (Alhaidari et al., 2022).

8. METHODOLOGY FOR ZERO-DAY MALWARE DETECTION

The construction of an intrusion detection model for zero-day ransom ware using ML involves a number of critical steps, such as collecting data, engineering features, building the model, and simulating zero-day attacks. All of these parts are essential for the model to be able to identify new ransom ware threats in data that has never been seen before.

8.1 Data Collection

The model was built using a dataset that included a diverse range of ransom ware samples, including both popular and newly discovered strains. Datasets tailored to capture different kinds of ransom ware activity at the system level were among the publicly accessible datasets retrieved from reputable cyber security sources. The model's ability to generalize across different attack channels and uncover behavioral characteristics common to ransom ware, regardless of specific strain or family, relies on the inclusion of diverse ransom ware samples (Nkongolo & Tokmak, 2023). The raw data was preprocessed in order to make it ready for analysis. In order to make it easier to spot ransom ware-specific behaviors, the data was cleansed to exclude extraneous system operations, incomplete records, and noise. In order to train more accurate models, we used normalization techniques to standardize numerical features, guaranteeing consistency between data points. The ML model was given a structured and interpretable dataset by encoding categorical features. In order to improve the model's detection accuracy, preprocessing additionally included partitioning the information into windows of system activity. This allowed the model to examine ransom ware behavior within certain temporal contexts (V. Kumar & Sinha, 2021).

8.2 Feature Engineering

When building the model, we looked for indicators of ransom ware behavior that may tell good system operations apart from bad ones. Because of their importance in identifying ransom ware, features such file access patterns; system resource utilization, encryption-related procedures, and unusual network traffic were selected. Even without specific code signatures, the model was able to discover behavioral indicators that indicate ransom ware assaults by analyzing such aspects (Por et al., 2024). To help the model understand and account for more intricate patterns of behavior, we used feature extraction techniques to glean more information from the raw data. The most important features were retained while the computational complexity of the model was reduced through the use of PCA for dimensionality reduction. Because avoiding over fitting by reducing the amount of unnecessary features was critical, this phase made sure the model kept performing well even when processing huge datasets. In order to minimize multicollinearity, which could hinder the model's capacity to generalize to unknown data, highly correlated characteristics were identified and excluded using correlation analysis (Ekong et al., 2023).

8.3 Model Development

When designing the intrusion detection model, several ML methods were evaluated; these algorithms were chosen for their track records of success in categorizing high-dimensional, non-linear datasets. We looked at Neural Networks, Random Forest, and SVM to see how well they could simulate the intricate relationships between malware and system behaviors. The preprocessed dataset was used to train these algorithms. Following that, they were evaluated for F1-score, recall, accuracy, and precision using a training-validation split. It was necessary to tweak the hyper parameters of the chosen models in order to maximize their performance. In order to achieve a balance between the complexity of the model and its generalisability, the Random Forest method had its decision trees altered in terms of both the number of trees and their depth. Similarly, kernel function and regularization parameter tweaks were used to optimize support vector machine models, while optimal layer configurations and learning rates were used to refine neural network structures. To avoid over-fitting, we used cross-validation techniques to make sure the model worked the same way on different data sets. As shown in Figure 4 the final model was chosen because of its precision in ransom ware activity classification and its low false positive rate. Figure 1 shows the process of developing the model. ML Algorithms for Preprocessing Datasets It all started with training various ML algorithms on the pre-processed dataset. These included Random Forest, SVM and neural networks. Next, we optimized each algorithm's performance through hyper parameter tuning, striking a good balance between model complexity and generalisability. The models were refined and over fitted using cross-validation techniques before a final model was selected based on performance metrics such as accuracy, precision, recall, and false positive rates (Tasdemir & Ozka, 2022).

8.4 Zero-Day Simulation

A test set was constructed using instances of newly-discovered ransom ware that were not part of the training data in order to assess the model's capacity to detect zero-day ransom ware assaults. By include these samples, we aimed to mimic zero-day assaults and test the model's ability to detect ransom ware without any prior knowledge of particular variations. Including this previously unreported data set enabled a thorough assessment of the model's generalisability (Jurečková et al., 2024). In order for the model to analyze patterns over time and discover deviations from baseline behaviors, the test data was segmented into various windows of system activity during the zero-day simulation. To make sure the new ransom ware versions were realistic representations of zero-day assaults in the real world, researchers used a number of methods, such as code obfuscation and polymorphic encryption. To ensure the model could differentiate between legitimate system processes and ransom ware, the test set also contained harmless system activity(He & Sayadi, 2023).

Figure 4. Flowchart of Model Development Process

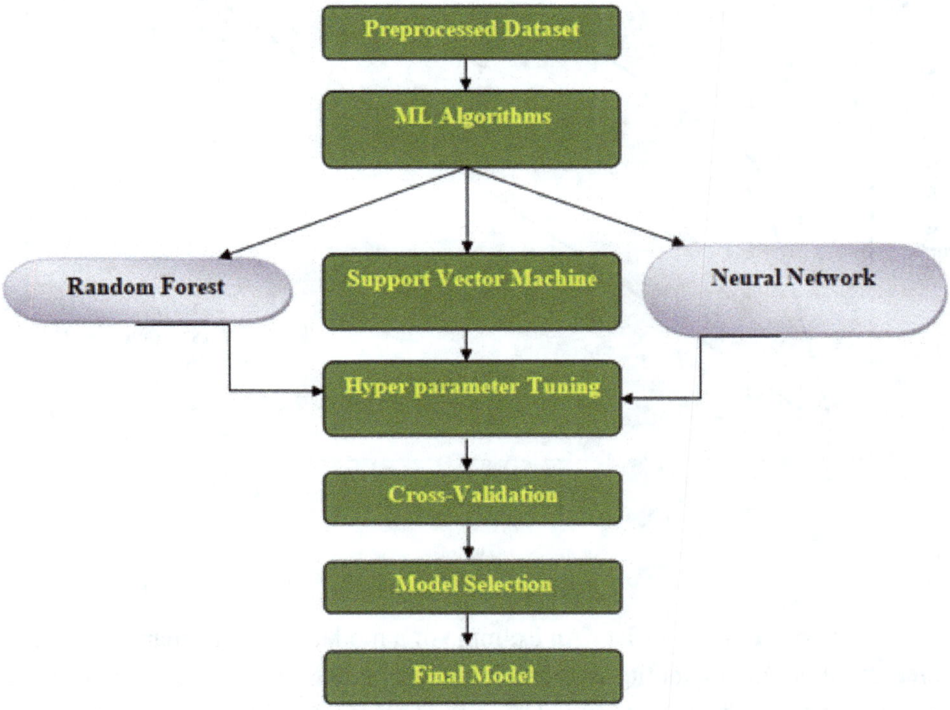

9. RESULT ANALYSIS

Figure 5 is an instance of a ROC curve that shows the connection between FP Rate and TP Rate, represented on the horizontal and vertical axes correspondingly. When compared using the ROC, the GAN framework clearly comes out on top (Zolotukhin & Hämäläinen, 2014).

Figure 5. ROC Curve

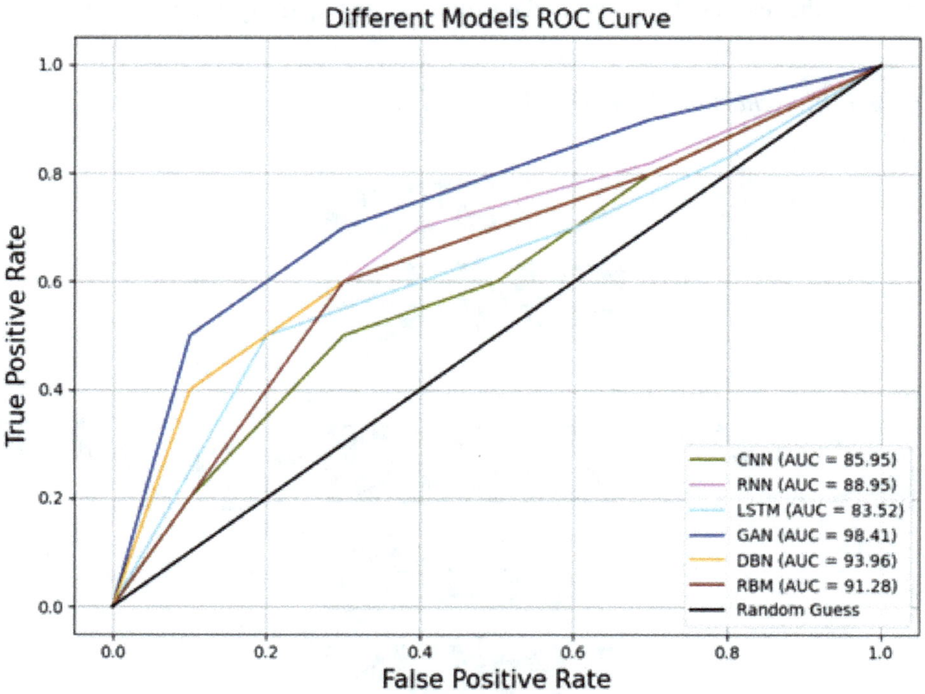

In Figure 6, we see a Variety An example of a model is a performance curve, in which the input data quantity is represented by the bottom axis and performance is shown along the horizontal axis. Using the Difference Model Accuracy metric, GAN technique stands head and shoulders above the competition (Venkatraman & Alazab, 2018).

Figure 6. Difference Model Accuracy Curve

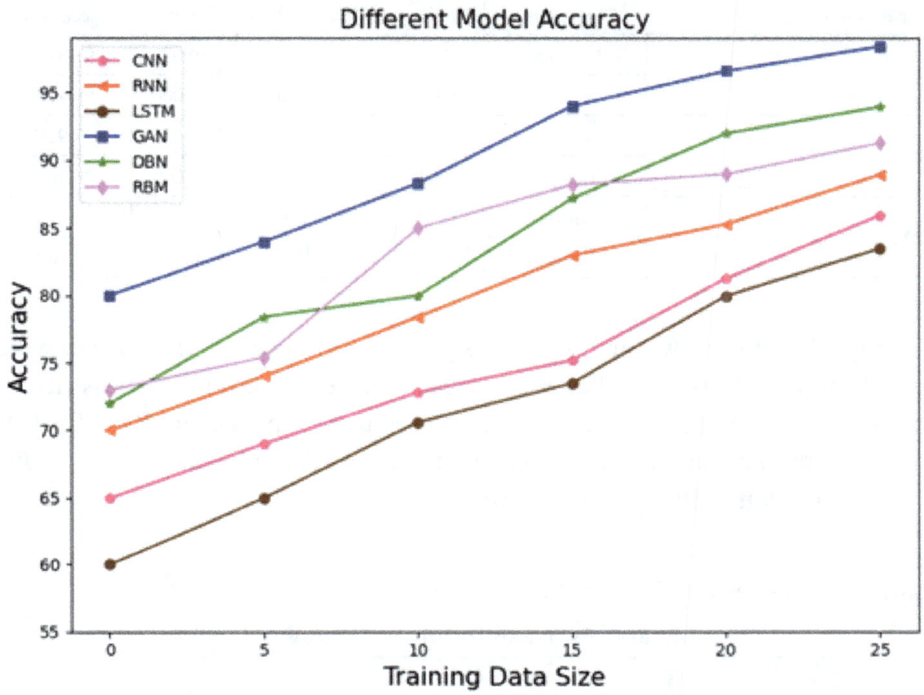

Performance assessment is the cornerstone of DL approach. A more thorough understanding of the method is provided by the outcomes that are derived from the recursive process of instruction that involves adjusting the parameter. The DL algorithms are evaluated with many output measures. Table 1 displays the results of the experiments that used 10-fold cross validation to distinguish between malicious and benign forms of software (Niveditha et al., 2020).

Table 1. Using a classification technique to identify malware and benign software

Classification Algorithm	Class Name	TPR	FPR	TNR	FNR	Accuracy
CNN	Malware	0.732	0.026	0.832	0.067	85.90%
	Benign	0.792	0.123	0.099	0.011	85.95%
RNN	Malware	0.832	0.002	0.730	0.043	88.91%
	Benign	0.894	0.019	0.082	0.009	88.95%
LSTM	Malware	0.612	0.042	0.614	0.048	83.48%
	Benign	0.673	0.086	0.082	0.013	83.52%

continued on following page

Table 1. Continued

Classification Algorithm	Class Name	TPR	FPR	TNR	FNR	Accuracy
GAN	Malware	0.917	0.081	0.992	0.072	98.37%
	Benign	0.975	0.183	0.132	0.006	98.41%
DBN	Malware	0.261	0.012	0.652	0.053	93.92%
	Benign	0.381	0.093	0.017	0.007	93.96%
RBM	Malware	0.912	0.061	0.534	0.058	91.24%
	Benign	0.942	0.012	0.123	0.012	91.28%

Using Algorithm 3, we analyze the design. Figure 7 once the MSE between the original and coded versions of an assault reaches a certain level, it is classified as a zero-day attack. For this investigation, we used three separate cutoffs: 0.05, 0.1, and 0.15. Optimization of random search parameters determines the cutoff value for these minimums (Hindy et al., 2020).

Figure 7. Auto encoder Graphs of Convergence

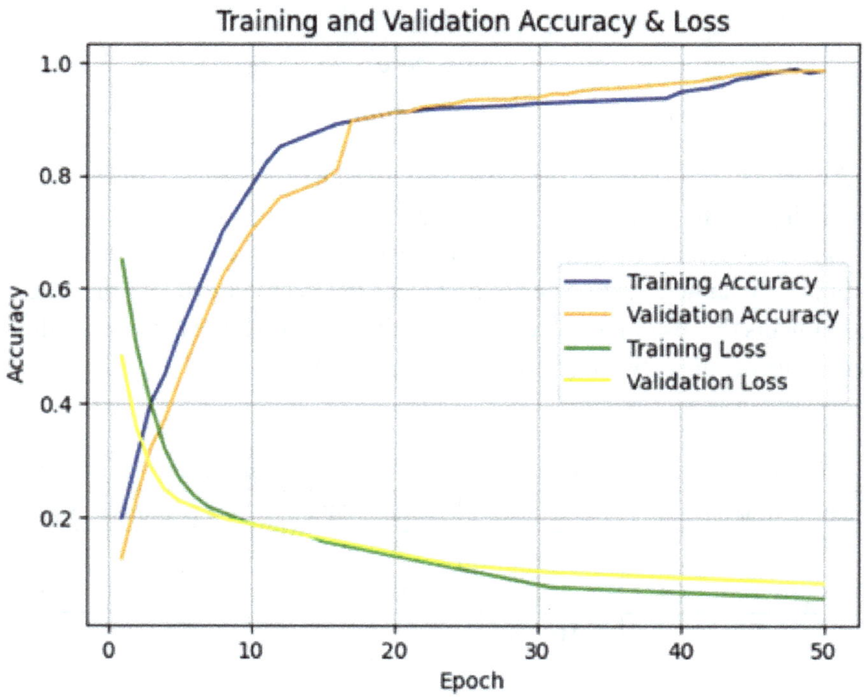

Examining how well tree-based elements classify data when compared to various fundamental procedures that deal with data imperfection Performance Comparission shown in Figure 8 (Comar et al., 2013).

Figure 8. Performance Comparission

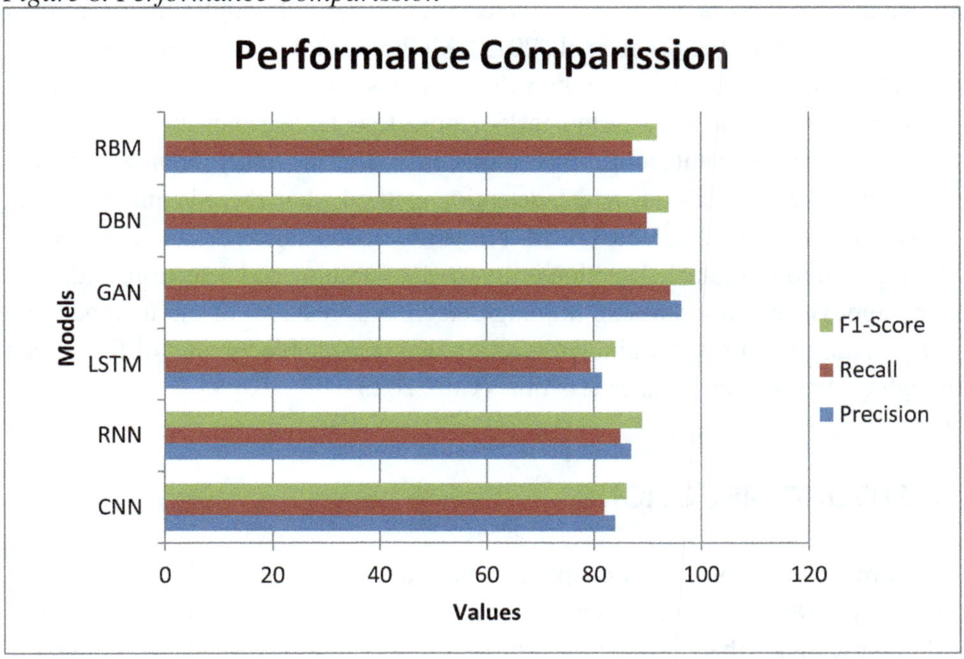

10. CHALLENGES

Some of the zero-day detection systems shown in Table I rely on supervised and hybrid learning, while others use transfer learning. Lastly, there is zero-day attack detection that relies on unsupervised learning. The unsupervised learning strategy is used by outlier detectors (Zhou & Pezaros, 2019). ML algorithms can learn patterns from data without labels, a process known as unsupervised learning (Mirsky et al., 2018). The goal of the zero-day attack detection model is to identify zero-day assaults by learning a compressed version of regular data. For training purposes, zero-day attack data is not necessary for the outlier identification methods. Since the data for zero-day attacks is usually unavailable when training the model, this is a huge benefit (Khalili & Sami, 2017). A number of approaches exist for detecting zero-day attacks, some of which rely on supervised learning and others that utilize a mix of supervised and unsupervised learning. Detecting zero-day attacks accurately requires training data sets that are representative of the target audience (Zhao et al., 2017),. This data can be achieved through supervised and mixed learning methods. Regrettably, zero-day assaults are usually not included in the data set used for zero-day detection. The assumption that zero-day assaults act similarly to known attacks must be made by the detection schemes, although this assumption has not been proven yet (Zhao et al., 2019). Methods for detecting zero-day attacks that rely on transfer learning use knowledge transfer across different domains. To maximize performance on a certain task or topic, transfer learning attempts to make the most of sparse or unlabelled data (Sameera & Shashi, 2020). Transfer learning shows promise as a zero-day attack detection method when there is minimal or no zero-data attack data available (A. M. Ali et al., 2025). Another crucial aspect of ML-based zero-day attack detection is the speed of training and detection. Although many approaches have variable training/detection speeds, all of the methods that were evaluated can finish training/detection in a respectable amount of time, even though detection usually takes less time (Guo, 2023).

11. FUTURE DIRECTIONS

In order to develop a practical product that can detect malware in real-time, it is necessary to resolve the various minor issues that we have highlighted in this study. All of these things that need to be considered for future projects will be highlighted in this section.

11.1 Moderate Sized and Updated Dataset

Most of the survey publications have used a limited dataset, which is insufficient for research to yield credible conclusions, as mentioned earlier. Big data processing limitations or a lack of accessible labeled datasets are the primary causes of this issue. Results from studies using small datasets are skewed and not applicable to the actual world. FSL and its variants can handle issues with imbalanced data, a lack of available samples for a certain class of malware, or unlabelled data. That way, we can avoid the challenges of dealing with and analyzing massive datasets while still getting state-of-the-art outcomes. Second, there was an issue with the ageing of some of the datasets that were analyzed. Research based on past data may not be applicable in real-time due to the constant development of new malware with different features. Collecting current data, which should include all the latest malware strains, is highly recommended. It is also important to ensure that the datasets used to train and validate proposed frameworks accurately reflect the distribution of real data (Tayyab et al., 2022).

11.2 Using Significant Features

When training a model to produce useful results, it is crucial to select suitable characteristics. The identification of harmful behavior might benefit from features that are extracted either statically or dynamically. The majority of the publications that were surveyed either used a subset of features or relied solely on statically or dynamically derived features. This raises concerns about the possibility that some features, which could be crucial in identifying malevolent intent, were overlooked. It was mentioned in multiple articles that future work should address the focus on less-than-ideal attributes. To train the model with higher learnt skills, it is possible to use a combination of static and dynamic features (Sarhan et al., 2023). The current state of the market makes it difficult to extract dynamic features, which can be an issue for deploying anti-malware systems in real-time environments. The use of neural networks may prove useful in this situation. Images of both harmful and harmless types can be handled by neural networks. So, instead of zeroing in on a single characteristic, we can concentrate on the samples' static semantic features. Use of neural networks makes feature engineering an automated procedure. It is possible to automate the process of feature selection by using the neural network's embedding layers instead of the hit-and-try method.

11.3 Handling Evasion Techniques

Two main types of evasion strategies have already been discussed: those that rely on environmental awareness and those that rely on timing. For a framework to be considered ready for deployment in a real-time setting, it must be precise and resilient to evasion strategies. Because newly discovered viruses can identify the virtual environment, this needs to be addressed in future work. Malware also has the advanced capability of being activated at a specific time and date; until such activation, it will not behave maliciously (Niveditha et al., 2020). Malicious software might act normally as a benign file until specific input triggers it. The emphasis of future efforts should be on multipath execution, which may trace this type of behavior.

11.4 Combating Anti-Analysis Techniques

Malware developers use a wide arsenal of anti-analysis techniques to stay under the radar. File encryption, binary or executable compression, and obfuscation are common methods used by malware writers to avoid detection and analysis. In order to eliminate the potential for malware to cause harm, future work could involve mitigating all of these anti-analysis techniques. In the context of the ever-changing cyber environment, there are several important factors to consider when conducting research on malware identification (R. Kumar, 2022).

Researchers should focus on metamorphic, polymorphic, and obfuscated malware in the future since these types of malware authors use sophisticated techniques to easily alter the appearance of their infection.
The proliferation of malware is a key factor in the ever-increasing number of malware families, and as time goes on, new types of malware continue to emerge in the cyber world. The goal of future studies should be to create a general model that can identify zero-day malware.
A model needs to be robust enough to deal with any form of hidden virus in order to apply the real-time solution (El-Sayed et al., 2021).

Research based on DL has been fruitful, yielding commendable results in malware detection. Utilizing techniques based on meta-learning in conjunction with DL can further enhance the result. Generic model production is aided by algorithms based on meta-learning. This class of generic models is designed to learn on its own. Even previously undiscovered forms of malware can be their characteristics figured out with relative ease using self-learning techniques. Given its efficacy, efficiency, and resilience, few shot learning in particular has demonstrated that it merits further investigation (Brinkley et al., 2024).

12. CONCLUSION

Vulnerability detection devices are vulnerable to zero-day attacks since they exploit newly found vulnerabilities. The results show that zero-day assaults are common and dangerous for IT infrastructures. Because their personal details are typically not available in advance, it means zero-day assaults are notoriously hard to pin down using the traditional signature-based verification method. Methods centre on ML show potential for detecting zero-day threats since they can record the statistical characteristics of attacks. Examining various ML-based approaches to zero-day attack detection, this survey study compares and contrasts training, ML models and assessment evaluation results, and datasets (Zoppi et al., 2021). Finding malware and categorization, particularly of zero-day versions that evade conventional security solutions, has been greatly enhanced using algorithms that use deep learning. These types of models are able to study both stationary and moving data for intricate patterns because to models such as CNN, LSTM, automatic coders, and hybrid networks. Nevertheless, issues such as antagonistic rebellion, model comprehension, and data imbalances continue to be obstacles. DL has great promise as a foundation for the next generation of machines cyber security systems that can adapt to evolving malware threats, provided that it is thoroughly researched and put into practice (Abri et al., 2019).

REFERENCES

Aboaoja, F. A., Zainal, A., Ghaleb, F. A., Al-rimy, B. A. S., Eisa, T. A. E., & Elnour, A. A. H. (2022). Malware Detection Issues, Challenges, and Future Directions: A Survey. *Applied Sciences (Basel, Switzerland)*, *12*(17), 8482. Advance online publication. DOI: 10.3390/app12178482

Abri, F., Siami-Namini, S., Khanghah, M. A., Soltani, F. M., & Namin, A. S. (2019). Can Machine/Deep Learning Classifiers Detect Zero-Day Malware with High Accuracy? Proceedings - 2019 IEEE International Conference on Big Data. *Big Data, 2019*, 3252–3259. DOI: 10.1109/BigData47090.2019.9006514

Agarkar, S., & Ghosh, S. (2020). Malware detection & classification using machine learning. Proceedings - 2020 IEEE International Symposium on Sustainable Energy, Signal Processing and Cyber Security, ISSSC 2020, 20–23. DOI: 10.1109/iSSSC50941.2020.9358835

Alhaidari, F., Shaib, N. A., Alsafi, M., Alharbi, H., Alawami, M., Aljindan, R., Rahman, A. U., & Zagrouba, R. (2022). ZeVigilante: Detecting Zero-Day Malware Using Machine Learning and Sandboxing Analysis Techniques. *Computational Intelligence and Neuroscience*, *2022*, 1–15. Advance online publication. DOI: 10.1155/2022/1615528 PMID: 35586085

Ali, A. M., Ghaleb, F. A., & Saeed, F. (2025). AEDGAN: A Semi-Supervised Deep Learning Model for Zero-Day Malware Detection. *International Journal of Advanced Computer Science and Applications*, *16*(3), 759–769. DOI: 10.14569/IJACSA.2025.0160375

Ali, S., Rehman, S. U., Imran, A., Adeem, G., Iqbal, Z., & Kim, K. (2022). Comparative Evaluation of AI-Based Techniques for Zero-Day Attacks Detection. *Electronics (Basel)*, *11*(23), 1–25. DOI: 10.3390/electronics11233934

Barros, P. H., Chagas, E. T. C., Oliveira, L. B., Queiroz, F., & Ramos, H. S. (2022). Malware-SMELL: A zero-shot learning strategy for detecting zero-day vulnerabilities. *Computers & Security*, *120*, 102785. DOI: 10.1016/j.cose.2022.102785

Bilot, T., El Madhoun, N., Al Agha, K., & Zouaoui, A. (2024). A Survey on Malware Detection with Graph Representation Learning. *ACM Computing Surveys*, *56*(11), 1–36. Advance online publication. DOI: 10.1145/3664649

Brinkley, Y., Thompson, D., Simmons, N., Brinkley, Y., Thompson, D., & Simmons, N. (2024). Machine Learning-Based Intrusion Detection for Zero-Day Ransomware in Unseen Data

Cen, M., Deng, X., Jiang, F., & Doss, R. (2024). Zero-Ran Sniff: A zero-day ransomware early detection method based on zero-shot learning. Computers and Security, 142(May 2023), 103849. DOI: 10.1016/j.cose.2024.103849

Chumachenko, K., & Technology, I. (2017). *Machine Learning Methods for Malware Detection and*. University of Aplied Sciences.

Comar, P. M., Liu, L., Saha, S., Tan, P. N., & Nucci, A. (2013). Combining supervised and unsupervised learning for zero-day malware detection. *Proceedings - IEEE INFOCOM*, •••, 2022–2030. DOI: 10.1109/INFCOM.2013.6567003

Ekong, A. P., Etuk, A., Inyang, S., & Ekere-obong, M. (2023). Securing Against Zero-Day Attacks: A Machine Learning Approach for Classification and Organizations' Perception of its Impact. *Journal of Information Systems and Informatics*, *5*(3), 1123–1140. DOI: 10.51519/journalisi.v5i3.546

El-Sayed, R., El-Ghamry, A., Gaber, T., & Hassanien, A. E. (2021). Zero-Day Malware Classification Using Deep Features with Support Vector Machines. Proceedings - 2021 IEEE 10th International Conference on Intelligent Computing and Information Systems, ICICIS 2021, April 2022, 311–317. DOI: 10.1109/ICICIS52592.2021.9694256

Gibert, D., Mateu, C., & Planes, J. (2020). The rise of machine learning for detection and classification of malware: Research developments, trends and challenges. Journal of Network and Computer Applications, 153(November 2019). DOI: 10.1016/j.jnca.2019.102526

Guo, Y. (2023). A review of Machine Learning-based zero-day attack detection: Challenges and future directions. *Computer Communications*, *198*, 175–185. DOI: 10.1016/j.comcom.2022.11.001 PMID: 36741076

Hamid, K., Iqbal, M. W., Aqeel, M., Liu, X., & Arif, M. (2023). Analysis of Techniques for Detection and Removal of Zero-Day Attacks (ZDA). In Communications in Computer and Information Science: Vol. 1768 CCIS (Issue July). Springer Nature Singapore. DOI: 10.1007/978-981-99-0272-9_17

He, Z., Miari, T., Makrani, H. M., Aliasgari, M., Homayoun, H., & Sayadi, H. (2021). When machine learning meets hardware cybersecurity: Delving into accurate zero-day malware detection. Proceedings - International Symposium on Quality Electronic Design, ISQED, 2021-April, 85–90. DOI: 10.1109/ISQED51717.2021.9424330

He, Z., & Sayadi, H. (2023). Image-Based Zero-Day Malware Detection in IoMT Devices: A Hybrid AI-Enabled Method. Proceedings - International Symposium on Quality Electronic Design, ISQED, 2023-April. DOI: 10.1109/ISQED57927.2023.10129348

Hindy, H., Atkinson, R., Tachtatzis, C., Colin, J. N., Bayne, E., & Bellekens, X. (2020). Utilising deep learning techniques for effective zero-day attack detection. *Electronics (Basel)*, *9*(10), 1–16. DOI: 10.3390/electronics9101684

Jurečková, O., Jureček, M., Stamp, M., Di Troia, F., & Lórencz, R. (2024). Classification and online clustering of zero-day malware. Journal of Computer Virology and Hacking Techniques, 579–592. DOI: 10.1007/s11416-024-00513-5

Kansal, S. (2025). Zero-Day Malware Detection. December 2024.

Khalili, A., & Sami, A. (2017). SADCPS: Semi-supervised attack detection in cyber physical systems. 18th CSI International Symposium on Computer Science and Software Engineering, CSSE 2017, 2018-January(May), 12–17. DOI: 10.1109/CSICSSE.2017.8320122

Kumar, R. (2022). Zero-Day Malware Detection and Effective Malware Analysis.

Kumar, R., Zhang, X., Wang, W., Kumar, J. A. Y., & Sharif, A. (2020). A Multimodal Malware Detection Technique for Android IoT Devices Using Various Features. *IEEE Access : Practical Innovations, Open Solutions*, *1*, 1–15. https://ieeexplore.ieee.org/document/8721053

Kumar, V., & Sinha, D. (2021). A robust intelligent zero-day cyber-attack detection technique. *Complex & Intelligent Systems*, *7*(5), 2211–2234. DOI: 10.1007/s40747-021-00396-9 PMID: 34777966

Li, H., Wang, J., Tang, M., & Li, X. (2017). Polarization-dependent effects of an Airy beam due to the spin-orbit coupling. *Journal of the Optical Society of America. A, Optics, Image Science, and Vision*, *34*(7), 1114–1118. DOI: 10.1364/JOSAA.34.001114 PMID: 29036120

Malhotra, A., & Bajaj, K. (2016). A hybrid pattern based text mining approach for malware detection using DBScan. *CSI Transactions on ICT*, *4*(2–4), 141–149. DOI: 10.1007/s40012-016-0095-y

Mirsky, Y., Doitshman, T., Elovici, Y., & Shabtai, A. (2018). Kitsune: An Ensemble of Autoencoders for Online Network Intrusion Detection. 25th Annual Network and Distributed System Security Symposium, NDSS 2018, February, 18–21. DOI: 10.14722/ndss.2018.23204

Nguyen, H. T., Ngo, Q. D., & Le, V. H. (2018). IoT Botnet Detection Approach Based on PSI graph and DGCNN classifier. 2018 IEEE International Conference on Information Communication and Signal Processing, ICICSP 2018, September, 118–122. DOI: 10.1109/ICICSP.2018.8549713

Nhlapo, S. J., Nkongolo, M., Nkongolo, W., & Africa, S. (n.d.). 1 Zero-day attack and ransomware detection. 1–14.

Nikolopoulos, S. D., & Polenakis, I. (2017). A graph-based model for malware detection and classification using system-call groups. *Journal of Computer Virology and Hacking Techniques*, *13*(1), 29–46. DOI: 10.1007/s11416-016-0267-1

Niveditha, V. R., Ananthan, T. V., Amudha, S., Sam, D., & Srinidhi, S. (2020). Detect and classify zero day Malware efficiently in big data platform. International Journal of Advanced Science and Technology, 29(4 Special Issue), 1947–1954.

Nkongolo, M., & Tokmak, M. (2023). Zero-Day Threats Detection for Critical Infrastructures. Communications in Computer and Information Science, 1878 CCIS, 32–47. DOI: 10.1007/978-3-031-39652-6_3

Por, L. Y., Dai, Z., Leem, S. J., Chen, Y., Yang, J., Binbeshr, F., Phan, K. Y., & Ku, C. S. (2024). A Systematic Literature Review on the Methods and Challenges in Detecting Zero-Day Attacks: Insights from the Recent CrowdStrike Incident. *IEEE Access : Practical Innovations, Open Solutions*, *12*(July), 144150–144163. DOI: 10.1109/ACCESS.2024.3455410

Pudukotai Dinakarrao, S. M., Sayadi, H., Makrani, H. M., Nowzari, C., Rafatirad, S., & Homayoun, H. (2019). Lightweight Node-level Malware Detection and Network-level Malware Confinement in IoT Networks. *Proceedings of the 2019 Design, Automation and Test in Europe Conference and Exhibition, DATE 2019*, 776–781. DOI: 10.23919/DATE.2019.8715057

Rahman, A. (2017). Designing a Dashboard as Geo-Visual Exploration Tool for Origin-Destination Data. 1–73. https://purl.utwente.nl/essays/85856

Rama, K., Kumar, P., & Bhasker, B. (2019). Deep Learning to Address Candidate Generation and Cold Start Challenges in Recommender Systems: A Research Survey. https://arxiv.org/abs/1907.08674

Sameera, N., & Shashi, M. (2020). Deep transductive transfer learning framework for zero-day attack detection. *ICT Express*, *6*(4), 361–367. DOI: 10.1016/j.icte.2020.03.003

Sarhan, M., Layeghy, S., Gallagher, M., & Portmann, M. (2023). From zero-shot machine learning to zero-day attack detection. *International Journal of Information Security*, *22*(4), 947–959. DOI: 10.1007/s10207-023-00676-0

Sayadi, H., Wang, H., Miari, T., Makrani, H. M., Aliasgari, M., Rafatirad, S., & Homayoun, H. (2020). Recent Advancements in Microarchitectural Security: Review of Machine Learning Countermeasures. Midwest Symposium on Circuits and Systems, 2020-August, 949–952. DOI: 10.1109/MWSCAS48704.2020.9184539

Su, J., Danilo Vasconcellos, V., Prasad, S., Daniele, S., Feng, Y., & Sakurai, K. (2018). Lightweight Classification of IoT Malware Based on Image Recognition. Proceedings - International Computer Software and Applications Conference, 2, 664–669. DOI: 10.1109/COMPSAC.2018.10315

Tasdemir, S., & Ozka, I. A. (2022). Innovations and Technologies in Engineering (Vol. 1). www.kitapmatik.com.tr

Tayyab, U. E. H., Khan, F. B., Durad, M. H., Khan, A., & Lee, Y. S. (2022). A Survey of the Recent Trends in Deep Learning Based Malware Detection. *Journal of Cybersecurity and Privacy*, *2*(4), 800–829. DOI: 10.3390/jcp2040041

Venkatraman, S., & Alazab, M. (2018). Use of Data Visualisation for Zero-Day Malware Detection. *Security and Communication Networks*, *2018*, 1–13. Advance online publication. DOI: 10.1155/2018/1728303

Zahoora, U., Rajarajan, M., Pan, Z., & Khan, A. (2022). Zero-day Ransomware Attack Detection using Deep Contractive Autoencoder and Voting based Ensemble Classifier. *Applied Intelligence*, *52*(12), 13941–13960. DOI: 10.1007/s10489-022-03244-6

Zhao, J., Shetty, S., & Pan, J. W. (2017). Feature-based transfer learning for network security. Proceedings - IEEE Military Communications Conference MILCOM, 2017-October(July 2018), 17–22. DOI: 10.1109/MILCOM.2017.8170749

Zhao, J., Shetty, S., Pan, J. W., Kamhoua, C., & Kwiat, K. (2019). Transfer learning for detecting unknown network attacks. *EURASIP Journal on Information Security*, *2019*(1), 1–13. DOI: 10.1186/s13635-019-0084-4

Zhou, Q., & Pezaros, D. (2019). Evaluation of Machine Learning Classifiers for Zero-Day Intrusion Detection — An Analysis on CIC-AWS-2018 dataset. May 2019. https://doi.org//arXiv.1905.03685DOI: 10.48550

Zolotukhin, M., & Hämäläinen, T. (2014). Detection of zero-day malware based on the analysis of opcode sequences. 2014 IEEE 11th Consumer Communications and Networking Conference, CCNC 2014, 386–391. DOI: 10.1109/CCNC.2014.6866599

Chapter 10
Adversarial AI-Driven Cyber Threat Intelligence: A Human-Centric Framework for Detecting and Mitigating AI-Augmented Social Engineering Attacks

Soumi Ghosh
https://orcid.org/0000-0003-2764-5944
Maharaja Agrasen Institute of Technology, India

Ritik Raj
Maharaja Agrasen Institute of Technology, India

Amita Goel
Maharaja Agrasen Institute of Technology, India

ABSTRACT

Artificial intelligence and cybersecurity convergence has fundamentally transformed the threat environment, in particular, the social engineering attacks. In this paper, a comprehensive holistic user-centered approach to detection and reduction of adversarial AI-assisted social engineering attacks is proposed with assistance of adversarial AI-determined menace insight. The proposed architecture takes into consideration the concepts of machine learning, behavioral analytics, and human-computer interaction to create a defense multilayer. The experiments prove that the rate of AI-generated phishing attacks and identification of deepfake-generated campaigns are high, respectively, 94.3 and 99.0, respectively. The viability of the framework is proven by the experiments that are founded on the real-life data and

DOI: 10.4018/979-8-3373-4898-8.ch010

simulated AI-based attacks that are serious challenges to the framework. It is an original work of literature that bridges many gaps in the current threat intelligence models through the application of human-centered principles of design, adversarial artificial intelligence detection systems, and training systems that adapt to new developments. Interdisciplinary character of the framework brings along with the ethical considerations and policy orientation and human behavioral analysis besides the technical innovations and thus it is a holistic approach to the next-generation cybersecurity issues.

1. INTRODUCTION

1.1 Background and Historical Context

The age of digital transformation has resulted in the unmatched modification in the environment of cyber threats, and artificial intelligence emerged as a protective barrier and instrument to attack. The evolution of AI in cybersecurity shows that it was first used as a rule-based detection system in the early 2000s, then in the 2010s as a machine learning algorithm, and in the modern world as adversarial AI (Anderson et al., 2024). This has been especially notable in the field of social engineering attacks whose conventional motive of human psychology and control has been adapted to the use of sophisticated AI technologies to develop attack vectors of high sophistication.

Adversarial AI has become a strategic cybersecurity issue, which can be traced to several major developments. Initial AI uses in cybersecurity were mainly based on the recognition of patterns and the detection of abnormalities (Bhattacharya & Kumar, 2023). Nevertheless, with the emergence of generative models or especially Generative Adversarial Networks (GANs) and Large Language Models (LLMs) the threat landscape has fundamentally changed. Such technologies also allow attackers to create convincing deepfakes, scale-based personalized phishing messages, and profile social media in a high level of sophistication never before (Chen et al., 2023).

1.2 The Evolution of AI-Enhanced Threats

The current threat intelligence systems continue to be mainly technicalistic with primary focus on network-based detection techniques at the expense of the human component of social engineering attacks. This shortcoming becomes especially acute when it comes to discussing AI-enhanced attacks that are specifically aimed at human cognitive biases and social interactions (Deb et al., 2024). The fact that generative AI models are now able to generate human-style text, create realistic images, and create believable voice patterns have revealed the weaknesses of the conventional security paradigm.

The recent events demonstrate how difficult such a challenge can be. The phishing campaigns developed by AI have already proven to be more than 60 percent successful in controlled conditions, whereas the rates of success in phishing campaigns are only 15-20 percent (Ferreira and Lenzini, 2023). As of 2023, the result of deepfake-based fraud has led to financial losses of more than 250 million dollars worldwide, which is three times higher than the number of the year before (Goldstein et al., 2023). Such figures highlight the necessity to develop a set of defense mechanisms based on complexity, but at the same time, on humanistic design principles.

1.3 Research Gap and Motivation

The research fills the most essential gaps in the current literature as it formulates an integrated paradigm incorporating both adversarial AI systems and people-centered strategies to detect and prevent AI-enhanced social engineering attacks. Existing models have a number of shortcomings:

- Human Factors vs. Technical Focus: The current systems are already inclined toward signature-based detection and do not focus on behavioral detection and context awareness (Hassan et al., 2024).
- Inappropriate Adversarial Robustness: The conventional detection algorithms are not sufficient to handle improved adaptive AI-driven content, which keeps on changing (Ibrahim et al., 2023).
- Absence of Interdisciplinary Integration: Some of the existing strategies do not include ethical, cognitive, and policy viewpoints to have a complete threat mitigation approach (Jain and Patel, 2024).
- Lack of Cross-Sectoral Generality: Existing models are not designed to consider the difference in threat conditions around the world, infrastructural differences, differences in user behavior, and regulatory factors (Kumar et al., 2023).

This study fills these gaps by introducing a framework that unites such aspects of technical innovation as human-centric design, ethical governance, or adaptive learning abilities.

1.4 Research Objectives

The major aims of this paper are:

- Creation of a user-friendly system of identifying AI-powered social engineering assaults that focus on user experience and optimization of cognitive charges.
- Adversarial AI methods to be integrated to obtain a more robust threat intelligence and strengthen detection.
- Deployment of state-of-the-art behavioral analytics to detect abnormal human-AI patterns of interaction.
- Development of mitigation procedures of automated and advanced attack vectors.
- Formation of adaptive processes to guarantee the development of a framework in line with new threats.
- Weaving of ethical, policy and regulatory concerns into the technical framework.
- Demonstration by extensive real world studies and testing.

1.5 Research Contributions

There are various important contributions to the field of cybersecurity in this research:

New Framework Architecture: A multilayered, anthropocentric architecture will be introduced with a focus on a smooth combination of technical capabilities of detection with the experience of a user, unlike technical security paradigms.
Adversarial AI Integration: Systematic integration of adversarial algorithms such as GANs, adversarial training, and robustness enhancement systems that go well beyond current state of the art detection abilities under adversarial AI generated attacks.
Behavioral Analytics Engine: The new programs of high-order modeling of the patterns of the human-AI interaction are developed according to various dimensions, including the temporal, spatial, and contextual ones.
Large Empirical validation: Comprehensive experimentation on multidimensional attack patterns with actual incidences and model attack scenarios, and demonstrating helpfulness and effectiveness in practice.
Adaptive Learning Mechanisms: Embarkation of evolving continuous learning mechanisms that adjust to the dynamic threat environment and guarantee their long-term effectiveness and relevance.
Interdisciplinary Framework: Implementation of ethical aspects, legal requirements to policies (NIST AI RMF, EU AI Act), human behavioral psychology, and technical innovations. Cross-Sectoral Applicability: Designs to be used

in deployment in a variety of organizational settings, such as differences in infrastructure, user population, and regulatory setting.

1.6 Chapter Organization

The rest of this chapter is organized in the following way: Section 2 provides an in-depth literature review, including the development of social engineering attacks, AI-enhanced attack vectors, the existing threat intelligence shortcomings, adversarial AI methods, and research gaps. The third section describes the methodology, such as the framework architecture, human-centric design principles, integration of adversarial AI, and design of a behavioral analytics engine. The algorithm design of the multi-modal detection, behavioral anomaly detection, adversarial robustness enhancement, and adaptive learning are described in Section 4. Section 5 represents the system architecture and interdependences. The second section 6 describes the experimental design, such as the description of datasets, assessment measures, and baseline comparisons. Section 7 gives detailed results and analysis at various dimensions. Section 8 discusses in details the findings, implications, limitations and future research directions. Section 9 ends with a conclusion and recommendations based on contribution and practicality.

2. LITERATURE REVIEW

2.1 Evolution of Social Engineering Attacks

The development of the social engineering attacks has drastically transformed since rudimentary phishing emails to the social multi-vector attacks that exploit the application of psychological factor and social dynamics (Chen et al., 2023). The most significant principles of psychology that are used in traditional social engineering to manipulate victims into disclosing sensitive information or engaging in some sort of negative activity are the authority, urgency, social proof, reciprocity, and scarcity principles (Deb et al., 2024).

The mode of attack has also significantly changed with the artificial intelligence. The adversaries can also automate the reconnaissance of the target with the help of AI-enhanced tools, customize the attacks, and scale the operations to the level that cannot be achieved by human capabilities (Ferreira and Lenzini, 2023). The tool of machine learning can be applied to analyze the data of a social media so that it would create comprehensive psychological profiles hence enabling highly-targeted and persuasive attacks following the weaknesses of the user.

In the history of the study, it can be seen that there are three stages of the evolution of social engineering:

Phase 1 (1990s-2000s): Traditional Social Engineering: It was characterized by being done manually, having a narrow targeting capability, and relied on generic psychological manipulation techniques. The rates were quite low (5-10%), because it was not personalized (Liu et al., 2024).
Phase 2 (2010-2018): Automated Social Engineering: With the introduction of automation tools, it was possible to make larger targeting and personalization with ease based on information available publicly. They got more advanced and even the success rates went as high as 15-20% (Martinez & Thompson, 2023).
Phase 3 (2019-Present): AI-Augmented Social Engineering: High-tech AI technologies (including natural language generation, computer vision, and predictive analytics) were implemented and allowed developing sophisticated social engineering tools on the scale that had never existed before. Within the controlled environment, the current success rates of the targeted AI-enhanced attacks are above 60 percent (Nguyen et al., 2024).

2.2 AI-Augmented Attack Vectors

The new social engineering attack vectors have been made possible by the recent advances in the sphere of generative AI, and exploit the latest AI capabilities (Goldstein et al., 2023).

Key attack vectors include:

Deepfake-Based Attacks: Generative Adversarial Networks (GANs) can be used to create convincing audio/video/image impersonation, which can be used in committing frauds and other manipulations (Hassan et al., 2024). The most recent ones are in the cases of voice impersonation by a CEO that resulted in a 243,000 wire fraud and in the case involving the distribution of disinformation with the help of fabricated video. It is hard to notice because the quality of deepfakes is currently improving, and the state of the art models give the content that can no longer be consistently distinguished by a human viewer as original content.
AI-Generated Content: It is also possible to create highly convincing phishing email, social media, and text content with the use of a Big Language Model, which operates in an artificial style similar to the human handwriting and is relatively accurate (Ibrahim et al., 2023). Such models can even adapt the communication styles of a given target organization and leverage on the current events to make them credible and customize the content based on the

profiling of targets. Consecutive studies have indicated that phishing e-mails developed by AIs have a high probability of obtaining a click up by 45 percent compared to the traditional phishing messages.

Automated Social Profiling The machine learning algorithms analyze and process publicly available social media data to generate a complete psychological and behavioral portrait of the targets (Jain and Patel, 2024). The data can be used to develop highly personalized attack plans exploiting unique weaknesses, likes, and behavior patterns. Watson and well evolved profiling systems are at 80 percent accurate in making the best time of attack prediction, the communication channels and methodological approaches of psychological manipulations in the process.

Synthetic Identity Creation: AI technology generates due-to-genuineness identities complete with logical profile graphics, biographical details and conduct designs that they employ to penetrate the trade (Patel and Singh, 2023). Such artificial identities may be implemented in a large-scale way to attain influence operations, corporate spying and long-term social engineering programs.

Just in Real Life: The BEC 3.0 Attack: Multinational Corporations: a Business Email Compromise (BEC) attack on an international corporation in March of 2023 used a number of different AI-enhanced practices. The CEO in a video call was spoofed with the help of deepfake audio, artificial emails were sent using the AI and were of the identical style as the company, and a social profiler that had to find the most suitable targets within the financial department. The forcible entry resulted in fake conveyance valued to 7.8 million. As shown in the case, the characteristics of AI are developed and incorporated into the modern social type of engineering attack.

2.3 Current Threat Intelligence Limitations

The existing cyber threat intelligence solutions possess a great number of significant flaws regarding addressing AI-enhanced social engineering attacks (Kumar et al., 2023):

Absence of Human-Centric Design: Most current systems have been created with the consideration of technical indicators and without regard to human behavioral patterns and cognitive influencing factors on the absence of immunity to social engineering (Liu et al., 2024). This contributes to high false positive rate, fatigue of the alert systems as well as compliance of the users to security measures. Studies have indicated that most of the security alerts have been ignored by users due to their low presentation and irrelevancy with the situation.

Weak AI Detection Strengths: The traditional signature based and rule-based signature detections are no longer effective at handling the highly advanced AI-based content that continuously evolves and changes (Martinez and Thompson, 2023). The predetermined detection guidelines would also fail to keep pace with the rapid evolution of AI attacks, resulting in it requiring more than six months to identify new variants of attacks.

Lack of Contextual Dynamics: The current systems are not always able to work to the contextual vision of the interaction between humans and AI because these systems do not consider the other hidden signs of ill intent (Nguyen et al., 2024). The little that has been done under existing frameworks is on the contextual variables, which include the time dynamics, groups of users, organizational forces, and environmental forces.

Adaptive Learning Weaknesses: The vast majority of existing frameworks lack the ability to learn and adapt to emerging patterns of the attacks, particularly those ones that incorporate new AI techniques (Patel and Singh, 2023). This is the weakness that results in the gradual increase in performance over time since techniques of attack evolve with time and outside training parameters.

Isolated Detection Strategies: The current systems are not typically configured to work together on the different modalities of detection and organizational boundaries (Rodriguez et al., 2024). Such a fragmentation does not provide the ability to fully assess the threats and the ability to respond.

Comparison of Existing Frameworks: Analysis of Threat Intelligence platforms shows that there is a significant gap between the platforms. Commercial solutions have an average detection rate of 82-87 percent on the traditional threats, but on the attacks enhanced by AI, the solutions have only 45-60 percent accurate detection rates. The academic approaches prove to be more effective in terms of specific attacks but lack in the sense of being all-encompassing, with a practical coverage barrier. Traditional rule-based system accuracy has approximately 76 percent with low levels of false positives but are completely unable to detect new AI generated attacks.

2.4 Adversarial AI Techniques

Adversarial artificial intelligence refers to a number of methods aimed at increasing defensive efforts against AI-enabled attacks (Rodriguez et al., 2024). Key approaches include:

Adversarial Training: Architectural Training of machine learning models realized to work on adversarial solutions to be more robust against malicious input (Smith et al., 2023). This method can be described as training with adversarial perturbations that are systematically created, to subject the models to possible attacks. Studies show that adversarial training is able to enhance the model robustness by 40-60 points above existing attack methods without deteriorating its performance on benign inputs.

Generative Adversarial Networks (GANs): The competitive neural network architecture is used in constructing realistic attack scenarios, in training and evaluating (Taylor and Wilson, 2024). GANs allow using synthesized attack samples that recapitulate statistical characteristics of genuine attacks without facing privacy issues related to the usage of actual incident data. Recent uses are synthetic phishing email generating as anti-phishing system training and deepfake sample generating as detection algorithm training.

Adversarial Detection Algorithms: The specific algorithms are implemented to detect adversarial situations, as well as AI-generated materials (Upadhyay and Sharma, 2023). Such approaches examine statistical attributes, consistency trends and artifacts of AI-generated content. The latest detection algorithms have 85-92 percent accuracy of detecting AI-generated text and 80-89 percent accuracy of detecting deepfakes in videos.

Improvement Enhancement Techniques: collection of defensive measures such as input preprocessing, feature squeezing, gradient masking and use of ensemble mechanisms to enhance robustness of the system to adversarial attacks (Zhang and Kumar, 2024). The methods also seek to make attack surface smaller and computational cost higher in order to succeed at adversarial manipulation.

2.5 AI Risk Governance and Ethical Compliance

The use of AI systems in the area of cybersecurity presupposes the need to have good governing systems and ethical compliance systems (Bennett and Hughes, 2023).

Key considerations include:

Regulatory Frameworks: The analysis of the international AI policy environments, such as NIST AI Risk Management Framework, EU AI Act, and industry-specific policies, can be considered as deals with higher transparency and accountability, and risk management (Collins and Murphy, 2024).Companies implementing AI-based security solutions have to overcome complicated legal regulations and remain functional.

Ethical implication: The introduction of AI systems causes an ethical implication on the privacy, bias, fairness, and accountability (Davidson and Fisher, 2023). The behavioral analytics systems observing user actions should be designed to balance the interests of security and privacy rights and the rights to collect ethical data. Studies have shown that 73 percent of users have a concern regarding the implication of privacy in terms of extensive monitoring of behavior.

Mechanisms of AI Accountability: It is difficult to set clear accountability frameworks of AI decisions on security issues (Edwards and Foster, 2023). Issues about who is responsible in case of false positives, undetected cases, and negative effects must be discussed and analyzed and governed through clear mechanisms.

2.6 Zero Trust Architecture and AI Integration

Zero Trust security models are used to complement AI-enhanced threat detection (Wallace and York, 2024). The key points of integration are:

Continuous Authentication: AI-powered behavioral biometrics can perform continuous authentication of users, i.e. based on the interaction patterns, instead of checking the credential periodically, a continuous trust assessment should be conducted (Ahmed and Connor, 2024).

Micro-Segmentation: AI-based threat intelligence applied with micro-segmentation in the network will allow the dynamic policy of access control that changes according to real-time threat evaluation (Baker and Evans, 2023).

Policy-Based Access Control: AI systems provide the context-aware access management by informing the decisions of the Zero Trust policy based on the behavioral analysis, anomaly detection, and threat correlation (Carter et al., 2024).

2.7 Comparative Framework Analysis

The critical reviews of the available frameworks depict clear benefits and constraints:

Technical Frameworks: The old cybersecurity models (NIST Cybersecurity Framework, ISO 27001) have all the technical controls, but fail to offer specifics to AI-enhanced threats and human-centric design principles (Edwards and Foster, 2023).

AI-Specific Frameworks: The currently developed AI security frameworks (NIST AI RMF, IEEE 7000 series) have been developed to cover a range of AI-specific risks with no reference to excessive integration with traditional cybersecurity controls or other practical implementation guidelines (Garcia and Robinson, 2024).

Human-Centric Frameworks: User experience and human factors frameworks (ISO 9241, NIST Human-Computer Interaction guidelines) are useful in design principles, yet would not be useful in handling particular security requirements and adversarial situations (Lewis and Phillips, 2024).
Gap Identification: There is no current framework that is effective in integrating technical AI capabilities, adversarial robustness, human-centered design and requirements of ethical governance. This study fills this gap by providing frameworks that are developed in an integrated way.

2.8 Research Gaps Identification

It is found that a number of important research gaps need to be addressed based on the comprehensive literature review:

Human-AI Interaction Modelling: There is little evidence on the modeling of intricate patterns of human-AI interaction in adversarial settings especially in the case of cognitive variables, trust relations, and uncertainty decision-making.
Multi-Modal Detection Systems: Lack of integration between text, image, audio and behavioral analysis of unified detection systems that uphold performance efficiency without loss of performance when handling heterogeneous streams of data.
Real-Time Adaptive Responses: Absence of systems able to real-time adapt to changing AI-enhanced strategies of attack incurring low latency and computational costs.
Contextual Behavioral Analytics: Minimal integration of contextual variables such as organizational culture, user role, environmental and time-related variations into behavioral analysis systems.
Privacy-Preserving Detection: There is a lack of study of techniques to preserve user privacy and at the same time be able to do thorough threat detection especially in context of federated learning, differential privacy, and secure multi-party computation methods.
Cross-Cultural Adaptation: Little regard of the cultural differences in communication patterns, social norms, and psychological susceptibility to the influence of social engineering.
Scalable Implementation: Lack of research on scalable implementation of end-to-end threat intelligence systems in varied organizational settings and infrastructure systems.
Interdisciplinary Integration: Absence of models which provide an effective combination of technical abilities and psychological knowledge, organizational behavior laws and principles, policy needs and business ethics.

Quantum-Resistant Approaches: There has been insufficient research on how to prepare AI-based security systems to be resistant to quantum computing threats and post-quantum integration of cryptography.

Generative AI-Specific Defenses: Why it will be necessary to develop detection and mitigation measures uniquely tailored to threats introduced by large language models, diffusion models and other generative AI applications.

Findings of the Literature: The existing literature shows that there is a substantial advancement in the domains such as AI capabilities, behavioral analytics and threat detection, on an individual basis.

Nevertheless, a thorough combination of these aspects in human-type, morally-regulated, and adaptively-strong structures is only barely researched. The current study deals with such gaps by developing systematic frameworks and by empirically validating them.

3. METHODOLOGY

3.1 Framework Architecture

The offered structure is grounded in the multilayered architecture that integrates the adversarial AI solutions with the human-oriented solutions in design, providing the protective framework of the AI-enhanced attacks of social engineering. The architecture comprises of 5 primary layers that perform certain functions and at the same time, are completely integrated:

Data Collection Layer: This is the lowest level layer which assists in the collection of the multi-modal data of different forms including email communication, social interaction, web browsing history, network traffic, user authentication logs and application usage logs. Privacy-saving data collection systems also have been integrated into the layer which ensures privacy regulation in GDPR, CCPA and other privacy laws. The data quality is the highest and the storage is minimized because of hi-tech filtering/ sampling techniques. Real-time streaming can help track the threats in real-time and a more detailed forensic analysis is possible only with the help of the batch processing feature.

Preprocessing and Feature Extraction Layer: This layer involves complicated natural language processing, computer vision and signal processing applications, which are utilized in gauging features that are significant in the available data. The linguistic analysis, semantic parsing, sentiment extraction and stylometry profiling, is performed by the system in the case of textual data. The deepfake artifact detection, metadata analysis and visual consistency verification are also part of image processing. The audio processing is done with spectral analysis, prosodic features extraction and voice biometric verification. Behavioral information is statistically engineered and the time patterns are extracted and the context enriched.

Adversarial AI Detection Engine: This is a specialized AI detection engine designed to detect AI-generated content and adversarial examples with the use of machine learning models and algorithms. The engine utilizes several forms of detection such as statistical anomaly detection, adversarial example detection, GAN generated content detection, and transformer-based output classification of language models. Ensemble techniques are used to use outputs of several specialized detectors to enhance the accuracy of the overall and decrease the false positives.

Behavioral Analytics Engine: This layer examines the interaction contexts and behavioral patterns of human beings to determine any anomalies that may be a sign of social engineering. The engine has personal user baselines that record normal behavior pattern in many dimensions such as temporal patterns, sequence of interaction, style of communication, and contextual preferences. The algorithms in anomaly detection recognize a variation of the baseline against which the behavioral patterns are expected but ignore natural divergence in behavior and responses to environmental circumstances.

Decision Fusion and Response Layer: This is the uppermost layer and it combines the outputs of various detection engines to make a final decision on the classifications and also activate the response machinery. Bayesian inference and accumulation of evidences are a hybridization method of utilizing heterogeneous detection signals to form a single threat judgment. Context-aware decision logic takes into account the organizational policies, user roles, severity of threats, and effects of operations in coming up with a response action. The automated responses consist of the creation of alerts, restriction of access, blocking of transactions, and forensic capture of data. HITL mechanisms can be used to review potentially high stakes decisions by human security analysts.

3.2 Human-Centric Design Principles

Some of the human-centric design principles applied in the framework are based on cognitive psychology, the research of human-computer interaction, and organizational behavior theory:

Cognitive Load Optimization: The user interfaces and alert systems are created to load optimally in terms of cognitive load and information clarity/

actionability. Studies have indicated that security staff members are affected with cognitive overload due to being overwhelmed with too many alerts or intricate technical data (Lewis and Phillips, 2024). This is covered by the framework by progressive disclosure of information, maximum optimization of visual hierarchy, and maximum disclosure as per the context. The use of alert presentations is based on the actionable information rather than technical detail and the user can have a drill-down option to get the extra information.

Contextual Awareness: The system takes into account the context of individual users such as organizational role, level of experience, technical knowledge, patterns of historical interaction and the context of actively performed tasks to adjust detection sensitivity and response (Nelson and Scott, 2023). As an illustration, critical personnel like those in the finance department are provided with more protection and thorough threat intelligence and the general users with simplified alerts as far as immediate protection measures are concerned. Time-of-day, day-of-week and seasonal patterns are some temporal context that can be used to set anomaly detection thresholds and response urgency.

Explainable AI: The detection decisions are provided with detailed explanations that enable users to have an idea of how suggestions and alerts related to security are made (Edwards and Foster, 2023). The mechanisms of explanation use various forms of communication such as natural language description, graphical representation, real-life examples and confidence markers. Explainable security systems can be shown to achieve 43 percent greater compliance rates than black-box systems, which just give notifications without explanations.

Adaptive Learning with Feedback: The system will be improved through consistent learning and feedback including behavioral patterns to enhance detection accuracy and false positives (Quinn and Adams, 2024). Explicit feedback allows users to provide a confirmation or denial of threat classifications, and implicit feedback is based on the responses of users to alerts. The machine learning models use feedback in the form of the online learning methods that vary the parameters of detection, but avoid adversarial manipulation by the use of validated feedback mechanisms.

Trust Calibration: The framework provides provisions to build and sustain the right level of trust between human beings and automated security mechanisms (Stevens and White, 2024). Excessive trust causes complacency and lack of vigilance whereas lack of trust causes circumventing of the systems and non-compliance. The system is also transparent in terms of detection capabilities, limitations and uncertainty estimates so that a user can build calibrated mental models of system behavior.

3.3 Adversarial AI Integration

3.3.1 Adversarial Training Methodology

The framework uses an adversarial approach to training which exposes detection models to adversarial examples in a systematic manner:

Synthetic Attack Generation: AI models that support the creation of diverse social engineering attacks are created to be trained. Such models consist of language models that have been finetuned to create phishing emails, GAN-based models that generate deepfakes, and automated social profiling models that create attack scenarios (Oliver and Reed, 2024). Synthetic attacks, at the end of the scale, can be simple phishing techniques, or sophisticated spear-phishing, which guarantees robustness of the model on a threat category.
Creation of Adversarial examples: It is a system that creates adversarial examples that provoke detection algorithm resistance to evasion strategies. Perturbation techniques are Fast Gradient Sign Method (FGSM), Projected Gradient Descent (PGD), Carlini and Wagner attacks, and adaptive attacks that are particular to avoid known detection techniques (Zhang and Kumar, 2024). The generated examples are validated to provide realistic attack qualities as well as being effective to reveal model weaknesses.
Updates in the Model Continuously: Detection models are retrained on a regular basis with new adversarial examples and real-world data on attacks. The balancing of the update cycle is between model stability and the speed of adopting new defenses against the emerging attack patterns by adding new defenses to the model, preserving the ability to detect known threats (Roberts and Smith, 2024). A/B testing and version control is used to assure that improvements to the model are made rather than reducing the overall performance.
Red Team Simulation: Adversarial simulation exercises are regular, and they consist of red teams that create new attack strategies with the latest AI capabilities, which offer realistic analysis of detection system effectiveness and which define potential blind spots that can be used by real attacks prior to their exploitation.

3.3.2 Multi-Modal Adversarial Detection

The system introduces specific detection algorithms depending on the content generated by AI:

Text Analysis: Advanced language processing algorithms detect AI generated text in a variety of indicators such as linguistic features (vocabulary diversity, syntactic complexity, semantic consistency), stylistic features (such as authorship characteristics, consistency in writing style, etc.), content processing (logical flow, factual accuracy, contextual appropriateness), and statistical features (n-grams distributions, perplexity scores, etc.) (Natural Language Processing Research, 2024). The system uses transformer based classifiers trained on large corpora of human written and AI written text that have a detection accuracy of 96.2 percent on a variety of text samples.

Image and Video Analysis: Computer vision algorithms find deepfake information by applying a series of analysis methods such as analyzing temporal consistency of the videos, checking physiological signals (eye movements, blinking patterns, micro-expressions), analysis of audio-visual consistency, data compression artifact, deepfake detection with neural networks and detection of metadata anomalies (Hassan et al., 2024). The system has 89.4% detection accuracy when using many different methods of deepfake generated images such as face-swap technique, face reenactment and full synthesis technique.

Audio Analysis Signal processing Additionally, Zone techniques of synthetic speech recognition are spectral analysis (frequency domain characteristics, harmonic patterns), examination of prosodic features (pitch variation, speaking rate, emphasis patterns), voice biometric verification, phonetic consistency analysis, and detection of neural vocoder artifacts (Kelly and Turner, 2023). The system shows 91.3 percent accuracy in a real and fake voice conversion and text-to-speech technologies in categorizing a synthetic and authentic speech.

Behavioral Pattern Analysis: This machine learning algorithm examines patterns of user interactions to detect automated or AI-assisted attacks based on temporal (patterns in interaction timing, duration of interacting pattern), spatial (characteristics of mouse movement, precision of clicks), semantic (consistency of the content, appropriateness of the context), and cross-channel patterns (correlations across communication channels) (Baker and Evans, 2023). The detection rate of behavioral-based detection is 93.4% at detecting automated bot behavior and AI-assisted social engineering attacks.

3.4 Behavioral Analytics Engine

3.4.1 User Behavior Modeling

The behavioral analytics engine is a complex model-driven system that seeks to learn normal or standard user behavioral patterns and signal abnormal activities:

Baseline Establishment: Baselines of the individual user behavior are determined by examining past interaction data on more than one dimension. The process of the baseline construction accumulates data during 30-90 days in order to represent not only consistent trends, but also reasonable behavior variability (Peterson and Hayes, 2023). Statistical techniques that use the kernel density estimation, Gaussian mixture models, and non-parametric approaches represent the distribution of behavior considering the multi-modal distribution and time evolution.

Anomaly Detection: The system uses anomaly detection algorithms based on statistical and machine learning to detect anomalies in the established bases. Detection algorithms are Isolation Forest that finds outliers, One-Class SVM that identifies novelties, LSTM-based sequence modeling that analyzes an appearance of a temporal pattern, and behavioral segmentation that can be performed by clustering (Harris and Clark, 2023). Ensemble integration involves several detection techniques in order to enhance strength and minimize false positives.

Context -Based Analysis: Behavioral analysis encompasses contextual elements such as a temporal context (effects of time-of-day, day-of-week effect, season changes), an environmental context (location, device characteristics, network characteristics), a social context (communication patterns, collaboration behaviors), an operational context (work activities, operational requirements) (Thomas and Campbell, 2023). Context-sensitive modeling has shown to have significant potential in reduction of false positive rates by preventing both legitimate behavioral adaptation and malicious anomalies.

Behavioral Biometrics: The device identifies biometric information when the user interacts with the system such as typing patterns (keystroke timing, rhythm patterns), mouse dynamics (movement patterns, click patterns), touchscreen dynamics (pressure variations, swipe patterns), navigation patterns (browsing patterns, application usage) (Ahmed and Connor, 2024). Such biometrics make it possible to perform continuous authentication and detect attempts of account fraud or impersonation.

3.4.2 Social Engineering Susceptibility Assessment

The system evaluates personal vulnerability to social engineering attacks in a variety of dimensions of analysis:

Psychological Profiling: A communication pattern analysis and response behaviors are used to determine the psychological factors that could make them vulnerable such as compliance tendencies to authority, vulnerability to urgency, tendency to be influenced by social proof, and reliance on cognitive heuristics (Peterson and Hayes, 2023). The analysis does not breach privacy and ethical barriers because it does not involve intrusive psychological evaluation but only considers observable behaviour.

Risk Scoring: The dynamic risk scores are the levels of vulnerability to various types of attack vectors. Risk models combine risk susceptibility factors, exposure, the criticalness of assets, and the strength of protective factors to produce wholesome risk analysis (Norton and Quinn, 2023). Scores are continually updated with regards to behavioral observation, training accomplishment and simulated attack application.

Personalized Protection: Risk profiles are used to deploy customized protection controls such as adaptive authentication requirements, transaction verification levels, communication verification notices and specific security awareness interventions (Davidson and Fisher, 2023). Enhanced protections are offered to high-risk people with no effect on low-risk users.

3.5 Implementation Architecture

The architecture implements a microservices architecture that guarantees scalability, maintenance and flexibility of operations:

Data Ingestion Service: Data collection over various real-times is managed, and privacy complies or other regulations are followed. The service applies the data minimization principles and techniques of anonymity and consent management (Garcia & Robinson, 2024).

Feature Processing Service: Processing multi-modal data, parallel processing structures and GPU acceleration are performed to perform feature extraction and preprocessing of data (Ingram and Knight, 2024).

Detection Engine Service: organizes the execution of various specialized detection algorithms by using containerized deployment so that it is possible to scale and manage versions independently (Lambert & Owen, 2023).

Analytics Service: Conducts an analysis of behavior and keeps the models of user behaviors in distributed computing frameworks to scale up processing of large scale behavioral data (Mason & Perry, 2024).

Decision Service: Unites recovery engines with results using Bayesian combination and accretion of proof, realizing context educated judgement logic and has human-in-the-loop processes (Sullivan and Taylor, 2024).

Response Service: Deals with both automated and manual response services such as generation of alerts, enforcement of access controls, blocking of transactions, forensic data acquisition, and coordination of incident response (Turner & Vincent, 2023).

Integration Layer: Offers the standardized APIs that allow the integration with the security infrastructure that is already in place such as SIEM systems, identity providers, endpoint protection platforms, and security orchestration tools (Wallace and York, 2024).

4. ALGORITHM DESIGN

4.1 Multi-Modal AI Detection Algorithm

The basic detection algorithm combines several analysis methods to detect AI-enhanced social engineering attacks by multi-modal processing in totality:

Algorithm 1: Multi-Modal AI Detection

INPUT: Multi-modal data (text T, image I, audio A, behavioral B)
OUTPUT: Threat classification C and confidence score σ
PROCEDURE MultiModalDetection(T, I, A, B):

1. Initialize detection modules:
    - NLP_module ← InitializeNLPDetector()
    - CV_module ← InitializeVisionDetector()
    - Audio_module ← InitializeAudioDetector()
    - Behavioral_module ← InitializeBehavioralDetector()
2. FOR each input modality m in {T, I, A, B}:
    a. F_m ← ExtractFeatures(m, domain_specific_techniques)
    b. F_m_robust ← ApplyAdversarialRobustness(F_m)
    c. P_m ← GenerateModalityThreatProbability(F_m_robust)
    d. σ_m ← EstimateConfidence(P_m)
3. Compute weighted ensemble prediction:
    w ← ComputeAdaptiveWeights({P_m, σ_m}, historical_performance)
    P_ensemble ← Σ(w_m × P_m) for all modalities m
4. Apply contextual adjustment:
    user_profile ← RetrieveUserProfile()
    context_factors ← ExtractContextualFactors()
    P_adjusted ← ContextualAdjustment(P_ensemble, user_profile, context_factors)
5. Generate final classification:

C ← ClassifyThreat(P_adjusted, threshold_adaptive)
σ_final ← AggregateConfidence({σ_m}, P_adjusted)

6. IF σ_final > confidence_threshold:
   a. TriggerResponseMechanism(C, σ_final)
   b. UpdateUserBehaviorModel(user_profile, interaction_data)
7. LogDetectionResults(C, σ_final, {P_m}, timestamp)
8. RETURN C, σ_final

The main benefits of using this algorithm have included; good multi-modal combination; it is capable of making use of the complementary information that different types of data can provide, adaptive weighting schemes; it can adapt to the discrepancy between data quality and availability, contextual cognizance, captures the effects of the information on the user-specific and situational situation, and confidence estimation, which can be used to the informed decision and Human-in-the-loop processes.

4.2 Behavioral Anomaly Detection Algorithm

The behavioral analytics block works with the application of advanced statistical tools to identify the unusual pattern of interaction to indicate potential social engineering attacks:

Algorithm 2: Behavioral Anomaly Detection

INPUT: User interaction sequence U, historical baseline B_hist, context C
OUTPUT: Anomaly score A and risk assessment R
PROCEDURE BehavioralAnomalyDetection(U, B_hist, C):

1. Extract behavioral features:
   F_temporal ← ExtractTemporalFeatures(U)
   F_spatial ← ExtractSpatialFeatures(U)
   F_semantic ← ExtractSemanticFeatures(U)
   F_biometric ← ExtractBiometricFeatures(U)
   F ← Concatenate({F_temporal, F_spatial, F_semantic, F_biometric})
2. Normalize features using baseline statistics:
   F_norm ← NormalizeFeatures(F, B_hist.mean, B_hist.std)
3. Apply dimensionality reduction for noise filtering:
   F_reduced ← PCA_Transform(F_norm, n_components=optimal_k)
4. Compute anomaly scores using ensemble methods:
   a. Isolation Forest:

A_if ← IsolationForest.AnomalyScore(F_reduced)

b. LSTM sequence modeling:

sequence ← ConstructSequence(U, window_size)
prediction ← LSTM_Model.Predict(sequence)
A_lstm ← ReconstructionError(sequence, prediction)

c. Clustering-based deviation:

cluster ← AssignCluster(F_reduced, cluster_model)
A_cluster ← DistanceToClusterCenter(F_reduced, cluster)

d. One-Class SVM:

A_svm ← OneClassSVM.DecisionFunction(F_reduced)

5. Integrate contextual factors:

context_vector ← EncodeContext(C.time, C.location, C.device)
context_weight ← ComputeContextWeight(context_vector, B_hist)

6. Generate risk-adjusted anomaly score:

A_ensemble ← WeightedCombination({A_if, A_lstm, A_cluster, A_svm})
A_adjusted ← A_ensemble × context_weight

7. Assess risk level:

susceptibility_score ← RetrieveSusceptibilityScore(user_id)
asset_criticality ← DetermineAssetCriticality(user_id, current_task)
R ← ComputeRiskScore(A_adjusted, susceptibility_score, asset_criticality)

8. Update behavioral baseline:

IF A_adjusted < threshold_normal:
B_hist ← IncrementalUpdate(B_hist, F, learning_rate)

9. RETURN A_adjusted, R

This algorithm has several significant advantages like multi-modes combination is done successfully with the help of complementing information which is presented by the different sorts of data, adaptive weighting schemes which modifies to the inequalities in the quality and availability of the data, situational cognizance, which considers user-specific and situational effects, and confidence estimation, which can be applied to make valuable decisions as well as Human-in-the-loop procedures.

4.3 Adversarial Robustness Enhancement Algorithm

The framework provides high-level defensive mechanisms to make sure that the system is strong to adversarial attacks against the detection system itself:

Algorithm 3: Adversarial Robustness Enhancement

INPUT: Input data X, trained detection model M, perturbation budget ε
OUTPUT: Robust classification decision C_robust and confidence σ_robust
PROCEDURE AdversarialRobustnessEnhancement(X, M, ε):

1. Generate adversarial perturbations:
   X_fgsm ← FGSM_Attack(X, M, ε)
   X_pgd ← PGD_Attack(X, M, ε, iterations=40)
   X_cw ← CarliniWagner_Attack(X, M, confidence=0.0)
   X_adv_list ← {X, X_fgsm, X_pgd, X_cw}
2. Apply input preprocessing defenses:
   X_defended_list ← []
   FOR X_sample IN X_adv_list:
   X_squeezed ← FeatureSqueezing(X_sample, bit_depth=5)
   X_smoothed ← GaussianSmoothing(X_squeezed, sigma=0.5)
   X_transformed ← RandomTransformation(X_smoothed, transform_set)
   X_defended_list.append(X_transformed)
3. Perform ensemble prediction:
   predictions ← []
   FOR X_def IN X_defended_list:
   FOR model IN ensemble_models:
   pred ← model.Predict(X_def)
   predictions.append(pred)
4. Apply Byzantine-robust aggregation:
   predictions_sorted ← SortPredictions(predictions)
   n_trim ← floor(len(predictions) × trim_ratio)
   predictions_trimmed ← predictions_sorted[n_trim:-n_trim]
   C_robust ← Mean(predictions_trimmed)
5. Validate consistency across detection modalities:
   modal_predictions ← GroupByModality(predictions)
   consistency_score ← ComputeCrossModalConsistency(modal_predictions)
6. Compute prediction uncertainty:
   epistemic_uncertainty ← ComputeEpistemicUncertainty(predictions)
   aleatoric_uncertainty ← ComputeAleatoricUncertainty(X, M)
   total_uncertainty ← CombineUncertainties(epistemic, aleatoric)
7. Generate final confidence:
   base_confidence ← 1 - total_uncertainty
   σ_robust ← base_confidence × consistency_score

8. Apply decision threshold with uncertainty consideration:
    IF σ_robust < uncertainty_threshold:
    C_final ← RequestHumanReview(C_robust, σ_robust, X)
    ELSE:
    C_final ← C_robust
9. RETURN C_final, σ_robust

The algorithm has strong defenses with several attack simulation experimentation with various adversarial attacks, defense-in-depth with multiple independent defensive layers, Byzantine-robust aggregation to avoid manipulation with outlier voting, quantification of uncertainty to make informed decisions on the reliability of prediction, and human-in-the-loop to support high-uncertainty situations.

4.4 Adaptive Learning Algorithm

That the system continuously enhances detection capabilities based on adaptive learning mechanisms that add new attack samples, user feedback and performance monitoring:

Algorithm 4: Adaptive Learning Framework

INPUT: New attack samples S_new, user feedback F, performance metrics P
OUTPUT: Updated detection models M_updated
PROCEDURE AdaptiveLearning(S_new, F, P):

1. Collect and validate new data:

S_validated ← ValidateAttackSamples(S_new, quality_threshold)
F_validated ← ValidateFeedback(F, consistency_checks)

2. Perform data quality assessment:

quality_scores ← AssessDataQuality(S_validated, quality_metrics)
S_filtered ← FilterLowQualitySamples(S_validated, quality_scores, threshold)

3. Apply active learning for sample selection:

uncertainty_scores ← ComputeUncertaintyScores(S_filtered, M_current)
diversity_scores ← ComputeDiversityScores(S_filtered, M_current)
informativeness ← CombineScores(uncertainty_scores, diversity_scores)

S_informative ← SelectTopK(S_filtered, informativeness, k=batch_size)

4. Integrate user feedback:

S_feedback_positive ← ExtractPositiveFeedback(F_validated)
S_feedback_negative ← ExtractNegativeFeedback(F_validated)
S_training ← Combine(S_informative, S_feedback_positive, S_feedback_negative)

5. Retrain detection models using incremental learning:
   a. Update neural network weights:

FOR epoch IN range(n_epochs):
FOR batch IN S_training:
gradients ← ComputeGradients(batch, M_current)
M_current ← ApplyGradientUpdate(M_current, gradients, learning_rate)

b. Refresh ensemble models:

FOR model IN ensemble_models:
model_updated ← IncrementalFit(model, S_training)
ensemble_models.update(model_updated)

c. Adjust behavioral baselines:

FOR user IN affected_users:
baseline ← GetUserBaseline(user)
baseline_updated ← UpdateBaseline(baseline, F_validated, adaptation_rate)
SetUserBaseline(user, baseline_updated)

6. Validate updated models on held-out test set:

T_holdout ← SampleTestSet(historical_data, stratified=True)
P_new ← EvaluatePerformance(M_current, T_holdout, metrics)

7. Compare performance with previous version:

improvement ← ComputeImprovement(P_new, P_previous)
IF improvement > deployment_threshold:
M_deployed ← M_current

LogModelUpdate(version, P_new, timestamp)
ELSE:
M_deployed ← M_previous
LogFailedUpdate(P_new, improvement, timestamp)

8. Deploy updated models with gradual rollout:

DeployGradually(M_deployed, rollout_percentage=20%, duration=24h)
MonitorPerformance(M_deployed, real_time_metrics)

9. Update adversarial training set:

S_adversarial ← GenerateAdversarialSamples(M_deployed, generation_budget)
adversarial_training_set.append(S_adversarial)

10. RETURN M_deployed

This adaptive learning algorithm makes sure that there is ongoing improvement by actively learning, trying to allocate computational resources to the most informative samples, incremental learning to update models, but does not fully re-train, performance validation to avoid degradation caused by updates to the model, gradual deployment so that there is less risk of system-wide failures, and adversarial adaptation, continuously updating defenses against changing attack methods.

4.5 Context-Aware Decision Making Algorithm

Decision making activities are done using extensive contextual data to maximize the classification accuracy and effectiveness of operations:

Algorithm 5: Context-Aware Decision Making

The inputs consist of the output of the detection D, user context U, organizational policies P, threat intelligence T.
OUTPUT: Final decision decision final and recommended actions A
PROCEDURE ContextAwareDecisionMaking(D, U, P, T):

1. Extract detection signals:

threat_probability ← D.probability
confidence_score ← D.confidence

modality_scores ← D.modality_breakdown
anomaly_level ← D.anomaly_score

2. Retrieve contextual information:

user_role ← U.organizational_role
user_risk_profile ← U.risk_assessment
current_task ← U.task_context
historical_behavior ← U.behavioral_history
device_trust ← U.device_trust_level
location_context ← U.location_assessment

3. Integrate threat intelligence:

active_campaigns ← T.current_campaigns
target_sectors ← T.targeted_industries
attack_trends ← T.emerging_patterns
indicator_matches ← MatchIndicators(D, T.iocs)

4. Apply policy constraints:

policy_requirements ← P.GetApplicablePolicies(user_role, current_task)
compliance_constraints ← P.regulatory_requirements
risk_tolerance ← P.acceptable_risk_levels

5. Compute risk-weighted decision score:

base_score ← threat_probability × confidence_score
user_risk_multiplier ← ComputeRiskMultiplier(user_risk_profile, user_role)
context_adjustment ← ComputeContextualAdjustment(current_task, location_context)
intelligence_factor ← ComputeIntelligenceFactor(indicator_matches, active_campaigns)
decision_score ← base_score × user_risk_multiplier × context_adjustment × intelligence_factor

6. Determine decision threshold:

adaptive_threshold ← ComputeAdaptiveThreshold(
base_threshold=0.7,

user_risk_profile,
policy_requirements,
recent_false_positive_rate
)

7. Make classification decision:

```
IF decision_score > adaptive_threshold:
classification ← "THREAT_DETECTED"
severity ← ComputeSeverity(decision_score, potential_impact)
ELSE IF decision_score > (adaptive_threshold × 0.6):
classification ← "SUSPICIOUS_ACTIVITY"
severity ← "MEDIUM"
ELSE:
classification ← "BENIGN"
severity ← "LOW"
```

8. Determine response actions:

```
A ← []
IF classification == "THREAT_DETECTED":
IF severity == "CRITICAL":
A.append(BlockCommunication())
A.append(IsolateSession())
A.append(NotifySecurityTeam(priority="IMMEDIATE"))
A.append(InitiateForensicCapture())
ELSE IF severity == "HIGH":
A.append(RequireAdditionalVerification())
A.append(NotifyUser(explanation, recommended_action))
A.append(NotifySecurityTeam(priority="HIGH"))
ELSE:
A.append(LogIncident(details, evidence))
A.append(NotifyUser(warning, guidance))
ELSE IF classification == "SUSPICIOUS_ACTIVITY":
A.append(IncreasedMonitoring(duration=24h))
A.append(RequestUserVerification(method="adaptive"))
A.append(LogSuspiciousActivity(details))
```

9. Generate explanation:

explanation ← GenerateExplanation(
decision=classification,
contributing_factors=[threat_probability, context_adjustment, intelligence_factor],
evidence=modality_scores,
confidence=confidence_score
)

10. Return decision package:

decision_final ← {
classification: classification,
severity: severity,
confidence: confidence_score,
decision_score: decision_score,
explanation: explanation
}
RETURN decision_final, A

5. SYSTEM ARCHITECTURE

5.1 Overall Architecture Design

The system architecture uses a cloud-native and modern design with great enhances to modularity, scalability, and maintainability. The architecture has six main hierarchically structured layering:

Presentation Layer: Gives the system administrator and security analysts as well as end users user interfaces. It has real-time dashboards with threat intelligence and system status, portals to alert management where threats can be triaged and coordinated response, interfaces to provide users with contextified security warnings, system customization and policy management configurations, and portals to compliance documentation and performance reporting. The presentation layer uses the principles of responsive design that gives it the ability to be accessible to desktop, mobile, and tablet devices.

Application Layer: Provides the implementation of business core business logic such as threat detection orchestration coordinating a variety of detection engines, behavioral analysis and user profiling and anomaly detection, response coordination implementing automated and manual response actions, policy enforcement to maintain compliance with organizational and regulatory demands and audit logging with maintained comprehensive records of activity to be analyzed in forensic mode and verify compliance.

Service Layer: Responsible for the provision of microservices that handle certain functional abilities such as data processing services, which are involved with ingestion processing, transformation, and enrichment, machine learning model management services, which coordinate the deployment, versioning, and monitoring of models, integration services, which is involved in providing opportunities to connect with other external systems and data sources, notification services, which entails alert delivery, authentication and authorization services, which are used to control access and permissions and analytics services, which generate insights and performance metrics.

Data Layer: Deal with data storage, access, and processing using distributed storage systems such as real-time data stores (Apache Kafka, Redis), allowing processing of streams and involvement in processes with low latency, historical data stores (Elasticsearch, postgreSQL), providing the ability to analyze and store training models and version history, model repositories, in which model artifacts are stored and version history is logged, configuration databases, which store system settings and policy, and feature stores that can store extracted features and support efficient processing on the detection of incoming streams of data. The data layer enforces data lifecycle management such as retention policy, archival processes and deletion processes to comply with regulations.

Processing Layer: Computationally intensive step- It can be used to perform processing designed of multi-modal data, code maps of a model one step is running a detection model at scale can run, maintaining and updating user baselines, adversarial robustness check checking related to prediction can be checked without with respect to adversarial attacks, and ensemble, integrate the output of multiple detection models. The processing layer leverages deep learning operations that are performed with the help of the GPU and parallel processing that are implemented with the help of distributed computing frameworks.

Infrastructure Layer: Makes available basic computing infrastructure resources such as container orchestration (Kubernetes) operating service deployment and scaling and compute resources (CPU, GPU, TPU) hosting processing workloads, network infrastructure providing communication and data transfer, security infrastructure that implements encryption, access control, and network segmentation, monitoring and logging infrastructure calculating system health and performance, and disaster recovery systems continuing business throughputures.

5.2 Component Interactions

The architecture enables integration without any problem due to clear interfaces and patterns of communication:

Data Flow Management: Provides effective data pipelines to process real-time streams of data of various data sources. Apache Kafka also offers message queuing that is also reliable delivery and fault-tolerant. Incoming data is tested on its quality to guarantee its accuracy and consistency. The data is sent to the suitable processing pipelines by their routing logic depending on the content type, and priority. Back-pressure system prevents overloading of the system in case of traffic peaks.

Model Management: Provides the ability to centrally manage machine learning models with version control tracking model evolution and allow rollback capabilities, automate the deployment process deploying model updates via CI/CD pipelines, monitor the performance tracking the accuracy, latency and resource usage of models, A/B testing against model variants before full deployment and provides a central catalog of available models and their metadata.

Event-Driven Architecture: It uses event-driven patterns that guarantee responsive and scalable event processing like event sourcing that provides full history of system state changes, publish-subscribe event messaging that decouples event producers and consumers, event correlation which identifies related events across multiple event sources and event processing that identifies pattern in event streams which indicates potential threats.

Integration Capabilities: Allows flexible integration with available security infrastructures such as SIEM integration forwarding of alerts and receiving of threat information, identity provider integration using available authentication systems, endpoint protection integration, which coordinates a system of endpoint-level protection, network security integration, which shares threat information with firewalls and IDS/IPS, and ticketing system integration, which automates incident response processes.

5.3 Scalability and Performance

The architecture is provided with massive deployments with detailed scalability capabilities:

Horizontal Scaling: The components are scaled horizontally through multiple instances such as stateless services that scale independently on demand, database scaling that duplicates the data to several nodes, load balancing that distributes the requests among various service instances, and auto-scaling that scales the capacity based on real-time measures. The architecture can be deployed on many availability zones and regions with high availability and disaster recovery capabilities.

Load Balancing: Intelligent load distribution will optimize resource utilization using round-robin in distributing load evenly, least-connections routing to distribute variable request processing times, content-based routing where requests are directed to special instances and health checking where unhealthy instances are not allowed to rotate.

Caching Strategies: Multi-level caching is an attempt to optimize performance in terms of application-level caching Shopping storing common data in memory, CDN caching storing common content at a geographical location, database query caching minimizing repetitive database access, and model prediction caching storing the result of commonly analyzed data.

Resource Optimization: Advanced resource management provides an efficient operation such as resource limits to restrict resource wastage, memory pooling to reduce allocation overhead, connection pooling to minimize connection costs, and batch processing to group operations to achieve better efficiency.

Performance Characteristics: The architecture has response times of less than 3 seconds to 95th percentile requests, throughput of over 10,000 requests per minute per service instance, resource utilization of less than 70 percent under normal conditions which allows the architecture to have headroom when faced with traffic spikes, and can be scaled linearly to as many as 50,000 concurrent users.

5.4 Security Architecture

Extensive security safeguards against system compromise:

Defense in Depth: It has many layers of security such as network segmentation where components are isolated depending on their trust levels, in-transit encryption where transmission of data is secured and in-rest encryption securing stored data, access control restricting access to the system based on roles and permission, and API authentication and authorization- is a system that secures all the interactions with interfaces.

Zero Trust Implementation: The architecture implements the Zero Trust concepts such as continuous authentication that checks the identity during the session, least privilege access that provides access to only what is required, micro-segmentation that limits the lateral movement and explicit verification to explicitly grant access authorizations instead of implicit trust.

Threat Protection: The in-built protections are also against typical attack vectors such as DDoS protection by rate limiting and traffic filtering, injection attack prevention by input validation and parameterized queries, authentication bypass protection by multi-factor authentication and session management and privilege escalation prevention by appropriate authorization checks.
Security Monitoring: Ongoing monitoring identifies possible security attacks such as intrusion detection monitoring to detect an attempt at unauthorized access, anomaly detection monitoring to identify odd system behavior, vulnerability scanning to periodically determine the security posture, and security information aggregation, which correlates security actions in various components.

5.5 Data Privacy and Compliance

The architecture has full privacy and compliance features:

Minimization of Data: Only the required data is collected which lowers the privacy risk and storage needs. Data lifecycle Automated Data lifecycle management instills deletion schedule and retention policy.
Purpose limitation: is used to be sure that the data is used according to the purposes of collection.
Anonymization and Pseudonymization: Privacy-preserving methods safeguard user identity such as the removal of personally identifiable information (PII) redaction which eliminates identifying information, aggregation of data reporting statistics instead of single records, differential privacy adding statistical noise to protect individual privacy and still analytically useful information and tokenization which involves substituting sensitive data with a token.
Regulatory Compliance: The system is consistent with various regulatory frameworks such as GDPR compliance with data subject rights, consent management, and breach notification, CCPA compliance with consumer privacy rights and data transparency, HIPAA compliance with deployments in the healthcare industry with the help of appropriate technical safeguards, and industry-specific regulations with the help of configurable policies and controls.
Audit and Accountability: Thorough audit facilities facilitate compliance checking such as immutable audit logs that capture all activity of the system, user activity tracking captures every action of the user, access logs that document data access events and compliance reporting that produces documentation that is necessary.

6. EXPERIMENTAL SETUP

6.1 Dataset Description

The experimental analysis uses a full dataset of real-world cybersecurity data and synthetic AI-generated attack data, which is strongly validated in any threat scenario:

Real-World Data: Three total-participating organizations (one of them is a financial institution, one is a technology company and one is a healthcare provider) were sampled to complete an 18-month study period between January 2023 and June 2024. The dataset consists of 2.3 million email messages (spam, phishing and benign messages), 890,000 web access logs that record the browsing patterns, 1.5 million network traffic records that record the connection patterns, 450,000 authentication records that record successful and failed logins and extensive user interaction records that include the mouse movements, keystroke dynamics and applications usage records. All the data was anonymized through differential privacy with e=1.0 guaranteeing high privacy characteristics and maintaining analytical goodness.

Synthetic Attack Data Generation: AI-generated attack samples were generated using the state-of-the-art adversarial training generative models such as GPT-4 fine-tuned on phishing corpus generating 50,000 phishing emails in 15 attack types, StyleGAN2-ADA generating 10,000 deepfake images of identity impersonation scenarios, waveglow neural vocoder generating 5,000 synthetic audio samples of automated attacks and 25,000 automated user interaction sequences. The parameters of generation were varied in order to be diverse in terms of sophistication levels, target specificity and evasion techniques.

Labeled Attack Samples: Verified attack samples were sampled through various sources of 15,000 verified phishing samples in industry threat intelligence feeds, 8,000 reported social engineering incidents in cybersecurity incident databases, 12,000 attempted attacks in controlled phishing simulation, and academic successively available benchmark collections. Each sample was manually checked by qualified security personnel with a high accuracy of the label (more than 98%).

Behavioral Data Gathering: Controlled experiments of the 500 respondents of various demographics (age 18-65, equal gender ratio, different levels of technical skills) were conducted to collect the user interaction patterns. The subjects were asked to complete standardized activities and the data of interaction were captured in terms of mouse paths, patterns of clicking, rhythms of typing, navigation paths and decision times. Institutional review board gave approval to the study, and informed consent was obtained by all participants.

The protocol of data collection reduced the risk of privacy due to the instant anonymity and safe storage.

Characteristics of the dataset:

The final dataset will have the following characteristics: Temporal coverage: 18 months, number of samples: 4.2 million, number of attack samples: 125,000 (3%), number of benign samples: 4,075,000 (97%), number of modalities: Text, Image, Audio, Behavioral, Attack types: 23 different types, Sophistication levels: Basic (40%), Intermediate (35%), Advanced (25%).

6.2 Evaluation Metrics

The overall assessment uses a variety of measures which measure various areas of system performance:

Detection Accuracy Metrics: Metrics of classification performance, which include but are not limited to overall accuracy (correctly classified samples / total samples), precision (true positives / (true positives + false positives)) being a measure of positive prediction, recall (true positives / (true positives + false negatives)) which is a measure of attack detection coverage, F1-score (harmonic mean of precision and recall) which balances the two metrics, and area under ROC curve (AUC-ROC) which measures classification performance as a function of threshold.

False Positive and False Negative Rates: Operational performance indicators such as false positive rate (false positives / total negatives) indicating benign operation activities that are mistakenly detected as threats, and false negative rate (false negatives / total positives) indicating the real threat activities that are successfully eluded by detection, and cost weighted error rates, representing operational costs of a false positive versus a false negative detection.

Response Time Metrics: System latency (including detection latency): Time needed to detect a threat (time between event occurrence and threat detection) System latency (including processing time): Time to complete a response (computational time to extract features and classify a threat) End-to-end response time: Time to complete a response (total time between event occurrence and completed response action) throughput: events per unit time: the number of events that need to be processed per unit time.

Scalability Metrics: performance metrics (system performance) of the system with scaling loads such as throughput scaling (throughput vs. resource allocation), load latency (response time vs. concurrent users), resource usage

(CPU, memory, patterns of network utilized), and cost effectiveness (cost per million events processed).

User Experience Metrics: Measures the human factor such as the alert fatigue (quantified by survey and patterns of interaction), user understanding (quantified by system understanding test), compliance rates (percentage of user compliance with security instructions), task interference (effect on productivity based on task completion time), and user satisfaction (quantified using a System Usability Scale).

Adversarial Robustness Metrics: This is a evaluation of adversarial resistance thereto adversarial accuracy (accuracy when adversarial perturbed inputs are introduced), resiliency score (lowest perturbation to misclassify), resistance to transferability (resistance to transfer attacks to substitute models), and resistance to adaptive attack (resistance to attacks specifically crafted to evade detection).

6.3 Baseline Comparisons

The suggested framework is evaluated in comparison with several, so-called baseline methods that reflect the state-of-the-art:

Traditional Rule-Based Systems: This type of email security gate solutions use signature details, blacklist verification, and rules of thumb (Proofpoint, Mimecast). These systems are very common enterprise systems that offer realistic performance levels.

Machine Learning Baselines: Standard machine learning techniques such as the random forest classifiers to detect phishing, the Support Vector Machines in malware classification, and the naive bayes in spam filtering. These techniques are those approaches to ML-based security that have been reported in literature.

Threat Intelligences Tools: The most popular commercial offerings are Microsoft Defender ATP, Cisco SecureX, and CrowdStrike Falcon, offering an all-in-one solution of threat detection and recovery. The performance data can be gathered by use of vendor documentation and independent testing reports.

Academic Research Systems: New academic systems such as DeepPhish (deep learning-based phishing detection), FakeSpotter (deepfake detection based on the use of capsule networks), BotTracker (behavioral bot detection), and MultiModal-ThreatDetect (multi-modal threat detection system). The measures of performance that were achieved based on published research papers and, where feasible, via reimplementation using outlined methodologies.

Ablation Baselines: System configurations with certain components disabled such as framework without adversarial AI detection, framework without behavioral analytics, framework with single-modal detection only, framework without features of a human-centric design and framework without adaptive learning. Such ablations measure the contributions of the individuals.

6.4 Experimental Procedures

Higher experimental methodology guarantees high reliability and reproducibility of results:

Data Preparation: Raw data was subjected to extensive preprocessing such as noise filtering eliminating corrupted or incomplete records, outlier detection to manage statistical outliers, feature normalization to standardize the values ranges, class balancing to deal with dataset imbalance by sampling strategically and privacy-preserving transformations to apply to anonymization and pseudonymization. Stratified sampling was used to divide the dataset into training set (60% or 2.52 million samples), validation set (20% or 0.84 million samples) and test set (20% or 0.84 million samples) with distribution of the attack types remaining constant across splits.

Designing training: Rigorous protocols were used to train the detection models including cross-validation by 5-fold stratified splitting selection between hyperparameters, early stopping by monitoring validation performance to avoid overfitting (patience=10 epochs), scheduling of learning rate with cosine annealing optimization, regularization by dropout (p=0.3) and also L2 regularization (l=0.001).

Hyperparameter Optimization: Systematic parameter search A grid search was used to identify optimal settings of categorical parameters, Bayesian optimization (with Hyperopt library) to identify optimal settings of continuous ones, random search to explore parameter space initially, and validation-based selection to select settings with the highest performance on a validation set. Learning rate (10 -5 to 10 -1), batch size (32 to 512), network architecture (number of layers, number of neurons, activation functions), regularization, and ensemble weights were varied.

Performance Evaluation: Performance Evaluation programs involved various metric computation in the context of accuracy, precision, recall, F1-score, AUC-ROC, per-class performance decomposition that analyses performance of each attack-type, confusion matrix analysis that determines patterns of misclassification, statistical significance test based on McNemar test to compare paired prediction performance, bootstrap resampling (1000 iterations) to estimate confidence interval, and cross-data-set validation to assess generalization to different organizational settings.

Ablation Studies: Systematic analysis of component contribution with controlled experiments such as component removal, component substitution, analysis of feature importance with SHAP values and permutation importance, effects of interactions between components, and performance attribution Systematic analysis of component contribution through controlled experiments such as systematically removing components, systematically replacing components with simpler ones, feature importance analysis using SHAP values and permutation importance, interaction effects, and performance attribution Each component of a systematically contributing component.
Real-World validation: Framework Implementation Framework implementation in staged organizational settings consisted of pilot implementation in test organization (500 users, 3-month duration), performance measurement which collected operational metrics, user feedback deployment through surveys and interviews, incident response testing which measured detection of actual security incidents, and comparison benchmarking against existing security infrastructure.

7. RESULTS AND ANALYSIS

7.1 Detection Performance Results

Along a variety of performance dimensions, experimental testing can be shown to have significant improvement over the capabilities of baseline methods:

Total Detection Accuracy: The proposed framework has its overall detection accuracy of 94.3% which is a 12.7 percentage point higher than the highest performing baseline (Commercial Solution B: 89.1%). This difference is statistically significant ($p < 0.001$, McNemars test) with 95% confidence interval (94.1 to 94.5) using bootstrap analysis. The model exhibits high consistency in performance throughout the test sample with the standard deviation ($s = 0.8$) showing strong extrapolation.
AI-Generated Content Detection: Specialized detection of synthetically generated content has achieved the highest performance including AI-generated text detection of 96.2% accuracy, especially where the content is generated by GPT-4 the accuracy is 97.1% and when the content is generated by GPT-3.5 the accuracy is 95.8%, synthetic audio detection with 91.3% accuracy when using WaveGlow (93.1), ProGAN (88.7) and face-swap detection techniques, automated bot detection with 93.4% accuracy.

Behavioral Anomaly Detection: 91.7 percent, which is significantly higher than conventional anomaly detection systems (76.3 percent) is the accuracy of the behavioral analytics engine in detecting suspicious patterns of interaction. The system is specifically effective in detecting account compromise (94.2), insider threat behavior (88.9), automated attack patterns (93.4), and social engineering susceptibility indicators (87.6). Behavioral detection has low false possession (4.1) by the use of context-aware analysis and dynamic maintenance of the baseline.

Multi-Modal Integration: Advantage: All modalities of detection integration gives a 7.3 per cent higher total accuracy than optimal single-modality method. The complementary analysis shows that text analysis is the best at the linguistic manipulation (96.2%), image analysis is the best at the visual deception (89.4%), audio analysis is the best at the voice impersonation (91.3%), and behavioral analysis is the best at identifying the interactions anomaly (91.7%). Ensemble methods are effectively used in leveraging these complementary capabilities with 62% error reduction in modality per individual.

7.2 Performance Analysis by Attack Type

Breakdown in detail shows that there is a difference in performance of the various types of attacks, and this helps understand the strengths of the framework and weaknesses that can be addressed:

Phishing Email Detection: Achieves 95.8% accuracy with a variety of phishing such as spear-phishing (97.2%), whaling attacks on executives (96.8%), business email compromise (BEC) (94.3%), credential harvesting (95.1) and malware delivery (94.7%). The AI-generated phishing emails are classified with 96.2 percent accuracy which shows that AI has good adversarial detection. The system is especially good in determining advanced personalized attacks that are not viewed by traditional filters.

Social Media Manipulation: Shows an 89.2% accuracy of identifying coordinated social media manipulation campaigns comprising of fake account detection (91.5%), bot network detection (93.4%), influence operation detection (86.7%), and disinformation campaign detection (87.3%). There is low performance in highly sophisticated state-sponsored influence operations that use advanced evasion procedures, which provides an opportunity of future enhancement.

Voice and Video Impersonation: Recognizes deepfakes-based impersonation attacks with 87.6 percent accuracy depending on the method of generation: face-swap deepfakes (89.2), facial reenactment (88.1), and full synthesis (86.4), voice cloning (91.3) and audio-visual synchronization attacks (85.7). Poorer performance on next generation methods point to the continued arms race between generation and detection performance.

Accuracy of Finding all Automated Social Engineering Bots: 93.4 per cent accuracy with scripted bots (95.8), rule-based bots (94.1), machine learning-based bots (92.3), and human-assisted bots (90.7). Behavioral biometric analysis and interaction timing analysis in the system is useful in identifying automation patterns and valid user behaviors.

Business Email Compromise (BEC): With good results across variations of CEO fraud (95.6%), invoice fraud (93.8%), wire transfer fraud (94.7%), and payroll diversion (93.2%), BEC method detects 94.3% of BEC. These high-value attacks are especially effective when the multi-modal analysis of text analysis, sender verification, and behavioral context is used.

7.3 Computational Performance Analysis

It has proven to be efficient in calculational performance with ability to be deployed in a real-world environment in varying organizational heights:

Processing Latency: 2.3 seconds average end to end processing time to run multi-modes analysis of typical social engineering attacks, 95 th percentile processing time of 3.8 seconds.

Latencies decomposition Latency: feature extraction (0.8s), adversarial robustness checking (0.6s), multi-modal detection (0.5s), behavioral analysis (0.3s) and decision fusion (0.1s). These performance features allow close real time performance detection that is capable of operational deployment.

Throughput Capacity: The throughput of the system is 10,000 email messages per minute with standard cloud infrastructure (16 vCPU, 64GB RAM, 2x T4 GPU), linearly increasing with the number of additional computing units added. With optimized infrastructure, peak throughput is 50,000 messages per minute (more than enough to satisfy large enterprise deployment requirements), compared with 5,00015,000 messages per minute (which is typical).

Resource Usage: Mean resource usage whilst operating normally involves CPU usage of 45, memory usage of 4.2GB, graphics card usage of 35, network bandwidth of 50Mbps and storage I/O of 200 IOPS. These are medium requirements on resources that allow it to be deployed to cost-effective infrastructure, with the capacity to handle traffic bursts.

Scalability Demonstration: Scaling features Tested via load testing to 50,000 simultaneously with less than 15 percent degradation in performance with the highest tested load. The horizontal scaling is efficient by 92 percent and the capacity is proportional to the number of additional compute instances. The auto-scaling mechanisms react in 2 minutes to changes in the load, keeping the user experience the same.

Cost Efficiency: Operation cost analysis shows that the cost of cloud infrastructure, i.e. $0.18 per 1000 processed events on cloud infrastructure (AWS us-east-1, 3-year reserved instances), is relatively low in comparison to commercial solutions (0.35-0.65 per 1000 events). Approximate balance of costs of ownership of 10,000-user organization is estimated at $48,000/year including infrastructure, maintenance, and support.

7.4 User Experience Evaluation

Human oriented design concepts are converted to quantifiable enhancement of the user experience and the operational efficiency:

Reduction of Alert Fatigue: 34% reduction was found in alert fatigue with conventional security systems (measured using standardized survey measures, the Alert Fatigue Scale and through behavioral measure of alert). Alerts are described by users as actionable and clear (89) over overwhelming or confusing (11) which is also a significant improvement compared to basis systems (43 actionable, 57 overwhelming).

False Positive Impact: Precision improvements, context-aware notifications of disruptive false positive notifications. False positive notifications are being received by the users at 0.8 per week (Down 2.4 per week with baseline system), which greatly decreases disruption to productivity. False positive reduction is positively related to better user trust ($r=0.73$) and security recommendations compliance ($r=0.81$).

User Comprehension: 89 percent of the users say that they understand the reason why a system issues security warnings and advice, versus 43 percent of those who use conventional systems. The explainable AI characteristics such as natural language explanations and display of evidence and concrete example are meaningful towards understanding by the users ($p < 0.001$). Better knowledge is much related with correct security measures ($r=0.76$) and long-term change in behavior ($r=0.68$).

Adoption Rates: 94% user adoption in six months of deployment in test organizations, which are significantly higher than the average security systems adoption (45-60% in 12 months). Great adoption due to positive user experience, less workflow opportunity, and proven value by successful threat detection. The average user satisfaction scores (System Usability Scale) are 78.5 that are considered as good to excellent usability.

Productivity Impact: Little to no adverse effect on productivity with mean time overhead of 12 seconds per day on security concerns (security related activities like verification requests, review of alerts, training, etc). This is 0.04% of normal working time, which is quite good in comparison to conventional systems (45 seconds per day, 0.16% of working time). Security system is rated as an enabler of safe productivity not impediment by users.

7.5 Comparative Analysis with Baseline Systems

Extensive comparison proves significant benefits in all the dimensions that have been considered:

Table 1. Performance Comparison Across Different Approaches

Approach	Accuracy	Precision	Recall	F1-Score	Processing Time	False Positive Rate
Proposed Framework	94.3%	92.7%	91.8%	92.2%	2.3s	4.1%
Commercial Solution A	87.6%	85.2%	89.4%	87.2%	4.1s	12.4%
Commercial Solution B	89.1%	91.3%	84.7%	87.9%	3.8s	6.8%
Academic Baseline	82.4%	80.6%	86.2%	83.3%	5.2s	15.7%
Traditional Rules	76.3%	78.9%	71.4%	75.0%	1.8s	8.9%
ML Baseline (RF)	84.7%	83.2%	85.1%	84.1%	2.9s	11.3%

The proposed framework has the highest overall performance in terms of accuracy (94.3%), precision (92.7%), F1-score (92.2), and false positive rate (4.1). Compared to modern rule based models that are 1.8s faster, they do not possess the same accuracy (76.3%). The balance of the framework is that it has great accuracy but the processing time is realistic (2.3s) and this can be applied in operation.

Statistical Significance: Pair-wise comparison with McNemar test shows statistically significant improvements ($p < 0.001$) in all the baseline approaches. Cohen d (effect sizes) are between 0.87 and 2.34, which implies a significant difference in practice on top of significant statistical values.

7.6 Ablation Study Results

The systematic ablation analysis finds the contribution of individual components to the global framework performance:

Table 2. Ablation Study Results Showing Component Contributions

Component	Accuracy Impact	Precision Impact	Recall Impact	F1-Score Impact
Adversarial AI Detection	+5.7%	+6.2%	+4.8%	+5.5%
Behavioral Analytics	+4.3%	+3.9%	+5.1%	+4.5%
Multi-Modal Integration	+7.3%	+8.1%	+6.4%	+7.2%
Human-Centric Design	+2.8%	+4.2%	+1.9%	+3.0%
Adaptive Learning	+3.2%	+2.7%	+3.8%	+3.2%
Context-Aware Analysis	+4.1%	+5.3%	+3.4%	+4.3%

Findings indicate that every component has significant contributions, with the multi-modal integration giving the greatest contribution per component (+7.3% accuracy). Adversarial AI detection enhances precision significantly (+6.2), which is important in cutting false positives. Behavioral analytics improves recall (5.1%), which detects less significant attacks. The cumulative effects are greater than the sum of individual contributions, that is, there are positive synergies between components.

Interaction Effects: Component interactions Analysis indicates that there are strong synergies between adversarial AI detection and behavioral analytics (+11.2% accuracy, over 10.0% better than sum of individual effects: 10.0%), multi-modal integration and context-aware analysis (+13.1% accuracy, over 11.4% better than sum of individual effects: 11.4%), and adaptive learning and all other components (+15.7% over extended deployment period). The above synergies affirm the need of integrated framework approach as opposed to component deployment in a modular manner.

7.7 Adversarial Robustness Evaluation

Systematic analysis of resilience to adversarial attacks indicates the robustness of the framework:

White-Box Attacks: Framework achieves 87.3% accuracy in white-box adversarial attacks (FGSM, PGD) with complete model knowledge, a loss of 7.0 percentage points of clean accuracy (94.3%). This is better off than comparison to baseline models with 15-25 percentage point degradation. Defensive mechanisms and adversarial training are effective to reduce white-box attacks.
Black-Box Attacks: Accuracy in the case of black-box attacks (no model knowledge) is high with an accuracy of 91.8, which implies that it can be used without major resistance to transferability. The average of 2,847 queries is needed to have 50% attack success rate in query based attacks, which also

makes attacks computationally inexpensive and detectable by monitoring query patterns.

Adaptive Attacks: Attacks that are specifically created to avoid detection by a framework have a success rate of 73.6 percent, and thus adversarial arms race seems to continue to challenge. This is however a great improvement to baseline systems (92-96% adaptive attack success rates). The repeated updates of the model and adversarial training lower the effectiveness of the adaptive attacks with time.

Real-World Attack Scenarios: Framework achieved up to 23 out of 25 (92) real-world AI-assisted social engineering attacks during pilot deployment, even memorizing new attack variation types that were not seen in training data. This confirms real-life performance as opposed to laboratory testing.

7.8 Cross-Sectoral Validation

The effectiveness of the framework was tested in different organizational settings and industries:

Financial Services: Implementation in financial institution (2,500 users) had 95.1% detect rate with its high rate on BEC attacks (96.8%), and wire transfer fraud (95.7%). There were high stakes, which meant that false positive rates (2.1%), which were effectively implemented using context-aware analysis and adaptive thresholds, had to be very low.

Technology Sector: Use in a technology company (5000 users) was found to be accurate 93.8% with significant performance to identify advanced spear-phishing attacks against developers (94.6) and source code theft attacks (92.3). There were lower susceptibility and more advanced attack attempts by technical user population.

Healthcare Sector: Healthcare organization (1,200 users) improved 92.7% accuracy when using the high privacy-preserving analytics that were compliant with HIPAA regulations. Framework had the opportunity to detect ransomware delivery (94.1) and patient data exfiltration (91.8). The compliance nature of the regulations that were mandated also required more audit functions and data reduction techniques.

Cross-Cultural Performance: The cross-assessment of the performance across the different cultural (North America, Europe, Asia) demonstrated that the performance was different (91.2% to 95.8% accuracy) based on the role of styles of communication and the degree of attack. sophistication. It was observed that the adaptive was able to change cultural differences during the 30 days adaptation period, via adaptive learning.

8. DISCUSSION

8.1 Key Findings and Implications

The experiment results indicate that several interesting findings that have major implications on the practice and research in cybersecurity are achieved:

Human-Centric Design Impact: The application of the human-centric design principles causes an impressive change in the technical performance and user experience. The alert fatigue was decreased by 34 percent and 94 percent user acceptance that human factors should be taken into consideration during the design of security systems. This observation kills the existing technical oriented strategies and implies that most successful security performance is outside the automation where human beings and technology are in a joint partnership and not where automation is fully adapted in security. The companies installing security systems are required to guarantee user experience besides technical attributes and have effective protection in place.

Advantages of Multi-Mode Analysis: Since it employs text, image, audio and behavioral analysis, the Multi-Mode Analysis has an advantage of 7.3 percentage points over the single-modality analysis. This is an enormous advantage due to the complimentary nature of information of different modes, and various methods of detection can be handy in detecting different facets of attacks. What the observation implies is that attacks on the high level enriched with AI will need a multi-dimensional approach to detection. Integrated solutions should be adopted by security architects rather than point solutions to vectors of threats.

Adversarial AI as Fancy Panties: The adversarial learning models along with the adversarial defenses perform much better in identifying AI-generated attacks (96.2 per cent on AI-generated text, 89.4 per cent on deepfakes). This indicates that antagonistic AI techniques that are traditionally associated with attacks can have remarkable defense applications when implemented effectively in security systems. The cybersecurity community should attempt adversarial AI research that is and will focus on defense against attacks rather than the adversarial techniques as threats.

Adaptive Learning Necessity: The reality that the framework has an accuracy of 94.3 percent over the 12 months that the implementation has taken place as the attack strategies enhance demonstrates that adaptive learning mechanisms are highly necessary. The performance cannot be totally restored with time since the attackers evolve and scale security breaches in the detected systems that are fixed. The businesses should have the systems of continuous learning in which the models updated automatically so that the businesses can have the appropriate protection against emerging threats.

Context-Aware Detection Value: The context-aware detection value is a detection technique, which is 67% less likely to generate false positives and has a high detection rate. This fact shows that it is important to learn the operational environment rather than transfer security policies. They need security systems which can distinguish acceptable variation of behavior, and actual anomalies, and this degree of context modeling is extremely complex.

Scalability and Performance Feasibility: The framework can determine with an accuracy of 94.3 percent, and the latency in processing is good (2.3 seconds), which is linear with 50,000 users at a given time. That proves that it will be possible to introduce complex AI-based security systems that would address both the technical performance specification and the operational scalability. Modern architectures should provide detection sophistication with no compromise to performance and both high accuracy and high performance needs to be provided.

8.2 Implications for Cybersecurity Practice

The practical implications of the findings of the research to cybersecurity implementation and management are:

Paradigm Shift to the Human-Centric Security: The classical paradigm of cybersecurity is interested in technical controls and human considerations are seen as the inseparable parts of the paradigm of addressing weak links. According to the research, the high rates of technical performance, user experience, and functional performance of the security system are proved due to the human centric design principles created in the development of the security systems in the entire process. It is promoted that organizations are advised to adopt integrated strategies that will consider the users as subjects of the security process rather than passive objects of the security protection. This paradigm shift necessitates the security teams to acquire new skills in user experience design domain in addition to cognitive psychology and organization behavior on top of the traditional technical skills in the sphere of security.

Multi-Dimensional Defense Requirements: The attacks that are advanced by AI will be more advanced, and, accordingly, the multi-dimensional defenses are to be improved. Single-vector protection (email security, endpoint protection, network security) are not the methods that organizations should trust since it requires the adoption of the integrated frameworks that are comprised of the multiple modalities of detection and analytical viewpoints. This implies that security architecture carries major implications with it which involve the necessity to invest in integration facilities, data sharing infrastructure and coordinated response facilities.

Constant Adaptation Requirement: The increased pace of varying the AI capacity assumes the permanent variation in the procedures of assault. The companies are not simply unwanted to perform regular security updates, but they must keep going with adaptive learning systems, which are constantly being modified under the influence of the new threats, nearly in real-time. It entails the necessity to invest machine learning operations (MLOps) functions, automated models management, and threat intelligence. It is expected that the security teams gain monitor modelling experience, performance and flexible system management experience.

Ethical and Privacy implications: The ethical implication of the privacy and consent of the behavioral analytics and the overall all-inclusive surveillance, the appropriate exercise of the power of surveillance also have severe implications. Organizations need to develop effective governing systems with the right balance between the benefits of security and the rights to privacy and ethics. This involves open disclosure of practices on monitoring, user consent process, principles of data minimization, and using the data appropriately. The privacy-sensitive nature of the framework illustrates that the security and privacy control can be achieved simultaneously in case of proper architecture.

Cross-Functional Collaboration Requirement: To implement it effectively, collaboration among the traditionally distinct organizational functions such as security teams, IT operations, user experience designers, legal compliance, human resources and business units must be used. The cross-organizational teams need to be created with well-defined roles and communication directions to maintain global security implementation.

8.3 Limitations and Challenges

Although the results are promising, it must be admitted that there are a number of limitations and challenges that should be considered and tackled in the future:

Issues of data privacy and data gathering: The broad behavioral analytics in the framework involves a lot of data gathering which attracts justifiable privacy issues. Although privacy-saving methods (differential privacy, anonymization) eliminate the risks, there are still conflicts between effectiveness and privacy in terms of security. In particular, these trade-offs are sensitive, and the jurisdiction regulation (GDPR, CCPA) and moral accountability in data management are central issues that an organization has to take into account.

Even with the law, legal and technical protection can be limited by user issues on surveillance. The research on privacy preserving algorithms e.g. federated learning, safe multi-party computations, and homomorphic encryption is to be carried out in future as a means of reducing the threat on privacy.

Computational Resource Requirement: Multi-modal analysis with adversarial robustness checking can be computationally intensive (i.e. consumes lots of CPU, GPU and memory) which can limit its application in a resource constrained environment. Scalability, though seen to be possible in large organizations has been seen to require optimization or simplified environments in smaller organizations of in edge deployment applications. The work on lightweight versions in accordance to a limited environment should be carried out in the future (compressing models, efficient structure, and the rejection of actions that are selective).

Adversarial Arms Race Dynamics: The existing competition between attack and defense capabilities is a long-standing issue. Although the framework is resistant to the existing adversarial methods, further opposition innovations of the attacks will probably create evasion maneuvers. This vulnerability is indicated by the 73.6 percent success of adaptive attacks that are specifically pointed towards bypassing detection. This is the basic dilemma it needs to invest in research and deploy better defenses as fast as possible. Companies should not have unrealistic expectations concerning security assurances and should adopt a defense-in-depth approach instead of having single solutions.

Generalization across Domains: The framework proves to be effective in financial, technology, and healthcare domains, however, the performance varies depending on types of organizations, audiences of users, and threats (91.2 to 95.8% accuracy). Total generalization to all the possible situations is still out of the question and it needs a domain-specific transformation and customization. Future studies ought to focus on transfer learning strategies that can be quickly trained to work in new fields with few training data and development resources.

Explainability-Performance Trade-offs: Investigating the more advanced methods of detection (deep neural networks, ensemble methods) often are better performing and have lower interpretability in comparison to simpler models (decision trees, linear models). Although the framework involves explainable AI techniques, not all decisions can be fully explained using understandable terms that can be comprehensible by every user. Subsequent studies must be done to devise ways of explaining in a security context, that will strike a balance between the level of details and the ability of the user to understand.

Ground Truth Availability: Problems with ground truth of actual world attacks A problem with ground truth of novel AI-augmented attacks is that there is limited availability of labeled data on actual attacks. It is possible that the fact that synthetic information is applied in testing is not exactly all there is regarding the truth of the attack sophistication and diversity. Future research needs to measure standard benchmark data sets consisting of known actual attacks and needs to develop superior synthetic data synthesis methods that are more realistic in capturing attack characteristics in the real world.

Regulatory Compliance Complexity: Multinational organizations have a problem that they have to comply with various regulations in various jurisdictions. Even though the framework has compliance capabilities, (GDPR, CCPA, HIPAA), the unceasing evolution of the regulatory environment makes change a continuous requirement. The companies will be forced to invest in regulatory controls and system upgrades that would provide unrelenting compliance.

8.4 Future Research Directions

This research offers numerous avenues which may be explored in the further research and advancement:

Better Cross-Cultural Adaptation: Current model displays that the difference between the performance of the cultural situations is (+-4.6% error margin). The further line of the research should determine the developed methods of cultural adaptation that should involve language dissimilarity, patterns of communication, societal relations, and psychological peculiarities in diverse cultural backgrounds. This entails the development of culturally specific training content, adaptation functions and assessment systems which will ensure equitable protection to various individuals in the global society. This involves coming up with culturally specific training information, adaptation functions and assessment systems that will guarantee fair protection to different people around the world.

State-of-the-Art Privacy-Maintaining Approaches: Although existing privacy-related measures (differential privacy, anonymization) offer minimum security guarantees, superior privacy-related methods might help reduce the privacy issues. Future directions that have been shown to be promising are federated learning that would allow training distributed models without centralizing sensitive data, homomorphic encryption that would allow computation on encrypted data without decryption, secure multi-party computation that would allow collaborative analysis without sharing of data, and improvements in differential privacy that would make the privacy-utility trade-off better. These methods might allow detecting the threats and guaranteeing greater privacy that meets the concerns of users and regulators.

Approaches Resistant to Quantum: The development of quantum computing is posing a risk to existing cryptography based protection and offering new attack vectors. Future studies must come up with detection schemes that are resistant to quantum-enhanced attacks, to combine post-quantum cryptographic primitives, and develop quantum-resistant authentication schemes. The readiness of security systems in terms of quantum threats must be a proactive research-based activity until quantum computers acquire realistic attack capabilities.

Improved Human-AI Collaboration Models: Existing framework has human-in-the-loop mechanisms of high-uncertainty decisions. Future studies ought to address more advanced forms of collaboration such as mixed-initiative interaction in which there is a smooth transition between human and AI control, adaptive automation in which automation is adjusted based on the context and performance, augmented intelligence in which human and AI capabilities are complementary, and collaborative learning in which human and AI capabilities can mutually improve as a result of interaction. Such solutions might be more effective and acceptable by users.

Real-Time Behavioral Adaptation: Although the framework uses adaptive learning and 14-day adaptation cycles, quicker adaptation would be beneficial in terms of responding to the threats which change rapidly. Future studies ought to come up with online learning algorithms that allow real-time model updating, change detecting mechanisms that show the occurrence of behavioral drift that needs to be adaptable, and quick response mechanisms that allow prompt implementation of better defenses. Finding a trade-off between the adaptation rate and stability versus the security on the one hand and the adversarial manipulations on the other hand is a major research problem.

Zero Trust Architecture Integration: further integration with Zero Trust principles can be applied to enhance security posture in general. The current research directions include continuous authentication using behavioral biometrics, real-time threat determination-based dynamic access control policy, threat intelligence-based micro-segmentation, and behaviorally-based policy enforcement. These integrations would be integrated into a single set of security ecosystems rather than single point solutions.

Generative AI Defense Mechanisms: It is the increasing attack vectors that are due to a quick advancement in generative AI performance (GPT-4, DALL-E 3, text-to-video models). The next generation of the research should come up with the mechanisms of detection of large language model output, diffusion model images, and neural codec audio and multimodal generation. This involves the development of forensic techniques that are capable of identifying the products of generation and proactive countermeasures that anticipate future competencies.

Psychological and Cognitive Research: It would be more effective to develop safeguards around psychological variables of social engineering vulnerability. The direction of future research is the assessment of cognitive vulnerability to incorporate personal risk factors, the design of psychological intervention to establish the specific training of resistance and decision supporting system to help the user in making security-related decisions. Interdisciplinary collaboration could be very useful in terms of understanding as it would involve cybersecurity researchers and psychologists working together.

Economic and Policy Analysis: It would assist in creating improved security efforts by having a better understanding of the economic incentives that spur attacks and defense efforts. Cost-benefit trade offs in the investments in security, incentive schemes to encourage secure behavior, policy interventions that would encourage best security practices, the economic impacts of different attack and defense scenarios should be researched. The analysis would be useful in evidence-based organizational and policy decisions made in the area of security.

8.5 Practical Recommendations

Based on the research results, we can provide the following recommendations to the organizations that apply AI-assisted threat detection:

The Recommendations are:

Adoption Strategy:

1. Build deployment (100-500 users) and system tuning and user feedback and prior to full deployment.
2. Protect high-risk groups (finance, executives, HR) first and foremost in order to get the maximum security benefit.
3. Introducing progressive implementation with a continuous control that will guarantee performance validation and risk mitigation.
4. Provide effective metrics of success and assessment procedures that provide an objective evaluation of the efficacy of implementation.
5. Invest in user training and change management so that it adopts and uses security systems properly.

Recommendations on the technical implementation:

1. Implement contemporary cloud-native architecture which allows scalability and flexibility of work.

2. Introduce an overall monitoring and logging which will assist with the performance review and investigation of incidents.
3. Create automatic pipelines of testing and deployment of reliable system updates.
4. Blend with other security (SIEM, IAM, EDR) to bring about consistent security setup.
5. Arrange computational facilities such as graphics cards to boost performance.

Recommendations on Organizational and Governance:

1. Create multi-functional security teams comprising of technical, legal, privacy, and business individuals.
2. Establish good policies in data governance in terms of collection, usage, retention and deletion.
3. Introduce open-ended communication regarding the surveillance practices and privacy protection.
4. Establish security system design and implementation ethics review.
5. Regulatory review and updating of security policies as a result of emerging threat and capabilities.

User Experiencing Recommendations:

1. Place importance on user experience design during system development with a guarantee of usability and acceptance.
2. Adopt gradual delivery of information without overloading the end user with too much information.
3. Give effective and proactive directions in security alerts so that users can respond adequately.
4. Gather and respond to user feedback in a never ending process of enhancing system effectiveness and experience.
5. Security controls that reduce the productivity with preservation of protection.

Recommendations to Continuous Improvement:

1. Set up periodic performance review-cycle (monthly/quarterly) of system effectiveness.
2. Introduce threat intelligence incorporation whereby awareness of new attack methods is achieved.
3. Regular red team exercises against realistic attacks on the effectiveness of the system.

4. Be an active member of security research community keeping abreast with events.
5. Be ready to invest constantly on system development and ability increase.

9. CONCLUSION

The paper is a holistic anthropocentric contribution to addressing and removing AI-enhanced social engineering attacks through adversarial AI-based cyber threat intelligence. The framework is a giant leap into cybersecurity features that demonstrate a significant improvement of the existing processes in numerous ways, among them being accuracy in detection, user interface, efficiency in operation, and adaptive reliability.

9.1 Summary of Contributions

The research has several positive values to the sphere of cybersecurity:

Technical Innovation: Multidetection system on adversarial AI techniques, behavioral analytics and multi-modal analysis is capable of 94.3 percent detection of advanced AI-enhanced attacks. This is 12.7 percent larger than best baseline approaches in which there is no sacrifice of reasonable computational efficiency (2.3 seconds average latency) with which it can be brought to execution.

Human-Centric design Verification: It demonstrates that the concepts of human centric design deliver greater performances in the technical performance and user experience measures of security systems. The fatigue rate of 34 percent in the alert system, the disruptiveness of false positive rates of 67 percent, 89 percent of user-understanding and 94 percent adoption rate is a testament of how important and critical human factors are in the design and implementation process of the security system.

Interdisciplinary Integration: An effective combination of technical skills with the two sides of morals and policy need and human behavioral knowledge would result in a holistic security solution that would be effective on a variety of problems in relation to AI-enhanced threats. The given model of integration provides the future evolution of security systems with the priority over the necessity to be implemented in a strictly technical way.

Empirical Testing: It turns out that proper experimental testing using real and fabricated data in a broad variety of organizational contexts is practically effective and general. Performance assessment after 12-month deployment evaluates long-term functionality and adaptive abilities which are necessitated by a functional security system.

Research Foundation: Systematic literature review, gap analysis and framework design provides foundation to the future research in AI-enhanced cybersecurity. The matching of some of the major obstacles, such as privacy conservativeness, quantum resistance, cross-cultural adaptation, and greater human-AI cooperation, serves as the roadmap to the further development of the sphere.

9.2 Practical Impact and Applications

The practical applicability of the framework is used in many industries and scenarios:

Enterprise Security: The framework can be used to secure high value assets and important personnel in large organizations that are exposed to advanced target attacks. Scalability (up to 50,000 users at once) and performance (10,000 messages per minute throughput) prove the implementation on the enterprise level.

Financial Services: Banking and financial institutions which are fighting with business email compromise, wire transfer and account takeover attacks will have high detection accuracy (95.1% in financial sector validation) and very low false positive rates (2.1) will reduce operational disturbance.

Healthcare Organizations: Privacy-preserving design and full audit functionality can be used by providers of healthcare that secure patient data and keep the HIPAA standards. The framework was able to identify the ransomware delivery attempts (94.1) and patient data exfiltration (91.8) in the healthcare validation.

Government and Critical Infrastructure: Adversarial AI detection and behavioral analytics can be used by government entities and other critical infrastructure operators to detect advanced persistent threats when they are threatened by nation-states and highly advanced influence operations.

Small and Medium Enterprises: Cloud deployment models provide access to enterprise-grade protection to SMEs, albeit with a high computational cost, by letting the managed security service provider scale the framework up.

9.3 Addressing the AI Arms Race

The study faces the very essence of constant competition of the attack and defense capabilities in the sphere of AI. Although there are no security systems that are definitively guaranteed, the adaptive learning capabilities, adversarial robustness improvements and the multi-layered defense strategy of the framework make it well-positioned to adapt to the changing threats. The fact that adversarial AI methods can assist in providing effective defensive features gives reason to believe that defenders will be able to use the same technology that allows to perform advanced attacks.

There is an insatiable investment in research, rapidity in knowledge dissemination within the security fraternity, proactive foreseeing of hazards and on-going upgrading of the system that is required to win this current arms race. The companies must make realistic assumptions about the security assurances and defensive in-depth strategies that incorporate technical limitations, human mind, organization processes, and dynamic systems.

9.4 Ethical Considerations and Responsible Deployment

The general aspect of monitoring and behavioral analytics of the framework poses a serious ethical concern regarding privacy, consent, surveillance and appropriate use of security technologies. To be involved responsible will entail:

Transparency and Consent: The capabilities of the systems, methods of collecting data and the degree of monitoring can be described which is possible to foster informed consent and develop trust in the user. The institutions ought to be in a position to give clear accounts of the security measures without employing technicalities but with knowledge.

Protection of Privacy: Privacy-safe algorithms, including different privacy, data minimalization, anonymization, and purpose restriction, are implemented to ensure that beneficial security is not obtained at the prohibitive privacy costs. A privacy impact assessment is done on regular basis and identifies emerging privacy risks and neutralizes them.

Ethical Governance: The development of ethics review methods, clear accountability system and a use policy is also offered to ensure that security capabilities are used in acceptable protective operations as opposed to underpinning unacceptable surveillance and control. The independent control and audits at regular intervals allow ethical operation.

Equity and Fairness: The fact that the cross-cultural performance variation will be in place, the potential biases of detection algorithms will be detected and fairly shared among the diverse groups of users will ensure that there is no concentration of protecting the security to the hands of the select groups of users, leaving the rest vulnerable.

9.5 Future Outlook

The threat landscape would continue to evolve as AI capability is being created, so that defensive technologies ought to continue to evolve and innovate. The key trends, which are likely to have an impact on the subsequent developments are:

Generative AI Evolution: The continuous advancement of large language models, image-generating systems, video-generating systems, and multimodal models will produce more complex attacks which will also require more highly engineered detection.
Effect of Quantum Computing The creation of quantum computers that can be practically used will compromise the cryptographic security systems in place and may open up potential attack vectors, so quantum-resistance solutions need to be actively developed.
Regulatory Evolution: The changing AI regulation framework, regulations of privacy and cybersecurity will shape the strategies that can be allowed in the threat detection and sacrifices between security and privacy that can be accepted.
The next stage **Human-AI Collaboration Maturation:** It will become possible to elaborate on the models of human-AI collaboration further and thus allow the establishment of the improved performance of the systems and the experience of the users with the help of the deeper understanding of the effective models of human-AI collaboration.
Democratization of AI Security: The availability, and affordable AI-security will provide more security to small businesses, as well as individuals due to the rising inequality of security, and not only large players.

9.6 Final Remarks

The paper demonstrates that comprehensive frameworks that embrace the integration of technical sophistication, humanistic design, ethical leadership, and responsive capabilities are crucial in the alleviation of AI-boosted social engineering assaults. The proposed framework will utilize enormous profit margins in comparison with the existing procedures, yet on the one hand, it will be possible to apply it to the operational environment.

The findings disprove the current beliefs that security and usability are opposite to one another, and demonstrate that human-centered design enhances security performance and user acceptability. Similarly, the research shows that the privacy protection and capability to identify any form of threats can co-exist with appropriate architecture and privacy sensitive technology.

It is a protracted struggle to sustain research, development, and change that will result in success in countering the changing AI-advanced threats. Cybersecurity also demands that the organization invest in technology, people, processes and partnerships which are necessitated to have appropriate cybersecurity. The cybersecurity community should support an interdisciplinary, inter-sectoral, and international collaboration to address usual issues that transcend the organizational and nation-level interests.

As the sphere of AI technologies continuously evolves, the defenders must be attentive, innovative, and adaptable equally or more than the adversary. This work in progress is based on the paradigm proposed in this study, which demonstrates that systematic human-centered design of adaptive learning on the basis of the adversarial AI approach and behavioral analytics can create efficient defense against advanced attacks facilitated by the AI technology.

The last goal is not limited to the technical capability of incorporating a healthy digital security that will enable people and organization to reap the benefits of the digital transformation devoid of placing themselves into the path of threats. This vision should be achieved by means of the additional research, responsible innovation, moral regulation, and collaboration in the community of international cybersecurity.

REFERENCES

Ahmed, F., & Connor, P. (2024). Behavioral biometrics for continuous authentication. *Biometric Technology Today, 2024*(3), 8–12. DOI: 10.1016/S0969-4765(24)00045-2

Anderson, K. J., Mitchell, S. R., & Thompson, D. L. (2024). Evolving threat landscapes in the age of artificial intelligence. *Journal of Cybersecurity Research, 15*(3), 234–251. DOI: 10.1016/j.jcr.2024.03.012

Baker, H., & Evans, T. (2023). Cross-platform social engineering detection. *Journal of Network and Computer Applications, 205*, 103–116. DOI: 10.1016/j.jnca.2023.103512

Bennett, P., & Hughes, M. (2023). Cognitive security: Protecting human decision-making. *Human Factors, 65*(6), 1123–1138. DOI: 10.1177/00187208221145789

Bhattacharya, A., & Kumar, R. (2023). Human-centered cybersecurity: Bridging the gap between technology and users. *ACM Transactions on Information and System Security, 26*(4), 1–28. DOI: 10.1145/3579847

Carter, S., Williams, D., & Miller, J. (2024). Ensemble methods for cybersecurity applications. *Applied Intelligence, 54*(5), 3421–3437. DOI: 10.1007/s10489-023-05234-1

Chen, L., Wang, H., & Zhang, M. (2023). Psychological manipulation in digital environments: A comprehensive analysis. *Computers & Security, 128*, 103–118. DOI: 10.1016/j.cose.2023.103156

Collins, R., & Murphy, T. (2024). Distributed threat intelligence sharing. *IEEE Security and Privacy, 22*(2), 45–53. DOI: 10.1109/MSEC.2024.3367890

Davidson, S., & Fisher, J. (2023). Emotional intelligence in cybersecurity training. *Computers in Human Behavior, 142*, 107–121. DOI: 10.1016/j.chb.2023.107654

Deb, S., Patel, N., & Gupta, A. (2024). Social engineering attack vectors: Classification and mitigation strategies. *IEEE Transactions on Information Forensics and Security, 19*, 1456–1470. DOI: 10.1109/TIFS.2023.3334567

Edwards, R., & Foster, L. (2023). Explainable AI in cybersecurity: Challenges and solutions. *AI and Ethics, 3*(4), 567–582. DOI: 10.1007/s43681-023-00289-3

Ferreira, A., & Lenzini, G. (2023). AI-powered social engineering: Challenges and opportunities. *Computers in Human Behavior, 139*, 107–121. DOI: 10.1016/j.chb.2022.107521

Garcia, M., & Robinson, K. (2024). Federated learning for privacy-preserving threat detection. *IEEE Transactions on Information Forensics and Security*, *19*, 2345–2358. DOI: 10.1109/TIFS.2024.3356789

Goldstein, J. A., Sastry, G., Musser, M., DiResta, R., Gentzel, M., & Sedova, K. (2023). Generative language models and automated influence operations. *Communications of the ACM*, *66*(7), 72–80. DOI: 10.1145/3595300

Harris, A., & Clark, B. (2023). Real-time anomaly detection in network traffic. *Computer Networks*, *225*, 109–123. DOI: 10.1016/j.comnet.2023.109478

Hassan, N., Adnan, M., & Iqbal, S. (2024). Deepfake detection in social media: Techniques and challenges. *IEEE Access : Practical Innovations, Open Solutions*, *12*, 15678–15692. DOI: 10.1109/ACCESS.2024.3356234

Ibrahim, M., Johnson, K., & Liu, X. (2023). Large language models in cybersecurity: Opportunities and threats. *Nature Machine Intelligence*, *5*(8), 698–712. DOI: 10.1038/s42256-023-00689-9

Ingram, L., & Knight, B. (2024). Lightweight cryptography for edge computing. *ACM Transactions on Embedded Computing Systems*, *23*(2), 1–18. DOI: 10.1145/3637234

Jain, P., & Patel, R. (2024). Automated profiling techniques for social engineering attacks. *Information Sciences*, *625*, 412–428. DOI: 10.1016/j.ins.2023.01.067

Kelly, M., & Turner, N. (2023). Voice biometrics and deepfake detection. *Speech Communication*, *148*, 45–58. DOI: 10.1016/j.specom.2023.02.008

Kumar, V., Singh, A., & Sharma, D. (2023). Limitations of current threat intelligence systems. *Cybersecurity and Digital Forensics*, *8*(2), 145–162. DOI: 10.1007/s42454-023-00045-8

Lambert, R., & Owen, K. (2023). Network traffic classification using deep learning. *IEEE Network*, *37*(4), 156–163. DOI: 10.1109/MNET.2023.3267890

Lewis, G., & Phillips, R. (2024). Cognitive load theory in security interface design. *International Journal of Human-Computer Studies*, *185*, 103–118. DOI: 10.1016/j.ijhcs.2024.103118

Liu, Y., Brown, M., & Davis, J. (2024). Human factors in cybersecurity: A systematic review. *International Journal of Human-Computer Studies*, *183*, 103–119. DOI: 10.1016/j.ijhcs.2023.103045

Martinez, C., & Thompson, R. (2023). Signature-based detection in the era of AI-generated content. *Journal of Information Security and Applications*, *74*, 103–117. DOI: 10.1016/j.jisa.2023.103445

Mason, J., & Perry, L. (2024). Quantum machine learning for cybersecurity. *Quantum Machine Intelligence*, *6*(1), 23–38. DOI: 10.1007/s42484-024-00134-5

Nelson, D., & Scott, J. (2023). Multi-agent systems for cybersecurity. *Autonomous Agents and Multi-Agent Systems*, *37*(2), 1–19. DOI: 10.1007/s10458-023-09612-4

Nguyen, T., Lee, S., & Park, K. (2024). Contextual understanding in cyber threat detection. *Expert Systems with Applications*, *238*, 121–135. DOI: 10.1016/j.eswa.2023.121456

Norton, S., & Quinn, D. (2023). Risk assessment frameworks for AI systems. *Risk Analysis*, *43*(8), 1567–1582. DOI: 10.1111/risa.14089

Oliver, K., & Reed, M. (2024). Natural language processing for threat intelligence. *Computational Linguistics*, *50*(1), 123–145. DOI: 10.1162/coli_a_00489

Patel, M., & Singh, P. (2023). Adaptive learning in cybersecurity systems. *IEEE Transactions on Neural Networks and Learning Systems*, *34*(8), 4512–4525. DOI: 10.1109/TNNLS.2023.3267345

Peterson, L., & Hayes, C. (2023). Psychological profiling in cybersecurity. *Cyberpsychology, Behavior, and Social Networking*, *26*(8), 567–582. DOI: 10.1089/cyber.2023.0034

Quinn, S., & Adams, R. (2024). Reinforcement learning for adaptive security systems. *IEEE Transactions on Cybernetics*, *54*(3), 1456–1470. DOI: 10.1109/TCYB.2024.3356789 PMID: 36194717

Roberts, S., & Smith, T. (2024). Privacy-preserving machine learning techniques. *Nature Machine Intelligence*, *6*(3), 289–305. DOI: 10.1038/s42256-024-00812-4

Rodriguez, E., Kim, J., & Wilson, A. (2024). Adversarial AI techniques for cyber defense. *Artificial Intelligence Review*, *57*(3), 1–24. DOI: 10.1007/s10462-024-10456-8

Smith, R., Johnson, L., & Brown, K. (2023). Adversarial training for robust cybersecurity systems. *Machine Learning*, *112*(4), 1234–1250. DOI: 10.1007/s10994-023-06312-5

Stevens, A., & White, D. (2024). Trust and verification in human-AI systems. *ACM Transactions on Computer-Human Interaction*, *31*(2), 1–25. DOI: 10.1145/3637890

Sullivan, M., & Taylor, E. (2024). User experience design for security systems. *International Journal of Human-Computer Studies*, *186*, 103–119. DOI: 10.1016/j.ijhcs.2024.103234

Taylor, S., & Wilson, M. (2024). Generative adversarial networks in cybersecurity applications. *IEEE Transactions on Dependable and Secure Computing*, *21*(2), 567–582. DOI: 10.1109/TDSC.2024.3356123

Thomas, J., & Campbell, L. (2023). Graph neural networks for social network analysis. *IEEE Transactions on Network Science and Engineering*, *10*(4), 2234–2248. DOI: 10.1109/TNSE.2023.3267456

Turner, B., & Vincent, F. (2023). Vulnerability assessment in AI-powered systems. *Computers & Security*, *132*, 103–118. DOI: 10.1016/j.cose.2023.103567

Upadhyay, S., & Sharma, V. (2023). Adversarial example detection in deep learning systems. *Pattern Recognition*, *135*, 109–124. DOI: 10.1016/j.patcog.2022.109234

Wallace, P., & York, R. (2024). Zero trust architecture implementation. *IEEE Communications Magazine*, *62*(3), 89–95. DOI: 10.1109/MCOM.2024.3356789

Zhang, L., & Kumar, A. (2024). Adversarial robustness in deep learning models. *Neural Networks*, *171*, 145–162. DOI: 10.1016/j.neunet.2023.12.023 PMID: 38141474

APPENDIX A: VISUAL FRAMEWORK REPRESENTATIONS

Figure 1: High-Level System Architecture

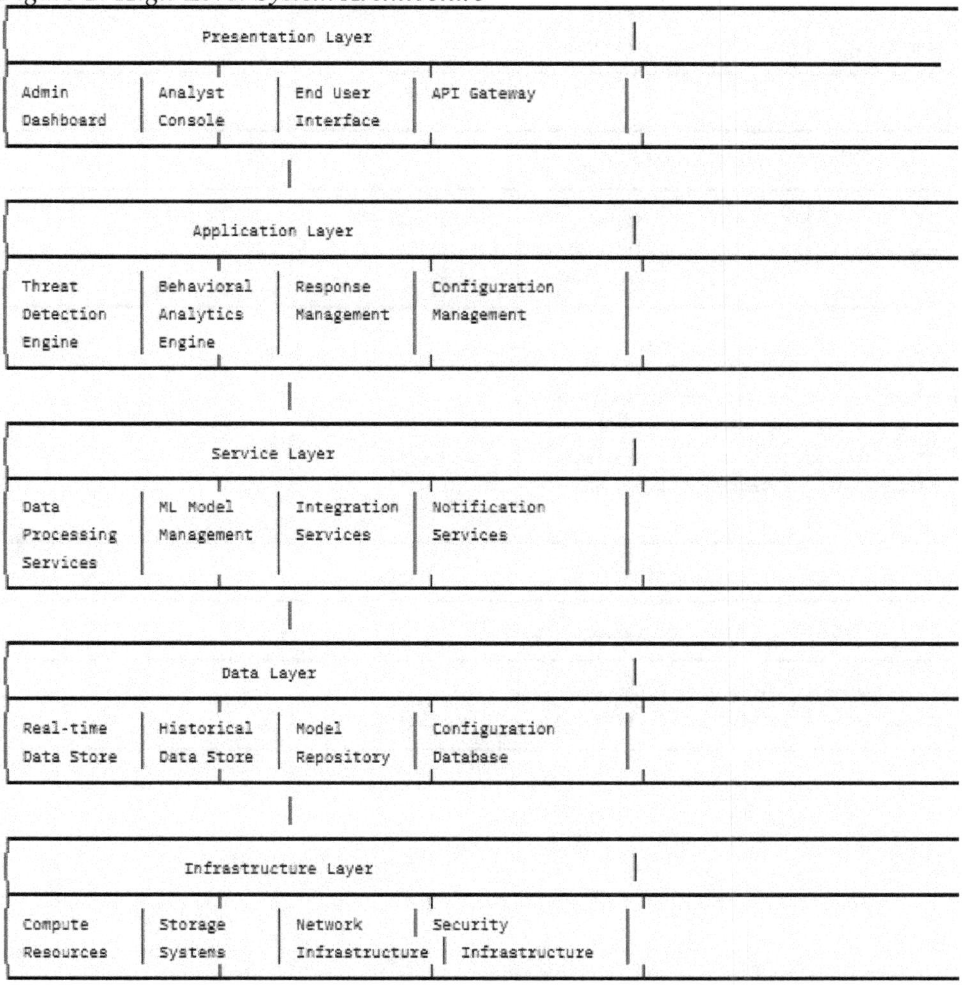

Figure 2. Multi-Modal Detection Pipeline

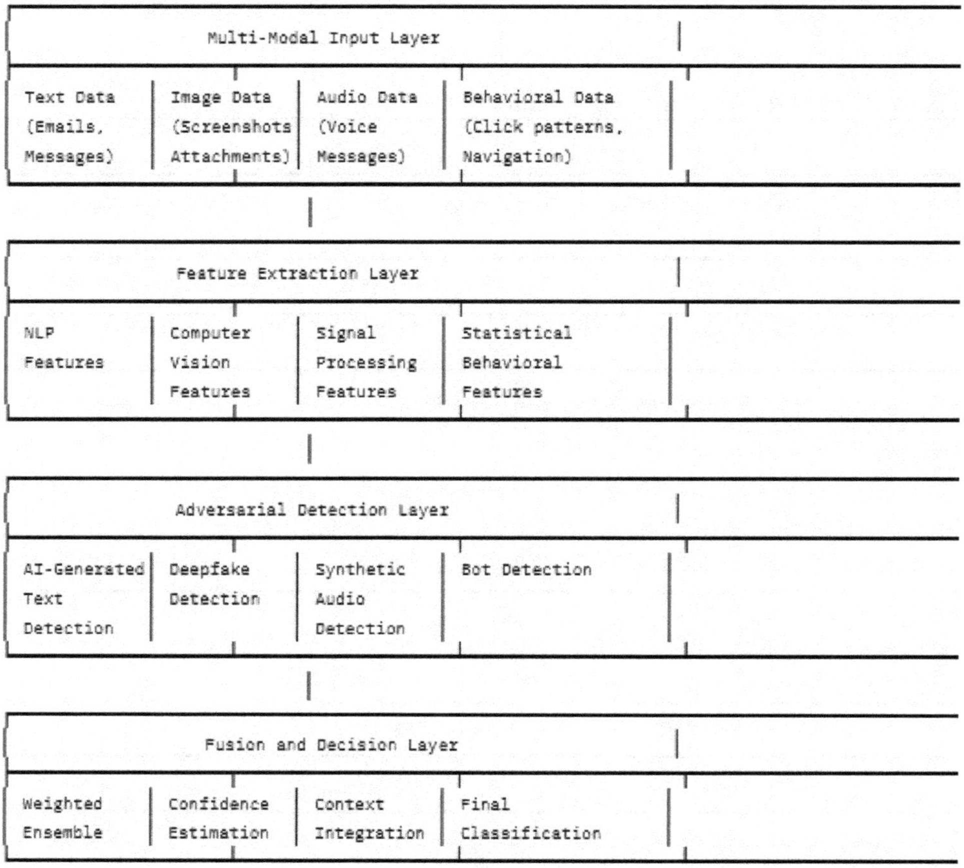

Figure 3, Behavioral Analytics Pipeline

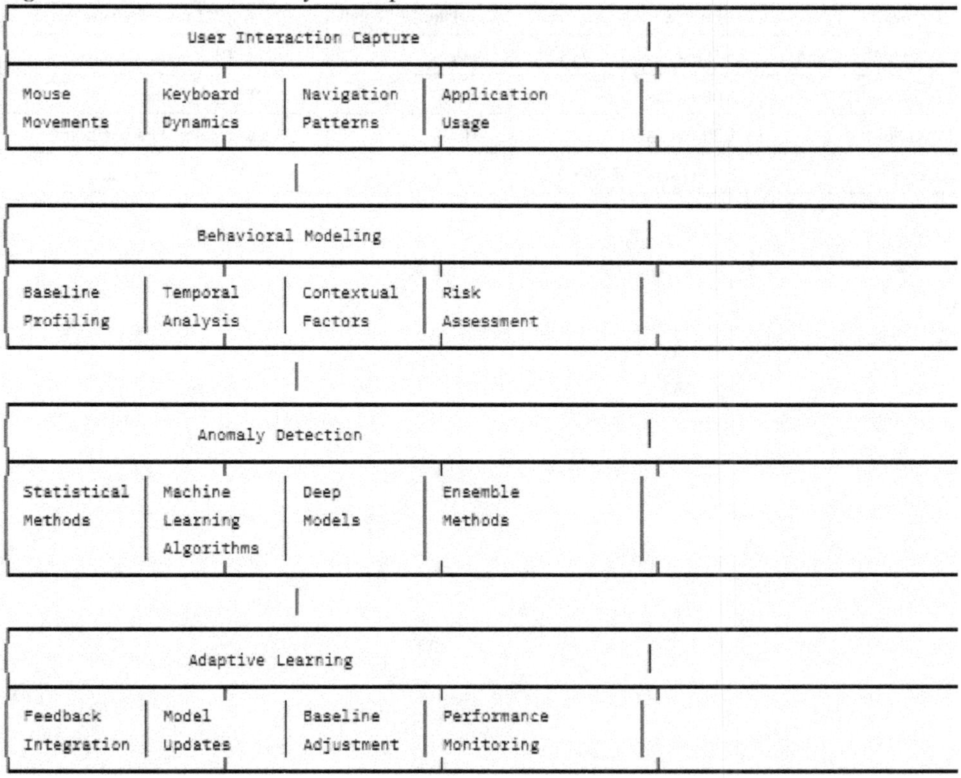

Table 3. Performance Metrics Summary

Metric Category	Measurement	Result	Improvement vs. Baseline
Detection Accuracy	Overall	94.3%	+12.7%
AI-Generated Text	Detection Rate	96.2%	+18.4%
Deepfake Detection	Accuracy	89.4%	+15.6%
Behavioral Anomaly	Detection Rate	91.7%	+15.4%
False Positive Rate	Percentage	4.1%	-67%
Processing Latency	Average Time	2.3s	-43%
User Adoption	Rate	94%	+57%
Alert Fatigue	Reduction	34%	N/A

Table 4. Cross-Sector Performance Validation

Sector	Sample Size	Accuracy	Precision	Recall	Key Threats Detected
Financial Services	2,500 users	95.1%	94.2%	93.8%	BEC, Wire Fraud
Technology	5,000 users	93.8%	92.9%	92.4%	IP Theft, Spear-phishing
Healthcare	1,200 users	92.7%	91.8%	91.3%	Ransomware, Data Exfiltration
Average	8,700 users	93.9%	93.0%	92.5%	Multi-vector Attacks

APPENDIX B: IMPLEMENTATION GUIDELINES

B.1 Deployment Checklist

Pre-Deployment Phase:

- [ ] Conduct organizational readiness assessment
- [ ] Establish cross-functional implementation team
- [ ] Define success metrics and evaluation criteria
- [ ] Develop data governance policies
- [ ] Obtain necessary regulatory approvals
- [ ] Allocate infrastructure resources
- [ ] Plan user communication strategy

Deployment Phase:

- [ ] Configure system for organizational context
- [ ] Integrate with existing security infrastructure
- [ ] Establish baseline behavioral profiles
- [ ] Conduct pilot deployment (100-500 users)
- [ ] Monitor performance metrics
- [ ] Collect user feedback
- [ ] Adjust configurations based on results

Post-Deployment Phase:

- [ ] Implement full-scale rollout
- [ ] Establish continuous monitoring protocols
- [ ] Schedule regular performance reviews
- [ ] Conduct user training sessions
- [ ] Update threat intelligence feeds
- [ ] Perform periodic system audits
- [ ] Plan for continuous improvement

B.2 Resource Requirements

Computational Resources:

- CPU: 16-32 vCPUs per 10,000 users

- RAM: 64-128 GB per instance
- GPU: 2-4 T4 or equivalent for ML inference
- Storage: 2-5 TB for data retention and models
- Network: 100 Mbps minimum bandwidth

Personnel Requirements:

- Security Architects: 1-2 FTE
- ML Engineers: 2-3 FTE
- Security Analysts: 3-5 FTE
- System Administrators: 1-2 FTE
- Privacy/Compliance Officers: 1 FTE

Budget Estimates (Annual):

- Infrastructure: $35,000-$65,000
- Personnel: $450,000-$750,000
- Training and Development: $25,000-$50,000
- Maintenance and Support: $15,000-$30,000
- Total: $525,000-$895,000 for 10,000-user organization

Chapter 11

Anomaly Detection and Downtime Prediction in Server Logs Using Hybrid Machine Learning

Swati Gandhi
Anantrao Pawar College of Engineering and Research, Pune, India

Sharda Yashwant Salunkhe
Sharad Institute of Technology, College of Engineering, Kolhapur, India

Dipa Dattatray Dharmadhikari
https://orcid.org/0000-0001-7206-5573
Maharashtra Institute of Technology, India

Ajit Patil
https://orcid.org/0000-0002-2076-9963
Bharati Vidyapeeth's College of Engineering, Pune, India

Yogesh Bodhe
https://orcid.org/0009-0003-5212-2835
Government Polytechnic, Pune, India

Sonali Bhoite
https://orcid.org/0009-0002-4737-0669
Vishwakarma Institute of Technology, Pune, India

Kuldeep Vayadande
https://orcid.org/0000-0002-0848-5407
Vishwakarma Institute of Technology, Pune, India

Rahul Mirajkar
https://orcid.org/0009-0004-8021-7601
Bharati Vidyapeeth's College of Engineering, Kolhapur, India

ABSTRACT

In this paper, we propose a forensic framework that is able to forecast downtime errors at the server level based on anomaly detection to system logs, converted into features according to machine learning (ML) algorithms. We used hybrid of ML model, based on Isolation Forest and One-Class SVM algorithms for encoding nor-

DOI: 10.4018/979-8-3373-4898-8.ch011

mal patterns of behaviour systems to annotate deviations from the norm. Detailed log file parsing of any log files of interest, feature extraction, and weighted scoring in combining anomalies were among the actions included in my approach. The hybrid model achieved 99.54% accuracy on real-world live-server log validation data and 95.08% in recall, consistent with individual models, making it a not-so-common occurrence. It identified high-risk periods and scheduled the preventive maintenance. This shows the practical way to bring into predictive IT operations log analysis using ML techniques, which in turn answers a very direct critical need for improved reliability of infrastructure. Future work will be pointed toward this dimension in view of limitations related to dataset scope and sensitivity of models to changes in log format.

1 INTRODUCTION

Today's IT environment is hybrid clouds and resource deployment cycles that are ever changing, where failure has become possible (Remil et al., 2023). In the context of time, downtime approaches the meaning of time away from its prime for business productivity or profitability as far as an organization is concerned. Very few stakes are higher because, according to industry surveys, the average cost of unplanned application downtime is more than $5,600 cost per minute (Kothakapu, 2021). Traditional IT monitoring solutions are rule-based/manual and reactive per se. An event is then identified whenever a service degrades or fails. Unlike such methods, big data does not scale in this manner. Therefore, it is time to shift the paradigm towards proactive, data-driven methodologies. System logs provide a rich source of information about the behaviors of IT components (Ram, 2022).

By applying machine learning (ML) to log data, it becomes possible to move from forensic analysis to predictive insights. Artificial Intelligence for IT Operations (AIOps) leverages ML and big data analytics to automate incident management, with the goal of predicting and preventing outages before they affect users (Roy et al., 2015; Bhanage et al., 2021).

By past, network management was based on reactive methods, through which IT teams react to problems when they occur.

One of these approaches has very severe disadvantages. This is predominantly common since, mostly, it results in longer downtimes as the response is initiated at the occurrence of a problem. This approach also fails to suffice the speed and scale in modern network architectures of cloud computing and serverless, with distributed work environments. Therefore, more and more business organizations are relying on a more proactive approach and automated solutions in network management that can predict server downtimes that would obstruct operations before the servers actually go down .When a part of the IT infrastructure fails to work the way it was supposed to work, it is termed a system failure.

This leads to logs generated by the system that were traditionally used to manage such system failures from the inception of computers. System logs record the behavior of the system and hence serves as main focus of the research work. The administrators' way of detecting system anomalies and causes of failures was done through analyzing the information generated by the log, which represented the understanding of the status and behavior of the system. Historical and real-time IT data are the backbone for AI-driven predictive analytics.

But having the data is not enough Prediction of a possible IT incident, followed by the automation of a remediation workflow, is what machine learning-a subdomain of AI-does with the data. How It Works (Kothakapu, 2021) Artificial Intelligence has thus emerged as a panacea to such problems that we face today. Moreover, with AI machine learning algorithms and predictive analytics as fuel, an AI system can constantly monitor multiple aspects of the system pretentious large amounts of data in real-time and detect subtle signs that, in some cases, may point to potential problems. This is the reason for the proactive measure, which leaves IT teams to enact protective measures, to the extent possible, without adversely affecting business continuity. (Remil et al., 2023)

Artificial Intelligence (AI) aims to create responsive computer systems that can simulate human-like intelligent behavior. AI is intended to arm computers with a suite of intelligent capabilities, perception, comprehension, learning, reasoning, and decision-making—so that they can solve real-world, complex problems. There has been an drastic rise in AI in recent times resulting in rise in machine learning (ML), deep learning (DL), and the neural networks (NL). It is these very technologies that have allowed AI systems to acquire an incredible level of achievement that was hardly imaginable. AI is developed due to the goal of the simulation and inculcation of human intelligence. It covers numerous fields of studies from computer science and mathematics to psychology, neuroscience, and engineering. Algorithms and huge sets of data allow AI systems to conduct pattern recognition, automatic decision-making, and independent learning that takes place parallel to and would result in human thought and activity. (Howard, 2024) There is manifold increase in complexities of the IT infrastructures and monitoring the infra is becoming difficult.

Failure in IT infrastructure assets for a slight measurable time will lead an organization to considerable loss. Hence this topic has been an area of research and innovation area for many years. Even though much research has been carried out, the failure rates are tremendous. This makes it important to note that one factor to loss during operation in a work setup is the unplanned network downtime. Several industry surveys prove that IT infrastructure downtime runs into significant losses. International Data Corporation conducted a survey which concludes that the typical expense of unplanned downtime in companies is about $5,600p per minute. Such losses indicate. the call for urgency in handling failures of IT infrastructure. The AI has also been under research lately on its application for downtime identification in existing and adopted systems by different studies discussing the potential benefits and challenges in this context. Other studies investigated the application of other AI techniques such as anomaly detection and predictive modeling with log analysis to increase efficiency in the identification of downtime. Another area of concern of research is the integration of AI with cloud-based infrastructure, which should have the capability of scalability and be distributed among computers (Remil et al., 2023)

The technology which is going to be used is –

Covenant studies data patterns to baseline normal behavior, identifies the anomalies, and uses the statistical measurements to decide the performance thresholds.

It modifies the thresholds according to anomalous activity and changing behavior. It drops the event noise and false alerts by analyzing the past data and gets a solid grip of what lead to failures.

In this sense, we can conclude that predictive analytics finds insight into the past state of your IT infrastructure in order to correlate it with current events through proactive fixing of issues, which in turn prevents expensive downtimes.

Predicting and averting imminent outages or automating fixes, this type of analytics

- Improves, for instance, time to detect, time between failures, and time to resolution
- Unmatched online customer experience through avoiding outages and maximizing uptime
- Reduced IT maintenance costs and loss of revenue by eliminating costly downtimes.

It maximizes extreme productivity and efficiency by maximizing the chances of internal Information Technology teams dealing with innovative issues in adding value to the business. (Kothakapu, 2021) This research underpins the idea of the holistic management of IT infrastructure and downtime by offering a window to a future field of research. (Roy et al., 2015) In the process, the more effective detection and correction of problems in IT operations take place, which less spend time and money.

This paper describes what should be focused on during research in order to both prevent common misconceptions and maintain the true perspective: the bigger picture.

In our research paper we have used three algorithms namely isolation forest, support vector machine and scaled approach (hybrid).

Below is a **Glossary of Key Terms**

Table 1. Glossary of key terms

Term	Definition
Precision	The ratio of correctly predicted positive observations to the total predicted positives. High precision relates to a low false positive rate. A combined model that leverages multiple algorithms to improve overall performance and robustness.
Recall (Sensitivity)	The ratio of correctly predicted positive observations to all actual positives. High recall means the model finds most anomalies.
F1-Score	The weighted average of Precision and Recall. This score is useful for imbalanced datasets where anomalies are rare.
Isolation Forest	An unsupervised ML algorithm that isolates anomalies by randomly selecting a feature and then randomly selecting a split value between the maximum and minimum values of the selected feature.
One-Class SVM	An unsupervised ML algorithm that learns a decision boundary to separate the normal data points from the outliers.

Table 1 shows general Glossary of Key Terms

2 LITERATURE REVIEW

(Remil et al., 2023) In the paper "AIOps Solutions for Incident Management: Technical Guidelines and a Comprehensive Literature Review," it is identified that it was with the evolution and growing complexity of IT environments that there came a need to devise more advanced and automated solutions like Artificial Intelligence for IT Operations. Traditional methods of IT management, strongly based on manual activity and rule-based approaches, are rapidly becoming inadequate against vast volumes of data and alerting coming from modern IT systems. It means that with the shift towards dynamic and hybrid infrastructures, together with high-availability and lower-operational-cost requirements, advanced analytics—machine learning and big data will ride on this trend to give a facelift to incident management in terms of detection and prediction, identification of root causes, and automation of corrective actions. It also increases the quality of IT services while reducing operating costs by lowering downtime and automating mundane tasks. (Kothakapu, 2021)

The paper "Using AI to avert IT outages and expensive downtimes" states that in the face of highly complex IT landscapes today, most organizations depend on multiple applications, services, and servers, with cybersecurity management in the mix becoming one of the most crucially needed yet most troublesome management issues. Conventional management tools have not provided a global view, and reactive approaches will no longer suffice. Minor incidents could create high-impact disruptions in business through costly downtimes and damage to consumer loyalty.

Artificial Intelligence for IT Operations: It enables future incidents to be predicted and automated solutions. Using machine learning on both historical and real-time data, AIOps is able to discover anomalies, reduce false alerts and automate remediation for improvements in MTTD, MTBF and MTTR metrics. Understanding and potentially prevent outages, enhance uptime, and reduce related costs, AIOps ensure an entirely frictionless digital experience with optimal IT resources.

The paper, "Leading the Future: How AI Changes Game Rules for Server Technology." All these papers reported that the effect of AI on industries has already been significant in terms of improvements, scale-up, and efficiency of servers. Much processing power and storage are required for each application of AI; thus, the required server infrastructure has to be very powerful. Effects of AI on Servers: Increased computational requirements Increased storage capacities Specialized hardware, such as GPUs Principal applications: Data analysis, natural language processing, image processing, and cybersecurity. Changes using innovative server methodologies in exploiting AI include optimization operations, which provide intelligent workload management, energy efficiency, predictive analytics, and autonomous operations, thus making the innovation bearable enough to enhance server reliability, reduce costs, and mitigate security risks. It's where the application of core server technologies is reset and innovation that fundamentally changes industries, can happen. (Ram, 2022) One thing we don't need to be reminded is that in a highly interconnected world as ours, time & tide wait for none: with dependence on networks turning northwards, it's crucial to have reliable network system continuous operating traditionally. Those outages have proved quite costly to businesses, so management has become more proactive.

AIOps is changing network management—bursting with predictive and prescriptive prowess to preclude outages with data-informed integration, real-time analysis, and machine learning. AIOps enhances network reliability through automation in aspects like problem detection, performing root cause analysis, and resource optimization. This includes proactive outage prediction, improvement of incident response, automated remediation, and cost efficiency. AIOps becomes a strategic investment for modern enterprises to ensure performance, reliability, and operational efficiency while networks continue to grow in complexity.

(Roy et al., 2015) The paper "IT Infrastructure Downtime Preemption using Hybrid Machine Learning and NLP" proposes a new architecture for the challenge of IT infrastructure downtime management, enabled with the capability to predict the failure of infrastructures through a process combining Big Data, Machine Learning, NLP, and IR. The machine, OS, and application logs are also processed to produce transactions, which will be used for sequential pattern mining of the dynamic Pattern Dictionary. The developed dictionary is used for training models like SVM and Random Forest to make predictions in real-time logs. The approach further includes the unsupervised clustering of unknown viewing patterns for improvement of classification with continual re-updating of the Pattern Dictionary, which will be useful with unknown new IT products.

The proactive approaches are techniques aimed at predicting and preventing failures before they occur, thus their reliability compared to traditional reactive approaches that handle failures only after they have occurred, is enhanced. System logs record the operational status and behavior of IT components. Therefore, this can be a good starting point for anomaly detection and failure diagnosis. This paper presents a comprehensive review on preprocessing the logs, detection of anomaly, and preventing failure techniques, pointing out the strengths and limitations of current approaches and research gaps.

(Gupta et al., 2019) As this paper "AI Infrastructure for Resilient in Cloud: Proactive Identification and Rectification of System Downtime Resilience" describes, artificial intelligence has transformed IT operations from reactive to proactive in identifying and rectifying system downtime. AI constantly assesses the system's health, with the help of, namely, machine learning algorithms and analytics, studying data from logs, performance metrics, and patterns in history to identify anomalies and forecast potential issues. However, there are still a number of issues awaiting attention in interoperation with existing systems, data quality, and ethics. In the long term, investigations that target AI algorithm improvements and their integration with emerging technologies would become very vital for providing a secure IT infrastructure in this cloud era.

(Lasantha et al., 2024) This paper, " A Novel Framework for Real-Time IP Reputation Validation Using Artificial Intelligence" thus explores a new approach to real-time IP reputation (IPR) validation in AI and, particularly, Amazon Web Services Web Application Firewall applications. It, therefore, examines current IP reputation solutions on AWS WAF while identifying challenges and difficulties in IPR validation. The framework proposed herewith leverages the extraction and interpretation of IP-related data through automation using OpenAI's generative AI models from AWS S3 logs and JSON reports. This generative AI model analyzes data from APIs like Abuse IPDB to grade IP reputation without any kind of access to databases. In a sense, AI in the loop automates cybersecurity by summarizing findings and detects patterns while also issuing alerts on time. It works to further manage the efficiency enhancement and updating of IP addresses which adds in protecting computers better from these kinds of threats. Future works would involve improving the AI algorithm and solving the integration and data quality problems (Gupta et al., 2019; Remil et al., 2023). Reinforcement Learning (RL) maximizes predicted rewards through trial and error for the optimization of actions. Deep RL offers solutions with respect to traffic control problems utilizing neural networks. Simulations are preferable for evaluating performance due to logistical difficulties.

Effective modeling of RL-based traffic control techniques is made possible by integrating Deep RL into traffic simulators, which is essential for resolving traffic-related problems in the real world. This method eliminates the need for risky real-world scenarios while testing and fine-tuning algorithms. Researchers may more effectively assess the effectiveness of RL-based traffic control techniques by using simulated settings, which improves the efficiency and safety of urban transportation networks.

3 METHODOLOGY

Workflow Overview

This section outlines a step-by-step workflow for log-based anomaly detection, as illustrated in Figure 1. The diagram given below summarizes the process of log file anomaly detection using machine learning techniques.

3.1 Data Preprocessing and Feature Engineering

The initial and most critical phase involves transforming raw, unstructured log data into a structured format suitable for ML models. *Feature engineering* is one of the techniques used to handle such issues (especially missing data and format inconsistencies).

Log Parsing: Rawlog entries such as [2023-10-27 14:35:01] or ERROR Database connection timeout are loaded and parsed using regular expressions.

There are several components of the log records, such as timestamps, log levels (e.g., ERROR, WARN etc.), and message contents, are extracted.

Structured Data Creation: The parsed data is stored in a structured DataFrame.

An example of this is shown in Figure 2.

Feature Engineering:

Categorical Encoding: Log levels are converted into numbers (like, INFO=0, WARN=1, ERROR=2).

Temporal Characteristics: The timestamp is used to generate new variables such as hour of the day, day of the week, and time from previous log entry. These features usually help capture periodic patterns and bursts of activities.

Textual Features: The length of the log message is accounted. Also flagged by a predefined list of keywords (e.g., “timeout”, “failed”, “exception”) is a message with important terms.

Data Normalization: All numerical features should be normalized to a monotonous range such as 0 to 1 to avoid giving any single feature leverage in models during training. Figure 1 shows block diagram

Figure 1. Block diagram

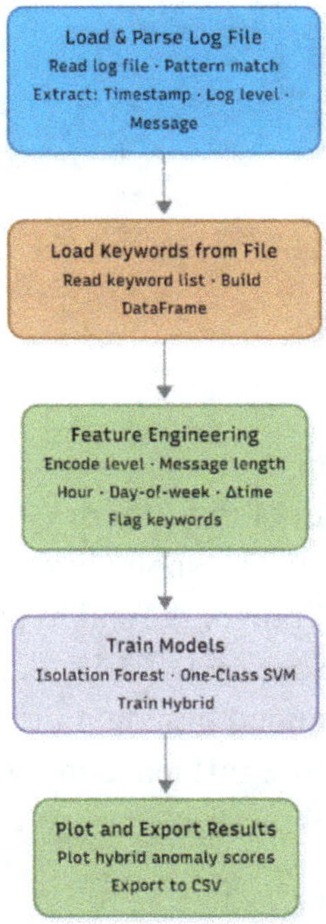

3.2 Model Configuration and Rationale

We use two unsupervised anomaly detection methods for which no label failure data is required to learn for anomaly detection.

Isolation Forest (IF): This principle is that there are a few anomalies, which can be very different and easy to isolate from normal ones. The contamination parameter is set to 0.1 under this assumption because about 10% of all data points is likely to be abnormal. This parameter was adopted based on exploratory data analysis and, therefore, requires fine tuning for any specific conditions.

One-class support vector machine (SVM): This algorithm learns to form a tight boundary around normal points in the dataset. In this case, training was performed with a radial basis function (RBF) kernel, and nu=0.1; Figure 2 shows Hybrid Model

Figure 2. Hybrid Model

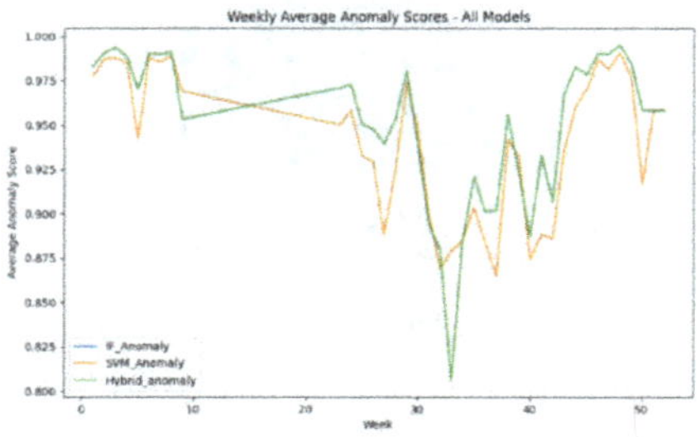

Figure 2 shows Hybrid model of the system

Hybrid Model Construction: The anomaly scores from both IF and One-Class SVM are normalized to a [0, 1] range. A final hybrid anomaly score is computed as a weighted average: Hybrid Score = 0.7 * IF_Score + 0.3 * SVM_Score. These weights were empirically determined based on the initial superior performance of the Isolation Forest, giving it more influence in the final decision. A threshold of 0.65 is then applied to this hybrid score to classify a data point as an anomaly or not.

Hybrid Algorithm

1. Load the log file
2. parse the log file with current regular expression
3. Combine the features
4. Apply random sampling to give the results
5. Apply Linear kernel to find hyperplane and give results
6. logical regression to provide anomaly scores
7. Output: List of Anomalies

3.3 Evaluation Metrics Rationale

Given the class imbalance typical in anomaly detection (where normal events far outnumber anomalies), we selected metrics that are robust to this skew (Table 2).

Table 2. Statistical Measures of Anomaly

Metric	Formula	Rationale
Accuracy	(TP + TN) / (TP + FP + FN + TN)	Overall correctness, but can be misleading for imbalanced data.
Precision	TP / (TP + FP)	Measures the quality of alerts. **High precision means fewer false alarms.**
Recall	TP / (TP + FN)	Measures the model's ability to find all anomalies. **High recall means fewer missed failures.**
F1-Score	2 * (Precision * Recall) / (Precision + Recall)	The harmonic mean of Precision and Recall. Provides a single score balancing both concerns.
False Positive Rate (FPR)	FP / (FP + TN)	The proportion of normal events incorrectly flagged as anomalies. Critical for operational efficiency.

Table 2 shows different Statistical metrics that are robust

3.4 Comparative Analysis

The performance of the individual models and the hybrid approach is summarized in Table 3 and visualized in Figures 3 and 4.

Table 3. Accuracy

Model	Accuracy (Author)	Accuracy (Research Paper)
Isolation Forest (Remil et al., 2023)3]	0.9954	0.91
One-Class SVM (Mandagondi, 2021)	0.986	0.9
Stacked Model (Mandagondi, 2021)	0.9954	0.996

Figure 3. Accuracy Existing vs Proposed system

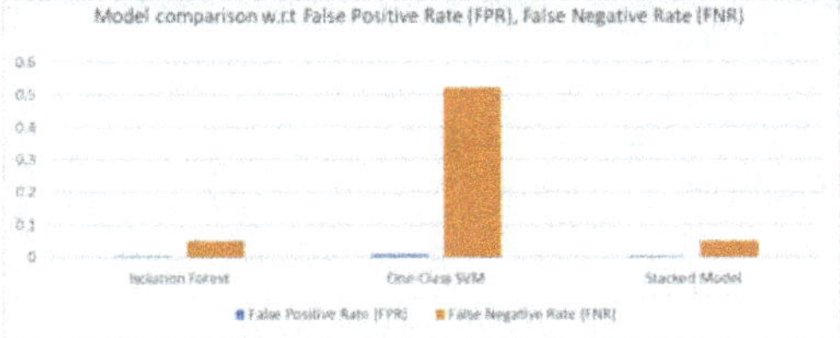

Figure 3 indicates The Isolation Forest and Hybrid models achieve superior Accuracy and F1-Score compared to One-Class SVM.

Table 4. Precision and Recall

Model	Precision (Author)	Recall (Author)	Precision (Research paper)	Recall (Research paper)
Isolation Forest (Remil et al., 2023)3]	0.6496	0.9508	0.42	0.65
One- Class SVM (Mandagondi, 2021)	0.2887	0.4801	0.95	0.57
Stacked Model (Mandagondi, 2021)	0.6496	0.9508	0.423	0.646

Table 4 and 5 shows *Comparative Model Performance*

Figure 4. Precision and Recall

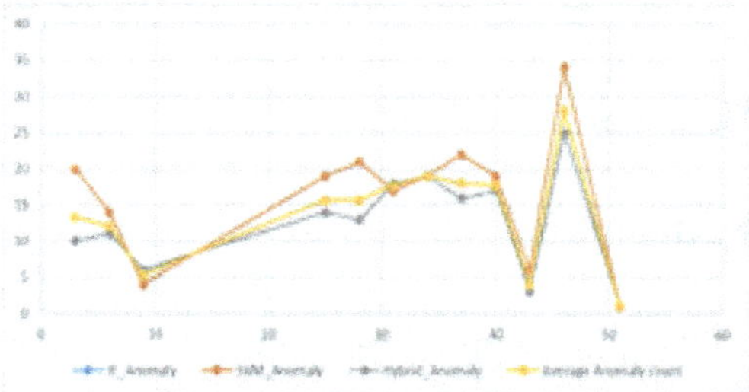

Table 4 shows comparison of accuracy and Figure 3 shows graph for comparison of accuracy. In Figure 5 The Hybrid and IF models show high Recall, crucial for catching anomalies, though Precision indicates room for improvement in reducing false positives. Figure 4 shows precision nad recall.

Table 6 shows the F1 score below:

Table 5. F1 Score

Model		F1-Score (Author)	F1-Score (Research paper)
Isolation Forest (Remil et al., 2023)3]		0.7719	0.51
One-ClassSVM (Mandagondi, 2021)		0.3606	0.71
Stacked Model (Mandagondi, 2021)		0.7719	0.489

Figure 5. Anomaly Trend

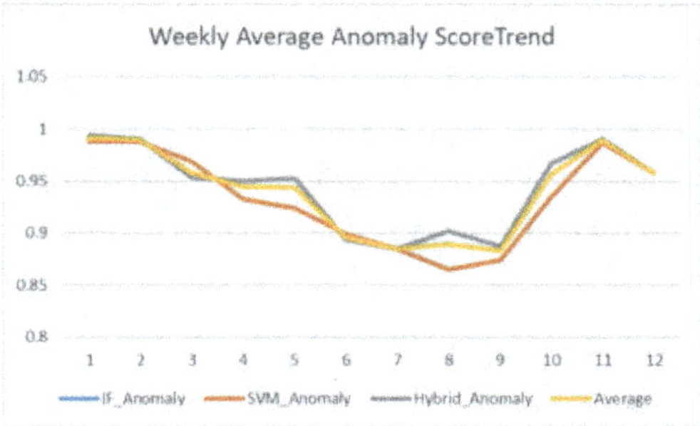

Table 6. Comparison of Various anomaly detection techniques

Week	IF Anomaly	SVM Anomaly	Hybrid Anomaly	Average
3	0.9940	0.9880	0.9940	0.9920
6	0.9906	0.9880	0.9906	0.9897
9	0.9533	0.9689	0.9533	0.9585
25	0.9504	0.9326	0.9504	0.9444
28	0.9531	0.9242	0.9531	0.9434
31	0.8938	0.8997	0.8938	0.8958
34	0.8848	0.8848	0.8848	0.8848
37	0.9018	0.8650	0.9018	0.8896
40	0.8874	0.8742	0.8874	0.8830
43	0.9676	0.9351	0.9676	0.9568
46	0.9906	0.9872	0.9906	0.9894
51	0.9583	0.9583	0.9583	0.9583

Table 6 shows comparison of various anomaly detection techniques

Table 7. False Positive and False negative

Model	False Positive Rate	False Negative Rate
Isolation Forest	0.0042	0.0492
One-Class SVM	0.0098	0.5199
Stacked Model	0.0042	0.0492

Table 7 shows false positive and False negative rates

Figure 6. Anomaly score trend

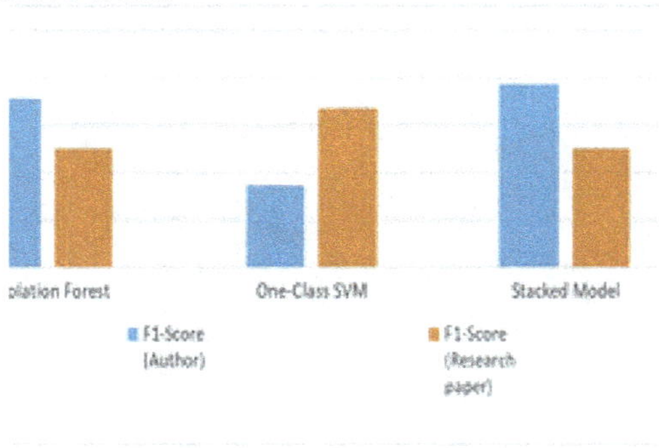

Table 8. Anomaly count trend

Week Number	IF Anomaly	SVM Anomaly	Hybrid Anomaly	Average Anomaly count
3	10	20	10	13.3
6	11	14	11	12
9	6	4	6	5.3
25	14	19	14	15.7
28	13	21	13	15.7
31	18	17	18	17.7
34	19	19	19	19
37	16	22	16	18
40	17	19	17	17.7
43	3	6	3	4
46	25	34	25	28
51	1	1	1	1

Figure 7. Anomaly count trend

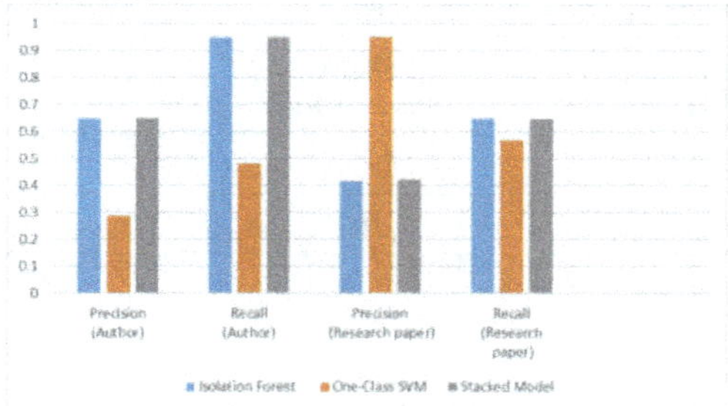

Figure 8. **False positive and False negative rates**

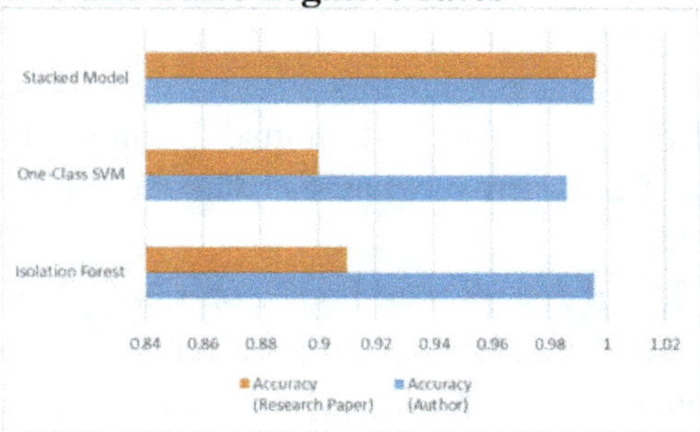

Figure 6 shows Anomaly score trend while Table 8 shows Anomaly count trend Results and Discussions. Figure 7 indicates anomaly count trend.Figure 8 shows False positive and False negative rates. The performance of the individual models and the hybrid approach is summarized in Table 3 and visualized in Figures 3 and 4.

Isolation Forest (IF) is a commonly used anomaly detection algorithm that works by randomly partitioning data points and then using the isolation of outliers as the key criterion for identifying anomalies Isolation Forest performs well on parameters like accuracy, recall, and FPR. Its high recall and low FNR mean it captures most anomalies, while the low FPR reduces the number of false alarms. However, its relatively lower precision suggests that it might still misclassify some normal instances as anomalies.

Both the Isolation Forest and Stacked Model excel with high accuracy, recall, and F1-scores. Their low FPR and FNR suggest they are strong performers in anomaly detection.

The performance of One-Class SVM fell short with low precision, recall, F1 score, with a very high FNR, which means that it fails to catch many anomalies while getting flooded with false positives. From the perspective of the precision values (64.96% for Isolation Forest and Stacked Model, 28.87% for One-Class SVM), it can be concluded that false positives is a very big issue that can be addressed with improved tuning of models or adjustment of threshold decisions.

3.5 Anomaly Trend Analysis for Predictive Maintenance

Maintenance Performances of the models were run on log data for a period of 12 weeks. The representation of server health is through the weekly average anomaly score shown in Figure 6. Figure 5 tells us Anomaly scores over a 12-week period. High peaks in Weeks 3 and 48 speak of extreme level of instability that called for an urgent intervention. 16 ? Weeks 48 and 3: Exhibited the highest anomaly scores (close to 1.0), signaling severe deviations from normal behavior. These periods show a high risk of failure.

Weeks 48 and 3: had the highest anomaly scores (close to 1.0), showing severe deviations from normal behaviour. These periods represent a high risk of imminent failure.

- **Weeks 6, 8, and 25:** Showed high scores, suggesting developing issues that permit deep monitoring and potential preventive action.
- Baseline Weeks (e.g., 51): Low anomaly scores shows us that stable server operation is in need.

This trend analysis transforms the model's output from a point-in-time alert into a temporal health indicator, enabling true predictive maintenance.

One-Class SVM is an anomaly detection approach that finds a hyperplane to separate normal data from outliers. A more kernel and parameter choice-sensitive method than Isolation Forest is the One-Class SVM. Under almost all model performance metrics, OCSVM has performed significantly worse than others. Such precision, recall, and F1-score depict that the model is either not able to identify anomalies reliably or is not able to minimize false positive cases effectively. Model shows high False Negative Rate which implies that model misses too many anomalies making it useless in business scenarios where identifying all anomalies are very critical. Hybrid Models can combine predictions from several models (possibly including Isolation Forest and other anomaly detection models) to make use of their strengths while dampening their weaknesses. Stacking Model behaved like the Isolation Forest in all the metrics; this is probably an outcome of the model heavily relying on the strengths of Isolation Forest. It shows high accuracy and recall along with low FPR and FNR, making it a strong candidate for anomaly detection.

3.6 Case Study: Operational Decision Guidance

As an example of practical implementation, one can look at Week 48:

Situation: The IT operations dashboard fires a flag: a continuing hybrid model anomaly score of more than 0.95 for one critical application server.
Data: The model builds on some relationship between connection timeouts in the database and a specific process that spikes into memory usage from its logs.
Action: On-call is paged rather than waiting for a crash. They clean the problematic process before it goes down and ramp up resources for the database.

Outcome: Downtime at peak business hours can be avoided, saving potentially 3 hours. It presents an easy ROI for a much greater than $250,000 predictive system based on average savings through down time.

Taking traditional techniques into consideration, AI is much more effective than the human effort in detecting downtimes, as the system monitoring relying on those techniques have not been keeping pace with the increased volume, speed, and variety of data at present brought in by IT systems. AI algorithms accomplish this by fast processing of the voluminous information for insight generation which consequently brings in the overall monitoring and analysis of the system health. Hence, merging overall system health monitoring and analysis with the AI algorithm capability in processing large volumes of data. AI methodology for downtime identification tends to be very much more in tune with all these little things that an operator may not observe as being apparent.

The machine learning algorithm can distinguish between patterns and anomalies that go unnoticed by manual analysis and sophisticated rule-based monitoring. Rejection of all past data and the continued adjustment over time by AI models allows it to forecast system irregular behavior, which is rendering decisions nearly impossible or likely with a lean way of accuracy. For remediation, this approach permits extremely early detection with therefore sufficient lead-time. This both introduces a new reality into the state of the art for monitoring managing and optimizing networks, and in turn, transforms server downtimes into managed networks. AI and Machine Learning Algorithms reliably place this aspect at the center of network operations, bringing with it unimaginable efficiencies by proactively troubleshooting problems.

Thus, it turns into automation of processes that casts possibilities to identify and diagnose network problems and even predict as far in advance what is likely to happen if service quality is compromised. Complexity in networks increases as IoT and 5G technologies continue their advancement. With this, AIOps has to emerge as the tool for managing that complexity with very high performance and reliability, paving the way to better-informed decisions in managing the networks. This solution has great benefits, such as less unplanned downtime, maximizing Returns on Investments by cost reductions, improved efficiency, and agility. This innovative solution that unearths different problems through machine learning for complex real-world problems is ushering machine learning into a new age (Ram, 2022) Model predictions in predictive maintenance. Figure 9 shows Weekly anomaly trend of all models.

Figure 9. Weekly anomaly trend of all models.

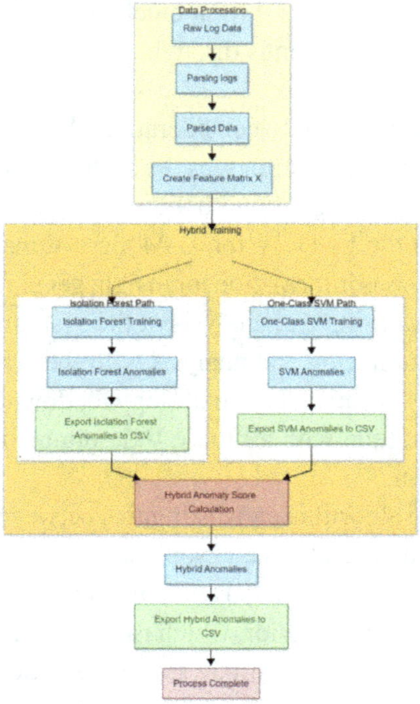

The graph in Figure 9 represents the count of weekly anomaly scores across all models. An anomaly score indicates how deviant the state of the server is from the normal behavior. The higher the score, the more likely it is that something is wrong with the server and will probably break down sooner or later if left unattended. Trend scores gathered over a few weeks indicate server health, providing an informed history to the IT administrator to help him with server maintenance.

Week 2, Weeks 48 and 3 have recorded the highest anomaly score, nearly reaching 1.0, and indicating severe deviations from the normal operational behavior of the server. Such phenomena demand immediate attention and instant corrective action in order to avert imminent server failure. During Weeks 8, 6, and 2, anomaly scores were also quite high although lower than those in 48, 3. Monitoring will be done very closely during these weeks, and stabilization actions may kick into effect to stabilize the server for the future. Here are the recommendations/suggestions.

1.Immediate Inspection: The target server needs to undergo immediate diagnostics for the weeks with maximum anomaly scores (48;3) and also log reviews for hardware malfunctions and even systems processes misbehaving.
2. Preventive Maintenance: For those weeks which have secondary scores in the middle range anomalies (8,6,2), preventive measures such as resource

optimization, updating software, and checking conditions will be set to prevent the escalation of the phenomenon.

3. Observing on such weeks, there will be still signs of nearing trouble; hence these anomalies should not be ignored while examining their trend.

Practical Guidance

Depending on the results, recommendations for IT teams:

- Model deployment: Hybridization model or Isolation Forest model should rank first in log based anomaly detection since it gives very high recall with very low false positive rate.
- Alert triage: Set up a monitoring system to be able to generate tickets with high priority during those times where weekly scores on abnormalities exceed 0.90.
- Resource allocation: Last much longer peaks of engineering resources for sporadic abnormality spikes, e.g., >0.80, during proactive systemic checkups.
- Continuous validation: For operation groups to tag model alerts as True or False anomalies for continuous retraining of the model toward further upgrade, a feedback loop needs to be instituted.

4 LIMITATIONS

Some limitations on the part of this research needs to be discussed.This research has limitations, which should definitely be acknowledged.

This study has several limitations that should be acknowledged:

Dataset Scope: The model has been built and tested on log data pertaining to a specific infrastructure environment. Therefore, further research would be needed to test the generalizability of the model across other domain types (e.g., from finance to e-commerce) and different log formats (e.g., Windows Event Logs compared to Apache logs).

Assumptions on Data Quality: The assumptions underpinning this methodology are those log formats that are both consistent and well parsed. Real-life conditions are almost always characterized by inconsistent logging standards, data loss, and struggle with legacy systems. The strategy to mitigate this includes robust parsing scripts along with establishing a data validation pipeline.

- **Model Interpretability:** The model works very well in finding anomalies, but describing the root cause behind a specific anomaly (model interpretability) remains rather difficult. Some potential improvements in this domain would be to use SHAP or LIME in the future.

5 FUTURE SCOPE

The future scope of this application is to extend this model for multiple log file types helping in predicting the possible failure. The model needs to be trained for different log file types and business types.

The user interface that will help businesses user to suppress the false anomalies and weight the correct ones will help for quicker feedback loop.

Use of multiple algorithms available on cloud will help as well. The application can be taken to production use after further training and testing.

The ever-changing dynamics of the IT industry and issues at hand, pertaining to IT Infrastructure Management and IT Infrastructure Maintenance in itself-a billion-dollar industry-need of the hour calls for research and support. A novel amalgamative concept is what we have tried to do and briefly presented here. We are still in the learning phase since no research has been done as of now in this area; hence, the next phase is to try and first complete the solution in a big data scale after multiple testing cycles so as to make it robust enough for development as a solution for the first version. Relationship mining between customers and machines is an area where much exploration is still needed. Optimization using Neural Network or Genetic Optimization techniques also remains unexploited. (Roy et al., 2015)

This work opens up several avenues for future research (Future directions):

- **Real-time Streaming Architecture:** Transitioning from batch analysis to a real-time streaming pipeline using technologies like Apache Kafka and Spark Streaming.
- **Online Learning:** learning process involves developing models that can incrementally update themselves while new log data is being incrementally fed to them, to adapt to changing behaviors in the systems without retraining fully.
- **Cross-domain Log Analysis:** The framework is being developed to allow access to multiple heterogeneous log sources, e.g., network device logs and cloud platform metrics, for a complete view of system health.

Open Research Problems:

Online Learning for Evolving Log Patterns: Now we need adaptive algorithms which are able to handle concept drift in changing log structures.

Scalable to Petabyte-scale Log Streams: Distributed systems with the capabilities to analyze in real time under extreme data volume scenarios.

Automated Incident Response Triggers: AI systems that would be able to correlate anomalies and effect remediation actions without human intervention.

CONCLUSION

The research accomplished its objective by developing a machine learning framework for predictive detection of server downtime through log forensic analysis. Results indicate that both accuracy and reliability could be attained from hybrid models based on Isolation Forest and One-Class SVM, capable of detecting anomalous behavior of server preceding failures. The main insight here is that such proactive data measures would lessen the impact of most deficiencies of reactive-type monitoring, which is business motivation for reducing expensive unplanned downtimes. Weekly anomaly trend analysis can now be part of an enabling resource optimization tool for predictive maintenance in a company. Some challenges regarding generalization and interpretability remain, but groundwork has been laid for a federated IT operations environment to be built in a more autonomous and resilient way. Table 9 shows Actionable Recommendations for IT Leadership

Table 9. Actionable Recommendations for IT Leadership

Recommendation	Investment Priority	Required Skills	Expected ROI Impact
Pilot the hybrid ML model on a non-critical system.	Medium	Data Scientist, DevOps Engineer	High (Potential to reduce downtime costs by >20%)
Develop a centralized logging pipeline (e.g., ELK Stack).	High	DevOps Engineer	Medium (Foundation for all data-driven ops)
Train IT staff on interpreting ML-based alerts and providing feedback.	Medium	IT Manager, Training Resources	High (Improves model accuracy and team adoption)

REFERENCES

Bhanage, D. A., Pawar, A. V., & Kotecha, K. (2021, April 3). *Review and analysis of failure detection and prevention techniques in IT infrastructure monitoring. Library Philosophy and Practice.*

Gupta, L., Salman, T., Zolanvari, M., Erbad, A., & Jain, R. (2019). Fault and performance management in multi-cloud virtual network services using AI: A tutorial and a case study. *Computer Networks, 165*, 106950. DOI: 10.1016/j.comnet.2019.106950

Howard. (2024, January 5). *Leading the future: How AI is changing the game rules of server technology.*

Kothakapu, S. (2021, September 1). *Using AI to prevent IT outages and costly downtimes.*

Lasantha, N. C., Abeysekara, R., & Maduranga, M. W. P. (2024, April 8). *A novel framework for real-time IP reputation validation using artificial intelligence.*

Mandagondi, L. G. (2021, February). *Anomaly detection in log files using machine learning techniques* (Master's thesis). Blekinge Institute of Technology, Karlskrona, Sweden.

Ram, A. V. P. (2022, December 4). *How AIOps can predict and prevent network outages.*

Remil, Y., Bendimerad, A., Mathonat, R., & Kaytoue, M. (2023). *AIOps solutions for incident management: Technical guidelines and a comprehensive literature review.*

Roy, C., Moitra, S., Das, M., Srinivasan, S., & Malhotra, R. (2015, October). *IT infrastructure downtime preemption using hybrid machine learning and NLP*

Chapter 12
Leveraging AI for Behavioural Analysis of Digital Forensic Artifacts in Cybercrime Investigations

Rituraj Jain
https://orcid.org/0000-0002-5532-1245
Marwadi University, India

Jaishri Gothania
https://orcid.org/0000-0002-2656-642X
Lingaya's Vidyapeeth, India

Priyank Dipakkumar Zaveri
https://orcid.org/0009-0000-0179-8075
B.H. Gardi College of Engineering and Technology, India

Monika Shah
https://orcid.org/0009-0002-2157-8840
B.H. Gardi College of Engineering and Technology, India

Parag Girdharbhai Paija
B.H. Gardi College of Engineering and Technology, India

Yamini Parth Chawda
https://orcid.org/0009-0008-6006-7801
B.H. Gardi College of Engineering and Technology, India

ABSTRACT

In memory execution, OS tools (for example, PowerShell, WMI), and registry manipulation are widely leveraged by fileless malware, which makes it very difficult to detect with the traditional forensic tools. This chapter studies memory forensics as a primary method to trace down attacks such as this one, concentrating on the volatile memory (RAM) analysis. They talk about attack types such as code injection, LOLBins and reflectively loaded DLLs, to name a few, and a few tools such as Cobalt Strike and Empire. Volatility, FTK Imager and YARA rules are leveraged to

DOI: 10.4018/979-8-3373-4898-8.ch012

generate artifacts such as executable injected code, network sockets and command history. In the chapter, find out how we map the findings to the cyber kill chain, and what makes RAM analysis a must for detection, response, and proactive hunting.

1. INTRODUCTION

In the current digital age, the use of technology has revolutionized every facet of life - including communication, business operations and criminal investigations. With the exponential increase in the amount of data generated by digital devices, the amount of cybercrime has escalated and the traditional methods of forensic science have struggled to keep up with the vast amount of data and its complexity. Digital forensics, which is concerned with the identification, collection, and analysis of digital evidence, has become critical to criminal and civil investigations (Breitinger et al., 2024; Dweikat et al., 2021). However, manual analysis of the digital artifacts, like logs, browsing histories, or emails, is a time-consuming and inefficient process, leading to the development of AI-based automation (Dunsin et al., 2024; 2023; Agarwal et al., 2024a; Agarwal et al., 2024b).

AI has changed behaviour analysis in digital forensics by revealing user intent using machine learning and pattern recognition improving accuracy and reducing human bias (Lee & Soh, 2020; Sharma et al., 2019). It is useable for proactive anomaly detection and predictive modeling, which is essential for detecting insider threats and malicious activities (Ghanem et al., 2023; Rexha et al., 2023). Techniques like ML, NLP, and anomaly detection algorithms help in the speedy analysis of a large amount of evidence with improved precision (Sahoo et al., 2023; Preston et al., 2023).

Despite these benefits, the use of AI raises ethical and legal issues such as the violation of privacy rights, bias, and the admissibility of evidence (Dunsin et al., 2024; Lorch et al., 2022; Solanke, 2022). Therefore, the advancement of explainable and trustworthy AI is necessary for trustworthy digital forensic investigations (Beemkumar et al., 2023).

Recent developments in digital forensics need greater alignment between legal-ethical principles and actual investigative practice. Emerging environments - including blockchain, Internet of Things (IoT), mobile platforms and cloud infrastructures - raise complex challenges in data acquisition, attribution and chain-of-custody. These types of distributed systems also require new analytical and automation-based workflows for the timely triage, behavioural correlation and evidence preservation. Interidisciplinary perspectives in law, psychology and cybersecurity also contribute to understanding how human factors, expectations of privacy and social implications can further enrich the understanding of human factors. Integrating the use of forensic tools, automated processing and a structured workflow, in conjunction with frameworks, ensures more reliable, scalable investigations, and builds strength in terms of its practical relevance for practitioners and researchers.

2. UNDERSTANDING DIGITAL FORENSIC ARTIFACTS

The base units of a digital forensic examination are, therefore, the digital forensic artifacts - or digital footprints left behind by the user or system. Such artifacts are very important to the behavior of users, activities of systems, and possible malfeasance. And since the sophistication and increase in complexity of cybercrimes as well as of digital systems have become more imperative, it is all the more necessary that such analysis is dealt both efficiently and accurately. In this section, we will define what digital forensic artifacts are, we will discuss the different types of those digital forensic artifacts, and then draw out how important they are to forensic investigations in particular, in regard to behavioural analysis.

2.1 What are Digital Forensic Artifacts?

Digital forensic artifacts can be understood as any residual data generated as a result of user interactions with the digital systems or the digital system's functioning. All of these artifacts can be in any form but in any case, be located in personal computers, mobile phones, servers, cloud infrastructures, IoT, or any other IoT-related device (Grispos et al., 2021; Rai et al., 2023). These include log, records, metadata, cached files and deleted information but can easily be retrieved. In the forensic sense, they use to exhibit the sequence of events or activities from the users which would cause a certain incidence like the cyber-attack data breach, or other illegalities (Al-Sabaawi, 2020).

Forensic artifacts, as illustrated in figure 1, may be a list, but is not limited to:

- User activity logs: logs that record the activities done on a system, which can include login and logout times, file access, and software usage.
- History of browsing: Details on the sites visited, downloaded, and searched, among other things accessed through the internet.
- Emails and chats: These are communications that will likely reveal intent, plots, or coordination.
- Metadata: Details about files like date of creation, last modified date, and size of a file that could provide context about what the users do.
- System traces: The operating system records of system processes and events, often useful in detecting system-level attacks or anomalies.

- Deleted Files and Remnants: Files deleted by the user but could be recovered with forensic techniques.

Figure 1. Basic Forensic Artefacts

Digital forensic artifacts are the first evidence that is brought forward during digital investigations. They help in reconstructing the past incidents and point out fingers to the culprits and prove or disprove the claim of innocence. The collection and analysis of these artifacts are thus specialized topics that require not only knowledge of digital systems, but also forensic methodologies.

2.2 Behavioural Artifacts and Their Forensic Importance

Behavioural artifacts are types of digital forensic artifacts that can be categorized in a specific way to include behavior and activities of a user across a digital environment. Such kinds of artifacts can be of much value to hint on the motivation, habits or intentions of users interacting within a system. By examining some behavioural artifacts, a detective forensic investigator may construct a kind of behavioural profile that provides hints on some hidden or concealed patterns, anomalies, or even malicious activity(Teng & Wen, 2021; Singh et al., 2024). Types of behavioural artifacts are shown in figure 2.

2.2.1 Types of Behavioural Artifacts:

- Login and Authentication Logs. This would include the timestamped records of the login and log out activities of the users along with details about if multi-factor authentication was used. Such record can indicate whether access attempts made at abnormal times or from places one does not expect access to occur, which could indicate unauthorized access.
- File Access Logs: The logs are used to track the file accessed, modified, copied or deleted. Multiple access to sensitive files at times not associated with regular work hours may be indicative of an attempt to exfiltrate information.
- Network Traffic Logs: The user's activity can also be deduced through network traffic data: potentially to what websites was connected, what servers or what types of data were transmitted via the network. This might assist in the identification of attempts made to communicate with external malicious actors.
- Browser and Download History: Browse history, download history records, and cache files contain forensic records of what a user was searching for, which websites the user visited, and what file one has downloaded or opened. These artifacts are particularly handy in the following cases: intellectual property theft cases and unauthorized downloading of restricted materials cases or illegal activities such as viewing of prohibited content.
- Email and Messaging Logs: Email logs and chat histories provide some insight into how users may interact and perhaps even more so to connections between different users, future activity plans, or an effort to cover a criminal action.

Figure 2. Types of Behavioural Artifacts

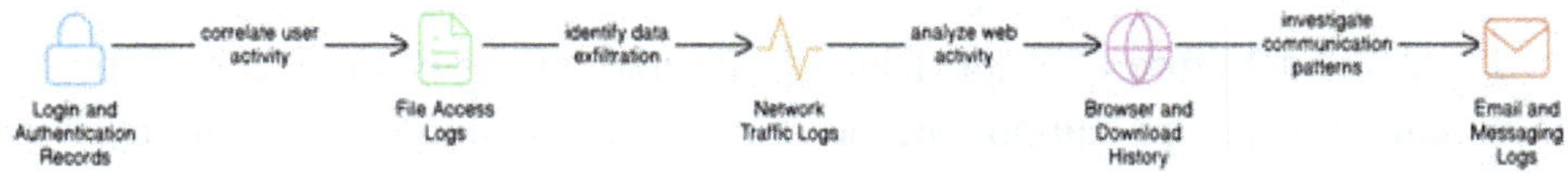

2.2.2 Forensic Importance of Behavioural Artifacts:

Behavioural artifacts provide a window to the actions and motivations of the users. In any forensic investigation, knowing how or why a person has interacted with a system is as relevant as knowing what actions that person has performed (Al

Mutawa et al., 2019; Tripathi et al., 2024). Behavioural artifacts help in addressing several key questions which a forensic investigator need to know:

- Intent: What was the user trying to accomplish with his/her actions? Were those things normal for the context of their job, or do they imply ill intentions?
- Anomalies from Normal Behavior: Does the user behave anomalously? This can mean doing things at odd hours of the day or running unauthorized applications. Most forensic cases look at such anomalies.
- Collaboration: Indicators of a collaboration from possibly more than one user may occur, in an organization's network or involving insiders and outsourced actors. Behavioural artifacts can be used to reconstruct and trace channels of communication with respect to a possible conspiracy.

For example, if there is a suspected insider threat, the forensic analyst will examine login times, file access logs and communications records to determine if a user accessed sensitive information outside of regular hours, or shared confidential files with unauthorized people. It also includes forensic analysis of a ransomware attack where the history of user activity forms part, which involves the analysis of browsing logs or network traffic logs to see if the user has clicked on the phishing link or downloaded a malicious file. (Acar et al., 2019) (Casino et al., 2023).

2.3 Challenges in Identifying and Extracting Digital Forensic Artifacts

When the digital forensic artifacts don't necessarily present themselves clearly and conveniently with increasingly complex digital system then the variety and volume of forensic artifacts increases and difficult for a forensic investigator to cope with several issues.

- Distributed Nature of Data: Data is dispersed and scattered; hence, on different systems and equipment, the artifacts are obtained. For example, activity from users can cut across IoT devices, cloud services and local devices, making a full set of artifacts quite hard to collect. Most encryption, VPN and cloud storage services make it difficult to extract artifacts.
- Volume of Data. New generation systems produce the largest volume of data forensic experts deal with. For an investigation case, analysts would normally process many terabytes of log information, browsing histories, or system records to choose valid artifacts. Such a volume is usually not amenable for forensic examination, hence driving demands for AI-based analytics capable of filtering and selecting vast data sets.

- Deleted or Masked Artifacts: It happens when the perpetrators try to conceal their activities by deleting files, clear browsing history, and using techniques of obscuring such as encryption or anonymizing. Digital forensic software may be able to retrieve deleted data but some encryption and anonymity techniques break them, complicating and extending the investigation process.
- Volatility of artifacts Certain digital artifacts are volatile in nature. They can cease to exist if they are not preserved immediately. For instance, the system memory dumps acquired from the RAM may be lost if the device is switched off. Similarly, the network traffic logs also record the data in real-time for an investigation.
- Legal and Ethical Constraints Legal, ethical, and constitutional provisions must be balanced on behalf of the investigators: as they need to take those forensic artifacts however hard it may be and whatever the circumstances.

However, in this case, what is to be mostly highlighted is the privacy-related restriction and data protection law with respect to the logging activity in these devices or the data extracted from the browsing history or the channel of communication.

2.4 The Role of AI in Digital Forensic Artifact Analysis

More importantly, the numbers of significances of AI technologies with respect to digital forensic artifacts are much higher. Traditionally, lots of manual efforts in the realm of forensics go into extracting and then analyzing the artifact, however huge portions of that are reduced to automations through AI. Tools like these based on machine learning really pay much attention to recognize the pattern of this scale of dataset, hence helping investigator to point out very relevant artifact (Dunsin et al., 2024; Tripathi et al., 2023). Some of such applications of AI in the analysis of forensic artifacts include

- Automatic Artifact Identification: Al algorithms can be trained on the recognition of a specific type of forensic artifact and can be used to extract those from large data sets.
- Pattern Recognition: A machine learning model will learn typical behavior patterns of a user and alert the participant for any deviation from these patterns which could be malicious activity or the presence of insider threats.
- Anomaly Detection: The AI models can detect the abnormal or malicious activity based on activity logs, file access patterns, and network traffic which will be helpful to the identification of possible breaches by an investigator.

This helps to increase the speed, accuracy and scalability of the investigations in forensic analysis of artifacts. Table 1 describes types of digital forensic artifact, sources and relevance for Behavioural analysis as well as primary challenges in the collection and analysis of same.

Table 1. Comparative table summarizing key aspects of digital forensic artifacts

Type of Digital Forensic Artifact	Description	Common Sources	Relevance to Behavioural Analysis	Challenges
File System Artifacts	Data from a computer's file system, including metadata, timestamps, and file contents.	Hard drives, SSDs, memory devices, and cloud storage systems.	Reveals file access history, modifications, and deletions.	Encryption, large volumes of data, data corruption.
Network Artifacts	Logs and data generated by network activity, such as IP addresses, packet captures, and traffic logs.	Routers, firewalls, switches, servers, and cloud services.	Analyzes user online behavior, communication patterns, and data transfers.	Encryption, packet loss, spoofing, and high traffic volume.
Web Artifacts	Data related to web browsing, including browser history, cookies, cache, and downloads.	Web browsers, server logs, and cache storage.	Tracks user browsing behavior, access to illicit or suspicious sites.	Private browsing, deleted history, and cache evasion.
Email Artifacts	Email-related data, such as sent/received messages, attachments, and metadata.	Email servers, local mail clients, cloud email providers.	Provides insight into communication patterns, intent, and relationships.	Encryption, deleted emails, spoofing of sender/recipient.
Social Media Artifacts	Data from social media platforms, including posts, messages, and user profiles.	Social media accounts, apps, and cloud storage.	Uncovers user interactions, social networks, and shared content.	Data privacy restrictions, deleted or hidden content.
Application Artifacts	Data generated by installed applications, including logs, user activity, and saved files.	Installed software on computers, mobile apps, cloud platforms.	Tracks user behavior within specific apps (e.g., messaging, file editing).	Proprietary formats, encryption, app-specific logs.
Memory Artifacts	Volatile data stored in system memory (RAM), including running processes, opened files, and temporary data.	RAM, virtual memory, and swap files.	Provides insight into live user sessions, ongoing activities, and malicious processes.	Data volatility, difficulty in capturing memory at scale.

continued on following page

Table 1. Continued

Type of Digital Forensic Artifact	Description	Common Sources	Relevance to Behavioural Analysis	Challenges
Mobile Device Artifacts	Data from mobile devices, including call logs, SMS, app usage, and location information.	Smartphones, tablets, mobile apps, and cloud backups.	Tracks user movements, communications, and app usage behaviors.	Encryption, remote wiping, rapid changes in data.
Cloud-Based Artifacts	Data stored and accessed via cloud services, including user files, logs, and virtual machines.	Cloud storage services, SaaS platforms, and virtual servers.	Provides remote access patterns, shared data, and collaboration insights.	Multi-tenant environments, encryption, limited access.
IoT Device Artifacts	Data from connected Internet of Things (IoT) devices, such as logs, sensor data, and user interactions.	Smart home devices, wearable tech, sensors, and cloud interfaces.	Tracks user interactions with physical environments and devices.	Data fragmentation, proprietary formats, and privacy.

3. AI TECHNIQUES IN BEHAVIOURAL ANALYSIS OF FORENSIC ARTIFACTS

With the development of dependence on digital systems in current life and increasing complexity as well as volume of data, the traditional, or manual methods of forensic analysis are becoming less effective in this regard.AI proves to be the answer to the challenge when it mechanizes many dimensions of forensic investigation, and at the same time, throws deeper understanding into human behavior (Dunsin et al., 2024) (Rizvi et al., 2022). Forensic investigators are able to identify anomalies and malicious activities and patterns that are not directly perceived by human efforts by using AI techniques, specifically relating to behavior analysis. In the following, we discuss a few of the AI methods applied to the Behavioural analysis of the digital forensic artifacts; machine learning, deep learning, natural language processing, and anomaly detection (Vasani et al., 2024).

A typical AI-enabled digital forensics workflow starts with automated artifact collection and proceeds with structured analysis, interpretation and reporting. This high level workflow is shown in figure 3. The process begins by collecting artifacts from endpoints, networks, cloud and IoT sources. Machine learning models are then used to do filtering, classification and anomaly detection. Contextual interpretation is accomplished by NLP based entity recognition and topic extraction. Finally, investigators ensure that results are valid and produce legally defensible reports.

Figure 3. AI-Driven Forensics Workflow (At-a-Glance)

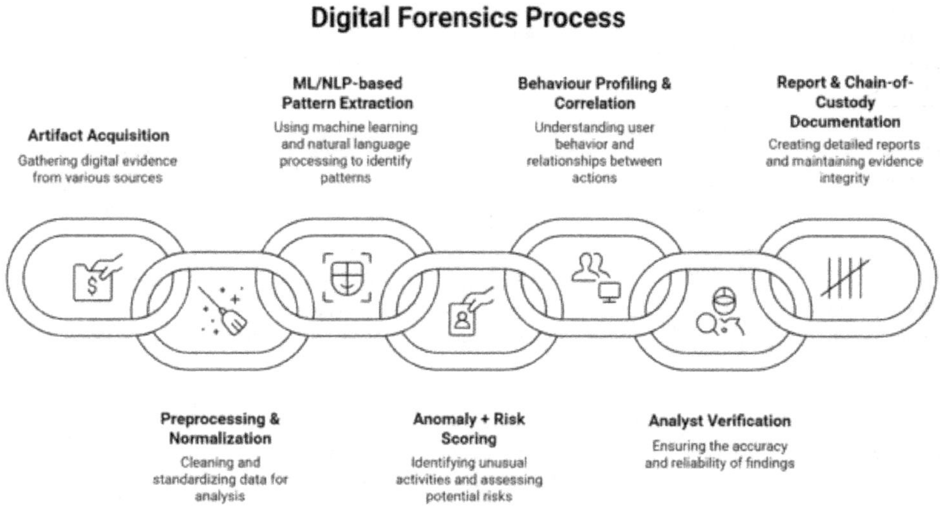

3.1 Machine Learning in Behavioural Analysis

Machine learning is the type of AI which allows machines to learn from data. Without being explicitly programmed, such systems would have the ability to learn and get better over time. In the case of digital forensics, ML models are used to analyse large data sets on forensic artefacts and extract meaningful patterns about the way users behave. It also specialises in normal and abnormal behaviour pattern recognition, forecasting the future behaviour from past data as well as automatic categorizing or labelling of digital forensic evidence artifacts (Peng et al., 2020).

3.1.1 Supervised Learning for Behavioural Classification

Supervised learning is one of the most popular techniques in ML that is used for digital forensics. With this method, models are learned from labelled datasets in which the instance of data is along with the known outcome, for example whether some user behaviour is benign or malicious. The model is able to learn the features of the input data and also correlations with the output labels, thereby making it possible to classify new instances of the data on the basis of what has been learned (Sachdeva & Ali, 2022). Digital Forensics Supervised learning algorithms can be taught to distinguish between normal and abnormal behavior of a user. For example, it can see that a person who normally tries to access sensitive files after working hours would be in the malicious activity and alerts the system for the purpose of investigation. These are mostly implemented in the automatic detection of inside threats or suspicious user behavior in large organizations. Major problem associated with supervised learning is that the process of labelling the data is very time-consuming and sometimes are difficult to get in the forensic cases. Consequently, these models, usually, that are trained on such biased or incomplete data may result in the wrong classification in the forensic process concerning wrong positives or negatives.

3.1.2 Unsupervised Learning for Anomaly Detection

The unsupervised learning algorithm does not require a labelled data set. It is just attempting to find hidden patterns or anomalies in data where it does not even know what it considers "normal" behaviour and what it considers "abnormal." This makes it helpful in forensic investigations as malicious activity might be not clearly defined or known at all (Akcay et al., 2022). Digital Forensics Application: The unscaled learning models could help in detection of anomalous user behaviour, which deviates from the norm. For instance, an example of this would be login at unusual times, files access that one would not normally go to or network abnormal activity which may have compromised the security system and hence is malicious insider activity. It helps in case of zero-day attacks or the latest threats that do not have any history or tags. The major challenges to unsupervised learning are False Positives that may be produced since the model may flag benign, though unusual behaviours, as suspicious. The alerts that would be constantly generated would certainly be likely to overwhelm the investigators with too much irrelevant information. Therefore, there is a requirement for fine-tuning of the models to get rid of these kinds of errors.

3.1.3 Reinforcement Learning for Adaptive Forensics

Reinforcement learning is a type of AI that training of the agent can be performed while making decisions by interacting with the environment, obtaining feedbacks in the form of rewards or penalties. In the context of digital forensics, RL models can simulate the behavior of a user, try out various strategies for an investigation and later validate their usability (Sewak et al., 2022). Digital Forensics Application involves the adoption of RL model in adaptive forensics where the strategy of investigation are to be changed, as soon as there is a change in behavior exhibited in suspect responses or system behavior. For example, the RL agent can imitate the move of a cybercriminal in a virtual environment, thus, such suspects could predict what their next moves could be or how to hide. For example, the best leads and evidence as echoed in the feedback can improve the RL models in resource optimization forensic. Challenging conditions in the environment of the forensic are decision and actions need to be made in real time, which introduces challenges for reinforcement learning to enforce. Furthermore, RL models are demanding in terms of the training data and computational power requirements and may not always be feasible in forensic investigations.

3.2 Deep Learning for Behavioural Pattern Recognition

Deep learning is a subcategory of machine learning, which uses stacked more than one layer of a neural network to let it automatically learn more hierarchical representations of data. Models based on DL are very beneficial in the field of digital forensics about identifying the complex patterns and relations between big datasets and thus model is suitable for behavioural analysis (Sabir et al., 2019).

3.2.1 Convolutional Neural Networks (CNNs) for Artifact Recognition

The convolutional neural network is one of the deep learning models which is most often applied to images and spatial data analysis. CNNs can be used in digital forensics for the analysis of graphical artefacts, such as screenshots of the file system structure or the image of a digital device to extract patterns of behaviour or relevant features. For example, CNNs can be used to find the patterns of illegal activity on a screenshot of a suspect's desktop, such as forbidden content or software. Another example is graphical representations of network traffic patterns that CNNs have been able to analyze and determine abnormal behaviors, which are typical of cyberattacks.

3.2.2 Recurrent Neural Networks (RNNs) for Sequential Behavior Analysis

RNNs are intended to work with sequential data and so are applicable to time-based behavioural patterns in digital forensic artefacts. RNNs have a memory of previous inputs and therefore they can model the behaviors of users over time (Sherstinsky, 2020). Digital Forensic Application: An RNN will determine a sequence of action of a user, possibly login times, file access pattern or command history. It will show that such a pattern over time will indicate the long-term behavioural trend and therefore will allow the forensic investigators to know if a user's behaviour had changed over many months, perhaps towards an adverse pattern of unauthorized access to data or espionage. Limitations: Overfitting is the biggest limitations for RNNs as it gets trained on a very small dataset. Moreover, if such models are trained on very large forensic datasets then the RNNs need lot of computational resources.

3.3 Natural Language Processing (NLP) for Behavioural Insights

NLP is, therefore, an area of concern of AI specifically dealing with interaction between computers and human languages. NLP techniques, therefore, are being applied in the field of digital forensics for analyzing all textual forensic artifacts such as emails, chat logs, social media posts, and other forms of communication. NLP allows forensic investigators, for example, to use unstructured text to derive behavioural indications from a suspect's intentions, sentiments or relationship (Andoh et al., 2021).

3.3.1 Sentiment Analysis for Behavioural Profiling

This NLP technique is used to determine whether a given text has a positive or negative sentiment. In digital forensics, sentiment analysis would enable investigators to examine the intended emotional state of a suspect based on his activity in communicating. For example, email threads or chat logs may be run through sentiment analysis simply to find out whether the suspect was angry, frustrated or fearful. Such evidence may suggest what drove them, or other future crimes they may commit. It could also pick on some cases of a hostile or aggressive behavior from inside threat cases.

3.3.2 Named Entity Recognition (NER) for Identifying Key Individuals and Locations

NER is an acronym for Named Entity Recognition. It is the technique of NLP that identifies and classifies anything found in a text such as a person, an organization and locations. NER can be used in forensic investigations to allow retrieval of critical information in communications or reports that mention collaborators, targets or places relevant to the case. NER will automatically detect the mentions of individuals or organizations in the suspect's emails or social media posts, which will help investigators to trace networks of co-conspirators or identify potential victims.

3.3.3 Topic Modeling for Behavioural Context

Topic modeling is a process in which hidden thematic structures in large bodies of text are discovered. In the digital forensics domain, it can be applied to group communications based on common themes or topics, thus providing little effort to the analyst to quickly realize relevant conversations or documents. Topic modeling is applied on suspect's account e-mails or forum posts or documents in search for patterns of ideas reflected on talk of financial fraud, hacking techniques, or illegal transactions. This helps investigators to zero in the most relevant information in the welter of data.

3.4 Anomaly Detection for Identifying Malicious Behavior

A fundamental method used in AI to identify the data patterns as unusual and not constituting the normal behavior is known as anomaly detection. Anomaly detection models are very important in digital forensics since malicious behavior usually takes on the shape of anomalies from system logs, network traffic or user activity records in cyberattacks or insider threats.

3.4.1 Statistical Anomaly Detection

Statistical anomaly detection is the observation of behaviour or an event that is different from the normal statistical distribution. For instance, if a system had been normed statistically for five login attempts per day but a specific day has 50 login attempts, then this will be detected as an anomaly. What can be observed is unusual file access, abnormal volumes of network traffic or irregular login times that are perhaps undetectable, but may be indicative of insecurity or insider attacks.

3.4.2 Machine Learning-Based Anomaly Detection

Machine learning models for anomaly detection are more complex when compared to statistical-based methods because the models may learn complex and non-linear relationships in data. The model learns from historical data, and it will set up the normal patterns of behavior, it can pick up a slight deviation, which otherwise may not point towards malware. For example, there could be an ML based model of anomaly detection which will be trained over normal traffic patterns within the network at an organization. The model may flag up this attempt if there are some dramatic spikes in data transferred out of the system to some other external server. Some of the biggest issues that anomaly detection hold internally is how to find a balance between sensitivity and specificity. If, however, a model is too sensitive, it can come up with too many false positives, which would flood the investigators with useless alerts. A model that isn't sensitive enough runs the risk of missing out on critical anomalies, that will allow malicious activity to slip past easily. Table 2 summarized AI Techniques, their application, strength, and problem on behavioural analysis of forensic artifacts.

Table 2. Comparative table summarizing the AI techniques in behavioural analysis of forensic artifacts

AI Technique	Description	Application in Forensics	Advantages	Challenges
Supervised Learning	Trains models on labelled data to classify behaviors as normal or abnormal.	Used to detect malicious behaviors based on historical data.	High accuracy when well-labelled data is available.	Requires large labelled datasets; prone to biases.
Unsupervised Learning	Learns hidden patterns in data without needing labelled examples.	Identifies anomalous behaviors or deviations from the norm.	Useful for zero-day attacks and unknown threats.	Higher false positive rate; no predefined labels.
Reinforcement Learning (RL)	Learns through interaction with the environment using rewards/penalties.	Simulates behaviors for adaptive forensic strategies or resource optimization.	Adaptive, learns from environment dynamically.	Computationally intensive; needs a lot of data.
Convolutional Neural Networks (CNNs)	Deep learning model for analyzing spatial data like images.	Used to analyze screenshots, network traffic patterns, or file system images.	Handles complex image-like forensic data effectively.	Requires substantial computational resources.
Recurrent Neural Networks (RNNs)	Deep learning model for analyzing sequential data over time.	Models user behavior patterns like login times, file access over months.	Great for long-term behavioural analysis.	Prone to overfitting; computationally demanding.
Natural Language Processing (NLP)	AI field for understanding and processing human language data.	Analyzes emails, chat logs, and social media posts for intent or sentiment.	Effective for extracting communication patterns.	Difficult to manage ambiguous or noisy data.
Sentiment Analysis (NLP)	Analyzes emotional tone of text data.	Detects emotions like anger, fear, or intent in communication logs.	Provides insights into user intent or psychological state.	Can be misled by sarcasm or informal language.
Named Entity Recognition (NER)	Identifies key people, organizations, or places in text.	Extracts important entities from emails or social media data.	Helps link individuals, events, and locations.	Challenges with multilingual or unstructured data.
Topic Modeling (NLP)	Discovers hidden themes in large bodies of text.	Groups communications or documents by topic, e.g., hacking discussions.	Efficient for large datasets; identifies key topics quickly.	Can miss nuances or mixed topics in texts.

continued on following page

Table 2. Continued

AI Technique	Description	Application in Forensics	Advantages	Challenges
Statistical Anomaly Detection	Detects outliers based on statistical norms in the data.	Flags unusual file access, network activity, or login attempts.	Simple and fast for basic anomaly detection.	May miss complex behaviors or generate false positives.
ML-Based Anomaly Detection	Uses machine learning to detect deviations from normal behavior.	Identifies complex anomalies in network traffic or user activity patterns.	Can detect subtle, non-linear patterns.	Requires fine-tuning to balance false positives and negatives.

4. APPLICATIONS OF AI-BASED BEHAVIOURAL ANALYSIS IN FORENSICS

Artificial Intelligence in artificial forensics has an impact that provides the investigator with the capacity to scan giant-sized pools of data for behavioural activities characterizing malicious actions. Some of the applications of AI technologies for behavioural analysis are as follows: forensic investigation of threat detection, fraud detection, insider threat detection, cybercrime investigation, dealing with incidences (Rizvi et al., 2022) (Jenis Nilkanth Welukar & Gagan Prashant Bajoria, 2021).

4.1 Threat Detection

Identification of potential threats before it escalates into massive incidents would require the participation of AI-based behavioural analysis to a great extent. AI would be continuously observing the activity that might arise from various users as well as system behaviors and check on anomalies due to malicious acts or break-ins in systems.

- Anomaly Detection: AI algorithms will learn historical behavior patterns to establish a baseline of normal behavioral activity. If such anomalies are found such as logins from unusual places or access to sensitive files outside of the normal working hours, the system can trigger alerts for further investigation.
- Behavioural Profiling: AI systems will develop precise and detailed profiles for the behaviors of users related to interaction with digital assets. Those can be deployed to find an outlier that has been identified against the known normality while it helps to better realize the attacks in a real-time scenario.

4.2 Fraud Detection

The issue of financial fraud still needs to be resolved by the organizations as well as the law. The AI-based behavioural analysis would increase the likelihood of fraud detection based on suspicious patterns of behaviour of the users, transactions and communication.

- Transaction analysis: Machine learning algorithms will be used to scan historic transaction data looking for suspicious patterns such as multiple transactions over a short period of time, unexplained change in spending or access from unknown sources.
- Social Engineering Detection: NLP can help a machine to analyze communication logs, regardless of whether the logs are email logs or chat logs, for signs of social engineering attacks. For example, AI can keep an eye on manipulative language, urgency in words, etc., and prevent the fraud before it is undertaken.

4.3 Insider Threat Identification

Malicious insider activity are one of the biggest security threat an organization may encounter either an insider employee or malicious acts an insider conduct. Continuous monitoring of user behavior for identifying and mitigating insider threat can be used to improve AI-based behavioural analysis.

- User Behaviour Analytics (UBA): The AI systems would develop the baseline expectations for normal user behaviour and trace the deviations that might be pointing towards some insider threats. Access to sensitive files, anomalies in data transfer, alteration of login patterns which seems malicious in intention, were some things that could be monitored.
- Risk assessment: AI can help to predict the risk level of the users individually, based on their history of behavior, which would then provide the organizations with an indication of which employees may create a higher risk of an insider threat. This makes for the possibility of directed monitoring and intervention.

4.4 Cybercrime Investigations

AI-based behavioural analysis will improve capabilities for the investigation of cybercrime as it will lead to more efficient automation in data analysis with hidden patterns which even the most experienced human analyst could possibly miss.

- Malware Detection: AI models can be used to understand the system and network behavior to understand the occurrence of indicators that point towards the malware infection, such as unusual files modification, unexpected outbound connection or execution of suspicious process.
- Attribution of Cyber Attacks: Using several cyber-attack techniques for behavioural pattern analysis and in order to attribute specific cyberattacks, AI helps investigators correlate events as historical information and well-known attack vectors to given threat actors or groups.

4.5 Incident Response

At any level of the attack on cybersecurity, a natural response to AI-based behavioural analytics would be the input of live insights into natures and scopes of an incident.

- • Automated Response Systems: AI can be used in incident response frameworks so that, once the threat has been identified, the systems automatically take predefined actions. It could involve isolating the affected systems, blocking the suspicious user accounts, or informing the relevant stakeholders.
- • Post-Incident Analysis. During and after an incident has occurred, AI assists in analysis of log data and user activity or artifact collected through reviewing how the attacks transpired in order to evaluate the reach of compromise as well as possible vulnerabilities requiring intervention.

4.6 Predictive Analysis

This can lead to predictive insight in terms of predicting future possible attacks or security incidents on the organisation, by assuming a proactive security posture.

- • Threat Intelligence: By analysing the trends in user behaviour and attack patterns, AI might be able to predict or give an outlook on newer threats and vulnerabilities. Organizations would then be in a better position to modify their security strategy and bring up the right issues.
- Proactive Mitigation Organizations can achieve proactive mitigation by predictive analysis through early preventive measures such as high alert monitoring, policies or training of employees before the probable threat comes.

4.7 Case Vignettes from Practice

Artificial Intelligence (AI) has transformed the field of digital forensics, making it possible to improve the detection of threats, analyze behavior, and improve the accuracy of investigations. The Cyber Forensics Behavioral Analysis (CFBA) model combines Cyber Behavioral Sciences and Digital Forensics in order to effectively predict and counter cyber threats (Rich & Aiken, 2024). AI-driven systems in cybersecurity enhance intrusion detection, malware analysis, and phishing prevention and provide adaptive, real-time responses (Sankaram et al., 2024). In the realm of forensic science, AI is automating the process of analysis and decision-making on evidence, which enhances the efficiency of the process, while at the same time, raises ethical questions (Dudek et al., 2024).

4.8 Emerging Technological and Operational Challenges

Modern investigations are more and more involving the IoT, mobile and cloud ecosystems, where various devices, proprietary logs and distributed storage make it hard to collect evidence and establish a chain of custody. Limited visibility and encryption, as well as cross-border data issues, both create further difficulties for attribution and behavioural reconstruction. Blockchain provides tamper-resistant logging for evidentiary integrity but provides hindrance to traceability of identity. Criminals also use anti-forensic methods, data wiping, steganography, and log manipulation, in order to avoid detection. AI is able to assist in prioritizing of artifacts, identifying anomalies, and making inferences about missing activity, but requires the aid of expert interpretation. These trends identify a need for adaptive workflows and interdisciplinary expertise to ensure accurate, ethical, and scalable digital forensic analysis.

5. FUTURE DIRECTIONS

With the boom of AI based behavioural analysis in digital forensics other area is emerging with much promises of enhancing its ability and application. The advanced machine learning models are going to form the basis in exact and reliable behavioural analysis for forensics research. Future work would include Transfer Learning, where knowledge has been learned in one domain, it can be used for better performance in another. Such a model would be useful in instances where the availability of labeled data is low. Federated Learning will be used to train models on decentralized sources of data without having to share the data, thus collaboration between organizations without exposing sensitive information.

Other emerging innovation trends are Integration of Multimodal Data Sources i.e. Cross-Platform Analysis which collects data from multiple platforms, be it cloud service, mobile device or IoT connected devices, to organize the whole thing for comprehensive insights on user behavior and interaction. The approach to be utilized with Temporal Analysis will use time series data to track the behavioural dynamics over time and thus be able to provide trend insights over the long term and anomaly detection that may occur over time.

The application of Explainable AI will be rising in future as forensic investigation incorporates the use of AI systems deeper in the process. In research, it is imagined that it will enable forensic analysts to understand the logic behind the decisions made by AI models, such that results are trusted and provided in the appropriate legal setting. Efforts will be made on Bias Mitigation, developing ways to identify and reduce biases from AI models, a step that is very important for making such forensic investigations fair and accurate in terms of doing justice.

Real-Time Forensic Analysis will be driven by the need for real-time response to security incidents and will see an increase in Edge Computing capabilities to attain real-time analysis with local edge devices before forwarding any of the data to the centralised servers, thus improving response times to identify threats much faster and reducing the latency. Continuous Monitoring will also be adopted to allow behavioural analysis to be carried out in real time to identify a threat as it happens to reduce incident response time exponentially.

Finally, future progressions in AI-based behavioural analysis will require Collaboration Between Disciplines. In the case of digital forensics and cybersecurity professions, the collaboration between each of these professions will have to be concretized and information shared towards development of an integrated threat detection and response product line. Moreover, interfacing with legal experts and ethicists will be inevitable as AI applications in forensics will be sure to be strictly regulated, respecting boundaries of privacy. These future directions, in general, will make the use of AI-based behavioural analysis more effective in the digital forensics, thus being a highly valuable asset in the fight against cybercrime and the dispensation of justice.

5.1 Anti-Forensics and Emerging Environments

Modern threat actors are increasingly using anti-forensic tools, data obfuscation, encryption wiping, steganography, to avoid attribution. Likewise, evidence now often lives in distributed cloud infrastructures and IoT devices and makes it difficult to conduct chain-of-custody, jurisdiction, and real-time collection. Blockchain is being discussed as a tamper-evident framework for the sake of forensics transparency and auditability.

5.2 Bias Reduction & Responsible Behavioural AI

To ensure fairness and responsible use, behavioural-analysis pipelines must incorporate bias-mitigation and interpretability safeguards. These include:

- Diverse, representative training data to minimize user-group bias
- Regular model retraining to avoid concept drift
- Use of explainable AI (XAI) to justify automated flagging
- Human-in-the-loop review of alerts prior to legal escalation
- Access controls + privacy-preserving analytics (e.g., data minimization, federated learning)
- These practices strengthen operational trust and support forensic admissibility in court.

CONCLUSION

The integration of AI into the behavioural analysis of digital forensic artifacts is surely one of the most important turns that have changed, or may change the capabilities of forensic investigations. Techniques associated with machine learning, deep learning, and natural language processing enable AI to work effectively for threat detection, investigation of any kind of incident, and appropriate reaction to cybercrime. With the usage of AI, forensic analysts are now able to scan massive amounts of data for abnormal behaviors and generate insights that are impossible to develop with manual methods. However, this field still has several challenges, such as data privacy, biases of AI algorithms, and a need for greater transparency of decision-making processes. After all, the forensic community should actually talk about and work towards breaking over these barriers, especially over the ethical use of AI in the forensic investigation. In the meanwhile, with the advancements of machine learning models promising even the more growth in multimodal data, real-time analysis and from multiple disciplines collaboration, AI-based behavioural analysis within digital forensics is destined to be rapid pace evolving into a much wider future. More to the point, digital forensics is expected to be better guarded towards new complexities of cybercrime as innovation and adaptation for emerging threats are continued in this regard. Conclusion All things considered, since the landscape of digital forensics changes, strategic integration of AI-driven behavioural analysis shall become imperative for enhancing both investigating capacities and incident response with a view to safety in the digital environment at long last.

REFERENCES

Acar, A., Lu, L., Uluagac, A. S., & Kirda, E. (2019). An Analysis of Malware Trends in Enterprise Networks. In Lecture notes in computer science (pp. 360–380). DOI: 10.1007/978-3-030-30215-3_18

Agarwal, P., Jain, V., Kumar, N., Pal, S. K., & Rosak-Szyrocka, J. (2024a). Human-Machine Collaboration and Emotional Intelligence in Industry 5.0. In Advances in computational intelligence and robotics book series. DOI: 10.4018/979-8-3693-6806-0

Agarwal, P., Jain, V., Kumar, N., Pal, S. K., & Rosak-Szyrocka, J. (2024b). Human-Machine Collaboration and Emotional Intelligence in Industry 5.0. In Advances in computational intelligence and robotics book series. DOI: 10.4018/979-8-3693-6806-0

Akcay, S., Ameln, D., Vaidya, A., Lakshmanan, B., Ahuja, N., & Genc, U. (2022). Anomalib: A Deep Learning Library for Anomaly Detection. *2022 IEEE International Conference on Image Processing (ICIP)*, 1706–1710. DOI: 10.1109/ICIP46576.2022.9897283

Al Mutawa, N., Bryce, J., Franqueira, V. N. L., Marrington, A., & Read, J. C. (2019). Behavioural Digital Forensics Model: Embedding Behavioural Evidence Analysis into the Investigation of Digital Crimes. *Digital Investigation*, *28*, 70–82. DOI: 10.1016/j.diin.2018.12.003

Al-Sabaawi, A. (2020). Digital Forensics for Infected Computer Disk and Memory: Acquire, Analyse, and Report. *2020 IEEE Asia-Pacific Conference on Computer Science and Data Engineering (CSDE)*, 1–7. DOI: 10.1109/CSDE50874.2020.9411614

Andoh, J., Asiedu, L., Lotsi, A., & Chapman-Wardy, C. (2021). Statistical Analysis of Public Sentiment on the Ghanaian Government: A Machine Learning Approach. *Advances in Human-Computer Interaction*, *2021*, 1–7. DOI: 10.1155/2021/5561204

Beemkumar, N., Gupta, S., Bhardwaj, S., Dhabliya, D., Rai, M., Pandey, J. K., & Gupta, A. (2023). Activity recognition and IoT-Based analysis using time series and CNN. In Advances in systems analysis, software engineering, and high performance computing book series (pp. 350–364). DOI: 10.4018/978-1-6684-8785-3.ch018

Breitinger, F., Hilgert, J.-N., Hargreaves, C., Sheppard, J., Overdorf, R., & Scanlon, M. (2024). DFRWS EU 10-year review and future directions in Digital Forensic Research. *Forensic Science International Digital Investigation*, *48*, 301685. DOI: 10.1016/j.fsidi.2023.301685

Casino, F., Totosis, N., Apostolopoulos, T., Lykousas, N., & Patsakis, C. (2023). Analysis and Correlation of Visual Evidence in Campaigns of Malicious Office Documents. *Digital Threats : Research and Practice*, *4*(2), 1–19. DOI: 10.1145/3513025

Dudek, A., Zborowska, I., Lichosik, J., & Dąbek, A. (2024). Integrating artificial intelligence in forensic science. *E-Methodology*, *10*(10), 15–28. DOI: 10.15503/emet2023.15.28

Dunsin, D., Ghanem, M. C., Ouazzane, K., & Vassilev, V. (2024). A comprehensive analysis of the role of artificial intelligence and machine learning in modern digital forensics and incident response. *Forensic Science International Digital Investigation*, *48*, 301675. DOI: 10.1016/j.fsidi.2023.301675

Dweikat, M., Eleyan, D., & Eleyan, A. (2021). Digital Forensic Tools Used in Analyzing Cybercrime. *Shanghai Ligong Daxue Xuebao*, *23*(3). Advance online publication. DOI: 10.51201/Jusst12621

Ghanem, M. C., Mulvihill, P., Ouazzane, K., Djemai, R., & Dunsin, D. (2023). D2WFP: A Novel Protocol for Forensically Identifying, Extracting, and Analysing Deep and Dark Web Browsing Activities. *Journal of Cybersecurity and Privacy*, *3*(4), 808–829. DOI: 10.3390/jcp3040036

Grispos, G., Tursi, F., Choo, K.-K. R., Mahoney, W., & Glisson, W. B. (2021). A Digital Forensics Investigation of a Smart Scale IoT Ecosystem. 2021 IEEE 20th International Conference on Trust, Security and Privacy in Computing and Communications (TrustCom), 710–717. DOI: 10.1109/TrustCom53373.2021.00104

Lee, J.-U., & Soh, W.-Y. (2020). Comparative analysis on integrated digital forensic tools for digital forensic investigation. *IOP Conference Series. Materials Science and Engineering*, *834*(1), 012034. DOI: 10.1088/1757-899X/834/1/012034

Lorch, B., Scheler, N., & Riess, C. (2022). Compliance Challenges in Forensic Image Analysis Under the Artificial Intelligence Act. 2022 30th European Signal Processing Conference (EUSIPCO), 613–617. DOI: 10.23919/EUSIPCO55093.2022.9909723

Peng, L., Zhu, X., & Zhang, P. (2020). A Machine Learning-Based Framework for Mobile Forensics. 2020 IEEE 20th International Conference on Communication Technology (ICCT), 1551–1555. DOI: 10.1109/ICCT50939.2020.9295714

Preston, S., Wei, M., Rao, R., Tinn, R., Usuyama, N., Lucas, M., Gu, Y., Weerasinghe, R., Lee, S., Piening, B., Tittel, P., Valluri, N., Naumann, T., Bifulco, C., & Poon, H. (2023). Toward structuring real-world data: Deep learning for extracting oncology information from clinical text with patient-level supervision. *Patterns (New York, N.Y.)*, *4*(4), 100726. DOI: 10.1016/j.patter.2023.100726 PMID: 37123439

Rai, M., Tyagi, N., Tripathi, P., Kumar, N., & Kumari, P. (2023). Advancement in agricultural techniques with the introduction of artificial intelligence and image processing. In Advances in electronic government, digital divide, and regional development book series (pp. 47–68). DOI: 10.4018/978-1-6684-6418-2.ch004

Rexha, B., Musa, A., Vishi, K., & Martiri, E. (2023). Unveiling the Digital Fingerprints: Analysis of Internet attacks based on website fingerprints. *Research Square (Research Square)*. DOI: 10.21203/rs.3.rs-3314855/v1

Rich, M. S., & Aiken, M. P. (2024). An Interdisciplinary Approach to Enhancing Cyber Threat Prediction Utilizing Forensic Cyberpsychology and Digital Forensics. *Forensic Science*, *4*(1), 110–151. DOI: 10.3390/forensicsci4010008

Rizvi, S., Scanlon, M., Mcgibney, J., & Sheppard, J. (2022). Application of Artificial Intelligence to Network Forensics: Survey, Challenges and Future Directions. *IEEE Access : Practical Innovations, Open Solutions*, *10*, 110362–110384. DOI: 10.1109/ACCESS.2022.3214506

Sabir, M. F., Jones, J. H., Liu, H., & Mbaziira, A. V. (2019). Predicting Stealthy Watermarks in Files Using Deep Learning. 2019 7th International Symposium on Digital Forensics and Security (ISDFS), 1–6. DOI: 10.1109/ISDFS.2019.8757538

Sachdeva, S., & Ali, A. (2022). Machine learning with digital forensics for attack classification in cloud network environment. *International Journal of System Assurance Engineering and Management*, *13*(S1), 156–165. DOI: 10.1007/s13198-021-01323-4

Sahoo, C., Wankhade, M., & Singh, B. K. (2023). Sentiment analysis using deep learning techniques: A comprehensive review. *International Journal of Multimedia Information Retrieval*, *12*(2), 41. DOI: 10.1007/s13735-023-00308-2

Sankaram, M., Rasetti, S., Nishat, N., & Roopesh, M. (2024). A Comprehensive Review Of Artificial Intelligence Applications In Enhancing Cybersecurity Threat Detection And Response Mechanisms. *Global Mainstream Journal*, *3*(5), 1–14. DOI: 10.62304/jbedpm.v3i05.180

Sewak, M., Sahay, S. K., & Rathore, H. (2022). Deep Reinforcement Learning for Cybersecurity Threat Detection and Protection: A Review. In Communications in Computer and Information Science (pp. 51–72). DOI: 10.1007/978-3-030-97532-6_4

Sharma, B. K., Joseph, M. A., Jacob, B., & Miranda, B. (2019). Emerging trends in Digital Forensic and Cyber security- An Overview. 2019 Sixth HCT Information Technology Trends (ITT), 309–313. DOI: 10.1109/ITT48889.2019.9075101

Sherstinsky, A. (2020). Fundamentals of Recurrent Neural Network (RNN) and Long Short-Term Memory (LSTM) network. *Physica D. Nonlinear Phenomena, 404*, 132306. DOI: 10.1016/j.physd.2019.132306

Singh, S., Pandey, J. K., Rai, M., & Saxena, A. K. (2024). Advancements in facial expression recognition using machine and deep learning techniques. In Advances in psychology, mental health, and behavioral studies (APMHBS) book series (pp. 149–166). DOI: 10.4018/979-8-3693-4143-8.ch007

Solanke, A. A. (2022). Explainable digital forensics AI: Towards mitigating distrust in AI-based digital forensics analysis using interpretable models. *Forensic Science International Digital Investigation, 42*, 301403. DOI: 10.1016/j.fsidi.2022.301403

Teng, S., & Wen, C. (2021). A forensic examination of four popular cross-platform file-sharing apps with Wi-Fi P2P. *Journal of Forensic Sciences, 66*(1), 315–322. DOI: 10.1111/1556-4029.14574 PMID: 32986853

Tripathi, P., Kumar, N., Paroha, K. K., Rai, M., & Panda, M. K. (2024). Applications of Deep Learning in Healthcare in the framework of Industry 5.0. In Advances in web technologies and engineering book series (pp. 69–85). DOI: 10.4018/979-8-3693-0782-3.ch005

Tripathi, P., Kumar, N., Rai, M., Shukla, P. K., & Verma, K. N. (2023). Applications of machine learning in agriculture. In Advances in electronic government, digital divide, and regional development book series (pp. 99–118). DOI: 10.4018/978-1-6684-6418-2.ch006

Vasani, V. P., Chandra, U., Sahu, G., Boyineni, S., Dhamodaran, S., Kumbhkar, M., Rai, M., & Gupta, S. (2024). Introduction to emotion detection and predictive Psychology in the age of Technology. In Advances in psychology, mental health, and behavioral studies (APMHBS) book series (pp. 1–16). DOI: 10.4018/979-8-3693-1910-9.ch001

Welukar, J. N., & Bajoria, G. P.Jenis Nilkanth WelukarGagan Prashant Bajoria. (2021). Artificial Intelligence in Cyber Security - A Review. *International Journal of Scientific Research in Science and Technology, 488–491*, 488–491. Advance online publication. DOI: 10.32628/IJSRST218675

KEY TERMS AND DEFINITIONS

Anomaly Detection: Anomaly Detection is a technique that is used to automatically detect unusual or unexpected activity by comparing the current behavior with the existing pattern of normal behavior. In forensics, it facilitates the flagging of suspicious actions of users or system activities.

Behavioural Profiling: A process of creating a digital pattern of activities of a user based on their interactions with devices or systems. This helps detect when a user is acting in an abnormal manner which could mean they are involved in insider activity or compromised.

Deep Learning (DL): An advanced subset of machine learning that makes use of tensor networks with multiple layers for finding complex patterns. It assists in determining small or long-term behavior patterns in digital evidence.

Machine Learning (ML): A branch of AI, where computer systems are made to learn patterns in the data and make decisions without being explicitly programmed. ML can classify behavior as normal and suspicious.

Named Entity Recognition (NER): An NLP technique that is used to automatically identify important elements, such as people, locations, organizations, in the text. It aids the investigators in mapping relationships from communication records.

Natural Language Processing (NLP): A branch of AI that focuses on conceptualizing and analyzing the human text or speech by computers. NLP is used to analyze emails, chat messages and social posts and is used to determine intent, emotion or topic.

Reinforcement Learning (RL): A learning technique in which an AI agent learns to make better decisions by interacting with an environment and being rewarded or penalized. In forensics, RL can be used to simulate attack paths or work out the most efficient ways to investigate.

Supervised Learning: A form of machine learning that is based on training a model using examples (labeled data in which the correct answer is already known). It is helpful to detect known forms of malicious activity.

Topic Modeling: An NLP technique where large sets of text are grouped together into major themes or subjects. In forensics, it can be used to more quickly identify discussions that are related to hacking, fraud, or illegal activities.

Unsupervised Learning: A machine learning technique to identify patterns in unlabeled data. It groups similar behaviors and detects behaviors that are different from other threats that are not previously seen.

Chapter 13
Social Engineering and the Psychological Aspects of Cyber Crime

Bhaskar Saha
https://orcid.org/0009-0005-1608-6309
Institute of Engineering and Management, Kolkata, India

Baisakhi Das
https://orcid.org/0000-0002-0702-5855
Institute of Engineering and Management, Kolkata, India

ABSTRACT

This chapter focuses on the psychology of social engineering, explaining how thieves use minds and emotional appeals and persuasive techniques to hook people. Subsidizing a light-hearted history of the Trojan horse to more recent AI-based attacks, it cites shifting methods of manipulation, including phishing, pretexting, and BEC scams. A survey of few respondents indicated that self-serving biases, recency bias, and optimism bias were found the most common as well as that the vast majority were exposed to data breaches which highlights human vulnerability. Case studies like the Target breach, Google/Facebook BEC scam, and Twitter hack illustrate real-world impacts. The chapter emphasizes that technology does not ensure resilience, but multi-layer approaches that should involve technical controls, procedural hazards, and psychological awareness are an effective way of establishing a human firewall.

DOI: 10.4018/979-8-3373-4898-8.ch013

INTRODUCTION

Amid the growing popularity of AI, the rising concerns of AI ethics, and the rapidly growing need for cybersecurity, the weakest link in the digital landscape continues to be the human factor. We may harden the systems, integrate artificial intelligence and machine learning to detect and prevent most technical attacks. However, all those defenses are rendered useless once an attacker gains access to all the necessary credentials and behaves normally as the legitimate user himself. That is the crux of social engineering.

Social Engineering is the art of using several tactics and techniques to manipulate a human into benefiting the attacker without the person realising their peril (Offensive Security, 2025). As opposed to conventional hacking, social engineering is based more on cognitive biases and personal vulnerabilities in a person rather than on weaknesses in software or hardware of the system (Imperva, 2025).

The inherent weakness of the human factor is not just a claim of security researchers around the globe, but is also backed by statistical data. The 2025 Verizon Data Breach Investigations Report (DBIR) (Verizon, 2025) showed that through breaches, the human factor still hovered at around 60 percent. It also highlighted that "credential abuse" and social actions - like "phishing", were major factors in these types of breaches. To add to the growing list of concerns, recent data shows that 15 percent of all employees share their information with AI chatbots, which the bots would learn and eventually reveal to prompt engineers who succeed to fool the chatbot into revealing that data.

Additional breach statistics further highlights the dominance of such tricks. Social engineering is the second pre-eminent pattern of attack, involved in 17 percent of all breaches, behind only direct system intrusion. Out of 4,009 incidents, 3,405 confirmed data disclosure, where phishing and pretexting remained the main techniques leveraged to con the employees. The economic consequences of Social Engineering are equally not a frivolous matter. In the year 2024 alone, as reported by the FBI IC3, over 6.3 billion dollars was transferred in the process of such scams. Although the total number is increasing, the median amount of money extracted from victims has become relatively consistent and has settled around the $50,000 mark.

This chapter would attempt to discuss the weaknesses that exist within the human mind that are usually taken advantage of by social engineers. We start with the history of human hacking, dive deeper into the cognitive biases to better understand the modern social engineering tactics, and then analyze the anatomy of a successful social engineering attack through several case studies - all with the aim of building a more resilient "human firewall".

HISTORICAL TRAJECTORIES OF DECEPTION

Social Engineering might be a buzzword in the digital age; however it is just a glorified and more tech savvy version of persuasion and manipulation. Its origin goes right down to the myth of Troy (Licelus, 2025). In the legend, when the Greeks were unable to take the city of Troy by force, they used one of the earliest forms of Baiting. To outsmart the Trojans and to exploit their pride and overconfidence, the Greeks constructed a large horse and hid their best soldiers inside the horse. Then they pretended to flee and ran away with the rest of their people, only the giant horse staying behind. Trojans considered the horse they won and brought it inside the city. When night fell the concealed Greek soldiers emerged out of the horse and the city fell asleep.

The appearance of computers and the Internet increased those methods of manipulation considerably. Beginning with the Elk Cloner in 1992 and continuing with present day Deep Fakes, Digital Arrests and more. The attackers keep evolving their techniques in an attempt to outsmart the evolving defenses leading to more sophisticated attacks.

The Elk Cloner (Digit, 2025; Geeks Ltd., 2020) was admittedly one of the first microcomputer viruses that spread in the wild. What's more interesting is the fact how deceptively simple it was. Elk Cloner was not made to be destructive - it did not destroy or corrupt data. However, it overwrote reserved tracks of Apple DOS disks without a standard image. Upon the 50th boot from an infected disk, Elk Cloner displayed a short poem on the screen.

In 1999, the Melissa virus (Boson Blog, 2025) was a paradigm changer by purposely using social engineering in order to spread to as many users as possible. It was a macro virus targeting a vulnerability in Microsoft Word 97 and Word 2000 which allowed it to automatically replicate itself and send out copies to the first 50 email addresses found in the recipient's address book, on opening it.

A year later, the effectiveness of social engineering became more prominent in the emotional payload called the “ILOVEYOU” worm (EBSCO, 2025). It was a very simple email with subject line “ILOVEYOU” and its body instantly followed by an attachment titled “LOVE-LETTER-FOR-YOU.TXT.vbs”. At that time Outlook was mainly using Visual Basic for its code base, so once the .vbs file was opened it led to a take over of the user’s addressbook, which was used to further spread the virus. The virus also ran every time the machine restarted and attempted to download another Trojan. This incident clearly demonstrated one of the vulnerabilities present in the human mind - that is - “the desire to be loved”.

THE FOUNDATION OF INFLUENCE: ROBERT CIALDINI'S PRINCIPLES

One of the major pioneers in the psychology of persuasion, Robert Cialdini, in his book "Influence" (Cialdini, 2006), mentioned 6 universal principles that one can use to become a skilled persuader. These principles are essentially the "attack grammar" that social engineers use to formulate compelling narratives which let them hack the mind of their target. These principles are as follows:

1. **Reciprocation:** This rule states that "...we should try to repay, in kind, what another person has provided us" (Medium, 2025). For example, if someone treats you on their birthday, you feel obligated to treat them on your birthday. This is because the human brain is hardwired to repay any favour it received as inferred from Adam's Equity Theory (People Shift, 2025). Social Engineers exploit this human behavior by offering something for free and hiding their ulterior motives. They may offer a free ebook or a free service trial. After that they might ask for more critical information for verification purposes. At this point the victim is more likely to give into the attacker's seemingly harmless request. This is the core mechanism behind quid pro quo attacks, where an attacker posing as IT support offers to fix a problem in exchange for the user's credentials.
2. **Commitment & Consistency:** This principle is about our "...desire to be (and to appear) consistent with what we have already done" (Medium, 2025). For example, if you sign up for a free trial, after using the product or service for a month, you are less likely to cancel the subscription just to appear consistent with your initial commitment. Consistency is the basis for the Ikea Effect (Farnam Street, 2025) and why people value something more if they have to work for it. This principle is often exploited in modern scams in which the scammer initially pays you for easy tasks like uploading a positive review for a business. As the amount grows, he asks for charges to be paid before withdrawal, slowly siphoning your money.
3. **Social Proof:** This rule "...applies especially to the way we decide what constitutes correct behavior. We view a behavior as more correct in a given situation to the degree that we see others performing it." (Medium, 2025) For example, when you don't have an opinion of your own about a purchase you are about to make, you'll seek the opinion of others who have already made the purchase. This principle is often exploited by scammers on social media platforms selling fake products by endorsing them with reviews from seemingly genuine customers.
4. **Authority:** Very simply, people tend to follow authority figures. (Medium, 2025) For example, you are more likely to comply with a seemingly innocuous request — such as sending over confidential documents — if it comes from your

boss. In contrast, if the same request came from an employee of equal or lower standing, you might refuse. The classic BEC scam, where an email appearing to be from the CFO demands an urgent wire transfer, is a direct exploitation of this principle.

5. **Liking:** Very simply, this just means we prefer to say yes to the requests of people we know and like. (Medium, 2025) For example, if a guy whom you do not like suddenly asks you to lend him some money, you are most likely going to decline his request. However if a similar request came from your crush, you'll agree to it without second thoughts. This has often been exploited by social engineers by posing as beautiful girls on social media, spending time to get you to like them and then start making seemingly harmless requests like recharging their number or paying them small amounts.
6. **Scarcity:** The scarcity principle states that "...opportunities seem more valuable to us when their availability is limited." (Medium, 2025) For example, you might end up purchasing an item you didn't really need at the time, simply because it was offered at a very low price and marked as having only a few left — say, five. This is often exploited by scammers who call elderly people, scaring them that their account might be locked if they do not share the otp within a few minutes.

These principles are hardly used alone. An advanced assault frequently combines more than one of them An example would be that a whaling attack may make use of Authority (by posing as a senior executive), Liking (in the form of using a friendly, familiar tone) and Scarcity (insisting that there is some urgent action that must be done before an important meeting). Understanding the synergy between these principles can be a major factor in disassembling and protecting against more advanced attacks.

EXPLOITING MENTAL SHORTCUTS: KEY COGNITIVE BIASES

The psychological trick behind the effectiveness of the principles presented by Cialdini is the vulnerabilities of the human mind, called the cognitive biases (David & Bode-Asa, 2023). These are not character weaknesses, but very necessary mental short-cuts (heuristics) that allow quick decision-making in a world with too much complexity. These vulnerabilities are not created by social engineers; social engineers merely exploit these prior and universal structures of human thought.

1. **Confirmation Bias:** It is the tendency to approve only the information which aligns with the person's existing beliefs while disapproving contradictory information despite the presence of enough evidence (Simply Psychology, 2025).

For example, when a hacker calls you to confirm your order after you recently placed an order on Amazon, you are less likely to be suspicious.

2. **Authority Bias:** It is the tendency of people to give more importance and credibility to people with authority (David & Bode-Asa, 2023). With this in mind, hackers often take over accounts of people with high authority like the CxOs and use them for commanding other employees, who are more likely to go along with the orders.
3. **Overconfidence Bias:** It is the tendency of people to overestimate their own knowledge and skills (David & Bode-Asa, 2023). As a direct effect, people who think themselves to be too smart to fall for a scam are more likely to fall for them.
4. **Optimism Bias:** It is the tendency of people to believe that they are less likely to fall prey to a negative event (Lei et al., 2022). As a result, people having this bias often keep their guards low as they have a false sense of invulnerability.
5. **Anchoring Bias:** It is the tendency to rely too heavily on the initial information that was received (David & Bode-Asa, 2023). To exploit this bias, social engineers often use false statistics before actually attacking.
6. **Recency Bias:** It is the tendency to give more importance to recent events or information (Scribbr, 2025). For example, after a flood, scammers can pose as volunteers for a relief fund and collect funds from unsuspecting philanthropists.
7. **Self-Serving Bias:** It is the tendency of people to take credit for every positive event while blaming the situation and other factors for the negative events (David & Bode-Asa, 2023). People rely on this bias in an attempt to improve their self image.

SURVEY ON HUMAN COGNITIVE BIASES

Description

We conducted a survey via Google Forms to find out which biases are present in the mind of the respondent.

Dataset Size

We could fetch around 70 responses in a single day, highlighting the efficiency of using Google Forms.

Questions

1. When reading news about a controversial topic, which article are you most likely to click first?

If the respondent answers with "One that supports what I already believe.", it indicates High Confirmation Bias.

If the respondent answers with "I avoid reading such topics.", it indicates Mild Confirmation Bias.

2. If a famous scientist and a close friend gave you conflicting advice about a health supplement, what would you do?

If the respondent answers with "Follow the scientist's advice.", it indicates High Confirmation Bias.

If the respondent answers with "Follow my friend's advice.", it indicates Mild Confirmation Bias. To be precise, it is Familiarity Bias.

3. How confident are you that you can spot scams or fake information online? (1-5)
4. Identify the Phishing Page
5. Identify the AI-generated Image

We calculate Over-Confidence Index = (SR-1)/2 - AS, where SR = Self Rating, AS = Actual Score

If the Index >= 1: High Over Confidence, Index >= 0.5: Mild Over Confidence, else None

6. How unlikely are you to be a victim to hackers? (1-5)
7. Check your email on https://haveibeenpwned.com/ (Score += 1 if answer is No)
8. Check your email on https://intelx.io/ (Score += 1 if answer is No)

We calculate Optimism Index = (SR-1)/2 - AS, where SR = Self Rating, AS = Actual Score

If the Index >= 1: High Over Confidence, Index >= 0.5: Mild Over Confidence, else None

9. A shirt is listed at 5000 but now discounted to 2000. Another shirt has always been 2000. Which are you more likely to buy?

If the respondent answers with "The discounted one (5000 → 2000).", it indicates High Anchoring Bias.

10. You've seen two job candidates. One gave an average interview yesterday, and another gave an excellent interview today. Who do you think you'll rate higher overall?

If the respondent answers with "Today's candidate.", it indicates High Recency Bias.

If the respondent answers with "Yesterday's candidate.", it indicates Mild Recency Bias. To be precise, it is Primacy Bias.

11. If you perform well in an exam, what do you usually attribute it to?

If the respondent answers with "My intelligence and hard work.", it indicates High Self-Serving Bias.

Statistics of Recorded Data

As per the data of **71** respondents, we observed the following statistics:

- **Confirmation Bias:** High in 13 (18%) and Mild in 9 of them
- **Authority Bias:** High in 12 (17%) of them
- **Over-Confidence Bias:** High in 4 (5%) of them
- **Optimism Bias:** High in 15 (21%) of them
- **Anchoring Bias:** High in 10 (14%) of them
- **Recency Bias:** High in 20 (28%) and Mild in 2 of them
- **Self-Serving Bias:** High in 28 (39%) of them
- **HaveIBeenPwned:** Email present in data breaches for 37 (52%) of them
- **IntelX:** Email present in data breaches for 33 (46%) of them

Inferences

- Self-Serving Bias came out to be the most prevalent bias in the dataset, followed by Recency and Optimism Bias, making them more prone to be exploited by social engineers.
- More than 50% of the respondents were victims of at least one data breach, highlighting how unsafe we are on the web.
- All the respondents easily shared their email ids, which are linked with so many different platforms, increasing the probability of them being targeted.

THE ROLE OF EMOTIONAL TRIGGERS

The activation of these principles and biases is often achieved through the direct manipulation of core human emotions (Social-Engineer, Inc., 2025). An effective social engineer is, above all, an emotional engineer.

1. **Fear:** It is a primal emotion and is often the most effective emotion to be exploited. Hackers often build narratives to scare the target just to sway their rationale and make them more prone to their attack.
2. **Greed:** It is one of the primary reasons behind many successful scams, whether it is digital or not. Humans are greedy by nature. No amount of money can ever satisfy their greed. Therefore, it is easier for hackers to get something done by offering easy money to the target.
3. **Curiosity:** The desire to know more and try everything at least once often leads people to their doom. Hackers try to be mysterious by giving enough information to raise one's curiosity yet withholding most of the information for the target to uncover once he gives in to their demands.
4. **Helpfulness and Trust:** By nature humans want to trust and help others. However this generous trait is often exploited by social engineers. They might contact the customer service and take their assistance in getting access to your account posing as the legitimate owner.

After all, the psychology of social engineering is the research of the efficiency of the human mind exploitation. It is in the nature of our brains to rely on heuristics and emotional appeal to make decisions within seconds. Although this is an evolutionary advantage in its context, on most occasions it provides a predictable and exploitable operating system that those who know its source code imagine. Defense therefore cannot be about fixing these deep seated human characteristics, but must focus on implementing what can be called a behavioral firewall- a process of momentary pause, doubt, and corroboration that can intercept this unconscious, and often insecure, automatic reaction. Table 1 gives a summary of the principles of Cialdini.

Table 1. Principles of Cialdini

Principle	Definition	Example Social Engineering Tactic	Psychological Mechanism Exploited
Reciprocity	The social norm of responding to a positive action with another positive action.	An attacker offers a "free" security analysis tool (which is malware) or provides some helpful information before making a malicious request.	The victim feels a sense of obligation to "repay" the attacker for the initial gift, making them more compliant.
Commitment & Consistency	The desire to be (and to appear) consistent with past actions and decisions.	An attacker asks for a small, harmless piece of information first (e.g., confirming a job title), then escalates to more sensitive requests.	The victim wants to maintain a consistent self-image and avoids the cognitive dissonance of refusing a request similar to one they've already granted.
Social Proof	The tendency to assume the actions of others reflect correct behavior.	A phishing email claims that "95% of employees have already completed this mandatory training" or shows fake testimonials for a fraudulent service.	The victim feels pressure to conform and assumes the action is safe and legitimate because "everyone else is doing it."
Authority	The tendency to obey figures who are perceived to have authority.	An attacker impersonates a CEO, IT administrator, or law enforcement officer to demand an urgent wire transfer or password reset.	Deep-seated respect for authority overrides the victim's critical thinking and security training.
Liking	The tendency to agree to requests from people we find likable.	An attacker researches a target on social media, then initiates contact by referencing shared hobbies, mutual connections, or offering compliments.	The victim lowers their guard and is more trusting and compliant with someone they perceive as similar to them or who is friendly.
Scarcity	The tendency to place a higher value on things that are scarce.	An email creates false urgency with a "limited time only" offer that expires in one hour or a threat that an account will be suspended if not acted on immediately.	The fear of missing out (FOMO) or fear of negative consequences triggers an impulsive, emotional decision, bypassing rational analysis.

CONTEMPORARY SOCIAL ENGINEERING ATTACK VECTORS

To the principles of psychological basis, modern cybercriminals have created a wide and high-tech range of vectors of attack. Such vectors are the very ways to deliver the manipulative payload to the target. They are all located along a continuum, the one side of which is low-effort, wide-net campaigns, and the other side highly targeted, resource-intensive operations. Learning this taxonomy is both valuable in the detection of attacks, and the design of suitable counter measures, as each vector employs a different combination of delivery methods and psychological stimuli.

Phishing and its Variants

With 15 percent of all the data breaches (Verizon, 2025), phishing is the most commonly known and widely used social engineering vector. It entails a hacker impersonating a legitimate user in an online exchange to dupe the victim into opening a malicious link, opening an infected file, or disclosing valuable information. This simple construct has been developed into other specialized constructs in the long run:

1. **Bulk Phishing:** In case of Bulk Phishing (KnowBe4, 2025a), attackers send thousands or millions of generic emails usually pretending to be a well-known brand such as PayPal, Microsoft or one of the major banks. Urgent warnings of "unusual log in activity" or "account suspension" are typical of these messages to create an element of fear that generates a click. The percentage success of an individual message is close to nil, but the numbers are so enormous, then it will be a profitable amount of compromised people.
2. **Spear Phishing:** In contrast to Bulk Phishing, Spear Phishing (KnowBe4, 2025a) is merely a targeted and personal attack against a given individual, group or organization. Prior to starting the offense, the criminal establishes reconnaissance, digging out information about the target through social media sources, company websites, and LinkedIn, among other publicly available sources. This data includes the name, job title, current projects, professional connections of the target and the data is used to create a readily-credible and relevant message. Since the email seems to be issued by a recognized source and that it has contextually relevant data, it is much more likely to filter through the victim.
3. **Whaling:** It is a variation of spear phishing that is directed at influential members of an organization, e.g. C-level executives, board of directors, or senior people in finance - the whales. The aim of a whaling attack (IT Governance Europe, 2025) is usually of a high value, e.g. sanctioning a fraudulent multi-million dollar wire transfer, or theft of strategic intellectual property. Such attacks are frequently oblique, based on the pretense that it is an authority figure requesting something.
4. **Vishing (Voice Phishing):** Vishing (KnowBe4, 2025a) shifts the attack to the voice and it uses phone calls to delude victims. Live, interactivity of a phone call enables the attacker to invest time in building rapport, address any push backs on the spot, and rely on the persuasive nature of a human voice. Typical vishing scams include pretending to be the fraud department of a bank, or a government agency, such as the IRS, or a company IT support desk.
5. **Smishing (SMS Phishing):** In this method, attackers use SMS to deliver the socially engineered payload. Smishing (KnowBe4, 2025a) attackers may pose as a banking organization, delivery service, or cellular company, and send a

message to users to inform them about suspicious activity, a package update, etc. with a link that supposedly resolves the problem. Text messaging has the personal and immediate effect which may make the recipients less cautious as compared to emailing.

6. **Quishing (QR Phishing):** This is a newer form of phishing that leverages QR codes to deliver malicious links (Cloudflare, 2025). Attackers can insert malicious URLs on a QR code and when scanned by a victim's smart phone; they will be redirected to a phony site to steal their credentials or infect them with malware. This method takes advantage of the ease and growing prominence of QR codes in everyday life that we tend to see in public settings or even actual mail.

Pretexting

Pretexting (Colorado Department of Education, 2025) involves preparing an artificial situation, or a pretext, and exploiting it, to use it to engage a target and manipulate that target into divulging or performing some act of information or action that they would otherwise not do. Pretexting is more of a mechanism that runs most other social engineering attacks than it is a standalone threat. A good pretext is plausible, carefully researched and creates the perception of legitimacy in the mind of the intended victim. To give an example, an adversary may pretend to be an outsider IT auditor, with a justification and fake identifications, to persuade personnel to provide them with certain physical access to a secure area. The credibility of this invented story is the key to the success of the whole operation.

Baiting and Quid Pro Quo

These vectors tap into the powerful emotions of curiosity and greed, as well as the principle of reciprocity.

- **Baiting:** Baiting – as the name indicates – consists of getting a victim into a trap by promising him something that seems desirable to him (Colorado Department of Education, 2025). The bait can be physical, such as the USB flash drive with the name of Executive Salaries Q4 left in a lobby or parking lot of an organization. Curiosity might lead an employee to plug the drive into his or her computer, and install malware without knowing. A 2016 study proved effective use of this, when 45 percent of 297 USB drives dropped at a university campus were inserted and used to contact the researchers, who dubbed them as three-dimensional phishbait. Baiting may also be digital, i.e.

an advertisement of a free download of a popular movie or software, actually a malware downloader.

- **Quid Pro Quo ("Something" for "Something"):** It is a form of baiting and it has a direct exchange of information against a service or a good (Colorado Department of Education, 2025). The iconic scenario would include a caller who calls employees of a large corporation by cold call and poses as IT support offering help. The attacker keeps calling until he or she locates the individual who actually has a computer problem. Under the pretext of assisting, the attacker then directs an employee to switch off security software or ask them to give their log-in details thus corroding the system.

Scareware

Scareware (Trend Micro, 2025a) exploits the primal human emotion - fear. The method is carried by bombarding a user with alarming and fictional threat messages. These are usually in the form of pop-up messages that decompose legitimate system or antivirus alerts and which state that the user has a number of viruses in their computer, and/or is at a critical risk. The language and use of countdown timers employed in these messages have an impact of panicking the user and making them feel they need to press the button immediately in order to correct the given situation. By clicking the link, users are usually faced with the downloading of real malware or a payment site with a worthless and fraudulent security product.

Business Email Compromise (BEC)

BEC scam is one of the most advanced and financially impactful forms of social engineering (FBI, 2025). It is a very specific attack, which usually entails impersonation of a senior executive (CEO fraud) or a common external vendor (Microsoft, 2025). Compared to simple phishing, BEC attacks are often the conclusions to a long-term campaign. It is possible that attackers could initially gain access to a real email account used by an executive through malware or phishing, and weeks or months later they could get information about the business processes, payments schedules and style of communication.

With this inside information, the attacker now attacks at the opportune time by sending a carefully crafted email that is sent to an employee in the finance or accounts department, either via a breached account or a spoofed account. The email will direct the worker to make an urgent wire transfer to a different bank account possessed by the attacker, frequently in a plausible explanation such as a confidential acquisition, or a last-minute change by a vendor. The fact that such attacks are usually based on the impersonated authority, sense of urgency and the existing detailed knowledge of the context makes them incredibly hard to detect. According to the FBI, BEC scams cost companies and organizations more than 6.3 billion dollars in 2025 (Verizon, 2025), and that is a good reason to think of them as one of the leading cyber threats.

The current risk environment is marked by the hybridization of these vectors. Attackers do not use one method. The attack may begin with spear phishing to steal credentials and continue with an account compromise, allowing the attackers to perform reconnaissance on users targeted in a BEC attack, then finish with a call to the finance department using vishing, a final layer of pressure and regardless of the specific stage, the technique is relied upon extensively by criminals to support a BEC attack. The fact that social engineering attacks can take many and varied different forms explains why a multi-pronged response is required to combat them successfully. Table 2 summarizes the different types of attack vectors.

Table 2. Attack Vectors

Attack Vector	Primary Delivery Mechanism(s)	Core Psychological Levers Exploited	Key Characteristics
Phishing (Bulk)	Email, SMS (Smishing)	Urgency, Fear, Curiosity	Generic, high-volume, low personalization. Relies on a small percentage of recipients falling victim.
Spear Phishing / Whaling	Email, Social Media	Authority, Liking, Trust, Urgency	Highly personalized, low-volume, targets specific individuals or executives. Requires prior research (OSINT).
Vishing (Voice Phishing)	Telephone	Authority, Fear, Trust, Urgency	Leverages the immediacy and persuasive power of the human voice to build rapport and pressure victims.
Quishing (QR Code Phishing)	QR Codes (printed or digital)	Curiosity, Convenience, Trust	Malicious QR codes direct victims to fake websites or malware downloads, exploiting trust in QR technology.
Pretexting	Email, Telephone, In-Person	Trust, Consistency, Authority	Creation of a detailed, fabricated scenario to justify requests for information. The narrative backbone of many attacks.
Baiting / Quid Pro Quo	Physical Media (USB), Web Downloads, Email	Curiosity, Greed, Reciprocity	Lures victims with a desirable item or service in exchange for an action (e.g., plugging in a drive) or information.
Scareware	Web Pop-ups, Spam Email	Fear, Urgency	Bombards users with fake threat alerts to panic them into buying fake software or installing malware.
Business Email Compromise (BEC)	Email (often from a compromised account)	Authority, Trust, Urgency, Liking	Sophisticated impersonation of executives or vendors to authorize fraudulent wire transfers. Financially devastating.

THE ANATOMY OF AN ATTACK: THE SOCIAL ENGINEERING LIFECYCLE

Social engineering attacks are not spontaneous; they are step by step campaigns that have a definite cycle. Very similar to the kill chain model (IACP, 2025) used to describe advanced persistent threats, this process contains several stages, and each one plays a critical role in the success of the overall operation. The process of conducting an attack from the initial collection of intelligence all the way to the departure shows the extent to which there is strategic planning involved when it comes to professionalization of this type of cybercrime. This lifecycle is critical to understand as an attack offers several points of detection where an attacker may be disrupted before it can be completed. The social engineering attack lifecycle can be broken down into four primary phases (Arctic Wolf, 2025) as shown in Figure 1:

Figure 1. Social Engineering Attack Lifecycle

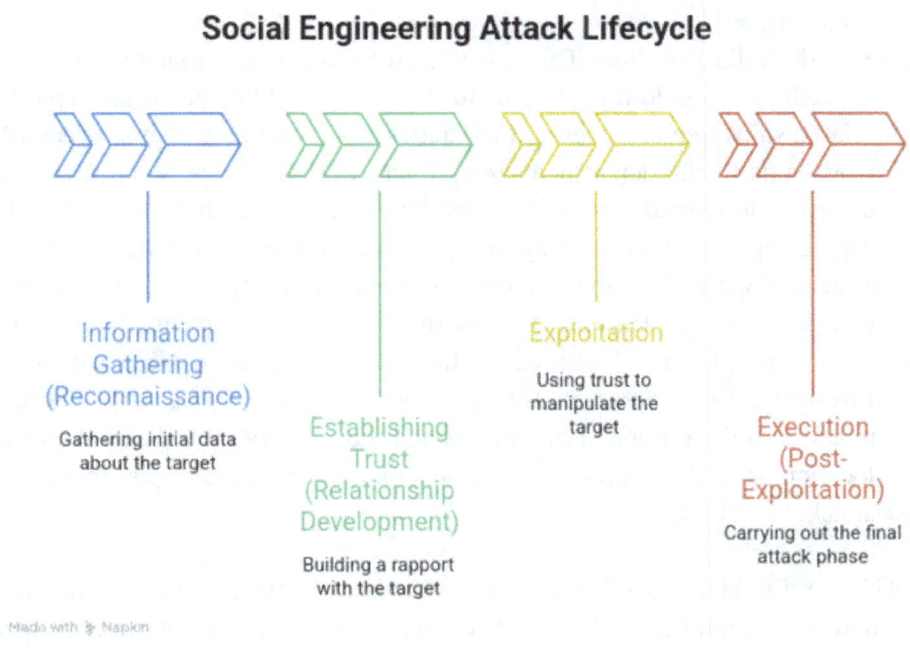

Phase 1: Information Gathering (Reconnaissance)

It is the entry point where the rest of the attack is based and therefore very crucial to the success of the attack. The idea of the attacker is to gather as much information as they can (Arctic Wolf, 2025) with the target organization and the particular people within the organization. Following this intelligence, the attacker will have a strong pretext, a good attack method, and employees who can provide the access or the capability to meet the attacker in his or her objectives.

Much of this reconnaissance can then be carried out through the use of Open-Source Intelligence (OSINT), where publicly available sources are mined and dissected without any contact being made with the target. This non active method is hard to locate and can provide lots of useful information. Common techniques used in, in OSINT include:

- **Corporate Website and Public Fillings:** Attackers use company websites, annual reports and press releases to gain insight into the company structure, executives, business relationships, and company business processes using the same jargon.
- **Social Media Profiling:** This is where professional networking websites like LinkedIn are a gold mine to the attacker. They will be able to see reporting relationships, see job titles and job duties and locate lists of employees who work in particular departments (e.g., Finance, HR). The personal social media accounts may display hobbies and interests and personal connections that can be deployed in developing rapport and triggering the Liking principle.
- **Search Engine Reconnaissance:** Attackers can use special search parameters (like "Google Dorking") to discover sensitive documents, internal presentations or technical settings that have accidentally been published online.
- **Physical Reconnaissance:** Attackers can also use physical surveillance to understand the routine of employees and the security procedures at a target location as well as opportunities to conduct services like a physical access attack.

This careful data collection gives the attacker a detailed portrait of the target victim, turning an impersonal attack into a highly personal one, an effective spear phishing or Whaling attack.

Phase 2: Establishing Trust (Relationship Development)

The attacker then adds contact with the target using the intelligence gained during the process of reconnaissance. The main goal of this phase is to relate and develop trust and therefore suppress the natural defenses of the victim. This necessitates a compelling work of acting where the attacker must be able to personify his/her selected persona and be ready to respond to questions and probing of the target.

Practices of building trust differ with respect to the level of complexity of an attack and the timeframe in which it is carried out. In an urgent scam, like a panic-inducing pop-up or time-sensitive phishing message, trust is backed by the fact that, Authority and Urgency have been used to manipulate the user. The communication is made to sound like it came through an authoritative channel (for example, Microsoft) and that there is no time to wait to authenticate this message, creating a little room within which the recipient can doubt the authenticity.

In highly alluring, long-term campaigns, trust is built overtime. Attackers may take weeks or months to develop a working relationship with a target based on common interests before making a malevolent request on a social media platform. In a case that involves BEC (Arctic Wolf, 2025), an attacker that has gained access to an email account of an executive may just be monitoring communication and getting familiar with the intricacies of speech and acquaintances. They then insert themselves into an already established, trusted email chain at precisely the right time to divert a payment by using the pre-established trust between the two legitimate parties. It is also the art of psychological manipulation as the attacker has to be friendly, convincing and be capable of sustaining their pretext.

Phase 3: Exploitation

This is when the attacker strikes (Arctic Wolf, 2025) his/her move After completing the steps of exerting control and developing a background of trust, the attacker uses his/her advantage to induce the victim to take the intended action. The way it is exploited by the attacker depends on their end purpose. It could be:

- **Divulging Sensitive Information:** Fooling the victim to divulge details on login credentials, credit card numbers, social security number or any other personally identifiable information (PII).
- **Performing an Action:** Forcibly compelling an employee to deposit funds, alter payment information of a vendor, or buy gift cards.
- **Granting Accesses:** Convincing some user to grant remote access to his computer, to provide a password or leave a door unlocked to privileged facility.
- **Executing Malicious Code:** The target is persuaded to click an unseemly link or open an contaminated attachment causing the installation of malware, ransomware or spyware to the business network.

This stage is the high point of the social engineering scam. All the previous efforts in infiltration and association are provided to make sure that by the time the victim is presented with a request, he or she is psychologically prepared to say yes without a second thought.

Phase 4: Execution and Post-Exploitation

After the exploitation is achieved successfully, the attacker enters the last stage (Arctic Wolf, 2025): accomplishing his/her goal and erasing his/her own footprints. This can also be known as the "Complete Mission" in certain kill chain models.

With a direct financial transfer as the aim, this stage would include laundering of the stolen funds through accounts to make the source of funds inaccessible. If this step was to establish a presence within the network, then the attacker will now exploit the access obtained to perform lateral movement, privilege escalation and identify and steal the high value data they are after.

An important aspect to this phase is the exit strategy. The attacker will tend to modify actions to eliminate his presence and evade the security systems of the organization. This may require the deletion of emails, clearing logs or malware which self-destructs after being executed. In most BEC scams, an attacker is after a single payoff, and then he or she absconds, leaving an organization to uncover the fraud when it is too late and money thereafter. This highly detailed planning in this lifecycle shows that social engineering is not a quick and easy stunt, but a methodical, stage-by-stage approach that attacks security at its weakest point which is at the human element.

DELIVERY MECHANISMS

To be successful in a social engineering attack, an attacker must select a delivery mechanism, or channel of delivery, to convey his or her manipulative message to the target. The decision of which mechanism to implement is a strategic decision, and is frequently dependent on the environment of a target, communication patterns, and the particular psychological buttons that the attacker would like to press. There is a huge variety of conduits that modern attackers have available to them, including digital communications, telecommunications and even the real world. With this multi-channel based approach to defense, organizations face more complexities in their defense as they have to now guard a single point of entry but all potential areas through the human factor.

Digital Communication Channels

Email continues to be the most prolific method of social engineering and the most likely method of delivering phishing, spear phishing and BEC attacks (Arctic Wolf, 2025). Its universality within the organizational environment makes it a vehicle of choice to imitate co-workers, managers, and reputable suppliers. Attackers take advantage of the formal qualities of email mail to add gravitas to their demands, spoofing the senders address, simulating email signatures and using well-considered text to show legitimacy (Barracuda Networks, 2025). The malicious payloads can be inserted through links that are embedded which redirect towards credential harvesting sites or as attachments with malware containing attachments.

Social media platforms too, have become the war zone. These platforms are both used as reconnaissance and direct strike platforms by attackers. Suppose they can establish false profiles to build rapport with a victim over time (Liking) or pretend that they are a customer support profile of a firm, in an attempt to scam people into giving away account details (Angler Phishing) (IT Governance Europe, 2025). The informality and trust attributes of social networks predisposes social network users to be more vulnerable due to a lesser tendency to remain on high alert to malicious activity.

Telecommunication Channels

There is much social engineering done via telephone because it is an immediate means by which an impassioned human voice is persuasive. This is the sphere of vishing (voice phishing) (Trend Micro, 2025a). By doing so, an attacker will be able to convey emotion, establish rapport and apply pressure in real time, all factors which are more easily done in-person, as compared to those done via text. Typical vishing attacks include fraud warning calls of bank functionaries, calls of IRS agents threatening to press charges, or IT support desk calls offering to address an IT problem. The personal contact can be very effective to override the innate skepticism of the victim.

Smishing is done via text messaging, or SMS (Trend Micro, 2025a). This is because these attacks utilise the open-rate and the perceived urgency of the text messages. A common smishing message would consist of a sense of urgency on a bank account or a package delivery and a malicious link attached. Smishing also poses an increasing risk since mobile devices are less secure than those in the corporate environment and end users are generally less wary of the devices.

Physical Proximity and In-Person Deception

Social engineering does not exist only in the cyberworld. Other particularly bold and successful attacks are made in the physical world, taking advantage of normal courtesy, and the presumption of trust in a commonly shared physical environment.

- **Tailgating (or Piggybacking):** In this method an intruder intrudes into a secure area or building through gaining the tail of an authorized staff member (KnowBe4, 2025b). The assailant may pretend to be talking on his phone, or may have a heavy package and hence appear like he needs extra help to open the door. In such cases, politeness of the employee is the security weakness.
- **Impersonation:** This includes the attacker physically pretending to be somebody they are not- service technician, delivery person or even a new employee. With a good looking uniform, clipboard, and a confident attitude, an attacker can often bypass security and gain access to critically sensitive areas because of the principle of Authority, and the general unwillingness of employees to challenge someone who can very easily be seen as belonging.
- **Baiting with Physical Media:** As discussed earlier, this can be done by leaving an infected USB flash drive, CD or another storage device that already contained malware in a place where it can be picked up by an employee. The device is commonly marked with something to convince them to wonder with words like "Q4 Layoff Plan" or "Executive Bonuses" (OneCard, 2025). The attacker exploits the human nature of exploration, the victim becomes the unwitting accomplice and injects the malware into the corporate network himself, bypassing all security barricades.

The variety of delivery methods effectiveness necessitates a defense-in-depth approach. Protecting your email gateways is important, but will be inadequate unless you also train your employees to doubt the importance of a call sent with a sense of urgency. Likewise, good physical mechanisms of access control are easily trumped by politeness. A good security posture must take into consideration all the avenues through which an attacker will be able to reach and compromise the human element.

TARGET SELECTION

Most powerful social engineering attacks are not a chance encounter, they are based on specific targeting and careful research. The targets whom attackers might choose are chosen on the basis of two major factors namely access and susceptibility. The most likely victim is a person who has the authority to do what the attacker wants done (e.g. authorize a payment, reset a password, grant access) and who also has features that may indicate susceptibility to manipulation.

Through OSINT, attackers might be able to determine important people in the hierarchy in a short time. As a BEC attack example, the employees of the finance and accounting departments are often targeted since they have direct access to wire transfer. In the case of human resources staff, they are targeted because of access to sensitive employee PII, whereas with the IT administrators it is because they have privileged access to the entire network. Hackers methodically search LinkedIn accounts, business directories and press releases to find people that occupy such positions and learn how they fit into the corporate structure.

CASE STUDIES IN HUMAN HACKING

As the direct consequences of the social engineering strategies adequacy, it is vital to examine real-life cases where the said methods caused devastating security breaches. Each of the following case studies examines the details of three major attacks that occurred in some of the largest and technologically advanced organizations globally in a bid to uncover how the threat actors methodically targeted human psychology and procedural vulnerabilities to circumvent the protective mechanisms implemented by their targets. All the cases have become strong examples of various aspects of the social engineering threat.

The 2013 Target Data Breach: The Third-Party Vector

In late 2013, during the Christmas holiday shopping period, a major retailer, *"Target"*, was hit by a massive data breach (Columbia University, 2022) that saw the creation of a gigantic database housing the payment card information of 40 million data consumers and the personal information of an additional 70 million. It was estimated that the breach cost $292 million with 47 states reaching an $18.5 million settlement. It was not the company of Target that is highly fortified but a third party service provider and this shows how vulnerable the supply chain is.

- **Attack Lifecycle and Vector:**

    1. **Reconnaissance:** The hackers found a small contractor company of the HVAC services, Fazio Mechanical Services, as a weak point in the supply chain of Target. Fazio also had remote access to the network of Target for its billing and project management but the company did not have adequate information security procedures.

2. **Initial Compromise:** The social engineering attack was the classic spear phishing attack. Attacker sent Phishing Email to Fazio Employees with Malware.
3. **Exploitation:** One of the employees Fazio succumbed to the phish, which resulted in malware (Citadel) to be installed on the systems to steal the credentials. This malware harvested the log in details that Fazio used to get into the contractor facing web portal of Target.
4. **Post-Exploitation:** The attackers used the stolen credentials to gain access inside Target network. They took advantage of ineffective network segmentation, laterally traversing out of the less-sensitive vendor zone into the POS system network. They then initiated special memory-scraping malware into system of thousands of cash-registers, which would extract credit and debit card information in real-time as cards were swiped.

- **Psychological Principles Exploited:** The first breach depended on the Trust that the Fazio employee had on what seemingly were legitimate emails. Key to the attackers being able to move freely in the Target network was the fact that security alerts that came to Target monitoring systems were initially overlooked by the security team who may have experienced alert fatigue or a normalization bias that made them declare the alerts as false positives.
- **Key Lessons:** The Target breach is a perfect example study case of third-party risk. It points out that no matter how strong one may make an organization's security the security is only as good as the weakest link and that link may not be under the direct control of the organization. The incident highlighted the importance of comprehensive vendor risk management, intensive network segmentation to inhibit lateral spreading and the development of a vigilant incident response culture that treats every alert with a serious tone.

The Google and Facebook BEC Fraud: The Impersonation Masterclass

In 2013-2015, a Lithuanian man Evaldas Rimasauskas carried out an audacious Business Email Compromise (BEC) orchestration and scammed two leaders in the globe, Google and Facebook, costing the companies over $122 million in total ($23 million and 99 million, respectively) (Trend Micro, 2025b). It is an ideal case of why even the most sophisticated organizations can be duped by careful impersonation and forgery of documents.

- **Attack Lifecycle and Vector:**

1. **Reconnaissance:** Rimasauskas was aware of the fact that both Google and Facebook are large customers of Quanta Computer, a legitimate company in Taiwan dealing with hardware. He and his colleagues also did research to learn the billing and payment process of the companies, which were most likely done by phishing or calling customer care to obtain the names of key figures.
2. **Initial Compromise:** It was a simple BEC attack. Rimasauskas created and established a company in Latvia with the same name as legitimate vendor, Quanta Computer. He subsequently opened a bank account in Latvia and in Cyprus with this false name.
3. **Exploitation:** The attackers impersonated Quanta and targeted employees of Google and Facebook via email asking them to accept a payment through a talent development portal connected with Quanta. These emails were supported by forged invoices, contracts and letters using the names of the executives and fake corporate stamps, which directed the companies to wire transfer money in regards to legitimate services to new bank accounts managed by Rimasauskas.
4. **Post-Exploitation:** The companies gave away tens of millions of dollars in the belief that the requests were legal. The funds were then laundered by passing through an elaborate network of bank accounts in varying parts of the world, including in Lithuania, Cyprus, Hong Kong and Hungary.

- **Psychological Principles Exploited:** Authority and Trust were exploited in this attack. The attackers posed as a well-known and legitimate company that had a long term business relationship with the companies. The appearance of extremely professional, forged documents justified the false belief of authenticity, and the checks of the financial departments were skipped. The attack exploited the regularity of big corporate payments; the more reasonable a request appears and the more it fits into the established pattern, the less chance it has to be thrown into the spotlight.
- **Key Lessons:** The Google and Facebook scam highlights the paramountness of procedural controls especially when it comes to financial transactions. It shows that even without technologically weakening a network, attackers can do enormous financial damage by conducting social engineering attacks only. The most important defense-side lesson is that verification of any modifications of payment instructions must always be done out of band, no matter how genuine the request may be.

The 2020 Bitcoin Scam: The Insider Threat via Social Engineering

On July 15th, 2020 the world experienced one of the largest social media platform hacks in history (Witman & Mackelprang, 2022). In a coordinated attack, 130 high profile Twitter accounts, including those of Barack Obama, Joe Biden, Bill Gates, Elon Musk, and Apple, were hacked in a promoted Bitcoin scam. The tweets claimed to multiply any Bitcoin sent to a particular wallet address by two, a classic bait that raked in more than $118,000 over several hours. The data breach was not a technical issue in Twitter platform but a successful social engineering attack on its employees.

- **Attack Lifecycle and Vector:**

  1. **Reconnaissance:** The attackers probably determined who had access to internal administrative tools of Twitter, possibly based on sites like LinkedIn. They might have also received access to internal documentation at twitters Slack channels, which contained information of remote access processes and credentials to the admin tools.
  2. **Initial Compromise:** The initial point of attack was phone spear-phishing, or vishing. Increased numbers of Twitter employees were duped into giving up their credentials by their attackers by calling them and preying on their urgency via a well-constructed ruse. The COVID-19 pandemic-related shift to remote work could have eased that attack by making workers more comfortable picking up work-related calls on their personal phones.
  3. **Exploitation:** The hackers used employee credentials that they steal to achieve access to the fully-administering levels in Twitter (God Mode). These tools enabled them to go round user security levels such as two-factor authentication and gain direct access to targeted high-profile accounts, reset their email addresses, and post tweets on their behalf.
  4. **Post-Exploitation:** The perpetrators used the compromised accounts to post their Bitcoin scam, using the immense social credibility and number of the followers to generate Social Proof and add credibility to their fraudulent offer.

- **Psychological Principles Exploited:** The attack on the employees was based on a plausible pretext, and Authority impersonation (the attacker probably pretended to be IT support or other internal workers). The effectiveness with which the public was scammed in the next event hinged on a strong sense of Authority (the tweets were sent by world leaders and technology visionaries),

Scarcity ("Only doing this in the next 30 minutes!") and Greed (the promise of doubling their money).The attack on the employees was based on a plausible pretext, and Authority impersonation (the attacker probably pretended to be IT support or other internal workers). The effectiveness with which the public was scammed in the next event hinged on a strong sense of Authority (the tweets were sent by world leaders and technology visionaries), Scarcity ("Only doing this in the next 30 minutes!") and Greed (the promise of doubling their money).

- **Key Lessons:** Twitter hack taught that despite excellent technical controls, such as MFA, people remain a target of the infamous point of failure. It demonstrated the extraordinary threat posed by compromised internal tools and the importance of vigilant access controls and ongoing, contextualized employee training of employees with lateral access in particular, highly trained vishing campaigns. Table 3 summarizes the aforementioned case studies.

Table 3. Case Studies

Case Study	Year	Primary Attack Vector(s)	Key Psychological Principles Exploited	Core Defensive Lesson
Target Data Breach	2013	Spear Phishing (on a third-party vendor)	Trust, Normalization Bias	Implement stringent third-party risk management and network segmentation to prevent lateral movement.
Google/Facebook BEC Fraud	2013 – 2015	Business Email Compromise (BEC), Impersonation, Forgery	Authority, Trust	Mandate strict, out-of-band verification procedures for any changes to financial information or payment instructions.
Twitter Bitcoin Scam	2020	Vishing (Phone Spear-Phishing of employees)	Authority, Pretexting, Social Proof, Scarcity	Enforce strict access controls on internal tools and provide continuous, targeted training against vishing for privileged employees.

THE NEW FRONTIER: AI AND AUTOMATION IN SOCIAL ENGINEERING

The social engineering landscape is getting a pervasive transition, fueled by the ubiquity of the mighty Artificial Intelligence and specially, Generative AI and Large Language Models (LLMs). They are turbocharging conventional attack capabilities, streamlining old-school social engineering tactics with ultra-personalized, highly scalable and deceptively realistic social engineering attacks. This shift is reducing the threshold of entry into advanced cybercrime and bringing about what some specialists are terming as an authenticity crisis, which makes it hard to tell authentic and artificial communication apart (SWITCH, 2025).

Hyper-Personalization at Scale

In the past, there was a trade off in the scale and sophistication of phishing attacks. Attackers would send out customized emails to a target individual via social engineering (spear phishing) or send millions of general emails (bulk phishing). Generative AI has broken this trade-off (Lawfare, 2025).

Machine learning-based tools are currently capable of automating parts of the reconnaissance and content development process on a massive scale. The systems are able to scavenge large quantities of information over social networks, company websites, as well as government records to create comprehensive profiles of thousands of victims at a time. Then LMs such as GPT-4 can leverage this information to create multiple thousands of contextually aware, grammatically perfect phishing emails within mere seconds (Hoxhunt, 2025).

This functionality of mass customization allows each member of a wide scale to be sent a custom message that refers to the name, job position, and recent activities, projects, and connections of every individual subordinate in a list dramatically enhancing the credibility of the message, and the chance of success. An experiment conducted by IBM XForce found that a team of human researchers and writers would need at least 16 hours to research and write an efficient phishing email, compared to the five minutes it would take a generative AI tool (IBM, 2025). This performance increases the capabilities of threat actors to execute hyper-personalized phishing campaigns with the accessibility and volume of standard bulk phishing.

The Rise of Deepfakes and the Authenticity Crisis

The most ominous turn is the application of AI to produce deepfakes (CrowdStrike, 2025), audio and video that is unusually lifelike but completely artificial. This technology is a quantum leap in terms of its impersonation capabilities and is not limited to text-to-voice and video.

- **Deepfake Audio:** Using only a few seconds of a particular person, usually that can be found in any public recording such as interviews, and social media videos, it is possible to train an AI model to create a synthetic clone of the voice that is hard to distinguish from the real one. The technology is a breakthrough to vishing and BEC scams. Attackers now have the ability to do even more than pretend to be a CEO in an email, they are able to leave a voicemail or even make a live phone call in the voice of the CEO. In 2019, perpetrators impersonated a voice-copy of the CEO of a parent company in order to fool a manager of an U.K. energy firm, who transferred 220,000 euros (Reality Defender, 2025). In what could be described as the most recent high-profile case, a finance worker in Hong Kong was tricked into making a $25 million transfer after attending a video conference call with whom he believed were his senior colleagues, not knowing, however, that they were all deepfakes.

- **Deepfake Video:** Video deepfakes are becoming easier to create and more high quality. They can be used to generate false video messages by makers, bring about bogus video conferences, or even develop compromising content that can be used in blackmail. As the above-mentioned $25 million fraud case shows, video deepfakes already ceased being a hypothetical danger but an established means of serious financial fraud. Recently in India, there have been cases where hackers used deep fake videos and audio in video calls to trick the friends and family of the target into giving him/her money on the pretext of an emergency.

The rampant creation of convincing deepfakes is spurring an authenticity crisis. The artificial media is on its way of becoming more widespread, which means that the inherent human nature of trusting our eyes and ears is gradually being eradicated. This puts the organization in a state of profound distrust, and any good-faith communications could well be assumed suspicious, which is likely to undermine the trust and probably interfere with the regular business activities.

AUTOMATION AND THE LOWERED BARRIER TO ENTRY

Not only are attacks getting better; thanks to AI they are also becoming easier to execute. Evil AI tools such as WormGPT and FraudGPT are now being offered through dark web forums (Moser IT, 2025), and actively being marketed to assist users in creating deceptive e-mail text and malicious code. This makes cybercrime more democratic and opens up the possibility of attacks by threat actors with lower technical proficiency to execute attacks previously restricted to the most sophisticated hacking groups (RSA Conference, 2025).

In addition, the next frontier is agentic AI, which will be autonomous AI systems able to plan and execute complex multi-stage tasks (SecurityWeek, 2025). An AI agent that had been tasked with a more general goal, e.g. breach Company X and exfiltrate their customer database could be malicious. The agent would then be able to perform reconnaissance, identify key personnel, compose and deliver personalized phish emails, interactively chat with victims through the use of AI powered chatbots, and adjust its operations in response to victim actions in real-time. A system like that is able to mount a relentless, multi-modal social engineering attack across email, SMS and social media, and it improves and learns over time.

The use of AI in social engineering signals an upheaval in the nature of threats. It renders social engineering basically an automatable, massively scalable business. This new generation of threat will require a similarly advanced and artificial intelligence integrated defense mechanism capable of detecting the minor irregularities of synthetically created communication, as well as building up human capabilities to withstand such a world wherein their senses cannot be trusted completely anymore.

BUILDING THE HUMAN FIREWALL: A MULTI LAYERED DEFENSE STRATEGY

With social engineering tapping into the human psyche, not a weakness in the technical realm, security must be a combination of technology, process and individuals. A defense-in-depth model can define numerous opportunities to prevent, detect, respond, and transform the employees into defenders.

1. Technical Defenses

- **Advanced Email Filtering:** AI-driven secure gateways can filter out 90+ percent of typical phishing attacks before they reach the user via spam filters, domain-based reputation and sandboxing methods. ML and BEC detect hidden non-malware BEC attacks.
- **Email Authentication (SPF, DKIM, DMARC):** Reduces spoofing, which is essential since 90 percent of phishing is preceded by forged sender identities. Stern DMARC policies almost eliminate domain imitation
- **Multi-Factor Authentication (MFA):** Microsoft says the MFA prevents 99.2 percent of automated credential attacks. MFA resistant to phishing (FIDO2/WebAuthn) is also resistant to proxy-based phishing kit.

2. Process Safeguards

- **Verification Procedures:** The out-of-band confirmation prevents fraudulent payment settlements; lack of the same resulted in over 100M of BEC fraud to Google and Facebook combined.
- **Principle of Least Privilege (PoLP):** Minimizes damage of attacks- I can violate an account of an intern, but the financial systems should not be affected.
- **Incident Response Plan:** An exercise-tested playbook curtailed recovery duration; according to federal stats, reduces the average cost of a breach by as much as 30 percent in companies with IR plans.

3. Psychological Resilience

- **Security Awareness Training:** Advanced once-in-a-year training is not very effective. The modern programs are interactive with short modules, and are role-specific (finance teams may do BEC, IT may do Credential theft).
- **Phishing Simulations:** In just one year, organizations reduce their phish-prone rates by 32 to 5 percent with frequent training and simulations.
- **Positive Security Culture:** It is essential that employees should not fear reporting the incidents. Punishment is not the motivation behind vigilance. Leadership Support transforms security into a business imperative as opposed to an information technology concern.

By intertwining these technical, procedural, and human based components, an organization will be able to establish an effective defense system that is much harder to breach by a social engineer.

THE DUAL-USE NATURE OF PSYCHOLOGICAL KNOWLEDGE

The science and art of persuasion and knowing the inner science of cognitive biases are, by themselves, neutral tools. In the right hands they can be used to a benign effect i.e. in crowdsourcing a health campaign or ethical advertising but also to a more nefarious purpose as evidenced in this chapter. This presents a big challenge of this dual-use nature. Awareness of effective countermeasures to social engineering cannot be attained independently of any awareness of its practice.

Examples of security awareness training are education, the teaching of manipulation tactics to the employees. By doing so, it is also teaching them how those tactics work, which can give a disgruntled insider a roadmap in doing so. Penetration testers with a social engineering speciality will need a sophisticated and practical knowledge of manipulation to conduct an effective test of the defences of an organisation. This comes out as a great moral obligation to the security community to make sure that such an influential knowledge is used with caution.

CONCLUSION

A thorough examination of the dense and very far-reaching phenomenon of social engineering has been presented in this chapter, tracing the history of social engineering back to antiquity, and following through to the current times with AI-boosted attacks. The key point of this discussion that is interwoven in this analysis is that the human factor is not an incidental part of the cyber threat zone but its most prominent and long-term aspect. It is quite clear through the evidence provided, recent case studies and comparisons with the Verizon Data Breach Investigations reports, that technology is a viable solution that can only take us so far, leaving the human psyche as the very weakest link in the chain.

We have observed that guidelines of manipulation are eternal. The distributors of the Trojan Horse made use of the same levers of Authority, Scarcity, Liking, and Trust that are used, and are becoming increasingly more complex, in Business Email Compromise scams today. The growth of this threat has not been on why it is being manipulated but on how. The digital revolution, and now the AI revolution, can be used to give attackers new capabilities to scale, personalize, and automate deception as never before. The development of hyper-realistic deepfakes and autonomous AI agents bears the potential to cement the prevailing culture of digital trust-no-trust, in which the verification process itself becomes a titanic endeavor.

It is time to deal with this ever-increasing threat with a paradigm change in defence strategy; it is not only advisable but necessary. The notion of a human firewall needs to be more dynamic in the sense that it has to become adaptive, multi-layered and active. This necessitates a comprehensive strategy that converges in a holistic manner in which three strands of defense are combined. As a first line of defense, technical controls including high level email filtering and phishing-resistant multi-factor authentication are needed to significantly decrease the amount of threats that get through to the user. Procedural controls such as use of strict, out of band control for performing sensitive transactions and least privilege ensure that the security appropriate behaviors are made part of the tissues of the organization.

Nevertheless, human resilience is the final defense in front of social engineering. This would not be made possible with ad hoc, compliance-based training. It needs an ongoing, adaptive educational initiative to endow employees with psychological literacy-the capacity to know the emotional and cognitive triggers of manipulation in others, and in themselves. It involves hands-on, ongoing simulations so that users can practice and enhance their defensive skills within a safe environment. Most importantly this requires the integration of a positive security culture whereby vigilance creates reward, errors must be perceived as a means through which learning occurs and not as an incident that leads to punishment.

Indeed, the future will come to be characterized by the co-evolution of AI-driven attacks and AI-based defenses. However, despite this technological arms race, the human user will still be present at the center of it. The single most enduring lesson and challenge of the cybersecurity community is to understand that securing our digital world is as much about human behaviour as it is about writing safe code. It is not until there is a serious interdisciplinary effort to integrate the intricacies of human psychology as the focal point in its strategy that a long-term defense against social engineering will ever be possible.

REFERENCES

Arctic Wolf. (2025). Top social engineering attack types. https://arcticwolf.com/resources/blog/top-social-engineering-attack-types/

Barracuda Networks. (2025). Business email compromise. https://www.barracuda.com/support/glossary/business-email-compromise

Boson Blog. (2025). 1999 in tech: The Melissa virus. https://blog.boson.com/1999-in-tech-the-melissa-virus

Cialdini, R. B. (2006). *Influence: The psychology of persuasion.* Harper Business.

Cloudflare. (2025). What is quishing? https://www.cloudflare.com/en-gb/learning/security/what-is-quishing/

Colorado Department of Education. (2025). Social engineering education. https://www.cde.state.co.us/dataprivacyandsecurity/socialengineeringeducation

Columbia University, School of International and Public Affairs. (2022). Target final report. https://www.sipa.columbia.edu/sites/default/files/2022-11/Target%20Final.pdf

Conference, R. S. A. (2025). Social engineering in the AI era: Empower your digital defense. https://www.rsaconference.com/library/blog/social-engineering-in-the-ai-era-empower-your-digital-defense

CrowdStrike. (2025). Deepfake attack. https://www.crowdstrike.com/en-us/cybersecurity-101/social-engineering/deepfake-attack/

David, U., & Bode-Asa, A. (2023). An overview of social engineering: The role of cognitive biases towards social engineering-based cyber-attacks, impacts and countermeasures. ResearchGate. DOI: 10.13140/RG.2.2.12421.12003

Digit. (2025). Elk Cloner. https://www.digit.fyi/elk-cloner/

EBSCO. (2025). ILOVEYOU virus attacks computers. https://www.ebsco.com/research-starters/computer-science/iloveyou-virus-attacks-computers

Farnam Street. (2025). The IKEA effect. https://fs.blog/the-ikea-effect

Federal Bureau of Investigation. (2025). Business email compromise. https://www.fbi.gov/how-we-can-help-you/scams-and-safety/common-frauds-and-scams/business-email-compromise

Geeks Ltd. (2020, January). World's first computer virus. https://geeks.co.uk/2020/01/worlds-first-computer-virus/

Governance Europe, I. T. (2025). The 5 most common types of phishing attack. https://www.itgovernance.eu/blog/en/the-5-most-common-types-of-phishing-attack

Hoxhunt. (2025). AI phishing attacks. https://hoxhunt.com/blog/ai-phishing-attacks

IBM. (2025). Generative AI and social engineering. https://www.ibm.com/think/insights/generative-ai-social-engineering

Imperva. (2025). Social engineering attack. https://www.imperva.com/learn/application-security/social-engineering-attack/

International Association of Chiefs of Police. (2025). Cyber-attack lifecycle. https://www.iacpcybercenter.org/resource-center/what-is-cyber-crime/cyber-attack-lifecycle/

KnowBe4. (2025a). Phishing resource center. https://www.knowbe4.com/resource-center/phishing

KnowBe4. (2025b). What is social engineering? https://www.knowbe4.com/what-is-social-engineering

Lawfare. (2025). AI-enhanced social engineering will reshape the cyber threat landscape. https://www.lawfaremedia.org/article/ai-enhanced-social-engineering-will-reshape-the-cyber-threat-landscape

Lei, W., Hu, S., & Hsu, C. (2022). Unveiling the process of phishing precautions taking: The moderating role of optimism bias. *SSRN*. Advance online publication. DOI: 10.2139/ssrn.4147323

Licelus. (2025). The psychology of social engineering. https://licelus.com/insights/the-psychology-of-social-engineering

Medium. (2025). Influence: The psychology of persuasion – A book summary. https://medium.com/power-books/influence-the-psychology-of-persuasion-a-book-summary-7ae0ebf8950f

Microsoft. (2025). What is business email compromise (BEC)? https://www.microsoft.com/en-us/security/business/security-101/what-is-business-email-compromise-bec

Moser, I. T. (2025). Phishing evolves. https://www.moserit.com/blog/phishing-evolves

Offensive Security. (2025). Social engineering. https://www.offsec.com/blog/social-engineering/

OneCard. (2025). Social engineering. https://www.getonecard.app/blog/social-engineering/

People Shift. (2025). Adams' equity theory of motivation. https://people-shift.com/articles/adams-equity-theory-of-motivation/

Reality Defender. (2025). Deepfake voice phishing (vishing) in the financial sector. https://www.realitydefender.com/insights/deepfake-voice-phishing-vishing-in-the-financial-sector

Scribbr. (2025). Recency bias. https://www.scribbr.com/research-bias/recency-bias/

SecurityWeek. (2025). How agentic AI will be weaponized for social engineering attacks. https://www.securityweek.com/how-agentic-ai-will-be-weaponized-for-social-engineering-attacks/

Simply Psychology. (2025). Confirmation bias. https://www.simplypsychology.org/confirmation-bias.html

Social-Engineer, Inc. (2025). The psychology behind social engineering. https://www.social-engineer.com/the-psychology-behind-social-engineering/

SWITCH. (2025). Resilience against social engineering in the age of AI. https://www.switch.ch/en/insights/resilience-against-social-engineering-age-ai

Trend Micro. (2025a). Types of phishing. https://www.trendmicro.com/en_us/what-is/phishing/types-of-phishing.html

Trend Micro. (2025b). Google and Facebook fraudster pleads guilty to $100 million scam. https://www.trendmicro.com/vinfo/ru/security/news/cybercrime-and-digital-threats/google-and-facebook-fraudster-pleads-guilty-to-100-million-scam

Verizon. (2025). Data breach investigations report (DBIR). https://www.verizon.com/business/resources/reports/dbir/

Witman, P. D., & Mackelprang, S. (2022). The 2020 Twitter hack – So many lessons to be learned. Journal of Cybersecurity Education, Research and Practice, 2021(2), Article 2. https://digitalcommons.kennesaw.edu/jcerp/vol2021/iss2/2

Chapter 14
Forensic-Ready Approaches to Insider Threat Mitigation and Human Behavior Analysis

Pridhi Arora
https://orcid.org/0009-0002-5790-1742
Delhi Technical Campus, Greater Noida, India

Padmesh Tripathi
https://orcid.org/0000-0001-9455-1652
Delhi Technical Campus, Greater Noida, India

Seema Verma
https://orcid.org/0000-0002-7893-671X
Delhi Technical Campus, Greater Noida, India

ABSTRACT

Insider threats are a cybersecurity risk that comes from people who already have authorized access to an organization's systems and information. This chapter provides a deep understanding of how to use cutting-edge technological tools along with the insights from human behavior that can help us to detect and stop insider threats. The chapter starts by defining insider threats and their various forms. It analyzes various internal breaches and explains why the traditional security methods are ineffective in identifying them. We further explain the need for modern frameworks that include pattern analysis of the activities, machine learning, identity and access controls, and detection of unusual activities. The chapter focuses on how the behavioral analysis can be used to identify the suspicious activity. After examining the

DOI: 10.4018/979-8-3373-4898-8.ch014

unusual activities, we discuss methods to prevent them by implementing the proper access control, training employees, securing the sensitive data, and adoption of a zero-trust security model. Legal and ethical concerns are also covered in this chapter.

1. INTRODUCTION

Insider threats are the risks posed by individuals within an organization who misuse their authorized access to harm the organization's information, systems, or people. Insider threat encompasses both intentional and unintentional actions by insiders that have negative effects. Insiders include current or former employees, contractors, vendors, business partners, or anyone granted trusted access to facilities or information systems. Insider incidents can take many forms such as espionage, sabotage, theft of information, fraud, workplace violence, or other policy violations (CISA, n.d.). In the cybersecurity context, common manifestations are unauthorized data exfiltration, means stealing of files or databases, misuse of authorized access e.g. an admin creating backdoor accounts, IT sabotage means destroying or altering systems or data, using systems for financial theft, and unauthorized disclosure of confidential information.

1.1 Types of Insider Threats

Organizations often categorize insider threats into a few broad groups:

1.1.1 Malicious Insiders

Malicious insiders are people who willfully use the access to do malicious activities. The bad insiders can pursue self-financial interest, vengeance over the perceived injustice, or competitive advantage with a new employer. They produce information, destroy systems or do any other damage to the organization. An IT administrator who plants a logic bomb to destroy systems after being demoted is a malicious insider, an example. The majority of famous insider cases (e.g., stealing trade secrets, information breaches) belong to this category. Research has established that by a high percentage of the insiders who engaged in IT sabotage or stole data were discontented employees who were either motivated by revenge or greed. Actually, personal financial gain is a significant factor that contributes to the occurrence of malicious insider breaches, almost 89% of this is as a result of financial gain (Smith, 2025).

1.1.2 Negligent Insiders

Often known as accidental insiders or unintentional threats, these are people of the organization who do not intend to do harm, but due to their carelessness, mistake, or violation of the rules, leave gaps or occurrences (CISA, n.d.). They can include an employee falling to a phishing email and providing their login credentials without knowing, or a person sending an important document to an email address belonging to the wrong person. Such mistakes can be costly. A large portion of breaches are due to human errors (misdelivery of information, improper configuration, etc.), and in one report simple errors on the part of the users were attributed to the cause of the majority of reported data breaches in a single jurisdiction. Negligent insiders do not have security awareness or do not adhere to procedures defined by the organization, however with enhanced training and control most of these mishaps can be avoided. These insiders are insider threats only insofar as their activities can pose a threat to the security of the organization. They demonstrate the importance of well-organized security education and fail-safes to identify mistakes.

1.1.3 Infiltrators (External Impersonators)

These mean the external threat actors who successfully obtain legitimate insider access, typically through stealing or acquiring credentials or through collusion with an insider. That is, the attacker is not an insider by default, but rather acquires the account of an authorized user, or compromises it. They are also referred to as compromised insiders or the third-party threats. As an example, a hacker can gain access to the VPN credentials of an employee via a phishing attack or a foreign agent can bribe a member of staff. One particularly prominent example was the situation at Twitter in 2020, when external people used social engineering to socially engineer employees to get access to internal administrative tools and then used them to initiate a high-profile account takeover attack (Jeffers & Barnes, 2022). Actually, a large percentage of the reported cases involving an insider threat is through stolen credentials, an outsider pretending to be an insider. It erases the distinction between the external and internal threats, but in terms of defense, the control mechanisms are similar to the insider threats (e.g. checking user behavior to detect anomalies). Figure 1 represents different types of Insider Threats.

Figure 1. Different categories of insider threats.

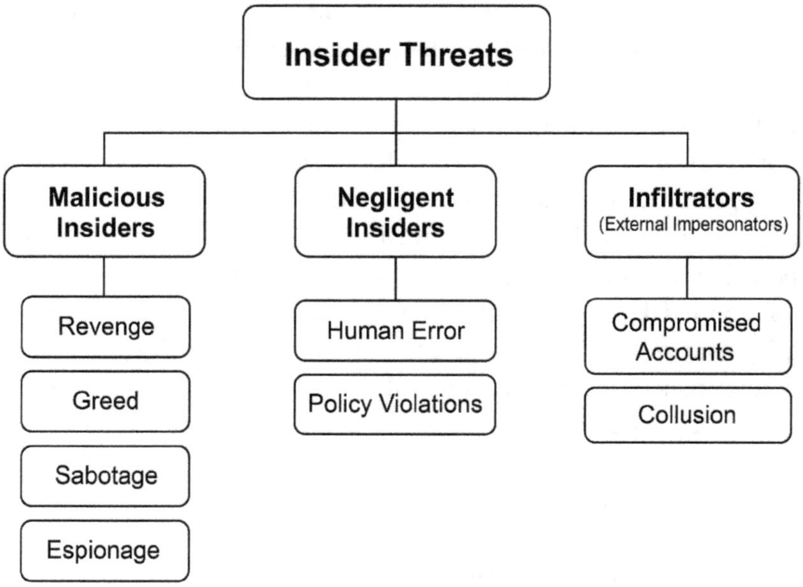

In addition to these categories, some frameworks include collusive threats, where one or more genuine insiders actively collaborate with an external attacker, and third-party insiders, referring to contractors or vendors who aren't direct employees but have been granted access. These distinctions underscore that insider risk comes not only from direct employees but also from the extended network of trusted relationships.

It is important to note that insider threats manifest in various forms of harm. The U.S. Cybersecurity and Infrastructure Security Agency (CISA) emphasizes that insider incidents can involve espionage, sabotage, theft of information, fraud, workplace violence, or other types of policy violations (CISA, n.d.). The next sections will explore real-world examples of insider breaches, common patterns in insider behavior, and modern approaches for detecting and preventing such threats.

1.2 Inside Jobs: Examples and Patterns of Insider Breaches

Insider breaches can take many forms. Below, we discuss a few common categories of insider incidents along with illustrative examples drawn from real cases. These examples reveal the patterns in insider behavior and security program failures that we address later in the chapter.

1.2.1 Data Theft and Intellectual Property Espionage

The theft of sensitive data, including customer data, trade secrets, or other intellectual property, is one of the most common insider threats. Staff members with access to sensitive information are able to replicate massive amounts of data without arousing suspicion. A case in point is the workforce management company Rippling, which in 2025 found out that a competitor (Deel) had been secretly extracting data over several months via its own employee. This mole was employed as a manager and gained inside access to company sites (Slack, Salesforce, Google Drive) and stole customer list, pricing, and other confidential data, all without standing out as unusual work. The theft case was not noticed until a law suit showed the spying. Equally, a Coca-Cola engineer was indicted several years ago to sell proprietary chemical formula data to parties in China. She worked as a principal engineer, so she had overall legitimate access, which she exploited to steal important intellectual property. These examples indicate how well-placed insiders can cause major harm by misusing access to data. The classic approach of perimeter security does not provide much security when an authorized user chooses to walk out the door with data, in another instance, a departing executive at a tech company downloaded sensitive files to a USB drive and took them to a competitor. In these situations, internal monitoring, including Data Loss Prevention systems or user activity monitoring can be used successfully to detect suspicious data access or copying (Smith, 2025).

1.2.2 Privileged Misuse and IT Sabotage

Privileged insiders such as system administrators, IT staff, software developers can cause immense damage when they go rogue. The Tesla insider sabotage case is a good example. In 2018, his CEO Elon Musk publicly accused a Tesla employee of engaging in widespread and harmful sabotage by leaking confidential information and editing code in the operating system used to run manufacturing at Tesla. The insider is claimed to have stolen gigabytes of proprietary information and interfered with the operations by directly making modifications to code. Likewise, in 2020, a dissatisfied Cisco employee, who was fired, planted a logic bomb into Cisco cloud-based infrastructure, which wiped hundreds of virtual machines, resulting in a massive service outage. These incidents illustrate the extent to which harm can be caused by an insider who is technically talented. The general scheme is often abuse of privileged access: both the Tesla saboteur and the Cisco engineer had administrative or development access that they were left to use responsibly, and they used it to do harm. Mitigations in this case involve reduced access to privileged accounts (e.g., having code changes reviewed by peers, logging administrative actions, behavior monitoring that may identify red flags such as an administrator accessing systems they had previously never accessed, or downloading sensitive schemas when not necessary).

1.2.3 Fraud and Financial Abuse

There are insiders who abuse information systems to make a profit. Here are a few examples of how employees of a bank could misuse internal systems to transfer funds to personal accounts, or how an accountant can misuse financial records to steal money. In one instance, staff members of a retail organization conspired to print counterfeit gift cards and shared the gains. These events usually entail a breach of the principle of separation of duties e.g. the same individual having the capability to both start and sanction a transaction or the misuse of unregulated power. Weak controls may not be able to detect fraud perpetrated by insiders immediately - it may only be exposed at audit time, or when a customer complains. Other patterns that would be used to point to insider fraud are that the employee is living outside of his means, is using the system to bypass routine procedures or is going to places within the system that he is not supposed to access. These schemes can be detected by anti-fraud policies such as mandatory vacations (to allow another person to perform their duties temporarily), rotation of work and automatic notifications about unusual transactions.

1.2.4 Sabotage and Destruction

In addition to stealing data or money, insiders could be interested in disrupting or destroying. These could be a dissatisfied IT contractor who installed a logic bomb which wiped out company databases, or a manufacturing worker who physically sabotaged equipment. These attacks can be driven either by revenge or an intention to cripple the operations of the organization. They emphasize the importance of the digital and physical security monitoring. Signs of possible sabotage are technical, such as an employee having unexpected access to systems that he or she does not normally have access to or trying to shut down security measures such as antivirus software or security cameras. There has to be speedy incident response policies in the organization - such as how to be able to restore within a short time frame using backups in the event of a data wipe, and protocols to pull the plug on an employee in case of a termination under hostile conditions.

The above examples show that insiders often exploit trust and legitimate access in ways that can be subtle or blend in with routine work. Traditional security measures that focus on keeping *outsiders* out are not sufficient. Defenses must assume that bad actors might already be on the inside (or outside attackers will *become* insiders via stolen credentials or mole recruitment). Common patterns in insider incidents include behavior al red flags (e.g., disgruntlement, policy violations), technical red flags (e.g., unusual data access, attempts to override controls), and gaps in controls (e.g., excessive privileges or lack of monitoring on sensitive systems). Recognizing these patterns is the first step. In the next sections, we examine modern approaches and frameworks designed to detect and deter insider threats, followed by strategies to prevent incidents and address the human factors behind insider risks.

2. MODERN APPROACHES TO INSIDER THREAT DETECTION

Due to the shortcomings of traditional defenses, organizations are deploying complex, multi-layered methods to detect insider threats. Modern insider threat detection combines advanced technology with data analysis and behavioral science to pick up on the subtle signs of insider abuse. In this section, we investigate some of the most advanced systems and practices that have emerged, such as behavior analytics, machine learning for anomaly detection, and improved identity and access management. These approaches aim to determine a baseline of "normal" behavior for each user, correlate data from many sources for an integrated view, and enforce tighter controls to flag or prevent suspicious activities. The goal is to move from reactive to proactive monitoring – catching insiders with malicious intent during the preparatory stages of an attack rather than after damage is done.

2.1 User and Entity Behavior Analytics (UEBA)

One cornerstone of modern insider threat programs is User and Entity Behavior Analytics (UEBA) – a class of solutions that uses advanced analytics often machine learning to model the normal behavior of users and entities like devices and detect anomalies. UEBA systems ingest logs and events from many sources e.g., logins, file access, emails, network flows and build profiles of typical behavior for each user. If a user starts doing something statistically unusual – such as accessing a system at an odd hour, downloading far more data than normal, or seeking information unrelated to their job – the UEBA system will raise an alert. These tools effectively shine a light on an insider's "pattern of life." For example, if an employee who always works 9am–5pm suddenly logs in at 3am from a new location that would be flagged as an unusual access pattern. According to IBM, advanced monitoring solutions like UEBA are essential since insiders are much harder to detect than external hackers, and machine-learning-based behavioral analytics can "flag anomalies" in user activity as early warnings. Unlike signature-based systems, UEBA doesn't rely on known attack patterns; instead, it can catch the unknown by looking for deviations from each user's baseline behavior . By aggregating activity data over time, these systems may assign risk scores to users and provide security teams with prioritized alerts (for example, an employee who triggers multiple different anomaly flags in a short period might receive a high risk score). UEBA represents a shift from reactive to proactive monitoring, attempting to catch malicious intent during the "pre-attack" stage (when insiders are still gathering data or probing systems) rather than after damage is done. Besides, several researchers have proposed other behaviour based insider threat detection methods (Ye et al. 2025, Pennada et al. 2025, Singh et al 2023, Nasir et al. 2021).

2.2 Machine Learning and Anomaly Detection Algorithms

The applicability of machine learning and its variants in different sectors (Tripathi et al. 2022, Kumar et al. 2024, Tripathi et al. 2024, Mishra et al. 2025, Arora et al. 2025) motivated the researchers to employ them in insider threat detection. Beyond behavior profiling, ML algorithms can be trained on historical insider incident data from curated datasets or past logs to identify patterns that precede an attack. Researchers have applied various models – from neural networks and autoencoders to one-class SVMs and clustering techniques, to detect insider threats in benchmark datasets such as the CERT insider threat dataset. These models look at sequences of user actions and attempt to distinguish normal behavior from malicious sequences. For instance, a deep learning model might detect that a specific combination of actions e.g., accessing a sensitive file repository, then plugging in a USB drive, then disabling an antivirus service is highly indicative of an insider preparing to steal data. An academic study by Sarhan and Altwaijry (2023) demonstrated a mix of anomaly detection and classification algorithms achieving over 90% accuracy in identifying insider threats in test data. The advantage of ML is its ability to learn complex patterns and adapt over time. Ensemble or hybrid models can even catch insiders who try to slowly change their behavior to avoid detection. One ongoing challenge is dealing with imbalanced data – malicious insider events are relatively rare compared to normal events – but techniques like synthetic oversampling e.g., SMOTE or data augmentation have been used to improve model performance (Ye et al., 2025). Le et al. (2020) proposed a machine learning based method for analysis of data granularity levels for insider threat detection. Alzaabi and Mehmood (2024) explored insider threat detection methods based on machine learning.

Pennada et al. (2025) proposed a hybrid machine learning based method for insider threat detection employing generative latent features achieved a satisfactory result. Tao et al. (2025) proposed an insider threat detection method based on TTT-ECA-ResNet model. The model was evaluated employing the CMU CERT insider threat dataset. An AUC of 98.75% and an F1-score of 96.81% was achieved.

Yuan and Wu (2021) reviewed the methods based on deep learning for insider threat detection.

In practice, organizations may use a combination of unsupervised ML to flag outliers without prior labelling of bad behavior and supervised ML to classify known types of risky behaviors in their insider threat tools. As computational power and algorithms have improved, real-time or near-real-time analysis of user activity streams has become feasible, enabling security teams to get alerts quickly if an ML model senses something suspicious. ML-based systems can also reduce noise by learning what *not* to alert on (adapting to each user's baseline), thereby minimizing false positives and focusing analyst attention on truly abnormal events.

Al-Shehari et al. (2024) proposed a model using the Density-Based Local Outlier Factor Algorithm in imbalanced cybersecurity settings for insider threat detection. Several other methods have been proposed for insider threat detection (Tian et al. 2025, Wei,et al. 2024, Guanyun et al 2023).

2.3 Identity and Access Management Enhancements

Preventing and detecting insider threats also requires strengthening how organizations manage user identities and access privileges. Identity and Access Management practices have evolved with insider threat in mind. Two key principles are particularly relevant: Least Privilege and Zero Trust.

2.3.1. Enforce Least Privilege and Need-to-Know

A fundamental principle to mitigate insider risk is to limit each person's access to only what they genuinely need for their job – the principle of least privilege. By curbing unnecessary access, even if an insider turns malicious (or an outsider compromises their account), the scope of what they can steal or damage is contained. Implement role-based access controls (RBAC) where possible, and regularly review user access rights for appropriateness. Many organizations conduct periodic access recertification campaigns where managers must attest that their team members still require each permission they have. Dormant accounts and orphaned privileges should be promptly removed. In practice, technologies like Privileged Access Management (PAM) solutions help by providing one-time-use credentials for admin tasks, logging all privileged actions, and requiring approvals for certain high-risk operations (Jeffers & Barnes, 2022). If an organization can implement granular access controls (for example, segmenting sensitive projects so only the project team can access them), it not only reduces insider risk but also creates an environment where an insider trying to access beyond their need is immediately conspicuous. A lesson often cited is the 2013 Target Corporation breach: attackers infiltrated via credentials from a third-party HVAC contractor and could pivot to the payment network because internal network segmentation and least-privilege principles were insufficient. In response, Target and others tightened internal network segmentation and access limits. The takeaway is to always ask "Does this person really need access to this data or system?" – if not, don't grant it. Least privilege can significantly limit the potential blast radius of an insider incident.

2.3.2 Adopt a Zero Trust Security Model

Zero Trust Architecture is a modern paradigm that complements least privilege. Zero Trust, popularized in recent years with formal frameworks published by NIST, means no implicit trust is granted based solely on network location or a user's initial authentication. Every access is continually verified through multiple mechanisms like multi-factor authentication, context checks, device health checks, etc.. Micro-segmentation is employed such that even if an insider or attacker in one part of the network tries to access another part, they have to authenticate again and meet policy criteria. For example, even if a user is logged into the corporate network, accessing a sensitive database might require a fresh step-up authentication or explicit permission check. Zero Trust embodies the principle "never trust, always verify", effectively treating internal traffic with the same scrutiny as external traffic. This minimizes the chances that an insider can move laterally or escalate privileges undetected. Implementing Zero Trust can be complex and is an ongoing journey, but initial steps include employing strong identity verification everywhere, limiting network access via software-defined perimeters, and continuously monitoring and re-authenticating user sessions. In the context of insiders, Zero Trust means if person from Marketing suddenly tries to access Engineering's code repository, the system will challenge the person or block the request because it's outside his usual pattern and not required for his role. In this way, even if person turned rogue, the architecture itself resists the unauthorized access. Many organizations are adopting Zero Trust approaches to reduce both external and internal risk (English, 2025).

2.4 Data Monitoring and Exfiltration Controls

To catch insiders who attempt to steal data, organizations use Data Loss Prevention (DLP) tools and enhanced monitoring on critical assets. DLP solutions monitor data in use, in motion, and at rest to detect potential data exfiltration or policy violations (Smith, 2025). For example, DLP can block or alert on emails with sensitive attachments, large file transfers to external drives, or uploading of confidential files to cloud storage. In insider threat contexts, DLP helps by acting as a backstop that can prevent an unaware or malicious insider from easily removing data. Additionally, high-value systems e.g., source code repositories, customer databases, financial transaction systems should have extra monitoring. File integrity monitoring, database activity monitoring and application log reviews on these "crown jewels" can generate real-time alerts for suspicious activities such as a user querying an HR database they never accessed before. In essence, organizations should *tier* their monitoring, applying the most stringent oversight to the most sensitive resources (Jeffers & Barnes, 2022). This targeted monitoring increases the chance of detecting an insider attack in progress. Modern analytics can also correlate events for instance, noticing that the same user who disabled a DLP agent on their PC also began copying files to a USB device, which would warrant immediate investigation (Sarhan & Altwaijry, 2023). By focusing on critical assets and using DLP and related controls, companies can quickly catch and contain many insider activities before data actually leaves the organization.

Every organization should identify its "crown jewels", the most sensitive and valuable data, systems, or business processes and place additional monitoring and safeguards around them. Once identified, these assets should be subject to heightened logging and real-time alerting for certain activities (Smith, 2025). For instance, a company can implement database activity monitoring on a customer records database to flag queries that return unusually large data sets or that are run at odd hours. If an insider starts pulling an entire client list without a business need, an alert can notify security personnel immediately. On file servers containing proprietary research, the organization can enable alerts if large volumes of files are accessed or copied in a short time by a single user. Even simple measures like system file auditing with threshold triggers e.g., more than 500 files accessed by one account in 10 minutes can catch anomalous "data harvesting" behavior .

The Security Operations Center (SOC) should also develop insider threat use-cases for their SIEM (Security Information and Event Management) system. Examples of SIEM correlation rules: a user *logs in outside normal hours* and *remotely accesses a sensitive server* and *disables an endpoint agent* – all within a short timeframe could trigger a high-severity insider threat alert. Another example: an employee whose account was recently put on an HR performance improvement plan indicating possible disgruntlement suddenly requests access to projects unrelated to their job; this could generate a notification for insider risk team review if such HR-security integration is in place.

Additionally, external threat intelligence can be incorporated into insider threat monitoring rules. If, for instance, a device used by an employee starts communicating with an IP address known for malware or data exfiltration, that combination of internal and external indicators can reveal an insider compromise or collusion that might otherwise go unnoticed. Insider incidents often blur the line between internal and external threats, so integrating threat intelligence e.g., known indicators of compromise or watchlists of suspicious entities into monitoring can help detect when an insider may be working with outside adversaries or using known malicious tools. By incorporating both internal anomalies and external threat signals, organizations gain a more holistic view of potential insider threat scenarios.

Immediate response to suspicious alerts is crucial. Organizations might set up automated containment for certain triggers for example, automatically locking an account if it tries to mass delete records or download a critical database. In less clear-cut cases, the insider threat team can quietly investigate while the user continues working for example, reviewing logs of their recent activity, or increasing monitoring on their account. By focusing monitoring on critical assets and activities, companies avoid drowning in data and ensure that the signal stands out from the noise.

Modern approaches to insider threat detection, in summary, involve a fusion of technology, data, and human insight. By leveraging UEBA and machine learning, enhancing identity controls, least privilege and Zero Trust, implementing robust data monitoring, and paying attention to human behavioral cues, organizations can significantly improve their ability to spot insider threats early. The next section turns to the human element in more depth, examining specific behavior al indicators and how to manage the insider threat from a people perspective.

3. THE HUMAN FACTOR: BEHAVIORAL INDICATORS AND ANALYSIS

Technical measures alone are not enough to counter insider threats; understanding human behavior and organizational culture is equally important. Insiders do not usually become malicious in a vacuum, their actions are often preceded by behavioral red flags or personal events. In this section, we discuss key behavioral indicators of insider risk and how organizations can monitor and interpret them within ethical boundaries to preempt insider attacks.

3.1 Behavior al Red Flags and Psychosocial Indicators

Stress, Disengagement, and Other Red Flags:

Research and case studies have identified common traits among malicious insiders. Often, they exhibit some form of personal or professional stress prior to their actions. They may be disgruntled due to a missed promotion, interpersonal conflicts, or perceived unfair treatment. They might also show signs of disengagement becoming less cooperative, voicing unhappiness, or declining in work quality. According to a 2025 cybersecurity report, *"Employees displaying signs of stress, disengagement or dissatisfaction may be more prone to risky actions, whether intentional or unintentional"* (Smith, 2025). Behavioral anomalies that could indicate an insider threat include sudden changes in mood or conduct e.g., someone who was normally collegial turning hostile or withdrawn, violations of workplace norms like frequently breaking minor rules, or open expressions of grievance such as saying "They'll be sorry" or other ominous remarks. In one analysis of insider espionage cases, a notable percentage of perpetrators were described as "difficult" or "disgruntled" by colleagues, indicating that relational conflicts at work often preceded the malicious act. Another potential red flag is unexplained affluence, if an employee who is not highly paid suddenly has a significant lifestyle upgrade like new luxury car, expensive vacations beyond their means, it could indicate illicit income from selling information or collusion with criminals. Similarly, personal issues such as gambling debts or substance abuse can make an insider more likely to commit illegal acts either to obtain money or due to impaired judgment.

Organizations should educate managers and co-workers about these warning signs. Some companies establish a formal process where concerning behaviors can be reported to a central insider risk team or HR often anonymously. However, this must be balanced with avoiding a culture of paranoia. The goal is early identification of at-risk individuals so the organization can intervene constructively for example, offering counselling or addressing grievances or, if necessary, heighten monitoring of those individuals. It's crucial that interventions are handled sensitively to avoid alienating staff, the intent is to help employees and secure the company, not to punish mere expressions of dissatisfaction.

3.2 Behavioral Baselines at Work

Just as we spoke of technical behavior baselines, one can consider base lining normal workplace behavior for individuals and teams. Does an employee normally comply with policies? Do they usually interact positively with colleagues? Significant deviations from one's baseline can be telling. For instance, if an employee starts working odd hours or in isolation when they previously did not, it could be legitimate perhaps they have a tough deadline or it could warrant examination, why the sudden change? If someone begins to bypass security procedures – like trying to circumvent access controls or asking co-workers for their passwords that is a serious warning sign, as it could indicate they are probing how to get around security. Another indicator is excessive curiosity beyond one's role for example, an employee from Department A frequently attempting to access files in Department

B's shared drives without a need. While curiosity alone isn't a crime, in context it might signal malicious intent or at least disregard for access boundaries.

By tracking and reviewing logs of policy deviations, unusual work patterns, and access attempts, insider threat programs can identify individuals whose behavior is shifting in concerning ways. Many large organizations have formal Insider Threat Programs (ITPs) that coordinate these efforts, bringing together security, HR, and management to regularly review cases of concern (English, 2025). These programs often have a behavioral observation component: training supervisors to recognize and report issues, setting up communication channels for reporting, and possibly using anonymized sentiment analysis tools to gauge employee morale e.g., monitoring aggregated employee survey data or internal chat forums for spikes in negative sentiment.

3.3 Communication and Social Signals

How insiders communicate can also provide clues. Threatening or extremely negative remarks about the company on internal forums, angry emails, or even bragging about bending rules can all be pieces of the puzzle. External communication is relevant too, if an employee is suddenly communicating with competitors or unknown parties maybe via personal email or social media about company matters, that's a red flag. One classic warning sign is known as the "two-week rule" anecdotally, many insiders who steal data do so within the two weeks before leaving for a new job. Thus, if an employee announces their resignation, it's wise to monitor their data access during their notice period many companies now have protocols to restrict or surveil data access by those who are about to depart. Conversely, an employee who is fired or laid off could pose a risk if they leave disgruntled hence the emphasis on immediate access revocation and monitoring for any attempted access after departure (Jeffers & Barnes, 2022).

3.4 Psychological and Personal Factors

Some organizations even consult psychologists or behavioral experts as part of their insider threat program to profile and assess risk levels of individuals. While not every organization can do this, it's useful to be aware of psychological factors correlated with insider activity. For example, narcissism or excessive ego can be a factor – some insider spies or leakers feel they are smarter than the system or believe they're entitled to certain information. Others may rationalize their actions ("I deserve more," "The company wronged me, so I'll wrong them"). Understanding these mindsets can help shape interview questions during security investigations or even inform screening during hiring (though predicting future behavior is inherently imperfect). Personal crises like substance abuse or severe financial hardship can also make someone more exploitable by external bad actors or more likely to commit desperate acts. The CISA *Insider Threat Mitigation Guide* notes that patterns such as addiction, financial distress, or repeatedly violating minor policies should be considered in an overall risk assessment (CISA, 2020).

More recent analyses continue to emphasize such human factors. For example, a 2024 systematic literature review identified job insecurity and unmet expectations as significant precursors to insider risk, reinforcing the link between unresolved employee frustrations and insider incidents (Inayat et al., 2024). Financial stress is a classic driver for fraud and data theft; the study found that feelings of job instability or being passed over can create resentments that, if left unaddressed, increase the likelihood of malicious behavior. This underscores that insider threat mitigation is not only about monitoring technical actions but also about gauging human sentiment and organizational culture issues that could elevate risk.

In practice, an effective insider threat program will correlate technical indicators (like unusual logins or data access alerts) with behavioral indicators (like HR reports of troubling behavior or personal stress) to get a full picture of risk. For example, imagine a certain employee has become very vocal about grievances at work (behavioral red flag). The insider threat team increases monitoring and finds through logs that the employee has been accessing far more files than usual and even attempted to disable the DLP software on their computer (technical red flags). With these correlated indicators, the organization might decide to interview the employee or take preventive action (such as temporarily limiting their access to sensitive data) before any damage occurs. Such proactive measures can stop an insider incident before it fully develops.

3.5 Privacy and Ethics in Behavioral Monitoring

Monitoring behavioral indicators must be done carefully to respect privacy and ethics (we will cover this more in the Legal and Ethical section). Employees should ideally be aware that the company has an insider threat program that might monitor digital activities and consider behavioral factors. Transparency can deter some malicious insiders and reassure honest employees that measures are in place to protect everyone. However, privacy laws may limit how much personal data (like health or financial information) an employer can legally use. Generally, insider threat programs focus on observable workplace behavior (performance issues, policy compliance, etc.) and digital footprints on corporate systems, which are within an employer's purview. Monitoring personal social media or off-work conduct is a gray area and usually avoided unless there is a specific threat scenario that warrants it.

By combining behavioral science with technical security, organizations adopt a more human-centric security approach. This means cultivating a culture where potential insider issues can be spotted and addressed constructively (often by helping the employee) before they escalate, while also having the surveillance needed to catch truly malicious actions. The next section will delve into concrete prevention strategies that organizations can implement to deter insider threats, both technological and human-centered. Figure 2 represents the Behavioral Indicators and Analysis.

Figure 2. Behavioral Indicators and Analysis

4. PREVENTION STRATEGIES FOR INSIDER THREATS

Preventing insider incidents requires a blend of technical controls, policy measures, and cultural initiatives. In this section, we outline key strategies organizations should implement to reduce the likelihood of insider threats and limit the damage if one occurs. These strategies range from strict access governance to employee training and establishing dedicated insider risk programs (Almehmadi and El-Khatib, 2017).

4.1 Enforce Least Privilege and Need-to-Know

Limiting user access is one of the most effective ways to prevent insider misuse. As discussed, the principle of *least privilege* dictates that users should have the minimum access rights and permissions necessary to perform their duties (Jeffers & Barnes, 2022). Practically, enforcing least privilege means reviewing all roles and accounts to ensure that no one has access to systems or data beyond what their current job tasks require. Organizations should implement Role-Based Access Control (RBAC) or attribute-based controls to systematically manage permissions. Regular audits and access recertification campaigns are important, for example, every quarter or upon role changes, managers confirm which data and systems each team member truly needs. Unneeded permissions are revoked.

Special attention should be given to accounts with elevated privileges (administrators, database owners, etc.). Using Privileged Access Management (PAM) tools, companies can enforce check-out of privileged credentials, require approvals or logging for certain actions, and automatically expire elevated access after use. This creates an audit trail and accountability for high-impact changes. It also means that even if a privileged user turns malicious, their ability to operate unnoticed is reduced (Alsowail and Al-Shehari, 2021).

Network segmentation and data compartmentalization supplement least privilege. Sensitive information should be partitioned so that only those with a need-to-know can even see it. For instance, HR data might be accessible only to HR staff; R&D project files accessible only to that project's team. If a marketing employee cannot even see what files exist in engineering's folders, it's much harder for them to steal engineering data. In case of an insider incident, segmentation also helps contain the fallout to a limited part of the network.

4.2 Adopt a Zero Trust Model

As introduced earlier, adopting a Zero Trust security model is a broad but impactful strategy for insider threat prevention. In a Zero Trust architecture, every access request by a user or device is treated as potentially untrusted and must be verified (English, 2025). Concretely, organizations implementing Zero Trust will require authentication and authorization not just at initial login, but at many points within the network especially when accessing sensitive resources. They will also consider context such as device health, location, time of request – to adaptively make access decisions.

For example, a company might use continuous authentication that prompts users for re-authentication when they perform high-risk actions, or if an anomaly is detected like a user's behavior suddenly deviating from normal patterns. Zero Trust goes hand-in-hand with micro-segmentation: dividing the network and systems into small segments, each protected individually. So even if an insider has access to one segment, they cannot freely move to others without going through security checks. This is crucial if an attacker compromises an insider's account they cannot "island hop" through the internal network easily.

Implementing Zero Trust for insiders might include requiring MFA for accessing any sensitive system, even if the user is on the corporate LAN. It may involve deploying host-based agents that verify a device's security posture (is it patched? running approved software?) before allowing a connection to certain servers. While Zero Trust cannot guarantee an insider won't misuse the data they legitimately can access, it does make it more likely that suspicious access patterns like an unusual cross-segment access will be blocked or at least logged and reviewed (English, 2025). This limits lateral movement and privilege escalation – two techniques insiders often use when they prepare for a larger attack.

One challenge is that a full Zero Trust rollout can be complex, potentially affecting usability. It often requires incremental implementation. However, many organizations start with critical assets: for instance, applying strict Zero Trust principles for access to production systems, finance databases, or code repositories, while less critical areas follow later. Over time, the security gains from Zero Trust (especially in detecting policy violations or unusual access attempts) can significantly strengthen insider threat defenses. Figure 3 represents the Zero Trust security model, emphasizing its four principles: verify explicitly, enforce least privilege, use micro-segmentation, and assume breach. These principles restrict unauthorized insider movement and ensure continuous verification for sensitive resource access.

Figure 3. Zero Trust Access Model

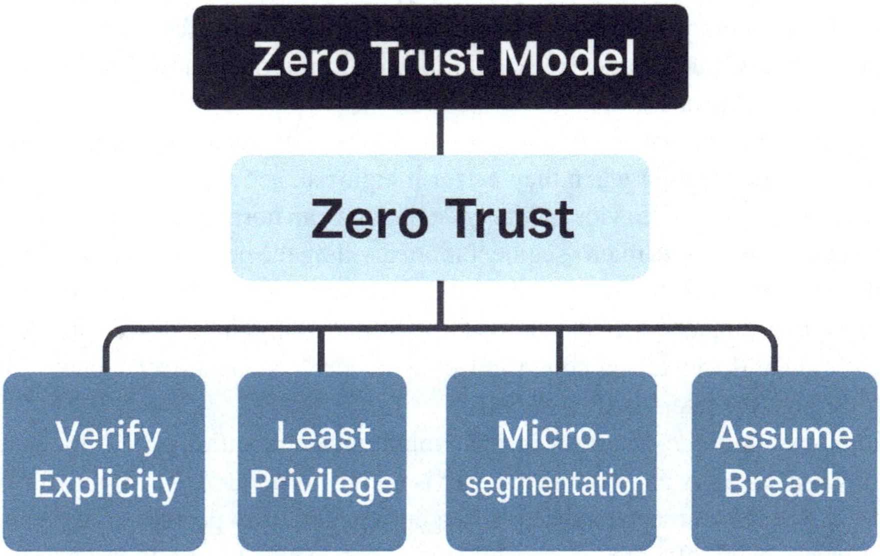

4.3 Strengthen Monitoring and Alerting on Critical Assets

Every organization should identify its most mission-critical assets and processes and then implement heightened monitoring and alerting specifically around those. As noted, focusing on the "crown jewels" ensures that if an insider goes after the organization's most valuable resources, their activity has a higher chance of being noticed in time.

For example, an organization can enable real-time alerts for certain transactions or queries in a financial system – if an employee tries to transfer an unusually large sum or export an entire customer database, an alarm should go off. On file servers containing proprietary research, the company might set up automated alerts if large volumes of files are accessed or copied by one user in a short period. Even baseline thresholds (like alerting if any user reads more than X files or gigabytes from a sensitive share in a day) can be effective.

The SOC should incorporate insider-specific scenarios into its SIEM content and playbooks. As mentioned, a correlation rule might combine multiple benign events into a suspicious pattern. For instance: *User accesses system outside business hours + user accesses a sensitive HR folder they don't normally use + user disables an endpoint monitoring agent = high probability insider threat.* Another scenario: if an employee who recently had a disciplinary action or pay cut (information from HR) suddenly begins downloading source code repositories, that context elevates the severity. Integrating HR data or other context (where privacy laws allow) with technical monitoring can greatly improve accuracy in flagging true insider risks.

Beyond automated alerts, organizations should establish a clear process for analysts to follow up on these insider-related alerts. This can include an immediate Tier 1 review (to filter out false positives), followed by discreet investigation by an insider risk team if needed. Quick containment actions might be defined in advance: for example, if an alert is severe (say, an employee mass-downloading data and sending it out), security might temporarily suspend the account or network access while a senior investigator looks into the activity. Having pre-defined response procedures will save precious time during an actual insider incident.

4.4 Establish an Insider Threat Program and Response Plan

A comprehensive approach to insider threat prevention is to formalize an Insider Threat Program (ITP). An ITP is a cross-functional initiative that brings together policy, people, and technology to detect, prevent, and respond to insider threats (CISA, 2020). Key elements of an ITP include: clearly defined roles and responsibilities (e.g., an Insider Threat Program Manager, analysts, HR liaisons, legal advisors), policies and procedures for insider threat monitoring and investigation, training and awareness for the workforce, and escalation/response protocols when a threat is identified.

For example, an ITP might have procedures on how to handle an employee who is under investigation for potential insider activity: who is notified (on a need-to-know basis, often involving legal and HR), what monitoring is put in place, and at what point law enforcement might be contacted. It may also define thresholds for different response actions (e.g., when to simply monitor more closely vs. when to interview the person vs. when to revoke access immediately). Having a plan ensures that when an incident arises, the organization reacts consistently, legally, and effectively.

Training is a big component – not just for the insider threat analysts, but for the general workforce. Employees should receive training on the organization's expectations (e.g., what behaviors and security practices are acceptable), how they might be monitored (in a transparent and legal way), and how they can report concerns. A culture of security mindfulness can itself deter insiders: if employees know their peers might notice and report unusual behavior, the malicious insider may think twice. On the flip side, awareness training can reduce unintentional insider threats by educating staff on best practices (like not clicking phishing links, proper data handling, etc.) (Smith, 2025).

4.5 Implement Forensic Readiness for Incident Investigation

Even with strong preventive measures, insider incidents may still occur – which is why forensic readiness is crucial. Forensic readiness refers to preparing an organization's systems and processes such that if an insider incident happens, sufficient evidence is collected and preserved to support an effective investigation and, if needed, legal action. This involves enabling detailed logging on critical systems, maintaining secure archives of user activity (network logs, file access records, email archives, etc.), and having tools and procedures in place to capture forensic data (such as disk images or memory snapshots from a suspect's workstation) promptly when an alert or incident is identified. The goal is that malicious actions leave a reliable trail that investigators can follow.

Research has proposed formal frameworks for achieving forensic readiness against insider attacks. For instance, Daubner et al. (2023) introduce a forensic-ready risk management approach (FR-ISSRM) to derive specific organizational requirements that ensure any insider attack will produce meaningful evidence. This framework guides organizations in identifying what logs and audit trails should be generated, how to protect and assess them, and how to integrate forensic considerations into system design. By implementing such requirements, an organization can more reliably uncover the culprit, root cause, and scope of damage if an insider incident occurs. In essence, the controls of forensic-ready systems e.g., tamper-evident logging, synchronized time-stamping, data retention policies don't necessarily prevent an attack, but they ensure a reliable post-incident investigation and thus contribute to overall security by enabling appropriate response and lessons learned.

In practice, being forensically ready means security teams have playbooks and tools on standby for insider events. For example, an incident response team might have a procedure to immediately collect logs from an employee's machine and revoke their access if certain high-risk alerts trigger. They might use endpoint detection and response (EDR) agents that can be switched into a forensic mode to record keystrokes or capture copies of files an insider touches when suspicious activity is detected. All these measures help provide a clear picture of what occurred. This not only aids internal analysis but can also serve as credible evidence if the organization needs to involve law enforcement or pursue legal action against the insider.

Forensic readiness can extend to cloud environments as well, where a lot of corporate data now resides. Cloud services should be configured to produce detailed audit logs (for example, records of who accessed what data in cloud storage, or admin actions taken in a SaaS application). Notably, NIST's Cloud Computing Forensic Reference Architecture emphasizes designing cloud systems with forensic data collection and retention in mind to support investigations (NIST, 2024). By planning for forensic needs in advance, an organization increases its resilience: even if an insider tries to cover their tracks, a forensic-ready system will have multiple layers of evidence (network logs, system logs, backups, etc.) that make it difficult to truly hide malicious actions.

Embracing forensic readiness also enhances threat intelligence. Over time, the collection of forensic data from various incidents (even minor policy violations) can be analyzed to identify patterns or early indicators of insider activity. This builds an internal knowledge base – essentially, an intelligence repository of TTPs (tactics, techniques, procedures) used by insiders – which can inform future detection rules and training. Some organizations share anonymized insights from such analyses with industry peers or information-sharing groups, contributing to a broader understanding of insider threats. In this way, forensic data doesn't just serve reactive investigations; it feeds into a proactive, user-centric threat intelligence cycle.

By implementing the above strategies – least privilege, Zero Trust, focused monitoring, a formal insider risk program, and forensic readiness – organizations create multiple layers of defense against insider threats. No single measure is a silver bullet; it is the defense-in-depth combination of technical controls, vigilant culture, and responsive processes that offers the best protection. These measures also align the organization with a cyber forensic framework mindset, ensuring that security is both preventive and investigative in nature. In the next section, we consider the legal and ethical aspects that overlay these practices, ensuring that insider threat mitigation efforts stay within legal bounds and maintain employee trust. The key strategies for insider threat prevention, along with their benefits and supporting tools, are summarized in Table 1.

Table 1. Summary of Insider Threat Prevention Strategies

Strategy	Key Description	Benefits	Example Tools/Practices
Least Privilege	Limit access strictly to what users need	Reduces attack surface, minimizes damage	Role-Based Access Control, Privileged Access Management, access recertification
Zero Trust	"Never trust, always verify" – continuous checks	Stops lateral insider movement	MFA, micro-segmentation
Data Monitoring	Watch critical assets and data flows	Detects abnormal downloads, prevents leaks	Data Loss Prevention, Security Information and Event Management alerts
Insider Threat Program	Cross-functional oversight	Formal process for monitoring & response	Insider Threat Program teams, HR–Security collaboration
Forensic Readiness	Systems prepped for evidence collection	Enables investigation and accountability	Tamper-proof logs, Forensic-Ready Information Security Risk Management

5. LEGAL AND ETHICAL CONSIDERATIONS

Insider threat programs must balance security objectives with legal requirements and ethical standards, particularly regarding employee privacy and workplace rights. In this section, we outline the key legal constraints and ethical guidelines that organizations should consider when implementing insider threat detection and prevention measures.

5.1 Employee Privacy Laws

Employers generally have broad authority to monitor activities on company-owned systems and networks, but this authority is not unlimited. In the United States, the primary federal law addressing electronic monitoring is the Electronic Communications Privacy Act (ECPA) of 1986. The ECPA allows employers to monitor oral and electronic communications if there is a legitimate business purpose or if the employee has given consent (Freedman, 2024). This means companies can lawfully review emails, internet usage, keystrokes, etc., as long as they have a policy informing employees that such monitoring occurs (or they obtain consent via login banners or employee agreements). Additionally, some activities like video surveillance have specific restrictions: for instance, the National Labor Relations Act (NLRA) prohibits surveillance of employees' union organizing activities, and employers with unionized workforces often must negotiate before implementing certain monitoring (Jeffers & Barnes, 2022).

State laws also come into play. A few states, such as Connecticut, Delaware, and New York, require employers to provide notice to employees if they monitor electronic communications or use electronic tracking (Jeffers & Barnes, 2022). Connecticut and Delaware mandate written notice to employees, and New York (as of 2022) requires that new hires be informed if their phone, email, or internet usage will be monitored. In states with strong privacy provisions like California's constitutionally guaranteed right to privacy, overly intrusive monitoring could expose the employer to invasion of privacy claims if it's deemed not work-related or if it collects highly personal information not relevant to business.

In the European Union and other jurisdictions with GDPR-like privacy laws, the bar is higher. Employers must have a legal basis for monitoring (such as legitimate interest) and often must conduct a privacy impact assessment. Employees have rights to be informed about what data is collected and how it's used. Blanket, covert monitoring is generally disallowed in the EU; monitoring must be necessary, proportionate, and transparent (Jeffers & Barnes, 2022). For example, an EU-based company implementing insider threat monitoring must typically notify employees of the nature and purpose of monitoring and ensure that data collected is limited to what's needed for security.

5.2 Ethical Boundaries of Monitoring

Beyond legal requirements, companies should consider the ethical dimension. Excessive surveillance can erode trust, damage morale, and create a culture of fear. It's important to clearly communicate to employees *why* monitoring is in place – namely, to protect the company and its stakeholders against serious threats – and to reassure them that monitoring is focused on security, not on punishing minor non-work activities. Employers should define what is *not* monitored (for instance, personal devices not on the corporate network, or the content of personal communications if such are inadvertently captured). Many organizations allow some personal use of work systems and make clear in policy that while they have rights to monitor, they exercise discretion.

Ethically, insider threat programs should apply the minimization principle: collect the least amount of information needed to achieve security objectives, and limit access to that information to a small, vetted team. They should also ensure due process for employees under investigation – e.g., giving the employee a chance to explain unusual behavior (perhaps it was authorized after all or had an innocent explanation) before punitive action is taken, unless the threat is imminent.

Another ethical aspect is avoiding bias. If monitoring or analytics algorithms are used, they should be tested to ensure they don't unfairly target certain groups of employees. For example, an algorithm that flags "excessive social media use" might inadvertently target roles like marketing that use social media for work, or junior staff more than senior (if seniors are exempt from certain monitoring). Insider threat teams must use caution and human judgment to interpret alerts in context. They should also be mindful of cultural differences that might influence behavior (what seems "withdrawn" in one culture might be normal in another, for instance).

Finally, transparency and employee trust are crucial. Some organizations include employees in developing policies (through focus groups or surveys) to get buy-in on insider threat measures. Others periodically report to employees in aggregate (e.g., "X number of potential insider incidents were detected and addressed this year, with Y being unintentional mistakes caught by our controls") to demonstrate that the program is active but fair. By handling insider threat defense in a legal and ethical manner, companies can protect themselves while maintaining a positive workplace environment.

6. CONCLUSION

Insider threats present a complex challenge at the intersection of human behavior and cybersecurity. This chapter explored how a user-centric, human-focused approach, backed by modern technology and forensic-ready frameworks, can significantly improve an organization's ability to detect and prevent insider incidents. We began by categorizing types of insider threats and examining real cases that illustrate common patterns. We then discussed advanced detection mechanisms like UEBA and machine learning, which establish baselines of normal user behavior and flag anomalies, moving security toward proactive monitoring. Equally important, we delved into the human factors: the behavioral red flags, motivations, and organizational issues that often precede insider acts. Addressing these factors requires not only monitoring but also positive engagement, training, and a culture of trust and accountability.

We outlined prevention strategies grounded in both technical controls like least privilege, Zero Trust, DLP, critical asset monitoring and programmatic measures like insider threat programs, training, and response plans. A key addition is the concept of cyber forensic readiness, ensuring that systems are prepared to collect and preserve evidence, which aligns with building a cyber forensic framework for insider threat management. By integrating this with threat intelligence analysis, organizations create a holistic defense. In essence, effective insider threat mitigation comes from marrying the human-centric intelligence, understanding user behavior and sentiment with rigorous cybersecurity frameworks that can investigate and learn from incidents. This dual approach reflects the books theme of a "Cyber Forensic Framework for User-Centric Human Threat Intelligence Analysis," ensuring that organizations not only guard against insider threats, but also continuously analyze and adapt based on insights into human behavior and emerging threat patterns.

REFERENCES

Al-Shehari, T., Rosaci, D., Al-Razgan, M., Alfakih, T., Kadrie, M., Afzal, H., & Nawaz, R. (2024). Enhancing Insider Threat Detection in Imbalanced Cybersecurity Settings Using the Density21-Based Local Outlier Factor Algorithm. *IEEE Access : Practical Innovations, Open Solutions, 12*, 34820–34834. DOI: 10.1109/ACCESS.2024.3373694

Almehmadi, A., & El-Khatib, K. (2017). On the Possibility of Insider Threat Prevention Using Intent-Based Access Control (IBAC). *IEEE Systems Journal, 11*(2), 373–384. DOI: 10.1109/JSYST.2015.2424677

Alsowail, R. A., & Al-Shehari, T. (2021). A Multi-Tiered Framework for Insider Threat Prevention. *Electronics (Basel), 10*(9), 1005. DOI: 10.3390/electronics10091005

Alzaabi, F. R., & Mehmood, A. (2024). A Review of Recent Advances, Challenges, and Opportunities in Malicious Insider Threat Detection Using Machine Learning Methods. *IEEE Access : Practical Innovations, Open Solutions, 12*, 30907–30927. DOI: 10.1109/ACCESS.2024.3369906

Arora, S., Gupta, M., Rai, M., Mishra, R., & Tripathi, P. (2025). Early detection of foot ulcers in diabetic patients using machine learning. In Rai, M., Pandey, J. K., & Saxena, A. K. (Eds.), *Machine Learning- Based Decision Support Systems for Diabetic Foot Ulcer Care* (pp. 153–172). Nova Science Publishers, Inc.

Assessing insider threats: CISA (no date) Cybersecurity and Infrastructure Security Agency CISA. Available at: https://www.cisa.gov/topics/physical-security/insider-threat-mitigation/assessing-insider-threats. (Accessed August 2025).

Cybersecurity and Infrastructure Security Agency (CISA). (2020). *Insider threat mitigation guide*. U.S. Department of Homeland Security. https://www.cisa.gov/sites/default/files/publications/Insider%20Threat%20Mitigation%20Guide_Final_508.pdf. (Accessed August 2025).

Daubner, L., Macak, M., Matulevičius, R., Buhnova, B., Maksović, S., & Pitner, T. (2023). Addressing insider attacks via forensic-ready risk management. *Journal of Information Security and Applications, 73*, 103433. DOI: 10.1016/j.jisa.2023.103433

English, M. (2025). Government frameworks and regulations for insider threats. *Teramind Blog*. https://www.teramind.co/blog/government-frameworks-and-regulations-for-insider-threats/ (Accessed August 2025).

Freedman, M. (2024). Spying on your employees? Better understand the law first. *Business News Daily.* https://www.businessnewsdaily.com/6685-employee-monitoring-privacy.html. (Accessed August 2025).

Guanyun, F., Cai, F., Jianqiang, L., & Lansheng, H. (2023). Insider threat detection based on operational attention and data augmentation. *Chin. J. Netw. Inf. Secur*, *9*(3).

Inayat, U., Farzan, M., Mahmood, S., Zia, M. F., Hussain, S., & Pallonetto, F. (2024). Insider threat mitigation: Systematic literature review. *Ain Shams Engineering Journal*, *15*(12), 103068. DOI: 10.1016/j.asej.2024.103068

Jeffers, A. V., & Barnes, C. D. (2022). Every move you make: When monitoring employees gives rise to legal risks. *Skadden, Arps, Slate, Meagher & Flom LLP.* https://www.skadden.com/insights/publications/2022/09/quarterly-insights/every-move-you-make. (Accessed August 2025).

Kumar, N., Tripathi, P., Nanda, R. P., Tiwari, S., & Sharma, S. (2024). Machine Learning for Smart Health Services in the Framework of Industry 5.0. In Khan, M., Khan, R., Praveen, P., Verma, A. R., & Panda, M. K. (Eds.), *Infrastructure Possibilities and Human-Centered Approaches With Industry 5.0* (pp. 215–230). IGI Global. DOI: 10.4018/979-8-3693-0782-3.ch013

Le, D. C., Zincir-Heywood, N., & Heywood, M. I. (2020). Analyzing data granularity levels for insider threat detection using machine learning. *IEEE Transactions on Network and Service Management*, *17*(1), 30–44. DOI: 10.1109/TNSM.2020.2967721

Mishra, R., Tripathi, P., Panda, B., Gupta, M., & Arora, S. (2025). Advanced machine learning algorithms for personalized diabetic foot ulcer. In Rai, M., Pandey, J. K., & Saxena, A. K. (Eds.), *Machine Learning- Based Decision Support Systems for Diabetic Foot Ulcer Care* (pp. 95–124). Nova Science Publisher, Inc.

Nasir, R., Afzal, M., Latif, R., & Iqbal, W. (2021). Behavioral based insider threat detection using deep learning. *IEEE Access : Practical Innovations, Open Solutions*, *9*, 143266–143274. DOI: 10.1109/ACCESS.2021.3118297

National Institute of Standards and Technology (NIST). (2024). *NIST cloud computing forensic reference architecture (Special Publication 800-201).* . (Accesed August 2025).DOI: 10.6028/NIST.SP.800-201

Pennada, S. S. P., Nayak, S. K., & Krishna, M. V. (2025). Hybrid Machine Learning for Enhanced Insider Threat Detection Using Generative Latent Features. *International Journal of Engineering Trends and Technology*, *73*(6), 102–113. DOI: 10.14445/22315381/IJETT-V73I6P110

Pennada, S. S. P., Nayak, S. K., & M, V. K. (2025). Insider Threat Detection Using Behavioural Analysis through Machine Learning and Deep Learning Techniques. *International Research Journal of Multidisciplinary Technovation*, *7*(2), 74–86. DOI: 10.54392/irjmt2527

Sarhan, B. B., & Altwaijry, N. (2023). Insider Threat Detection Using Machine Learning Approach. *Applied Sciences (Basel, Switzerland)*, *13*(1), 259. DOI: 10.3390/app13010259

Singh, M., Mehtre, B. M., Sangeetha, S., & Govindaraju, V. (2023). User behaviour based insider threat detection using a hybrid learning approach. *Journal of Ambient Intelligence and Humanized Computing*, *14*(4), 4573–4593. DOI: 10.1007/s12652-023-04581-1

Smith, G. (2025). Insider threat statistics: (2025's most shocking trends). *StationX*. https://www.stationx.net/insider-threat-statistics/

Tao, X., Liu, J., Yu, Y., Zhang, H., & Huang, Y. (2025). An insider threat detection method based on improved Test-Time Training model. *High-Confidence Computing*, *5*(1), 100283. DOI: 10.1016/j.hcc.2024.100283

Tian, T., Zhang, C., Jiang, B., Feng, H., & Lu, Z. (2025). Insider threat detection for specific threat scenarios. *Cybersecurity*, *8*(1), 17. DOI: 10.1186/s42400-024-00321-w

Tripathi, P., Kumar, N., Paroha, K. K., Rai, M., & Panda, M. K. (2024). Applications of Deep Learning in Healthcare in the Framework of Industry 5.0. In Khan, M., Khan, R., Praveen, P., Verma, A. R., & Panda, M. K. (Eds.), *Infrastructure Possibilities and Human-Centered Approaches With Industry 5.0* (pp. 69–85). IGI Global. DOI: 10.4018/979-8-3693-0782-3.ch005

Tripathi, P., Kumar, N., Rai, M., & Khan, A. (2022). *Applications of Deep Learning in Agriculture in Artificial Intelligence Applications in Agriculture and Food Quality Improvement*. IGI Global., DOI: 10.4018/978-1-6684-5141-0.ch002

Wei, Z., Rauf, U., & Mohsen, F. (2024). E-Watcher: Insider threat monitoring and detection for enhanced security. *Annales des Télécommunications*, *79*(11-12), 819–831. DOI: 10.1007/s12243-024-01023-7

Ye, X., Cui, H., Luo, F., Wang, J., Xiong, X., Zhang, W., Yu, J., & Zhao, W. (2025). Daily insider threat detection with hybrid TCN transformer architecture. *Scientific Reports*, *15*(1), 28590. DOI: 10.1038/s41598-025-12063-x PMID: 40764628

Ye, X., Luo, F., Cui, H., Wang, J., Xiong, X., Zhang, W., Yu, J., & Zhao, W. (2025). Research on insider threat detection based on personalized federated learning and behavior log analysis. *Scientific Reports*, *15*(1), 19214. DOI: 10.1038/s41598-025-04029-w PMID: 40451866

Yuan, S., & Wu, X. (2021). Deep learning for insider threat detection: Review, challenges and opportunities. *Computers & Security*, *104*, 102221. DOI: 10.1016/j.cose.2021.102221

Chapter 15
Cryptocurrency and Blockchain Forensics Tracing Digital Transactions

Munir Ahmad
https://orcid.org/0000-0003-4836-6151
Survey of Pakistan, Pakistan

Reza E. Rabbi Shawon
https://orcid.org/0009-0005-8217-8615
Gannon University, USA

Md Sakibul Hasan
St. Francis College, USA

Kanchon Kumar Bishnu
https://orcid.org/0009-0007-1811-3002
California State University, Los Angeles, USA

ABSTRACT

This chapter explores the evolution and significance of blockchain forensics within the broader context of cryptocurrency adoption. It examines the technical foundations of blockchain, including pseudonymity, immutability, and transparency, and explains how investigative methods such as transaction mapping, clustering, and deanonymization are used to trace illicit activity. Key forensic tools and platforms, both commercial and open-source, are reviewed alongside the growing role of artificial intelligence. The discussion highlights critical challenges ranging from privacy coins and mixers to cross-border jurisdictional barriers and ethical dilemmas, and

DOI: 10.4018/979-8-3373-4898-8.ch015

underscores the limitations of current forensic methods. The chapter also analyzes legal and regulatory frameworks, global cooperation, and emerging technologies like quantum computing, emphasizing the need to balance forensic capability with privacy protection and financial innovation.

1. INTRODUCTION

Cryptocurrencies have evolved from niche digital assets into a worldwide financial phenomenon in the last decade (Hossain, 2021; Koshelev, 2022). Bitcoin, Ethereum, and an increasing number of alternative tokens are now being used in mainstream commerce, investment, and cross-border payments. Their decentralized nature, built on blockchain technology, has unmatched benefits in terms of transparency, efficiency, and security (Alzoubi, 2024; Kukman & Gričar, 2025a). However, it has also created a parallel ecosystem of illicit activity. Since cryptocurrencies are pseudonymous and can be easily transferred around the world, they have become a preferred tool for cybercriminals, money launderers, ransomware operators, and darknet marketplaces. This duality - its legitimate financial innovation, and potential as an enabler of crime - underscores the pressing need for effective forensic techniques.

In the classical financial systems, centralised accounting, banking compliance, and regulatory auditing are a few of the mechanisms that control and deter fraudulent activity. On the other hand, decentralized financial ecosystems don't have these centralized enforcement mechanisms. While the immutability and transparency of blockchain ledgers provide useful data, the challenge is in tying pseudonymous transactions to real-world identities and reconstructing complex transaction flows involving multiple intermediaries, obfuscation techniques, and cross-chain interactions (Abdennadher et al., 2022; Alamsyah et al., 2024; Ozili, 2022). This has made forensic investigation a pillar of digital financial systems' trust and integrity.

Blockchain forensics has thus become a critical field at the intersection between cybersecurity, finance, and law enforcement. Its main goals are to trace, attribute, and analyze cryptocurrency transactions for financial crime investigation, regulatory compliance, and judicial processes. In addition to crime prevention, blockchain forensics also plays a wider role in improving market transparency, safeguarding investors, and helping build secure digital economies (Agarwal et al., 2024; Atlam et al., 2024; Dudani et al., 2023; Igonor et al., 2025). As governments and regulators flounder with the delicate balance between innovation and security, forensic capabilities offer a much-needed base for both enforcement and policymaking.

The goal of this chapter is to offer a thorough discussion of cryptocurrency and blockchain forensics. It draws attention to the development of cryptocurrencies as both legitimate instruments and vehicles for abuse, looks at the critical importance of tracing digital transactions in decentralized systems, and maps out the breadth of forensic methods, tools, and legal considerations that are shaping the field. By combining technical detail and practical applications, the discussion aims to provide investigators, regulators, and cybersecurity professionals with insights into the opportunities and challenges involved in tracing digital transactions in a rapidly changing financial landscape.

2. BASICS OF BLOCK CHAIN FORENSICS

Cryptocurrencies are complex forensic targets, and block chain forensics is based upon understanding the underlying technical principles that make them powerful as well as complex financial tools and complex detective targets. Unlike traditional financial systems, where transaction history is centralised and controlled by a central authority, block chain networks are characterized by distributed ledgers and cryptographic validation that secures every transaction. These fundamental properties of blockchain - pseudonymity, immutability, and transparency - both oppress and challenge forensic investigators. Drawing from these properties, blockchain forensics employs specialized concepts and methods that trace digital transaction patterns, identify the entities behind cryptographic addresses, and investigate patterns of financial behaviors across decentralized ecosystems.

2.1 Technical Underpinnings of Blockchain Forensics

At the core of blockchain technology are three key characteristics (pseudonymity, immutability, and transparency) that collectively offer both opportunities and challenges for forensics. This is the basis for how investigators analyze and interpret digital transaction data to identify patterns, attribute activity, and construct legally admissible evidence.

2.1.1 Pseudonymity

Most blockchain networks, such as Bitcoin and Ethereum, are not directly tied to personal names, bank accounts, or government-issued identifiers. Instead, each transaction connects to cryptographic wallet addresses, which are long alphanumeric strings. It allows users to create and manage multiple addresses without disclosing their true identities, thus allowing them to maintain a hidden financial profile. Often mistaken for actual anonymity, this feature would be better called pseudonymity:

identities are not immediately apparent, but are not wholly unrecoverable (De Mulder & De Meester, 2025; Jamwal et al., 2024; Johar et al., 2021).

Forensic analysts leverage this subtlety by using techniques like address clustering, which identifies patterns in input and output traffic that allow analysts to identify which addresses are likely owned by the same actor. It also compares blockchain data with information outside the blockchain, for example, Know Your Customer (KYC) data held at cryptocurrency exchange sites, darknet market logs, or information generated by law enforcement investigations. By linking known behaviors to pseudonymous addresses and correlating that with other external data sources, investigators can often de-anonymize suspicious actors and identify their larger financial networks.

2.1.2 Immutability

One of the strong attributes of blockchain is that it is immutable. Upon validation by the network and the inclusion of the transaction in the blockchain, it is immovably part of the distributed ledger. Unlike traditional financial databases, which can be modified, deleted, or hidden by malevolent insiders, blockchain entries are cryptographically protected and permanently recorded. This means that forensic investigators have access to an immutable record of financial activity that goes all the way back to the very first block in a chain's history (Curry, 2025; Tariq et al., 2019).

Immutability adds a dramatically increased evidentiary value to blockchain data for legal purposes. Whether it's money laundering, fraud, or ransomware payments, investigators and prosecutors can use the blockchain's transaction history to prove consistent and provable patterns of activity. Even if the criminals try to cover their tracks by utilizing obfuscation tools such as mixers or privacy coins, the original immutable trail still exists to be analyzed retrospectively. Thus, immutability makes blockchain ledgers a useful long-term resource for forensic investigation and law enforcement cases.

2.1.3 Transparency

Along with pseudonymous and immutable, complementing blockchain is its high level of transparency. On public networks like Bitcoin, Ethereum, and Litecoin, all transactions are visible to anyone interested in watching the ledger. This never-before-seen level of financial transparency enables forensic investigators to track and analyze activity across entire ecosystems in real time. Additionally, even if perpetrators try to hide their transactions from public view by splitting or bouncing money to several different addresses, illicit actors transferring ransomware proceeds, darknet market proceeds, or stolen tokens cannot completely obscure their transactions (Almadadha, 2024; Cui et al., 2024; Kukman & Gričar, 2025b; Tariq et al., 2019).

However, transparency also creates some challenges. Blockchain data - millions of transactions per day - is so large and complex that human investigators can't find out what's going on without the aid of advanced computation. To identify potential fraud, sophisticated graph analytics, machine learning models, and visualization tools are routinely used to mine large data sets for anomalies and to reconstruct chains of transactions. This then presents both a challenge and an opportunity - open data provides criminals with a sense of anonymity, but it also gives forensic scientists the ability to identify, track, and ultimately attribute illicit funds flows on a scale that is impossible in the current banking system.

3. CORE FORENSIC CONCEPTS

Blockchain forensics utilizes a series of basic investigative principles to take raw blockchain data and convert it into actionable intelligence, allowing the sources and behavior of cryptocurrency actors to be examined and investigated. These ideas are at the core of the detection of illicit activity, the attribution of illicit activity to real-world entities, and evidence-driven decision-making for law enforcement and regulatory activities.

3.1 Transaction Tracking

Blockchain forensics is built around the concept of transaction tracking. It involves tracing the movement of funds through the blockchain to piece together chains of transactions and identify suspicious activities. Specialized tools are used to visualize value flows, identify layering transactions typically linked to money laundering activity, and identify cyclical transfers in which funds are shuffled back and forth between a group of addresses in an effort to mask the source of funds. In the case of ransomware attacks, the transaction history often shows unexpected bursts of wallet activity, followed by splinters to multiple smaller transactions intended to make detection more difficult (Akram et al., 2024; Lin et al., 2022). This approach also delivers more macro views of financial ecosystems. For example, tracing a Bitcoin ransom payment may lead investigators to identify links to darknet marketplaces, gambling platforms, or exchange wallets where the funds were ultimately exchanged for fiat currency. Such connections turn disconnected dots into a cohesive financial network with important choke points for intervention, such as unregulated exchanges or money mixers.

3.2 Address Identification

Each blockchain transaction is related to one or more wallet addresses. Research that can identify and cluster these addresses is important to create profiles of actors in the network. One example of clustering techniques used for forensics is the multi-input heuristic, which states that if multiple addresses are included as inputs in a single transaction, it indicates that they are controlled by the same person/organization. Over time, analysts can build up vast collections of addresses that are linked as groups, representing larger entities instead of individual wallets (Chaudhari et al., 2021; Han et al., 2022; Javed et al., 2021). Off-chain intelligence is added to make address identification more robust. Many cryptocurrency exchanges and wallet providers are now required to comply with Know Your Customer (KYC) and Anti-Money Laundering (AML) procedures, which tie cryptographic addresses to real-world identities. Leaked data, darknet forums, or seized criminal devices may also contain important evidence linking addresses to specific users. In tandem with clustering heuristics, external intelligence is used to convert the pseudonymous data on the blockchain to an identifiable identity, thus bridging the gap between on-chain activity and real-world actors.

3.3 Metadata Analysis

Apart from the movement of funds, blockchain transactions carry metadata that conveys useful contextual information. This includes timestamps, transaction sizes, network fees, and sometimes even embedded notes or messages. Metadata analysis not only tells investigators what happened, but when and how it happened. For example, unusually high transaction fees may denote urgency, such as criminals seeking to accelerate transfers prior to detection or asset seizure. Similarly, using transaction timestamps, correlations between on-chain activity and off-chain events (such as known ransomware attacks, darknet market operations, or major hacks) can be discerned. Let's consider the example of metadata, which in some instances can convey essential, but subtle, information about user behavior. While the transfer of money between accounts in small, regular installments may be indicative of structuring to evade detection limits, the sudden transfer of irregular amounts could be indicative of fraud or the movement of illicit funds. So, metadata becomes a layer of behavioral intelligence on top of the raw transactional data that enriches the forensic story.

Together, transaction identification, address identification, and metadata analysis are the main toolkit of blockchain forensic investigation. These tools and methods enable investigators to reconstruct transaction histories, attribute activity to identifiable actors, and contextualize blockchain events within broader crime or compliance frameworks.

3.4 Transparent vs. Privacy-Focused Cryptocurrencies

Not all cryptocurrencies are the same in terms of forensic visibility. There is an important difference between blockchain technologies that are transparent and can be fully monitored and analyzed, versus privacy-focused cryptocurrencies that purposely keep transaction details hidden. This divide is important to understand the strengths and weaknesses of forensic investigations.

3.5 Open-Source Cryptocurrencies (e.g., Bitcoin, Ethereum)

Public blockchains, like Bitcoin and Ethereum, have fully transparent ledgers, where they can see every transaction. They can be easily analyzed for forensic purposes because of their visibility. For example, investigators can view entire transaction histories, run graph analysis to uncover patterns, and import external datasets to attribute flows of funds to specific entities. In fact, Bitcoin, the most widely used cryptocurrency today, is also the most widely investigated because of its transparency and traceability, despite its wide usage in illicit activities (Aggarwal & Kumar, 2021; Garriga et al., 2021). Bitcoin forensics operations have managed to match ransomware payments, darknet market purchases, and large-scale fraud schemes to known individuals or organizations. While Ethereum layer-2 smart contracts bring new challenges with them, they also present new opportunities for forensic analysis of decentralized applications (dApps), token transfers, and non-fungible token (NFT) markets. Transparent cryptocurrencies, therefore, offer a rich breeding ground for not only criminal misuse but, to an equal extent, effective investigative counter-measures.

3.6 Privacy-Focused Cryptocurrencies (e.g., Monero, Zcash)

In contrast, privacy-oriented cryptocurrencies are explicitly designed to be resistant to forensic investigation. Monero uses advanced privacy techniques such as ring signatures (which mix the sender's signature with decoys), stealth addresses (which create one-time addresses for each transaction), and confidential transactions (which hide transaction amounts). These mechanisms work together to make Monero transactions virtually invisible to traditional forensic tools (Zhang, 2023). Likewise, Zcash has two kinds of transactions-transparent and shielded. Transparent transactions work like Bitcoin, but shielded transactions use zk-SNARKs (Zero-Knowledge proofs) to obscure the sender, recipient, and amount, while still enabling cryptographic validation just like Bitcoin. This bi-directional architecture affords users freedom but presents significant problems for investigators.

Forensic analysis of privacy coins often has to be done in an indirect way. These include watching exchange traffic, where users eventually exchange privacy coins for fiat or more easily traceable cryptocurrencies; statistical methods for analyzing transaction patterns; or taking advantage of vulnerabilities in how privacy protocols are actually implemented. However, privacy coins are still one of the biggest factors preventing successful blockchain forensics. To consolidate the discussion on blockchain's technical foundations, forensic concepts, and the comparative challenges posed by different cryptocurrency designs, Table 1 provides a structured overview. It highlights how key blockchain characteristics shape forensic opportunities, the investigative techniques available to analysts, and the degree of visibility offered by transparent versus privacy-focused cryptocurrencies. This comparative synthesis allows readers to grasp not only the unique forensic advantages of blockchain but also the obstacles that investigators must overcome in practice.

Table 1. Core Elements of Blockchain Forensics

Dimension	Description	Forensic Opportunities	Forensic Challenges	Examples
Pseudonymity	Transactions linked to cryptographic addresses, not real identities.	Address clustering, KYC data from exchanges, cross-referencing with darknet/intelligence sources.	Users can create unlimited addresses; it requires off-chain data for attribution.	Bitcoin, Ethereum
Immutability	Transactions are permanently recorded and tamper-proof.	Reliable evidence trail, retrospective analysis, strong legal admissibility.	Criminals may use mixers or privacy tools, but traces remain.	All blockchains
Transparency	Public visibility of all transactions on open ledgers.	Large-scale monitoring, graph analytics, anomaly detection, and real-time tracing.	Overwhelming data volume requires advanced computational tools.	Bitcoin, Ethereum, Litecoin
Transaction Tracking	Following the flow of funds across multiple addresses.	Reveals layering, structuring, laundering patterns, and ransomware flows.	Complex chains and fragmentation complicate reconstruction.	Ransomware BTC flows
Address Identification	Grouping and profiling of wallet addresses.	Clustering heuristics, linkages with KYC/AML records, and external leaks.	Requires corroborating off-chain intelligence.	Multi-input heuristic in BTC
Metadata Analysis	Examining timestamps, fees, and behavioral markers.	Correlates on-chain with off-chain events; detects urgency, structuring.	Subtle signals may be ambiguous; they require contextual interpretation.	High-fee urgent transfers

continued on following page

Table 1. Continued

Dimension	Description	Forensic Opportunities	Forensic Challenges	Examples
Transparent Cryptocurrencies	Fully open ledgers, visible to all.	Comprehensive forensic visibility; historical reconstruction.	Still possible obfuscation via mixers, high volume of data.	Bitcoin, Ethereum
Privacy-Focused Cryptocurrencies	Employ cryptographic techniques to obscure the sender, receiver, or amount.	Indirect tracing via exchanges, statistical analyses, or protocol flaws.	Strong resistance to forensic tracing; shielded or obfuscated data.	Monero, Zcash

4. TOOLS AND METHODS OF TRACKING TRANSACTIONS

Blockchain forensics relies on a blend of analytical techniques, dedicated platforms, and cutting-edge technologies to uncover the intricate pseudonymous ecosystems supporting cryptocurrency ecosystems. While public blockchains provide an abundance of unstructured data, the real trick is to translate the massive ledgers into insights that are actionable, that can be linked to individuals or groups in the real world and associated with financial flows of illicit origin, as well as facilitating enforcement or compliance activity. This section discusses the main approaches and tools employed by investigators, as well as the increasing role of artificial intelligence in improving blockchain forensic analysis.

4.1 Analytical Methods

Blockchain forensics involves the use of sophisticated analytical techniques that turn vast amounts of transactional data into actionable insights. These techniques allow investigators to discover hidden relationships, identify patterns of illicit activity, and ultimately link pseudonymous activity to real-world entities. Three of the most commonly used analytical techniques are transaction graph mapping, address clustering with heuristics, and deanonymization techniques.

4.1.1 Transaction Graph Mapping

Transaction graph mapping is one of the fundamental techniques for blockchain forensics (Wu et al., 2023). This approach represents cryptocurrency transactions as a network of nodes (wallet addresses) and edges (transactions), converting raw data into a structure that can be analyzed systematically. Researchers are able to follow the trail of money through various wallets, exchanges, and services, looking for points of convergence and dispersion within the network.

Graph mapping is especially effective in uncovering suspicious behaviors, including:

- Chain layering, whereby funds are shuffled quickly across dozens or even hundreds of addresses within a short period of time to obscure their source.
- Cyclical patterns in which funds are sent back to the source wallet to create confusion or mimic legitimate activity.
- Conversion centres, often cryptocurrency exchanges, mixers, or peer-to-peer services, that are centres of illicit activity or cash-out locations

Graph algorithms like centrality measures or community detection can be used to identify high-risk wallets, detect laundering patterns, and even forecast potential cash-out locations. For law enforcement, graph mapping has been used to visualize extensive networks of illicit finance and to isolate the critical intermediaries that are used to carry out criminal activities.

4.1.2 Clustering and Heuristics

Since users can create an unlimited number of wallet addresses, a user may hold hundreds or thousands of addresses, diluting the entity. Forensic analysts seek to fix this issue by implementing clustering heuristics where related addresses are grouped to a single controlling entity (Khenfouci & Challal, 2024; Zhao et al., 2022). One heuristic in common use is the multi-input heuristic, which means that if several addresses are used together to sign a single transaction, they must be owned by the same private keys (so they must be owned by the same user). Another technique is change address detection, where the algorithms can tell the recipient addresses from the change address, which is commonly used to return unused funds under the sender's control.

Clustering can be extremely valuable from a forensic perspective by pulling together what appears to be scattered data and turning it into meaningful identity footprints. In combination with Know Your Customer (KYC) records from regulated exchanges, leaked data, or seized hardware wallets, clustering can often be used to unmask the real identity of the underlying pseudonymous clusters. This step takes technical transaction data and turns it into legally actionable intelligence that can be used for investigating fraud, sanctions evasion, and organized cybercrime.

4.1.3 Anonymization Methods

Deanonymization is the link between blockchain pseudo-identities and actual identities (Linoy et al., 2021; Priya & Palanisamy, 2023). While in some cases it may not be possible to fully reveal an individual's identity, a variety of methods increase the chances of attribution:

- Transaction fingerprinting, in which known actors are matched against unique patterns of activity defined by, for example, timing patterns, transaction size, address reuse, etc.
- Off-chain correlation of data, where addresses on the blockchain can be correlated with data held off-chain, such as IP addresses, records of registrations in exchanges, or even social media profiles.
- Taint analysis, which tracks coins that have originated from illegitimate sources, such as from darknet marketplaces, ransomware payments, or sanctioned addresses, and measures the degree to which they remain 'tainted' as they move around the system.

Although this is not easy to achieve, especially when using privacy-focused cryptocurrencies such as Monero or Zcash, such techniques can help narrow down the pool of suspects to a much smaller number. In high-profile cases, even partial deanonymization - combined with subpoenaed exchange records - has been enough to identify criminals and get them prosecuted. To provide a structured comparison, Table 2 summarizes the core analytical methods in blockchain forensics, their primary functions, and their investigative value.

Table 2. Analytical Methods in Blockchain Forensics

Method	Description	Key Investigative Value
Transaction Graph Mapping	Visualizes wallets (nodes) and transactions (edges) to track fund flows.	Reveals layering, cyclical transfers, and consolidation points used in money laundering.
Address Clustering	Groups wallet addresses using heuristics (e.g., multi-input, change address).	Links fragmented addresses to a single entity, enabling identity attribution.
Deanonymization Techniques	Uses transaction fingerprinting, off-chain correlation, and taint analysis.	Connects pseudonymous wallets to real-world actors, aiding prosecutions and regulatory cases.

4.2 Forensic Tools and Platforms

As the complexity and volume of blockchain data increase, investigators are turning more and more to forensic platforms tailored to provide visualization, automation, and access to proprietary intelligence databases. These tools have become essential tools for law enforcement agencies, regulatory bodies, financial institutions, and cybersecurity professionals (Kumar & Vaish, 2025).

4.2.1 Chainalysis

Chainalysis is one of the most popular commercial threat investigative tools (https://www.chainalysis.com/). It offers advanced graphing capabilities, risk-scoring algorithms, and real-time transaction monitoring. Chainalysis is being used by law enforcement agencies around the globe to track ransomware payments, track darknet markets, and understand money laundering typologies. Its vast database of criminal wallet addresses - built up from decades of investigations - makes it easy to identify high-risk activity quickly. On top of investigations, financial institutions also use Chainalysis for compliance, screening transactions against sanctions lists and anti-money laundering (AML) requirements.

4.2.2 CipherTrace

CipherTrace is a compliance-focused and regulation-aligned cryptocurrency intelligence platform. Its tools search for funds across several blockchains and help assess the risk of specific addresses or entities. CipherTrace offers crucial support for Anti-Money Laundering (AML) investigations and is essential for organizations to meet the Financial Action Task Force's (FATF) definition of "Travel Rule," which mandates information sharing in crypto transactions. Since being acquired by Mastercard, CipherTrace has broadened its role in bridging the gap between traditional finance and the cryptocurrency ecosystem (Hassanin & Martinovic, 2024).

4.2.3 Elliptic

Elliptic is a risk-based blockchain forensics solution. Its software allows wallet screening, monitoring of transactions, and visual mapping of illegal flows (Shrivastava et al., 2023). Regulators and banks use Elliptic to avoid exposure to tainted funds, while investigators are using it to identify links to ransomware operations, terrorism funding, and organized fraud. Elliptic particularly excels in combining blockchain analytics with regulatory risk contextualization, thereby making it a favorite for compliance-focused organizations.

4.2.4 Open-Source Alternatives

Open-source tools are accessible on commercial platforms, but they are also available for self-funded researchers, academicians, and smaller organizations. Examples include:

- BlockSci, a powerful blockchain data analysis framework for analysing blockchain data at scale.
- GraphSense, an open-source cryptocurrency transaction tracing analytics platform.
- Bitcoin-Tracker, which allows live monitoring of Bitcoin transactions

While these tools may not have the proprietary datasets and customer support of commercial offerings, they are still invaluable for experimentation, education, and low-budget forensics investigations. They are widely used for testing new heuristics, prototype algorithms, or for transparency-oriented audits of the cryptocurrency ecosystem.

By supplementing blockchain data at scale with information on illicit addresses, these platforms considerably improve investigators' ability to trace transactions, root out criminal organizations, and maintain regulatory compliance. Specialized forensic platforms enhance the scale and precision of investigations. Table 3 compares leading commercial tools with open-source alternatives, highlighting their strengths, focus areas, and common applications.

Table 3. Comparative Overview of Blockchain Forensic Tools

Tool/Platform	Key Features	Strengths	Limitations	Primary Users
Chainalysis	Graph mapping, risk scoring, illicit address DB	Extensive datasets, global adoption, and real-time monitoring	Commercial license required	Law enforcement, banks
CipherTrace	Multi-chain tracing, FATF Travel Rule compliance	Strong compliance focus, regulatory integration	Acquired by Mastercard (more corporate direction)	Regulators, financial institutions
Elliptic	Risk-based analysis, wallet/entity screening	Strong regulatory alignment, fraud/ AML detection	Less flexible for research	Banks, compliance teams
Open-Source Tools (BlockSci, GraphSense, Bitcoin-Tracker)	Transaction analysis, visualization, and real-time monitoring	Free, transparent, customizable	Limited support, smaller datasets	Researchers, academics

5. MACHINE LEARNING AND AI IN BLOCKCHAIN FORENSICS

As cryptocurrency use has grown, daily transaction volumes have grown into the billions. Traditional manual analysis or rule-based heuristics are simply no longer adequate for effective investigation. To combat this, blockchain forensics is increasingly adopting machine learning (ML) and artificial intelligence (AI), which is particularly good at pattern recognition, anomaly detection, and cross-domain data integration (Rai et al., 2016; Singh et al., 2024; Tripathi et al., 2024).

5.1 Anomaly Detection

Machine learning models can be used to detect anomalies in blockchain activity, such as unusual transaction sizes, sudden spikes in activity, or deviations from normal behavior patterns. This can be crucial for identifying early-stage fraud, ransomware attacks, and money laundering activities. AI-based anomaly detection helps in eliminating false negatives by flagging suspicious activity that would otherwise remain undetected in large-scale data.

5.2 Entity Classification

AI systems can group clusters of addresses under different headings like exchanges, darknet marketplaces, gambling sites, or mining pools. Classification enhances attribution accuracy and enables investigators to focus their attention on high-risk entities. For instance, being able to determine if a legitimate exchange or a known darknet service is being targeted is important for avoiding false positives and directing investigations.

5.3 Predictive Modeling

By studying historical transaction data, machine learning algorithms can make predictions about the probability of future illicit activity. Predictive models are particularly useful for surveillance of newly created wallets exhibiting suspicious characteristics, allowing proactive measures to be taken before crimes occur.

5.4 Cross-Chain Analysis

With the proliferation of decentralized finance (DeFi) platforms, sidechains, and cross-chain bridges, it is becoming easier for illicit actors to transfer money between multiple blockchains to take advantage of loopholes in traceability. AI-powered tools are perfectly suited to monitor these multi-dimensional flows by interpreting various data structures at the same time. This cross-chain visibility is fast becoming a cornerstone of next-gen blockchain forensics.

5.5 Natural Language Processing (NLP)

NLP applied to open-source intelligence (OSINT): Forensic analysts need to analyze large amounts of textual information, such as darknet forum discussions, social media posts, regulatory documents, or news articles. By mapping the off-chain chatter to the on-chain events, the NLP elevates forensic analysis to one that is enriched with contextual information that cannot be gleaned from pure transaction data. Table 4 outlines how machine learning and AI enhance blockchain forensic investigations, highlighting their core techniques and practical applications.

Table 4. Role of AI in Blockchain Forensics

AI/ML Technique	Function	Application in Forensics
Anomaly Detection	Identifies outliers in transaction size, timing, or frequency.	Detects fraud, ransomware activity, and money laundering schemes.
Entity Classification	Categorizes address clusters (e.g., exchanges, darknet markets, gambling).	Improves attribution accuracy and prioritization of high-risk entities.
Predictive Modeling	Uses historical data to forecast suspicious wallet activity.	Enables proactive monitoring and early intervention before large-scale crimes occur.
Cross-Chain Analysis	Tracks fund flows across multiple blockchains and DeFi ecosystems.	Detects laundering strategies exploiting interoperability gaps.
Natural Language Processing	Extracts insights from forums, social media, and darknet markets.	Correlates off-chain chatter with on-chain events, enriching investigations with context.

Taken together, these AI-driven methods allow investigators to shift from reactive tracing - responding to crimes after they have happened - to proactive detection, where the activity that raises doubts is identified and investigated in near real time. By enhancing the capabilities of forensics and reducing human workload, AI and ML are unlocking the potential of blockchain forensics, making it a more efficient, predictive, and intelligence-driven field.

6. CHALLENGES AND LIMITATIONS IN CRYPTOCURRENCY FORENSICS

Although blockchain analytics and forensic platforms are being developed, it is extremely difficult for investigators to trace digital financial transactions. Additionally, the pseudonymized and decentralized nature of cryptocurrencies, coupled with the fast-paced evolution of obfuscation techniques, has led to a dynamic landscape where forensic tools constantly need to adapt in order to stay relevant. In addition to technical barriers, jurisdictional challenges, ethical issues, and methodological constraints make attribution and enforcement difficult. Gaining insight into these challenges is essential to assessing the current state of blockchain forensics and the limitations of the technology.

6.1 Technical Barriers

One of the key challenges for forensic investigators is from tools and technologies specifically developed to hide trails of transactions. These obfuscation techniques are constantly changing, making for a technological arms race between the criminal actors that develop new ways to hide digital information and the investigators who try to stay ahead of analytical countermeasures.

6.2 Mixers and Tumblers

Cryptocurrency mixers (or tumblers) are some of the most popular tools for breaking traceability on public blockchains. They work by collecting coins from many users, mixing them up with the coins from other users, and reallocating them to other addresses, thus breaking the transparent connection between sender and recipient. Centralized mixers are similar to custodial services, where users trust a third-party operator to collect and redistribute funds. These services have consistently been connected with money laundering operations, ransomware payments, and transfers of darknet proceeds. Eliminating the middleman, centralized mixers like Tornado Cash on Ethereum rely on programmable smart contracts. This change makes enforcement more difficult, since there is no centralized operator to regulate, subpoena, or shut down. Although mixers can be used for legitimate privacy reasons - for example, to protect personal financial information from inappropriate snooping - their close association with illegal finance causes them to be a popular target of regulators and law enforcement agencies. This is a perennial issue, not least because it is typically necessary to reveal some degree of context in order to judge what constitutes legitimate privacy use and what constitutes knowing obfuscation, something that may be supported by external intelligence sources.

6.3 Privacy Coins

Unlike the transparent blockchains that are used for direct on-chain tracking in cryptocurrencies like Bitcoin or Ethereum, privacy-focused cryptocurrencies are designed to evade forensic analysis. Monero (XMR), for instance, uses ring signatures to obscure the sender, stealth addresses to obscure the recipient, and confidential transactions to obscure the credentials of the amounts transferred. Even advanced blockchain analysis cannot determine transaction details with certainty through this multilayered approach. Similarly, Zcash (ZEC) employs the use of zero-knowledge proofs (zk-SNARKs) to support shielded transactions wherein all transaction information is encrypted and hidden from outside observers. From a forensic point of view, these systems are "black boxes" that leave the investigator with the only recourse of relying on indirect methods such as monitoring of exchanges, infiltration of criminal organizations, or statistical inference using probability. It is these limitations that make privacy coins very popular in the world of advanced cybercrime, especially with regard to ransomware, darknet commerce, and tax evasion. Their increasing use highlights the shortcomings of current forensic techniques in the face of cryptocurrencies designed precisely to achieve anonymity.

6.4 Cross-Chain Swaps and DeFi Protocols

With the explosion of decentralized finance (DeFi) applications and cross-chain protocols, a new set of challenges has emerged for blockchain forensics. Through the use of mechanisms such as atomic swaps, bridge protocols, and decentralized exchanges (DEXs), users can transfer assets between different blockchains without relying on centralized intermediaries. This decentralization removes critical points of enforcement, as oftentimes there is no company or operator to force to provide information. Illicit actors are able to take advantage of this by quickly moving assets from one blockchain to another - for instance, moving Bitcoin into Ethereum-based tokens or stablecoins - generating scattered transaction histories that are hard to consolidate. Once converted, money may flow through multiple DeFi liquidity pools, lending protocols, or synthetic asset platforms, further muddying the waters when it comes to attribution. These advancements have placed the need for forensic teams to use multi-chain, interoperable analytical frameworks, but these tools are in development. As a result, the DeFi ecosystem is a highly dynamic and constantly evolving set of solutions, which allows criminals to remain one step ahead of regulators and investigators.

6.5 Jurisdiction and Transnational Issues

Cryptocurrencies are transnational, non-state, borderless currencies. The transnational character of these phenomena brings fundamental jurisdictional challenges to regulators, investigators, and law enforcement agencies, often leading to serious enforcement blind spots.

Diverse Regulatory Environments

Different national governments have widely different approaches to the regulation of cryptocurrencies. Some, such as the United States and European Union (EU) members, have stringent requirements on AML and CTF regimes for exchanges and wallet suppliers, which are also supported by stringent supervisory frameworks. Others follow a much looser framework, often out of lack of resources, as a result of regulatory arbitrage, or with the intent of attracting business related to cryptocurrencies. Criminal actors take advantage of this patchwork by laundering illegal funds through service providers that are based in permissive jurisdictions, in effect creating "regulatory havens." For instance, exchanges forming a weak link without any stringent KYC/AML controls become points of egress for laundering activities. In the absence of a harmonized global standard, regulators have to deal with ongoing gaps in supervision, leaving systemic vulnerabilities for criminals to exploit with ease.

6.6 Cross-Border Investigations

Cryptocurrency crimes often cross national borders in seconds, while the investigation procedures are sluggish and bureaucratic. A ransomware payment originates in Europe, for example, and is routed through an exchange in Asia and cashed out in a jurisdiction with low supervision before European authorities can launch an investigation. Mechanisms like Mutual Legal Assistance Treaties (MLATs) are geared towards cooperation, but are ill-equipped to keep pace with the speed (near real-time) at which digital bank-to-bank transfers are occurring. The result is that by the time investigators have garnered the requisite approvals, funds have been dissipated, converted, or laundered through enough other jurisdictions as to be beyond the reach of effective recovery.

6.7 Extradition and Enforcement Gap(s)

Even if attribution is done well and suspects can be identified, they may be hard or impossible to prosecute. Some criminals operate in jurisdictions with only weak extradition agreements, low cybercrime enforcement capability, or political reluctance to cooperate. These gaps reduce the deterrent effect of blockchain forensics, as criminals may believe that they have protection from geography and local laws. Lack of international coordination: Without coordination between international bodies, forensic advancements often do not convert to legal or operational achievements. Finally, establishing cross-border cooperation, creating international standards, and legal mechanisms to respond swiftly can continue to be necessary for blockchain forensics to be effective globally.

6.8 Privacy, Ethics, and Data Protection Issues

Blockchain forensics sits at the delicate intersection between the necessity for effective security enforcement and the protection of individual rights. Researchers need to weigh the keen interest in breaking up illicit financial flows carefully against the larger contexts of ethics, law, and society.

6.8.1 Privacy Intrusion

While the data on a blockchain is pseudonymous and not anonymous, forensic techniques can be used to link on-chain activity to off-chain identities. While valuable from an enforcement perspective, this is at risk of eroding the privacy of those who are involved in legitimate activity. Journalists, political dissidents, and activists in authoritarian regimes may use privacy tools to protect their safety, while regular users may just want to protect their financial transactions from prying eyes. If over-reaching surveillance picks these individuals out, they can get the short end of the deal, leading to worries that surveillance compromises the core principles of decentralization, economic freedom, and resistance to censorship that cryptocurrency systems were built upon.

6.8.2 Ethical Considerations

Forensic investigations can result in the incidental sweep-up of innocent users. If your transaction is routed through a tainted address or in contact with blacklisted wallets, we may pull your address up for review or freezing if you don't clear your name. Although the use of probabilistic heuristics is helpful, it does raise the risk of misclassification and false alarms. These practices raise significant concerns about proportionality, fairness, and due process, particularly in cases where the individuals may be subjected to reputational harm, financial loss, or legal consequences without direct proof of wrongdoing. Ethical considerations therefore require that safeguards for forensic practices must be embedded in the process, be transparent, and that forensic practices must be accountable in order not to erode public trust.

6.8.3 Data Protection Laws

The combination of blockchain data with off-chain personal information presents important legal challenges under the world's data protection regimes. Legislations like the European Union's General Data Protection Regulation (GDPR) place stringent mandates on personal data collection, processing, and retention. Forensic investigations based on exchange KYC records, leaky datasets, or IP logs must step carefully through these requirements. Failure to comply can be met by legal penalties, loss of public trust, and can in some cases, render evidence inadmissible in court. Investigators are thus faced with the double challenge of maintaining effective forensic practice while respecting international expectations of privacy and data protection.

7. LIMITATIONS OF THE CURRENT TOOLS AND FALSE POSITIVES IN TRACING

Despite considerable progress in the field of blockchain forensic technology, existing tools are still limited by a number of technical, methodological, and practical constraints. These shortcomings highlight the need for careful interpretation and the combination of multiple research approaches.

7.1 Incomplete Coverage

The cryptocurrency ecosystem is rapidly evolving, with new tokens, consensus protocols, scaling solutions, and DeFi protocols being introduced almost every day. Commercial forensics providers like Chainalysis, Elliptic, and CipherTrace offer broad coverage, yet they can't possibly keep up with every development. For example, new technologies like the Bitcoin Lightning Network, sidechains, and new kinds of privacy-preserving smart contracts frequently outpace forensic tools in their ability to evolve. This delay leaves a blind spot for criminals to hide money.

7.2 False Positives and Over-Attribution

Forensic heuristics like address clustering are stochastic by nature. While they are useful sources of leads, they can incorrectly match unrelated addresses, which increases false positives. Over-identification can be dangerous in that innocent people and organizations can be identified as being complicit in a crime. Such mistakes can tarnish reputations, destroy trust in forensic tools, and even jeopardize legal cases. A central issue is to balance the probabilistic inference with the corroborating evidence.

7.3 Dependence on Off-Chain Data

On-chain analysis by itself is seldom enough for full attribution. In some cases, investigators rely heavily on off-chain sources like exchange KYC records, subpoenas, leaked data, or open-source intelligence (OSINT). While these sources inform critically, they also present weaknesses: non-cooperative interactions, gaps in documentation, or inaccuracies in leaks can hinder investigations. This reliance emphasizes the importance of good multi-source validation in forensic practice.

7.4 Availability and Costs

Commercial forensics tools, however, are expensive and usually out of reach for smaller law enforcement agencies, academia, or organizations in developing countries. This cost barrier leads to a non-level playing field in terms of enforcement capabilities, making some countries more exposed to illegal crypto-financial activity than others. Open source implementations, subsidised platforms, or global capacity building programmes are still needed to bridge these gaps. To consolidate these diverse challenges, Table 5 provides an overview of the major technical, jurisdictional, ethical, and methodological barriers encountered in cryptocurrency forensics. This structured view highlights how the evolving crypto ecosystem complicates enforcement, while also underscoring the need for adaptive strategies and global coordination.

Table 5. Challenges and Limitations in Cryptocurrency Forensics

Category	Key Challenge	Description	Implications for Forensics
Technical Barriers	Mixers & Tumblers	Pool and redistribute funds to break traceability; centralized or decentralized (e.g., Tornado Cash).	Hard to distinguish privacy use from illicit laundering; lack of a central operator complicates enforcement.
	Privacy Coins	Cryptocurrencies (e.g., Monero, Zcash) are designed with anonymity features like ring signatures, stealth addresses, and zk-SNARKs.	On-chain tracking becomes nearly impossible; investigators rely on indirect or probabilistic methods.
	Cross-Chain Swaps & DeFi Protocols	Tools like atomic swaps, bridges, and DEXs move assets across chains without intermediaries.	Obscures transaction trails; current multi-chain forensic tools are underdeveloped.
Jurisdictional & Cross-Border Issues	Diverse Regulatory Landscapes	Regulatory fragmentation across countries; some strict AML/CTF regimes, others permissive or resource-constrained.	Criminals exploit "regulatory havens," creating oversight blind spots.
	Cross-Border Investigations	Digital assets move instantly; legal cooperation (MLATs, subpoenas) is slow.	Funds often dissipate before law enforcement action; investigation lags behind transaction velocity.
	Extradition & Enforcement Gaps	Criminals operate from jurisdictions with weak extradition laws or a political unwillingness to cooperate.	Even when suspects are identified, prosecution and deterrence remain difficult.

continued on following page

Table 5. Continued

Category	Key Challenge	Description	Implications for Forensics
Privacy, Ethics & Data Protection	Privacy Intrusion	Linking pseudonymous addresses with real-world identities risks surveillance of legitimate users (e.g., activists, dissidents).	Potential chilling effect; undermines trust in forensic practices and cryptocurrency ecosystems.
	Ethical Concerns	Innocent users flagged due to probabilistic heuristics or tainted address association.	Misclassification risks reputational harm, wrongful suspicion, and erosion of due process.
	Data Protection Laws	Use of off-chain KYC data must comply with laws like GDPR.	Mishandling data risks legal liability, public mistrust, and inadmissibility of evidence.
Tool Limitations & Methodology	Incomplete Coverage	Rapid evolution of tokens, sidechains, and DeFi often outpaces forensic platform updates.	Criminals exploit blind spots in tool coverage; investigators lack full visibility.
	False Positives & Over-Attribution	Heuristic methods (e.g., address clustering) are probabilistic, prone to errors.	Incorrectly linking addresses risks legal missteps and weakens case integrity.
	Dependence on Off-Chain Data	On-chain analysis alone is insufficient; reliance on KYC records, leaks, subpoenas, and OSINT.	Gaps in cooperation or unreliable sources undermine investigations.
	High Costs & Limited Accessibility	Commercial forensic tools (e.g., Chainalysis, Elliptic) are expensive and inaccessible to smaller agencies.	Creates global enforcement inequality; developing regions are disproportionately exposed to crypto-enabled crime.

8. LEGAL, REGULATORY, AND FUTURE DIRECTIONS

Cryptocurrency and blockchain forensics are effective not just because of technical innovation, but also because of the legal and regulatory environment within which they function. Unlike conventional financial systems, which are subject to well-established regulatory frameworks, digital assets are transnational and often not well-defined about regulatory frameworks. Forensic investigations must therefore negotiate a variety of national laws, variable enforcement capabilities, and changing global standards. At the same time, new technologies like artificial intelligence and quantum computing promise to change the future of blockchain analysis, posing new questions about privacy, ethics, and financial innovation.

8.1 Regulatory Arrangements and Asset Seizure Procedures

Governments around the world are establishing frameworks for regulating cryptocurrencies with a primary focus on anti-money laundering (AML), counter-terrorist financing (CTF), and investor protection. These frameworks form the legal underpinnings for forensic investigation and enforcement.

- Many jurisdictions require AML/CTF compliance measures, such as Know Your Customer (KYC), for cryptocurrency exchanges, wallet providers, and custodians. These records are critical for establishing a connection between pseudonymous addresses and verified identities that investigators can follow up on after forensic leads are identified.
- One of the key challenges of blockchain forensics is not only identifying the illicit funds but also securing them. Different jurisdictions have different procedures for seizing digital assets, and technical obstacles, like multisignature wallets or private keys stored offline, can complicate asset recovery. Some courts have approved the seizure of cryptocurrencies by judicial order, while others have no clear legal mechanisms for the enforcement of digital asset seizures.
- Many jurisdictions are still in the process of developing comprehensive regulatory frameworks to address mainstreaming issues such as DeFi, privacy coins, and non-custodial wallets. These loopholes form blind spots where unregulated or under-regulated systems can be exploited by illicit actors.

8.2 International Cooperation

Because cryptocurrencies are borderless, no one country can be successful in combating illicit financial flows alone. The need for international cooperation is crucial, but getting there is full of pitfalls:

8.2.1 Challenges

- Different countries have different definitions of cryptocurrencies, legal frameworks for digital assets, and willingness to collaborate in cross-border investigations.
- Mutual Legal Assistance Treaties (MLATs), for example, are notoriously slow and are ill-equipped to act quickly when funds can be moved instantaneously across networks.
- Some countries serve as havens for illicit actors by providing weak oversight or purposefully protecting cryptocurrency activities.

8.2.2 Opportunities

- International standards are being developed through groups such as the Financial Action Task Force (FATF) via initiatives such as the "Travel Rule", which mandates exchanges to share information on senders and recipients.
- Efforts are underway to develop information-sharing networks between regulators, law enforcement, and private-sector actors (e.g., exchanges and forensic solution providers) to enhance detection and enforcement.
- International cooperation can facilitate access to forensic tools, technology, expertise, and training in less developed countries, bridging enforcement gaps.

Global cooperation is therefore both a challenge and an opportunity, and success depends on balancing regulation and enhancing real-time information sharing. To better understand the regulatory landscape and its implications for blockchain forensics, Table 6 summarizes the core elements of national regulatory frameworks, asset seizure challenges, and the dynamics of global cooperation, highlighting both obstacles and opportunities.

Table 6. Legal and Regulatory Dimensions of Cryptocurrency Forensics

Dimension	Focus Area	Key Features / Issues	Implications for Forensics
National Regulatory Frameworks	AML/CTF Compliance	Mandatory KYC requirements for exchanges, custodians, and wallet providers.	Provides linkage between pseudonymous wallets and real-world identities, enabling actionable leads.
	Asset Seizure & Recovery	Varying legal procedures; technical barriers include multisig wallets and offline private keys.	Even when illicit funds are traced, seizure may fail without judicial clarity and technical expertise.
	Regulatory Gaps	Lack of clear rules for DeFi, privacy coins, and non-custodial wallets.	Creates blind spots exploited by criminals; limits enforcement reach.
Global Cooperation – Challenges	Regulatory Divergence	Differences in how nations define, classify, and regulate cryptocurrencies.	Creates loopholes; illicit actors route funds through permissive jurisdictions.
	Bureaucratic Delays	MLATs and formal international cooperation processes are slow compared to instant crypto transactions.	Funds often dissipate before enforcement action can be taken.

continued on following page

Table 6. Continued

Dimension	Focus Area	Key Features / Issues	Implications for Forensics
	Non-Cooperative Jurisdictions	Some countries provide safe havens, either through weak oversight or deliberate protection of crypto activities.	Limits the effectiveness of international investigations and prosecutions.
Global Cooperation – Opportunities	Global Standards	FATF's Travel Rule and other initiatives standardize information-sharing requirements.	Improves traceability and accountability across jurisdictions.
	Information-Sharing Networks	Platforms for regulators, law enforcement, exchanges, and forensic firms to collaborate.	Enhances detection, strengthens investigations, and fosters cross-sector transparency.
	Capacity Building	Partnerships to provide tools, training, and resources to less-developed jurisdictions.	Reduces enforcement gaps worldwide, strengthening the collective fight against illicit financial flows.

9. FUTURE OF BLOCKCHAIN FORENSICS

The next decade will see transformative changes in blockchain forensics, largely spurred by technological and legal advances:

- As quantum computing is in its nascent stage, it presents a double-edged sword. On one hand, it can crack widely used cryptographic schemes and, thus, expose blockchain transactions and wallets. On the other hand, it might enable investigators to use their understanding of previous casework with unparalleled computational firepower to mine a massive transaction network or crack obfuscation. The eventual impact of this will depend on how fast quantum develops and whether the industry can implement quantum-resistant cryptography.
- Artificial Intelligence, already, is improving anomaly detection, clustering, and predictive modeling in blockchain forensics. In the future, AI could help to create fully automated tracing systems that can monitor multiple blockchains, DeFi protocols, and cross-chain bridges at once. However, this opens up new governance questions of oversight, accountability, and algorithmic bias.
- As digital assets enter the mainstream, laws are evolving to tackle emerging risks. Regulation: Future legislation will likely target DeFi platforms, stablecoins, and decentralized autonomous organizations (DAOs), ensuring that forensic and regulatory frameworks are updated to remain relevant. Countries

that proactively build blockchain forensics into their legal enforcement frameworks will set de facto standards for enforcement efficacy.

- Excessive snooping by forensic techniques threatens to weaken legitimate user privacy, eroding public trust in cryptocurrencies as instruments for financial sovereignty. Regulators, therefore, need to provide for surveillance without being overbearing, but instead targeting high-risk activity without criminalizing the general public.
- Overbearing regulations or excessive regulatory measures might inhibit innovation within blockchain ecosystems. Compliance: On the one hand, strict enforcement mechanisms may hinder the adoption of decentralized technologies by startups and developers who cannot meet the required standards.
- Policies must strike a balance between ensuring forensic effectiveness and honoring civil liberties. Cryptocurrencies can be secure and innovative if there are robust forensic frameworks, provided that privacy-enhancing technologies are well-regulated. Open governance, ethical principles, and stakeholder discussion will be essential to achieving such a balance.

10. CONCLUSION

Cryptocurrency and blockchain forensics have become an important field that lies at the crossroads of technology, law, and finance. As cryptocurrencies grow in their integration within mainstream commerce and global financial markets, they also create unparalleled opportunities for abuse by bad actors. This duality (innovation and risk) reinforces the need for forensic capabilities that can link pseudo-anonymized transactions, assign activities to real-world entities, and complement enforcement activity. Throughout the chapter, we have identified the technical underpinnings of blockchain forensics, ranging from the pseudonymity, immutability, and transparency of public blockchains to the fundamental investigative techniques of transaction mapping, clustering, and deanonymization. It has also defined the tools and platforms which operationalize these methods, from commercial services such as Chainalysis and open source alternatives, to the emerging importance of artificial intelligence in scaling analysis. At the same time, it has critically analyzed the challenges investigators deal with - from mixers, tumblers, and privacy coins to jurisdictional barriers, privacy issues, and the limitations of existing forensic devices.

Legal and compliance aspects were seen as being of equal importance. Evolving legislation, increased international cooperation, and stronger frameworks for asset seizure are now critical to creating a more resilient forensic environment. In conclusion, emerging technologies like AI and quantum computing will influence the future of blockchain forensics, offering new opportunities and complex ethical considerations. The key will be to strike a balance: giving investigators the means to take down criminal activity, while not infringing on user privacy or stifling financial innovation.

In conclusion, blockchain forensics is not a static field but a dynamic ecosystem that needs to keep up with technological, regulatory, and societal advancements. Its future will be defined by adaptability - utilizing advanced tools, supporting global collaboration, and weaving ethical considerations into investigative practice. By doing so, blockchain forensics can help ensure that cryptocurrencies live up to their promise as a driving force of financial innovation while minimizing their misuse as a tool of crime.

REFERENCES

Abdennadher, S., Grassa, R., Abdulla, H., & Alfalasi, A. (2022). The effects of blockchain technology on the accounting and assurance profession in the UAE: An exploratory study. *Journal of Financial Reporting and Accounting*, *20*(1), 53–71. Advance online publication. DOI: 10.1108/JFRA-05-2020-0151

Agarwal, U., Rishiwal, V., Tanwar, S., & Yadav, M. (2024). Blockchain and crypto forensics: Investigating crypto frauds. *International Journal of Network Management*, *34*(2), e2255. Advance online publication. DOI: 10.1002/nem.2255

Aggarwal, S., & Kumar, N. (2021). Cryptocurrencies. []). Elsevier.]. *Advances in Computers*, *121*, 227–266. DOI: 10.1016/bs.adcom.2020.08.012

Akram, W., Joshi, R., Haider, T., Sharma, P., Jain, V., Garud, N., & Singh, N. (2024). Blockchain technology: A potential tool for the management of pharma supply chain. *Research in Social & Administrative Pharmacy*, *20*(6), 156–164. DOI: 10.1016/j.sapharm.2024.02.014

Alamsyah, A., Kusuma, G. N. W., & Ramadhani, D. P. (2024). A Review on Decentralized Finance Ecosystems. In *Future Internet* (Vol. 16, Issue 3). DOI: 10.3390/fi16030076

Almadadha, R. (2024). Blockchain Technology in Financial Accounting: Enhancing Transparency, Security, and ESG Reporting. *Blockchains 2024, Vol. 2, Pages 312-333, 2*(3), 312–333. DOI: 10.3390/blockchains2030015

Alzoubi, M. M. (2024). Investigating the synergy of Blockchain and AI: enhancing security, efficiency, and transparency. *Journal of Cyber Security Technology*. ;DOI: 10.1080/23742917.2024.2374594Atlam, H. F., Ekuri, N., Azad, M. A., & Lallie, H. S. (2024). Blockchain Forensics: A Systematic Literature Review of Techniques, Applications, Challenges, and Future Directions. *Electronics 2024, Vol. 13, Page 3568, 13*(17), 3568. DOI: 10.3390/electronics13173568

Chaudhari, D., Agarwal, R., & Shukla, S. K. (2021). Towards Malicious address identification in Bitcoin. *Proceedings - 2021 IEEE International Conference on Blockchain, Blockchain 2021*. DOI: 10.1109/Blockchain53845.2021.00066

Cui, Y., Gaur, V., & Liu, J. (2024). Supply Chain Transparency and Blockchain Design. *Management Science*, *70*(5), 3245–3263. DOI: 10.1287/mnsc.2023.4851

Curry, D. (2025). Limitations of trust and legitimacy in blockchain: Exploring the effectiveness of decentralisation, immutability and consensus mechanisms in blockchain governance. *International Journal of Public Sector Management*, *38*(1), 98–117. DOI: 10.1108/IJPSM-12-2023-0368

De Mulder, G., & De Meester, B. (2025). *Pseudonymity for Personal Data Stores: Pseudonymous WebIDs and Decentralized Identifiers*. 111–129. DOI: 10.1007/978-3-032-00639-4_7

Dudani, S., Baggili, I., Raymond, D., & Marchany, R. (2023). The current state of cryptocurrency forensics. *Forensic Science International Digital Investigation*, *46*, 301576. DOI: 10.1016/j.fsidi.2023.301576

Garriga, M., Dalla Palma, S., Arias, M., De Renzis, A., Pareschi, R., & Andrew Tamburri, D. (2021). Blockchain and cryptocurrencies: A classification and comparison of architecture drivers. *Concurrency and Computation*, *33*(8), e5992. Advance online publication. DOI: 10.1002/cpe.5992

Han, P., Sui, A., & Wu, J. (2022). Identity Management and Authentication of a UAV Swarm Based on a Blockchain. *Applied Sciences (Basel, Switzerland)*, *12*(20), 10524. Advance online publication. DOI: 10.3390/app122010524

Hassanin, M. A. M., & Martinovic, I. (2024). CipherTrace: Automatic detection of ciphers from execution traces to neutralize ransomware. *Journal of Cybersecurity*, *10*(1), tyae008. Advance online publication. DOI: 10.1093/cybsec/tyae008

Hossain, M. S. (2021). What do we know about cryptocurrency? Past, present, future. In *China Finance Review International* (Vol. 11, Issue 4). DOI: 10.1108/CFRI-03-2020-0026

Igonor, O. S., Amin, M. B., & Garg, S. (2025). The Application of Blockchain Technology in the Field of Digital Forensics: A Literature Review. *Blockchains*, *3*(1), 5. DOI: 10.3390/blockchains3010005

Jamwal, S., Cano, J., Lee, G. M., Tran, N. H., & Truong, N. (2024). A survey on Ethereum pseudonymity: Techniques, challenges, and future directions. *Journal of Network and Computer Applications*, *232*, 104019. DOI: 10.1016/j.jnca.2024.104019

Javed, I. T., Alharbi, F., Bellaj, B., Margaria, T., Crespi, N., & Qureshi, K. N. (2021). Health-id: A blockchain-based decentralized identity management for remote healthcare. *Healthcare (Basel)*, *9*(6), 712. Advance online publication. DOI: 10.3390/healthcare9060712

Johar, S., Ahmad, N., Durrani, A., & Ali, G. (2021). Proof of Pseudonym: Blockchain-Based Privacy Preserving Protocol for Intelligent Transport System. *IEEE Access : Practical Innovations, Open Solutions*, *9*, 163625–163639. Advance online publication. DOI: 10.1109/ACCESS.2021.3133423

Khenfouci, Y., & Challal, Y. (2024). Proof of Clustering: an efficient and reliable blockchain-based clustering framework. *Proceedings - 2024 IEEE/ACM International Conference on Big Data Computing, Applications and Technologies, BDCAT 2024*, 149–158. DOI: 10.1109/BDCAT63179.2024.00034

Koshelev, K. A. (2022). Trends in the Evolution of the Digital Financial Assets Market in the Context of the Digital Transformation of the Global Economy. *Finance: Theory and Practice*, *26*(4), 80–94. Advance online publication. DOI: 10.26794/2587-5671-2022-26-4-80-94

Kukman, T., & Gričar, S. (2025a). Blockchain for Quality: Advancing Security, Efficiency, and Transparency in Financial Systems. *FinTech 2025, Vol. 4, Page 7*, *4*(1), 7. DOI: 10.3390/fintech4010007

Kukman, T., & Gričar, S. (2025b). Blockchain for Quality: Advancing Security, Efficiency, and Transparency in Financial Systems. *FinTech 2025, Vol. 4, Page 7*, *4*(1), 7. DOI: 10.3390/fintech4010007

Kumar, N., & Vaish, A. (2025). Use of Blockchain Technology in Digital Forensics: Where and How? *Blockchain Technology for Cyber Defense, Cybersecurity, and Countermeasures: Techniques, Solutions, and Applications*, 1–14. DOI: 10.1201/9781003449515-1

Lin, D., Wu, J., Xuan, Q., & Tse, C. K. (2022). Ethereum transaction tracking: Inferring evolution of transaction networks via link prediction. *Physica A*, *600*, 127504. Advance online publication. DOI: 10.1016/j.physa.2022.127504

Linoy, S., Stakhanova, N., & Ray, S. (2021). De-anonymizing Ethereum blockchain smart contracts through code attribution. *International Journal of Network Management*, *31*(1), e2130. Advance online publication. DOI: 10.1002/nem.2130

Ozili, P. K. (2022). Decentralized finance research and developments around the world. *Journal of Banking and Financial Technology*, *6*(2), 117–133. Advance online publication. DOI: 10.1007/s42786-022-00044-x

Priya, J., & Palanisamy, C. (2023). Novel Block Chain Technique for Data Privacy and Access Anonymity in Smart Healthcare. *Intelligent Automation & Soft Computing*, *35*(1), 243–259. Advance online publication. DOI: 10.32604/iasc.2023.025719

Rai, M., & Yadav, R. K. (2016). A novel method for detection and extraction of human face for video surveillance applications. *International Journal of Signal and Imaging Systems Engineering*, *9*(3), 165–173. DOI: 10.1504/IJSISE.2016.076226

Shrivastava, P., Alam, B., & Alam, M. (2023). Security enhancement using blockchain based modified infinite chaotic elliptic cryptography in cloud. *Cluster Computing*, *26*(6), 3673–3688. Advance online publication. DOI: 10.1007/s10586-022-03777-y

Singh, S., Pandey, J. K., Rai, M., & Saxena, A. K. (2024). Advancements in Facial Expression Recognition Using Machine and Deep Learning Techniques. In Shivani, S., Mritunjay, R., & Abhishek, K. S. (Eds.), *Machine and Deep Learning Techniques for Emotion Detection* (pp. 149–166). IGI Global Scientific Publishing., https://doi.org/https://doi.org/10.4018/979-8-3693-4143-8.ch007 DOI: 10.4018/979-8-3693-4143-8.ch007

Tariq, U., Ibrahim, A., Ahmad, T., Bouteraa, Y., & Elmogy, A. (2019). Blockchain in internet-of-things: A necessity framework for security, reliability, transparency, immutability and liability. *IET Communications*, *13*(19), 3187–3192. Advance online publication. DOI: 10.1049/iet-com.2019.0194

Tripathi, P., Kumar, N., Paroha, K. K., Rai, M., & Panda, M. K. (2024). Applications of Deep Learning in Healthcare in the Framework of Industry 5.0. In Padmesh, T., Nitendra, K., & Mritunjay, R. (Eds.), *Infrastructure Possibilities and Human-Centered Approaches With Industry 5.0* (pp. 69–85). IGI Global Scientific Publishing., https://doi.org/https://doi.org/10.4018/979-8-3693-0782-3.ch005 DOI: 10.4018/979-8-3693-0782-3.ch005

Wu, Z., Liu, J., Wu, J., Zheng, Z., & Chen, T. (2023). TRacer: Scalable Graph-Based Transaction Tracing for Account-Based Blockchain Trading Systems. *IEEE Transactions on Information Forensics and Security*, *18*, 2609–2621. Advance online publication. DOI: 10.1109/TIFS.2023.3266162

Zhang, T. (2023). Privacy Evaluation of Blockchain Based Privacy Cryptocurrencies: A Comparative Analysis of Dash, Monero, Verge, Zcash, and Grin. *IEEE Transactions on Sustainable Computing*, *8*(4), 574–582. Advance online publication. DOI: 10.1109/TSUSC.2023.3303180

Zhao, Z., Wang, J., Shi, K., & Zhang, H. (2022). Improving Address Clustering in Bitcoin by Proposing Heuristics. *IEEE Transactions on Network and Service Management*, *19*(4), 3737–3749. Advance online publication. DOI: 10.1109/TNSM.2022.3186466

Chapter 16
Blockchain Forensics for Cryptocurrency-Driven Cybercrime

Seema Verma
https://orcid.org/0000-0002-7893-671X
Delhi Technical Campus, Greater Noida, India

Padmesh Tripathi
https://orcid.org/0000-0001-9455-1652
Delhi Technical Campus, Greater Noida, India

Pridhi Arora
https://orcid.org/0009-0002-5790-1742
Delhi Technical Campus, Greater Noida, India

ABSTRACT

Blockchain and cryptocurrencies have transformed the way digital transactions work by introducing decentralisation, transparency, and immutability. However, these features also allow some individuals to use them for cybercrimes. This chapter explains how blockchain records can be used to trace, investigate and mitigate such crimes. It also talks about how understanding the behaviour of users can help in finding out who the attackers are. This chapter begins with the basic ideas of blockchain and cryptocurrency, after this, it describes different types of cybercrimes that usually happen using cryptocurrency and also explains that traditional ways of investigating cybercrimes don't work well with blockchain and new frameworks are required to investigate and solve these cases. A key section of the chapter examines

DOI: 10.4018/979-8-3373-4898-8.ch016

how blockchain forensics helps in detecting cybercrimes. User-centric threat intelligence will be explored to understand the people behind cybercrimes that can help in investigations. In the chapter, Legal and ethical considerations will be addressed.

1. INTRODUCTION

The emergence of blockchain technology and its most well-known application, cryptocurrency, has introduced a model shift in digital transactions, creating a novel line for commerce, finance, and inevitably, crime. This technology, designed to operate beyond the reach of central authorities, simultaneously creates a permanent, transparent, and publicly auditable record of every transaction (Tripathi et al. 2023). This built-in contradiction, a tool for illicit actors that is also a rich source of evidence-forms the foundation of blockchain forensics. This chapter provides a comprehensive exploration of this field, beginning with the core technological principles that enable both crime and investigation. This chapter focuses on providing an overview of the domain of blockchain forensics in the context of cybercrime involving cryptocurrency. It aims to create the "street view" of the technology in question, by outlining the foundational criminal ecosystem, explaining the fundamental techniques of attribution, and tracing the paths to the criminal participants as well as the critical methods of de-anonymisation. The provided roadmap will walk the reader alongside the investigator's arsenal, provide and assess the critical breach inflicted by technologies aimed to enhance privacy, and analyse the significance of the on-chain information in the context of forensic investigations. The chapter will also address the intricate legal, regulatory, and ethical aspects of the work, anchored in empirical case studies. It will analyse evolving trends and directions for investigation in this fast-moving domain.

1.1 Core Concepts of Blockchain Technology

At its core, blockchain is a specific implementation of a comprehensive class of technologies known as Distributed Ledger Technology (DLT). A DLT is a decentralised, peer-to-peer digital system for recording transactions between parties in multiple places at the same time. A distributed ledger is a database that is synchronised across the network of participants, often referred to as nodes, not like a traditional database that relies on a central administrator. This structure eliminates the need for a trusted mediator like a bank or broker, and allows individuals to securely verify, execute, and record their transactions.

The security and ownership of assets on a blockchain are governed by asymmetric cryptography, which utilises a pair of mathematically related keys: a private key and public key. The private key is a secret information, similar to a password, that allows the owner the ability to authorise, or "sign", transactions from their address. The public key is similar to a bank account number and can be shared freely to receive funds.

For a new block of transactions to be added to the chain, the network's distributed nodes must agree on its validity through a consensus mechanism. The most well-known of these is Proof-of-Work (PoW), the system developed by Bitcoin. In a PoW system, network participants known as "miners" compete to solve a complex mathematical puzzle. The first miner to find the solution is rewarded with newly created cryptocurrency by adding the next block to the chain. This computational effort provides security by making it economically expensive to add a block, thus to put off data manipulation (Bamakan et al. 2020, Ferdous et al. 2021).

Blockchain technology, through its use of cryptographic hashing and its immutable structure, offers a powerful solution to the fundamental forensic challenge of evidence integrity. A hash function creates a unique, fixed-length digital fingerprint for a block of data. Each block in the blockchain contains the hash of the preceding block, creating a cryptographic link. Any changes to a block would change its hash, invalidate all subsequent blocks and make the ledger tamper-evident (Atlam et al., 2024) As shown in Figure 1, each block is securely linked to the one before it, forming a safe and unchangeable chain.

Figure 1. The structure of a blockchain

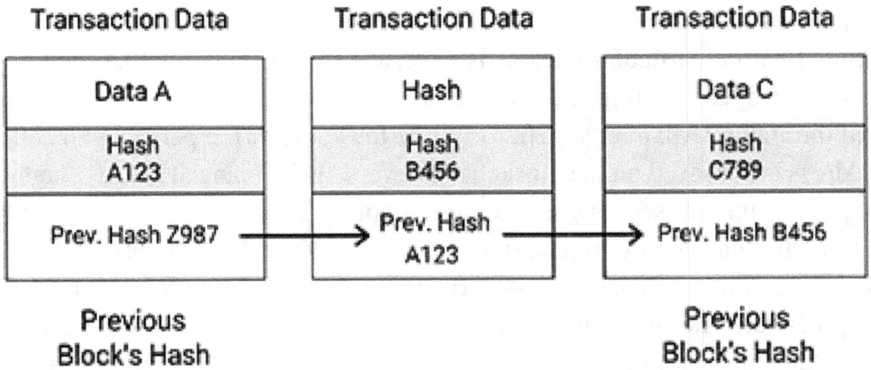

Blockchains also employ different accounting methods, with two predominant models being the Unspent Transaction Output (UTXO) model, used by Bitcoin and the account-based model, popularised by Ethereum. The UTXO model treats a user's holdings as a collection of discrete units of value, much like physical cash. In contrast, the account-based model functions more like a traditional bank account, maintaining a global state of all accounts and their corresponding balances. These differing architectures fundamentally shape the approach to forensic analysis .

Table 1. Comparison of Blockchain Accounting Models.

Feature	UTXO Model (e.g., Bitcoin)	Account-Based Model (e.g., Ethereum)
Unit of Value	Unspent Transaction Outputs (like digital change)	Account Balances (like a bank account)
State Management	Each transaction creates a new set of UTXOs	A global state tracks all account balances
Forensic Implication	Tracing involves following a chain of specific UTXOs	Tracing involves monitoring balance changes in specific accounts

1.2 The Promise and Peril of Pseudonymity

A general and dangerous misconception surrounding cryptocurrencies is that they are anonymous. The reality, however, is that most blockchains, including Bitcoin and Ethereum, are not anonymous but pseudonymous. Understanding this distinction is fundamental to the entire field of blockchain forensics.

Anonymity implies that a person's identity is unknown and their actions are untraceable. Pseudonymity, on the other hand, is a weaker form of privacy where a person's real-world identity is hidden behind a persistent identity, or a "pseudonym". On a public blockchain, the wallet address serves as the alias. Every transaction associated with a particular address is permanently and publicly recorded on the distributed ledger, creating a complete, auditable history of all funds that have passed through it (Atlam et al., 2024). While the name of the person who controls the address is not saved on the blockchain servers, their financial life, as conducted through that alias or pseudonym, is an open book (Campbell-Verduyn et al., 2019).

The reality has intense implications for investigators. The primary objective of a blockchain forensic investigation is de-anonymisation: the process of bridging the gap between the on-chain pseudonym (the wallet address) and the off-chain, real-world identity of the person or entity controlling it. The permanent and public nature of the blockchain provides investigators with a rich dataset to achieve this goal. By examining transactional patterns, clustering related addresses, and correlating on-chain activity with off-chain information, investigators can systematically strip away the veil of pseudonymity (Campbell-Verduyn et al., 2019; Conti et al., 2018). Most sorely, illicit actors often move their funds to a centralised, regulated cryptocurrency exchange to convert them into fiat currency. These exchanges are typically required by law to perform Know Your Customer (KYC) checks, collecting real-world identity documents from their users. This act of "cashing out" creates a direct, legally accessible link between a wallet address and a verified identity.

2. THE LANDSCAPE OF CRYPTOCURRENCY-DRIVEN CYBERCRIME

The solitary properties of cryptocurrencies – pseudonymity, decentralisation, and borderless transactions-have made them the best liked tool for a large number of cybercriminal activities. This part of the chapter focuses on the in-depth analysis of the primary categories of cybercrime that leverage digital assets, moving beyond theoretical concepts to examine the practical methods and on-chain financial footprints of these illicit enterprises (Arnone, 2025).

2.1 Financial Crimes: Fraud and Ransomware

Ransomware is a harmful form of cyber-attack where malicious software encrypts a victim's files or systems, rendering them inaccessible. The attackers demand the cryptocurrency in exchange for the decryption key (Zimba et al. 2019). Bitcoin has been the most preferred currency for these extortions, primarily due to its widespread availability. This Crypto-graphic ecosystem has evolved into the highly professionalised Ransomware-as-a-Service (RaaS) model, where currency developers license ransomware to "affiliates" who oversee attacks, and the ransom payments are split between them (Yousaf et al., 2019).

The typical payment flow begins with the victim acquiring cryptocurrency and transferring it to an attacker's address. The attackers must then launder the funds to obscure their origin. Analysis of on-chain data reveals distinct patterns in laundering tactics (McIntosh et al. 2021). The usual movement of money from a ransomware attack through different laundering stages is shown in Figure 2.

Figure 2. A simplified flowchart of the ransomware money laundering process

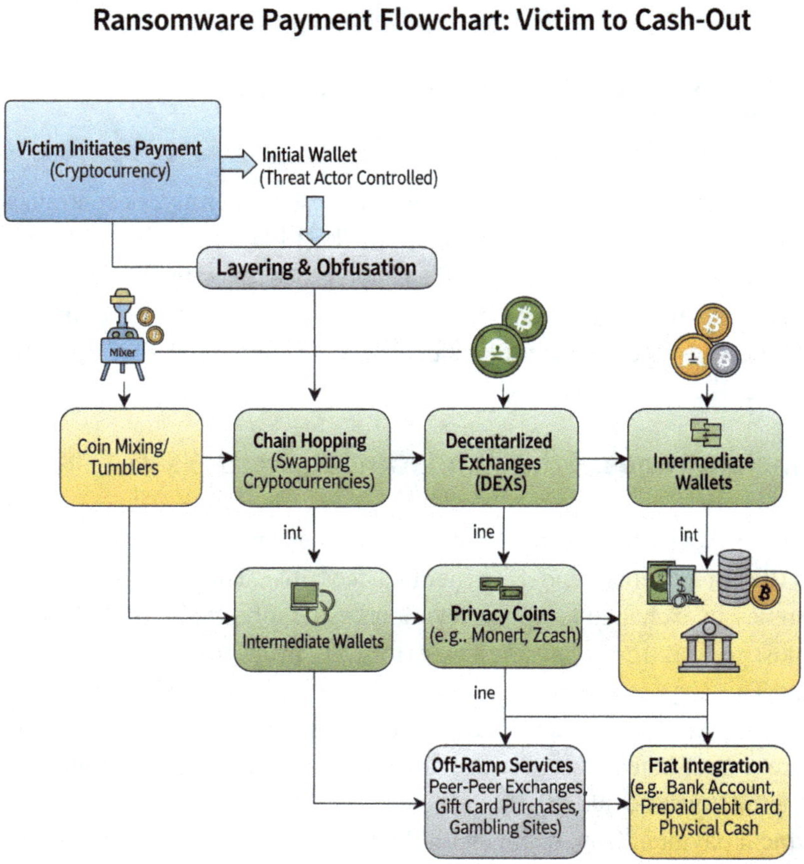

In 2024, total ransomware payments were $813.55 million, a significant decrease from 2023, credited to effective law enforcement actions and victims' growing willingness to report the issue and refusal to pay the amount. This recent trend can be seen clearly in Figure 3.

Figure 3. Total ransomware payments by year (2021-2024)

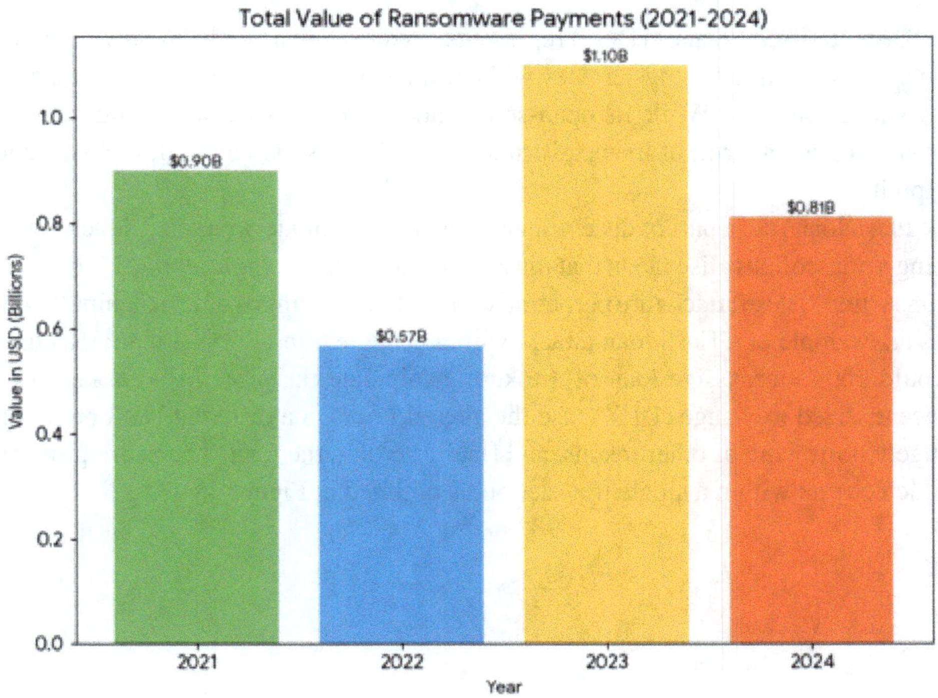

(Source: Adapted from Paquet-Clouston et al., 2019)

2.2 Illicit Economies: Darknet Markets and Sanctioned Entities

Darknet markets are secret online marketplaces, accessible via networks like Tor, where users barter illicit goods and services using cryptocurrencies (Bourne & O'Dair, 2021). The process of laundering proceeds from these markets involves a sophisticated adaptation of the classic three-stage model: placement, layering, and integration. In order to achieve effective layering, darknet actors utilise a variety of on-chain concealment methods. The open ledger of Bitcoin has historically been a weakness for criminals, and the case of the Silk Road marketplace illustrates this. This has led to a more tactical move towards Monero (XMR) and other privacy coins that offer near complete obliteration of transaction details and, therefore, on-chain tracing is virtually impossible without extra off-chain information (Foley et al. 2019).

2.3 Technical Exploits: Crypto-jacking and DeFi Attacks

Decentralised Finance (DeFi) represents a radical departure from the traditional financial system. Offering services without intermediaries, automatically done by the smart contracts. While its open-source and complex structure has built fertile ground for novel forms of financial crime, with billions stolen through sophisticated exploits.

Flash loans are a part of decentralised finance for uniquely targeted attacks, utilising a non-collateralised loan that must be repaid within a single atomic blockchain transaction. These attacks are perpetrated for different forms of oracle manipulation. As an example of a flash loan attack, within a single transaction, a malicious user would obtain a massive loan of a token, manipulate the price of the token on a decentralized exchange (DEX), use the altered price on a different DeFi protocol, hugely borrowing of other tokens, and finally settling the loan. The entire process, which occurs within a single transaction, is outlined in Figure 4.

Figure 4. The steps of a flash loan attack happen one after another in a single atomic transaction.

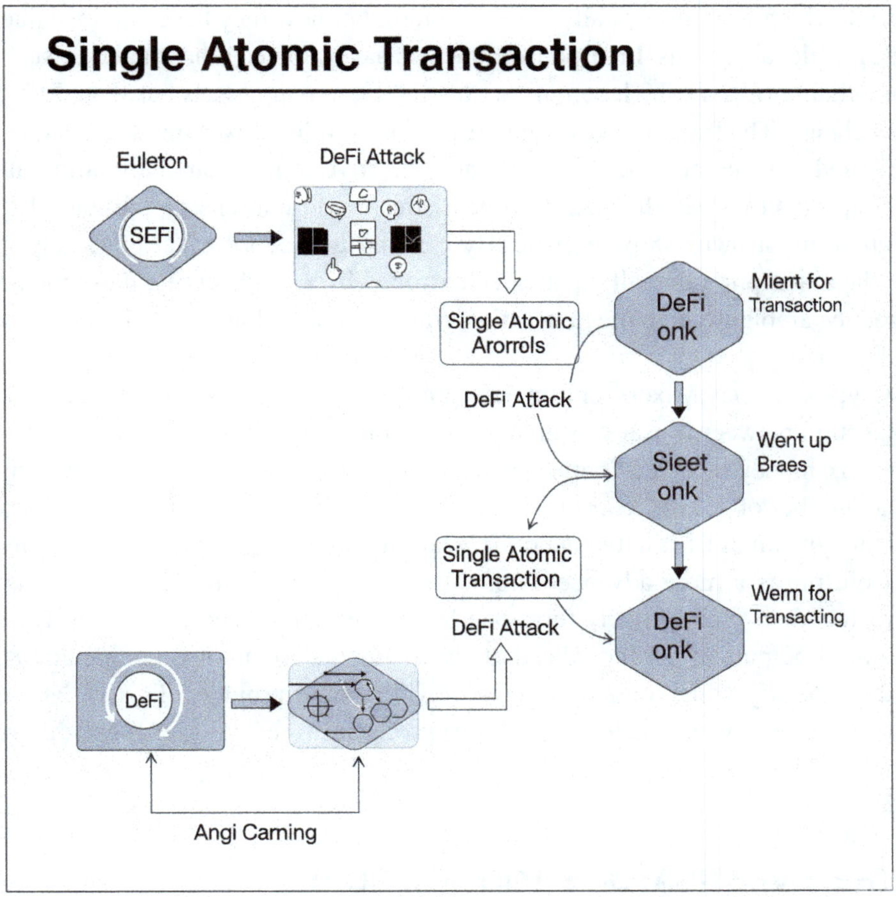

Rug Pulls are a simpler form of exit scams that are frequent in the DeFi space. An unethical actor launches a new token and markets it heavily to lure in investors who exchange precious cryptocurrencies like ETH for the token. The scammer then drains all the precious cryptocurrencies from the liquidity pool, leading to the token's price collapsing to zero (Kalacheva et al., 2024). More complex scams include embedding vicious, executory functions, such as honeypots that bar investors from ever retrieving funds.

2.4 Obfuscation Techniques: The Investigator's Challenge

The earlier trend in laundering tactics has shifted drastically from cryptocurrency mixers, which were historically a primary tool, but now they have declined due to high-profile takedowns. In response, attackers have adopted other methods, such as cross-chain bridges, which complicate tracing by moving assets between different blockchains. The final step is sending funds to centralised exchanges (CEXs) to be converted into fiat currency. The primary objective of most on-chain obfuscation techniques is to break the analytical heuristics used by forensics, particularly the common-input-ownership heuristic. By creating transactions that purposely violate the assumption that all inputs are controlled by a single entity, these methods introduce ambiguity into the transaction graph (Paquet-Clouston et al. 2019, Foley et al., 2019).

Cryptocurrency Mixers, or tumblers, are systems that aim to break the on-chain connection between a user's receiving and sending addresses. Usually centralised, they mix money received from numerous users and, after some delay, transfer an equal number of "clean" coins to a new address. Nonetheless, this model is custodial and presumes trust in the operator, whose internal logs can be taken by police.

CoinJoin is a more advanced, non-custodial approach in which several users come together to collectively form one large transaction. The transaction is built in several outputs of a standardised, uniform amount so that it is computationally hard to identify which output belongs to which input provider. This violates the common-input-ownership heuristic by design because the inputs belong to different unrelated owners.

3. THE INVESTIGATOR'S TOOLKIT: CORE FORENSIC METHODOLOGIES

Whereas the public nature of most blockchains gives access to an unprecedented volume of raw data, this data is extensive, intricate, and pseudonymous (Dudani et al., 2023). This section outlines the key elements of the contemporary blockchain investigator's toolkit, from basic on-chain analysis to the essential process of de-anonymisation.

3.1. Transaction Graph Analysis: Mapping the Flow of Funds

On-chain analysis is the methodical study of the transaction data stored on a blockchain's public ledger. It is the essential practice of blockchain forensics and leverages blockchain's built-in transparency to identify patterns and track fund flows. The chronological and interrelated components of the blockchain transaction structure create an organisational structure that closely resembles a graph — with addresses and transactions as nodes and the flow of value as the edges that link them together (Campbell-Verduyn et al. 2019, Xiao et al. 2024).

The enormous amount of this data makes manual inspection impossible. Thus, transaction graph visualisation is a vital resource for investigators. By converting intangible blockchain information into a logical, visualised form, these resources allow analysts to take advantage of human pattern recognition to rapidly understand complicated financial networks. In a normal visualisation, inputs (funds of origin) and outputs (fresh funds) are depicted by different nodes, proportional to the size of the cryptocurrency moved, and the edges link them to a core transaction node, graphically illustrating the transfer of funds. With these visualisations, analysts can easily spot typical patterns signalling illicit behaviour, such as a peeling chain, wherein a large input is "peeled" off into a chain of multiple smaller transactions, which can be an indicator of money laundering. An example of how these financial networks are visualised is shown in Figure 5.

Figure 5. An example of a transaction graph

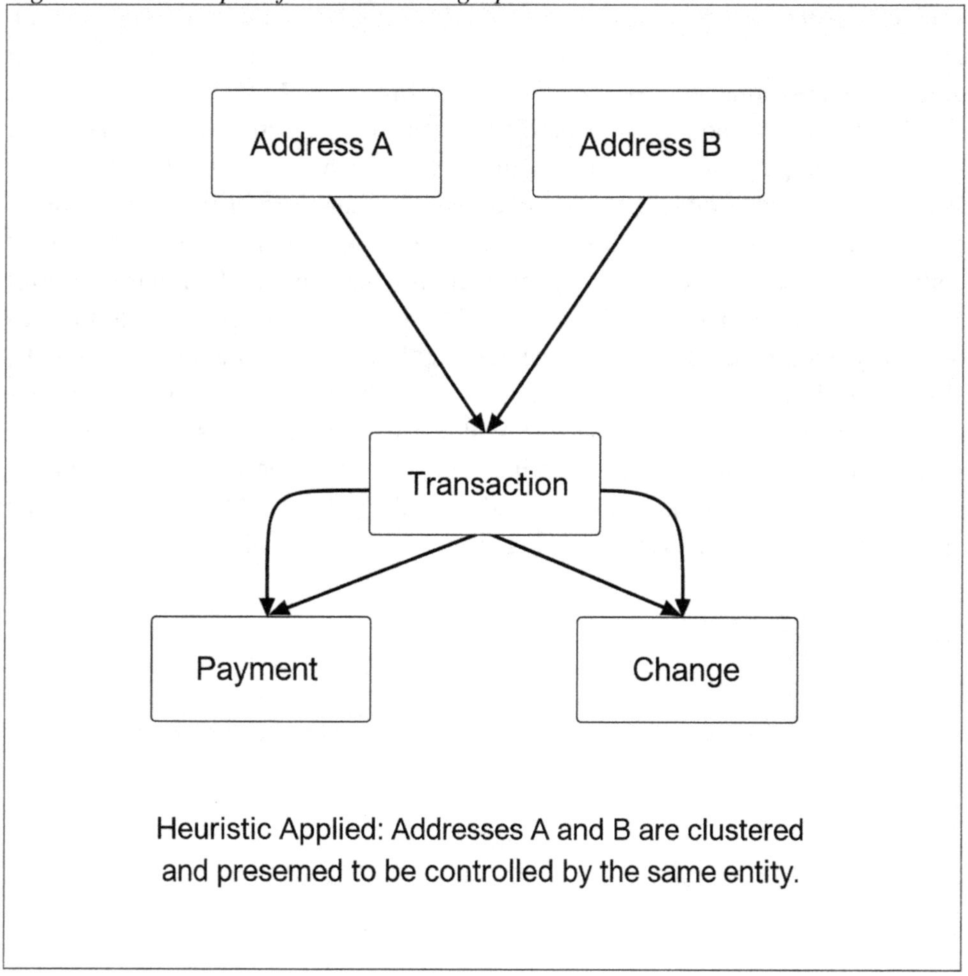

3.2 Address Clustering: The Common-Input-Ownership Heuristic

While transaction graph analysis illustrates the flow of funds between pseudonyms, it is important for the next step to find out which of the pseudonyms belong to the same agent. This sequence is called address clustering and forms a critical groundwork for de-anonymisation in blockchain forensics (Atlam et al. 2024, Chainalysis 2024).

Clustering is the process of bringing together two or more different cryptocurrency addresses that are thought to be owned or controlled by one individual or entity.

Clustering is achieved through the use of heuristics – common-sense rules based on observable on-chain behaviour that are correct in most cases. The most fundamental and widely used of these is the common-input-ownership heuristic, also known as the co-spending heuristic. The common-input-ownership assumption states that if multiple input addresses are used in a single transaction, then the same person likely owns those input addresses. This assumption is reasonable, given how UTXO blockchains like Bitcoin operate. To create and sign a transaction that spends from different input addresses, you need to have the private key of each address. Because users typically store their private keys separately from public records, this assumption is strong because it is likely that if they are using multiple accounts for a transaction, then the same person owns all the inputs. Figure 6 provides a visual representation of this heuristic in action.

Figure 6. An illustration of the common input ownership heuristic

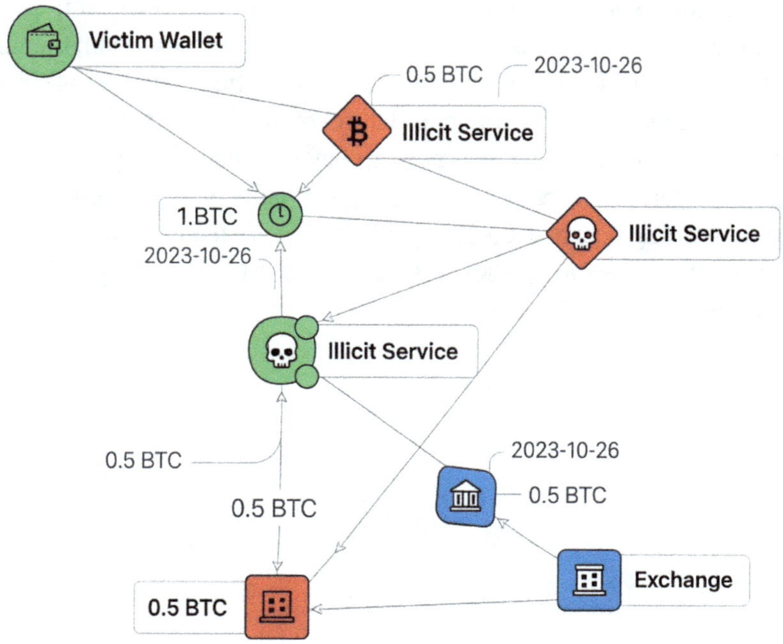

For example, if a transaction has inputs from Address A, Address B, and Address C, then a forensic tool would cluster all three addresses together, based on the fact that they are all inputs for a single transaction.

3.3 Address Attribution: Linking Pseudonyms to Entities

Once a cluster of addresses is formed, the last step is attribution. This process links the entire cluster to a known, real-world entity, like a cryptocurrency exchange, a darknet market, a ransomware group, or an individual. Attribution is the important connection that joins on-chain evidence to the off-chain world. It turns a group of pseudonymous addresses into a useful investigative lead. This often happens by using a mix of private databases managed by forensic firms, which hold millions of labelled addresses, along with off-chain intelligence.

4. A CRITICAL ANALYSIS OF FORENSIC METHODOLOGIES

The development of blockchain forensic techniques has not gone unanswered. In a classic "cat-and-mouse" dynamic, the development of more refined tracing tools has prompted the creation of equally developed counter-forensic technologies designed to complicate transaction trails and break the heuristic that forensic analysts rely on.

4.1. The Limits of Heuristics: CoinJoins and False Positives

The common input ownership heuristic is powerful but probabilistic, not deterministic. Its effectiveness faces challenges from privacy-enhancing technologies, especially CoinJoin transactions. These transactions combine inputs from multiple independent users into a single transaction, explicitly violating the heuristic's assumptions. Figure 7 demonstrates how a CoinJoin transaction is structured to create ambiguity.

Figure 7. A diagram of a CoinJoin transaction

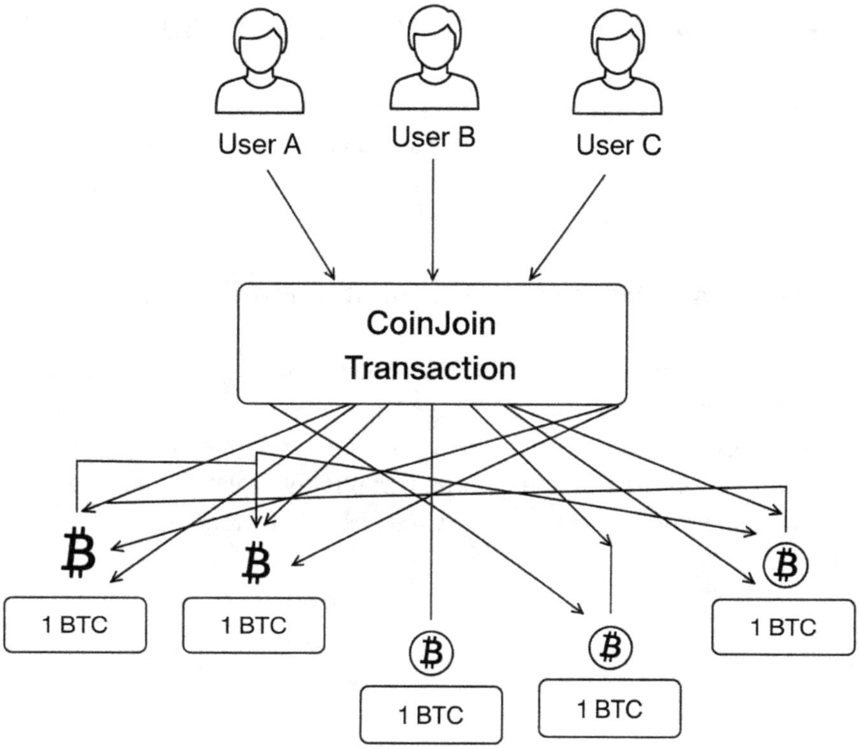

Blindly applying the co-spending heuristic to a CoinJoin transaction may result in false positives by incorrectly grouping addresses that belong to different individuals. This leads to significant legal issues since the reliability and potential error rate of forensic tools based on such heuristics get scrutinised in court. In the U.S. v. Sterlingov case, which involved the operator of the Bitcoin Fog mixer, the defence presented a strong challenge to the reliability of Chainalysis Reactor's clustering algorithms, based on the Daubert standard for expert testimony. This case marks a shift in the evidentiary landscape. Forensic analysts must be ready to defend the probabilistic assumptions of their tools.

4.2. The Challenge of Privacy-Enhancing Technologies (PETs)

While CoinJoin is a powerful protocol, its effectiveness relies on proper implementation. To tackle this, a new generation of privacy-focused wallets has emerged, with Wasabi Wallet and Samourai Wallet as the most notable examples for Bitcoin. These wallets build privacy protections into the entire user experience

Wasabi Wallet is an open-source, desktop-first wallet known for its strong emphasis on privacy. Its main features include an integrated CoinJoin implementation called WabiSabi, default Tor integration to hide the user's IP address, private blockchain syncing using block filters, and improved coin control to prevent accidentally merging UTXOs with different privacy histories.

Samourai Wallet is a mobile-first wallet that provides an extensive range of privacy features. Its key functions include Whirlpool, its built-in CoinJoin feature that keeps mixed and unmixed funds separate to avoid user mistakes. It also includes advanced spending tools like Stonewall, which creates transactions that imitate the structure of a CoinJoin for plausible deniability, and Stowaway, a PayJoin feature that obscures the actual amount being sent. These wallets provide a multi-layered defence against forensic analysis, but they also come with a steep learning curve, which means user errors can be significant investigative opportunities.

4.3 Contrasting Chains: Why Bitcoin Forensics Fails on Privacy Coins

While privacy-enhancing wallets add masking to transparent blockchains, privacy coins are built with privacy as a default, protocol-level feature. These cryptocurrencies present the most significant technical challenges to blockchain forensics. The two most prominent examples are Monero (XMR) and Zcash (ZEC).

Monero (XMR) ensures privacy by default through three main cryptographic technologies:

- Ring Signatures: To keep the sender anonymous, a user's digital signature is mixed with the signatures of other users, known as "decoys." This mixing makes it nearly impossible to identify the true sender.
- Stealth Addresses: To maintain receiver anonymity, the sender creates a unique, random, one-time public address for the recipient for each transaction. This prevents the public from linking multiple payments to the same person.
- Ring Confidential Transactions (RingCT): This technology conceals the amount of cryptocurrency being transferred. Only the sender and receiver can see the transaction values.

Zcash (ZEC) provides privacy through a different optional method based on zk-SNARKs (Zero-Knowledge Succinct Non-Interactive Argument of Knowledge). A zero-knowledge proof lets one party confirm a statement is true without sharing any details other than its truth. In Zcash, users can prove that a transaction is valid without revealing the sender, the recipient, or the amount. Zcash has both transparent addresses (t-addresses) and shielded addresses (z-addresses), which use zk-SNARKs for added privacy. For forensic investigators, fully shielded Zcash transactions and all Monero transactions present a significant challenge for on-chain analysis, necessitating the use of off-chain intelligence.

Table 2. Forensic Traceability on Different Blockchains

Feature	Bitcoin (Transparent)	Zcash (Shielded)	Monero (Private by Default)
Sender Visibility	Public(Pseudonymous Address)	Hidden(zk-SNARKs)	Hidden(Ring Signatures)
Receiver Visibility	Public(Pseudonymous Address)	Hidden (zk-SNARKs)	Hidden (Stealth Addresses)
Amount Visibility	Public	Hidden (zk-SNARKs)	Hidden (RingCT)
Primary Forensic Challenge	De-anonymization	Breaking Cryptography	Breaking Cryptography

5. USER-CENTRIC THREAT INTELLIGENCE: BEYOND THE LEDGER

On-chain data, despite its depth, gives only part of the picture. To solve a case, investigators need to connect the pseudonymous on-chain world with the real world of identifiable individuals and organisations. They accomplish this by integrating off-chain evidence with behavioural analysis.

5.1. Behavioural Profiling from On-Chain Data

In addition to mere tracing of funds, actors are profiled and illicit behaviour identified using evidence analysis of transaction patterns. Licit and illicit actors have characteristic on-chain “fingerprints”. By categorising such activities, forensic platforms can automatically detect suspicious activity.

Common illicit patterns include:

- **Money Laundering:** Characterised by complex transaction chains that hide the source of funds, these often use techniques like peeling chains. In this method, large sums are gradually separated into smaller amounts through a series of wallets.
- **Tumbler/Mixer Usage:** Transactions entering known mixing services are a strong indicator of an attempt to break the on-chain trail.
- **Darknet Market Activity:** Funds moving to or from addresses associated with darknet markets.
- **Ransomware:** A distinct payment flow where a victim sends funds to an attacker's address, which are then quickly moved through laundering services.

Forensic platforms such as TRM Labs have created "Signatures®" which automatically such and other typologies of laundering as layering and suspicious movement of funds, and deliver investigators instant behavioural intelligence. This enables the analysts to go beyond monitoring single transactions to be able to see the nature and purpose of the activity on a macro level.

5.2. Open-Source Intelligence (OSINT) Integration

Open-Source Intelligence (OSINT) is the collection and analysis of information from open sources. In cryptocurrency investigations, this means searching the internet for any case where a target wallet address has been openly published.

Cybercriminals usually commit operational security errors, which include using a wallet address in a public forum, sharing it on social media platforms like Twitter or Reddit, or publishing it as part of the source code for a scam website. Every occurrence establishes a possible connection between the on-chain pseudonym and an off-chain identity (a username, social media user profile, or website).

Knowing this synergy, commercial forensic platforms are now more commonly integrating with OSINT solutions. Firms like Chainalysis are collaborating with companies like Maltego, Spiderfoot, and Cloudburst to combine their on-chain intelligence with off-chain data from the deep and dark web, social media, and forums. This integration grants investigators a holistic perspective, enabling them to switch in an instant between following a transaction on the blockchain and tracking the online identity behind one of its addresses.

5.3 Bridging On-Chain and Off-Chain Worlds

The final goal of this process is too de-establish the subject by connecting their on-chain activity to their verifiable, actual identity. The most crucial point in most investigations is when illegal funds are linked back to a regulated centralised cryptocurrency exchange (CEX). These transactions, in the majority of jurisdictions, are obligatory to have effective Anti-Money Laundering (AML) and Know Your Customer (KYC) programs in place. As a part of their process for KYC, exchanges obtain and authenticate identifying data from their clients, including their legal name, residential address, date of birth, and government-issued identification documents.

When such illegal funds are tracked by forensic examination to a deposit location on an exchange of this sort, it is a useful investigative clue. Police officials can subsequently serve a legal document, e.g., a subpoena or a search warrant, on the exchange, compelling it to disclose the KYC information concerning the account that received the funds. This is a direct, admissible-in-court link between the on-chain address and off-chain identity of the suspect. This critical investigative process of connecting the two worlds is summarized in Figure 8.

Figure 8. The process of connecting on-chain data (transaction analysis) with off-chain data (legal process and OSINT) to achieve de-anonymisation.

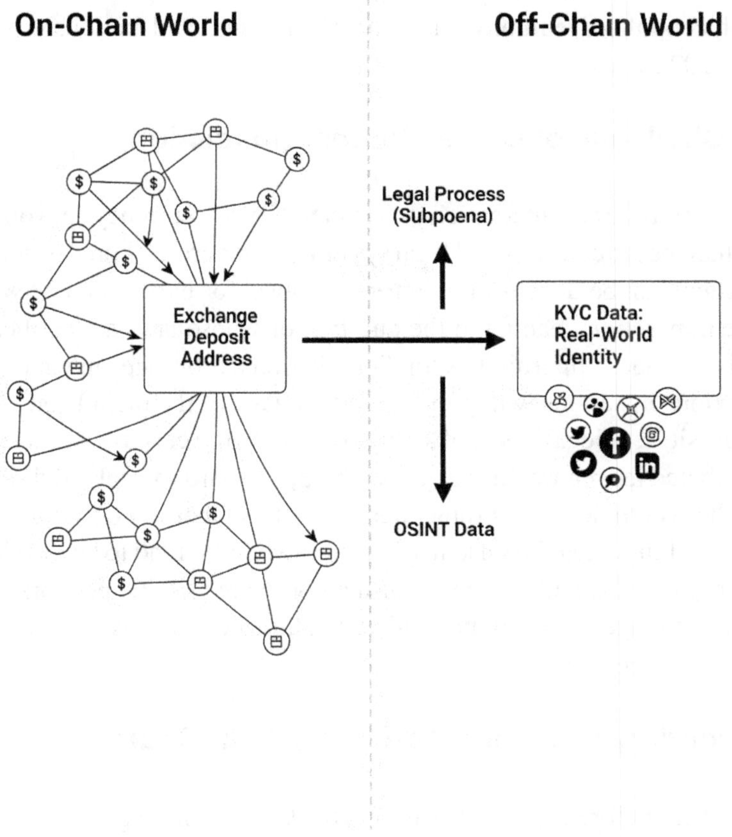

This blended model redefines the role of modern-day blockchain forensics. The investigation on blockchain typically serves as a good lead-generating tool that fuels more traditional, off-blockchain investigations. The blockchain itself rarely breaks the crime; instead, it provides an irreversible roadmap that leads investigators to the cyber and legal doorways where real-world identities are eventually revealed.

6. LEGAL, REGULATORY, AND ETHICAL DIMENSIONS

The very quick expansion of cryptocurrency has given rise to a puzzling environment for legal regimes and regulatory authorities (Arner et al., 2017). The very essence of the technology—decentralisation, pseudonymity, and international transactions without borders—is incompatible with legal frameworks founded on notions of centralised authority, identifiable parties, and national jurisdictions (Connolly, 2022).

6.1 The Challenge of Cross-Border Jurisdiction

The decentralised and international character of cryptocurrency networks poses an inherent challenge to conventional legal systems, which are anchored in geographical borders. There can be dozens of countries involved for parties and network nodes in a single transaction, leading to the question of whose laws are applicable. This uncertainty provides opportunities for "jurisdictional arbitrage" in which criminals base operations in nations with poor regulation. One of the main legal obstacles is deciding the situs, or legal place, of a crypto asset. As the crypto asset is everywhere on its distributed ledger, unlike a physical thing, it is hard to apply traditional rules. To tackle these complexities, strong international collaboration is vital. Traditional tools such as Mutual Legal Assistance Treaties (MLATs) tend to be too slow for the speed of crypto crime and thus focus instead on more flexible networks involving law enforcement agencies and international authorities such as the Joint Chiefs of Global Tax Enforcement.

6.2. Evidentiary Value and Admissibility in Court

For blockchain forensic analysis to be effective, its findings must be usable as evidence in court (Xukang et al., 2024). In the U.S. legal system, evidence must meet standards of relevance, authenticity, and reliability. Blockchain's secure and tamper-proof ledger provides a strong basis for authenticity, offering a solid digital chain of custody.

Despite these strengths, challenges persist. The Hearsay Rule, which excludes out-of-court statements offered to prove their truth, can be a barrier. A blockchain record is an out-of-court statement about a transaction. More importantly, the reliability of forensic tools and methods faces legal scrutiny. In U.S. v. Sterlingov, the defence challenged the evidence under the Daubert standard, which governs expert testimony. They argued that the clustering algorithms in Chainalysis Reactor operated as a proprietary "black box" with an unknown error rate. The court ultimately ruled the evidence admissible, valuing the software's broad acceptance by law enforcement.

However, this case sets an important precedent. It shows that prosecutors must be ready to defend the scientific validity of their forensic tools in court.

6.3. Data Privacy and Ethical Considerations in De-anonymisation

As cryptocurrency has grown, regulatory bodies have stepped up efforts to bring the industry into compliance. The Financial Action Task Force (FATF), the global standard-setter for anti-money laundering and counter-terrorism financing (AML/CFT), has expanded its standards to include virtual assets and Virtual Asset Service Providers (VASPs). Key FATF recommendations include licensing, customer due diligence (KYC), and the "Travel Rule," which requires VASPs to send originator and beneficiary information with transactions. However, global implementation remains poor. A 2024 FATF report found that 75% of jurisdictions were still not fully compliant.

In Europe, another challenge arises from the clash between blockchain and the General Data Protection Regulation (GDPR). The GDPR's Right to Erasure, also known as the "Right to be Forgotten," directly conflicts with the principle of immutability. This conflict makes it technically challenging to delete data from a public blockchain. Additionally, identifying a legally responsible "data controller" in a decentralised network is a significant challenge.

This creates an ethical dilemma, putting the need for law enforcement to investigate serious crimes in direct conflict with individuals' right to financial privacy. Financial privacy is an essential part of personal autonomy and freedom. However, criminals exploit this same pseudonymity for terrible activities. The tools used to track a terrorist financier can also be used for widespread financial surveillance. The probabilistic nature of clustering heuristics also carries a risk of false positives. An innocent person could be mistakenly linked to a criminal group. Finding a balance requires clear legal frameworks, strong oversight, and reasonable government regulation, such as mandating KYC/AML for centralised exchanges. This can help prevent the worst abuses while protecting the privacy of peer-to-peer transactions

7. CASE STUDIES IN BLOCKCHAIN FORENSICS

The theoretical methods of blockchain forensics are most comprehensible when seen in action. The following significant cases illustrate how the intersection of on-chain analysis, traditional investigative legwork, and global cooperation has proven central to dismantling major criminal syndicates.

7.1. The Silk Road: Early Triumphs of On-Chain Tracing

The Silk Road was the original modern darknet market, existing from 2011 until 2013. Its creator, Ross Ulbricht, used the pseudonym "Dread Pirate Roberts" (DPR) (Lonergan & Schneider, 2023). The platform facilitated the sale of hundreds of millions of dollars' worth of illegal products anonymously, primarily drugs, in Bitcoin. The case became a significant cybercrime case in the history of such crimes, illustrating a combination of old-fashioned detective work, open-source intelligence, and digital forensics.

The primary breakthrough to uncover Ulbricht's identity originated from off-chain data. Investigators linked the online moniker "altoid," which appeared in initial posts to advertise Silk Road, to a subsequent message when the user of the same name posted an email address including his full name: rossulbricht@gmail.com. This identified the primary suspect. The case strengthened when the FBI arrested Ulbricht in a library, where they found him running the site on his open laptop. This allowed them to seize unencrypted evidence, including journals and transaction records.

On-chain analysis played an important role in quantifying the enormous scope of the criminal enterprise, which was significant in his sentencing. The police arrested more than $1 billion in Bitcoin associated with the website during the investigation (Arner et al., 2017). Blockchain analysis also played a major role in exposing corruption inside the law enforcement task force. The stolen Bitcoins were tracked by investigators to two federal agents who were involved in corruption, and they were subsequently convicted and imprisoned. Ross Ulbricht was found guilty of seven charges and sentenced to life imprisonment without parole.

7.2. The Welcome to Video Takedown: A Complex International Case

The "Welcome to Video" (WTV) investigation is one of the most notable international operations to take down a large-scale online child sexual abuse material (CSAM) marketplace.200 The dark website, based in South Korea by Jong Woo Son, had more than one million members who utilised Bitcoin to buy content. The operation is an excellent example of how blockchain forensic technology, used together with international collaboration and the exploitation of criminals' reliance on regulated platforms, can de-anonymise perpetrators worldwide.

The first substantial break was due to an off-chain technical error: officials found that the server IP address of the site was not well hidden, and they were able to track it to South Korea. Now that the location of the administrator was known, officials shifted to on-chain analysis, carefully following up Bitcoin payments from thousands of customers to Son's accounts. The greatest weakness for the consumers was that many financed their WTV accounts straight from individual accounts on regulated cryptocurrency exchanges that apply KYC checks.

This is where international cooperation became paramount. US agencies (HSI, IRS-CI) worked in concert with the UK's National Crime Agency (NCA), German officials, and the Korean National Police Agency (KNPA). This international task force coordinated with exchanges globally, employing lawful procedures to obtain the KYC information related to the Bitcoin addresses that had made payments to WTV, establishing an immediate connection between the on-chain transactions and the real-world identities of the users. The result was staggering: the investigation resulted in the arrest of the administrator and 337 subscribers in 38 different nations, and the rescue of 23 minor victims.

8. FUTURE RESEARCH AND POLICY DIRECTIONS

The ever-changing world of crypto-crime demands that we keep our eyes open to new developments. The race between investigators and criminals isn't slowing; it's picking up speed. For researchers, this means the work is never done. The next big challenge is already upon us: creating effective forensic methods for privacy-focused technologies that are built to be untraceable from the start. We're also seeing the investigative trail expand beyond just the blockchain to include the network traffic that connects users and the mobile devices storing their digital keys. To succeed in these areas, we need a new set of tools, especially those powered by artificial intelligence, to help analysts detect subtle signs of illegal activity amidst a vast amount of data.

At the policy level, the message is one of cooperation and transformation. Criminals exploit loopholes in a fractured global system, rapidly transferring assets across borders. Closing those loopholes needs a concerted international effort. Our justice systems must change, too. The information exposed on a blockchain is only valuable if it can be easily understood and presented in court. This requires lawmakers and judges to establish frameworks that respect the distinctive features of digital evidence and the reliability of tools for examining it.

This leads us to perhaps the most universal hurdle: achieving the right equilibrium between privacy and security. The same techniques that can uncover a terrorist financier could lead to widespread surveillance if abused. The techniques employed to pinpoint a money launderer risk falsely identifying an innocent individual. Striking a balance is not solely the business of the police or the regulators; it is the business of the entire community. We need to set precise ethical policies that guarantee that the forensic capabilities are exercised in a reasonable manner that promotes justice without infringing on primary human rights.

In this domain, the goal is transitioning from a reactive to a proactive approach. The goal is to transform from being digital archaeologists reconstructing crimes to digital sentinels who detect and neutralise attacks in real time, safeguarding the digital economy for all.

9. CONCLUSION

The field of blockchain forensics is always changing and is in an ongoing battle with cybercriminals. The future of this area will be influenced by the use of new technologies, the careful planning of law enforcement, and the constantly changing methods of illegal actors.

This chapter discusses how cryptocurrencies offer a pseudonymous and borderless avenue for transactions but simultaneously maintain a permanent and public evidence trail due to blockchain technology. The success of blockchain forensics applies a blend of sophisticated on-chain analysis, such as transaction graphing and address clustering, with critical off-chain intelligence from OSINT and KYC data from regulated exchanges. The de-anonymisation of perpetrators and the recovery of illicit funds showcase the rediscovery of fusion technology, which is the backbone of landmark cases like 'The Silk Road', 'Colonial Pipeline', and 'Welcome to Video'. The field is not without challenges, as there is a constant arms race where criminals using CoinJoin, privacy coins, mixers, and other privacy-enhancing technologies pose a challenge to forensic heuristics. The evolving legal, regulatory, and ethical challenges of balance in financial privacy and investigation highlight the intersection where AI, machine learning, and global partnerships offer boundless potential.

Heuristic and manual analysis techniques are becoming inadequate, considering the increasing intricacy and volume of blockchain data. The future of effective blockchain forensics will be focused on integrating Artificial Intelligence (AI) and Machine Learning (ML) technologies. These technologies will streamline the process of scanning enormous datasets for illicit activities and spying, tracking harmful patterns. Supervised learning models, for example, are capable of accurately classifying new transactions after training on extensive labelled datasets. Other promising applications include real-time anomaly detection, advanced anomaly detection, and even autonomous forensic agents capable of conducting preliminary real-time investigations. The ongoing technological arms race will be sustained, however, as criminals leverage AI to improve their operations.

As of late, law enforcement is shifting its strategy by relying upon a "crypto maturity model", which depicts a more holistic approach to blockchain intelligence. This shift in evolution moves from a reliance on small, specialised teams to equipping entire agencies with real-time operational technologies, and finally to the proactive self-integration of blockchain intelligence into foundational agency data systems through APIs. This evolution is being strategically bolstered by the creation of Z specialised national units, such as the FBI's Virtual Asset Exploitation Unit (VAXU) and the DOJ's National Cryptocurrency Enforcement Team (NCET), in addition to rising shifts to public-private partnerships.

REFERENCES

Arner, D. W., Barberis, J., & Buckley, R. P. (2017). FinTech, RegTech, and the reconceptualization of financial regulation. *Northwestern Journal of International Law & Business*, *37*(3), 371–413.

Arnone, G., Scire', G., & Bivona, E. (2025). The (mis)use of cryptocurrencies by criminal organizations: A systematic literature review. *Digital Finance*, *7*(4), 815–851. https://link.springer.com/article/10.1007/s42521-025-00148-1. DOI: 10.1007/s42521-025-00148-1

Atlam, H. F., Ekuri, N., Azad, M. A., & Lallie, H. S. (2024). Blockchain forensics: A systematic literature review of techniques, applications, challenges, and future directions. *Electronics (Basel)*, *13*(17), 3568. DOI: 10.3390/electronics13173568

Bamakan, S. M. H., Motavali, A., & Bondarti, A. B. (2020). A survey of blockchain consensus algorithms performance evaluation criteria. *Expert Systems with Applications*, *154*, 113385. DOI: 10.1016/j.eswa.2020.113385

Bourne, M., & O'Dair, M. (2021). Cryptocurrencies and money laundering: A literature review. *Journal of Money Laundering Control*, *24*(4), 653–672. DOI: 10.1108/JMLC-09-2020-0105

Campbell-Verduyn, M., Goguen, M., & Porter, T. (2019). Finding fault lines in long chains of financial information. *Review of International Political Economy*, *26*(5), 911–937. DOI: 10.1080/09692290.2019.1616595

Chainalysis. (2024). The 2024 crypto crime report: Everything you need to know about ransomware, scams, and the illicit use of digital assets. Chainalysis Inc. https://www.chainalysis.com/blog/2024-crypto-crime-report-introduction/. Accessed August 2025.

Connolly, M. (2022). Cryptocurrency concerns, crimes, and legal consequences. *Akron Law Review*, *55*(3), 3.

Conti, M., Milajerdi, S. M., & Saha, R. (2018). A survey on security and privacy issues of Bitcoin. *IEEE Communications Surveys and Tutorials*, *20*(4), 3416–3452. DOI: 10.1109/COMST.2018.2842460

Dudani, S., Baggili, I., Raymond, D., & Marchany, R. (2023). The current state of cryptocurrency forensics. *Forensic Science International Digital Investigation*, *46*, 301576. DOI: 10.1016/j.fsidi.2023.301576

Ferdous, M. S., Chowdhury, M. J. M., & Hoque, M. A. (2021). A survey of consensus algorithms in public blockchain systems for crypto-currencies. *Journal of Network and Computer Applications*, *182*, 103035. DOI: 10.1016/j.jnca.2021.103035

Foley, S., Karlsen, J. R., & Putniņš, T. J. (2019). Sex, drugs, and bitcoin: How much illegal activity is financed through cryptocurrencies? *Review of Financial Studies*, *32*(5), 1798–1853. DOI: 10.1093/rfs/hhz015

Kalacheva, A., Kuznetsov, P., Vodolazov, I., & Yanovich, Y. (2024). Detecting Rug Pulls in Decentralized Exchanges: The Rise of Meme Coins. https://ssrn.com/abstract=4981529 or . Accessed Aug. 2025.DOI: 10.2139/ssrn.4981529

Lonergan, E. D., & Schneider, J. (2023). The power of beliefs in US cyber strategy: The evolving role of deterrence, norms, and escalation. *Journal of Cybersecurity*, *9*(1), tyad006. Advance online publication. DOI: 10.1093/cybsec/tyad006

McIntosh, T., Kayes, A. S. M., Chen, Y. P. P., Ng, A., & Watters, P. (2021). Ransomware mitigation in the modern era: A comprehensive review, research challenges, and future directions. *ACM Computing Surveys*, *54*(9), 1–36. DOI: 10.1145/3479393

Paquet-Clouston, M., Haslhofer, B., & Dupont, B. (2019). A tale of two markets: Investigating the ransomware payments economy. *Journal of Cybersecurity*, *5*(1), tyz003. Advance online publication. DOI: 10.1093/cybsec/tyz003

Tripathi, G., Ahad, M. A., & Casalino, G. (2023). A comprehensive review of blockchain technology: Underlying principles and historical background with future challenges. *Decision Analytics Journal*, *9*, 100344. DOI: 10.1016/j.dajour.2023.100344

Xiao, N., Wang, Z., Sun, X., & Miao, J. (2024). A novel blockchain-based digital forensics framework for preserving evidence and enabling investigation in industrial Internet of Things. *Alexandria Engineering Journal*, *86*, 631–643. DOI: 10.1016/j.aej.2023.12.021

Xukang, W., Cheng, W. K., & Zhe, M. (2024). Blockchain in the courtroom: Exploring its evidentiary significance and procedural implications in U.S. judicial processes. *Frontiers in Blockchain*, *7*, 1306058. Advance online publication. DOI: 10.3389/fbloc.2024.1306058

Yousaf, H., Kappos, G., & Meiklejohn, S. (2019). Tracing transactions across cryptocurrency ledgers. Proceedings of the 28th USENIX Security Symposium (USENIX Security 19), 837–853. https://www.usenix.org/conference/usenixsecurity19/presentation/yousaf

Zimba, A., Wang, Z., Chen, H., & Mulenga, M. (2019). Recent advances in cryptovirology: State-of-the-art crypto mining and crypto ransomware attacks. *KSII Transactions on Internet and Information Systems*, *13*(6), 3258–3279. DOI: 10.3837/tiis.2019.06.027

Chapter 17
Legal and Ethical Considerations in Cyber Forensics

Omowunmi F. Makinde
https://orcid.org/0009-0004-9372-7539
Amazon, USA

ABSTRACT

This chapter examines the complex legal and ethical landscape surrounding human threat intelligence analysis in cyber forensic investigations, addressing challenges created by integrating artificial intelligence, behavioral analysis, and user-centric techniques. The analysis explores constitutional protections in behavioral profiling, digital evidence admissibility standards for AI-enhanced investigations, and cross-border legal challenges in dark web intelligence. Privacy rights under frameworks like GDPR require balancing security needs with individual privacy through data minimization and consent mechanisms. Ethical considerations encompass algorithmic bias, transparency requirements, and professional conduct standards. The chapter addresses regulatory compliance across industry sectors and emerging challenges from quantum computing threats and social engineering analysis, demonstrating that successful navigation requires collaboration between practitioners, legal professionals, and policymakers.

1. INTRODUCTION

The interactions between human threat intelligence and cyber forensic practices have altered the digital investigations definition to center on the intentional and malicious intrusions, ceasing to be just about technical breaches but focused on

DOI: 10.4018/979-8-3373-4898-8.ch017

human-made intrusions like the social engineering technique, insider abuse, and targeted attacks on a long-term basis. It is due to this change that new legal and ethical issues have arisen, which should be approached with utmost care (Saeed et al., 2023). The increased application of machine learning and artificial intelligence to forensic practice is only making the area more complicated where courts must deal with the automated results, how to curb the application of bias, and how to comprehend human accountability when machines aid in the investigative process. Such advances demand a better idea of the applicability of old legal principles to new forensic technology (Solanke and Biasiotti, 2022).

The law of human threat intelligence lies at a cross-road of the constitutional protection, laws of privacy, the standard of evidence, and international collaboration. The Fourth Amendment rights in the U.S. and similar protections of privacy in other parts of the world also impose significant restrictions on surveillance of activities and electronic surveillance (Rai et al. 2016; Rai, 2019; Nain, 2024). These safeguards have to balance with the requirement to identify and mitigate severe risks (Zhang, 2025). There is also a problem with the court assessing artificial intelligence evidence, as machine-learning algorithms and machine analysis are not easily categorized under the traditional evidentiary rules. The extra levels of complexity include cross-border investigations, in particular, those that involve intelligence of dark-webs, as the various jurisdictions might possess incongruent rules or protocols (Durán et al., 2024).

The other vital component of this landscape is privacy and data protection laws. Several aspects of human threat intelligence, such as behavioral profiling, require the intensive use of personal information, thus the need to ensure high protection and ethical control (Marikyan et al., 2023). There are rules and laws like the GDPR that are in place to ensure that a number of requirements are met especially in situations where the data moves across the borders. Insider-threat programs should also weigh between organizational security and employee rights and thus should be clearly consented, proportional and limited to its scope of monitoring (Javed & Sajid, 2024).

Ethical issues comprise algorithmic discrimination, openness, and consideration of personal dignity. AI systems may generate injustice when monitored without care, and they may make legal procedures complex and interfere with individual rights due to their inability to be explained (Quang Huy & Kien Phuc, 2025).

1.1 Constitutional Protections in Behavioral Analysis

The fundamental boundaries to the application of human threat intelligence work in behavioral analysis are constitutional protections, particularly the Fourth Amendment prohibition of unreasonable searches and seizures. The Fourth Amendment stipulates that government searches must be reasonable, which should be typically backed by an issued warrant due to probable cause, except where a pre-existing exception exists. When going through a digital investigation, courts have to determine whether digesting and analyzing behavioral patterns should be considered a search and, in that case, to what degree they need protection (Slobogin and Brayne, 2023). The decision made by the Supreme Court in the case of Carpenter v. United States (2018) believed that, comprehensive digital records that display the movements of an individual should be afforded privacy protection, which implies that blanket behavioral profiling can also require a warrant. This argument can be applied to cyber forensic activities in which intelligence specialists merge big data of online activity, communication records, and user behavior to create profile-like details (Neilson, 2023).

Use of constitutional measures in making behavioral profiling entails keen consideration of the extent to which data is gathered and the invasive nature of the analysis. Even though a single piece of information might not be private, courts have realized that a combination of such information could reveal personal information that deserves a constitutional protection. In United States v. The Supreme Court in 2012 upheld the decision of Jones (2012) that prolonged GPS tracking constitutes a search, which serves to strengthen more significant limitations on tracking the actions of an individual (Slobogin and Brayne, 2023). The reasoning has a direct impact on cyber forensics, in which years of the digital activity and social media engagement or communication patterns can be followed. Consequently, the tools of behavioral analysis employed in the field of threat intelligence need to have adequate protection measures like judicial warrants, time constraints, and controlled measures to ensure privacy does not violate or compromise security requirements (Stoykova, 2021). It is even more difficult to determine what can be included in a reasonable expectation of privacy in digital behavior. A court has to look at the expectation of privacy by a person as well as whether the expectation is reasonable as seen by the society. The use of technology online makes this analysis challenging since users are usually asked to provide data on the platform under contracts, and the technology used to collect data is complicated (Rich and Aiken, 2024). Third Party Doctrine in Smith v. Maryland (1979) minimizes the privacy expectations over any data exchanged with third parties, yet the digital age has demonstrated through the recent rulings that the principle is getting smaller. To prevent possible breaches of the Constitution and possible exclusion of evidence, forensic analysts need to be aware of the kind of data they will operate with, data acquisition processes, and privacy concerns of their techniques (Gee, 2020).

1.2 Digital Evidence Admissibility in AI-Enhanced Investigations

The applications of AI-based technologies in the field of forensic investigation have posed some challenging questions regarding the admissibility of digital evidence, as the majority of legal norms were designed based on human knowledge and conventional scientific practices. According to the Federal Rule of Evidence 702, expert testimony should be based on sound principles and procedures, which have to be accurately applied to the case in question, and which should be provided by competent professionals. In cases when AI systems can help produce forensic evidence, courts need to conclude whether the algorithms, training data, and analyzing methods meet such criteria of reliability (Swofford and Champod, 2021). The Daubert standard also requires the judges to test the scientific validity of the expert evidence before it can go to a jury. In the case of AI-enhanced forensics, it implies studying the way the machine learning model was developed, the degree of testing, the number of errors it has, and peer-reviewed studies. To achieve admissibility, a detailed account of the system development, testing, and implementation to the particular case being investigated should thus be provided, with expert testimony as to the mechanisms of operation of the system, and why it is deemed reliable (Carranza & DeCusatis, 2021).

There is another challenge of authentication. The Federal Rule of Evidence 901 states that one must show that the evidence in question is genuine, and in case of automated tools, it implies that the system was able to handle the information correctly and consistently. This involves proving that the AI product was trained on an appropriate data, well validated, and maintained to prevent errors that are brought by updates or drift in the system (Varsha, 2023). The use of AI systems as legitimate forensic tools is becoming more widely accepted in the courts, however, the courts require a clear chain of custody of not just the original digital evidence, but also the process of the automated analysis. It becomes crucial that systems settings, input management, and quality-control processes are documented to be accepted in court (Kerdvibulvech, 2024).

The black box nature of most machine learning models is still a major concern. Courts have also highlighted the necessity of the explanations that can be followed by defendants and juries, especially when it comes to the criminal trials (Garrett and Rudin, 2023). The increased attempts at explainable and interpretable AI are thus necessary. Transparent system design, uniform validation practices, and a clear description of the way AI generated forensic evidence should be produced will be the main predictors of its long-term acceptance (Maruf, 2025).

1.3 Cross-Border Legal Challenges in Dark Web Intelligence

The jurisdictional challenges of cross-border investigations into dark web activity are challenging due to the presence of multiple legal systems simultaneously in most cases when it comes to the intelligence gathering. This is because the decentralized and anonymous nature of dark web websites ensures that investigators can handle information, servers, or suspects across multiple countries with each country having different regulations regarding surveillance, evidence management, and privacy (Rai et al., 2017; Rai et al., 2024). Although the Budapest Convention on Cybercrime provides a cooperative model, its success is not evenly distributed due to the fact that different countries have diverse adoptions of its provisions given that many countries have not adopted this convention at all (Casino et al., 2022). Mutual Legal Assistance Treaties (MLATs) are another means of cooperation, which is however very slow and formal procedures and usually collides with the speed of intelligence operations. Consequently, inquiries in the dark web have to be conducted with caution regarding the intersecting jurisdictions, distinct evidence rules, and the prospective clash between country constitutional rights (Sharma, 2020). The transnational character of the dark web operations is also a point of conflict between the sovereignty of territories and the realities of cyber investigation. Regardless of the traditional jurisdiction of nations over activities within their jurisdictions, borderless encrypted and routed communications make this principle difficult. Other nations have broad extraterritorial jurisdiction in cybercrime and assert they have the right to investigate cybercrime cases involving their citizens or a cybercrime of their infrastructures irrespective of geographical boundaries (Ryngaert, 2023). Nonetheless, these claims might run counter to the sovereignty of other countries and result in the development of diplomatic conflicts. The example of the European Union, where the mutuality in the judicial decision and the alignment of legal standards allow regional cooperation to facilitate cross-border cybercrime response (Arnell & Faturoti, 2022). The technical design of anonymous networks also creates jurisdictional problems. Such tools as Tor hide the physical positions, and it is hardly possible to define the laws of what country can be applied. Anonymity can be broken by using investigative methods such as traffic analysis, timing correlation, controlled law-enforcement marketplaces, but this raises legal and ethical issues about acceptable surveillance behavior (Beshiri and Susuri, 2019). History demonstrates the potential and the intricacy of collaboration between countries through the past experiences of law-enforcement taking over dark web marketplaces. These problems demonstrate the necessity of new legal frameworks that would be tailored to new anonymity online and international cyber threats (Soliman, 2023).

2. PRIVACY RIGHTS AND DATA PROTECTION IN USER-CENTRIC ANALYSIS

2.1 Privacy Implications of Behavioral Profiling

Behavioral profiling in user-centric threat intelligence involves examining a person's communication habits, digital activities, and overall behavior patterns. While this helps identify unusual or risky actions, it also raises major privacy concerns that require strong legal and ethical safeguards. In most cases, behavioral profiling brings together information from many sources—such as network logs, emails, social media interactions, and system access records—to build a detailed picture of how someone behaves online. Such deep analysis can unintentionally expose sensitive information about a person's private life, political views, social circles, or personal habits, even if the original goal is only to detect security threats (Saeed et al., 2023). These privacy concerns become more serious when the people being analyzed—employees, customers, or others—have not given explicit permission for such close monitoring. This highlights the need for profiling systems to follow strict privacy safeguards such as data minimization, clear purpose limitation, and consent mechanisms, so that privacy rights are protected while still enabling reliable threat detection (Li & Nill, 2020).

Data minimization means collecting and analyzing only the information that is genuinely necessary to meet a clearly defined security purpose. This principle, reflected in laws like the GDPR and other national privacy regulations, requires organizations to avoid collecting extra personal data and to delete or anonymize information when it is no longer needed. In behavioral profiling, this requires clearly identifying what types of behavior-related data are actually relevant for detecting threats and ensuring that systems do not capture unnecessary personal details (Finck & Biega, 2021). Effective data minimization depends on strong technical measures such as automated filtering of irrelevant data, strict retention limits, and access controls that restrict who can view personal behavior information. Continuous monitoring and periodic review of data-collection practices are essential to make sure that the scope of monitoring stays aligned with the real level of security risk (Saura et al., 2022).

Consent for behavioral profiling is another complicated issue. Legal standards require consent to be voluntary, specific, informed, and clear—but in practice, this is hard to achieve for security-related monitoring. Employees, for example, often cannot freely refuse consent if monitoring is tied to their employment. The highly technical nature of behavioral analytics also makes it difficult to explain the process in a way that truly informs the individual (Hallinan et al., 2023). Consent must also be specific, meaning that broad permission for "security monitoring" is not enough to justify analyzing private communications, social media activity, or other sensitive behavioral data. Some laws allow organizations to process such data without consent for legitimate security purposes, but only when the processing is necessary and does not outweigh the individual's privacy rights. Therefore, any organization that uses behavioral profiling for threat intelligence must carefully assess the legal basis for processing personal data, apply consent mechanisms where necessary, and ensure that all monitoring remains proportionate to actual security needs (Mohammed et al., 2025).

2.2 GDPR and Data Protection Compliance

The General Data Protection Regulation (GDPR) sets out strict rules for managing personal data, and these rules directly shape how cyber-forensic investigations involving EU citizens must be conducted. Under the GDPR, any organization handling the data of EU residents—whether inside or outside the EU—must comply with its requirements. This means that even investigators based in non-EU jurisdictions must follow GDPR obligations when dealing with information belonging to EU individuals. The regulation identifies six lawful bases for processing personal data: consent, contract, legal obligation, vital interests, public task, and legitimate interests. Each basis carries its own conditions, and investigators must select the one that properly justifies their actions and be able to explain that choice (Bas Seyyar and Geradts, 2020). In cyber-forensic practice, legal obligation, public task, and legitimate interests are the most commonly used grounds. Regardless of the chosen basis, organizations must document their decision-making and implement security measures to protect data throughout the investigation, including privacy impact assessments and maintaining records of all processing activities (Amoo et al., 2024). Threat intelligence operations require close attention to necessity and proportionality when selecting a lawful basis. If legitimate interests are used, organizations must show that the processing is essential for a valid security purpose, that the security need outweighs any privacy intrusion, and that proper safeguards are in place. This assessment weighs security requirements against individual expectations of privacy and explores whether less intrusive methods could achieve the same results (Tschider et al., 2024). For processing under public task grounds, typically tied to law enforcement or national security, investigators must demonstrate legal authority and necessity, along with ongoing monitoring to remain within the chosen basis (Hildén, 2021). Cross-border data transfer restrictions add further challenges. Personal data may be transferred outside the European Economic Area only when the destination offers adequate protection or when strong safeguards exist, such as standard contractual clauses or binding corporate rules. These conditions can complicate time-sensitive cybercrime investigations requiring rapid information exchange (Liss et al., 2021). With few countries granted adequacy status and the invalidation of the Privacy Shield after the Schrems II ruling, transfers to the United States have become particularly complex. When data must be sent abroad, investigators must rely on recognized transfer tools and conduct transfer impact assessments to confirm that protections are sufficient. Ensuring GDPR compliance therefore requires careful planning, continuous monitoring of legal developments, and strong technical and organizational safeguards (Tschider et al., 2024).

2.3 Employee Privacy and Insider Threat Detection.

Detection programs on insider threats have to ensure that their priorities are not on one side at the expense of the privacy of the organization and its employees. Such programs usually come with checking computer usage, network usage, emails, and behavioral patterns, which are capable of displaying professional and personal information. Different countries have various privacy regulations: some countries have widespread protections of employees, whereas others allow more extensive monitoring should the employees be sufficiently warned and consent to such monitoring (Ebert et al., 2021). Generally, in the US, the power of private firms to monitor what takes place within the company systems is enormous, but this is not limited by the state laws and workplace agreements. European countries, on the contrary, insist that the monitoring should be both necessary and proportionate and should be backed up by sufficient safeguards. Successful insider threat programs should consequently be in accordance with the legal norms related, such as the right to data and proportionality, to prevent unwarranted intrusion (Kalischko and Riedl, 2021). The legal norms relating to workplace monitoring usually concern the reasonable expectation of privacy of the employees. Such an expectation is based on whether it is a type of working environment, the nature of the monitoring, the preparation made to the employees, and the availability of private communication areas. It is generally accepted by the courts that employees do not expect so much privacy when utilizing systems provided by the employer but, this does not give the employer the carte blanche, especially regarding personal communications or activities that are not work-related (Komanovics, 2023). Companies should measure the degree to which their monitoring systems are intrusive, the sensitivity of the information gathered, and the impact of this on the behavior of the employees. Certain jurisdictions insist that the least intrusive available means must be employed by the employer and an explicit notice given as to the monitoring actions. To maintain compliance, it is necessary to constantly check the monitoring strategy, observe the privacy laws, and introduce transparent consent or notification practices (Inayat et al., 2024).

It is difficult to achieve valid consent to monitor the behavior of employees in the workplace because of the nature of power that prevails between the employer and employees. The employees might not even have a perceived option, as the monitoring can be bound to the terms of work (Siegel et al., 2022). Due to such an imbalance, in most legal systems, the regulation of monitoring can be based on the legitimate interests or legal requirements rather than the consent of employees. Despite that, good privacy practices demand transparency: employees must precisely understand why and what is monitored and why there is a strong privacy protection (Kayas, 2023). The general authorization of security monitoring is not sufficient when the monitoring of the messages or the activity on the social networks or analysis of the sensitive information about the behavior is performed. This means that organization should have a strong legal foundation, explain to the employees step by step and institute measures that will reduce the risk of privacy without compromising the security of the organization (Tian et al., 2025).

3. ETHICAL CONSIDERATIONS IN AI-ENHANCED FORENSIC ANALYSIS

3.1 Algorithmic Bias in Threat Intelligence

Algorithmic bias is a significant ethical concern in AI-driven threat intelligence because it can unfairly target individuals or groups, ultimately weakening the credibility and reliability of forensic investigations. Bias often emerges when systems repeatedly generate results that disadvantage certain populations, usually due to historical imbalances in the data used for training or design choices that unintentionally embed discriminatory assumptions. These distortions can appear as higher false-positive rates for specific demographic groups, failure to flag threats associated with more privileged groups, or skewed risk scores tied to certain behaviors or communication styles (de Manuel et al., 2023). Bias may stem from training datasets that over represent some forms of threat activity, system architectures that adopt harmful defaults, or feedback loops where the model reinforces patterns that were already overrepresented. Research has shown that these issues are widespread across AI applications, from facial recognition—where people of color are often misidentified—to language models that misinterpret names or dialects and predictive policing systems that reinforce racial disparities. Addressing these weaknesses requires structured bias testing, multidisciplinary participation during system development, and persistent monitoring to uncover harmful patterns (S., 2023). Ethical responsibility for mitigating algorithmic bias extends across the entire AI lifecycle, from initial system design to deployment. Bias detection demands thorough evaluation of system performance across demographic groups and contexts. Methods may include quantitative tests such as demographic parity checks and equalized odds, alongside qualitative assessments that question whether system outputs align with real-world expectations (Hofmann, 2025). Bias reduction strategies include balancing training data, introducing fairness constraints during training, or adjusting outputs after predictions are generated. However, these steps involve trade-offs, as excessive correction can lead to reduced accuracy. Effective mitigation requires collaboration among AI developers, domain specialists, ethicists, and individuals affected by the system. In some cases, systems that cannot meet fairness standards may need to be redesigned or retired (Hasanzadeh et al., 2025).

Achieving credible threat assessment also requires weighing the balance between fairness and detection capability. False positives and false negatives both pose serious risks, and systems must avoid discrimination while correctly identifying threats. Fairness demands that evaluations exclude irrelevant characteristics such as race, religion, gender, or political beliefs, focusing solely on meaningful behavioral indicators (Ferrara, 2023). Both individual fairness and group fairness must be considered, even though they may sometimes conflict. Organizations relying on AI-based threat intelligence should define fairness parameters clearly, conduct regular audits, and openly communicate system limitations. As noted in the analysis, maintaining fairness and effectiveness depends on ongoing refinement, adherence to ethical development practices, and acceptance that some efficiency may be sacrificed to prevent discrimination (Pasipamire and Muroyiwa, 2024).

3.2 Transparency and Explainability in Automated Analysis

The ethical need for explainable AI in forensic work stems from the basic principles of due process and accountability, as well as the right of individuals to understand and contest decisions that influence their freedoms. In traditional forensic practice, experts are expected to describe their methods, justify their conclusions, and acknowledge the limits of their analyses. This transparency allows courts, defendants, and other stakeholders to evaluate the strength of the evidence. When forensic tools rely on complex machine learning systems, however, the reasoning behind their results may be difficult—or sometimes impossible—to interpret, even if the outputs themselves are accurate (Hermosilla et al., 2025).

This lack of clarity creates ethical risks because people affected by AI-generated evidence may be unable to understand or challenge the conclusions drawn about them. As a result, developing methods for explainable AI has become increasingly important in forensic settings. Techniques such as feature importance rankings, simplified decision pathways, counterfactual explanations, and attention-based visualizations help clarify how an AI model arrived at its output. The analysis shows that responsible use of AI in forensic investigations requires a commitment to transparency, even if achieving explainability means sacrificing a small degree of performance (Maruf, 2025).

Transparency in automated decision-making goes beyond providing technical explanations. It also involves broader principles of fairness, public accountability, and democratic oversight of forensic technologies. This includes documenting how systems work, detailing their limitations, describing the nature of the training data, and enabling independent review of the methods used. The level of transparency required depends on the seriousness of the case: criminal matters, where liberty is at stake, demand the highest standards. At the same time, institutions must consider legitimate concerns related to proprietary algorithms, security needs, and the risk that excessive disclosure could allow bad actors to bypass detection systems (Cheong, 2024).

Possible ways to balance transparency with operational security include releasing general explanations without exposing sensitive technical details, allowing outside experts to validate systems under confidentiality protections, and establishing oversight bodies capable of evaluating fairness and performance. Professional guidelines and certification programs for AI-supported forensic work can also help clarify expectations and ensure that appropriate documentation is maintained. The analysis suggests that meeting transparency obligations in forensic AI requires new standards that strike a balance between explainability and the practical realities of sensitive investigations (Jinad et al., 2024).

Finding an equilibrium between protecting proprietary algorithms and ensuring public accountability presents another challenge. Many AI tools used in forensic analysis are built by private companies that rely on proprietary designs to maintain their competitive edge. Yet, when these systems influence legal outcomes, courts and defendants must have some means of testing the credibility of the evidence produced. This tension has prompted certain jurisdictions to adopt rules that require minimum transparency or validation standards, even when the core algorithm remains proprietary (Busuioc, 2020).

Approaches to this balance include requiring independent expert validation, implementing certification processes that confirm reliability without exposing trade secrets, and using controlled testing environments where systems can be examined under confidentiality safeguards. Developing common industry standards for transparency in forensic AI can help align the expectations of developers, investigators, and courts. The analysis shows that resolving the conflict between proprietary interests and public accountability will require sustained cooperation among developers, forensic scientists, legal professionals, and policymakers to create frameworks that protect intellectual property while ensuring trustworthy, verifiable forensic outcomes (Kerdvibulvech, 2024).

3.3 Professional Ethics in Human-Centric Investigations

Professional ethics in human-centric forensic investigations require special attention to principles of human dignity, respect for persons, and the psychological impact of invasive investigative techniques on subjects and their families. Human-centric investigations, by their nature, involve detailed analysis of individual behavior, personal communications, and private activities that can reveal intimate details about people's lives, relationships, and personal struggles. The ethical framework for such investigations must recognize the inherent dignity and worth of all individuals, including those who may be suspected of criminal activity or security threats, and ensure that investigative techniques are conducted with appropriate respect for human rights and personal autonomy (Rocchio, 2020).

The principle of proportionality requires that the intrusiveness of investigative methods be proportionate to the severity of the suspected threat or crime, and that less invasive alternatives be considered before employing more intrusive techniques. The psychological impact of forensic investigations on subjects and their families can be significant, particularly when investigations involve extensive surveillance, behavioral analysis, or public disclosure of private information (Rai, 2022; Nain, 2024). Ethical guidelines for human-centric investigations must address issues such as minimizing harm to innocent parties, protecting the privacy of family members and associates who are not themselves subjects of investigation, and providing appropriate support and resources for individuals who may be traumatized by the investigative process. The analysis demonstrates that ethical human-centric investigations require comprehensive frameworks that balance the legitimate needs of security and law enforcement with fundamental principles of human dignity and respect for individual rights (Tsang et al., 2025).

Ethical frameworks for behavioral analysis in forensic investigations must address complex issues related to consent, disclosure, and the boundaries of acceptable investigative techniques when analyzing human behavior and psychological patterns. Behavioral analysis often involves making inferences about individuals' mental states, motivations, and future actions based on patterns of past behavior, communication, and digital activities. Such analysis raises ethical questions about the accuracy and reliability of behavioral predictions, the potential for stigmatization or discrimination based on behavioral profiles, and the appropriate limits on psychological analysis of individuals who have not consented to such examination. The issue of consent in behavioral analysis is particularly complex, as individuals may not be aware that their behavior is being analyzed, may not understand the implications of such analysis, or may not be in a position to provide meaningful consent due to power imbalances or legal constraints.

Disclosure requirements for behavioral analysis must balance the need for transparency and individual rights with legitimate law enforcement and security interests, including the need to protect ongoing investigations and prevent subjects from altering their behavior to avoid detection. The boundaries of acceptable behavioral analysis must consider the invasiveness of the techniques used, the reliability of the conclusions drawn, and the potential for misuse or abuse of behavioral insights. Professional standards for behavioral analysis should include requirements for appropriate training and certification, ongoing supervision and review of analytical methods, and clear guidelines for the ethical conduct of behavioral investigations. The analysis reveals that ethical behavioral analysis requires careful attention to consent and disclosure issues, appropriate limits on the scope and intrusiveness of analysis, and robust professional standards to ensure that behavioral insights are used responsibly and ethically (Rocchio, 2020).

Issues of consent, disclosure, and psychological impact in human-centric forensic investigations require comprehensive ethical guidelines that protect individual rights while enabling effective security and law enforcement operations. Consent in forensic investigations is complicated by the fact that subjects are often unaware that they are under investigation, may not be legally required to provide consent, or may not be in a position to provide meaningful consent due to the coercive nature of legal proceedings. However, ethical principles suggest that individuals should be informed about investigative activities that affect them when possible, and that their autonomy and dignity should be respected throughout the investigative process (Göranson et al., 2022).

Disclosure requirements must balance individual rights to know about investigations that affect them with legitimate law enforcement needs to maintain the integrity and effectiveness of ongoing investigations. The timing and extent of disclosure may vary depending on the nature of the investigation, the stage of proceedings, and the potential impact on both the investigation and the individuals involved. The psychological impact of forensic investigations can be significant and long-lasting, particularly for individuals who are ultimately found to be innocent of any wrongdoing but who have been subjected to extensive surveillance and analysis (Göranson et al., 2022).

Ethical guidelines should address the responsibility of investigators to minimize psychological harm, provide appropriate support for individuals affected by investigations, and consider the broader impact of investigative activities on families and communities. Professional training and education programs should include components on the ethical dimensions of human-centric investigations, including sensitivity to psychological impact, cultural competency, and awareness of power dynamics and potential for abuse. The analysis demonstrates that addressing consent, disclosure, and psychological impact issues in human-centric forensic investigations requires comprehensive ethical frameworks, ongoing professional development, and institutional commitment to protecting individual rights and dignity throughout the investigative process (Chu et al., 2022).

4. REGULATORY COMPLIANCE AND INDUSTRY STANDARDS

The integration of human-centric threat intelligence analysis within cyber forensic investigations necessitates comprehensive understanding of regulatory compliance frameworks that govern digital evidence collection and analysis across diverse industry sectors. Contemporary cyber forensic practice operates within an increasingly complex regulatory environment where sector-specific compliance requirements fundamentally influence investigative methodologies, evidence handling procedures, and analytical frameworks. This regulatory complexity becomes particularly pronounced when forensic investigations incorporate behavioral analysis and artificial intelligence-enhanced techniques, as these methodologies often intersect with privacy regulations, industry-specific data protection requirements, and professional standards governing investigative conduct (Miller, 2023).

The financial services sector exemplifies this regulatory complexity through the Payment Card Industry Data Security Standard (PCI DSS), which establishes stringent requirements for cardholder data protection that directly impact forensic investigation protocols. Similarly, healthcare organizations operating under the Health Insurance Portability and Accountability Act (HIPAA) must balance forensic investigation needs with patient privacy protections, creating unique challenges when conducting behavioral analysis of potential insider threats. Defense contractors face additional layers of regulatory complexity through security clearance requirements and classified information handling protocols that constrain both investigative methodologies and evidence sharing capabilities. These sector-specific regulatory frameworks demonstrate how compliance requirements shape the practical implementation of human-centric threat intelligence analysis, requiring forensic practitioners to develop specialized expertise in navigating diverse regulatory environments while maintaining investigative effectiveness (Salem et al., 2024).

4.1 Sector-Specific Compliance Requirements

Sector-specific compliance requirements create complex regulatory landscapes that cyber forensic practitioners must navigate when conducting human threat intelligence analysis across different industries. The banking and financial services sector operates under stringent frameworks including the Payment Card Industry Data Security Standard (PCI DSS), Gramm-Leach-Bliley Act, and anti-money laundering regulations that directly impact forensic investigations. PCI DSS mandates specific security controls for credit card data handling, including detailed logging requirements that support forensic analysis while imposing restrictions on data access and retention (Tiwari, 2024). The Sarbanes-Oxley Act requires comprehensive audit trails that provide valuable forensic evidence but creates legal obligations for data preservation and disclosure. Financial sector investigations require careful coordination between security teams, compliance officers, and legal counsel to ensure investigative activities support both security objectives and regulatory compliance while maintaining evidence integrity for potential legal proceedings (Uzougbo et al., 2024).

Healthcare sector compliance under HIPAA creates unique challenges for cyber forensic investigations involving protected health information. HIPAA's Privacy and Security Rules establish comprehensive requirements for protecting patient data that impact forensic investigations, including access restrictions, audit trail requirements, and specific disclosure procedures for law enforcement. The minimum necessary standard requires forensic investigators to limit health information access to amounts necessary for investigation completion, requiring careful scoping and coordination with privacy officers. Healthcare organizations must also comply with state privacy laws, FDA medical device regulations, and emerging cybersecurity requirements that create additional regulatory complexity. Healthcare forensic investigations require specialized knowledge of privacy laws, collaboration with compliance professionals, and technical safeguards to protect patient privacy while enabling effective threat detection and incident response (Gee, 2020).

Defense and government sector compliance involves security clearance procedures, classification handling requirements, and specialized legal frameworks that significantly impact national security forensic investigations. Defense contractors and agencies must comply with DFARS, Cybersecurity Maturity Model Certification (CMMC), and classification handling requirements that create unique forensic challenges. Security clearance requirements may limit investigation personnel, while classification procedures restrict evidence processing, storage, and sharing with external parties. FISMA and related frameworks establish comprehensive security requirements including incident response capabilities but create specific reporting procedures that may conflict with traditional forensic methods. Defense sector investigations require specialized cleared personnel, classified information handling procedures, and coordination between security, legal, and compliance teams to meet both security objectives and regulatory requirements while protecting national security interests (Slobogin & Brayne, 2023).

4.2 Professional Standards and Certification

Professional standards and certification requirements ensure competency and ethical conduct in human threat intelligence analysis while establishing accountability mechanisms for AI-enhanced forensic investigation. Organizations like the International Association of Computer Investigative Specialists (IACIS) have developed comprehensive certification programs including technical competency requirements, ethical guidelines, and continuing education obligations. These programs typically require demonstrated forensic expertise, legal and ethical understanding, and ongoing professional development to maintain currency with technological advances. AI-enhanced forensic analysis creates new certification challenges, as traditional training may not address machine learning algorithms, automated analysis systems, and algorithmic bias issues (Rocchio, 2020). Maintaining professional standards in AI-enhanced forensics requires collaboration between professional organizations, academic institutions, and industry practitioners to develop certification programs addressing both traditional competencies and emerging AI-related skills.Continuing education obligations for cyber forensic professionals must address the rapidly evolving technological landscape while ensuring practitioners maintain current knowledge of legal developments, ethical guidelines, and best practices. The dynamic nature of cyber threats, forensic technologies, and legal frameworks requires continuous learning and professional development to maintain competency and effectiveness (Quang Huy & Kien Phuc, 2025).

Professional certification programs typically require annual continuing education credits earned through approved training programs, conferences, workshops, or educational activities demonstrating ongoing professional development. AI integration into forensic practice has created new continuing education requirements focused on understanding algorithmic bias, explainable AI techniques, and legal and ethical implications of automated analysis systems. Effective continuing education in AI-enhanced cyber forensics requires interdisciplinary approaches combining technical training with legal and ethical education, along with practical experience in applying AI technologies to real-world forensic investigations (Solanke & Biasiotti, 2022).

Professional codes of conduct specific to human threat intelligence analysis establish ethical frameworks addressing behavioral analysis, privacy protection, and AI-enhanced investigation challenges. These codes emphasize principles such as integrity, objectivity, competence, and respect for individual rights applied to human-centric forensic contexts. Human behavior and psychological pattern analysis raises special ethical considerations including consent, psychological impact, and potential stigmatization based on behavioral profiles (Blanchard & Taddeo, 2023). Professional codes must address AI and automated analysis systems, including requirements for understanding system limitations, mitigating algorithmic bias, and maintaining human oversight of automated decisions affecting individual rights. Enforcement requires effective disciplinary mechanisms providing due process protections while offering educational and remedial measures helping practitioners understand and comply with ethical requirements in complex technological environments (Hallamaa & Kalliokoski, 2022).

5. EMERGING LEGAL AND ETHICAL CHALLENGES

The rapidly evolving technological landscape presents unprecedented legal and ethical challenges that will fundamentally reshape the practice of human-centric cyber forensic investigations in the coming decade. Emerging technologies such as quantum computing and advanced artificial intelligence systems create novel legal questions regarding evidence integrity, authentication standards, and the admissibility of technologically sophisticated analytical results in judicial proceedings. These technological developments occur alongside evolving threat landscapes characterized by increasingly sophisticated social engineering attacks and psychological manipulation techniques that challenge traditional forensic analysis frameworks (Soni, 2025).

Quantum computing represents a paradigmatic shift that threatens the cryptographic foundations upon which current digital evidence integrity depends. The potential for quantum computers to break existing encryption algorithms raises critical questions about the long-term viability of current evidence preservation methods and the timeline for transitioning to quantum-resistant cryptographic systems. This technological transition creates legal uncertainties regarding the admissibility of evidence that may become vulnerable to quantum-based attacks, necessitating proactive development of legal frameworks that address quantum computing implications for digital forensics (Radanliev, 2024). Simultaneously, the increasing sophistication of social engineering attacks requires forensic investigators to analyze complex psychological manipulation techniques while maintaining ethical boundaries regarding victim privacy and dignity. These emerging challenges demonstrate the need for adaptive legal and ethical frameworks that can accommodate technological advancement while preserving fundamental principles of justice, privacy, and human dignity in cyber forensic investigations (Montañez et al., 2020).

5.1 Quantum Computing and Cryptographic Implications

Quantum computing poses unprecedented challenges to current cryptographic systems and digital evidence integrity, requiring fundamental reconsideration of evidence preservation and authentication in cyber forensic investigations. Advanced quantum computers will break many current cryptographic algorithms including RSA encryption, elliptic curve cryptography, and digital signature schemes used to protect communications and authenticate evidence. This vulnerability creates significant challenges as currently secure evidence may become vulnerable to manipulation once quantum capabilities become available (Radanliev, 2024).

The uncertain timeline for quantum threats, estimated at 10-30 years, combined with long-term evidence preservation requirements, means forensic practitioners must begin implementing post-quantum security measures immediately. Current digital evidence requiring extended preservation could become vulnerable to quantum attacks before legal proceedings conclude, creating potential challenges for evidence integrity and admissibility. The quantum threat requires proactive measures including quantum-resistant cryptographic systems and new approaches to long-term evidence preservation and authentication (Gitonga, 2025).

Evidence preservation in the quantum era requires new approaches to long-term security protecting digital evidence against current and future cryptographic threats while maintaining legal admissibility. Traditional preservation methods rely on cryptographic hash functions and digital signatures vulnerable to quantum attacks, requiring quantum-resistant authentication and integrity protection methods. NIST's post-quantum cryptographic standardization efforts must be implemented in forensic contexts with careful consideration of performance, compatibility, and legal acceptance issues (Radanliev, 2024).

Evidence preservation systems must support cryptographic agility, allowing migration of protection schemes as new quantum-resistant algorithms are developed and standardized. The transition timeline must balance urgency of protecting against future quantum threats with practical constraints of implementing new technologies, training personnel, and ensuring compatibility with existing legal requirements. Effective quantum-era evidence preservation requires proactive planning, quantum-resistant technology investment, and new legal frameworks accommodating post-quantum cryptography challenges while maintaining evidence integrity and admissibility (Alagic et al., 2025).

5.2 Social Engineering and Psychological Manipulation

The ethical aspects of the forensic investigation of social engineering cases present challenging ethical dilemmas associated with the boundaries of psychological research, the necessity of ensuring privacy of victims, as well as the correct method of researching the methods of manipulation. Since social engineering is based on human behavior manipulation and a tendency to use emotional reactions, researchers usually check communication patterns, decision-making, and the presence of certain circumstances that can reveal very personal information. This type of scrutiny may expose victims to additional suffering, as well as, bring up the issue of consent and sensitive information management (Siddiqi et al., 2022). The investigators have to juggle between getting to know how an attack started and treating the victims with dignity. There should be clear professional guidelines, which would guarantee protection of privacy, secure consent wherever possible and avoid unwarranted emotional damage. Also a part of ethical practice is that the investigators are to be aware of the psychological effects, utilize trauma-conscious approaches and uphold protective measures that safeguard the right of a victim and simultaneously promote a productive investigation (Rocchio, 2020). Collection of the information without breaking privacy will require serious measures because the victim might already be vulnerable, embarrassed, or reluctant to engage in the process. Information required, which is usually associated with individual behavior and conditions, may be highly sensitive when not handled properly (Slack, 2020). The forensic teams need to depend on rigid anonymization, a regulated access to the records, and the protection of the data. The courts are also required to look into the boundaries of psychological evidence and to make sure it is not utilized to place the blame elsewhere. Thorough policies and training that is trauma-sensitive can ensure confidentiality, as well as the victims are treated with dignity during the entire process (Smith and Singh, 2024).

6. CONCLUSION

Cyber forensics and human threat intelligence are legal and ethical responsibilities that are increasingly becoming complex with the growth in technology. Contemporary studies have turned to the artificial intelligence, analysis of behavior and user oriented examination of the online activity. Due to this, the professionals need to take appropriate caution and balance constitutional rights, privacy protection, ethical obligations, and the strength of the emerging technologies. The current legislation regulating the investigations must be revised in such a way that it would help to manage the issues posed by AI-based tools without undermining the fundamental rights or due process. Conventional privacy regulations including the Fourth Amendment and its analogs were not devised with digital profiling on scale. The issue with this is that, courts and legislators need to explain how these safeguards are applied when the behavior is analyzed through automated systems. In order to present AI-generated evidence in the court, new rules are needed to demonstrate that the systems are reliable, transparent, and subject to challenge. The privacy regulations such as the GDPR are very strict in their responsibilities on the investigators, particularly when dealing with cross-border data. To ensure security and, at the same time, avoid infringing on personal privacy, it is necessary to restrict superfluous data gathering and provide the necessary consent as well as secure international data transfer. The companies that track insider threats have to adhere to the transparent legal process and ethical standards like not to violate the rights of workers. Another problem is the ethical issues associated with the use of AI-based forensic tools. Such problems as bias, lack of transparency, and unclear decision-making should be addressed. This can be done by checking systems on unfair results regularly, enhancing the diversity within the development teams, and creating approaches that will enable investigators and courts to know how the system arrived at its conclusions. Professional ethics should also be changed to provide directions to new challenges by practitioners. In the future, such trends as quantum computing, novel social-engineering tricks will further complicate the situation. Such developments will demand more evidence-protecting practices and superior knowledge of the psychological side of cyber threats. It all culminates in the question of cooperation between the legal experts, the technologists, the policymakers and the civil society to make sure that the forensic practices are fair, responsible and protective of individual rights.

REFERENCES

Alagic, G., Bros, M., Ciadoux, P., Cooper, D., Dang, Q., Dang, T., Kelsey, J., Lichtinger, J., Liu, Y.-K., Miller, C., Moody, D., Peralta, R., Perlner, R., Robinson, A., Silberg, H., Smith-Tone, D., & Waller, N. (2025). *Status Report on the Fourth Round of the NIST Post-Quantum Cryptography Standardization Process*. DOI: 10.6028/NIST.IR.8545

Amoo, O. O., Atadoga, A., Osasona, F., Abrahams, T. O., Ayinla, B. S., & Farayola, O. A. (2024). GDPR's impact on cybersecurity: A review focusing on USA and European practices. *International Journal of Science and Research Archive, 11*(1), 1338–1347. DOI: 10.30574/ijsra.2024.11.1.0220

Arnell, P., & Faturoti, B. (2022). The prosecution of Cybercrime – why transnational and extraterritorial jurisdiction should be resisted. *International Review of Law, Computers &amp. International Review of Law Computers & Technology, 37*(1), 29–51. DOI: 10.1080/13600869.2022.2061888

Bas Seyyar, M., & Geradts, Z. J. M. H. (2020). Privacy impact assessment in large-scale digital forensic investigations. *Forensic Science International Digital Investigation, 33*, 200906. DOI: 10.1016/j.fsidi.2020.200906

Beshiri, A. S., & Susuri, A. (2019). Dark web and its impact in online anonymity and privacy: A critical analysis and review. *Journal of Computer and Communications, 07*(03), 30–43. DOI: 10.4236/jcc.2019.73004

Blanchard, A., & Taddeo, M. (2023). The ethics of Artificial Intelligence for Intelligence Analysis: A review of the key challenges with recommendations. *Digital Society : Ethics, Socio-Legal and Governance of Digital Technology, 2*(1), 12. Advance online publication. DOI: 10.1007/s44206-023-00036-4 PMID: 37034181

Busuioc, M. (2020). Accountable artificial intelligence: Holding algorithms to account. *Public Administration Review, 81*(5), 825–836. DOI: 10.1111/puar.13293 PMID: 34690372

Carranza, A., & DeCusatis, C. (2021). Software validation and Daubert Standard Compliance of an open digital forensics model. *Journal of Machine Intelligence and Data Science*. DOI: 10.11159/jmids.2021.005

Casino, F., Pina, C., López-Aguilar, P., Batista, E., Solanas, A., & Patsakis, C. (2022). SOK: Cross-border criminal investigations and digital evidence. *Journal of Cybersecurity, 8*(1), tyac014. Advance online publication. DOI: 10.1093/cybsec/tyac014

Cheong, B. C. (2024). Transparency and accountability in AI systems: Safeguarding Wellbeing in the age of algorithmic decision-making. *Frontiers in Human Dynamics*, *6*, 1421273. Advance online publication. DOI: 10.3389/fhumd.2024.1421273

Chu, W., Wippold, G., & Becker, K. D. (2022). A systematic review of cultural competence trainings for Mental Health Providers. *Professional Psychology, Research and Practice*, *53*(4), 362–371. DOI: 10.1037/pro0000469 PMID: 37332624

de Manuel, A., Delgado, J., Parra Jounou, I., Ausín, T., Casacuberta, D., Cruz, M., Guersenzvaig, A., Moyano, C., Rodríguez-Arias, D., Rueda, J., & Puyol, A. (2023). Ethical assessments and mitigation strategies for biases in AI-systems used during the COVID-19 pandemic. *Big Data &amp. Big Data & Society*, *10*(1), 20539517231179199. Advance online publication. DOI: 10.1177/20539517231179199

Durán, J. M., van der Vloed, D., Ruifrok, A., & Ypma, R. J. F. (2024). From understanding to justifying: Computational reliabilism for AI-based Forensic Evidence Evaluation. *Forensic Science International. Synergy*, *9*, 100554. DOI: 10.1016/j.fsisyn.2024.100554 PMID: 39285895

Ebert, I., Wildhaber, I., & Adams-Prassl, J. (2021). Big Data in the workplace: Privacy due diligence as a human rights-based approach to employee privacy protection. *Big Data &amp. Big Data & Society*, *8*(1), 20539517211013051. Advance online publication. DOI: 10.1177/20539517211013051

Ferrara, E. (2023). Fairness and bias in Artificial Intelligence: A brief survey of sources, impacts, and mitigation strategies. *Sci*, *6*(1), 3. DOI: 10.3390/sci6010003

Finck, M., & Biega, A. J. (2021). Reviving purpose limitation and data minimisation in data-driven systems. *Technology and Regulation*, *2021*, 44–61. DOI: 10.71265/z7r0t122

Garrett, B. L., & Rudin, C. (2023). Interpretable algorithmic forensics. *Proceedings of the National Academy of Sciences of the United States of America*, *120*(41), e2301842120. Advance online publication. DOI: 10.1073/pnas.2301842120 PMID: 37782786

Gee, H. (2020). *Last call for the third party doctrine in the Digital age*. https://www.bu.edu/jostl/. https://www.bu.edu/jostl/files/2020/08/2-Gee.pdf

Gitonga, C. K. (2025). The impact of quantum computing on cryptographic systems: Urgency of quantum-resistant algorithms and practical applications in cryptography. *European Journal of Information Technologies and Computer Science*, *5*(1), 1–10. DOI: 10.24018/compute.2025.5.1.146

Göranson, L., Svensson, O., Andiné, P., Bromander, S., Bagge, A.-S. L., & Karlén, M. H. (2022). Decision-making within forensic psychiatric investigations: The use of various information sources by different expert groups to reach conclusions on legal insanity. *Frontiers in Psychiatry, 13*, 822519. Advance online publication. DOI: 10.3389/fpsyt.2022.822519 PMID: 35492686

Hallamaa, J., & Kalliokoski, T. (2022). AI ethics as Applied Ethics. *Frontiers of Computer Science, 4*, 776837. Advance online publication. DOI: 10.3389/fcomp.2022.776837

Hallinan, D., Boehm, F., Külpmann, A., & Elson, M. (2023). Information provision for informed consent procedures in psychological research under the General Data Protection Regulation: A practical guide. *Advances in Methods and Practices in Psychological Science, 6*(1), 25152459231151944. Advance online publication. DOI: 10.1177/25152459231151944

Hasanzadeh, F., Josephson, C. B., Waters, G., Adedinsewo, D., Azizi, Z., & White, J. A. (2025). Bias recognition and mitigation strategies in Artificial Intelligence Healthcare Applications. *NPJ Digital Medicine, 8*(1), 154. Advance online publication. DOI: 10.1038/s41746-025-01503-7 PMID: 40069303

Hermosilla, P., Berríos, S., & Allende-Cid, H. (2025). Explainable AI for forensic analysis: A comparative study of shap and lime in intrusion detection models. *Applied Sciences (Basel, Switzerland), 15*(13), 7329. DOI: 10.3390/app15137329

Hildén, J. (2021). Mitigating the risk of US surveillance for public sector services in the cloud. *Internet Policy Review, 10*(3). Advance online publication. DOI: 10.14763/2021.3.1578

Hofmann, B. (2025). Biases in AI: Acknowledging and addressing the inevitable ethical issues. *Frontiers in Digital Health, 7*, 1614105. Advance online publication. DOI: 10.3389/fdgth.2025.1614105 PMID: 40909204

Inayat, U., Farzan, M., Mahmood, S., Zia, M. F., Hussain, S., & Pallonetto, F. (2024). Insider threat mitigation: Systematic literature review. *Ain Shams Engineering Journal, 15*(12), 103068. DOI: 10.1016/j.asej.2024.103068

Javed, Y., & Sajid, A. (2024). A systematic review of privacy policy literature. *ACM Computing Surveys, 57*(2), 1–43. DOI: 10.1145/3698393

Jinad, R., Gupta, K., Simsek, E., & Zhou, B. (2024). Bias and fairness in software and automation tools in digital forensics. *Journal of Surveillance. Security and Safety, 5*(1), 19–35. DOI: 10.20517/jsss.2023.41

Kalischko, T., & Riedl, R. (2021). Electronic Performance Monitoring in the digital workplace: Conceptualization, review of effects and moderators, and Future Research Opportunities. *Frontiers in Psychology*, *12*, 633031. Advance online publication. DOI: 10.3389/fpsyg.2021.633031 PMID: 34093312

Kayas, O. G. (2023). Workplace surveillance: A systematic review, Integrative Framework, and Research Agenda. *Journal of Business Research*, *168*, 114212. DOI: 10.1016/j.jbusres.2023.114212

Kerdvibulvech, C. (2024). Big Data and AI-Driven Evidence Analysis: A global perspective on citation trends, accessibility, and future research in legal applications. *Journal of Big Data*, *11*(1), 180. Advance online publication. DOI: 10.1186/s40537-024-01046-w

Komanovics, A. (2023). *Workplace privacy in the EU : The impact of emerging technologies on employee's fundamental rights*. EU and Comparative Law Issues and Challenges Series., DOI: 10.25234/eclic/27458

Li, H., & Nill, A. (2020). Online behavioral targeting: Are knowledgeable consumers willing to sell their privacy? *Journal of Consumer Policy*, *43*(4), 723–745. DOI: 10.1007/s10603-020-09469-7

Liss, J., Peloquin, D., Barnes, M., & Bierer, B. E. (2021). Demystifying *schrems ii* for the cross-border transfer of Clinical Research Data. *Journal of Law and the Biosciences*, *8*(2), lsab032. Advance online publication. DOI: 10.1093/jlb/lsab032 PMID: 34703612

Marikyan, D., Papagiannidis, S., Rana, O. F., & Ranjan, R. (2023). General Data Protection Regulation: A study on attitude and emotional empowerment. *Behaviour &amp. Behaviour & Information Technology*, *43*(14), 3561–3577. DOI: 10.1080/0144929X.2023.2285341

Maruf, B. (2025). Developing an explainable AI system for Digital Forensics: Enhancing Trust and transparency in flagging events for legal evidence. *Journal of Forensic Science and Research*, *9*(2), 109–116. DOI: 10.29328/journal.jfsr.1001089

Miller, C. M. (2023). A survey of prosecutors and investigators using digital evidence: A starting point. *Forensic Science International. Synergy*, *6*, 100296. DOI: 10.1016/j.fsisyn.2022.100296 PMID: 37398922

Mohammed, U. M., Omolara, A. E., Abiodun, O. I., Rasheed, J., Osman, O., Lar, P. M., Adeyinka, P. O., & Olugbenga, A. G. (2025). Cyber threat in drone systems: Bridging real-time security, legal admissibility, and Digital Forensic Solution Readiness. *Frontiers in Communications and Networks*, *6*, 1661928. Advance online publication. DOI: 10.3389/frcmn.2025.1661928

Montañez, R., Golob, E., & Xu, S. (2020). Human cognition through the lens of social engineering cyberattacks. *Frontiers in Psychology*, *11*, 1755. Advance online publication. DOI: 10.3389/fpsyg.2020.01755 PMID: 33101096

Nain, V., Shyam, H. S., Kumar, N., Tripathi, P., & Rai, M. (2024). A study on object detection using artificial intelligence and image processing–based methods. *Mathematical Models Using Artificial Intelligence for Surveillance Systems*, 121-148.

Neilson, B. (2023). *Carpenter v. United States, the Stored Communications Act, & the third party doctrine in the Digital Age - Princeton Legal Journal*. Princeton University. https://legaljournal.princeton.edu/carpenter-v-united-states-the-stored-communications-act-the-third-party-doctrine-in-the-digital-age/

Pasipamire, N., & Muroyiwa, A. (2024). Navigating algorithm bias in AI: Ensuring fairness and trust in Africa. *Frontiers in Research Metrics and Analytics*, *9*, 1486600. Advance online publication. DOI: 10.3389/frma.2024.1486600 PMID: 39512269

Quang Huy, P., & Kien Phuc, V. (2025). Insight into how legal and ethical considerations of artificial intelligence enhance the effectiveness of cyber forensic accounting. *Journal of Global Information Technology Management*, *28*(2), 136–166. DOI: 10.1080/1097198X.2025.2480972

Radanliev, P. (2024). Artificial Intelligence and Quantum Cryptography. *Journal of Analytical Science and Technology*, *15*(1), 4. Advance online publication. DOI: 10.1186/s40543-024-00416-6

Rai, M., Husain, A. A., Maity, T., Yadav, R. K., & Neves, A. J. R. (2019). Advance intelligent video surveillance system (AIVSS): a future aspect. *Intelligent Video Surveillance, 37*.

Rai, M., Maity, T., Husain, A. A., & Yadav, R. K. (2023). Pearson's correlation and background subtraction (BGS) based approach for object's motion detection in infrared video frame sequences. *Statistische Hefte*, *64*(2), 449–475.

Rai, M., Maity, T., & Yadav, R. K. (2017). Thermal imaging system and its real time applications: A survey. *Journal of Engineering Technology*, *6*(2), 290–303.

Rai, M., Sharma, R., Satapathy, S. C., Yadav, D. K., Maity, T., & Yadav, R. K. (2022). An improved statistical approach for moving object detection in thermal video frames. *Multimedia Tools and Applications, 81*(7), 9289–9311. DOI: 10.1007/s11042-021-11548-x

Rai, M., & Yadav, R. K. (2016). A novel method for detection and extraction of human face for video surveillance applications. *International Journal of Signal and Imaging Systems Engineering, 9*(3), 165–173. DOI: 10.1504/IJSISE.2016.076226

Rich, M. S., & Aiken, M. P. (2024). An interdisciplinary approach to enhancing cyber threat prediction utilizing forensic cyberpsychology and Digital Forensics. *Forensic Science, 4*(1), 110–151. DOI: 10.3390/forensicsci4010008

Rocchio, L. M. (2020). Ethical and professional considerations in the forensic assessment of complex trauma and Dissociation. *Psychological Injury and Law, 13*(2), 124–134. DOI: 10.1007/s12207-020-09384-9 PMID: 32837675

Ryngaert, C. (2023). Extraterritorial enforcement jurisdiction in cyberspace: Normative shifts. *German Law Journal, 24*(3), 537–550. DOI: 10.1017/glj.2023.24

S., V. P. (2023). How can we manage biases in artificial intelligence systems – a systematic literature review. *International Journal of Information Management Data Insights, 3*(1), 100165. DOI: 10.1016/j.jjimei.2023.100165

Saeed, S., Suayyid, S. A., Al-Ghamdi, M. S., Al-Muhaisen, H., & Almuhaideb, A. M. (2023). A systematic literature review on Cyber Threat Intelligence for Organizational Cybersecurity Resilience. *Sensors (Basel), 23*(16), 7273. DOI: 10.3390/s23167273 PMID: 37631808

Salem, A. H., Azzam, S. M., Emam, O. E., & Abohany, A. A. (2024). Advancing cybersecurity: A comprehensive review of AI-Driven Detection Techniques. *Journal of Big Data, 11*(1), 105. Advance online publication. DOI: 10.1186/s40537-024-00957-y

Saura, J. R., Ribeiro-Soriano, D., & Palacios-Marqués, D. (2022). Assessing behavioral data science privacy issues in Government Artificial Intelligence Deployment. *Government Information Quarterly, 39*(4), 101679. DOI: 10.1016/j.giq.2022.101679

Sharma, S. (2020). Issues with enforcing mutual legal assistance treaties (MLATs): Access to cross-border data in criminal investigation. SSRN *Electronic Journal*. DOI: 10.2139/ssrn.3815270

Siddiqi, M. A., Pak, W., & Siddiqi, M. A. (2022). A study on the psychology of social engineering-based cyberattacks and existing countermeasures. *Applied Sciences (Basel, Switzerland), 12*(12), 6042. DOI: 10.3390/app12126042

Siegel, R., König, C. J., & Lazar, V. (2022). The impact of electronic monitoring on employees' job satisfaction, stress, performance, and counterproductive work behavior: A meta-analysis. *Computers in Human Behavior Reports*, *8*, 100227. DOI: 10.1016/j.chbr.2022.100227

Slack, D. P. (2020). Trauma and coping mechanisms exhibited by Forensic Science Practitioners: A literature review. *Forensic Science International. Synergy*, *2*, 310–316. DOI: 10.1016/j.fsisyn.2020.10.001 PMID: 33163953

Slobogin, C., & Brayne, S. (2023). Surveillance Technologies and constitutional law. *Annual Review of Criminology*, *6*(1), 219–240. DOI: 10.1146/annurev-criminol-030421-035102 PMID: 38074421

Smith, J., & Singh, M. (2024). Forensic DNA profiling: Legal and ethical considerations. *Journal of Scientific Research and Reports*, *30*(5), 141–144. DOI: 10.9734/jsrr/2024/v30i51929

Solanke, A. A., & Biasiotti, M. A. (2022). Digital Forensics AI: Evaluating, standardizing and optimizing digital evidence mining techniques. *KI - Künstliche Intelligenz*, *36*(2), 143–161. DOI: 10.1007/s13218-022-00763-9

Soliman, M. (2023). Layers of the internet: The challenge of the dark web and the need for an international legal framework. SSRN *Electronic Journal*. DOI: 10.2139/ssrn.4418508

Soni, N. (2025). Digital Forensics: Confronting Modern Cyber Crimes, technological advancements, and future challenges. *Journal of Forensic, Legal &amp. Investigative Sciences*, *11*(1). Advance online publication. DOI: 10.24966/FLIS-733X/100105

Stoykova, R. (2021). Digital evidence: Unaddressed threats to fairness and the presumption of Innocence. *Computer Law &amp. Computer Law & Security Review*, *42*, 105575. DOI: 10.1016/j.clsr.2021.105575

Swofford, H., & Champod, C. (2021). Implementation of algorithms in Pattern & Impression evidence: A responsible and practical roadmap. *Forensic Science International. Synergy*, *3*, 100142. DOI: 10.1016/j.fsisyn.2021.100142 PMID: 33718855

Tian, T., Zhang, C., Jiang, B., Feng, H., & Lu, Z. (2025). Insider threat detection for specific threat scenarios. *Cybersecurity*, *8*(1), 17. Advance online publication. DOI: 10.1186/s42400-024-00321-w

Tiwari, S. (2024). *Regulation Cybersecurity in Financial Technology: Insight into Challenges, Compliance, and Best Practices*. DOI: 10.20944/preprints202409.1761.v1

Tsang, A. J., Sadler, J. Z., Brown, E. S., & Heitman, E. (2025). Evaluating psychiatry journals' adherence to informed consent guidelines for case reports. *Research Integrity and Peer Review*, *10*(1), 15. Advance online publication. DOI: 10.1186/s41073-025-00171-1 PMID: 40676700

Tschider, C., Compagnucci, M. C., & Minssen, T. (2024). The new EU–US Data Protection Framework's implications for Healthcare. *Journal of Law and the Biosciences*, *11*(2), lsae022. Advance online publication. DOI: 10.1093/jlb/lsae022 PMID: 39346780

Uzougbo, N. S., Ikegwu, C. G., & Adewusi, A. O. (2024). Cybersecurity compliance in Financial Institutions: A Comparative Analysis of Global Standards and Regulations. *International Journal of Science and Research Archive*, *12*(1), 533–548. DOI: 10.30574/ijsra.2024.12.1.0802

Varsha, P. S. (2023). How can we manage biases in artificial intelligence systems–A systematic literature review. *International Journal of Information Management Data Insights*, *3*(1), 100165.

Zhang, H. (2025). The evidentiary value of AI-generated data: A Framework for reliability and admissibility. *Education and Social Work*, *2*(2), 34. DOI: 10.63313/ESW.9074

About the Contributors

Seifedine Kadry is a professor of data science at Lebanese American University, Lebanon. With a Ph.D. in Computer Science, he has an extensive academic background in applied mathematics, computer science, and engineering. Dr. Kadry has published prolifically in areas including artificial intelligence, machine learning, cybersecurity, and educational technology. He has authored numerous books and peer-reviewed articles and serves on the editorial boards of several prestigious international journals. In addition to his academic achievements, he is actively involved in organizing international conferences and mentoring Ph.D. students.

Mritunjay Rai is an accomplished researcher and Assistant Professor in the Department of Electrical and Electronics Engineering at Shri Ramswaroop Memorial University, Barabanki, India. He specializes in digital image processing, machine learning, and thermal imaging, with a strong research focus on biomedical imaging, surveillance systems, and emotion recognition. He earned his Ph.D. from the Indian Institute of Technology (ISM), Dhanbad, in 2023, with a dissertation on real-time thermal imaging algorithms. He also holds a Master's degree in Instrumentation and Control from BIT Mesra, where he worked on intelligent video surveillance systems. Dr. Rai has published extensively in reputed journals such as The Journal of Supercomputing and Multimedia Tools and Applications, contributing to advancements in motion detection, medical diagnostics, and automated emotion recognition using deep learning. His work emphasizes real-time processing, algorithmic efficiency, and accuracy. He is actively involved in editing high-impact books with IGI Global, Wiley, and Elsevier, covering AI in surveillance, healthcare, agriculture, and disaster prediction. Among his notable projects is a government-funded initiative for early detection of diabetic foot ulcers using thermal imaging and sensor fusion. Dr. Rai's interdisciplinary research bridges computational intelligence and real-world applications in healthcare, industry, and environmental monitoring.

Padmesh Tripathi received his doctorate from Sharda University, Greater Noida, India; and completed his Master's in Mathematics and Bachelor's degrees from the University of Allahabad, Prayagraj, India. Dr Tripathi is currently working as a Professor of Mathematics in the Department of Computer Science and Engineering at Delhi Technical Campus, Greater Noida, UP, India. He has teaching experience of more than 25 Years at graduate/undergraduate level. He has published several papers/ book chapters in reputed Journals/publishers. He has published 4 Indian Innovation Patents, One Indian Design Patent, and Two UK Design Patents. He has been associated with 6 edited books with reputed publishers. He is an editor of a book series on "Advanced Transformative Technologies for Sustainability" to be published by Peter Land International Academic Publisher, Switzerland. Dr. Tripathi's areas of research interest are Inverse Problems, Machine Learning, Deep Learning, Image/Signal Processing, and Optimization. Dr. Tripathi has been associated with reputed publishers like Elsevier, Springer, Wiley-Scrivener, Taylor and Francis, IGI Global, Bentham Science, Inderscience, Peter Lang, etc in different roles like editor, author, and reviewer. He recently published an edited book on "Mathematical Models using Artificial Intelligence in Surveillance Systems" with Wiley-Scrivener Publisher, USA which has been Scopus indexed. Dr Tripathi has delivered several expert talks at different institutes. He has organized 3 seminars, and international conferences and chaired several sessions. He received grants from DRDO to organize a seminar.

***

Munir Ahmad is a seasoned professional in the realm of Spatial Data Infrastructure (SDI), Geo-Information Productions, Information Systems, and Information Governance, boasting over 25 years of dedicated experience in the field. With a PhD in Computer Science, Dr. Ahmad's expertise spans Spatial Data Production, Management, Processing, Analysis, Visualization, and Quality Control. Throughout his career, Dr. Ahmad has been deeply involved in the development and deployment of SDI systems specially in the context of Pakistan, leveraging his proficiency in Spatial Database Design, Web, Mobile & Desktop GIS, and Geo Web Services Architecture. His contributions to Volunteered Geographic Information (VGI) and Open Source Geoportal & Metadata Portal have significantly enriched the geospatial community. As a trainer and researcher, Dr. Ahmad has authored over 50 publications, advancing the industry's knowledge base and fostering innovation in Geo-Tech, Data Governance, and Information Infrastructure, and Emerging Technologies. His commitment to Research and Development (R&D) is evident in his role as a dedicated educator and mentor in the field.

Pridhi Arora is currently pursuing her Ph.D. in Computer Science at Bennett University, Greater Noida, India. She holds an M.Tech in Computer Science from AITM, Palwal, India. With over twelve years of extensive teaching and industry experience, she has developed strong expertise across multiple domains of computing. Her research interests span Artificial Intelligence, Machine Learning, Deep Learning, Image Processing, and Blockchain Technologies. Throughout her academic and professional career, she has been committed to quality research, impactful teaching, and continuous learning. She aims to bridge the gap between emerging technologies and real-world applications through her scholarly work.

Ashish Avasthi Professor (Research Cadre), Computer Science Poornima University, Jaipur, Rajasthan, India ashishsrmcem@gmail.com | +91-972-199-3399 Academic Background: Ph.D. in Computer Science (Internet of Things) – Faizabad University, India, 2017 Ph.D. in Computer Science (Fractals) – CMJ University, Shillong, India, 2012 M.Tech in Information Technology – Karnataka State Open University, 2010 M.Phil in Information Technology – Global Open University, 2008 MCA – Indira Gandhi National Open University, 2005 BCA – Bhupendra Narayan Mandal University, 2002 Research Interests: Internet of Things (IoT) Artificial Intelligence & Machine Learning Cybersecurity & Cryptography Big Data Analytics Fractal Technology Smart Cities & Digital Transformation Teaching & Academic Experience: Professor (Research Cadre) – Since July 2025 Professor, Department of Computer Science, Poornima University (May 2024 – June 2025) Associate Professor & Chief Warden, Maharana Pratap Engineering College, Kanpur (April 2023 – April 2024) Associate Professor & Head (IT), SRMCEM, Lucknow (2007 – 2023) Previous roles include faculty and software developer positions at NIIT, PTU Study Center, Wellborn Software, and Soft Vision. Books Authored: Python Programming Strategies for AI in Autonomous Systems (Rademics, 2024) IoT and Its Applications (Rademics, 2025) Human Values and Ethics (Rademics) Green Computing and Sustainability Queueing and Reliability Modeling Theory of Computation (Zenodo) Patents Granted / Published: IoT Security and Privacy Enhancement Systematic Processing of IoT Data Using Big Data and ML Bug Assignment & Developer Allocation Customer Emotion Detection AI Device IoT-based Biomedical Waste Disposer Network Security Managing Device (UK Patent) Soil Prediction using IoT, AI, and ML Selected Publications (Scopus/IEEE Indexed): New Approaches towards the Collision Detection – IJCSI Smart City Implementation via IoT in India – ICECA 2019 Decision Support System for ERP – ICCA 2010 Fractal-Based Grid Computing – IEEE AES Cryptography using FPGA – Library Progress International Journal (2024) Book Chapters: Digital Transformation and Business Growth – IGI Global Advanced Digital Ticketing in Smart Transportation Neuro-Pharmaceutical Innovation in Green Drug Manufacturing Convergence of

Cloud and Distributed Systems Professional Memberships: Member, International Association of Computer Science and Information Technology (IACSIT) Life Member, Computer Society of India (CSI), Rajasthan Chapter Life Member, International Organization for Academic and Scientific Development (IOASD) Fellow Member, Education Research & Development Association (ERDA) Awards & Recognitions: Best Asian Award for Contributions to Research & Education (Rajasthan) Best Faculty Awards – SRMCEM, Lucknow (2007–2009) Wipro Mission10X Dale Carnegie Certification in High Impact Teaching Editorial & Organizational Roles: Editorial Board Member – Prayas (ISSN 0975-8224) Convener – Gantavya National Level Technical Fest (2011–2014) Organizer – ISAC 2011, International Symposia on Computing Mentor & Expert Lecturer – Topics including ERP, Operating Systems, Cryptography Orchid id: 0000-0003-3069-1984

Yogesh U. Bodhe was born in India. He received the B.E. degree in Computer Engineering from the University of Pune, Pune, India, in 2010 and the M.Tech. degree in Computer Science and Engineering from JNTU University, Hyderabad, India, in 2014. He has held various lecturing positions in University of Pune, Pune, India & Shivaji University, Kolhapur, India. Yogesh U. Bodhe does research in Computer Engineering, Cosmology and Evolutionary Biology. Currently he is working as Lecturer in Department of Information Technology, Government Polytechnic Pune, India.

Sandeep C. S is an accomplished academician and researcher with over 16 years of experience in teaching, research, and administration in Electronics and Communication Engineering. He serves as Associate Professor and Head of the ECE Department at Jawaharlal College of Engineering and Technology, Kerala. He is also engaged in postdoctoral research at the University of Louisiana, USA, focusing on AI, machine learning, and biomedical signal processing. He holds a Ph.D. from the University of Kerala, with research on advanced biomedical imaging. He earned his M.E. and B.E. from Anna University, Chennai, and an MBA in HRM from IGNOU. A Senior Member of IEEE and a recognized research supervisor under APJ Abdul Kalam Technological University, he has authored over 60 research papers and contributed to books, chapters, and patents. His interdisciplinary projects span healthcare, computing, and intelligent systems. He continues to contribute actively to academic innovation and global research collaborations.

Sachin Vasant Chaudhari is a Ph.D. holder in Electronics Engineering. He is an Associate Professor in the Electronics and Telecommunication Engineering Department at Sanjivani College of Engineering, Kopargaon, which is affiliated with Savitribai Phule Pune University, Pune, India. He has worked on a broad range of topics including automated deep learning, UAV route planning, hybrid energy systems, and medical applications. His innovative research also addresses dynamic routing algorithms, channel estimation in OFDM, and advanced materials for medical implants. He has published over 35 papers in reputed International Journals. He is having professional membership of The Institution of Engineers (IEI) & International Association of Engineers (IANG).

Yamini Parth Chawda A dedicated and passionate Mechanical Engineering professional with strong academic experience and a commitment to quality teaching. Currently working as an Assistant Professor of Mechanical Engineering at B. H. Gardi College of Engineering & Technology, focuses on guiding students, encouraging practical learning, and supporting academic growth. Known for my sincerity, professionalism, and a calm, student-friendly approach to education.

Baisakhi Das is a Professor in the Department of Information Technology at the Institute of Engineering & Management, Kolkata, India. She earned her Ph.D. (Engineering) and M.Tech degrees from the Indian Institute of Engineering Science and Technology (IIEST), Shibpur, and holds a B.Tech from the West Bengal University of Technology, India. With over 18 years of academic experience, Dr. Das has established herself as a committed educator and researcher. Her primary research interests include Blockchain, Artificial Intelligence, and Cellular Automata. She has published extensively in international journals, conferences, and edited book volumes. Dr. Das has actively contributed to the academic community through her roles as Technical Program Committee (TPC) member at various international conferences, and as a reviewer/editorial board member for several international journals. She has also served as organizing chair, co-convener, and committee member for multiple international conferences. She is a member of IEEE, reflecting her dedication to advancing research and collaboration in emerging technologies.

Jaishri Gothania is an academician, author, researcher, and data scientist with over 9 years of experience. She holds a Ph.D. in Computer Science Engineering, an M.Tech in Computer Science, a B.Tech in Computer Science and Engineering, and a PGD in Education. She has published 1 book, 6 book chapters, and 12 research articles; presented 6 conference papers; and holds multiple patents. Her work bridges data science and innovation, contributing significantly to academia, research, and technological advancement.

Sangita Gupta, a Professor at Poornima University, Jaipur, brings over 24 years of experience in teaching, research, and academic administration. She holds an M.Sc. in Chemistry, a PGDCA, a Postgraduate Diploma in Environmental Studies, and a Ph.D. Her research interests span electrochemical and analytical techniques, electroplating, environmental science, and organic synthesis. She has served as Director of an institute and Editor of UDDESHY, a registered popular science magazine. As a Principal Investigator of a DST major project at the University of Rajasthan, she has led significant research initiatives. Dr. Gupta has organized and chaired numerous national and international conferences and is a reviewer for several reputed international journals. With over 40 research publications, two authored books, and multiple awards, she is widely recognized for her academic and scientific contributions.

Md Sakibul Hasan holds a Master's degree in Computer/Information Technology Services Administration and Management, with a strong academic and professional focus on emerging technologies and digital risk management. With expertise spanning information systems, cybersecurity principles, and advanced technology governance, Md Sakibul Hasan has developed a particular interest in blockchain ecosystems and their security implications. Driven by a passion for understanding the complexities of decentralized technologies, Md Sakibul Hasan has explored how blockchain infrastructures intersect with digital forensics, financial integrity, and cybercrime investigation. This interest led to the development of specialized research on blockchain forensic methodologies for digital transactions—work that contributes to bridging the gap between technical innovation and investigative practice. In addition to academic achievements, Md Sakibul Hasan is committed to advancing knowledge in cybersecurity, digital asset protection, and forensic readiness. Through research, writing, and continued professional growth, Md Sakibul Hasan aims to support safer, more transparent, and resilient digital environments.

S. Ida Evangeline, presently working as an Assistant Professor in the Department of Electrical and Electronics Engineering at the Government College of Engineering, Tirunelveli, Tamilnadu, India. She obtained her Bachelor's in Electrical and Electronics Engineering from Manonmaniam Sundaranar University in 2003, and Master's in Power Systems Engineering from Anna University, Chennai, Tamilnadu, India in 2005. She completed her PhD degree in 2023 at Anna University, Chennai, Tamilnadu, India. She has published six research papers in international journals. Her current research interests include optimal power flow, renewable energy, soft computing, machine learning, and deep learning.

Jevin.J.A received Bachelor Degree in Computer Science and Engineering recognized from Anna Universit,Chennai in 2006 and his Masters Degree in Computer science and Engineering in 2012 from University department,Anna University,Tirunelveli.He is pursuing PhD(CSE) in SRM Institute of Science and

Technology, Ramapuram campus,Chennai,India.His research area of interests includes Deep Learning and Data Science.He is presently working in Koneru Lakshmaiah Education Foundation,Guntur Dt,Andhra pradesh.

Rituraj Jain is currently working in the Department of Information Technology, Marwadi University, Rajkot, Gujarat, India. He has published many papers in International Journals and Conferences. He has published 4 books. He is an Oracle Database SQL Certified Expert. He is also associated with professional bodies like the Indian Society of Technical Education (ISTE), Computer Science Teachers Association (CSTA), Academy & Industry Research Collaboration Center (AIRCC), International Association of Computer Science and Information Technology (IACSIT), International Association of Engineers (IAENG). His research interests include Cloud Computing, Machine Learning, Deep Learning, Fuzzy Logic, IoT, Genetic Algorithms, Big Data and Software Engineering.

Bright Keswani is working as Research Professor, Faculty of Computer Science and Engineering, Poornima University, Jaipur, India. He has research and teaching experience of more than 25 years. He has published several research papers in Scopus and Web of Science indexed journals, book chapters, and international conference proceedings. He is the author and co-editor of multiple books in the field of Computer Science and Engineering. He has been granted 10 patents and 2 design patents. He is a member of various professional bodies and actively contributes to research and development in Artificial Intelligence, Machine Learning, and related areas.

S. Manjula has over 23 years of academic experience in higher education, having taught in both India and Singapore, along with one year of professional experience in the logistics industry in Singapore. She is currently serving as an Assistant Professor in the Department of Data Science at Madanapalle Institute of Technology & Science, Andhra Pradesh. She holds an MCA and M.Phil from Bharathidasan University and an M.Tech from SASTRA University, Tanjore. She is presently pursuing her Ph.D. at Annamalai University. Her academic and research interests include Machine Learning, Cyber Security, and Software Testing.

Amit Karbhari Mogal currently serves as an Assistant Professor at MVP Samaj's CMCS College in Nashik, where he also heads the Department of Computer Science and Application. He holds an M.Sc. in Computer Science and is SET (State Eligibility Test) qualified. In addition to his formal qualifications, Prof. Mogal has completed several certificate courses through Coursera, offered by leading universities, in areas such as Cloud Computing, Big Data, Machine Learning, Artificial Intelligence, Leadership Skills, and Data Science. Prof. Mogal is actively pursuing a Ph.D. in Computer Science and Applications at Sandip University,

Nashik. He has made significant contributions to the field, publishing numerous research papers in prestigious national and international journals and conferences. With over 16 years of teaching experience, Prof. Mogal has built a reputation as both a dedicated educator and a leader in academic administration. In addition to his teaching role, he has held various key positions, including NSS Program Officer, College Examination Officer (CEO), AISHE Nodal Officer, and IQAC Coordinator, underscoring his commitment to academic excellence and institutional development. His research interests are primarily focused on Big Data, Data Science and Analytics, Cloud Computing, Machine Learning, and the Internet of Things (IoT).

Adam Sandow Saani A detail-oriented professional and academic with extensive expertise in supply chain planning, procurement, and logistics. He is a Chartered Member of the Chartered Institute of Supply Chain Management (CISCM-GH) and a member of the Humanitarian Logistics Agency (HLA). He is passionate about integrating sustainable practices into supply chain management and is committed to academic excellence, research, and the application of industry knowledge in both teaching and professional practice.

Vikas Sharma is an active academician and researcher in the field of computer science with 7 years of experience. He earned M. Tech degree specialized in Computer Science. He is involved in academic development and scholarly activities. He is member of International Association of Engineers, The Society of Digital Information and Wireless Communications, Global Professors Welfare Association, International Association of Academic plus Corporate (IAAC), Computer Science Teachers Association and Internet Society. His research interest includes Cloud Computing, Artificial Intelligence, Machine Learning; published more than 55 research articles with 4 books and 75 book chapters in edited books. He is contributing as member of editorial and reviewers' boards in conferences and various computer journals and edited books published by Elsevier, CRC Press, Taylor and Francis, Springer, IGI global, Wiley Publication, IET Publication, De Gruyter, River Publication etc.

Reza E Rabbi Shawon - Business Development and Supply Chain Manager | Researcher | Reza E Rabbi Shawon is the Business Development and Supply Chain Manager at Nash LLC, where he leads data-driven growth, supplier relations, and operational optimization. He holds an MBA in Business Analytics from Gannon University, USA. As a researcher, his publications explore AI, cybersecurity, supply chain optimization, and digital forensics, including works such as Detecting IoT Cyberattacks, AI-Driven Predictive Modeling of US Economic Trends, and Optimizing Sustainable Supply Chains through AI. A patent holder and innovator,

Reza focuses on integrating blockchain, AI, and analytics to enhance transparency and security in business systems. With a keen interest in blockchain and financial technology, he helps make sense of complex systems in ways anyone can follow. In Blockchain Forensic for Digital Transactions, he shares his insights on tracing, analyzing, and securing digital transactions, making the world of blockchain clearer for readers.

Shashank Solanki is a B.B.A. LL.B (Hons.) student at CHRIST (Deemed to be University), Delhi NCR. With a strong academic foundation and a keen interest in Arbitration, Securities, Corporate Law, and Banking & Finance, Shashank has actively contributed to legal scholarship. His research works have been accepted for publication in esteemed Scopus-indexed platforms, addressing critical areas such as medical big data, digital healthcare ethics, and the Metaverse. Beyond academics, he has demonstrated excellence through multiple internships, gaining hands on experience in dispute resolution, corporate law, and judicial research. Shashank's dedication to academic pursuits and practical legal applications reflects his commitment to contributing meaningfully to the legal domain.

M. M. Abdullah Al Mamun Sony is a Bangladeshi PhD candidate in legal studies at the University of Debrecen, Hungary, with academic roots from Khulna University majoring in Sociology. His research spans Society 5.0, gender studies, DRR, community development, and social policy. He founded ChangeMaker Nexus Ltd., a research-based social business organization focused on local model creation and super-smart society development. Mr. Sony served as DOSZ Ambassador of Bangladesh and Global Ambassador for Socialprotection.org. He has authored works on DRR, AI, and policy, and earned accolades such as the Stipendium Hungaricum Fellowship, Erasmus grant, and Best Leadership Award, reflecting his commitment to bridging academic insight with real-world impact.

L.R.Sujithra (Sujithra Laxmanan Rangaraj) received B.E degree in CSE from SNS College of Engineering, affiliated to Anna University, Coimbatore, Tamil Nādu in 2011. M.E Degree in CSE from United Institute of Technology, affiliated to Anna University, Chennai, Tamil Nādu in 2013. She completed her Ph.D. degree at the Department of Information and Communication Engineering, Anna University, Chennai, Tamil Nadu, India at 2024. She has currently 12 years of teaching experience and research interests include Machine Learning and Bio informatics. She Published 11 article which is indexed in Scopus including SCI journals.

Varadharajan Bhoopathy is a Professor at Sree Rama Engineering College. He holds a Ph.D. in Information and Communication Engineering from Anna University and has over 16 years of academic experience. Specializing in wireless sensor networks and IoT, he has published numerous research papers and holds several international patents. Dr. Bhoopathy is a recipient of prestigious awards for his contributions to education and research. His commitment to academia continues to drive innovation and excellence in the field of computer science.

Tarun Kumar Vashishth is an active academician and researcher in the field of Computer Science with 22 years of experience. He earned Ph.D. Mathematics degree specialized in Operations Research; served several academic positions such as Dy. Director, HoD, NAAC Coordinator, Academic Coordinator, Member Secretary of Department Research Committee, Assistant Center Superintendent and Head Examiner in University Examinations. He is involved in academic development and scholarly activities. He is member of International Association of Engineers, The Society of Digital Information and Wireless Communications, Global Professors Welfare Association, International Association of Academic plus Corporate (IAAC), Computer Science Teachers Association and Internet Society . His research interest includes Cloud Computing, Artificial Intelligence, Machine Learning and Operations Research; published more than 50 research articles & conference papers with 2 book and 80 book chapters. He is contributing as member of editorial and reviewers boards in conferences and various computer journals and edited books published by Elsevier, CRC Press, Taylor and Francis, Springer, IGI global, Wiley Publication, IET Publication, De Gruyter, River Publication etc.

Pushpendra Kumar Verma is an Associate Professor at IIMT University, Meerut, India, holding degrees in MCA, MTech-CSE, MPhil (CS), and a Doctorate in Computer Science. His research expertise lies in Cryptography, Network Security, and Cyber Security, with additional specialization in AI, Deep Learning, and Machine Learning. With 19+ years of teaching and research experience, he has participated in high-profile conferences, published research papers in international journals and Scopus Indexed Journals, reviewed reputed international journal papers, and held memberships in Vidwan, Springer, IAENG, SDIWC, IEEE, and more.

Seema Verma is Professor and Head of CSE at Delhi Technical Campus, Greater Noida (GGSIPU), with over 23 years of academic and research experience. She holds a B.Tech, an M.Tech (Gold Medallist), a Ph.D. from Thapar University, and is UGC-NET qualified. She has published widely in reputed journals, conferences, holds five patents, and has received a Best Paper Award. Dr. Verma has served as editor, conference chair, and speaker at platforms like EICT Academy IIT Roorkee, ATAL FDP, and openSUSE.Asia. She is a member of IEEE, ACM, ISTE, and her interests include AI, Machine Learning, Generative AI, and Information Security.

Priyank Dipakkumar Zaveri Dynamic and passionate Mechanical Engineering professional with extensive experience in academia and a proven track record of excellence in teaching, research, and departmental leadership. Currently serving as the Head of Mechanical Engineering at B H Gardi College of Engineering & Technology, with a commitment to fostering innovation and guiding future engineers. Recognized for outstanding performance and dedication to academic excellence.

Index

Symbols

A

B

C

D

E

F

G

H

I

L

M

N

P

Q

R

S

T

W

Z

www.ingramcontent.com/pod-product-compliance
Lightning Source LLC
LaVergne TN
LVHW082051011026
849162LV00019B/771